Portales

José A. Blanco

VISTA®
HIGHER LEARNING
Boston, Massachusetts

INTRODUCTORY
Spanish

1

Publisher: José A. Blanco
Editorial Development: Armando Brito, Deborah Coffey, María Victoria Echeverri,
Jo Hanna Kurth, Raquel Rodríguez, Verónica Tejeda
Project Management: Hillary Gospodarek, Sharon Inglis, Sofía Pellón
Rights Management: Annie Pickert Fuller, Caitlin O'Brien
Technology Production: Egle Gutiérrez, Paola Ríos Schaaf
Design: Mark James, Andrés Vanegas
Production: Manuela Arango, Oscar Díez, Jennifer López

Student Text ISBN: 978-1-68004-041-8

Library of Congress Control Number: 2014948568

7 8 9 WC 21 20

THE VISTA HIGHER LEARNING STORY

Your Specialized Foreign Language Publisher

Independent, specialized, and privately owned, Vista Higher Learning was founded in 2000 with one mission: to raise the teaching and learning of world languages to a higher level. This mission is based on the following beliefs:

- It is essential to prepare students for a world in which learning another language is a necessity, not a luxury.

- Language learning should be fun and rewarding, and all students should have the tools necessary for achieving success.

- Students who experience success learning a language will be more likely to continue their language studies both inside and outside the classroom.

With this in mind, we decided to take a fresh look at all aspects of language instructional materials. Because we are specialized, we dedicate 100 percent of our resources to this goal and base every decision on how well it supports language learning.

That is where you come in. Since our founding in 2000, we have relied on the continuous and invaluable feedback from language instructors and students nationwide. This partnership has proved to be the cornerstone of our success by allowing us to constantly improve our programs to meet your instructional needs.

The result? Programs that make language learning exciting, relevant, and effective through:

- an unprecedented access to resources
- a wide variety of contemporary, authentic materials
- the integration of text, technology, and media, and
- a bold and engaging textbook design

By focusing on our singular passion, we let you focus on yours.

The Vista Higher Learning Team

table of contents

	contextos	fotonovela

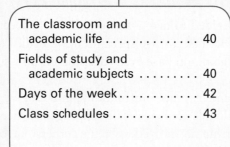

cultura	estructura	adelante

vi

| | contexts | fotonovela |

contextos	fotonovela

Lección 9
Las fiestas

Lección 10
En el consultorio

Lección 11
La tecnología

Lección 12
La vivienda

contextos	fotonovela

Lección 13

La naturaleza

Lección 14

En la ciudad

Lección 15

El bienestar

Lección 16

El mundo del trabajo

cultura	estructura	adelante

Icons

Familiarize yourself with these icons that appear throughout **PORTALES**.

 Listening activity/section

 Pair activity

acknowledgments

On behalf of its author and editors, Vista Higher Learning expresses its sincere appreciation to the many educators nationwide who contributed their ideas and suggestions to **PORTALES**.

We are grateful to the instructors who completed our survey about **En línea**, VHL's previous online Spanish program. Their insights and detailed comments were instrumental in shaping our new online program.

Reviewers

Amy M. Adrian
 Ivy Tech Community College, IN

Teresa Borden
 Columbia College, CA

Majel Campbell
 Pikes Peak Community
 College, CO

Beth Cardon
 Georgia Perimeter College, GA

Rafael Cherry
 Wayland Baptist University, TX

Jealynn Liddle Coleman
 Wytheville Community
 College, VA

Krista Croghan
 Northern State University, NE

Patricia Davis
 Darton State College, GA

Frederic Deloizy
 Harrisburg Area Community
 College, PA

Benjamin Earwicker
 Northwest Nazarene
 University, ID

Marianne Franco
 Modesto Junior College, CA

Margarita García-Notario
 SUNY Plattsburgh, NY

Aimee Guerin
 Mesa Community College, AZ

Loida Gutiérrez
 South Mountain Community
 College, AZ

Sergio A. Guzmán
 College of Southern Nevada, NV

Steven Hartlaub
 Inver Hills Community
 College, MN

Katie Heaps
 Western Texas College, TX

Yanina Hernández
 Texas State Technical
 College, TX

Stacy Jazán
 Glendale Community
 College, CA

Karen Jones
 Santa Fe College, TX

Roxana Levin
 St. Petersburg College, FL

Kenneth V. Luna
 California State University,
 Northridge, CA

Mirta Pagnucci
 College of DuPage, IL

Carolyn Perry
 West Kentucky Community and
 Technical College, KY

Bevin Rainwater
 Charter Oak State College, CT

Terese Ricard
 Spartanburg Community
 College, SC

Ramiro Rodriguez
 Texas State Technical College
 Harlingen, TX

Jorge Salvo
 Claflin University, SC

Albert Shank
 Scottsdale Community
 College, AZ

Gretcen Skivington
 Great Basin College, NV

James Bryant Smith
 Nicholls State University, LA

Andrea Van Vorhis
 Owens Community College, OH

Imelda Vázquez
 Ivy Tech Community College, IN

We gratefully acknowledge the instructors who class-tested **PORTALES**. Their comments and suggestions were invaluable to us.

Pilot Users

Leah Caceres Lutzow
Fox Valley Technical College, WI

Maria Coronel
Fresno City College, CA

Daniel Darrow
University of
Alaska-Fairbanks, AK

Cliff Escobedo
Diablo Valley College, CA

Mary Fatora-Tumbaga
Kauai Community College, HI

Kathryn C. Grovergrys
Madison Area Technical
College, WI

Roxana Levin
St. Petersburg College, FL

Jeff Ruth
East Stroudsburg University of
Pennsylvania, PA

Jacquelyn Sandone
University of
Missouri-Columbia, MO

Sara Villa
The New School, NY

Sarah Willoughby
Everett Community College, WA

Hola, ¿qué tal?

1

Communicative Goals

You will learn how to:

- Greet people in Spanish
- Say goodbye
- Identify yourself and others
- Talk about the time of day

contextos

fotonovela

cultura

estructura

adelante

A PRIMERA VISTA
- Guess what the people on the photo are saying:
  a. Adiós. b. Hola. c. salsa
- Most likely they would also say:
  a. Gracias. b. fiesta c. Buenos días.
- The women are:
  a. amigas b. chicos c. señores

Hola, ¿qué tal?

Más vocabulario

Buenos días.	*Good morning.*
Buenas noches.	*Good evening; Good night.*
Hasta la vista.	*See you later.*
Hasta pronto.	*See you soon.*
¿Cómo se llama usted?	*What's your name? (form.)*
Le presento a…	*I would like to introduce you to (name). (form.)*
Te presento a…	*I would like to introduce you to (name). (fam.)*
el nombre	*name*
¿Cómo estás?	*How are you? (fam.)*
No muy bien.	*Not very well.*
¿Qué pasa?	*What's happening?; What's going on?*
por favor	*please*
De nada.	*You're welcome.*
No hay de qué.	*You're welcome.*
Lo siento.	*I'm sorry.*
Gracias.	*Thank you; Thanks.*
Muchas gracias.	*Thank you very much; Thanks a lot.*

Variación léxica

Items are presented for recognition purposes only.

Buenos días.	⟷	Buenas.
De nada.	⟷	A la orden.
Lo siento.	⟷	Perdón.
¿Qué tal?	⟷	¿Qué hubo? *(Col.)*
Chau	⟷	Ciao; Chao

1

ELENA Patricia, le presento a Jorge Perales.
PATRICIA Encantada.
SEÑOR PERALES Igualmente. ¿De dónde es usted, señorita?
PATRICIA Soy de México. ¿Y usted?
SEÑOR PERALES De Puerto Rico.

2

TOMÁS ¿Qué tal, Alberto?
ALBERTO Regular. ¿Y tú?
TOMÁS Bien. ¿Qué hay de nuevo?
ALBERTO Nada.

3

SEÑOR VARGAS Buenas tardes, señora Wong. ¿Cómo está usted?
SEÑORA WONG Muy bien, gracias. ¿Y usted, señor Vargas?
SEÑOR VARGAS Bien, gracias.
SEÑORA WONG Hasta mañana, señor Vargas. Saludos a la señora Vargas.
SEÑOR VARGAS Adiós.

AYUDA

In Spanish, people can be addressed either formally or informally. Dialogues 1 and 3 are formal exchanges and use **usted** (*you*) forms. Dialogues 2, 4, and 5 are informal and use the familiar **tú** (*you*) form or other informal expressions. You will learn more about this in **Estructura 1.3.**

BERTA Hasta luego, Tere.
TERESA Chau, Berta. Nos vemos mañana.

CARMEN Buenas tardes. Me llamo Carmen.
　¿Cómo te llamas tú?
ANTONIO Buenas tardes. Me llamo Antonio.
　Mucho gusto.
CARMEN El gusto es mío. ¿De dónde eres?
ANTONIO Soy de los Estados Unidos, de California.

Práctica

1 Escuchar 🎧 Listen to each question or statement, then choose the correct response.

1. a. Muy bien, gracias.   b. Me llamo Graciela.
2. a. Lo siento.   b. Mucho gusto.
3. a. Soy de Puerto Rico.   b. No muy bien.
4. a. No hay de qué.   b. Regular.
5. a. Mucho gusto.   b. Hasta pronto.
6. a. Nada.   b. Igualmente.
7. a. Me llamo Guillermo Montero.   b. Muy bien, gracias.
8. a. Buenas tardes. ¿Cómo estás?   b. El gusto es mío.
9. a. Saludos a la Sra. Ramírez.   b. Encantada.
10. a. Adiós.   b. Regular.

2 Identificar 🎧 You will hear a series of expressions. Identify the expression (**a**, **b**, **c**, or **d**) that does not belong in each series.

1. ____   3. ____
2. ____   4. ____

3 Escoger For each expression, write another word or phrase that expresses a similar idea.

> **modelo**
> ¿Cómo estás? *¿Qué tal?*

1. De nada.   4. Hasta la vista.
2. Encantado.   5. Mucho gusto.
3. Adiós.

4 Ordenar Put this scrambled conversation in order.

—Muy bien, gracias. Soy Rosabel.
—Soy de México. ¿Y tú?
—Mucho gusto, Rosabel.
—Hola. Me llamo Carlos. ¿Cómo estás?
—Soy de Argentina.
—Igualmente. ¿De dónde eres, Carlos?

CARLOS   _____
ROSABEL   _____
CARLOS   _____
ROSABEL   _____
CARLOS   _____
ROSABEL   _____

5 **Completar** Complete these dialogues.

> modelo
> ¿Cómo estás?
> Muy bien, gracias.

1. — _____
   — Buenos días. ¿Qué tal?

2. — _____
   — Me llamo Carmen Sánchez.

3. — _____
   — De Canadá.

4. — Te presento a Marisol.
   — _____

5. — Gracias.
   — _____

6. — _____
   — Regular.

7. — _____
   — Nada.

8. — ¡Hasta la vista!
   — _____

6 **Cambiar** Correct the second part of each conversation to make it logical.

> modelo
> ¿Qué tal?
> ~~No hay de qué.~~ Bien. ¿Y tú?

1. — Hasta mañana, señora Ramírez. Saludos al señor Ramírez.
   — *Muy bien, gracias.*

2. — ¿Qué hay de nuevo, Alberto?
   — *Sí, me llamo Alberto. ¿Cómo te llamas tú?*

3. — Gracias, Tomás.
   — *Regular. ¿Y tú?*

4. — Miguel, te presento a la señorita Perales.
   — *No hay de qué, señorita.*

5. — ¿De dónde eres, Antonio?
   — *Muy bien, gracias. ¿Y tú?*

6. — ¿Cómo se llama usted?
   — *El gusto es mío.*

7. — ¿Qué pasa?
   — *Hasta luego, Alicia.*

8. — Buenas tardes, señor. ¿Cómo está usted?
   — *Soy de Puerto Rico.*

Comunicación

7

Diálogos With a partner, complete and role-play these conversations.

Conversación 1

—Hola. Me llamo Teresa. ¿Cómo te llamas tú?

—_____

—Soy de Puerto Rico. ¿Y tú?

—_____

Conversación 2

—_____

—Muy bien, gracias. ¿Y usted, señora López?

—_____

—Hasta luego, señora. Saludos al señor López.

—_____

Conversación 3

—_____

—Regular. ¿Y tú?

—_____

—Nada.

8

Conversaciones This is the first day of class. Write four short conversations based on what the people in this scene would say.

9

Situaciones With a partner, role-play these situations.

1. On your way to the library, you strike up a conversation with another student. You find out the student's name and where he or she is from before you say goodbye.
2. At the library you meet up with a friend and find out how he or she is doing.
3. As you're leaving the library, you see your friend's father, Mr. Sánchez. You say hello and send greetings to Mrs. Sánchez.
4. Make up a real-life situation that you and your partner can role-play with the language you've learned.

Bienvenida, Marissa

Marissa llega a México para pasar un año con la familia Díaz.

PERSONAJES MARISSA SRA. DÍAZ

MARISSA ¿Usted es de Cuba?

SRA. DÍAZ Sí, de La Habana. Y Roberto es de Mérida. Tú eres de Wisconsin, ¿verdad?

MARISSA Sí, de Appleton, Wisconsin.

MARISSA ¿Quiénes son los dos chicos de las fotos? ¿Jimena y Felipe?

SRA. DÍAZ Sí. Ellos son estudiantes.

DON DIEGO ¿Cómo está usted hoy, señora Carolina?

SRA. DÍAZ Muy bien, gracias. ¿Y usted?

DON DIEGO Bien, gracias.

DON DIEGO Buenas tardes, señora. Señorita, bienvenida a la Ciudad de México.

MARISSA ¡Muchas gracias!

MARISSA ¿Cómo se llama usted?

DON DIEGO Yo soy Diego. Mucho gusto.

MARISSA El gusto es mío, don Diego.

SRA. DÍAZ Ahí hay dos maletas. Son de Marissa.

DON DIEGO Con permiso.

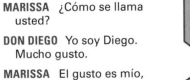

DON DIEGO **SR. DÍAZ** **FELIPE** **JIMENA**

SR. DÍAZ ¿Qué hora es?

FELIPE Son las cuatro y veinticinco.

SRA. DÍAZ Marissa, te presento a Roberto, mi esposo.

SR. DÍAZ Bienvenida, Marissa.

MARISSA Gracias, señor Díaz.

JIMENA ¿Qué hay en esta cosa?

MARISSA Bueno, a ver, hay tres cuadernos, un mapa... ¡Y un diccionario!

JIMENA ¿Cómo se dice mediodía en inglés?

FELIPE "Noon".

FELIPE Estás en México, ¿verdad?

MARISSA ¿Sí?

FELIPE Nosotros somos tu diccionario.

Expresiones útiles

Identifying yourself and others

¿Cómo se llama usted?
What's your name?

Yo soy Diego, el portero. Mucho gusto.
I'm Diego, the doorman. Nice to meet you.

¿Cómo te llamas?
What's your name?

Me llamo Marissa.
My name is Marissa.

¿Quién es...? / ¿Quiénes son...?
Who is...? / Who are...?

Es mi esposo.
He's my husband.

Tú eres..., ¿verdad?/¿cierto?/¿no?
You are..., right?

Identifying objects

¿Qué hay en esta cosa?
What's in this thing?

Bueno, a ver, aquí hay tres cuadernos...
Well, let's see, here are three notebooks...

Oye/Oiga, ¿cómo se dice *suitcase* en español?
Hey, how do you say suitcase in Spanish?

Se dice *maleta*.
You say maleta.

Saying what time it is

¿Qué hora es?
What time is it?

Es la una. / Son las dos.
It's one o'clock. / It's two o'clock.

Son las cuatro y veinticinco.
It's four twenty-five.

Polite expressions

Con permiso.
*Pardon me; Excuse me.
(to request permission)*

Perdón.
Pardon me; Excuse me. (to get someone's attention or excuse yourself)

¡Bienvenido/a! *Welcome!*

¿Qué pasó?

1 **¿Cierto o falso?** Indicate if each statement is **cierto** or **falso**. Then correct the false statements.

	Cierto	Falso
1. La Sra. Díaz es de Caracas.	○	○
2. El Sr. Díaz es de Mérida.	○	○
3. Marissa es de Los Ángeles, California.	○	○
4. Jimena y Felipe son profesores.	○	○
5. Las dos maletas son de Jimena.	○	○
6. El Sr. Díaz pregunta "¿qué hora es?".	○	○
7. Hay un diccionario en la mochila (*backpack*) de Marissa.	○	○

2 **Identificar** Indicate which person would make each statement. One name will be used twice.

1. Son las cuatro y veinticinco, papá.
2. Roberto es mi esposo.
3. Yo soy de Wisconsin, ¿de dónde es usted?
4. ¿Qué hay de nuevo, doña Carolina?
5. Yo soy de Cuba.
6. ¿Qué hay en la mochila, Marissa?

MARISSA   **FELIPE**   **SRA. DÍAZ**

DON DIEGO   **JIMENA**

3 **Completar** Complete the conversation between Don Diego and Marissa.

DON DIEGO Hola, (1)_____.

MARISSA Hola, señor. ¿Cómo se (2)_____ usted?

DON DIEGO Yo me llamo Diego, ¿y (3)_____?

MARISSA Yo me llamo Marissa. (4)_____.

DON DIEGO (5)_____, señorita Marissa.

MARISSA Nos (6)_____, don Diego.

DON DIEGO Hasta (7)_____, señorita Marissa.

4 **Conversar** Imagine that you are chatting with a traveler you just met at the airport. With a partner, prepare a conversation using these cues.

Estudiante 1	Estudiante 2
Say "good afternoon" to your partner and ask for his or her name.	Say hello and what your name is. Then ask what your partner's name is.
Say what your name is and that you are glad to meet your partner.	Say that the pleasure is yours.
Ask how your partner is.	Say that you're doing well, thank you.
Ask where your partner is from.	Say where you're from.
Say it's one o'clock and say goodbye.	Say goodbye.

Pronunciación

The Spanish alphabet

The Spanish and English alphabets are almost identical, with a few exceptions. For example, the Spanish letter **ñ (eñe)** doesn't occur in the English alphabet. Furthermore, the letters **k (ka)** and **w (doble ve)** are used only in words of foreign origin. Examine the chart below to find other differences.

¡LENGUA VIVA!

Note that **ch** and **ll** are digraphs, or two letters that together produce one sound. Conventionally they have been considered part of the alphabet, but **ch** and **ll** do not have their own entries when placing words in alphabetical order, as in a glossary.

Letra	Nombre(s)	Ejemplos	Letra	Nombre(s)	Ejemplos
a	a	adiós	m	eme	mapa
b	be	bien, problema	n	ene	nacionalidad
c	ce	cosa, cero	ñ	eñe	mañana
ch	che	chico	o	o	once
d	de	diario, nada	p	pe	profesor
e	e	estudiante	q	cu	qué
f	efe	foto	r	ere	regular, señora
g	ge	gracias, Gerardo, regular	s	ese	señor
h	hache	hola	t	te	tú
i	i	igualmente	u	u	usted
j	jota	Javier	v	ve	vista, nuevo
k	ka, ca	kilómetro	w	doble ve	walkman
l	ele	lápiz	x	equis	existir, México
ll	elle	llave	y	i griega, ye	yo
			z	zeta, ceta	zona

El alfabeto Repeat the Spanish alphabet and example words after your instructor.

AYUDA

The letter combination **rr** produces a strong trilled sound which does not have an English equivalent. English speakers commonly make this sound when imitating the sound of a motor. This sound occurs with the **rr** between vowels and with the **r** at the beginning of a word: **puertorriqueño, terrible, Roberto,** etc. See **Lección 7,** p. 233 for more information.

Práctica Spell these words aloud in Spanish.

1. nada
2. maleta
3. quince
4. muy
5. hombre
6. por favor
7. San Fernando
8. Estados Unidos
9. Puerto Rico
10. España
11. Javier
12. Ecuador
13. Maite
14. gracias
15. Nueva York

Refranes Read these sayings aloud

Ver es creer.[1]

En boca cerrada no entran moscas.[2]

1 Seeing is believing.
2 Silence is golden.

EN DETALLE

Saludos y besos en los países hispanos

In Spanish-speaking countries, kissing on the cheek is a customary way to greet friends and family members. Even when people are introduced for the first time, it is common for them to kiss, particularly in non-business settings. Whereas North Americans maintain considerable personal space when greeting, Spaniards and Latin Americans tend to decrease their personal space and give one or two kisses (**besos**) on the cheek, sometimes accompanied by a handshake or a hug. In formal business settings, where associates do not know one another on a personal level, a simple handshake is appropriate.

Greeting someone with a **beso** varies according to gender and region. Men generally greet each other with a hug or warm handshake, with the exception of Argentina, where male friends and relatives lightly kiss on the cheek. Greetings between men and women, and between women, generally include kissing, but can differ depending on the country and context. In Spain, it is customary to give **dos besos**, starting with the right cheek first. In Latin American countries, including Mexico, Costa Rica, Colombia, and Chile, a greeting consists of a single "air kiss" on the right cheek. Peruvians also "air kiss," but

strangers will simply shake hands. In Colombia, female acquaintances tend to simply pat each other on the right forearm or shoulder.

Tendencias

País	Beso	País	Beso
Argentina	💋	España	💋💋
Bolivia	💋	México	💋
Chile	💋	Paraguay	💋💋
Colombia	💋	Puerto Rico	💋
El Salvador	💋	Venezuela	💋/💋💋

ACTIVIDADES

1 **¿Cierto o falso?** Indicate whether these statements are true (**cierto**) or false (**falso**). Correct the false statements.

1. In Spanish-speaking countries, people use less personal space when greeting than in the U.S.
2. Men never greet with a kiss in Spanish-speaking countries.
3. Shaking hands is not appropriate for a business setting in Latin America.
4. Spaniards greet with one kiss on the right cheek
5. In Mexico, people greet with an "air kiss."
6. Gender can play a role in the type of greeting given.
7. If two women acquaintances meet in Colombia, they should exchange two kisses on the cheek.
8. In Peru, a man and a woman meeting for the first time would probably greet each other with an "air kiss."

Saludos y despedidas

¿Cómo te/le va?	How are things going (for you)?
¡Cuánto tiempo!	It's been a long time!
Hasta ahora.	See you soon.
¿Qué hay?	What's new?
¿Qué onda? (Méx., Arg., Chi.); ¿Qué más? (Ven., Col.)	What's going on?

Parejas y amigos famosos

Here are some famous couples and friends from the Spanish-speaking world.

- **Penélope Cruz** (España) y **Javier Bardem** (España) Both Oscar-winning actors, the couple married in 2010. They starred together in *Vicky Cristina Barcelona* (2008).

- **Gael García Bernal** (México) y **Diego Luna** (México) These lifelong friends became famous when they starred in the 2001 Mexican film *Y tu mamá también*. They continue to work together on projects, such as the 2012 film *Casa de mi padre.*

- **Salma Hayek** (México) y **Penélope Cruz** (España) These two close friends developed their acting skills in their home countries before meeting in Hollywood.

La plaza principal

In the Spanish-speaking world, public space is treasured. Small city and town life revolves around the **plaza principal**. Often surrounded by cathedrals or municipal buildings like the **ayuntamiento** (*city hall*), the pedestrian **plaza** is designated as a central meeting place for family and friends. During warmer months, when outdoor cafés usually line the **plaza**, it is

La Plaza Mayor de Salamanca

a popular spot to have a leisurely cup of coffee, chat, and people watch. Many town festivals, or **ferias**, also take place in this space. One of the most famous town squares

is the **Plaza Mayor** in the university town of Salamanca, Spain. Students gather underneath its famous clock tower to meet up with friends or simply take a coffee break.

La Plaza de Armas, Lima, Perú

Conexión Internet

What are the **plazas principales** in large cities such as Mexico City and Caracas?

Use the Web to find more cultural information related to this **Cultura** section.

2 Comprensión Answer these questions.
1. What are two types of buildings found on the **plaza principal**?
2. What two types of events or activities are common at a **plaza principal?**
3. How would Diego Luna greet his friends?
4. Would Salma Hayek and Gael García Bernal greet each other with one kiss or two?

3 Saludos Role-play these greetings with a partner.

1. friends in Mexico
2. business associates at a conference in Chile
3. friends meeting in Madrid's Plaza Mayor
4. Peruvians meeting for the first time
5. relatives in Argentina

1.1 Nouns and articles

Spanish nouns

ANTE TODO A noun is a word used to identify people, animals, places, things, or ideas. Unlike English, all Spanish nouns, even those that refer to non-living things, have gender; that is, they are considered either masculine or feminine. As in English, nouns in Spanish also have number, meaning that they are either singular or plural.

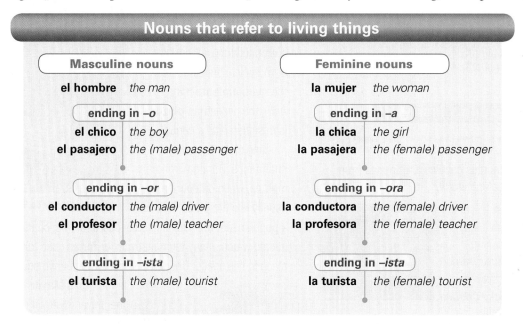

Nouns that refer to living things

Masculine nouns		Feminine nouns	
el hombre	*the man*	**la mujer**	*the woman*
ending in –o		*ending in –a*	
el chico	*the boy*	**la chica**	*the girl*
el pasajero	*the (male) passenger*	**la pasajera**	*the (female) passenger*
ending in –or		*ending in –ora*	
el conductor	*the (male) driver*	**la conductora**	*the (female) driver*
el profesor	*the (male) teacher*	**la profesora**	*the (female) teacher*
ending in –ista		*ending in –ista*	
el turista	*the (male) tourist*	**la turista**	*the (female) tourist*

▶ Generally, nouns that refer to males, like **el hombre**, are masculine, while nouns that refer to females, like **la mujer**, are feminine.

▶ Many nouns that refer to male beings end in **–o** or **–or**. Their corresponding feminine forms end in **–a** and **–ora**, respectively.

el conductor

la profesora

▶ The masculine and feminine forms of nouns that end in **–ista**, like **turista**, are the same, so gender is indicated by the article **el** (masculine) or **la** (feminine). Some other nouns have identical masculine and feminine forms.

el joven	**la** joven
the young man	*the young woman*
el estudiante	**la** estudiante
the (male) student	*the (female) student*

Nouns that refer to non-living things

Masculine nouns		Feminine nouns	
ending in –o		**ending in –a**	
el cuaderno	the notebook	la computadora	the computer
el diario	the diary	la cosa	the thing
el diccionario	the dictionary	la escuela	the school
el número	the number	la maleta	the suitcase
el video	the video	la palabra	the word
ending in –ma		**ending in –ción**	
el problema	the problem	la lección	the lesson
el programa	the program	la conversación	the conversation
ending in –s		**ending in –dad**	
el autobús	the bus	la nacionalidad	the nationality
el país	the country	la comunidad	the community

¡LENGUA VIVA!

The Spanish word for *video* can be pronounced with the stress on the **i** or the **e**. For that reason, you might see the word written with or without an accent: **video** or **vídeo**.

▶ As shown above, certain noun endings are strongly associated with a specific gender, so you can use them to determine if a noun is masculine or feminine.

▶ Because the gender of nouns that refer to non-living things cannot be determined by foolproof rules, you should memorize the gender of each noun you learn. It is helpful to learn each noun with its corresponding article, **el** for masculine and **la** for feminine.

▶ Another reason to memorize the gender of every noun is that there are common exceptions to the rules of gender. For example, **el mapa** (*map*) and **el día** (*day*) end in **–a**, but are masculine. **La mano** (*hand*) ends in **–o**, but is feminine.

Plural of nouns

▶ To form the plural, add **–s** to nouns that end in a vowel. For nouns that end in a consonant, add **–es**. For nouns that end in **z**, change the **z** to **c**, then add **–es**.

el chic**o** ⟶ los chic**os**   la nacionalida**d** ⟶ las nacionalida**des**

el diari**o** ⟶ los diari**os**   el paí**s** ⟶ los paí**ses**

el problem**a** ⟶ los problem**as**   el lápi**z** (*pencil*) ⟶ los lápi**ces**

CONSULTA

You will learn more about accent marks in **Lección 4, Pronunciación**, p. 123.

▶ In general, when a singular noun has an accent mark on the last syllable, the accent is dropped from the plural form.

la lecci**ón** ⟶ las lecci**ones**   el autob**ús** ⟶ los autob**uses**

▶ Use the masculine plural form to refer to a group that includes both males and females.

1 pasajer**o** + 2 pasajer**as** = 3 pasajer**os**   2 chic**os** + 2 chic**as** = 4 chic**os**

Spanish articles

ANTE TODO As you know, English often uses definite articles (*the*) and indefinite articles (*a, an*) before nouns. Spanish also has definite and indefinite articles. Unlike English, Spanish articles vary in form because they agree in gender and number with the nouns they modify.

Definite articles

▶ Spanish has four forms that are equivalent to the English definite article *the*. Use definite articles to refer to specific nouns.

Masculine		**Feminine**	
SINGULAR	PLURAL	SINGULAR	PLURAL
el diccionario	**los** diccionarios	**la** computadora	**las** computadoras
the dictionary	*the dictionaries*	*the computer*	*the computers*

Indefinite articles

▶ Spanish has four forms that are equivalent to the English indefinite article, which according to context may mean *a, an,* or *some*. Use indefinite articles to refer to unspecified persons or things.

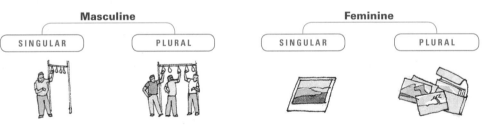

Masculine		**Feminine**	
SINGULAR	PLURAL	SINGULAR	PLURAL
un pasajero	**unos** pasajeros	**una** fotografía	**unas** fotografías
a (one) passenger	*some passengers*	*a (one) photograph*	*some photographs*

¡INTÉNTALO! Provide a definite article for each noun in the first column and an indefinite article for each noun in the second column.

¿el, la, los o las?

1. ___la___ chica
2. _____ chico
3. _____ maleta
4. _____ cuadernos
5. _____ lápiz
6. _____ mujeres

¿un, una, unos o unas?

1. ___un___ autobús
2. _____ escuelas
3. _____ computadora
4. _____ hombres
5. _____ señora
6. _____ lápices

Práctica

1 **¿Singular o plural?** If the word is singular, make it plural. If it is plural, make it singular.

1. el número
2. un diario
3. la estudiante
4. el conductor
5. el país
6. las cosas
7. unos turistas
8. las nacionalidades
9. unas computadoras
10. los problemas
11. una fotografía
12. los profesores
13. unas señoritas
14. el hombre
15. la maleta
16. la señora

2 **Identificar** For each drawing, provide the noun with its corresponding definite and indefinite articles.

modelo
las maletas, unas maletas

1. _____
2. _____

3. _____
4. _____
5. _____

6. _____
7. _____
8. _____

Comunicación

3 **Un juego** With a partner, play a game in which one of you names a noun and the other says a related noun (**un chico; un estudiante**). Keep the chain going until one of you can't think of another noun.

1.2 Numbers 0–30

Los números 0 a 30					
0	cero				
1	uno	**11**	once	**21**	veintiuno
2	dos	**12**	doce	**22**	veintidós
3	tres	**13**	trece	**23**	veintitrés
4	cuatro	**14**	catorce	**24**	veinticuatro
5	cinco	**15**	quince	**25**	veinticinco
6	seis	**16**	dieciséis	**26**	veintiséis
7	siete	**17**	diecisiete	**27**	veintisiete
8	ocho	**18**	dieciocho	**28**	veintiocho
9	nueve	**19**	diecinueve	**29**	veintinueve
10	diez	**20**	veinte	**30**	treinta

AYUDA

Though it is less common, the numbers 16 through 29 (except 20) can also be written as three words: **diez y seis, diez y siete…**

▶ The number **uno** (*one*) and numbers ending in **–uno**, such as **veintiuno**, have more than one form. Before masculine nouns, **uno** shortens to **un**. Before feminine nouns, **uno** changes to **una**.

un hombre ⟶ veinti**ún** hombres   **una** mujer ⟶ veinti**una** mujeres

▶ **¡Atención!** The forms **uno** and **veintiuno** are used when counting (**uno, dos, tres… veinte, veintiuno, veintidós…**). They are also used when the number *follows* a noun, even if the noun is feminine: **la lección uno**.

▶ To ask *how many people* or *things* there are, use **cuántos** before masculine nouns and **cuántas** before feminine nouns.

▶ The Spanish equivalent of both *there is* and *there are* is **hay**. Use **¿Hay…?** to ask *Is there…?* or *Are there…?* Use **no hay** to express *there is not* or *there are not*.

—**¿Cuántos** estudiantes **hay**?
How many students are there?

—**¿Hay** chicos en la fotografía?
Are there guys in the picture?

—**Hay** seis estudiantes en la foto.
There are six students in the photo.

—**Hay** tres chicas y **no hay** chicos.
There are three girls, and there are no guys.

¡INTÉNTALO! Provide the Spanish words for these numbers.

1. **7** _____
2. **16** _____
3. **29** _____
4. **1** _____

5. **0** _____
6. **15** _____
7. **21** _____
8. **9** _____

9. **23** _____
10. **11** _____
11. **30** _____
12. **4** _____

13. **12** _____
14. **28** _____
15. **14** _____
16. **10** _____

Práctica

1 **Contar** Following the pattern, write out the missing numbers in Spanish.

1. 1, 3, 5, ..., 29
2. 2, 4, 6, ..., 30
3. 3, 6, 9, ..., 30
4. 30, 28, 26, ..., 0
5. 30, 25, 20, ..., 0
6. 28, 24, 20, ..., 0

2 **Resolver** Solve these math problems.

modelo
5 + 3 =
Cinco más tres son ocho.

AYUDA

+ → más
– → menos
= → son

1. **2 + 15 =**
2. **20 – 1 =**
3. **5 + 7 =**
4. **18 + 12 =**
5. **3 + 22 =**

6. **6 – 3 =**
7. **11 + 12 =**
8. **7 – 2 =**
9. **8 + 5 =**
10. **23 – 14 =**

3 **¿Cuántos hay?** How many persons or things are there in these drawings?

modelo
Hay tres maletas.

1. _____ 2. _____

3. _____ 4. _____ 5. _____

6. _____ 7. _____ 8. _____

Comunicación

4

¿Cuántos? Answer your partner's questions about the place where you study.

1. ¿Cuántos estudiantes hay?
2. ¿Hay un video?
3. ¿Hay una computadora?
4. ¿Hay una maleta?
5. ¿Cuántos mapas hay?

6. ¿Cuántos lápices hay?
7. ¿Hay cuadernos?
8. ¿Cuántos diccionarios hay?
9. ¿Hay un diario?
10. ¿Cuántas fotografías hay?

5

Preguntas With a partner, take turns asking and answering questions about the drawing. Talk about:

1. how many children there are
2. how many women there are
3. if there are some photographs
4. if there is a boy
5. how many notebooks there are

6. if there is a bus
7. if there are tourists
8. how many pencils there are
9. if there is a man
10. how many computers there are

1.3 | Present tense of ser

Subject pronouns

ANTE TODO In order to use verbs, you will need to learn about subject pronouns. A subject pronoun replaces the name or title of a person and acts as the subject of a verb.

Subject pronouns			
SINGULAR		**PLURAL**	
yo	*I*	**nosotros**	*we* (masculine)
		nosotras	*we* (feminine)
tú	*you* (familiar)	**vosotros**	*you* (masc., fam.)
usted (Ud.)	*you* (formal)	**vosotras**	*you* (fem., fam.)
		ustedes (Uds.)	*you*
él	*he*	**ellos**	*they* (masc.)
ella	*she*	**ellas**	*they* (fem.)

¡LENGUA VIVA!

In Latin America, **ustedes** is used as the plural for both **tú** and **usted**. In Spain, however, **vosotros** and **vosotras** are used as the plural of **tú**, and **ustedes** is used only as the plural of **usted**.

• • •

Usted and **ustedes** are abbreviated as **Ud.** and **Uds.**, or occasionally as **Vd.** and **Vds.**

▶ Spanish has two subject pronouns that mean *you* (singular). Use **tú** when addressing a friend, a family member, or a child you know well. Use **usted** to address a person with whom you have a formal or more distant relationship, such as a superior at work, a professor, or an older person.

Tú eres de Canadá, ¿verdad, David?   **¿Usted** es la profesora de español?
You are from Canada, right, David?   *Are you the Spanish professor?*

▶ The masculine plural forms **nosotros**, **vosotros**, and **ellos** refer to a group of males or to a group of males and females. The feminine plural forms **nosotras**, **vosotras**, and **ellas** can refer only to groups made up exclusively of females.

nosotros, vosotros, ellos

nosotros, vosotros, ellos

nosotras, vosotras, ellas

▶ There is no Spanish equivalent of the English subject pronoun *it*. Generally *it* is not expressed in Spanish.

Es un problema.   Es una computadora.
It's a problem.   *It's a computer.*

The present tense of ser

ANTE TODO In **Contextos** and **Fotonovela**, you have already used several present-tense forms of **ser** (*to be*) to identify yourself and others, and to talk about where you and others are from. **Ser** is an irregular verb; its forms do not follow the regular patterns that most verbs follow. You need to memorize the forms, which appear in this chart.

The verb ser (*to be*)		
SINGULAR FORMS		
yo	**soy**	*I am*
tú	**eres**	*you are* (fam.)
Ud./él/ella	**es**	*you are* (form.); *he/she is*
PLURAL FORMS		
nosotros/as	**somos**	*we are*
vosotros/as	**sois**	*you are* (fam.)
Uds./ellos/ellas	**son**	*you are; they are*

Uses of *ser*

▶ Use **ser** to identify people and things.

—¿Quién **es** él?
Who is he?

—**Es** Felipe Díaz Velázquez.
He's Felipe Díaz Velázquez.

—¿Qué **es**?
What is it?

—**Es** un mapa de España.
It's a map of Spain.

Es Marissa.

Es una maleta.

▶ **Ser** also expresses possession, with the preposition **de**. There is no Spanish equivalent of the English construction [*noun*] + 's (*Maru's*). In its place, Spanish uses [*noun*] + **de** + [*owner*].

—¿**De** quién **es**?
Whose is it?

—**Es** el diario **de** Maru.
It's Maru's diary.

—¿**De** quién **son**?
Whose are they?

—**Son** los lápices **de** la chica.
They are the girl's pencils.

▶ When **de** is followed by the article **el**, the two combine to form the contraction **del**. **De** does *not* contract with **la**, **las**, or **los**.

—**Es** la computadora **del** conductor.
It's the driver's computer.

—**Son** las maletas **del** chico.
They are the boy's suitcases.

▶ **Ser** also uses the preposition **de** to express origin.

¿De dónde eres?

Yo soy de Wisconsin.

¿De dónde es usted?

Yo soy de Cuba.

—¿**De** dónde **es** Juan Carlos?
Where is Juan Carlos from?

—Es **de** Argentina.
He's from Argentina.

—¿**De** dónde **es** Maru?
Where is Maru from?

—**Es de** Costa Rica.
She's from Costa Rica.

▶ Use **ser** to express profession or occupation.

Don Francisco **es conductor**.
Don Francisco is a driver.

Yo **soy estudiante**.
I am a student.

▶ Unlike English, Spanish does not use the indefinite article (**un**, **una**) after **ser** when referring to professions, unless accompanied by an adjective or other description.

Marta **es** profesora.
Marta is a teacher.

Marta **es una** profesora excelente.
Marta is an excellent teacher.

Somos Perú

LanPerú

¡LENGUA VIVA!

Some geographic locations can be referred to either with or without a definite article:
Soy de Estados Unidos./Soy de los Estados Unidos.

• • •

Sometimes a definite article is a part of a proper name, as in **El Salvador, El Paso,** and **Los Ángeles**. In these cases, **de** and **el** do not contract:
Soy de El Salvador.

CONSULTA

You will learn more about adjectives in **Estructura 3.1**, pp. 88–90.

NOTA CULTURAL

Created in 1998, LAN Perú is an affiliate of the Chilean-based LAN Airlines, one of the largest carriers in South America. LAN Perú operates out of Lima, offering domestic flights and international service to select major cities in the Americas and Spain.

¡INTÉNTALO! Provide the correct subject pronouns and the present forms of **ser**.

1. Gabriel　_él_　_es_
2. Juan y yo　_____ _____
3. Óscar y Flora　_____ _____
4. Adriana　_____ _____
5. las turistas　_____ _____
6. el chico　_____ _____
7. los conductores　_____ _____
8. los señores Ruiz　_____ _____

Práctica

1 **Pronombres** What subject pronouns would you use to (a) talk *to* these people directly and (b) talk *about* them to others?

modelo

un joven   tú, él

1. una chica
2. el presidente de México
3. tres chicas y un chico

4. un estudiante
5. la señora Ochoa
6. dos profesoras

2 **Identidad y origen** Answer these questions about the people indicated: **¿Quién es?/¿Quiénes son?** and **¿De dónde es?/¿De dónde son?**

modelo

Selena Gomez (Estados Unidos)
¿Quién es?   ¿De dónde es?
Es Selena Gomez.   Es de los Estados Unidos.

1. Enrique Iglesias (España)

2. Robinson Canó (República Dominicana)

3. Eva Mendes y Marc Anthony (Estados Unidos)

4. Carlos Santana y Salma Hayek (México)

5. Shakira (Colombia)

6. Antonio Banderas y Penélope Cruz (España)

7. Taylor Swift y Demi Lovato (Estados Unidos)

8. Daisy Fuentes (Cuba)

3 **¿Qué es?** Indicate what each object is and to whom it belongs.

modelo

¿Qué es?   ¿De quién es?
Es un diccionario.   Es del profesor Núñez.

1.   2.   3.   4.

Comunicación

4

La clase Read Stephanie's description of one of her classes. Then indicate whether the following conclusions are **lógico** or **ilógico**, based on what you read.

> Yo soy Stephanie. Soy estudiante de la clase de la señora Rodríguez. Ella es de Uruguay y yo soy de los Estados Unidos. En la clase de la señora Rodríguez hay diez diccionarios de español y una computadora. Los diccionarios son de los estudiantes y la computadora es de la señora Rodríguez.

	Lógico	Ilógico
1. La señora Rodríguez es profesora.	○	○
2. Stephanie es de Madrid.	○	○
3. Es una clase de español.	○	○
4. Hay dos estudiantes en la clase.	○	○
5. La señora Rodríguez es de Miami.	○	○

5

Famosos Describe several famous people using the vocabulary and grammar you have learned. Use the list of professions to think of people from a variety of backgrounds.

actor *actor*	cantante *singer*	escritor(a) *writer*
actriz *actress*	deportista *athlete*	músico/a *musician*

modelo

> John Leguizamo es actor. Es de Colombia...

6

Preguntas Using the items in the word bank, ask your partner questions about the ad.

¿Cuántas?	¿De dónde?	¿Qué?
¿Cuántos?	¿De quién?	¿Quién?

SOMOS ECOTURISTA, S.A.
Los autobuses oficiales de la Ruta Maya

- 25 autobuses en total
- 30 conductores del área
- pasajeros internacionales
- mapas de la región

¡Todos a bordo!

1.4 # Telling time

ANTE TODO In both English and Spanish, the verb *to be* (**ser**) and numbers are used to tell time.

▶ To ask what time it is, use **¿Qué hora es?** When telling time, use **es + la** with **una** and **son + las** with all other hours.

Es la una.

Son las dos.

Son las seis.

▶ As in English, you express time in Spanish from the hour to the half hour by adding minutes.

Son las cuatro **y cinco**.

Son las once **y veinte**.

▶ You may use either **y cuarto** or **y quince** to express fifteen minutes or quarter past the hour. For thirty minutes or half past the hour, you may use either **y media** or **y treinta**.

Es la una **y cuarto**.

Son las nueve **y quince**.

Son las doce **y media**.
Son las siete **y treinta**.

▶ You express time from the half hour to the hour in Spanish by subtracting minutes or a portion of an hour from the next hour.

Es la una **menos cuarto**.

Son las tres **menos quince**.

Son las ocho **menos veinte**.

Son las tres **menos diez**.

▶ To ask at what time a particular event takes place, use the phrase **¿A qué hora (...)?** To state at what time something takes place, use the construction **a la(s)** + *time*.

¿A qué hora es la clase de biología?	La clase es **a las dos**.
(At) what time is biology class?	*The class is at two o'clock.*
¿A qué hora es la fiesta?	**A las ocho**.
(At) what time is the party?	*At eight.*

▶ Here are some useful words and phrases associated with telling time.

Son las ocho **en punto**.	Son las nueve **de la mañana**.
It's 8 o'clock on the dot/sharp.	*It's 9 a.m./in the morning.*
Es **el mediodía**.	Son las cuatro y cuarto **de la tarde**.
It's noon.	*It's 4:15 p.m./in the afternoon.*
Es **la medianoche**.	Son las diez y media **de la noche**.
It's midnight.	*It's 10:30 p.m./at night.*

¿Qué hora es?

Son las cuatro menos diez.

¿Qué hora es?

Son las cuatro y veinticinco.

¡INTÉNTALO!   Practice telling time by completing these sentences.

1. (1:00 a.m.) Es la _____una_____ de la mañana.
2. (2:50 a.m.) Son las tres _____ diez de la mañana.
3. (4:15 p.m.) Son las cuatro y _____ de la tarde.
4. (8:30 p.m.) Son las ocho y _____ de la noche.
5. (9:15 a.m.) Son las nueve y quince de la _____.
6. (12:00 p.m.) Es el _____.
7. (6:00 a.m.) Son las seis de la _____.
8. (4:05 p.m.) Son las cuatro y cinco de la _____.
9. (12:00 a.m.) Es la _____.
10. (3:45 a.m.) Son las cuatro menos _____ de la mañana.
11. (2:15 a.m.) Son las _____ y cuarto de la mañana.
12. (1:25 p.m.) Es la una y _____ de la tarde.
13. (6:50 a.m.) Son las _____ menos diez de la mañana.
14. (10:40 p.m.) Son las once menos veinte de la _____.

Práctica

1

Ordenar Put these times in order, from the earliest to the latest.

a. Son las dos de la tarde.
b. Son las once de la mañana.
c. Son las siete y media de la noche.
d. Son las seis menos cuarto de la tarde.
e. Son las dos menos diez de la tarde.
f. Son las ocho y veintidós de la mañana.

2

¿Qué hora es? Give the times shown on each clock or watch.

> *modelo*
> *Son las cuatro y cuarto/quince de la tarde.*

NOTA CULTURAL

Many Spanish-speaking countries use both the 12-hour clock and the 24-hour clock (that is, military time). The 24-hour clock is commonly used in written form on signs and schedules. For example, 1 p.m. is **13h**, 2 p.m. is **14h** and so on. See the photo on p. 33 for a sample schedule.

p.m.   p.m.   p.m.   a.m.

1. _____ 2. _____ 3. _____ 4. _____ 5. _____

a.m.   p.m.   a.m.   p.m.

6. _____ 7. _____ 8. _____ 9. _____ 10. _____

3

¿A qué hora? Indicate at what time these events take place.

> *modelo*
> la clase de matemáticas (2:30 p.m.)
> *La clase de matemáticas es a las dos y media de la tarde.*

1. el programa *Las cuatro amigas* (11:30 a.m.)
2. el drama *La casa de Bernarda Alba* (7:00 p.m.)
3. el programa *Las computadoras* (8:30 a.m.)
4. la clase de español (10:30 a.m.)
5. la clase de biología (9:40 a.m.)
6. la clase de historia (10:50 a.m.)
7. el partido (game) de béisbol (5:15 p.m.)
8. el partido de tenis (12:45 p.m.)
9. el partido de baloncesto (basketball) (7:45 p.m.)

NOTA CULTURAL

La casa de Bernarda Alba is a famous play by Spanish poet and playwright **Federico García Lorca** (1898–1936). Lorca was one of the most famous writers of the 20th century and a close friend of Spain's most talented artists, including the painter Salvador Dalí and the filmmaker Luis Buñuel.

Comunicación

4

Escuchar Listen to Laura and David talk about their schedules for the day. Then indicate whether the following conclusions are **lógico** or **ilógico**, based on what you heard.

		Lógico	Ilógico
1.	La clase es a las once y media de la mañana.	○	○
2.	Son las once y cuarto de la noche.	○	○
3.	La fiesta es a las nueve de la noche.	○	○
4.	Rafael es estudiante.	○	○

5

Preguntas Answer your partner's questions based on your own knowledge.

1. Son las tres de la tarde en Nueva York. ¿Qué hora es en Los Ángeles?

2. Son las ocho y media en Chicago. ¿Qué hora es en Miami?

3. Son las dos menos cinco en San Francisco. ¿Qué hora es en San Antonio?

4. ¿A qué hora es el programa *Saturday Night Live*?; ¿A qué hora es el programa *American Idol*?

6

Horas Write sentences about the times that your favorite TV shows are on. Mention at least three shows.

Síntesis

7

Situación With a partner, play the roles of a journalism student interviewing a visiting literature professor (**profesor(a) de literatura**) from Venezuela.

Estudiante	Profesor(a) de literatura
Ask the professor his/her name.	→ Ask the student his/her name.
Ask the professor what time his/her literature class is.	→ Ask the student where he/she is from.
Ask how many students are in his/her class.	→ Ask to whom the notebook belongs.
Say thank you and goodbye.	→ Say thank you and you are pleased to meet him/her.

Recapitulación

SUBJECT ↓ Javier   CONJUGATED FORM empiezo   Main clause   Dudan

Review the grammar concepts you have learned in this lesson by completing these activities.

1   **Completar** Complete the charts according to the models. **28 pts.**

Masculino	Femenino
el chico	la chica
	la profesora
	la amiga
el señor	
	la pasajera
el estudiante	
	la turista
el joven	

Singular	Plural
una cosa	unas cosas
un libro	
	unas clases
una lección	
un conductor	
	unos países
	unos lápices
un problema	

2   **En la clase** Complete each conversation with the correct word. **22 pts.**

 César   Beatriz

CÉSAR   ¿(1) _____ (Cuántos/Cuántas) chicas hay en la (2) _____ (maleta/clase)?

BEATRIZ   Hay (3) _____ (catorce/cuatro) [*14*] chicas.

CÉSAR   Y, ¿(4) _____ (cuántos/cuántas) chicos hay?

BEATRIZ   Hay (5) _____ (tres/trece) [*13*] chicos.

CÉSAR   Entonces (*Then*), en total hay (6) _____ (veintiséis/veintisiete) (7) _____ (estudiantes/chicas) en la clase.

 Ariana   Daniel

ARIANA   ¿Tienes (*Do you have*) (8) _____ (un/una) diccionario?

DANIEL   No, pero (*but*) aquí (9) _____ (es/hay) uno.

ARIANA   ¿De quién (10) _____ (son/es)?

DANIEL   (11) _____ (Son/Es) de Carlos.

RESUMEN GRAMATICAL

1.1   **Nouns and articles**   *pp. 12–14*

Gender of nouns

Nouns that refer to living things

	Masculine		Feminine
-o	el chico	-a	la chica
-or	el profesor	-ora	la profesora
-ista	el turista	-ista	la turista

Nouns that refer to non-living things

	Masculine		Feminine
-o	el libro	-a	la cosa
-ma	el programa	-ción	la lección
-s	el autobús	-dad	la nacionalidad

Plural of nouns

▶ ending in vowel + *-s*   la chica → las chicas

▶ ending in consonant + *-es*   el señor → los señores

    (-z → -ces un lápiz → unos lápices)

▶ Definite articles: el, la, los, las

▶ Indefinite articles: un, una, unos, unas

1.2   **Numbers 0–30**   *p. 16*

0	cero	8	ocho	16	dieciséis
1	uno	9	nueve	17	diecisiete
2	dos	10	diez	18	dieciocho
3	tres	11	once	19	diecinueve
4	cuatro	12	doce	20	veinte
5	cinco	13	trece	21	veintiuno
6	seis	14	catorce	22	veintidós
7	siete	15	quince	30	treinta

1.3   **Present tense of *ser***   *pp. 19–21*

yo	soy	nosotros/as	somos
tú	eres	vosotros/as	sois
Ud./él/ella	es	Uds./ellos/ellas	son

3   **Presentaciones** Complete this conversation with the correct form of the verb **ser**. `18 pts.`

JUAN	¡Hola! Me llamo Juan. (1) _____ estudiante en la clase de español.
DANIELA	¡Hola! Mucho gusto. Yo (2) _____ Daniela y ella (3) _____ Mónica. ¿De dónde (4) _____ (tú), Juan?
JUAN	De California. Y ustedes, ¿de dónde (5) _____ ?
MÓNICA	Nosotras (6) _____ de Florida.

1.4   Telling time   *pp. 24–25*

Es la una.	*It's 1:00.*
Son las dos.	*It's 2:00.*
Son las tres y diez.	*It's 3:10.*
Es la una y cuarto/quince.	*It's 1:15.*
Son las siete y media/treinta.	*It's 7:30.*
Es la una menos cuarto/quince.	*It's 12:45.*
Son las once menos veinte.	*It's 10:40.*
Es el mediodía.	*It's noon.*
Es la medianoche.	*It's midnight.*

4   **¿Qué hora es?** Write out in words the following times, indicating whether it's morning, noon, afternoon, or night. `28 pts.`

1. It's 12:00 p.m.

_____

2. It's 7:05 a.m.

_____

3. It's 9:35 p.m.

_____

4. It's 5:15 p.m.

_____

5. It's 1:30 p.m.

_____

6. It's 11:50 a.m.

_____

7. It's 3:10 p.m.

_____

5   **Canción** Use the two appropriate words from the list to complete this children's song. `4 pts.`

cinco	cuántas	cuatro	media	quiénes

" _____ patas°
tiene un gato°?
Una, dos, tres y
_____ . "

patas *legs*   tiene un gato *does a cat have*

Lectura

Antes de leer

Estrategia
Recognizing cognates

As you learned earlier in this lesson, cognates are words that share similar meanings and spellings in two or more languages. When reading in Spanish, it's helpful to look for cognates and use them to guess the meaning of what you're reading. But watch out for false cognates. For example, **librería** means *bookstore*, not *library*, and **embarazada** means *pregnant*, not *embarrassed*. Look at this list of Spanish words, paying special attention to prefixes and suffixes. Can you guess the meaning of each word?

importante	oportunidad
farmacia	cultura
inteligente	activo
dentista	sociología
decisión	espectacular
televisión	restaurante
médico	policía

Examinar el texto
Glance quickly at the reading selection and guess what type of document it is. Explain your answer.

Cognados
Read the document and make a list of the cognates you find. Guess their English equivalents.

Joaquín Salvador Lavado nació (*was born*) en Argentina en 1932 (mil novecientos treinta y dos). Su nombre profesional es **Quino**. Es muy popular en Latinoamérica, Europa y Canadá por sus tiras cómicas (*comic strips*). Mafalda es su serie más famosa. La protagonista, Mafalda, es una chica muy inteligente de seis años (*years*). La tira cómica ilustra las aventuras de ella y su grupo de amigos. Las anécdotas de Mafalda y los chicos también presentan temas (*themes*) importantes como la paz (*peace*) y los derechos humanos (*human rights*).

Después de leer

Preguntas
Answer these questions.

1. What is Joaquín Salvador Lavado's pen name?
2. What is Mafalda like?
3. Where is Mafalda in panel 1? What is she doing?
4. What happens to the sheep in panel 3? Why?
5. Why does Mafalda wake up?
6. What number corresponds to the sheep in panel 5?
7. In panel 6, what is Mafalda doing? How do you know?

Los animales

This comic strip uses a device called onomatopoeia: a word that represents the sound that it stands for. Did you know that many common instances of onomatopoeia are different from language to language? The noise a sheep makes is *baaaah* in English, but in Mafalda's language it is **béeeee**. Do you think you can match these animals with their Spanish sounds? First, practice saying aloud each animal sound in group B. Then, match each animal with its sound in Spanish. If you need help remembering the sounds the alphabet makes in Spanish, see p. 9.

A

 1. ___ **gato**

 2. ___ **perro**

 3. ___ **vacas**

 4. ___ **gallo**

 5. ___ **rana**

 6. ___ **pato**

 7. ___ **cerdo**

B

a. kikirikí   b. muuu   c. croac   d. guau

e. cuac cuac   f. miau   g. oinc

Escritura

Estrategia
Writing in Spanish

Why do we write? All writing has a purpose. For example, we may write an e-mail to share important information or compose an essay to persuade others to accept a point of view. Proficient writers are not born, however. Writing requires time, thought, effort, and a lot of practice. Here are some tips to help you write more effectively in Spanish.

DO

▶ Try to write your ideas in Spanish

▶ Use the grammar and vocabulary that you know

▶ Use your textbook for examples of style, format, and expression in Spanish

▶ Use your imagination and creativity

▶ Put yourself in your reader's place to determine if your writing is interesting

AVOID

▶ Translating your ideas from English to Spanish

▶ Simply repeating what is in the textbook or on a web page

▶ Using a dictionary until you have learned how to use foreign language dictionaries

Tema

Hacer una lista

Create a telephone/address list that includes important names, numbers, and websites that will be helpful to you in your study of Spanish. Make whatever entries you can in Spanish without using a dictionary. You might want to include this information:

▶ The names, phone numbers, and e-mail addresses of at least four other students

▶ Your professor's name, e-mail address, and office hours

▶ Three phone numbers and e-mail addresses of campus offices or locations related to your study of Spanish

▶ Five electronic resources for students of Spanish, such as chat rooms and sites dedicated to the study of Spanish as a second language

Nombre _Sally (la chica de Indiana)_
Teléfono _655-8888_
Dirección electrónica _sally@uru.edu_

Nombre _Profesor José Ramón Casas_
Teléfono _655-8090_
Dirección electrónica _jrcasas@uru.edu_
Horas de oficina _12 a 12:30_

Nombre _Biblioteca_ _655-7000_
Dirección electrónica _library@uru.edu_

Escuchar

Estrategia

Listening for words you know

You can get the gist of a conversation by listening for words and phrases you already know.

 To help you practice this strategy, listen to the following sentence and make a list of the words you have already learned.

Preparación

Based on the photograph, what do you think Dr. Cavazos and Srta. Martínez are talking about? How would you get the gist of their conversation, based on what you know about Spanish?

Ahora escucha

Now you are going to hear Dr. Cavazos's conversation with Srta. Martínez. List the familiar words and phrases each person says.

Dr. Cavazos	Srta. Martínez
1. _____	9. _____
2. _____	10. _____
3. _____	11. _____
4. _____	12. _____
5. _____	13. _____
6. _____	14. _____
7. _____	15. _____
8. _____	16. _____

Use your lists of familiar words as a guide to come up with a summary of what happened in the conversation.

TRANSPORTES
ECUADOR
★★★ SERVICIO PREFERENCIAL ★★★

HORARIOS QUITO-GUAYAQUIL

MAÑANA	TARDE	NOCHE
4:50	12:50	19:20
5:50	14:05	20:20
6:50	15:05	21:20
8:00	16:20	21:50
8:50	17:40	22:20
9:20	18:40	22:40
10:20		23:20
11:50		00:20

Comprensión

Identificar

Who would say the following things, Dr. Cavazos or Srta. Martínez?

1. Me llamo…
2. De nada.
3. Gracias. Muchas gracias.
4. Aquí tiene usted los documentos de viaje (*trip*), señor.
5. Usted tiene tres maletas, ¿no?
6. Tengo dos maletas.
7. Hola, señor.
8. ¿Viaja usted a Buenos Aires?

Contestar

1. Does this scene take place in the morning, afternoon, or evening? How do you know?
2. How many suitcases does Dr. Cavazos have?
3. Using the words you already know to determine the context, what might the following words and expressions mean?

   - boleto
   - pasaporte
   - un viaje de ida y vuelta
   - ¡Buen viaje!

En pantalla

Latinos form the largest-growing minority group in the United States. This trend is expected to continue; the Census Bureau projects that by the year 2050, the Latino population will grow to 30 percent. Viewership of the two major Spanish-language TV stations, **Univisión** and **Telemundo**, has skyrocketed, at times surpassing that of the four major English-language networks. With Latino purchasing power estimated at 1.5 trillion dollars a year, many companies have responded by adapting successful marketing campaigns to target a Spanish-speaking audience. Turn on a Spanish-language channel any night of the week, and you'll see ads for the world's biggest consumer brands, from soft drinks to car makers; many of these advertisements are adaptations of their English-language counterparts. Bilingual ads, which use English and Spanish in a way that is accessible to all viewers, have become popular during events such as the Super Bowl, where advertisers want to appeal to a diverse market.

Vocabulario útil

carne en salsa	*beef with sauce*
copa de helado	*cup of ice cream*
no tiene precio	*priceless*
plato principal	*main course*
un domingo en familia	*Sunday with the family*

Emparejar

Match each item with its price according to the ad. **¡Ojo!** (*Careful!*) One of the responses will not be used.

_____ 1. aperitivo   a. quince dólares

_____ 2. plato principal   b. ocho dólares

_____ 3. postre   c. treinta dólares

                                  d. seis dólares

Un comercial

Brainstorm and write a MasterCard-like TV ad about something you consider priceless. Use as much Spanish as you can.

Aperitivo *Appetizer* Postre *Dessert*

Anuncio de MasterCard

Aperitivo°...

Postre°...

Un domingo en familia...

The **Plaza de Mayo** in Buenos Aires, Argentina, is perhaps best known as a place of political protest. Aptly nicknamed **Plaza de Protestas** by the locals, it is the site of weekly demonstrations. Despite this reputation, for many it is also a traditional **plaza**, a spot to escape from the hustle of city life. In warmer months, office workers from neighboring buildings flock to the plaza during lunch hour. **Plaza de Mayo** is also a favorite spot for families, couples, and friends to gather, stroll, or simply sit and chat. Tourists come year-round to take in the iconic surroundings: **Plaza de Mayo** is flanked by the rose-colored presidential palace (**Casa Rosada**), city hall (**municipalidad**), a colonial era museum (**Cabildo**), and a spectacular cathedral (**Catedral Metropolitana**).

Vocabulario útil

abrazo	*hug*
¡Cuánto tiempo!	*It's been a long time!*
encuentro	*encounter*
plaza	*city or town square*
¡Qué bueno verte!	*It's great to see you!*
¡Qué suerte verlos!	*How lucky to see you!*

Preparación

Where do you and your friends usually meet? Are there public places where you get together? What activities do you take part in there?

Identificar

Identify the person or people who make(s) each of these statements.

1. ¿Cómo están ustedes?
2. ¡Qué bueno verte!
3. Bien, ¿y vos?
4. Hola.
5. ¡Qué suerte verlos!

a. Gonzalo
b. Mariana
c. Mark
d. Silvina

Encuentros en la plaza

Today we are at the Plaza de Mayo.

People come to walk and get some fresh air...

And children come to play...

Estados Unidos

El país en cifras°

- **Población°** de los EE.UU.: 317 millones
- **Población de origen hispano:** 50 millones
- **País de origen de hispanos en los EE.UU.:**

3,5% Cuba
10,9% otros
9,2% Puerto Rico
13,4% Centroamérica y Suramérica
63,0% México

SOURCE: U.S. Census Bureau

- **Estados con la mayor° población hispana:**

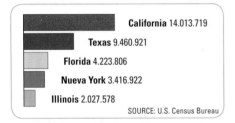

California 14.013.719
Texas 9.460.921
Florida 4.223.806
Nueva York 3.416.922
Illinois 2.027.578

SOURCE: U.S. Census Bureau

Canadá

El país en cifras

- **Población de Canadá:** 35 millones
- **Población de origen hispano:** 700.000
- **País de origen de hispanos en Canadá:**

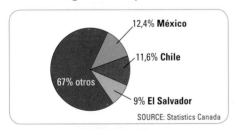

12,4% **México**
11,6% **Chile**
67% otros
9% **El Salvador**

SOURCE: Statistics Canada

- **Ciudades° con la mayor población hispana:**
  Montreal, Toronto, Vancouver

en cifras *by the numbers* Población *Population* mayor *largest*
Ciudades *Cities* creció *grew* más *more* cada *every* niños *children*
Se estima *It is estimated* va a ser *it is going to be*

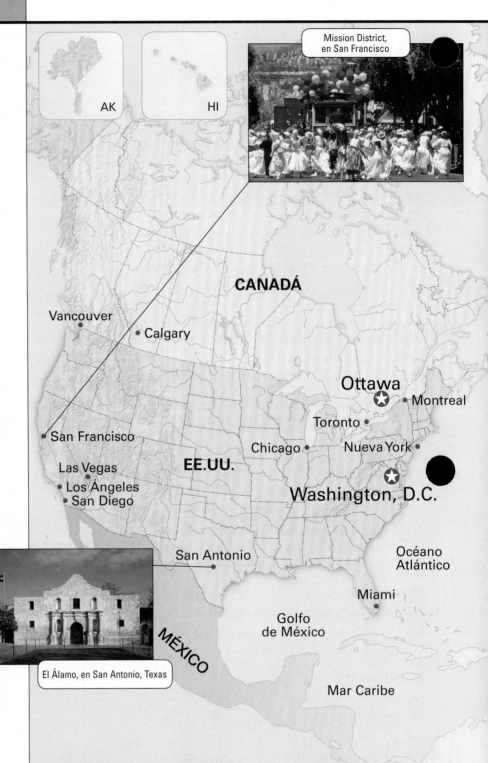

Mission District, en San Francisco

AK   HI

CANADÁ

Vancouver
• Calgary

Ottawa ✪
• Montreal
Toronto •
Chicago •
Nueva York •
• San Francisco
EE.UU.
Washington, D.C. ✪
Las Vegas
• Los Ángeles
• San Diego

San Antonio

MÉXICO

Océano Atlántico

Miami

Golfo de México

Mar Caribe

El Álamo, en San Antonio, Texas

Comida • **La comida mexicana**

La comida° mexicana es muy popular en los Estados Unidos. Los tacos, las enchiladas, las quesadillas y los frijoles frecuentemente forman parte de las comidas de muchos norteamericanos. También° son populares las variaciones de la comida mexicana en los Estados Unidos: el tex-mex y el cali-mex.

Lugares • **La Pequeña Habana**

La Pequeña Habana° es un barrio° de Miami, Florida, donde viven° muchos cubanoamericanos. Es un lugar° donde se encuentran° las costumbres° de la cultura cubana, los aromas y sabores° de su comida y la música salsa. La Pequeña Habana es una parte de Cuba en los Estados Unidos.

Costumbres • **Desfile puertorriqueño**

Cada junio, desde° 1958 (mil novecientos cincuenta y ocho), los puertorriqueños celebran su cultura con un desfile° en Nueva York. Es un gran espectáculo con carrozas° y música salsa, merengue y hip-hop. Muchos espectadores llevan° la bandera° de Puerto Rico en su ropa° o pintada en la cara°.

Comunidad • **Hispanos en Canadá**

En Canadá viven° muchos hispanos. Toronto y Montreal son las ciudades° con mayor° población hispana. Muchos de ellos tienen estudios universitarios° y hablan° una de las lenguas° oficiales: inglés o francés°. Los hispanos participan activamente en la vida cotidiana° y profesional de Canadá.

¿Qué aprendiste? Completa las oraciones con la información adecuada (*appropriate*).

1. Hay _____ de personas de origen hispano en los Estados Unidos.
2. Los cuatro estados con las poblaciones hispanas más grandes son (en orden) _____, Texas, Florida y _____.
3. Toronto, Montreal y _____ son las ciudades con más población hispana de Canadá.
4. Las quesadillas y las enchiladas son platos (*dishes*) _____.
5. La Pequeña _____ es un barrio de Miami.
6. En Miami hay muchas personas de origen _____.
7. Cada junio se celebra en Nueva York un gran desfile para personas de origen _____.
8. Muchos hispanos en Canadá hablan _____ o francés.

Conexión Internet Investiga estos temas en Internet.

1. Haz (*Make*) una lista de seis hispanos célebres de los EE.UU. o Canadá. Explica (*Explain*) por qué (*why*) son célebres.
2. Escoge (*Choose*) seis lugares en los Estados Unidos con nombres hispanos e investiga sobre el origen y el significado (*meaning*) de cada nombre.

comida *food* También *Also* La Pequeña Habana *Little Havana* barrio *neighborhood* viven *live* lugar *place* se encuentran *are found* costumbres *customs* sabores *flavors* Cada junio desde *Each June since* desfile *parade* con carrozas *with floats* llevan *wear* bandera *flag* ropa *clothing* cara *face* viven *live* ciudades *cities* mayor *most* tienen estudios universitarios *have a degree* hablan *speak* lenguas *languages* inglés o francés *English or French* vida cotidiana *daily life*

Saludos

Hola.	Hello; Hi.
Buenos días.	Good morning.
Buenas tardes.	Good afternoon.
Buenas noches.	Good evening; Good night.

Despedidas

Adiós.	Goodbye.
Nos vemos.	See you.
Hasta luego.	See you later.
Hasta la vista.	See you later.
Hasta pronto.	See you soon.
Hasta mañana.	See you tomorrow.
Saludos a...	Greetings to…
Chau.	Bye.

¿Cómo está?

¿Cómo está usted?	How are you? (form.)
¿Cómo estás?	How are you? (fam.)
¿Qué hay de nuevo?	What's new?
¿Qué pasa?	What's happening?; What's going on?
¿Qué tal?	How are you?; How is it going?
(Muy) bien, gracias.	(Very) well, thanks.
Nada.	Nothing.
No muy bien.	Not very well.
Regular.	So-so; OK.

Expresiones de cortesía

Con permiso.	Pardon me; Excuse me.
De nada.	You're welcome.
Lo siento.	I'm sorry.
(Muchas) gracias.	Thank you (very much); Thanks (a lot).
No hay de qué.	You're welcome.
Perdón.	Pardon me; Excuse me.
por favor	please

Títulos

señor (Sr.); don	Mr.; sir
señora (Sra.); doña	Mrs.; ma'am
señorita (Srta.)	Miss

Presentaciones

¿Cómo se llama usted?	What's your name? (form.)
¿Cómo te llamas?	What's your name? (fam.)
Me llamo...	My name is…
¿Y usted?	And you? (form.)
¿Y tú?	And you? (fam.)
Mucho gusto.	Pleased to meet you.
El gusto es mío.	The pleasure is mine.
Encantado/a.	Delighted; Pleased to meet you.
Igualmente.	Likewise.
Le presento a...	I would like to introduce you to (name). (form.)
Te presento a...	I would like to introduce you to (name). (fam.)
el nombre	name

¿De dónde es?

¿De dónde es usted?	Where are you from? (form.)
¿De dónde eres?	Where are you from? (fam.)
Soy de...	I'm from…

Palabras adicionales

¿cuánto(s)/a(s)?	how much/many?
¿de quién...?	whose…? (sing.)
¿de quiénes...?	whose…? (plural)
(no) hay	there is (not); there are (not)

Sustantivos

el autobús	bus
el chico	boy
la chica	girl
la computadora	computer
la comunidad	community
el/la conductor(a)	driver
la conversación	conversation
la cosa	thing
el cuaderno	notebook
el día	day
el diario	diary
el diccionario	dictionary
la escuela	school
el/la estudiante	student
la foto(grafía)	photograph
el hombre	man
el/la joven	young person
el lápiz	pencil
la lección	lesson
la maleta	suitcase
la mano	hand
el mapa	map
la mujer	woman
la nacionalidad	nationality
el número	number
el país	country
la palabra	word
el/la pasajero/a	passenger
el problema	problem
el/la profesor(a)	teacher
el programa	program
el/la turista	tourist
el video	video

Verbo

ser	to be

Numbers 0–30	See page 16.
Telling time	See pages 24–25.
Expresiones útiles	See page 7.

En la universidad

2

Communicative Goals

You will learn how to:

- Talk about your classes and school life
- Discuss everyday activities
- Ask questions in Spanish
- Describe the location of people and things

A PRIMERA VISTA
- ¿Hay un chico y una chica en la foto?
- ¿Hay una computadora o dos?
- ¿Son turistas o estudiantes?
- ¿Qué hora es, la una de la mañana o de la tarde?

En la universidad

Más vocabulario

la biblioteca	*library*
la cafetería	*cafeteria*
la casa	*house; home*
el estadio	*stadium*
el laboratorio	*laboratory*
la librería	*bookstore*
la residencia estudiantil	*dormitory*
la universidad	*university; college*
el/la compañero/a de clase	*classmate*
el/la compañero/a de cuarto	*roommate*
la clase	*class*
el curso	*course*
la especialización	*major*
el examen	*test; exam*
el horario	*schedule*
la prueba	*test; quiz*
el semestre	*semester*
la tarea	*homework*
el trimestre	*trimester; quarter*
la administración de empresas	*business administration*
el arte	*art*
la biología	*biology*
las ciencias	*sciences*
la computación	*computer science*
la contabilidad	*accounting*
la economía	*economics*
el español	*Spanish*
la física	*physics*
la geografía	*geography*
la música	*music*

Variación léxica

pluma ⟷ bolígrafo
pizarra ⟷ tablero (*Col.*)

el reloj

la ventana

la puerta

la profesora

el estudiante

la mesa

la calculadora

el libro

la pluma

la historia

el mapa

la pizarra

LAS MATERIAS | *COURSES*
la historia | *history*
las humanidades | *humanities*
el inglés | *English*
las lenguas extranjeras | *foreign languages*
la literatura | *literature*
las matemáticas | *mathematics*
el periodismo | *journalism*
la psicología | *psychology*
la química | *chemistry*
la sociología | *sociology*

el papel

el borrador

la tiza

la papelera

el escritorio

la mochila

la estudiante

la silla

Práctica

1 Escuchar Listen to Professor Morales talk about her Spanish classroom, then check the items she mentions.

puerta ○	tiza ○	plumas ○
ventanas ○	escritorios ○	mochilas ○
pizarra ○	sillas ○	papel ○
borrador ○	libros ○	reloj ○

2 Identificar You will hear a series of words. Write each one in the appropriate category.

Personas	Lugares	Materias
_____	_____	_____
_____	_____	_____
_____	_____	_____

3 Emparejar Match each question with its most logical response. **¡Ojo!** (*Careful!*) One response will not be used.

1. ¿Qué clase es?
2. ¿Quiénes son?
3. ¿Quién es?
4. ¿De dónde es?
5. ¿A qué hora es la clase de inglés?
6. ¿Cuántos estudiantes hay?

a. Hay veinticinco.
b. Es un reloj.
c. Es de Perú.
d. Es la clase de química.
e. Es el señor Bastos.
f. Es a las nueve en punto.
g. Son los profesores.

4 Escoger Identify the word that does not belong in each group.

1. examen • casa • tarea • prueba
2. economía • matemáticas • biblioteca • contabilidad
3. pizarra • tiza • borrador • librería
4. lápiz • cafetería • papel • cuaderno
5. veinte • diez • pluma • treinta
6. conductor • laboratorio • autobús • pasajero

5 ¿Qué clase es? Name the class associated with the subject matter.

modelo

los elementos, los átomos Es la clase de química.

1. Abraham Lincoln, Winston Churchill
2. Picasso, Leonardo da Vinci
3. Freud, Jung
4. África, el océano Pacífico
5. la cultura de España, verbos
6. Hemingway, Shakespeare
7. geometría, calculadora

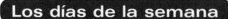

¿Qué día es hoy (today)?

Hoy es martes.

¿Cuándo (When) es el examen?

Es el viernes.

septiembre

lunes	martes	miércoles	jueves	viernes	sábado	domingo
	1	2	3	4	5	6
7	8	9	10			

¡LENGUA VIVA!

The days of the week are never capitalized in Spanish.

•••

Monday is considered the first day of the week in Spanish-speaking countries.

CONSULTA

Note that September in Spanish is **septiembre**. For all of the months of the year, go to **Contextos, Lección 5, p. 154.**

6

¿Qué día es hoy? Complete each statement with the correct day of the week.

1. Hoy es martes. Mañana es _____. Ayer fue (*Yesterday was*) _____.
2. Ayer fue sábado. Mañana es _____. Hoy es _____.
3. Mañana es viernes. Hoy es _____. Ayer fue _____.
4. Ayer fue domingo. Hoy es _____. Mañana es _____.
5. Hoy es jueves. Ayer fue _____. Mañana es _____.
6. Mañana es lunes. Hoy es _____. Ayer fue _____.

7

Analogías Use these words to complete the analogies. Some words will not be used.

arte	día	martes	pizarra
biblioteca	domingo	matemáticas	profesor
catorce	estudiante	mujer	reloj

1. maleta ←→ pasajero ⊜ mochila ←→ _____
2. chico ←→ chica ⊜ hombre ←→ _____
3. pluma ←→ papel ⊜ tiza ←→ _____
4. inglés ←→ lengua ⊜ miércoles ←→ _____
5. papel ←→ cuaderno ⊜ libro ←→ _____
6. quince ←→ dieciséis ⊜ lunes ←→ _____
7. Cervantes ←→ literatura ⊜ Dalí ←→ _____
8. autobús ←→ conductor ⊜ clase ←→ _____
9. los EE.UU. ←→ mapa ⊜ hora ←→ _____
10. veinte ←→ veintitrés ⊜ jueves ←→ _____

Comunicación

8

Horario Read Cristina's description of her schedule. Then indicate whether the following conclusions are **lógico** or **ilógico**, based on what you read.

> Hoy es lunes. Los lunes y los miércoles hay clase de sociología a las nueve. El profesor Núñez enseña (*teaches*) la clase de sociología. A las once hay clase de biología con la profesora Calderón. Tomo (*I take*) biología los lunes y los jueves. Los miércoles y los jueves tomo matemáticas a las tres. La profesora Salazar enseña la clase de matemáticas. Tomo química los martes y los viernes a la una y media. El profesor Fuentes enseña la clase de química.

	Lógico	Ilógico
1. Cristina es estudiante.	O	O
2. Cristina toma (*takes*) dos clases hoy.	O	O
3. Cristina toma una clase los lunes a las tres de la tarde.	O	O
4. La profesora Calderón enseña la clase de biología los lunes y los jueves.	O	O
5. Cristina toma clases los sábados.	O	O
6. Cristina toma clases de humanidades.	O	O

9

La semana Write a paragraph about what a typical week looks like for you. Describe your schedule for the week, including classes, times, and professors.

> **modelo**
>
> El lunes tomo la clase de matemáticas a las nueve con el profesor Smith. A las diez...

10

Nuevos amigos During the first week of class, you meet a new student in the cafeteria. With a partner, prepare a conversation using these cues.

Estudiante 1		Estudiante 2
Greet your new acquaintance.	→	Introduce yourself.
Find out about him or her.	→	Tell him or her about yourself.
Ask about your partner's class schedule.	→	Compare your schedule to your partner's.
Say nice to meet you and goodbye.	→	Say nice to meet you and goodbye.

¿Qué estudias?

Felipe, Marissa, Juan Carlos y Miguel visitan Chapultepec
y hablan de las clases.

PERSONAJES MARISSA FELIPE

1

FELIPE Dos boletos, por favor.

2

EMPLEADO Dos boletos son
64 pesos.

FELIPE Aquí están 100 pesos.

EMPLEADO 100 menos 64 son
36 pesos de cambio.

MIGUEL Marissa, hablas muy bien
el español... ¿Y dónde está tu
diccionario?

MARISSA En casa de los Díaz.
Felipe necesita practicar inglés.

MIGUEL ¡Ay, Maru! Chicos, nos
vemos más tarde.

3

FELIPE Ésta es la Ciudad
de México.

5

4

FELIPE Oye, Marissa, ¿cuántas
clases tomas?

MARISSA Tomo cuatro clases:
español, historia, literatura y
también geografía. Me gusta
mucho la cultura mexicana.

6

FELIPE Juan Carlos, ¿quién enseña
la clase de química este semestre?

JUAN CARLOS El profesor Morales.
Ah, ¿por qué tomo química
y computación?

FELIPE Porque te gusta la tarea.

JUAN CARLOS **MIGUEL** **EMPLEADO** **MARU**

FELIPE Los lunes y los miércoles, economía a las 2:30. Tú tomas computación los martes en la tarde, y química, a ver... Los lunes, los miércoles y los viernes ¿a las 10? ¡Uf!

FELIPE Y Miguel, ¿cuándo regresa?

JUAN CARLOS Hoy estudia con Maru.

MARISSA ¿Quién es Maru?

MIGUEL ¿Hablas con tu mamá?

MARU Mamá habla. Yo escucho. Es la 1:30.

MIGUEL Ay, lo siento. Juan Carlos y Felipe...

MARU Ay, Felipe.

MARU Y ahora, ¿adónde? ¿A la biblioteca?

MIGUEL Sí, pero primero a la librería. Necesito comprar unos libros.

Expresiones útiles

Talking about classes

¿Cuántas clases tomas?
How many classes are you taking?
Tomo cuatro clases.
I'm taking four classes.
Mi especialización es en arqueología.
My major is archeology.
Este año, espero sacar buenas notas y, por supuesto, viajar por el país.
This year, I hope / I'm hoping to get good grades. And, of course, travel through the country.

Talking about likes/dislikes

Me gusta mucho la cultura mexicana.
I like Mexican culture a lot.
Me gustan las ciencias ambientales.
I like environmental science.
Me gusta dibujar.
I like to draw.
¿Te gusta este lugar?
Do you like this place?

Paying for tickets

Dos boletos, por favor.
Two tickets, please.
Dos boletos son sesenta y cuatro pesos.
Two tickets are sixty-four pesos.
Aquí están cien pesos.
Here's a hundred pesos.
Son treinta y seis pesos de cambio.
That's thirty-six pesos change.

Talking about location and direction

¿Dónde está tu diccionario?
Where is your dictionary?
Está en casa de los Díaz.
It's at the Díaz house.
Y ahora, ¿adónde? ¿A la biblioteca?
And now, where to? To the library?
Sí, pero primero a la librería.
Está al lado.
Yes, but first to the bookstore.
It's next door.

¿Qué pasó?

1 **Escoger** Choose the answer that best completes each sentence.

1. Marissa toma (*is taking*) _____ en la universidad.
   a. español, psicología, economía y música   b. historia, inglés, sociología y periodismo
   c. español, historia, literatura y geografía
2. El profesor Morales enseña (*teaches*) _____.
   a. química   b. matemáticas   c. historia
3. Juan Carlos toma química _____.
   a. los miércoles, jueves y viernes   b. los lunes, miércoles y viernes
   c. los lunes, martes y jueves
4. Miguel necesita ir a (*needs to go to*) _____.
   a. la biblioteca   b. la residencia estudiantil   c. la librería

2 **Identificar** Indicate which person would make each statement. The names may be used more than once.

1. ¿Maru es compañera de ustedes? _____
2. Mi mamá habla mucho. _____
3. El profesor Morales enseña la clase de química este semestre. _____
4. Mi diccionario está en casa de Felipe y Jimena. _____
5. Necesito estudiar con Maru. _____
6. Yo tomo clase de computación los martes por la tarde. _____

MARU

JUAN CARLOS   MARISSA

MIGUEL

3 **Completar** These sentences are similar to things said in the **Fotonovela**. Complete each sentence with the correct word(s).

| Castillo de Chapultepec | estudiar | miércoles |
| clase | inglés | tarea |

1. Marissa, éste es el _____.
2. Felipe tiene (*has*) el diccionario porque (*because*) necesita practicar _____.
3. A Juan Carlos le gusta mucho la _____.
4. Hay clase de economía los lunes y _____.
5. Miguel está con Maru para _____.

4 **Preguntas personales** Answer your partner's questions about your classes.

1. ¿Qué clases tomas en la universidad?
2. ¿Qué clases tomas los martes?
3. ¿Qué clases tomas los viernes?
4. ¿Quién enseña la clase de español?
5. ¿Te gusta la clase de español?

Pronunciación
Spanish vowels

a   **e**   **i**   **o**   **u**

Spanish vowels are never silent; they are always pronounced in a short, crisp way without the glide sounds used in English.

Álex	**clase**	**nada**	**encantada**

The letter **a** is pronounced like the *a* in *father*, but shorter.

el	**ene**	**mesa**	**elefante**

The letter **e** is pronounced like the *e* in *they*, but shorter.

Inés	**chica**	**tiza**	**señorita**

The letter **i** sounds like the *ee* in *beet*, but shorter.

hola	**con**	**libro**	**don Francisco**

The letter **o** is pronounced like the *o* in *tone*, but shorter.

uno	**regular**	**saludos**	**gusto**

The letter **u** sounds like the *oo* in *room*, but shorter.

Práctica Practice the vowels by saying the names of these places in Spain.

1. Madrid   3. Tenerife   5. Barcelona   7. Burgos
2. Alicante   4. Toledo   6. Granada   8. La Coruña

Oraciones Read the sentences aloud, focusing on the vowels.

1. Hola. Me llamo Ramiro Morgado.
2. Estudio arte en la Universidad de Salamanca.
3. Tomo también literatura y contabilidad.
4. Ay, tengo clase en cinco minutos. ¡Nos vemos!

Refranes Practice the vowels by reading these sayings aloud.

Cada loco con su tema.²

Del dicho al hecho hay un gran trecho.¹

1 *Easier said than done.*
2 *To each his own.*

La elección de una
carrera universitaria

Since higher education in the Spanish-speaking world is heavily state-subsidized, tuition is almost free. As a result, public universities see large enrollments. Spanish and Latin American students generally choose their **carrera universitaria** (major) when they're eighteen—which is either the year they enter the university or the year before. In order to enroll, all students must complete a high school degree, known as the **bachillerato**. In countries like Bolivia, Mexico, and Peru, the last year of high school (**colegio***) tends to be specialized in an area of study, such as the arts or natural sciences.

Universidad Central de Venezuela en Caracas

Students then choose their major according to their area of specialization. Similarly, university-bound students in Argentina focus their studies on specific fields, such as the humanities and social sciences, natural sciences, communication, art and design, and economics and business, during their five years of high school. Based on this coursework, Argentine students choose their **carrera**. Finally, in Spain, students choose their major according to the score they receive on the **prueba de aptitud** (skills test or entrance exam).

University graduates receive a **licenciatura**, or bachelor's degree. In Argentina and Chile, a **licenciatura** takes four to six years to complete, and may be considered equivalent to a master's degree. In Peru and Venezuela, a bachelor's degree is a five-year process. Spanish and Colombian **licenciaturas** take four to five years, although some fields, such as medicine, require six or more.

> ### Estudiantes hispanos
> ### en los EE.UU.
>
> In the 2012–13 academic year, over 14,000 Mexican students (1.7% of all international students) studied at U.S. universities. Colombians were the second-largest Spanish-speaking group, with over 6,500 students.

*¡Ojo! El colegio is a false cognate. In most countries, it means *high school*, but in some regions it refers to an elementary school. All undergraduate study takes place at **la universidad**.

1 **¿Cierto o falso?** Indicate whether these statements are cierto or falso. Correct the false statements.

1. Students in Spanish-speaking countries must pay large amounts of money toward their college tuition.

2. **Carrera** refers to any undergraduate or graduate program that students enroll in to obtain a professional degree.

3. After studying at a **colegio**, students receive their **bachillerato**.

4. Undergraduates study at a **colegio** or an **universidad**.

5. In Latin America and Spain, students usually choose their majors in their second year at the university.

6. In Argentina, students focus their studies in their high school years.

7. In Mexico, the **bachillerato** involves specialized study.

8. In Spain, majors depend on entrance exam scores.

9. Venezuelans complete a **licenciatura** in five years.

10. According to statistics, Colombians constitute the third-largest Latin American group studying at U.S. universities.

Clases y exámenes

aprobar	*to pass*
la asignatura (Esp.)	la clase, la materia
la clase anual	*year-long course*
el examen parcial	*midterm exam*
la facultad	*department, school*
la investigación	*research*
el profesorado	*faculty*
reprobar; suspender (Esp.)	*to fail*
sacar buenas/ malas notas	*to get good/ bad grades*
tomar apuntes	*to take notes*

Las universidades hispanas

It is not uncommon for universities in Spain and Latin America to have extremely large student body populations.

- **Universidad de Buenos Aires** (Argentina)
  308.700 estudiantes

- **Universidad Autónoma de Santo Domingo** (República Dominicana)
  170.500 estudiantes

- **Universidad Complutense de Madrid** (España)
  84.900 estudiantes

- **Universidad Central de Venezuela** (Venezuela)
  62.600 estudiantes

La Universidad de Salamanca

The University of Salamanca, established in 1218, is the oldest university in Spain. It is located in Salamanca, one of the most spectacular Renaissance cities in Europe. Salamanca is nicknamed **La Ciudad Dorada** (*The Golden City*) for the golden glow of its famous sandstone buildings, and it was declared a UNESCO World Heritage Site in 1988.

Salamanca is a true college town, as its prosperity and city life depend on and revolve around the university population. Over 38,000 students from all over Spain, as well as abroad, come to study here each year. The school offers over 250 academic programs, as well

as renowned Spanish courses for foreign students. To walk through the university's historic grounds is to follow the footsteps of immortal writers like Miguel de Cervantes and Miguel de Unamuno.

Conexión Internet

To which **facultad** does your major belong in Spain or Latin America?

Use the Web to find more cultural information related to this **Cultura** section.

2 **Comprensión** Complete these sentences.

1. The University of Salamanca was established in the year _____.

2. A _____ is a year-long course.

3. Salamanca is called _____.

4. Over 300,000 students attend the _____.

5. An _____ occurs about halfway through a course.

3 **La universidad en cifras** Research a Spanish or Latin American university online and find five statistics about that institution (for instance, the total enrollment, majors offered, year it was founded, etc.). Using the information you found, create a dialogue between a prospective student and a university representative.

2.1 Present tense of -ar verbs

ANTE TODO In order to talk about activities, you need to use verbs. Verbs express actions or states of being. In English and Spanish, the infinitive is the base form of the verb. In English, the infinitive is preceded by the word *to*: *to study*, *to be*. The infinitive in Spanish is a one-word form and can be recognized by its endings: **-ar**, **-er**, or **-ir**.

-ar verb		*-er* verb		*-ir* verb	
estudiar	*to study*	**comer**	*to eat*	**escribir**	*to write*

▶ In this lesson, you will learn the forms of regular **-ar** verbs.

The verb estudiar (*to study*)

SINGULAR FORMS	yo	estudi**o**	*I study*
	tú	estudi**as**	*you* (fam.) *study*
	Ud./él/ella	estudi**a**	*you* (form.) *study; he/she studies*
PLURAL FORMS	nosotros/as	estudi**amos**	*we study*
	vosotros/as	estudi**áis**	*you* (fam.) *study*
	Uds./ellos/ellas	estudi**an**	*you study; they study*

Juan Carlos estudia ciencias ambientales.

Y tú, ¿qué estudias, Miguel?

▶ To create the forms of most regular verbs in Spanish, drop the infinitive endings (**-ar**, **-er**, **-ir**). You then add to the stem the endings that correspond to the different subject pronouns. This diagram will help you visualize verb conjugation.

Conjugation of *-ar* verbs

INFINITIVE	VERB STEM	CONJUGATED FORM
estudi**ar**	estudi-	yo estudi**o**
bail**ar**	bail-	tú bail**as**
trabaj**ar**	trabaj-	nosotros trabaj**amos**

Common *-ar* verbs

bailar	to dance	**estudiar**	to study
buscar	to look for	**explicar**	to explain
caminar	to walk	**hablar**	to talk; to speak
cantar	to sing	**llegar**	to arrive
cenar	to have dinner	**llevar**	to carry
comprar	to buy	**mirar**	to look (at); to watch
contestar	to answer	**necesitar (+ *inf.*)**	to need
conversar	to converse, to chat	**practicar**	to practice
desayunar	to have breakfast	**preguntar**	to ask (a question)
descansar	to rest	**preparar**	to prepare
desear (+ *inf.*)	to desire; to wish	**regresar**	to return
dibujar	to draw	**terminar**	to end; to finish
enseñar	to teach	**tomar**	to take; to drink
escuchar	to listen (to)	**trabajar**	to work
esperar (+ *inf.*)	to wait (for); to hope	**viajar**	to travel

▶ **¡Atención!** Unless referring to a person, the Spanish verbs **buscar**, **escuchar**, **esperar**, and **mirar** do not need to be followed by prepositions as they do in English.

Busco la tarea.
I'm looking for the homework.

Escucho la música.
I'm listening to the music.

Espero el autobús.
I'm waiting for the bus.

Miro la pizarra.
I'm looking at the blackboard.

COMPARE & CONTRAST

English uses three sets of forms to talk about the present: (1) the simple present (*Paco works*), (2) the present progressive (*Paco is working*), and (3) the emphatic present (*Paco does work*). In Spanish, the simple present can be used in all three cases.

Paco **trabaja** en la cafetería.
1. *Paco works in the cafeteria.*
2. *Paco is working in the cafeteria.*
3. *Paco does work in the cafeteria.*

In Spanish and English, the present tense is also sometimes used to express future action.

Marina **viaja** a Madrid mañana.
1. *Marina travels to Madrid tomorrow.*
2. *Marina will travel to Madrid tomorrow.*
3. *Marina is traveling to Madrid tomorrow.*

▶ When two verbs are used together with no change of subject, the second verb is generally in the infinitive. To make a sentence negative in Spanish, the word **no** is placed before the conjugated verb. In this case, **no** means *not*.

Deseo hablar con el señor Díaz.
I want to speak with Mr. Díaz.

Alicia **no** desea bailar ahora.
Alicia doesn't want to dance now.

▶ Spanish speakers often omit subject pronouns because the verb endings indicate who the subject is. In Spanish, subject pronouns are used for emphasis, clarification, or contrast.

—¿Qué enseñan?
What do they teach?

—**Ella** enseña arte y **él** enseña física.
She teaches art, and he teaches physics.

—¿Quién desea trabajar hoy?
Who wants to work today?

—**Yo** no deseo trabajar hoy.
I don't want to work today.

The verb gustar

▶ **Gustar** is different from other **-ar** verbs. To express your likes and dislikes, use the expression **(no) me gusta** + **el/la** + [*singular noun*] or **(no) me gustan** + **los/las** + [*plural noun*]. Note: You may use the phrase **a mí** for emphasis, but never the subject pronoun **yo**.

Me gusta la música clásica.
I like classical music.

Me gustan las clases de español y biología.
I like Spanish and biology classes.

A mí me gustan las artes.
I like the arts.

A mí no me gusta el programa.
I don't like the program.

▶ To talk about what you like and don't like to do, use **(no) me gusta** + [*infinitive(s)*]. Note that the singular **gusta** is always used, even with more than one infinitive.

No me gusta viajar en autobús.
I don't like to travel by bus.

Me gusta cantar y **bailar**.
I like to sing and dance.

▶ To ask a friend about likes and dislikes, use the pronoun **te** instead of **me**. Note: You may use **a ti** for emphasis, but never the subject pronoun **tú**.

—¿**Te gusta** la geografía?
Do you like geography?

—Sí, me gusta. Y a ti, ¿**te gusta** el inglés?
Yes, I like it. And you, do you like English?

▶ You can use this same structure to talk about other people by using the pronouns **nos**, **le**, and **les**. Unless your instructor tells you otherwise, only the **me** and **te** forms will appear on test materials until **Lección 7**.

Nos gusta dibujar. (nosotros)
We like to draw.

Nos gustan las clases de español e inglés. (nosotros)
We like Spanish class and English class.

**No le gusta trabajar.
(usted, él, ella)**
You don't like to work.
He/She doesn't like to work.

**Les gusta el arte.
(ustedes, ellos, ellas)**
You like art.
They like art.

¡ATENCIÓN!

Note that **gustar** does not behave like other **-ar** verbs. You must study its use carefully and pay attention to prepositions, pronouns, and agreement.

AYUDA

Use the construction **a** + [*name/pronoun*] to clarify to whom you are referring. This construction is not always necessary.
A Gabriela le gusta bailar.
A Sara y a él les gustan los animales.
A mí me gusta viajar.
¿**A ti** te gustan las clases?

CONSULTA

For more on **gustar** and other verbs like it, see **Estructura 7.4**, pp. 246–247.

¡INTÉNTALO! Provide the present tense forms of these verbs. The first items have been done for you.

hablar	gustar
1. Yo _hablo_ español.	1. _Me gusta_ el café. (a mí)
2. Ellos _____ español.	2. ¿_____ las clases? (a ti)
3. Inés _____ español.	3. No _____ el café. (a ti)
4. Nosotras _____ español.	4. No _____ las clases. (a mí)
5. Tú _____ español.	5. No _____ el café. (a mí)

Práctica

1

Completar Complete the conversation with the appropriate forms of the verbs in parentheses.

JUAN ¡Hola, Linda! ¿Qué tal las clases?

LINDA Bien. (1)_____ (Tomar) tres clases... química, biología y computación. Y tú, ¿cuántas clases (2)_____ (tomar)?

JUAN (3)_____ (Tomar) tres también... biología, arte y literatura. El doctor Cárdenas (4)_____ (enseñar) la clase de biología.

LINDA ¿Ah, sí? Lily, Alberto y yo (5)_____ (tomar) biología a las diez con la profesora Garza.

JUAN ¿(6)_____ (Estudiar) mucho ustedes?

LINDA Sí, porque hay muchos exámenes. Alberto y yo (7)_____ (necesitar) estudiar dos horas todos los días (*every day*).

2

Oraciones Form sentences using the words provided. Remember to conjugate the verbs and add any other necessary words.

1. ustedes / practicar / vocabulario
2. ¿preparar (tú) / tarea?
3. clase de español / terminar / once
4. ¿qué / buscar / ustedes?
5. (nosotros) buscar / pluma
6. (yo) comprar / calculadora

3

Gustos Read what these people do. Then use the information in parentheses to tell what they like.

> **modelo**
> Yo enseño en la universidad. (las clases)   *Me gustan las clases.*

1. Tú deseas mirar cuadros (*paintings*) de Picasso. (el arte)
2. Soy estudiante de economía. (estudiar)
3. Tú estudias italiano y español. (las lenguas extranjeras)
4. No descansas los sábados. (cantar y bailar)
5. Busco una computadora. (la computación)

4

Actividades Get together with a partner and take turns asking each other if you do these activities. Which activities does your partner like? Which do you both like?

> **modelo**
> tomar el autobús
> **Estudiante 1:** *¿Tomas el autobús?*
> **Estudiante 2:** *Sí, tomo el autobús, pero (but) no me gusta./ No, no tomo el autobús.*

bailar merengue	escuchar música rock	practicar el español
cantar en público	estudiar física	trabajar en la universidad
	mirar la televisión	viajar a Europa
dibujar bien		

Comunicación

5

Actividades Talk about the different activities you and your friends do in your daily life. Then specify which of those activities you like to do and which you don't. Use at least five of the **-ar** verbs you have learned.

> Yo bailo hip hop en una academia. Mary dibuja...
> Me gusta bailar. No me gusta dibujar.

6

Describir Write a description of what you see in each picture using the given verbs. Also mention whether or not you like the activities.

> enseñar
> La profesora enseña química. A mí me gusta la química.

1. caminar, hablar, llevar

2. buscar, descansar, estudiar

3. dibujar, cantar, escuchar

4. llevar, tomar, viajar

Síntesis

7

Conversación With a partner, pretend that you are friends who have not seen each other for a few days. Have a conversation in which you catch up on things. Mention how you're feeling, what classes you're taking, which professors teach those classes, and which classes you like and don't like.

2.2 Forming questions in Spanish

ANTE TODO There are three basic ways to ask questions in Spanish. Can you guess what they are by looking at the photos and photo captions on this page?

Te gusta mucho la tarea, ¿no?

¿Hablas con tu mamá?

¿Estudia Maru?

▶ One way to form a question is to raise the pitch of your voice at the end of a declarative sentence. When writing any question in Spanish, be sure to use an upside-down question mark (¿) at the beginning and a regular question mark (?) at the end of the sentence.

Statement	Question
Ustedes trabajan los sábados.	¿Ustedes trabajan los sábados?
You work on Saturdays.	*Do you work on Saturdays?*
Carlota busca un mapa.	¿Carlota busca un mapa?
Carlota is looking for a map.	*Is Carlota looking for a map?*

▶ You can also form a question by inverting the order of the subject and the verb of a declarative statement. The subject may even be placed at the end of the sentence.

Statement	Question
SUBJECT VERB	VERB SUBJECT
Ustedes trabajan los sábados.	¿**Trabajan ustedes** los sábados?
You work on Saturdays.	*Do you work on Saturdays?*
SUBJECT VERB	VERB SUBJECT
Carlota regresa a las seis.	¿**Regresa** a las seis **Carlota**?
Carlota returns at six.	*Does Carlota return at six?*

▶ Questions can also be formed by adding the tags **¿no?** or **¿verdad?** at the end of a statement.

Statement	Question
Ustedes trabajan los sábados.	Ustedes trabajan los sábados, **¿no?**
You work on Saturdays.	*You work on Saturdays, don't you?*
Carlota regresa a las seis.	Carlota regresa a las seis, **¿verdad?**
Carlota returns at six.	*Carlota returns at six, right?*

Question words

Interrogative words			
¿Adónde?	Where (to)?	**¿De dónde?**	From where?
¿Cómo?	How?	**¿Dónde?**	Where?
¿Cuál?, ¿Cuáles?	Which?; Which one(s)?	**¿Por qué?**	Why?
¿Cuándo?	When?	**¿Qué?**	What?; Which?
¿Cuánto/a?	How much?	**¿Quién?**	Who?
¿Cuántos/as?	How many?	**¿Quiénes?**	Who (plural)?

▶ To ask a question that requires more than a *yes* or *no* answer, use an interrogative word.

CONSULTA

You will learn more about the difference between **qué** and **cuál** in **Estructura 9.3**, p. 316.

¿Cuál de ellos estudia en la biblioteca?
Which of them studies in the library?

¿Adónde caminamos?
Where are we walking (to)?

¿Cuántos estudiantes hablan español?
How many students speak Spanish?

¿Por qué necesitas hablar con ella?
Why do you need to talk to her?

¿Dónde trabaja Ricardo?
Where does Ricardo work?

¿Quién enseña la clase de arte?
Who teaches the art class?

¿Qué clases tomas?
What classes are you taking?

¿Cuánta tarea hay?
How much homework is there?

▶ When pronouncing this type of question, the pitch of your voice falls at the end of the sentence.

¿Cómo llegas a clase?
How do you get to class?

¿Por qué necesitas estudiar?
Why do you need to study?

▶ Notice the difference between **¿por qué?**, which is written as two words and has an accent, and **porque**, which is written as one word without an accent.

¿Por qué estudias español?
Why do you study Spanish?

¡Porque es divertido!
Because it's fun!

▶ In Spanish **no** can mean both *no* and *not*. Therefore, when answering a yes/no question in the negative, you need to use **no** twice.

¿Caminan a la universidad?
Do you walk to the university?

No, no caminamos a la universidad.
No, we do not walk to the university.

¡INTÉNTALO! Make questions out of these statements. Use the intonation method in column 1 and the tag **¿no?** method in column 2.

Statement	Intonation	Tag questions
1. Hablas inglés.	¿Hablas inglés?	Hablas inglés, ¿no?
2. Trabajamos mañana.		
3. Ustedes desean bailar.		
4. Raúl estudia mucho.		
5. Enseño a las nueve.		
6. Luz mira la televisión.		

Práctica

1

Preguntas Change these sentences into questions by inverting the word order.

> Ernesto habla con su compañero de clase.
> ¿Habla Ernesto con su compañero de clase? /
> ¿Habla con su compañero de clase Ernesto?

1. La profesora Cruz prepara la prueba.

2. Sandra y yo necesitamos estudiar.

3. Los chicos practican el vocabulario.

4. Jaime termina la tarea.

5. Tú trabajas en la biblioteca.

2

Completar Irene and Manolo are chatting in the library. Complete their conversation with the appropriate questions.

IRENE   Hola, Manolo. (1)_____

MANOLO Bien, gracias. (2)_____

IRENE   Muy bien. (3)_____

MANOLO Son las nueve.

IRENE   (4)_____

MANOLO Estudio historia.

IRENE   (5)_____

MANOLO Porque hay un examen mañana.

IRENE   (6)_____

MANOLO Sí, me gusta mucho la clase.

IRENE   (7)_____

MANOLO El profesor Padilla enseña la clase.

IRENE   (8)_____

MANOLO No, no tomo psicología este (*this*) semestre.

IRENE   (9)_____

MANOLO Regreso a la residencia a las once.

IRENE   (10)_____

MANOLO No, no deseo tomar una soda. ¡Deseo estudiar!

3

Dos profesores Create a dialogue, similar to the one in **Actividad 2**, between Professor Padilla and his colleague Professor Martínez. Use question words.

> **Prof. Padilla:** ¿Qué enseñas este semestre?
> **Prof. Martínez:** Enseño dos cursos de sociología.

Comunicación

4

Muchas preguntas Listen to the conversation between Manuel and Ana. Then indicate whether the following conclusions are **lógico** or **ilógico**, based on what you heard.

	Lógico	Ilógico
1. Ana es profesora.	○	○
2. Diana es estudiante.	○	○
3. La profesora de España habla inglés.	○	○
4. Ana no toma la clase de administración de empresas porque hay mucha tarea.	○	○
5. Diana camina a la universidad.	○	○

5

Un juego With a partner, play a game (**un juego**) of Jeopardy®. Remember to phrase your answers in the form of a question.

> **Es algo que...**   **Es un lugar donde...**   **Es una persona que...**
> *It's something that...*   *It's a place where...*   *It's a person that...*

> **modelo**
>
> **Estudiante 1:** Es un lugar donde estudiamos.
> **Estudiante 2:** ¿Qué es la biblioteca?
>
> **Estudiante 2:** Es algo que escuchamos.
> **Estudiante 1:** ¿Qué es la música?
>
> **Estudiante 1:** Es un director de España.
> **Estudiante 2:** ¿Quién es Pedro Almodóvar?

6

El nuevo estudiante Imagine you are a transfer student and today is your first day of Spanish class. Ask your partner questions to find out all you can about the class, your classmates, and the university. Then switch roles.

> **modelo**
>
> **Estudiante 1:** Hola, me llamo Samuel. ¿Cómo te llamas?
> **Estudiante 2:** Me llamo Laura.
> **Estudiante 1:** ¿Quiénes son ellos?
> **Estudiante 2:** Son Melanie y Lucas.
> **Estudiante 1:** En la universidad hay cursos de ciencias, ¿verdad?
> **Estudiante 2:** Sí, hay clases de biología, química y física.
> **Estudiante 1:** ¿Cuántos exámenes hay en esta clase?
> **Estudiante 2:** Hay dos.

Síntesis

7

Entrevista Imagine that you are a reporter and you are writing an article about college life in your community. Write five questions you would ask students about college life.

CONSULTA

To review the forms of
ser, see **Estructura 1.3**,
pp. 19–21.

2.3 Present tense of **estar**

ANTE TODO In **Lección 1**, you learned how to conjugate and use the verb **ser** (*to be*).
You will now learn a second verb which means *to be*, the verb **estar**.
Although **estar** ends in **-ar**, it does not follow the pattern of regular **-ar** verbs. The **yo** form
(**estoy**) is irregular. Also, all forms have an accented **á** except the **yo** and **nosotros/as** forms.

The verb estar (*to be*)

SINGULAR FORMS	yo	est**oy**	*I am*
	tú	est**ás**	*you* (fam.) *are*
	Ud./él/ella	est**á**	*you* (form.) *are; he/she is*
PLURAL FORMS	nosotros/as	est**amos**	*we are*
	vosotros/as	est**áis**	*you* (fam.) *are*
	Uds./ellos/ellas	est**án**	*you are; they are*

¡Estamos en Perú!

María está en la biblioteca.

COMPARE & CONTRAST

Compare the uses of the verb **estar** to those of the verb **ser**.

Uses of *estar*	Uses of *ser*

Location
Estoy en casa.
I am at home.

Marissa **está** al lado de Felipe.
Marissa is next to Felipe.

Health
Juan Carlos **está** enfermo hoy.
Juan Carlos is sick today.

Well-being
—¿Cómo **estás**, Jimena?
How are you, Jimena?

—**Estoy** muy bien, gracias.
I'm very well, thank you.

Identity
Hola, **soy** Maru.
Hello, I'm Maru.

Occupation
Soy estudiante.
I'm a student.

Origin
—¿**Eres** de México?
Are you from Mexico?

—Sí, **soy** de México.
Yes, I'm from Mexico.

Telling time
Son las cuatro.
It's four o'clock.

AYUDA

Use **la casa** to express
the house, but **en casa**
to express *at home*.

CONSULTA

To learn more about
the difference between
ser and **estar**, see
Estructura 5.3,
pp. 170–171.

▶ **Estar** is often used with certain prepositions and adverbs to describe the location of a person or an object.

Prepositions and adverbs often used with estar

al lado de	next to	**delante de**	in front of
a la derecha de	to the right of	**detrás de**	behind
a la izquierda de	to the left of	**en**	in; on
allá	over there	**encima de**	on top of
allí	there	**entre**	between
cerca de	near	**lejos de**	far from
con	with	**sin**	without
debajo de	below	**sobre**	on; over

La tiza **está al lado de** la pluma.
The chalk is next to the pen.

Los libros **están encima del** escritorio.
The books are on top of the desk.

El laboratorio **está cerca de** la clase.
The lab is near the classroom.

Maribel **está delante de** José.
Maribel is in front of José.

La maleta **está allí**.
The suitcase is there.

El estadio no **está lejos de** la librería.
The stadium isn't far from the bookstore.

El mapa **está entre** la pizarra y la puerta.
*The map is between the blackboard and
the door.*

Los estudiantes **están en** la clase.
The students are in class.

La calculadora **está sobre** la mesa.
The calculator is on the table.

Los turistas **están allá**.
The tourists are over there.

Estamos lejos de casa.

La biblioteca está al
lado de la librería.

¡INTÉNTALO!   Provide the present tense forms of **estar**.

1. Ustedes ___están___ en la clase.
2. José _____ en la biblioteca.
3. Yo _____ bien, gracias.
4. Nosotras _____ en la cafetería.
5. Tú _____ en el laboratorio.
6. Elena _____ en la librería.
7. Ellas _____ en la clase.

8. Ana y yo _____ en la clase.
9. ¿Cómo _____ usted?
10. Javier y Maribel _____ en el estadio.
11. Nosotros _____ en la cafetería.
12. Yo _____ en el laboratorio.
13. Carmen y María _____ enfermas.
14. Tú _____ en la clase.

Práctica

1

Completar Daniela has just returned home from the library. Complete this conversation with the appropriate forms of **ser** or **estar**.

MAMÁ   Hola, Daniela. ¿Cómo (1)_____?

▶ DANIELA   Hola, mamá. (2)_____ bien. ¿Dónde (3)_____ papá?

     ¡Ya (*Already*) (4)_____ las ocho de la noche!

MAMÁ   No (5)_____ aquí. (6)_____ en la oficina.

DANIELA   Y Andrés y Margarita, ¿dónde (7)_____ ellos?

MAMÁ   (8)_____ en el restaurante La Palma con Martín.

DANIELA   ¿Quién (9)_____ Martín?

MAMÁ   (10)_____ un compañero de clase. (11)_____ de México.

DANIELA   Ah. Y el restaurante La Palma, ¿dónde (12)_____?

MAMÁ   (13)_____ cerca de la Plaza Mayor, en San Modesto.

DANIELA   Gracias, mamá. Voy (*I'm going*) al restaurante. ¡Hasta pronto!

2

Escoger Choose the preposition that best completes each sentence.

1. La pluma está (encima de / detrás de) la mesa.
2. La ventana está (a la izquierda de / debajo de) la puerta.
3. La pizarra está (debajo de / delante de) los estudiantes.
4. Las sillas están (encima de / detrás de) los escritorios.
5. Los estudiantes llevan los libros (en / sobre) la mochila.
6. La biblioteca está (sobre / al lado de) la residencia estudiantil.
7. España está (cerca de / lejos de) Puerto Rico.
8. México está (cerca de / lejos de) los Estados Unidos.
9. Felipe trabaja (con / en) Ricardo en la cafetería.

3

La librería Indicate the location of five items in the drawing.

modelo

▶   *Los diccionarios están debajo de los libros de literatura.*

Comunicación

4   **La ciudad universitaria** You are a student at a Spanish university. Tell where the different buildings are located.

> **modelo**
>
> La Facultad de Medicina está a la izquierda de la Facultad de Administración de Empresas...

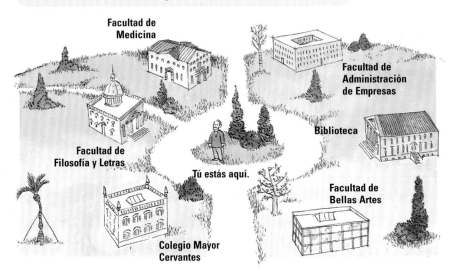

Facultad de Medicina

Facultad de Administración de Empresas

Biblioteca

Facultad de Filosofía y Letras

Tú estás aquí.

Facultad de Bellas Artes

Colegio Mayor Cervantes

¡LENGUA VIVA!

La Facultad (*School*) de Filosofía y Letras includes departments such as language, literature, philosophy, history, and linguistics. Fine arts can be studied in la Facultad de Bellas Artes. In Spain, the business school is sometimes called la Facultad de Administración de Empresas. Residencias estudiantiles are referred to as colegios mayores.

5   **¿Dónde estás...?** With a partner, take turns asking each other where you normally are at these times.

> **modelo**
>
> lunes / 10:00 a.m.
>
> **Estudiante 1:** ¿Dónde estás los lunes a las diez de la mañana?
>
> **Estudiante 2:** Estoy en la biblioteca.

1. sábados / 6:00 a.m.
2. miércoles / 9:15 a.m.
3. lunes / 11:10 a.m.
4. jueves / 12:30 a.m.
5. viernes / 2:25 p.m.
6. martes / 3:50 p.m.
7. jueves / 5:45 p.m.
8. miércoles / 8:20 p.m.

Síntesis

6   **Entrevista** Answer your partner's questions.

1. ¿Cómo estás?
2. ¿Dónde estás ahora?
3. ¿Dónde está tu (*your*) diccionario de español?
4. ¿Dónde está tu casa?
5. ¿Cuándo hay un examen?
6. ¿Estudias mucho?
7. ¿Cuántas horas estudias para (*for*) una prueba?

Numbers 31 and higher

ANTE TODO You have already learned numbers 0–30. Now you will learn the rest of the numbers.

Numbers 31–100

▶ Numbers 31–99 follow the same basic pattern as 21–29.

Numbers 31–100		
31 treinta y uno	**40** cuarenta	**50** cincuenta
32 treinta y dos	**41** cuarenta y uno	**51** cincuenta y uno
33 treinta y tres	**42** cuarenta y dos	**52** cincuenta y dos
34 treinta y cuatro	**43** cuarenta y tres	**60** sesenta
35 treinta y cinco	**44** cuarenta y cuatro	**63** sesenta y tres
36 treinta y seis	**45** cuarenta y cinco	**64** sesenta y cuatro
37 treinta y siete	**46** cuarenta y seis	**70** setenta
38 treinta y ocho	**47** cuarenta y siete	**80** ochenta
39 treinta y nueve	**48** cuarenta y ocho	**90** noventa
	49 cuarenta y nueve	**100** cien, ciento

▶ **Y** is used in most numbers from **31** through **99**. Unlike numbers 21–29, these numbers must be written as three separate words.

Hay **noventa y dos** exámenes.
There are ninety-two exams.

Hay **cuarenta y dos** estudiantes.
There are forty-two students.

Hay cuarenta y siete estudiantes en la clase de geografía.

Cien menos sesenta y cuatro son treinta y seis pesos de cambio.

▶ With numbers that end in **uno** (31, 41, etc.), **uno** becomes **un** before a masculine noun and **una** before a feminine noun.

Hay **treinta y un** chicos.
There are thirty-one guys.

Hay **treinta y una** chicas.
There are thirty-one girls.

▶ **Cien** is used before nouns and in counting. The words **un**, **una**, and **uno** are never used before **cien** in Spanish. Use **cientos** to say *hundreds*.

Hay **cien** libros y **cien** sillas.
There are one hundred books and one hundred chairs.

¿Cuántos libros hay? **Cientos.**
How many books are there? Hundreds.

Numbers 101 and higher

▶ As shown in the chart, Spanish uses a period to indicate thousands and millions, rather than a comma, as is used in English.

Numbers 101 and higher			
101	ciento uno	1.000	mil
200	doscientos/as	1.100	mil cien
300	trescientos/as	2.000	dos mil
400	cuatrocientos/as	5.000	cinco mil
500	quinientos/as	100.000	cien mil
600	seiscientos/as	200.000	doscientos/as mil
700	setecientos/as	550.000	quinientos/as cincuenta mil
800	ochocientos/as	1.000.000	un millón (de)
900	novecientos/as	8.000.000	ocho millones (de)

▶ Notice that you should use **ciento**, not **cien**, to count numbers over 100.

110 = **ciento diez**   118 = **ciento dieciocho**   150 = **ciento cincuenta**

▶ The numbers 200 through 999 agree in gender with the nouns they modify.

324 plum**as**   3.505 libr**os**
trescient**as** veinticuatro plum**as**   tres mil quinient**os** cinco libr**os**

▶ The word **mil**, which can mean *a thousand* and *one thousand*, is not usually used in the plural form to refer to an exact number, but it can be used to express the idea of *a lot*, *many*, or *thousands*. **Cientos** can also be used to express *hundreds* in this manner.

¡Hay **miles** de personas en el estadio!   Hay **cientos** de libros en la biblioteca.
There are thousands of people   *There are hundreds of books*
in the stadium!   *in the library.*

▶ To express a complex number (including years), string together all of its components.

55.422   cincuenta y cinco mil cuatrocientos veintidós

¡INTÉNTALO!   Write out the Spanish equivalent of each number.

1. **102** _____ciento dos_____
2. **5.000.000** _____
3. **201** _____
4. **76** _____
5. **92** _____
6. **550.300** _____
7. **235** _____
8. **79** _____
9. **113** _____
10. **88** _____
11. **17.123** _____
12. **497** _____

Práctica y Comunicación

1 **Baloncesto** Provide these basketball scores in Spanish.

1. Ohio State 76, Michigan 65
2. Florida 92, Florida State 104
3. Stanford 83, UCLA 89
4. Purdue 81, Indiana 78
5. Princeton 67, Harvard 55
6. Duke 115, Virginia 121

2 **Completar** Following the pattern, write out the missing numbers in Spanish.

1. 50, 150, 250 ... 1.050

2. 5.000, 20.000, 35.000 ... 95.000

3. 100.000, 200.000, 300.000 ... 1.000.000

4. 100.000.000, 90.000.000, 80.000.000 ... 0

3 **Resolver** Solve the math problems. Write out the numbers in Spanish.

AYUDA

+	→	**más**
–	→	**menos**
=	→	**son**

> **modelo**
> 200 + 300 =
> *Doscientos más trescientos son quinientos.*

1. 1.000 + 753 =
2. 1.000.000 – 30.000 =
3. 10.000 + 555 =
4. 15 + 150 =
5. 100.000 + 205.000 =
6. 29.000 – 10.000 =

4 **Los números de teléfono** Write a list of telephone numbers that are important to you. Write out the numbers.

> **modelo**
> *mi celular: 635-1951 seis-tres-cinco-diecinueve-cincuenta y uno*

Síntesis

5 **Preguntas** With a partner, ask each other questions that require numbers in the answers. The questions could be about phone numbers, the number of people in your city or state, the year you finish college, etc.

> **modelo**
> **Estudiante 1:** *¿Cuándo terminas la universidad?*
> **Estudiante 2:** *Termino la universidad en dos mil diecinueve.*

CONJUGATED FORM
SUBJECT
Javier empiezo
Main clause

Recapitulación

Dudan

Review the grammar concepts you have learned in this lesson by completing these activities.

1 **Completar** Complete the chart with the correct verb forms. `24 pts.`

yo	tú	nosotros	ellas
compro			
	deseas		
		miramos	
			preguntan

2 **Números** Write these numbers in Spanish. `16 pts.`

modelo

645: seiscientos cuarenta y cinco

1. **49:** _____
2. **97:** _____
3. **113:** _____
4. **632:** _____
5. **1.781:** _____
6. **3.558:** _____
7. **1.006.015:** _____
8. **67.224.370:** _____

3 **Preguntas** Write questions for these answers. `12 pts.`

1. —¿_____ Patricia?
   —Patricia es de Colombia.
2. —¿_____ él?
   —Él es mi amigo (*friend*).
3. —¿_____ (tú)?
   —Hablo dos idiomas (*languages*).
4. —¿_____ (ustedes)?
   —Deseamos tomar café.
5. —¿_____?
   —Tomo biología porque me gustan las ciencias.
6. —¿_____?
   —Camilo descansa por las mañanas.

2.1 **Present tense of -ar verbs** *pp. 50–52*

estudiar

estudio	estudiamos
estudias	estudiáis
estudia	estudian

The verb gustar

(no) me gusta + el/la + [*singular noun*]

(no) me gustan + los/las + [*plural noun*]

(no) me gusta + [*infinitive(s)*]

Note: You may use **a mí** for emphasis, but never **yo**.

To ask a friend about likes and dislikes, use **te** instead of **me**, but never **tú**.

¿Te gusta la historia?

2.2 **Forming questions in Spanish** *pp. 55–56*

▶ ¿Ustedes trabajan los sábados?

▶ ¿Trabajan ustedes los sábados?

▶ Ustedes trabajan los sábados, ¿verdad?/¿no?

Interrogative words

¿Adónde?	¿Cuánto/a?	¿Por qué?
¿Cómo?	¿Cuántos/as?	¿Qué?
¿Cuál(es)?	¿De dónde?	¿Quién(es)?
¿Cuándo?	¿Dónde?	

2.3 **Present tense of estar** *pp. 59–60*

▶ estar: estoy, estás, está, estamos, estáis, están

2.4 **Numbers 31 and higher** *pp. 63–64*

31	treinta y uno	101	ciento uno
32	treinta y dos	200	doscientos/as
	(and so on)	500	quinientos/as
40	cuarenta	700	setecientos/as
50	cincuenta	900	novecientos/as
60	sesenta	1.000	mil
70	setenta	2.000	dos mil
80	ochenta	5.100	cinco mil cien
90	noventa	100.000	cien mil
100	cien, ciento	1.000.000	un millón (de)

4　**Al teléfono** Complete this telephone conversation with the correct forms of the verb **estar**.

16 pts.

MARÍA TERESA　Hola, señora López. (1) ¿ _____ Elisa en casa?

SRA. LÓPEZ　Hola, ¿quién es?

MARÍA TERESA　Soy María Teresa. Elisa y yo (2) _____ en la misma (*same*) clase de literatura.

SRA. LÓPEZ　¡Ah, María Teresa! ¿Cómo (3) _____ ?

MARÍA TERESA　(4) _____ muy bien, gracias. Y usted, ¿cómo (5) _____ ?

SRA. LÓPEZ　Bien, gracias. Pues, no, Elisa no (6) _____ en casa. Ella y su hermano (*her brother*) (7) _____ en la Biblioteca Cervantes.

MARÍA TERESA　¿Cervantes?

SRA. LÓPEZ　Es la biblioteca que (8) _____ al lado del café Bambú.

MARÍA TERESA　¡Ah, sí! Gracias, señora López.

SRA. LÓPEZ　Hasta luego, María Teresa.

5　**¿Qué te gusta?** Form complete sentences with the information provided to indicate what is liked. **28 pts.**

> **modelo**
>
> yo: las ciencias
> Me gustan las ciencias.

1. yo: la clase de música _____
2. tú: las lenguas extranjeras _____
3. yo: escuchar la radio _____
4. tú: la historia _____
5. yo: las matemáticas _____
6. tú: viajar _____
7. yo: el arte _____

6　**Canción** Use the appropriate forms of the verb **gustar** to complete the beginning of a popular song by Manu Chao. **4 pts.**

❝Me _____ los aviones°,
me gustas tú,
me _____ viajar,
me gustas tú,
me gusta la mañana,
me gustas tú.❞

aviones *airplanes*

Lectura

Antes de leer

Estrategia
Predicting content through formats

Recognizing the format of a document can help you to predict its content. For instance, invitations, greeting cards, and classified ads follow an easily identifiable format, which usually gives you a general idea of the information they contain. Look at the text and identify it based on its format.

	lunes	martes	miércoles	jueves	viernes
8:30	biología		biología		biología
9:00		historia		historia	
9:30	inglés		inglés		inglés
10:00					
10:30					
11:00					
12:00					
12:30					
1:00					
2:00	arte		arte		arte

If you guessed that this is a page from a student's schedule, you are correct. You can now infer that the document contains information about a student's weekly schedule, including days, times, and activities.

Cognados
Make a list of the cognates in the text and guess their English meanings. What do cognates reveal about the content of the document?

Examinar el texto
Look at the format of the document entitled ***¡Español en Madrid!*** What type of text is it? What information do you expect to find in this type of document?

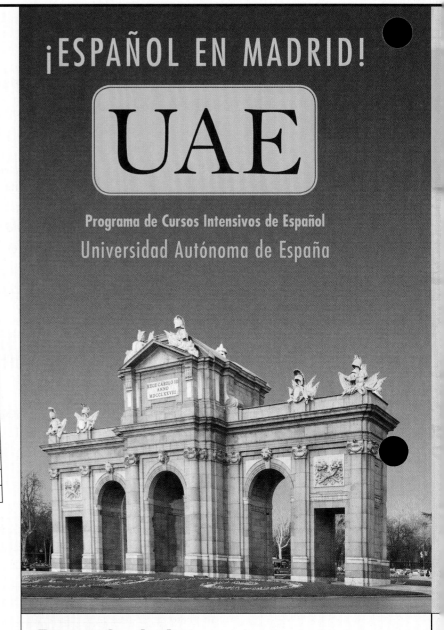

¡ESPAÑOL EN MADRID!

UAE

Programa de Cursos Intensivos de Español
Universidad Autónoma de España

Después de leer

Correspondencias

Provide the letter of each item in Column B that matches the words in Column A. Two items will not be used.

 A   B

A	B
1. profesores	a. (34) 91 523 4500
2. vivienda	b. (34) 91 524 0210
3. Madrid	c. 23 junio–30 julio
4. número de teléfono	d. capital cultural de Europa
5. Español 2B	e. 16 junio–22 julio
6. número de fax	f. especializados en enseñar español como lengua extranjera
	g. (34) 91 523 4623
	h. familias españolas

Universidad Autónoma de España

*Madrid, la capital cultural de Europa,
y la UAE te ofrecen cursos intensivos de verano°
para aprender° español como nunca antes°.*

¿Dónde?

En el campus de la UAE, edificio° de la Facultad de Filosofía y Letras.

¿Quiénes son los profesores?

Son todos hablantes nativos del español y catedráticos° de la UAE especializados en enseñar el español como lengua extranjera.

¿Qué niveles se ofrecen?

Se ofrecen tres niveles° básicos:

1. Español Elemental, A, B y C
2. Español Intermedio, A y B
3. Español Avanzado, A y B

Viviendas

Para estudiantes extranjeros se ofrece vivienda° con familias españolas.

¿Cuándo?

Este verano desde° el 16 de junio hasta el 10 de agosto. Los cursos tienen una duración de 6 semanas.

Cursos	Empieza°	Termina
Español 1A	16 junio	22 julio
Español 1B	23 junio	30 julio
Español 1C	30 junio	10 agosto
Español 2A	16 junio	22 julio
Español 2B	23 junio	30 julio
Español 3A	16 junio	22 julio
Español 3B	23 junio	30 julio

Información

Para mayor información, sirvan comunicarse con la siguiente° oficina:

Universidad Autónoma de España

Programa de Español como Lengua Extranjera
Calle del Valle de Mena 95, 28039 Madrid, España
Tel. (34) 91 523 4500, **Fax** (34) 91 523 4623
www.uae.es

verano *summer* aprender *to learn* nunca antes *never before* edificio *building* catedráticos *professors* niveles *levels* vivienda *housing* desde *from* Empieza *Begins* siguiente *following*

¿Cierto o falso?

Indicate whether each statement is **cierto** or **falso**.
Then correct the false statements.

	Cierto	Falso
1. La Universidad Autónoma de España ofrece (*offers*) cursos intensivos de italiano.	O	O
2. La lengua nativa de los profesores del programa es el inglés.	O	O
3. Los cursos de español son en la Facultad de Ciencias.	O	O
4. Los estudiantes pueden vivir (*can live*) con familias españolas.	O	O

	Cierto	Falso
5. La universidad que ofrece los cursos intensivos está en Salamanca.	O	O
6. Español 3B termina en agosto.	O	O
7. Si deseas información sobre (*about*) los cursos intensivos de español, es posible llamar al (34) 91 523 4500.	O	O
8. Español 1A empieza en julio.	O	O

Escritura

Estrategia
Brainstorming

How do you find ideas to write about? In the early stages of writing, brainstorming can help you generate ideas on a specific topic. You should spend ten to fifteen minutes brainstorming and jotting down any ideas about the topic. Whenever possible, try to write your ideas in Spanish. Express your ideas in single words or phrases, and jot them down in any order. While brainstorming, don't worry about whether your ideas are good or bad. Selecting and organizing ideas should be the second stage of your writing. Remember that the more ideas you write down while you're brainstorming, the more options you'll have to choose from later when you start to organize your ideas.

Me gusta

bailar
viajar
mirar la televisión
la clase de español
la clase de psicología

No me gusta

cantar
dibujar
trabajar
la clase de química
la clase de biología

Tema

Una descripción

Write a description of yourself to post in a chat room on a website in order to meet Spanish-speaking people. Include this information in your description:

▶ your name and where you are from, and a photo (optional) of yourself
▶ your major and where you go to school
▶ the courses you are taking
▶ where you work (if you have a job)
▶ some of your likes and dislikes

¡Hola! Me llamo Alicia Roberts. Estudio matemáticas en la Universidad de Toronto.

Escuchar

Estrategia
Listening for cognates

You already know that cognates are words that have similar spellings and meanings in two or more languages: for example, *group* and **grupo** or *stereo* and **estéreo**. Listen for cognates to increase your comprehension of spoken Spanish.

 To help you practice this strategy, you will now listen to two sentences. Make a list of all the cognates you hear.

Preparación

Based on the photograph, who do you think Armando and Julia are? What do you think they are talking about?

Ahora escucha

Now you are going to hear Armando and Julia's conversation. Make a list of the cognates they use.

Armando	Julia
_____	_____
_____	_____
_____	_____
_____	_____

Based on your knowledge of cognates, decide whether the following statements are **cierto** or **falso**.

	Cierto	Falso
1. Armando y Julia hablan de la familia.	○	○
2. Armando y Julia toman una clase de matemáticas.	○	○
3. Julia toma clases de ciencias.	○	○
4. Armando estudia lenguas extranjeras.	○	○
5. Julia toma una clase de religión.	○	○

Comprensión

Preguntas

Answer these questions about Armando and Julia's conversation.

1. ¿Qué clases toma Armando?

   _____

2. ¿Qué clases toma Julia?

   _____

Seleccionar

Choose the answer that best completes each sentence.

1. Armando toma _____ clases en la universidad.
   a. cuatro   b. cinco   c. seis
2. Julia toma dos clases de _____.
   a. matemáticas   b. lengua   c. ciencias
3. Armando toma italiano y _____.
   a. astronomía   b. japonés   c. geología
4. Armando y Julia estudian _____ los martes y jueves.
   a. filosofía   b. antropología   c. italiano

Preguntas personales

1. ¿Cuántas clases tomas tú este semestre?
2. ¿Qué clases tomas este semestre?
3. ¿Qué clases te gustan y qué clases no te gustan?

En pantalla

Christmas isn't always in winter. During the months of cold weather and snow in North America, the southern hemisphere enjoys warm weather and longer days. Since Chile's summer lasts from December to February, school vacation coincides with these months. In Chile, the school year starts in early March and finishes toward the end of December. All schools, from preschools to universities, observe this scholastic calendar, with only a few days' variation between institutions.

Vocabulario útil

quería	*I wanted*
pedirte	*to ask you*
te preocupa	*it worries you*
ahorrar	*to save (money)*
Navidad	*Christmas*
aprovecha	*take advantage of*
nuestras	*our*
ofertas	*offers, deals*
calidad	*quality*
no cuesta	*doesn't cost*

¿Qué hay?

For each item, write **sí** if it appears in the TV clip or **no** if it does not.

____ 1. papelera   ____ 5. diccionario
____ 2. lápiz   ____ 6. cuaderno
____ 3. mesa   ____ 7. tiza
____ 4. computadora   ____ 8. ventana

¿Qué quieres?

Write a list of things that you want for your next birthday. Use as much Spanish as you can.

> Lista de cumpleaños°
>
> Quiero°...

Viejito Pascuero°...

¿Cómo se escribe *mountain bike*?

M... O...

cumpleaños *birthday* Quiero *I want* Viejito Pascuero *Santa Claus (Chile)*

Mexican author and diplomat Octavio Paz (March 31, 1914–April 19, 1998) studied both law and literature at the **Universidad Nacional Autónoma de México** (**UNAM**), but after graduating he immersed himself in the art of writing. An incredibly prolific writer of novels, poetry, and essays, Paz solidified his prestige as Mexico's preeminent author with his 1950 book *El laberinto de la soledad*, a fundamental study of Mexican identity. Among the many awards he received in his lifetime are the **Premio Miguel de Cervantes** (1981) and Nobel Prize for Literature (1990). Paz foremost considered himself a poet and affirmed that poetry constitutes "**la religión secreta de la edad° moderna**".

Vocabulario útil

¿Cuál es tu materia favorita?	*What is your favorite subject?*
¿Cuántos años tienes?	*How old are you?*
¿Qué estudias?	*What do you study?*
el/la alumno/a	*student*
la carrera (de medicina)	*(medical) degree program, major*
derecho	*law*
reconocido	*well-known*

Preparación

What is the name of your school or university? What degree program are you in? What classes are you taking this semester?

Emparejar

Match the first part of the sentence in the left column with the appropriate ending in the right column.

1. En la UNAM no hay
2. México, D.F. es
3. La UNAM es
4. La UNAM ofrece

a. una universidad muy grande.
b. 74 carreras de estudio.
c. residencias estudiantiles.
d. la ciudad más grande (*biggest*) de Hispanoamérica.

Los estudios

—¿Qué estudias?
—Ciencias de la comunicación.

Estudio derecho en la UNAM.

¿Conoces a algún° profesor famoso que dé° clases... en la UNAM?

---

edad *age* ¿Conoces a algún...? *Do you know any...?* que dé *that teaches*

España

El país en cifras

- **Área:** 505.370 km² (kilómetros cuadrados) o 195.124 millas cuadradas°, incluyendo las islas Baleares y las islas Canarias
- **Población:** 47.043.000
- **Capital:** Madrid—5.762.000
- **Ciudades° principales:** Barcelona—5.029.000, Valencia—812.000, Sevilla, Zaragoza
- **Moneda°:** euro
- **Idiomas°:** español o castellano, catalán, gallego, valenciano, euskera

Plaza Mayor en Madrid

La Sagrada Familia en Barcelona

Gallego
Euskera
Catalán
Español
Valenciano

Regiones lingüísticas

Bandera de España

Españoles célebres

- **Miguel de Cervantes,** escritor° (1547–1616)
- **Pedro Almodóvar,** director de cine° (1949–)
- **Rosa Montero,** escritora y periodista° (1951–)
- **Fernando Alonso,** corredor de autos° (1981–)
- **Paz Vega,** actriz° (1976–)
- **Severo Ochoa,** Premio Nobel de Medicina, 1959; doctor y científico (1905–1993)

millas cuadradas *square miles* **Ciudades** *Cities* **Moneda** *Currency*
Idiomas *Languages* **escritor** *writer* **cine** *film* **periodista** *reporter*
corredor de autos *race car driver* **actriz** *actress* **pueblo** *town*
Cada año *Every year* **Durante todo un día** *All day long*
se tiran *throw at each other* **varias toneladas** *many tons*

Mar Cantábrico

FRANCIA

La Coruña

ANDORRA

San Sebastián

Pirineos

Zaragoza Río Ebro

Salamanca

Barcelona

ESPAÑA

Menorca

PORTUGAL

Madrid

Valencia

Mallorca

Ibiza

Islas Baleares

Sevilla

Sierra Nevada

Mar Mediterráneo

Estrecho de Gibraltar

Ceuta

Melilla

MARRUECOS

El baile flamenco

Islas Canarias

La Palma

Tenerife Gran Canaria

Lanzarote

Gomera

Hierro

OCÉANO ATLÁNTICO

EUROPA

ÁFRICA

ESPAÑA

¡Increíble pero cierto!

En Buñol, un pueblo° de Valencia, la producción de tomates es un recurso económico muy importante. Cada año° se celebra el festival de *La Tomatina*. Durante todo un día°, miles de personas se tiran° tomates. Llegan turistas de todo el país, y se usan varias toneladas° de tomates.

Gastronomía • **José Andrés**

José Andrés es un chef español famoso internacionalmente°. Le gusta combinar platos° tradicionales de España con las técnicas de cocina más innovadoras°. Andrés vive° en Washington, DC, es dueño° de varios restaurantes en los EE.UU. y presenta° un programa en PBS (foto, izquierda). También° ha estado° en *Late Show with David Letterman* y *Top Chef*.

Cultura • **La diversidad**

La riqueza° cultural y lingüística de España refleja la combinación de las diversas culturas que han habitado° en su territorio durante siglos°. El español es la lengua oficial del país, pero también son oficiales el catalán, el gallego, el euskera y el valenciano.

Sóc molt fan de la pàgina 335.

Póster en catalán

Ajuntament de Barcelona

Las meninas, Diego Velázquez, 1656

Artes • **Velázquez y el Prado**

El Prado, en Madrid, es uno de los museos más famosos del mundo°. En el Prado hay pinturas° importantes de Botticelli, de El Greco y de los españoles Goya y Velázquez. *Las meninas* es la obra° más conocida° de Diego Velázquez, pintor° oficial de la corte real° durante el siglo° XVII.

Comida • **La paella**

La paella es uno de los platos más típicos de España. Siempre se prepara° con arroz° y azafrán°, pero hay diferentes recetas°. La paella valenciana, por ejemplo, es de pollo° y conejo°, y la paella marinera es de mariscos°.

La costa de Ibiza

¿Qué aprendiste? Completa las oraciones con la información adecuada.
1. El chef español _____ es muy famoso.
2. El arroz y el azafrán son ingredientes básicos de la _____.
3. El Prado está en _____.
4. José Andrés vive en _____.
5. El chef José Andrés tiene un _____ de televisión en PBS.
6. El gallego es una de las lenguas oficiales de _____.

Conexión Internet Investiga estos temas en Internet.

1. Busca información sobre la Universidad de Salamanca u otra universidad española. ¿Qué cursos ofrece (*does it offer*)? ¿Ofrece tu universidad cursos similares?

2. Busca información sobre un español o una española célebre (por ejemplo, un[a] político/a, un actor, una actriz, un[a] artista). ¿De qué parte de España es y por qué es célebre?

....

internacionalmente *internationally* **platos** *dishes* **más innovadoras** *most innovative* **vive** *lives* **dueño** *owner* **presenta** *hosts* **También** *Also* **ha estado** *has been* **riqueza** *richness* **han habitado** *have lived* **durante siglos** *for centuries* **mundo** *world* **pinturas** *paintings* **obra** *work* **más conocida** *best-known* **pintor** *painter* **corte real** *royal court* **siglo** *century* **Siempre se prepara** *It is always prepared* **arroz** *rice* **azafrán** *saffron* **recetas** *recipes* **pollo** *chicken* **conejo** *rabbit* **mariscos** *seafood*

La clase y la universidad

el/la compañero/a de clase	classmate
el/la compañero/a de cuarto	roommate
el/la estudiante	student
el/la profesor(a)	teacher
el borrador	eraser
la calculadora	calculator
el escritorio	desk
el libro	book
el mapa	map
la mesa	table
la mochila	backpack
el papel	paper
la papelera	wastebasket
la pizarra	blackboard
la pluma	pen
la puerta	door
el reloj	clock; watch
la silla	seat
la tiza	chalk
la ventana	window
la biblioteca	library
la cafetería	cafeteria
la casa	house; home
el estadio	stadium
el laboratorio	laboratory
la librería	bookstore
la residencia estudiantil	dormitory
la universidad	university; college
la clase	class
el curso, la materia	course
la especialización	major
el examen	test; exam
el horario	schedule
la prueba	test; quiz
el semestre	semester
la tarea	homework
el trimestre	trimester; quarter

Las materias

la administración de empresas	business administration
la arqueología	archeology
el arte	art
la biología	biology
las ciencias	sciences
la computación	computer science
la contabilidad	accounting
la economía	economics
el español	Spanish
la física	physics
la geografía	geography
la historia	history
las humanidades	humanities
el inglés	English
las lenguas extranjeras	foreign languages
la literatura	literature
las matemáticas	mathematics
la música	music
el periodismo	journalism
la psicología	psychology
la química	chemistry
la sociología	sociology

Preposiciones y adverbios

al lado de	next to
a la derecha de	to the right of
a la izquierda de	to the left of
allá	over there
allí	there
cerca de	near
con	with
debajo de	below
delante de	in front of
detrás de	behind
en	in; on
encima de	on top of
entre	between
lejos de	far from
sin	without
sobre	on; over

Palabras adicionales

¿Adónde?	Where (to)?
ahora	now
¿Cuál?, ¿Cuáles?	Which?; Which one(s)?
¿Por qué?	Why?
porque	because

Verbos

bailar	to dance
buscar	to look for
caminar	to walk
cantar	to sing
cenar	to have dinner
comprar	to buy
contestar	to answer
conversar	to converse, to chat
desayunar	to have breakfast
descansar	to rest
desear	to wish; to desire
dibujar	to draw
enseñar	to teach
escuchar la radio/ música	to listen (to) the radio/music
esperar (+ inf.)	to wait (for); to hope
estar	to be
estudiar	to study
explicar	to explain
gustar	to like
hablar	to talk; to speak
llegar	to arrive
llevar	to carry
mirar	to look (at); to watch
necesitar (+ inf.)	to need
practicar	to practice
preguntar	to ask (a question)
preparar	to prepare
regresar	to return
terminar	to end; to finish
tomar	to take; to drink
trabajar	to work
viajar	to travel

Los días de la semana

¿Cuándo?	When?
¿Qué día es hoy?	What day is it?
Hoy es…	Today is…
la semana	week
lunes	Monday
martes	Tuesday
miércoles	Wednesday
jueves	Thursday
viernes	Friday
sábado	Saturday
domingo	Sunday

Numbers 31 and higher	See pages 63–64.
Expresiones útiles	See page 45.

La familia

3

Communicative Goals

You will learn how to:
- Talk about your family and friends
- Describe people and things
- Express possession

contextos

fotonovela

cultura

estructura

adelante

A PRIMERA VISTA
- ¿Cuántos chicos hay en la foto?
- ¿Hay una mujer detrás de la chica? ¿Y a la izquierda?
- ¿Hay una cosa en la mano del chico?
- ¿Conversan ellos? ¿Trabajan? ¿Descansan?
- ¿Están en su casa?

La familia

Más vocabulario

los abuelos	*grandparents*
el/la bisabuelo/a	*great-grandfather/ great-grandmother*
el/la gemelo/a	*twin*
el/la hermanastro/a	*stepbrother/stepsister*
el/la hijastro/a	*stepson/stepdaughter*
la madrastra	*stepmother*
el medio hermano/ la media hermana	*half-brother/ half-sister*
el padrastro	*stepfather*
los padres	*parents*
los parientes	*relatives*
el/la cuñado/a	*brother-in-law/ sister-in-law*
la nuera	*daughter-in-law*
el/la suegro/a	*father-in-law/ mother-in-law*
el yerno	*son-in-law*
el/la amigo/a	*friend*
el apellido	*last name*
la gente	*people*
el/la muchacho/a	*boy/girl*
el/la niño/a	*child*
el/la novio/a	*boyfriend/girlfriend*
la persona	*person*
el/la artista	*artist*
el/la ingeniero/a	*engineer*
el/la doctor(a), el/la médico/a	*doctor; physician*
el/la periodista	*journalist*
el/la programador(a)	*computer programmer*

Variación léxica

madre ←→ mamá, mami (*colloquial*)
padre ←→ papá, papi (*colloquial*)
muchacho/a ←→ chico/a

La familia de José Miguel Pérez Santoro

Juan Santoro Sánchez

mi abuelo (*my grandfather*)

Ernesto Santoro González

mi tío (*uncle*)
hijo (*son*) **de Juan y Socorro**

Marina Gutiérrez de Santoro

mi tía (*aunt*)
esposa (*wife*) **de Ernesto**

Silvia Socorro Santoro Gutiérrez

mi prima (*cousin*)
hija (*daughter*) **de Ernesto y Marina**

Héctor Manuel Santoro Gutiérrez

mi primo (*cousin*)
nieto (*grandson*) **de Juan y Socorro**

Carmen Santoro Gutiérrez

mi prima
hija de Ernesto y Marina

¡LENGUA VIVA!

In Spanish-speaking countries, it is common for people to go by both their first name and middle name, such as **José Miguel** or **Juan Carlos**. You will learn more about names and naming conventions on p. 86.

Socorro González
de Santoro

mi abuela (*my grandmother*)

Mirta Santoro
de Pérez

Rubén Ernesto
Pérez Gómez

mi madre (*mother*)
hija de Juan y Socorro

mi padre (*father*)
esposo de mi madre

José Miguel
Pérez Santoro

Beatriz Alicia
Pérez de Morales

Felipe Morales
Zapata

**hijo de Rubén
y Mirta**

mi hermana
(*sister*)

esposo (*husband*)
de Beatriz Alicia

Víctor Miguel
Morales Pérez

Anita Morales
Pérez

mi sobrino (*nephew*)
hermano (*brother*)
de Anita

mi sobrina (*niece*)
nieta (*granddaughter*)
de mis padres

los hijos (*children*) **de Beatriz Alicia y Felipe**

Práctica

1 **Escuchar** 🎧 Listen to each statement made by José Miguel Pérez Santoro, then indicate whether it is **cierto** or **falso**, based on his family tree.

	Cierto	Falso			Cierto	Falso
1.	○	○		6.	○	○
2.	○	○		7.	○	○
3.	○	○		8.	○	○
4.	○	○		9.	○	○
5.	○	○		10.	○	○

2 **Personas** 🎧 Indicate each word that you hear mentioned in the narration.

1. _____ cuñado
2. _____ tía
3. _____ periodista
4. _____ niño
5. _____ esposo
6. _____ abuelos
7. _____ ingeniera
8. _____ primo

3 **Emparejar** Provide the letter of the phrase that matches each description. Two items will not be used.

1. Mi hermano programa las computadoras.
2. Son los padres de mi esposo.
3. Son los hijos de mis (*my*) tíos.
4. Mi tía trabaja en un hospital.
5. Es el hijo de mi madrastra y el hijastro de mi padre.
6. Es el esposo de mi hija.
7. Es el hijo de mi hermana.
8. Mi primo dibuja y pinta mucho.
9. Mi hermanastra enseña en la universidad.
10. Mi padre trabaja con planos (*blueprints*).

a. Es médica.
b. Es mi hermanastro.
c. Es programador.
d. Es ingeniero.
e. Son mis suegros.
f. Es mi novio.
g. Es mi padrastro.
h. Son mis primos.
i. Es artista.
j. Es profesora.
k. Es mi sobrino.
l. Es mi yerno.

4 **Definiciones** Define these family terms in Spanish.

modelo

hijastro Es el hijo de mi esposo/a, pero no es mi hijo.

1. abuela
2. bisabuelo
3. tío
4. primas
5. suegra
6. cuñado
7. nietos
8. medio hermano

5

Escoger Complete the description of each photo using words you have learned in **Contextos**.

1. La _____ de Sara
   es grande.

2. Héctor y Lupita son _____.

3. Maira Díaz es _____.

4. Rubén habla con su _____.

5. Los dos _____ están
   en el parque.

6. Irene es _____.

7. Elena Vargas Soto es _____.

8. Don Manuel es el _____
   de Martín.

Comunicación

6 **Preguntas personales** Answer your partner's questions.

1. ¿Cuántas personas hay en tu familia?
2. ¿Cómo se llaman tus padres? ¿De dónde son? ¿Dónde trabajan?
3. ¿Cuántos hermanos tienes? ¿Cómo se llaman? ¿Dónde estudian o trabajan?
4. ¿Cuántos primos tienes? ¿Cuáles son los apellidos de ellos? ¿Cuántos son niños y cuántos son adultos? ¿Hay más chicos o más chicas en tu familia?
5. ¿Eres tío/a? ¿Cómo se llaman tus sobrinos/as? ¿Dónde estudian o trabajan?
6. ¿Quién es tu pariente favorito?
7. ¿Tienes novio/a? ¿Tienes esposo/a? ¿Cómo se llama?

AYUDA

tu, tus *your* (sing., pl.)
mi, mis *my* (sing., pl.)
tienes *you have*
tengo *I have*

7 **Árbol genealógico** Write about a family tree. Use your own family or invent a family.

> *modelo*
>
> *El abuelo se llama Robert Lange. Es de Nebraska...*

8 **Una familia** With a partner, identify the members in the family tree by asking questions about how each family member is related to Graciela Vargas García.

> *modelo*
>
> **Estudiante 1:** *¿Quién es Beatriz Pardo de Vargas?*
> **Estudiante 2:** *Es la abuela de Graciela.*

CONSULTA

To see the cities where these family members live, look at the map in **Panorama** on p. 112.

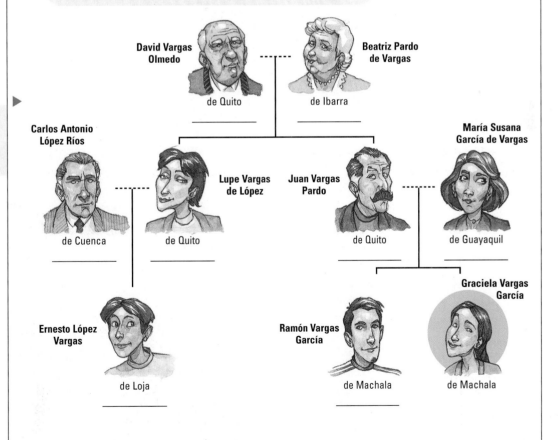

Un domingo en familia

Marissa pasa el día en Xochimilco con la familia Díaz.

PERSONAJES   FELIPE   TÍA NAYELI

JIMENA Hola, tía Nayeli.

TÍA NAYELI ¡Hola, Jimena! ¿Cómo estás?

JIMENA Bien, gracias. Y, ¿dónde están mis primas?

TÍA NAYELI No sé. ¿Dónde están mis hijas? ¡Ah!

MARISSA ¡Qué bonitas son tus hijas! Y ¡qué simpáticas!

MARISSA La verdad, mi familia es pequeña.

SRA. DÍAZ ¿Pequeña? Yo soy hija única. Bueno, y ¿qué más? ¿Tienes novio?

MARISSA No. Tengo mala suerte con los novios.

FELIPE Soy guapo y delgado.

JIMENA Ay, ¡por favor! Eres gordo, antipático y muy feo.

TÍO RAMÓN ¿Tienes una familia grande, Marissa?

MARISSA Tengo dos hermanos mayores, Zack y Jennifer, y un hermano menor, Adam.

MARISSA Tía Nayeli, ¿cuántos años tienen tus hijas?

TÍA NAYELI Marta tiene ocho años y Valentina doce.

JIMENA
 MARTA
 VALENTINA
 SRA. DÍAZ
 TÍO RAMÓN
 SR. DÍAZ
 MARISSA

7

SRA. DÍAZ Chicas, ¿compartimos una trajinera?

MARISSA ¡Claro que sí! ¡Qué bonitas son!

SRA. DÍAZ ¿Vienes, Jimena?

JIMENA No, gracias. Tengo que leer.

8

MARISSA Me gusta mucho este sitio. Tengo ganas de visitar otros lugares en México.

SRA. DÍAZ ¡Debes viajar a Mérida!

TÍA NAYELI ¡Sí, con tus amigos! Debes visitar a Ana María, la hermana de Roberto y de Ramón.

9

(*La Sra. Díaz habla por teléfono con la tía Ana María.*)

SRA. DÍAZ ¡Qué bien! Excelente. Sí, la próxima semana. Muchísimas gracias.

10

MARISSA ¡Gracias, Sra. Díaz!

SRA. DÍAZ Tía Ana María.

MARISSA Tía Ana María.

SRA. DÍAZ ¡Un beso, chau!

MARISSA *Bye!*

Expresiones útiles

Talking about your family

¿Tienes una familia grande?
Do you have a big family?
Tengo dos hermanos mayores y un hermano menor.
I have two older siblings and a younger brother.
La verdad, mi familia es pequeña.
The truth is, my family is small.
¿Pequeña? Yo soy hija única.
Small? I'm an only child.

Describing people

¡Qué bonitas son tus hijas!
Y ¡qué simpáticas!
Your daughters are so pretty!
And so nice!
Soy guapo y delgado.
I'm handsome and slim.
¡Por favor! Eres gordo, antipático y muy feo.
Please! You're fat, unpleasant, and very ugly.

Talking about plans

¿Compartimos una trajinera?
Shall we share a trajinera?
¡Claro que sí! ¡Qué bonitas son!
Of course! They're so pretty!
¿Vienes, Jimena?
Are you coming, Jimena?
No, gracias. Tengo que leer.
No, thanks. I have to read.

Saying how old people are

¿Cuántos años tienen tus hijas?
How old are your daughters?
Marta tiene ocho años y Valentina doce.
Marta is eight and Valentina twelve.

Additional vocabulary

ensayo *essay*
pobrecito/a *poor thing*
próxima *next*
sitio *place*
todavía *still*
trajinera *type of barge*

¿Qué pasó?

1 **¿Cierto o falso?** Indicate whether each sentence is **cierto** or **falso**. Correct the false statements.

		Cierto	Falso
1.	Marissa dice que (*says that*) tiene una familia grande.	○	○
2.	La Sra. Díaz tiene dos hermanos.	○	○
3.	Marissa no tiene novio.	○	○
4.	Valentina tiene veinte años.	○	○
5.	Marissa comparte una trajinera con la Sra. Díaz y la tía Nayeli.	○	○
6.	A Marissa le gusta mucho Xochimilco.	○	○

◀

NOTA CULTURAL

Xochimilco is famous for its system of canals and **chinampas,** or artificial islands, which have been used for agricultural purposes since Pre-Hispanic times. In 1987, UNESCO declared **Xochimilco** a World Heritage Site.

2 **Identificar** Indicate which person would make each statement. The names may be used more than once. **¡Ojo!** One name will not be used.

1. Felipe es antipático y feo.
2. Mis hermanos se llaman Jennifer, Adam y Zack.
3. ¡Soy un joven muy guapo!
4. Mis hijas tienen ocho y doce años.
5. ¡Qué bonitas son las trajineras!
6. Ana María es la hermana de Ramón y Roberto.
7. No puedo (*I can't*) compartir una trajinera porque tengo que leer.
8. Tus hijas son bonitas y simpáticas, tía Nayeli.

SRA. DÍAZ

JIMENA

MARISSA

FELIPE

TÍA NAYELI

NOTA CULTURAL

Trajineras are large passenger barges that you can rent in **Xochimilco.** Each boat is named and decorated and has a table and chairs so passengers can picnic while they ride.

3 **Escribir** Choose Marissa, Sra. Díaz, or tía Nayeli and write a brief description of her family. Be creative!

MARISSA

SRA. DÍAZ

TÍA NAYELI

Marissa es de los EE.UU.
¿Cómo es su familia?

La Sra. Díaz es de Cuba.
¿Cómo es su familia?

La tía Nayeli es de México.
¿Cómo es su familia?

4 **Conversar** Answer your partner's questions.

1. ¿Cuántos años tienes?
2. ¿Tienes una familia grande?
3. ¿Tienes hermanos o hermanas?
4. ¿Cuántos años tiene tu abuelo (tu hermana, tu primo, etc.)?
5. ¿De dónde son tus padres?

◀

AYUDA

Here are some expressions to help you talk about age.

Yo tengo… años.
I am… years old.

Mi abuelo tiene… años.
My grandfather is… years old.

Pronunciación
Diphthongs and linking

hermano   **niña**   **cuñado**

In Spanish, **a**, **e**, and **o** are considered strong vowels. The weak vowels are **i** and **u**.

---

ruido   **parientes**   **periodista**

A diphthong is a combination of two weak vowels or of a strong vowel and a weak vowel. Diphthongs are pronounced as a single syllable.

mi hijo   **una clase excelente**

Two identical vowel sounds that appear together are pronounced like one long vowel.

la abuela

---

con Natalia   **sus sobrinos**   **las sillas**

Two identical consonants together sound like a single consonant.

---

es ingeniera   **mis abuelos**   **sus hijos**

A consonant at the end of a word is linked with the vowel sound at the beginning of the next word.

---

mi hermano   **su esposa**   **nuestro amigo**

A vowel at the end of a word is linked with the vowel sound at the beginning of the next word.

Práctica Say these words aloud, focusing on the diphthongs.

1. historia	5. residencia	9. lenguas
2. nieto	6. prueba	10. estudiar
3. parientes	7. puerta	11. izquierda
4. novia	8. ciencias	12. ecuatoriano

Oraciones Read these sentences aloud to practice diphthongs and linking words.

1. Hola. Me llamo Anita Amaral. Soy del Ecuador.
2. Somos seis en mi familia.
3. Tengo dos hermanos y una hermana.
4. Mi papá es del Ecuador y mi mamá es de España.

Refranes Read these sayings aloud to practice diphthongs and linking sounds.

Cuando una puerta se cierra, otra se abre.[1]

Hablando del rey de Roma, por la puerta se asoma.[2]

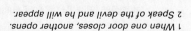

1 When one door closes, another opens. 2 Speak of the devil and he will appear.

¿Cómo te llamas?

In the Spanish-speaking world, it is common to have two last names: one paternal and one maternal. In some cases, the conjunctions **de** or **y** are used to connect the two. For example, in the name **Juan Martínez de Velasco**, *Martínez* is the paternal surname (**el apellido paterno**), and *Velasco* is the maternal surname (**el apellido materno**); **de** simply links the two. This convention of using two last names (**doble apellido**) is a European tradition that Spaniards brought to the Americas. It continues to be practiced in many countries, including Chile, Colombia, Mexico, Peru, and Venezuela. There are exceptions, however. In Argentina, the prevailing custom is for children to inherit only the father's last name.

When a woman marries in a country where two last names are used, legally she retains her two maiden surnames. However, socially she may take her husband's paternal surname in place of her inherited maternal surname. For example, **Mercedes**

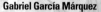

Gabriel García Márquez   **Mercedes Barcha Pardo**

Rodrigo García Barcha

Barcha Pardo, widow of Colombian writer **Gabriel García Márquez**, might use the names **Mercedes Barcha García** or **Mercedes Barcha de García** in social situations (although officially her name remains **Mercedes Barcha Pardo**). Adopting a husband's last name for social purposes, though widespread, is only legally recognized in Ecuador and Peru.

Most parents do not break tradition upon naming their children; regardless of the surnames the mother uses, they use the father's first surname followed by the mother's first surname, as in the name **Rodrigo García Barcha**. However, one should note that both surnames come from the grandfathers, and therefore all **apellidos** are effectively paternal.

Hijos en la casa

In Spanish-speaking countries, family and society place very little pressure on young adults to live on their own (**independizarse**), and children often live with their parents well into their thirties. For example, about 60% of Spaniards under 34 years of age live at home with their parents. This delay in moving out is both cultural and economic—lack of job security or low wages coupled with a high cost of living may make it impractical for young adults to live independently before they marry.

1 **¿Cierto o falso?** Indicate whether these statements are **cierto** or **falso**. Correct the false statements.

1. Most Spanish-speaking people have three last names.

2. Hispanic last names generally consist of the paternal last name followed by the maternal last name.

3. It is common to see **de** or **y** used in a Hispanic last name.

4. Someone from Argentina would most likely have two last names.

5. Generally, married women legally retain two maiden surnames.

6. In social situations, a married woman often uses her husband's last name in place of her inherited paternal surname.

7. Adopting a husband's surname is only legally recognized in Peru and Ecuador.

8. Hispanic last names are effectively a combination of the maternal surnames from the previous generation.

Familia y amigos

el/la bisnieto/a	*great-grandson/daughter*
el/la chamaco/a (Méx.); el/la chamo/a (Ven.); el/la chaval(a) (Esp.); el/la pibe/a (Arg.)	el/la muchacho/a
mi colega (Esp.); mi cuate (Méx.); mi parcero/a (Col.); mi pana (Ven., P. Rico, Rep. Dom.)	*my pal; my buddy*
la madrina	*godmother*
el padrino	*godfather*
el/la tatarabuelo/a	*great-great-grandfather/ great-great-grandmother*

Las familias

Although worldwide population trends show a decrease in average family size, households in many Spanish-speaking countries are still larger than their U.S. counterparts.

- **México** 4,0 personas
- **Colombia** 3,9 personas
- **Argentina** 3,6 personas
- **Uruguay** 3,0 personas
- **España** 2,9 personas
- **Estados Unidos** 2,6 personas

La familia real española

Undoubtedly, Spain's most famous family is **la familia real** (*Royal*). In 1962, the then prince **Juan Carlos de Borbón** married Princess **Sofía** of Greece. In the 1970s, **el Rey** (*King*) **Juan Carlos** and **la Reina** (*Queen*) **Sofía** helped transition Spain to democracy after a forty-year dictatorship. The royal couple has three children: las **infantas** (*Princesses*) **Elena** and **Cristina**, and a son, **el príncipe** (*Prince*) **Felipe**, whose official title was **el Príncipe de Asturias**. In 2004, Felipe married **Letizia Ortiz Rocasolano,** a journalist and TV presenter. They have two daughters, **las infantas Leonor** (born in 2005) and **Sofía** (born in 2007). In 2014, Juan Carlos decided to abdicate the throne in favor of his son.

Conexión Internet

What role do **padrinos** and **madrinas** have in today's Hispanic family?

Use the Web to find more cultural information related to this **Cultura** section.

2 **Comprensión** Complete these sentences.

1. Spain's royals were responsible for guiding in _____.
2. In Spanish, your godmother is called _____.
3. Princess Leonor is the _____ of Queen Sofía.
4. Uruguay's average household has _____ people.
5. If a Venezuelan calls you **mi pana**, you are that person's _____.

3 **Una familia famosa** Create a genealogical tree of a famous family, using photos or drawings labeled with names and ages. Explain who the people are and their relationships to each other.

Descriptive adjectives

ANTE TODO Adjectives are words that describe people, places, and things. In Spanish, descriptive adjectives are used with the verb **ser** to point out characteristics such as nationality, size, color, shape, personality, and appearance.

Forms and agreement of adjectives

COMPARE & CONTRAST

In English, the forms of descriptive adjectives do not change to reflect the gender (masculine/feminine) and number (singular/plural) of the noun or pronoun they describe.

*Juan is **nice**.*   *Elena is **nice**.*   *They are **nice**.*

In Spanish, the forms of descriptive adjectives agree in gender and/or number with the nouns or pronouns they describe.

   Juan es simpátic**o**.   Elena es simpátic**a**.   Ellos son simpátic**os**.

▶ Adjectives that end in **-o** have four different forms. The feminine singular is formed by changing the **-o** to **-a**. The plural is formed by adding **-s** to the singular forms.

Masculine		Feminine	
SINGULAR	PLURAL	SINGULAR	PLURAL
el muchach**o** alt**o**	los muchach**os** alt**os**	la muchach**a** alt**a**	las muchach**as** alt**as**

¡Qué bonitas son
tus hijas, tía Nayeli!

Felipe es gordo,
antipático y muy feo.

▶ Adjectives that end in **-e** or a consonant have the same masculine and feminine forms.

Masculine		Feminine	
SINGULAR	PLURAL	SINGULAR	PLURAL
el chico inteligent**e**	los chicos inteligent**es**	la chica inteligent**e**	las chicas inteligent**es**
el examen difíci**l**	los exámenes difíci**les**	la clase difíci**l**	las clases difíci**les**

▶ Adjectives that end in **-or** are variable in both gender and number.

Masculine		Feminine	
SINGULAR	PLURAL	SINGULAR	PLURAL
el hombre trabajad**or**	los hombres trabajad**ores**	la mujer trabajad**ora**	las mujeres trabajad**oras**

▶ Use the masculine plural form to refer to groups that include males and females.

Manuel es alt**o**.   Lola es alt**a**.   Manuel y Lola son alt**os**.

Common adjectives

alto/a	*tall*	**gordo/a**	*fat*	**mucho/a**	*much; many;*
antipático/a	*unpleasant*	**grande**	*big*		*a lot of*
bajo/a	*short (in*	**guapo/a**	*good-looking*	**pelirrojo/a**	*red-haired*
	height)	**importante**	*important*	**pequeño/a**	*small*
bonito/a	*pretty*	**inteligente**	*intelligent*	**rubio/a**	*blond(e)*
bueno/a	*good*	**interesante**	*interesting*	**simpático/a**	*nice; likeable*
delgado/a	*thin*	**joven**	*young*	**tonto/a**	*foolish*
difícil	*difficult*	**malo/a**	*bad*	**trabajador(a)**	*hard-working*
fácil	*easy*	**mismo/a**	*same*	**viejo/a**	*old*
feo/a	*ugly*	**moreno/a**	*brunet(te)*		

Adjectives of nationality

▶ Unlike in English, Spanish adjectives of nationality are **not** capitalized. Proper names of countries, however, are capitalized.

Some adjectives of nationality

alemán, alemana	*German*	**francés, francesa**	*French*
argentino/a	*Argentine*	**inglés, inglesa**	*English*
canadiense	*Canadian*	**italiano/a**	*Italian*
chino/a	*Chinese*	**japonés, japonesa**	*Japanese*
costarricense	*Costa Rican*	**mexicano/a**	*Mexican*
cubano/a	*Cuban*	**norteamericano/a**	*(North) American*
ecuatoriano/a	*Ecuadorian*	**puertorriqueño/a**	*Puerto Rican*
español(a)	*Spanish*	**ruso/a**	*Russian*
estadounidense	*from the U.S.*		

▶ Adjectives of nationality are formed like other descriptive adjectives. Those that end in **-o** change to **-a** when forming the feminine.

chin**o** ⟶ chin**a**   mexican**o** ⟶ mexican**a**

The plural is formed by adding an **-s** to the masculine or feminine form.

argentin**o** ⟶ argentin**os**   cuban**a** ⟶ cuban**as**

▶ Adjectives of nationality that end in **-e** have only two forms, singular and plural.

canadiens**e** ⟶ canadiens**es**   estadounidens**e** ⟶ estadounidens**es**

▶ To form the feminine of adjectives of nationality that end in a consonant, add **–a**.

alem**á**n ⟶ alema**na**   españo**l** ⟶ españo**la**

japoné**s** ⟶ japone**sa**   inglé**s** ⟶ ingle**sa**

Position of adjectives

▶ Descriptive adjectives and adjectives of nationality generally follow the nouns they modify.

El niño **rubio** es de España.
The blond boy is from Spain.

La mujer **española** habla inglés.
The Spanish woman speaks English.

▶ Unlike descriptive adjectives, adjectives of quantity precede the modified noun.

Hay **muchos** libros en la biblioteca.
There are many books in the library.

Hablo con **dos** turistas puertorriqueños.
I am talking with two Puerto Rican tourists.

▶ **Bueno/a** and **malo/a** can appear before or after a noun. When placed before a masculine singular noun, the forms are shortened: **bueno** ⟶ **buen; malo** ⟶ **mal.**

Joaquín es un **buen** amigo.
Joaquín es un amigo **bueno.** ⟶ *Joaquín is a good friend.*

Hoy es un **mal** día.
Hoy es un día **malo.** ⟶ *Today is a bad day.*

▶ When **grande** appears before a singular noun, it is shortened to **gran**, and the meaning of the word changes: **gran** = *great* and **grande** = *big, large.*

Don Francisco es un **gran** hombre.
Don Francisco is a great man.

La familia de Inés es **grande.**
Inés' family is large.

¡INTÉNTALO!   Provide the appropriate forms of the adjectives.

simpático

1. Mi hermano es ___simpático___.
2. La profesora Martínez es _____.
3. Rosa y Teresa son _____.
4. Nosotros somos _____.

alemán

1. Hans es ___alemán___.
2. Mis primas son _____.
3. Marcus y yo somos _____.
4. Mi tía es _____.

difícil

1. La química es ___difícil___.
2. El curso es _____.
3. Las pruebas son _____.
4. Los libros son _____.

guapo

1. Su esposo es ___guapo___.
2. Mis sobrinas son _____.
3. Los padres de ella son _____.
4. Marta es _____.

Práctica

1 **Emparejar** Find the words in column B that are the opposite of the words in column A. One word in B will not be used.

Marcos
Jorge

A	B
1. guapo	a. delgado
2. moreno	b. pequeño
3. alto	c. malo
4. gordo	d. feo
5. joven	e. viejo
6. grande	f. rubio
7. simpático	g. antipático
	h. bajo

2 **Completar** Indicate the nationalities of these people by selecting the correct adjectives and changing their forms when necessary.

NOTA CULTURAL

Alfonso Cuarón
(1961–) became the
first Mexican winner
of the Best Director
Academy Award for
his film *Gravity* (2013).

1. Penélope Cruz es _____.
▶ 2. Alfonso Cuarón es un gran director de cine de México; es _____.
3. Ellen Page y Avril Lavigne son _____.
4. Giorgio Armani es un diseñador de modas (*fashion designer*) _____.
5. Daisy Fuentes es de La Habana, Cuba; ella es _____.
6. Emma Watson y Daniel Radcliffe son actores _____.
7. Heidi Klum y Michael Fassbender son _____.
8. Serena Williams y Michael Phelps son _____.

3 **Describir** Look at the drawing and describe each family member using as many adjectives as possible.

Carlos Romero Sandoval
Josefina Barcos de Romero
Susana Romero Barcos
Tomás Romero Barcos
Alberto Romero Pereda

1. Susana Romero Barcos es _____.
2. Tomás Romero Barcos es _____.
3. Los dos hermanos son _____.
4. Josefina Barcos de Romero es _____.
5. Carlos Romero Sandoval es _____.
6. Alberto Romero Pereda es _____.
7. Tomás y su (*his*) padre son _____.
8. Susana y su (*her*) madre son _____.

Comunicación

4

Busco novio Read Cecilia's personal ad. Then indicate whether these conclusions are **lógico** or **ilógico**, based on what you read.

	Lógico	Ilógico
1. Cecilia es profesora.	○	○
2. Cecilia desea ser artista.	○	○
3. Cecilia dibuja.	○	○
4. Cecilia tiene novio.	○	○
5. El novio ideal de Cecilia es ingeniero.	○	○

SOY ALTA, morena y bonita. Soy cubana, de Holguín. Estudio arte en la universidad. Busco un chico similar. Mi novio ideal es alto, moreno, inteligente y muy simpático.

5

Preguntas Answer your partner's questions.

1. ¿Cómo eres tú?
2. ¿Cómo es tu casa?
3. ¿Cómo es tu universidad?
4. ¿Cómo es tu ciudad?
5. ¿Cómo es tu país?
6. ¿Cómo son tus amigos?

6

Anuncio personal Write a personal ad that describes yourself and your ideal boyfriend, girlfriend, or mate.

Síntesis

7

¿Cómo es? With a partner, take turns describing people, places, and things. You may want to use the items on the list. Tell your partner whether you agree (**Estoy de acuerdo**) or disagree (**No estoy de acuerdo**) with his/her descriptions.

> **modelo**
>
> San Francisco
> **Estudiante 1:** San Francisco es una ciudad (city) muy bonita.
> **Estudiante 2:** No estoy de acuerdo. Es muy fea.

Nueva York
Chicago
George Clooney
Taylor Swift
los médicos
los periodistas

las clases de español/física/
   matemáticas/química
el presidente de los Estados
   Unidos
la primera dama (first lady)
   de los Estados Unidos

3.2 Possessive adjectives

ANTE TODO Possessive adjectives, like descriptive adjectives, are words that are used to qualify people, places, or things. Possessive adjectives express the quality of ownership or possession.

Forms of possessive adjectives

SINGULAR FORMS	PLURAL FORMS	
mi	**mis**	*my*
tu	**tus**	*your* (fam.)
su	**sus**	*his, her, its, your* (form.)
nuestro/a	**nuestros/as**	*our*
vuestro/a	**vuestros/as**	*your* (fam.)
su	**sus**	*their, your*

COMPARE & CONTRAST

In English, possessive adjectives are invariable; that is, they do not agree in gender and number with the nouns they modify. Spanish possessive adjectives, however, do agree in number with the nouns they modify.

my cousin	*my cousins*	*my aunt*	*my aunts*
mi primo	**mis** primos	**mi** tía	**mis** tías

The forms **nuestro** and **vuestro** agree in both gender and number with the nouns they modify.

nuestr**o** prim**o**	nuestr**os** prim**os**	nuestr**a** tía	nuestr**as** tías

▶ Possessive adjectives are always placed before the nouns they modify.

—¿Está **tu novio** aquí?   —No, **mi novio** está en la biblioteca.
Is your boyfriend here?   *No, my boyfriend is in the library.*

▶ Because **su** and **sus** have multiple meanings (*your, his, her, their, its*), you can avoid confusion by using this construction instead: [*article*] + [*noun*] + **de** + [*subject pronoun*].

sus parientes ◀
los parientes **de él/ella**   *his/her relatives*
los parientes **de Ud./Uds.**   *your relatives*
los parientes **de ellos/ellas** *their relatives*

 **¡INTÉNTALO!** Provide the appropriate form of each possessive adjective.

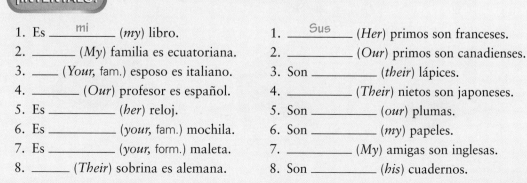

1. Es _____mi_____ (*my*) libro.
2. _____ (*My*) familia es ecuatoriana.
3. ____ (*Your*, fam.) esposo es italiano.
4. _____ (*Our*) profesor es español.
5. Es _____ (*her*) reloj.
6. Es _____ (*your*, fam.) mochila.
7. Es _____ (*your*, form.) maleta.
8. _____ (*Their*) sobrina es alemana.

1. ___Sus___ (*Her*) primos son franceses.
2. _____ (*Our*) primos son canadienses.
3. Son _____ (*their*) lápices.
4. _____ (*Their*) nietos son japoneses.
5. Son _____ (*our*) plumas.
6. Son _____ (*my*) papeles.
7. _____ (*My*) amigas son inglesas.
8. Son _____ (*his*) cuadernos.

Práctica

1 **La familia de Manolo** Complete each sentence with the correct possessive adjective from the options in parentheses. Use the subject of each sentence as a guide.

1. Me llamo Manolo, y _____ (nuestro, mi, sus) hermano es Federico.
2. _____ (Nuestra, Sus, Mis) madre Silvia es profesora y enseña química.
3. Ella admira a _____ (tu, nuestro, sus) estudiantes porque trabajan mucho.
4. Yo estudio en la misma universidad, pero no tomo clases con _____ (mi, nuestras, tus) madre.
5. Federico trabaja en una oficina con _____ (mis, tu, nuestro) padre.
6. _____ (Mi, Su, Tu) oficina está en el centro de la Ciudad de México.
7. Javier y Óscar son _____ (mis, mi, sus) tíos de Oaxaca.
8. ¿Y tú? ¿Cómo es _____ (mi, su, tu) familia?

2 **Clarificar** Clarify each sentence with a prepositional phrase. Follow the model.

> **modelo**
>
> Su hermana es muy bonita. (ella)
>
> *La hermana de ella es muy bonita.*

1. Su casa es muy grande. (ellos) _____
2. ¿Cómo se llama su hermano? (ellas) _____
3. Sus padres trabajan en el centro. (ella) _____
4. Sus abuelos son muy simpáticos. (él) _____
5. Maribel es su prima. (ella) _____
6. Su primo lee los libros. (ellos) _____

3 **¿Dónde está?** Look at the drawings and indicate where your belongings are. ◄

> **modelo**
>
> *Mi mochila está encima del escritorio.*

1.

2.

3.

4.

5.

6.

Comunicación

4

Noticias de familia Listen to Ana María talk about some family news. Then indicate whether the following conclusions are **lógico** or **ilógico**, based on what you heard.

	Lógico	Ilógico
1. Ana María es rubia.	○	○
2. Sus padres están en Bogotá.	○	○
3. Su primo es inteligente.	○	○
4. Su primo habla español.	○	○
5. La novia de su primo es doctora.	○	○

5

Describir With a partner, describe the people and places listed below.

> **modelo**
>
> la biblioteca de su universidad
> La biblioteca de nuestra universidad es muy grande. Hay muchos libros en la biblioteca.

1. tu profesor favorito
2. tu profesora favorita
3. tus clases
4. la librería de su universidad
5. tus padres
6. tus abuelos
7. tu mejor (*best*) amigo
8. tu mejor amiga

6

Una familia famosa Assume the identity of a member of a famous family, real or fictional (the Obamas, Clintons, Bushes, Kardashians, Simpsons, etc.), and write a description of "your" family. Reveal your identity at the end of your description.

> **modelo**
>
> Hay cuatro personas en mi familia. Mi padre es delgado y simpático. Él es de Philadelphia. Mi madre es muy inteligente y guapa. Mis padres son actores. Tengo una hermana menor. Nosotros también somos actores... Soy Jaden Smith.

Síntesis

7

Describe a tu familia With a partner, take turns asking each other questions about your families.

> **modelo**
>
> **Estudiante 1:** ¿Cómo es tu padre?
> **Estudiante 2:** Mi padre es alto, guapo y muy inteligente.

3.3 Present tense of -er and -ir verbs

ANTE TODO   In **Lección 2,** you learned how to form the present tense of regular -ar verbs. You also learned about the importance of verb forms, which change to show who is performing the action. The chart below shows the forms from two other important groups, **-er** verbs and **-ir** verbs.

CONSULTA

To review the conjugation of -ar verbs, see **Estructura 2.1**, p. 50.

Present tense of -er and -ir verbs		
	comer *(to eat)*	**escrib**ir *(to write)*
SINGULAR FORMS		
yo	com**o**	escrib**o**
tú	com**es**	escrib**es**
Ud./él/ella	com**e**	escrib**e**
PLURAL FORMS		
nosotros/as	com**emos**	escrib**imos**
vosotros/as	com**éis**	escrib**ís**
Uds./ellos/ellas	com**en**	escrib**en**

▶ **-Er** and **-ir** verbs have very similar endings. Study the preceding chart to detect the patterns that make it easier for you to use them to communicate in Spanish.

AYUDA

Here are some tips on learning Spanish verbs:
1) Learn to identify the verb's stem, to which all endings attach.
2) Memorize the endings that go with each verb and verb tense.
3) As often as possible, practice using different forms of each verb in speech and writing.
4) Devote extra time to learning irregular verbs, such as **ser** and **estar**.

Felipe y su tío comen.

Jimena lee.

▶ Like **-ar** verbs, the **yo** forms of **-er** and **-ir** verbs end in **-o.**

Yo com**o**.   Yo escrib**o**.

▶ Except for the **yo** form, all of the verb endings for **-er** verbs begin with **-e.**

-es	**-emos**	**-en**
-e	**-éis**	

▶ **-Er** and **-ir** verbs have the exact same endings, except in the **nosotros/as** and **vosotros/as** forms.

nosotros ◀ com**emos** / escrib**imos**   vosotros ◀ com**éis** / escrib**ís**

Common -er and -ir verbs

-er verbs		-ir verbs	
aprender (a + *inf.*)	*to learn*	**abrir**	*to open*
beber	*to drink*	**asistir (a)**	*to attend*
comer	*to eat*	**compartir**	*to share*
comprender	*to understand*	**decidir (+ *inf.*)**	*to decide*
correr	*to run*	**describir**	*to describe*
creer (en)	*to believe (in)*	**escribir**	*to write*
deber (+ *inf.*)	*should*	**recibir**	*to receive*
leer	*to read*	**vivir**	*to live*

Ellos **corren** en el parque.

Él **escribe** una carta.

¡INTÉNTALO! Provide the appropriate present tense forms of these verbs.

correr

1. Graciela ___corre___.
2. Tú _____.
3. Yo _____.
4. Sara y Ana _____.
5. Usted _____.
6. Ustedes _____.
7. La gente _____.
8. Marcos y yo _____.

abrir

1. Ellos ___abren___ la puerta.
2. Carolina _____ la maleta.
3. Yo _____ las ventanas.
4. Nosotras _____ los libros.
5. Usted _____ el cuaderno.
6. Tú _____ la ventana.
7. Ustedes _____ las maletas.
8. Los muchachos _____ los cuadernos.

aprender

1. Él ___aprende___ español.
2. Maribel y yo _____ inglés.
3. Tú _____ japonés.
4. Tú y tu hermanastra _____ francés.
5. Mi hijo _____ chino.
6. Yo _____ alemán.
7. Usted _____ inglés.
8. Nosotros _____ italiano.

Práctica

1 **Completar** Complete Susana's sentences about her family with the correct forms of the verbs in parentheses. One of the verbs will remain in the infinitive.

1. Mi familia y yo _____ (vivir) en Mérida, Yucatán.
2. Tengo muchos libros. Me gusta _____ (leer).
3. Mi hermano Alfredo es muy inteligente. Alfredo _____ (asistir) a clases los lunes, miércoles y viernes.
4. Los martes y jueves Alfredo y yo _____ (correr) en el Parque del Centenario.
5. Mis padres _____ (comer) mucha lasaña los domingos y se quedan dormidos (*they fall asleep*).
6. Yo _____ (creer) que (*that*) mis padres deben comer menos (*less*).

2 **Oraciones** Juan is talking about what he and his friends do after school. Form complete sentences by adding any other necessary elements.

> **modelo**
> yo / correr / amigos / lunes y miércoles
> *Yo corro con mis amigos los lunes y miércoles.*

1. Manuela / asistir / clase / yoga
2. Eugenio / abrir / correo electrónico (*e-mail*)
3. Isabel y yo / leer / biblioteca
4. Sofía y Roberto / aprender / hablar / inglés
5. tú / comer / cafetería / universidad
6. mi novia y yo / compartir / libro de historia

3 **Consejos** Mario and his family are spending a year abroad to learn Japanese. Use the words below to indicate what he and/or his family members are doing or should do to adjust to life in Japan. Then, create one more sentence using a verb not on the list.

> **modelo**
> recibir libros / deber practicar japonés
> *Mario y su esposa reciben muchos libros en japonés.*
> *Los hijos deben practicar japonés.*

aprender japonés	decidir explorar el país
asistir a clases	escribir listas de palabras en japonés
beber sake	leer novelas japonesas
deber comer cosas nuevas	vivir con una familia japonesa
¿?	¿?

Comunicación

4

Entrevista Answer your partner's questions.

1. ¿Dónde comes al mediodía? ¿Comes mucho?
2. ¿Dónde vives?
3. ¿Con quién vives?
4. ¿Qué cursos debes tomar el próximo (*next*) semestre?
5. ¿Lees el periódico (*newspaper*)? ¿Qué periódico lees y cuándo?
6. ¿Recibes muchos mensajes de texto (*text messages*)? ¿De quién(es)?
7. ¿Escribes poemas?
8. ¿Crees en fantasmas (*ghosts*)?

5

Deberes Talk about at least five things you should do to improve your life and the lives of others. Use **deber** (+ *inf.*) and other **-er** or **-ir** verbs.

> *modelo*
>
> *Yo debo correr más...*

6

Descripción With a partner, take turns choosing an action from the list. Then give a description. Your partner will have to guess the action you are describing.

abrir (un libro, una puerta, una mochila)	correr (en el parque, en un maratón)
aprender (a bailar, a hablar francés, a dibujar)	escribir (una composición, un mensaje de texto [*text message*], con lápiz)
asistir (a una clase de yoga, a un concierto de rock, a una clase interesante)	leer (una carta [*letter*] de amor, un mensaje electrónico [*e-mail message*], un periódico [*newspaper*])
beber (agua, Coca-Cola)	recibir un regalo (*gift*)
comer (pasta, un sándwich, pizza)	¿?
compartir (un libro, un sándwich)	

> *modelo*
>
> **Estudiante 1:** *Soy estudiante y tomo muchas clases. Vivo en Roma.*
> **Estudiante 2:** *¿Comes pasta?*
> **Estudiante 1:** *No, no como pasta.*
> **Estudiante 2:** *¿Aprendes a hablar italiano?*
> **Estudiante 1:** *¡Sí!*

Síntesis

7

Un día típico Write a description of a typical day in your life. Include at least six verbs.

> *modelo*
>
> *A las nueve de la mañana mis amigas y yo bebemos un café.*
> *Asisto a la clase de yoga a las nueve y media.....*

3.4 Present tense of **tener** and **venir**

ANTE TODO   The verbs **tener** (*to have*) and **venir** (*to come*) are among the most frequently used in Spanish. Because most of their forms are irregular, you will have to learn each one individually.

The verbs **tener** and **venir**

		tener	**venir**
SINGULAR FORMS	yo	ten**go**	ven**go**
	tú	tien**es**	vien**es**
	Ud./él/ella	tien**e**	vien**e**
PLURAL FORMS	nosotros/as	ten**emos**	ven**imos**
	vosotros/as	ten**éis**	ven**ís**
	Uds./ellos/ellas	tien**en**	vien**en**

▶ The endings are the same as those of regular **-er** and **-ir** verbs, except for the **yo** forms, which are irregular: **tengo, vengo.**

▶ In the **tú, Ud.,** and **Uds.** forms, the **e** of the stem changes to **ie,** as shown below.

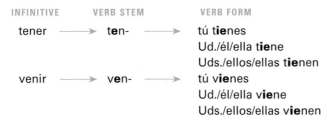

INFINITIVE	VERB STEM	VERB FORM
tener →	ten- →	tú t**ie**nes
		Ud./él/ella t**ie**ne
		Uds./ellos/ellas t**ie**nen
venir →	ven- →	tú v**ie**nes
		Ud./él/ella v**ie**ne
		Uds./ellos/ellas v**ie**nen

¿Tienes una familia grande, Marissa?

No, tengo una familia pequeña.

▶ Only the **nosotros** and **vosotros** forms are regular. Compare them to the forms of **comer** and **escribir** that you learned on page 96.

	tener	**comer**	**venir**	**escribir**
nosotros/as	ten**emos**	com**emos**	ven**imos**	escrib**imos**
vosotros/as	ten**éis**	com**éis**	ven**ís**	escrib**ís**

▶ In certain idiomatic or set expressions in Spanish, you use the construction **tener** + [*noun*] to express *to be* + [*adjective*]. This chart contains a list of the most common expressions with **tener**.

Expressions with tener

tener... años	*to be... years old*	tener (mucha) prisa	*to be in a (big) hurry*
tener (mucho) calor	*to be (very) hot*	tener razón	*to be right*
tener (mucho) cuidado	*to be (very) careful*	no tener razón	*to be wrong*
tener (mucho) frío	*to be (very) cold*	tener (mucha) sed	*to be (very) thirsty*
tener (mucha) hambre	*to be (very) hungry*	tener (mucho) sueño	*to be (very) sleepy*
tener (mucho) miedo (de)	*to be (very) afraid/ scared (of)*	tener (mucha) suerte	*to be (very) lucky*

—¿**Tienen** hambre ustedes? —Sí, y **tenemos** sed también.
Are you hungry? *Yes, and we're thirsty, too.*

▶ To express an obligation, use **tener que** (*to have to*) + [*infinitive*].

—¿Qué **tienes que** estudiar hoy? —**Tengo que** estudiar biología.
What do you have to study today? *I have to study biology.*

▶ To ask people if they feel like doing something, use **tener ganas de** (*to feel like*) + [*infinitive*].

—¿**Tienes ganas de** comer? —No, **tengo ganas de** dormir.
Do you feel like eating? *No, I feel like sleeping.*

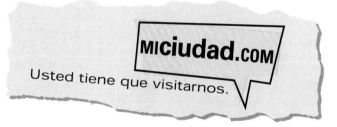
MIciudad.com
Usted tiene que visitarnos.

¡INTÉNTALO! Provide the appropriate forms of **tener** and **venir**.

tener	venir
1. Ellos ___tienen___ dos hermanos.	1. Mis padres ___vienen___ de México.
2. Yo _____ una hermana.	2. Tú _____ de España.
3. El artista _____ tres primos.	3. Nosotras _____ de Cuba.
4. Nosotros _____ diez tíos.	4. Pepe _____ de Italia.
5. Eva y Diana _____ un sobrino.	5. Yo _____ de Francia.
6. Usted _____ cinco nietos.	6. Ustedes _____ de Canadá.
7. Tú _____ dos hermanastras.	7. Alfonso y yo _____ de Portugal.
8. Ustedes _____ cuatro hijos.	8. Ellos _____ de Alemania.
9. Ella _____ una hija.	9. Usted _____ de Venezuela.

Práctica

1 **Emparejar** Find the expression in column B that best matches an item in column A. Then, come up with a new item that corresponds with the leftover expression in column B.

A	B
1. el Polo Norte	a. tener calor
2. una sauna	b. tener sed
3. la comida salada (*salty food*)	c. tener frío
4. una persona muy inteligente	d. tener razón
5. un abuelo	e. tener ganas de
6. una dieta	f. tener hambre
	g. tener 75 años

2 **Completar** Complete the sentences with the correct forms of **tener** or **venir**.

1. Hoy nosotros _____ una reunión familiar (*family reunion*).
2. Yo _____ en autobús de la Universidad de Quito.
3. Todos mis parientes _____, excepto mi tío Manolo y su esposa.
4. Ellos no _____ ganas de venir porque viven en Portoviejo.
5. Mi prima Susana y su novio no _____ hasta las ocho porque ella _____ que trabajar.
6. En las fiestas, mi hermana siempre (*always*) _____ muy tarde (*late*).
7. Nosotros _____ mucha suerte porque las reuniones son divertidas (*fun*).
8. Mi madre cree que mis sobrinos son muy simpáticos. Creo que ella _____ razón.

3 **Describir** Describe what these people are doing or feeling using an expression with **tener**.

1. _____ 2. _____ 3. _____

4. _____ 5. _____ 6. _____

Comunicación

4

Mi familia Listen to Francisco's description of his family. Then indicate whether the following conclusions are **lógico** or **ilógico**, based on what you heard.

	Lógico	Ilógico
1. Francisco tiene una familia grande.	○	○
2. A Francisco le gustan los números.	○	○
3. Francisco vive en la casa de sus padres durante el semestre.	○	○
4. Francisco desea ser artista.	○	○
5. Carlos y Dolores tienen gemelos.	○	○

5

Preguntas Answer your partner's questions.

1. ¿Tienes que estudiar hoy?
2. ¿Cuántos años tienes? ¿Y tus hermanos/as?
3. ¿Cuándo vienes a la universidad?
4. ¿Cuándo vienen tus amigos a tu casa, apartamento o residencia estudiantil?
5. ¿De qué tienes miedo? ¿Por qué?
6. ¿Qué tienes ganas de hacer esta noche (*tonight*)?

6

Obligaciones Talk about five things that you have to do but cannot do for various reasons, such as fear, lack of motivation, or being in a rush. Use expressions with **tener**.

> *modelo*
> Tengo que estudiar, pero no tengo ganas.

Síntesis

7

Minidrama Role-play this situation with a partner: you are introducing your boyfriend/girlfriend to your extended family. To avoid any surprises before you go, talk about who is coming and what each family member is like. Switch roles.

SUBJECT CONJUGATED FORM *Main clause*
Javier empiezo
Recapitulación
Dudan

Review the grammar concepts you have learned in this lesson by completing these activities.

1 **Adjetivos** Complete each phrase with the appropriate adjective from the list. Make all necessary changes. **18 pts.**

antipático	interesante	mexicano
difícil	joven	moreno

1. Mi tía es _____. Vive en Guadalajara.
2. Mi primo no es rubio, es _____.
3. Mi novio cree que la clase no es fácil; es _____.
4. Los libros son _____; me gustan mucho.
5. Mis hermanos son _____; no tienen muchos amigos.
6. Las gemelas tienen quince años. Son _____.

2 **Completar** For each set of sentences, provide the appropriate form of the verb **tener** and the possessive adjective. Follow the model. **36 pts.**

modelo
Él tiene un libro. Es su libro.

1. Esteban y Julio _____ una tía. Es _____ tía.
2. Yo _____ muchos amigos. Son _____ amigos.
3. Tú _____ tres primas. Son _____ primas.
4. María y tú _____ un hermano. Es _____ hermano.
5. Nosotras _____ unas mochilas. Son _____ mochilas.
6. Usted _____ dos sobrinos. Son _____ sobrinos.

3 **Oraciones** Arrange the words in the correct order to form complete logical sentences. **¡Ojo!** Don't forget to conjugate the verbs. **20 pts.**

1. libros / unos / tener / interesantes / tú / muy

   _____

2. dos / leer / fáciles / compañera / tu / lecciones

   _____

3. mi / francés / ser / amigo / buen / Hugo

   _____

4. ser / simpáticas / dos / personas / nosotras

   _____

5. a / clases / menores / mismas / sus / asistir / hermanos / las

   _____

RESUMEN GRAMATICAL

3.1 **Descriptive adjectives** *pp. 88–90*

Forms and agreement of adjectives

Masculine		Feminine	
Singular	**Plural**	**Singular**	**Plural**
alto	altos	alta	altas
inteligente	inteligentes	inteligente	inteligentes
trabajador	trabajadores	trabajadora	trabajadoras

► Descriptive adjectives follow the noun:
   el chico rubio

► Adjectives of nationality also follow the noun:
   la mujer española

► Adjectives of quantity precede the noun:
   muchos libros, dos turistas

► When placed before a singular masculine noun, these adjectives are shortened.

   bueno → buen   malo → mal

► When placed before a singular noun, **grande** is shortened to **gran**.

3.2 **Possessive adjectives** *p. 93*

Singular		Plural	
mi	nuestro/a	mis	nuestros/as
tu	vuestro/a	tus	vuestros/as
su	su	sus	sus

3.3 **Present tense of -er and -ir verbs** *pp. 96–97*

comer		escribir	
como	comemos	escribo	escribimos
comes	coméis	escribes	escribís
come	comen	escribe	escriben

3.4 **Present tense of tener and venir** *pp. 100–101*

tener		venir	
tengo	tenemos	vengo	venimos
tienes	tenéis	vienes	venís
tiene	tienen	viene	vienen

4 **Carta** Complete this letter with the appropriate forms of the verbs in the word list. Not all verbs will be used. **22 pts.**

abrir	correr	recibir
asistir	creer	tener
compartir	escribir	venir
comprender	leer	vivir

Hola, Ángel:

¿Qué tal? (Yo) (1) _____ esta carta (this letter) en la biblioteca. Todos los días (2) _____ aquí y (3) _____ un buen libro. Yo (4) _____ que es importante leer por diversión. Mi compañero de apartamento no (5) _____ por qué me gusta leer. Él sólo (6) _____ los libros de texto. Pero nosotros (7) _____ unos intereses. Por ejemplo, los dos somos atléticos; por las mañanas nosotros (8) _____. También nos gustan las ciencias; por las tardes (9) _____ a nuestra clase de biología. Nosotros (10) _____ en un apartamento que está cerca del laboratorio. Y tú, ¿cómo estás? ¿(Tú) (11) _____ mucho trabajo (work)?

5 **Proverbio** Complete this proverb with the correct forms of the verbs in parentheses. **4 pts.**

" **Dos andares°** _____ **(tener) el dinero°,**
_____ **(venir) despacio°**
y se va° ligero°. "

andares *speeds* dinero *money* despacio *slowly*
se va *it leaves* ligero *quickly*

Lectura

Antes de leer

Estrategia

Guessing meaning from context

As you read in Spanish, you'll often come across words you haven't learned. You can guess what they mean by looking at the surrounding words and sentences. Look at the following text and guess what **tía abuela** means, based on the context.

¡Hola, Claudia!

¿Qué hay de nuevo?

¿Sabes qué? Ayer fui a ver a mi tía abuela, la hermana de mi abuela. Tiene 85 años, pero es muy independiente. Vive en un apartamento en Quito con su prima Lorena, quien también tiene 85 años.

If you guessed *great-aunt*, you are correct, and you can conclude from this word and the format clues that this is a letter about someone's visit with his or her great-aunt.

Examinar el texto

Quickly read through the paragraphs and find two or three words you don't know. Using the context as your guide, guess what these words mean. Then glance at the paragraphs where these words appear and try to predict what the paragraphs are about.

Examinar el formato

Look at the format of the reading. What clues do the captions, photos, and layout give you about its content?

Gente... Las familias

1. Me llamo Armando y tengo setenta años, pero no me considero viejo. Tengo seis nietas y un nieto. Vivo con mi hija y tengo la oportunidad de pasar mucho tiempo con ella y con mi nieto. Por las tardes salgo a pasear° por el parque con él y por la noche le leo cuentos°.

Armando. Tiene seis nietas y un nieto.

2. Mi prima Victoria y yo nos llevamos muy bien. Estudiamos juntas° en la universidad y compartimos un apartamento. Ella es muy inteligente y me ayuda° con los estudios. Además°, es muy simpática y generosa. Si necesito cualquier° cosa, ¡ella me la compra!

Diana. Vive con su prima.

3. Me llamo Ramona y soy paraguaya, aunque° ahora vivo en los Estados Unidos. Tengo tres hijos, uno de nueve años, uno de doce y el mayor de quince. Es difícil a veces, pero mi esposo y yo tratamos° de ayudarlos y comprenderlos siempre°.

Ramona. Sus hijos son muy importantes para ella.

4. Tengo mucha suerte. Aunque mis padres están divorciados, tengo una familia muy unida. Tengo dos hermanos y dos hermanas. Me gusta hablar y salir a fiestas con ellos. Ahora tengo novio en la universidad y él no conoce a mis hermanos. ¡Espero que se lleven bien!

Ana María. Su familia es muy unida.

5. Antes quería° tener hermanos, pero ya no° es tan importante. Ser hijo único tiene muchas ventajas°: no tengo que compartir mis cosas con hermanos, no hay discusiones° y, como soy nieto único también, ¡mis abuelos piensan° que soy perfecto!

Fernando. Es hijo único.

6. Como soy joven todavía°, no tengo ni esposa ni hijos. Pero tengo un sobrino, el hijo de mi hermano, que es muy especial para mí. Se llama Benjamín y tiene diez años. Es un muchacho muy simpático. Siempre tiene hambre y por lo tanto vamos° frecuentemente a comer hamburguesas. Nos gusta también ir al cine° a ver películas de acción. Hablamos de todo. ¡Creo que ser tío es mejor que ser padre!

Santiago. Cree que ser tío es divertido.

salgo a pasear *I go take a walk* cuentos *stories* juntas *together* me ayuda *she helps me* Además *Besides* cualquier *any* aunque *although* tratamos *we try* siempre *always* quería *I wanted* ya no *no longer* ventajas *advantages* discusiones *arguments* piensan *think* todavía *still* vamos *we go* ir al cine *to go to the movies*

Después de leer

Emparejar
Glance at the paragraphs and see how the words and phrases in column A are used in context. Then find their definitions in column B.

A	B
1. me la compra	a. the oldest
2. nos llevamos bien	b. movies
3. no conoce	c. the youngest
4. películas	d. buys it for me
5. mejor que	e. borrows it from me
6. el mayor	f. we see each other
	g. doesn't know
	h. we get along
	i. portraits
	j. better than

Seleccionar
Choose the sentence that best summarizes each paragraph.

1. Párrafo 1
   a. Me gusta mucho ser abuelo.
   b. No hablo mucho con mi nieto.
   c. No tengo nietos.

2. Párrafo 2
   a. Mi prima es antipática.
   b. Mi prima no es muy trabajadora.
   c. Mi prima y yo somos muy buenas amigas.

3. Párrafo 3
   a. Tener hijos es un gran sacrificio, pero es muy bonito también.
   b. No comprendo a mis hijos.
   c. Mi esposo y yo no tenemos hijos.

4. Párrafo 4
   a. No hablo mucho con mis hermanos.
   b. Comparto mis cosas con mis hermanos.
   c. Mis hermanos y yo somos como (*like*) amigos.

5. Párrafo 5
   a. Me gusta ser hijo único.
   b. Tengo hermanos y hermanas.
   c. Vivo con mis abuelos.

6. Párrafo 6
   a. Mi sobrino tiene diez años.
   b. Me gusta mucho ser tío.
   c. Mi esposa y yo no tenemos hijos.

Escritura

Estrategia

Using idea maps

How do you organize ideas for a first draft? Often, the organization of ideas represents the most challenging part of the process. Idea maps are useful for organizing pertinent information. Here is an example of an idea map you can use:

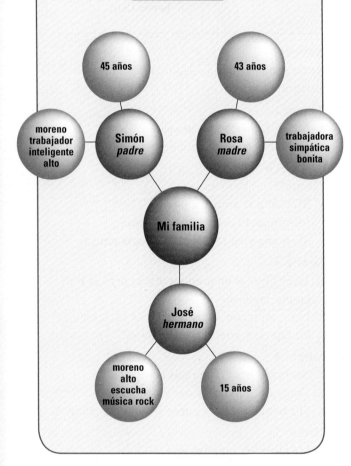

MAPA DE IDEAS

45 años — 43 años

moreno trabajador inteligente alto — **Simón** *padre* — **Rosa** *madre* — trabajadora simpática bonita

Mi familia

José *hermano*

moreno alto escucha música rock — 15 años

Tema

Escribir un mensaje electrónico

A friend you met in a chat room for Spanish speakers wants to know about your family. Using some of the verbs and adjectives you have learned in this lesson, write a brief e-mail describing your family or an imaginary family, including:

▶ Names and relationships
▶ Physical characteristics
▶ Hobbies and interests

Here are some useful expressions for writing an e-mail or letter in Spanish:

Salutations	
Estimado/a Julio/Julia:	*Dear Julio/Julia,*
Querido/a Miguel/Ana María:	*Dear Miguel/Ana María,*

Closings	
Un abrazo,	*A hug,*
Abrazos,	*Hugs,*
Cariños,	*Much love,*
¡Hasta pronto!	*See you soon!*
¡Hasta la próxima semana!	*See you next week!*

Escuchar

Estrategia

Asking for repetition/ Replaying the recording

Sometimes it is difficult to understand what people say, especially in a noisy environment. During a conversation, you can ask someone to repeat by saying **¿Cómo?** (*What?*) or **¿Perdón?** (*Pardon me?*). In class, you can ask your teacher to repeat by saying **Repita, por favor** (*Repeat, please*). If you don't understand a recorded activity, you can simply replay it.

 To help you practice this strategy, you will listen to a short paragraph. Ask your professor to repeat it or replay the recording, and then summarize what you heard.

Preparación

Based on the photograph, where do you think Cristina and Laura are? What do you think Laura is saying to Cristina?

Ahora escucha

Now you are going to hear Laura and Cristina's conversation. Use **R** to indicate which adjectives describe Cristina's boyfriend, Rafael. Use **E** for adjectives that describe Laura's boyfriend, Esteban. Some adjectives will not be used.

____ rubio   ____ interesante

____ feo   ____ antipático

____ alto   ____ inteligente

____ trabajador   ____ moreno

____ un poco gordo   ____ viejo

Comprensión

Identificar

Which person would make each statement: Cristina or Laura?

	Cristina	Laura
1. Mi novio habla sólo de fútbol y de béisbol.	○	○
2. Tengo un novio muy interesante y simpático.	○	○
3. Mi novio es alto y moreno.	○	○
4. Mi novio trabaja mucho.	○	○
5. Mi amiga no tiene buena suerte con los muchachos.	○	○
6. El novio de mi amiga es un poco gordo, pero guapo.	○	○

¿Cierto o falso?

Indicate whether each sentence is **cierto** or **falso**, then correct the false statements.

	Cierto	Falso
1. Esteban es un chico interesante y simpático.	○	○
2. Laura tiene mala suerte con los chicos.	○	○
3. Rafael es muy interesante.	○	○
4. Laura y su novio hablan de muchas cosas.	○	○

En pantalla

In the Spanish-speaking world, grandparents play an important role in the nuclear family structure. Even in the U.S., where retirement communities and nursing homes abound, in Latino families it is often expected that members of the older generation will live with their adult children and grandchildren. This living situation usually brings benefits—financial, emotional, and logistical—that improve the quality of life for everyone involved, and it facilitates the passing on of family history and culture.

Vocabulario útil

la canción	song
cocinar	to cook
el espíritu	spirit
los frijoles	beans
la lágrima	tear
el milagro	miracle
romántico/a	romantic
se aparece en	appears in
supersticioso/a	superstitious

Preparación

Have you or anyone in your family ever experienced a situation that seemed supernatural? What happened?

Preguntas

Choose the correct answer for each question.

1. ¿Qué hace (*is she doing*) la abuela?
   a. Prepara tortillas.   b. Come tortillas.

2. ¿Quién escucha una canción?
   a. la abuela   b. el nieto

3. ¿Quién se aparece en la tortilla?
   a. el nieto   b. el abuelo

4. ¿Qué tiene el nieto?
   a. sed   b. hambre

Los personajes

Choose one of the characters and write a description of him or her. Use as many adjectives as you can and mention the person's likes and dislikes. Be creative!

**Tears &
Tortillas**

Ay, Carlos. Nuestra canción.

¡Beto!... ¡Beto!...

Abuelita... ¿me llamaste?°

Tears & Tortillas forms part of a growing U.S. market for Latino cinema. Director Xóchitl Dorsey's narrative and documentary films have appeared on Showtime and PBS, as well as in various film festivals.

¿me llamaste? *you called me?*

If a Spanish-speaking friend told you he was going to a **reunión familiar,** what type of event would you picture? Most likely, your friend would not be referring to an annual event reuniting family members from far-flung cities. In Hispanic culture, family gatherings are much more frequent and relaxed, and thus do not require intensive planning or juggling of schedules. Some families gather every Sunday afternoon to enjoy a leisurely meal; others may prefer to hold get-togethers on a Saturday evening, with food, music, and dancing. In any case, gatherings tend to be laid-back events in which family members spend hours chatting, sharing stories, and telling jokes.

Vocabulario útil

el Día de la Madre	*Mother's Day*
estamos celebrando	*we are celebrating*
familia grande y feliz	*a big, happy family*
familia numerosa	*a large family*
hacer (algo) juntos	*to do (something) together*
el patio interior	*courtyard*
pelear	*to fight*
reuniones familiares	*family gatherings, reunions*

Preparación

What is a "typical family" like where you live? Is there such a thing? What members of a family usually live together?

Completar

Complete this paragraph with the correct options.

Los Valdivieso y los Bolaños son dos ejemplos de familias en Ecuador. Los Valdivieso son una familia (1) _____ (difícil/numerosa). Viven en una casa (2) _____ (grande/buena). En el patio, hacen (*they do*) muchas reuniones (3) _____ (familiares/con amigos). Los Bolaños son una familia pequeña. Ellos comen (4) _____ (separados/juntos) y preparan canelazo, una bebida (*drink*) típica ecuatoriana.

La familia

—Érica, ¿y cómo se llaman tus padres?
—Mi mamá, Lorena y mi papá, Miguel.

¡Qué familia tan° grande tiene!

Te presento a la familia Bolaños.

Ecuador

El país en cifras

▸ **Área:** 283.560 km² (109.483 millas²), *incluyendo las islas Galápagos, aproximadamente el área de Colorado*

▸ **Población:** 15.439.000

▸ **Capital:** Quito — 1.622.000

▸ **Ciudades° principales:** Guayaquil — 2.634.000, Cuenca, Machala, Portoviejo

▸ **Moneda:** dólar estadounidense

▸ **Idiomas:** español (oficial), quichua *La lengua oficial de Ecuador es el español, pero también se hablan° otras° lenguas en el país. Aproximadamente unos 4.000.000 de ecuatorianos hablan lenguas indígenas; la mayoría° de ellos habla quichua. El quichua es el dialecto ecuatoriano del quechua, la lengua de los incas.*

Bandera de Ecuador

Ecuatorianos célebres

▸ **Francisco Eugenio De Santa Cruz y Espejo,** médico, periodista y patriota (1747–1795)

▸ **Juan León Mera,** novelista (1832–1894)

▸ **Eduardo Kingman,** pintor° (1913–1997)

▸ **Rosalía Arteaga,** abogada°, política y ex vicepresidenta (1956–)

▸ **Iván Vallejo Ricafuerte,** montañista (1959–)

Ciudades *cities* se hablan *are spoken* otras *other* mayoría *majority* pintor *painter* abogada *lawyer* sur *south* mundo *world* pies *feet* dos veces más alto que *twice as tall as*

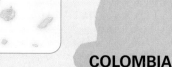

Las islas Galápagos

Indígenas del Amazonas

COLOMBIA

Río Esmeraldas

• Ibarra

Quito ★

Volcán Cotopaxi ▲   Río Napo

▲ Volcán Tungurahua

Río Pastaza

Portoviejo •

Río Daule

Cordillera de los Andes

Guayaquil •   ▲ Volcán Chimborazo

Océano Pacífico   • Cuenca

Muchos indígenas de Ecuador hablan quichua.

• Machala

• Loja

PERÚ

Catedral de Guayaquil

La ciudad de Quito y la Cordillera de los Andes

¡Increíble pero cierto!

El volcán Cotopaxi, situado a unos 60 kilómetros al sur° de Quito, es considerado el volcán activo más alto del mundo°. Tiene una altura de 5.897 metros (19.340 pies°). Es dos veces más alto que° el monte Santa Elena (2.550 metros o 9.215 pies) en el estado de Washington.

Lugares • Las islas Galápagos

Muchas personas vienen de lejos a visitar las islas Galápagos porque son un verdadero tesoro° ecológico. Aquí Charles Darwin estudió° las especies que inspiraron° sus ideas sobre la evolución. Como las Galápagos están lejos del continente, sus plantas y animales son únicos. Las islas son famosas por sus tortugas° gigantes.

Artes • Oswaldo Guayasamín

Oswaldo Guayasamín fue° uno de los artistas latinoamericanos más famosos del mundo. Fue escultor° y muralista. Su expresivo estilo viene del cubismo y sus temas preferidos son la injusticia y la pobreza° sufridas° por los indígenas de su país.

Deportes • El *trekking*

El sistema montañoso de los Andes cruza° y divide Ecuador en varias regiones. La Sierra, que tiene volcanes, grandes valles y una variedad increíble de plantas y animales, es perfecta para el *trekking*. Muchos turistas visitan Ecuador cada° año para hacer° *trekking* y escalar montañas°.

Lugares • Latitud 0

Hay un monumento en Ecuador, a unos 22 kilómetros (14 millas) de Quito, donde los visitantes están en el hemisferio norte y el hemisferio sur a la vez°. Este monumento se llama la Mitad del Mundo° y es un destino turístico muy popular.

Explosión del volcán Tungurahua

¿Qué aprendiste? Completa las oraciones con la información correcta.
1. La ciudad más grande (*biggest*) de Ecuador es _____.
2. La capital de Ecuador es _____.
3. Unos 4.000.000 de ecuatorianos hablan _____.
4. Darwin estudió el proceso de la evolución en _____.
5. Dos temas del arte de _____ son la pobreza y la _____.
6. Un monumento muy popular es _____.
7. La Sierra es un lugar perfecto para el _____.
8. El volcán _____ es el volcán activo más alto del mundo.

Conexión Internet Investiga estos temas en Internet.

1. Busca información sobre una ciudad de Ecuador. ¿Te gustaría (*Would you like*) visitar la ciudad? ¿Por qué?
2. Haz una lista de tres animales o plantas que viven sólo en las islas Galápagos. ¿Dónde hay animales o plantas similares?

....

verdadero tesoro *true treasure* **estudió** *studied* **inspiraron** *inspired* **tortugas** *tortoises* **fue** *was* **escultor** *sculptor* **pobreza** *poverty*
sufridas *suffered* **cruza** *crosses* **cada** *every* **hacer** *to do* **escalar montañas** *to climb mountains* **a la vez** *at the same time*
Mitad del Mundo *Equatorial Line Monument (lit. Midpoint of the World)*

La familia

el/la abuelo/a	grandfather/ grandmother
los abuelos	grandparents
el apellido	last name
el/la bisabuelo/a	great-grandfather/ great-grandmother
el/la cuñado/a	brother-in-law/ sister-in-law
el/la esposo/a	husband/wife; spouse
la familia	family
el/la gemelo/a	twin
el/la hermanastro/a	stepbrother/ stepsister
el/la hermano/a	brother/sister
el/la hijastro/a	stepson/ stepdaughter
el/la hijo/a	son/daughter
los hijos	children
la madrastra	stepmother
la madre	mother
el/la medio/a hermano/a	half-brother/ half-sister
el/la nieto/a	grandson/ granddaughter
la nuera	daughter-in-law
el padrastro	stepfather
el padre	father
los padres	parents
los parientes	relatives
el/la primo/a	cousin
el/la sobrino/a	nephew/niece
el/la suegro/a	father-in-law/ mother-in-law
el/la tío/a	uncle/aunt
el yerno	son-in-law

Otras personas

el/la amigo/a	friend
la gente	people
el/la muchacho/a	boy/girl
el/la niño/a	child
el/la novio/a	boyfriend/girlfriend
la persona	person

Profesiones

el/la artista	artist
el/la doctor(a), el/la médico/a	doctor; physician
el/la ingeniero/a	engineer
el/la periodista	journalist
el/la programador(a)	computer programmer

Adjetivos

alto/a	tall
antipático/a	unpleasant
bajo/a	short (in height)
bonito/a	pretty
buen, bueno/a	good
delgado/a	thin
difícil	difficult
fácil	easy
feo/a	ugly
gordo/a	fat
grande	big
guapo/a	good-looking
importante	important
inteligente	intelligent
interesante	interesting
joven (sing.), jóvenes (pl.)	young
mal, malo/a	bad
mismo/a	same
moreno/a	brunet(te)
mucho/a	much; many; a lot of
pelirrojo/a	red-haired
pequeño/a	small
rubio/a	blond(e)
simpático/a	nice; likeable
tonto/a	foolish
trabajador(a)	hard-working
viejo/a	old

Nacionalidades

alemán, alemana	German
argentino/a	Argentine
canadiense	Canadian
chino/a	Chinese
costarricense	Costa Rican
cubano/a	Cuban
ecuatoriano/a	Ecuadorian
español(a)	Spanish
estadounidense	from the U.S.
francés, francesa	French
inglés, inglesa	English
italiano/a	Italian
japonés, japonesa	Japanese
mexicano/a	Mexican
norteamericano/a	(North) American
puertorriqueño/a	Puerto Rican
ruso/a	Russian

Verbos

abrir	to open
aprender (a + *inf.*)	to learn
asistir (a)	to attend
beber	to drink
comer	to eat
compartir	to share
comprender	to understand
correr	to run
creer (en)	to believe (in)
deber (+ *inf.*)	should
decidir (+ *inf.*)	to decide
describir	to describe
escribir	to write
leer	to read
recibir	to receive
tener	to have
venir	to come
vivir	to live

Possessive adjectives	See page 93.
Expressions with *tener*	See page 101.
Expresiones útiles	See page 83.

Los pasatiempos

4

Communicative Goals

You will learn how to:

- Talk about pastimes, weekend activities, and sports
- Make plans and invitations

A PRIMERA VISTA

- ¿Es esta persona un atleta o un artista?
- ¿En qué tiene interés, en el ciclismo o en el tenis?
- ¿Es viejo? ¿Es delgado?
- ¿Tiene frío o calor?

Los pasatiempos

Más vocabulario

el béisbol	baseball
el ciclismo	cycling
el esquí (acuático)	(water) skiing
el fútbol americano	football
el golf	golf
el hockey	hockey
la natación	swimming
el tenis	tennis
el vóleibol	volleyball
el equipo	team
el parque	park
el partido	game; match
la plaza	city or town square
andar en patineta	to skateboard
bucear	to scuba dive
escalar montañas (f., pl.)	to climb mountains
esquiar	to ski
ganar	to win
ir de excursión	to go on a hike
practicar deportes (m., pl.)	to play sports
escribir una carta/ un mensaje electrónico	to write a letter/ an e-mail
leer el correo electrónico	to read e-mail
leer una revista	to read a magazine
deportivo/a	sports-related

Variación léxica

piscina	⟷	pileta (Arg.); alberca (Méx.)
baloncesto	⟷	básquetbol (Amér. L.)
béisbol	⟷	pelota (P. Rico, Rep. Dom.)

Lee el periódico. (leer)

Pasea en bicicleta. (pasear)

la pelota

el fútbol

la jugadora

Visitan el monumento. (visitar)

Pasean. (pasear)

Toma el sol. (tomar)

Nada. (nadar)

la piscina

Práctica

Patina en línea.
(patinar)

el baloncesto

el jugador

1 **Escuchar** 🎧 Indicate the letter of the activity in Column B that best corresponds to each statement you hear. Two items in Column B will not be used.

A   **B**

1. _____   a. leer el correo electrónico
2. _____   b. tomar el sol
3. _____   c. pasear en bicicleta
4. _____   d. ir a un partido de fútbol americano
5. _____   e. escribir una carta
6. _____   f. practicar muchos deportes
            g. nadar
            h. ir de excursión

2 **Ordenar** 🎧 Order these activities according to what you hear in the narration.

_____ a. pasear en bicicleta   _____ d. tomar el sol
_____ b. nadar   _____ e. practicar deportes
_____ c. leer una revista   _____ f. patinar en línea

3 **¿Cierto o falso?** Indicate whether each statement is **cierto** or **falso** based on the illustration.

	Cierto	Falso
1. Un hombre nada en la piscina.	○	○
2. Un hombre lee una revista.	○	○
3. Un chico pasea en bicicleta.	○	○
4. Dos muchachos esquían.	○	○
5. Una mujer y dos niños visitan un monumento.	○	○
6. Un hombre bucea.	○	○
7. Hay un equipo de hockey.	○	○
8. Una mujer toma el sol.	○	○

4 **Clasificar** Fill in the chart below with as many terms from **Contextos** as you can.

Actividades	Deportes	Personas

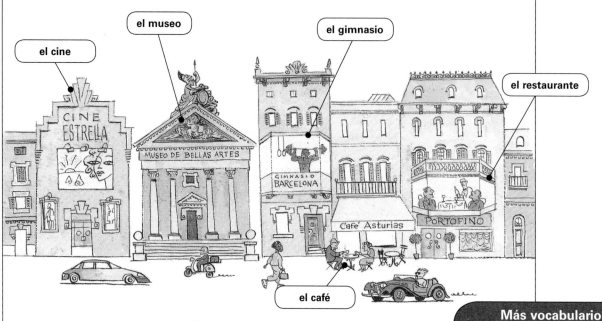

el cine

el museo

el gimnasio

el restaurante

el café

En el centro

Más vocabulario

la diversión	*fun activity; entertainment; recreation*
el fin de semana	*weekend*
el pasatiempo	*pastime; hobby*
los ratos libres	*spare (free) time*
el videojuego	*video game*
la iglesia	*church*
el lugar	*place*
ver películas (*f., pl.*)	*to watch movies*
favorito/a	*favorite*

5   **Identificar** Identify the place where these activities would take place.

modelo

> Esquiamos. Es una montaña.

1. Tomamos una limonada.
2. Vemos una película.
3. Nadamos y tomamos el sol.
4. Hay muchos monumentos.
5. Comemos tacos y fajitas.
6. Miramos pinturas (*paintings*) de Diego Rivera y Frida Kahlo.
7. Hay mucho tráfico.
8. Practicamos deportes.

6   **Lugares** Indicate what you do in the places mentioned below.

modelo

> una plaza
> *Camino por la plaza y miro a las personas.*

beber	escalar	mirar	practicar
caminar	escribir	nadar	tomar
correr	leer	patinar	visitar

1. una biblioteca
2. un estadio
3. una plaza
4. una piscina
5. las montañas
6. un parque
7. un café
8. un museo

Comunicación

7

Guadalajara Read this description of Guadalajara. Then indicate whether the following conclusions are **lógico** or **ilógico**, based on what you read.

> Guadalajara es una gran ciudad del estado de Jalisco, México. ¿Te gustan los parques? El Parque Mirador Independencia es un buen lugar para pasear en bicicleta, andar en patineta o tomar el sol. ¿Te gusta el cine? Guadalajara es un importante centro cultural, famosa por el Festival de Cine de Guadalajara. ¿Tienes hambre? Hay fabulosos restaurantes por toda la ciudad. ¿Te gustan los deportes? Debes asistir a un partido del Club Deportivo Guadalajara, uno de los equipos de fútbol más populares de México. ¿Te gusta el arte? Guadalajara es también muy famosa por sus museos y sus monumentos.

	Lógico	Ilógico
1. En el Parque Mirador Independencia, hay lugar para la diversión.	O	O
2. Asistes al Festival de Cine de Guadalajara para ver películas.	O	O
3. En Guadalajara, la gente come bien.	O	O
4. No hay estadios de fútbol en Guadalajara.	O	O
5. En Guadalajara, los turistas visitan monumentos.	O	O

8

Entrevista Answer your partner's questions.

1. ¿Hay un café cerca de tu casa?
2. ¿Cuál es tu restaurante favorito?
3. ¿Te gusta viajar y visitar monumentos?
4. ¿Te gusta ir al cine los fines de semana?
5. ¿Cuáles son tus películas favoritas?
6. ¿Te gusta practicar deportes?
7. ¿Cuáles son tus deportes favoritos?
8. ¿Cuáles son tus pasatiempos favoritos?

CONSULTA

To review expressions with **gustar,** see **Estructura 2.1**, p. 52.

9

Pasatiempos Write a paragraph about the pastimes three of your friends and family members enjoy.

> **modelo**
>
> Mi hermana pasea mucho en bicicleta, pero mis padres practican la natación. Mi hermano no nada, pero visita muchos museos.

10

Conversación Using the words and expressions provided, work with a partner to prepare a short conversation about pastimes.

¿a qué hora?	¿con quién(es)?	¿dónde?
¿cómo?	¿cuándo?	¿qué?

> **modelo**
>
> **Estudiante 1:** ¿Cuándo patinas en línea?
> **Estudiante 2:** Patino en línea los domingos. Y tú, ¿patinas en línea?
> **Estudiante 1:** No, no me gusta patinar en línea. Me gusta practicar el béisbol.

Fútbol, cenotes y mole

Maru, Miguel, Jimena y Marissa visitan un cenote, mientras
Felipe y Juan Carlos van a un partido de fútbol.

PERSONAJES

 MIGUEL

 PABLO

MIGUEL Buenos días a todos.

TÍA ANA MARÍA Hola, Miguel. Maru, ¿qué van a hacer hoy?

MARU Miguel y yo vamos a llevar a Marissa a un cenote.

MARISSA ¿No vamos a nadar? ¿Qué es un cenote?

MIGUEL Sí, sí vamos a nadar. Un cenote... difícil de explicar. Es una piscina natural en un hueco profundo.

MARU ¡Ya vas a ver! Seguro que te va a gustar.

(unos minutos después)

EDUARDO Hay un partido de fútbol en el parque. ¿Quieren ir conmigo?

PABLO Y conmigo. Si no consigo más jugadores, nuestro equipo va a perder.

ANA MARÍA Marissa, ¿qué te gusta hacer? ¿Escalar montañas? ¿Ir de excursión?

MARISSA Sí, me gusta ir de excursión y practicar el esquí acuático. Y usted, ¿qué prefiere hacer en sus ratos libres?

PABLO Mi mamá tiene muchos pasatiempos y actividades.

EDUARDO Sí. Ella nada y juega al tenis y al golf.

PABLO Va al cine y a los museos.

ANA MARÍA Sí, salgo mucho los fines de semana

FELIPE ¿Recuerdas el restaurante del mole?

EDUARDO ¿Qué restaurante?

JIMENA El mole de mi tía Ana María es mi favorito.

MARU Chicos, ya es hora. ¡Vamos!

ANA MARÍA

MARU

MARISSA

EDUARDO

FELIPE

JUAN CARLOS

JIMENA

DON GUILLERMO

7

(*más tarde, en el parque*)

PABLO No puede ser. ¡Cinco a uno!

FELIPE ¡Vamos a jugar! Si perdemos, compramos el almuerzo. Y si ganamos...

EDUARDO ¡Empezamos!

8

(*mientras tanto, en el cenote*)

MARISSA ¿Hay muchos cenotes en México?

MIGUEL Sólo en la península de Yucatán.

MARISSA ¡Vamos a nadar!

9

(*Los chicos visitan a don Guillermo, un vendedor de paletas heladas.*)

JUAN CARLOS Don Guillermo, ¿dónde podemos conseguir un buen mole?

FELIPE Eduardo y Pablo van a pagar el almuerzo. Y yo voy a pedir un montón de comida.

10

FELIPE Sí, éste es el restaurante. Recuerdo la comida.

EDUARDO Oye, Pablo... No tengo...

PABLO No te preocupes, hermanito.

FELIPE ¿Qué buscas? (*muestra la cartera de Pablo*) ¿Esto?

¿Qué pasó?

1 **Escoger** Choose the answer that best completes each sentence.

1. Marissa, Maru y Miguel desean _____.
   a. nadar   b. correr por el parque   c. leer el periódico

2. A Marissa le gusta _____.
   a. el tenis   b. el vóleibol   c. ir de excursión y practicar esquí acuático

3. A la tía Ana María le gusta _____.
   a. jugar al hockey   b. nadar y jugar al tenis y al golf   c. hacer ciclismo

4. Pablo y Eduardo pierden el partido de _____.
   a. fútbol   b. béisbol   c. baloncesto

5. Juan Carlos y Felipe desean _____.
   a. patinar   b. esquiar   c. comer mole

NOTA CULTURAL

Mole is a typical sauce in Mexican cuisine. It is made from pumpkin seeds, chile, and chocolate, and it is usually served with chicken, beef, or pork. To learn more about **mole**, go to page 272.

2 **Identificar** Identify the person who would make each statement.

1. A mí me gusta nadar, pero no sé qué es un cenote. _____

2. Mamá va al cine y al museo en sus ratos libres. _____

3. Yo voy a pedir mucha comida. _____

4. ¿Quieren ir a jugar al fútbol con nosotros en el parque? _____

5. Me gusta salir los fines de semana. _____

MARISSA

FELIPE

EDUARDO

PABLO

TÍA ANA MARÍA

NOTA CULTURAL

Cenotes are deep, freshwater sinkholes found in caves throughout the Yucatán peninsula.

They were formed in prehistoric times by the erosion and collapse of cave walls. The Mayan civilization considered the **cenotes** sacred, and performed rituals there. Today, they are popular destinations for swimming and diving.

3 **Preguntas** Answer the questions using the information from the **Fotonovela.**

1. ¿Qué van a hacer Miguel y Maru?

2. ¿Adónde van Felipe y Juan Carlos mientras sus amigos van al cenote?

3. ¿Quién gana el partido de fútbol?

4. ¿Quiénes van al cenote con Maru y Miguel?

4 **Conversación** With a partner, prepare a conversation in which you talk about pastimes and invite each other to do some activity together. Use these expressions and also look at **Expresiones útiles** on the previous page.

¿A qué hora?	¿Dónde? *Where?*	Nos vemos a las siete.
(At) What time?	No puedo porque...	*See you at seven.*
contigo *with you*	*I can't because...*	

▶ ¿Eres aficionado/a a...?   ▶ ¿Por qué no...?   ▶ ¿Qué vas a hacer esta noche?

▶ ¿Te gusta...?   ▶ ¿Quieres... conmigo?

Pronunciación
Word stress and accent marks

pe-lí-cu-la   **e-di-fi-cio**   **ver**   **yo**

Every Spanish syllable contains at least one vowel. When two vowels are joined in the same syllable they form a **diphthong***. A **monosyllable** is a word formed by a single syllable.

bi-blio-te-ca   **vi-si-tar**   **par-que**   **fút-bol**

The syllable of a Spanish word that is pronounced most emphatically is the "stressed" syllable.

pe-lo-ta   **pis-ci-na**   **ra-tos**   **ha-blan**

Words that end in **n, s**, or a **vowel** are usually stressed on the next-to-last syllable.

na-ta-ción   **pa-pá**   **in-glés**   **Jo-sé**

If words that end in **n, s**, or a **vowel** are stressed on the last syllable, they must carry an accent mark on the stressed syllable.

bai-lar   **es-pa-ñol**   **u-ni-ver-si-dad**   **tra-ba-ja-dor**

Words that do not end in **n, s**, or a **vowel** are usually stressed on the last syllable.

béis-bol   **lá-piz**   **ár-bol**   **Gó-mez**

If words that do not end in **n, s**, or a **vowel** are stressed on the next-to-last syllable, they must carry an accent mark on the stressed syllable.

*The two vowels that form a diphthong are either both weak or one is weak and the other is strong.

En la unión
está la fuerza.²

Práctica Pronounce each word, stressing the correct syllable. Then give the word stress rule for each word.

1. profesor	4. Mazatlán	7. niños	10. México
2. Puebla	5. examen	8. Guadalajara	11. están
3. ¿Cuántos?	6. ¿Cómo?	9. programador	12. geografía

Oraciones Read the conversation aloud to practice word stress.

MARINA Hola, Carlos. ¿Qué tal?
CARLOS Bien. Oye, ¿a qué hora es el partido de fútbol?
MARINA Creo que es a las siete.
CARLOS ¿Quieres ir?
MARINA Lo siento, pero no puedo. Tengo que estudiar biología.

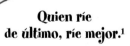

Quien ríe
de último, ríe mejor.¹

Refranes Read these sayings aloud to practice word stress.

1 He who laughs last, laughs best.
2 United we stand.

Real Madrid y Barça:
rivalidad total

Soccer in Spain is a force to be reckoned with, and no two teams draw more attention than **Real Madrid** and the **Fútbol Club Barcelona.** Whether the venue is Madrid's **Santiago Bernabéu** or Barcelona's **Camp Nou,** the two cities shut down for the showdown, paralyzed by **fútbol** fever. A ticket to the actual game is always the hottest ticket in town.

The rivalry between **Real Madrid** and **Barça** is about more than soccer. As the two biggest, most powerful cities in Spain, Barcelona and Madrid are constantly compared to one another and have a natural rivalry. There is also a political component to the dynamic. Barcelona, with its distinct language and culture, has long struggled for increased autonomy from Madrid's centralized government. Under Francisco Franco's rule (1939–1975), when repression of the Catalan identity was at its height, a game between **Real Madrid** and **FC Barcelona** was wrapped up with all the symbolism of the regime versus the resistance, even though both teams suffered casualties in Spain's civil war and the subsequent Franco dictatorship.

Although the dictatorship is long over, the momentum of all those decades of competition still transforms both cities into a frenzied, tense panic leading up to the game. Once the final score is announced, one of those cities is transformed again, this time into the best party in the country.

Rivalidades del fútbol

Argentina: Boca Juniors vs River Plate

México: Águilas del América vs Chivas del Guadalajara

Chile: Colo Colo vs Universidad de Chile

Guatemala: Comunicaciones vs Municipal

Uruguay: Peñarol vs Nacional

Colombia: Millonarios vs Independiente Santa Fe

1 **¿Cierto o falso?** Indicate whether each statement is **cierto** or **falso**. Correct the false statements.

1. People from Spain don't like soccer.
2. Madrid and Barcelona are the most important cities in Spain.
3. Santiago Bernabéu is a stadium in Barcelona.
4. The rivalry between Real Madrid and FC Barcelona is not only in soccer.
5. Barcelona has resisted Madrid's centralized government.
6. Only the FC Barcelona team was affected by the civil war.
7. During Franco's regime, the Catalan culture thrived.
8. There are many famous rivalries between soccer teams in the Spanish-speaking world.
9. River Plate is a popular team from Argentina.
10. Comunicaciones and Peñarol are famous rivals in Guatemala.

ASÍ SE DICE

Los deportes

el/la árbitro/a	referee
el/la atleta	athlete
la bola; el balón	la pelota
el campeón/ la campeona	champion
la carrera	race
competir	to compete
empatar	to tie
la medalla	medal
el/la mejor	the best
mundial	worldwide
el torneo	tournament

EL MUNDO HISPANO

Atletas importantes

World-renowned Hispanic athletes:

- **Rafael Nadal** (España) has won 14 Grand Slam singles titles and the 2008 Olympic gold medal in singles tennis.

- **Lionel Andrés Messi** (Argentina) is one of the world's top soccer players. He plays for **FC Barcelona** and for the Argentine national team.

- **Mireia Belmonte García** (España) won two silver medals in swimming at the 2012 Olympics.

- **Lorena Ochoa** (México) was the top-ranked female golfer in the world when she retired in 2010 at the age of 28. She still hosts an LPGA golf tournament, the Lorena Ochoa Invitational, every year.

PERFILES

Miguel Cabrera y Paola Espinosa

Miguel Cabrera, considered one of the best hitters in baseball, now plays first base for the Detroit Tigers. Born in Venezuela in 1983, he made his Major League debut at the age of 20. Cabrera has been selected for both the National League and American League All-Star Teams. In 2012, he became the first player since 1967 to win the Triple Crown.

Mexican diver **Paola Milagros Espinosa Sánchez**, born in 1986, has competed in three Olympics (2004, 2008, and 2012). She and her partner Tatiana Ortiz took home a bronze medal in 2008. In 2012, she won a silver medal with partner Alejandra Orozco. She won three gold medals at the Pan American Games in 2007 and again in 2011.

Conexión Internet

¿Qué deportes son populares en los países hispanos?

Use the Web to find more cultural information related to this **Cultura** section.

ACTIVIDADES

2 **Comprensión** Write the name of the athlete described in each sentence.

1. Es un jugador de fútbol de Argentina. _____
2. Es una mujer que practica el golf. _____
3. Es un jugador de béisbol de Venezuela. _____
4. Es una mujer mexicana que practica un deporte en la piscina. _____

3 **¿Quién es?** Write a short paragraph describing an athlete that you like. What does he/she look like? What sport does he/she play? Where does he/she live?

4.1 Present tense of **ir**

ANTE TODO The verb **ir** (*to go*) is irregular in the present tense. Note that, except for the **yo** form (**voy**) and the lack of a written accent on the **vosotros** form (**vais**), the endings are the same as those for regular present tense **-ar** verbs.

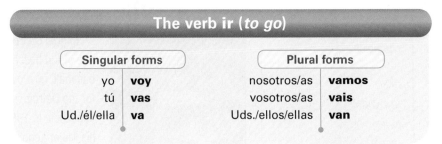

The verb **ir** (*to go*)			
Singular forms		**Plural forms**	
yo	**voy**	nosotros/as	**vamos**
tú	**vas**	vosotros/as	**vais**
Ud./él/ella	**va**	Uds./ellos/ellas	**van**

▶ **Ir** is often used with the preposition **a** (*to*). If **a** is followed by the definite article **el**, they combine to form the contraction **al**. If **a** is followed by the other definite articles (**la, las, los**), there is no contraction.

a + el = al

Voy **al** parque con Juan.   Mis amigos van **a las** montañas.
I'm going to the park with Juan.   *My friends are going to the mountains.*

CONSULTA

To review the contraction **de + el**, see **Estructura 1.3**, pp. 20–21.

▶ The construction **ir a** + [*infinitive*] is used to talk about actions that are going to happen in the future. It is equivalent to the English *to be going* + [*infinitive*].

Va a leer el periódico.   **Van a pasear** por el pueblo.
He is going to read the newspaper.   *They are going to walk around town.*

¡Voy a ir con ellos!

Ella va al cine y a los museos.

AYUDA

When asking a question that contains a form of the verb **ir**, remember to use **adónde**:

¿Adónde vas?
(To) Where are you going?

▶ **Vamos a** + [*infinitive*] can also express the idea of *let's (do something)*.

Vamos a pasear.   ¡**Vamos a** comer!
Let's take a walk.   *Let's eat!*

¡INTÉNTALO!   Provide the present tense forms of **ir**.

1. Ellos __van__.
2. Yo _____.
3. Tu novio _____.
4. Adela _____.

5. Mi prima y yo _____.
6. Tú _____.
7. Ustedes _____.
8. Nosotros _____.

9. Usted _____.
10. Nosotras _____.
11. Miguel _____.
12. Ellas _____.

Práctica

1

¿Adónde van? Everyone in your neighborhood is dashing off to various places. Say where they are going.

1. la señora Castillo / el centro
2. las hermanas Gómez / la piscina
3. tu tío y tu papá / el partido de fútbol
4. yo / el Museo de Arte Moderno
5. nosotros / el restaurante Miramar

2

¿Qué van a hacer? These sentences describe what several students in a college hiking club are doing today. Use **ir a** + [*infinitive*] to say that they are also going to do the same activities tomorrow.

> **modelo**
>
> Martín y Rodolfo nadan en la piscina.
>
> *Van a nadar en la piscina mañana también.*

1. Sara lee una revista.
2. Yo practico deportes.
3. Ustedes van de excursión.
4. El presidente del club patina.
5. Tú tomas el sol.
6. Paseamos con nuestros amigos.

3

Actividades Indicate where the people are going and what they are going to do there.

> **modelo**
>
> Estela va a la Librería Sol.
>
> *Va a comprar un libro.*

Estela

1. Álex y Miguel

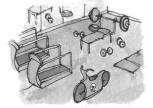

2. mi amigo

3. tú

4. los estudiantes

5. la profesora Torres

6. ustedes

Comunicación

4

Esta noche Listen to the conversation between Enrique and Rosa. Then indicate whether the following conclusions are **lógico** or **ilógico**, based on what you heard.

	Lógico	Ilógico
1. Rosa y Mercedes van a ver una película esta noche.	○	○
2. A Enrique le gustan los deportes.	○	○
3. Enrique va a ir al estadio esta noche.	○	○
4. Enrique y Pedro van a cenar mientras (*while*) miran el partido.	○	○
5. A Rosa no le gustan los restaurantes japoneses.	○	○
6. Rosa y Enrique conversan en el cine.	○	○

5

Situaciones Work with a partner and say where you and your friends go in these situations.

1. Cuando deseo descansar…
2. Cuando mi novio/a tiene que estudiar…
3. Si deseo hablar con mis amigos…
4. Cuando mis amigos y yo tenemos hambre…
5. En mis ratos libres…
6. Cuando mis amigos desean esquiar…
7. Si estoy de vacaciones…
8. Si tengo ganas de leer…

6

Entrevista With a partner, take turns asking each other where you are going and what you are going to do on your next vacation.

> **modelo**
>
> **Estudiante 1:** ¿Adónde vas de vacaciones (*on vacation*)?
> **Estudiante 2:** Voy a Guadalajara con mis amigos.
> **Estudiante 1:** ¿Y qué van a hacer (*to do*) ustedes en Guadalajara?
> **Estudiante 2:** Vamos a visitar unos monumentos y museos. ¿Y tú?

Síntesis

7

Planes Make a schedule of your activities for the weekend.

▶ For each day, list at least three things you have to do.
▶ For each day, list at least two things you will do for fun.

4.2 Stem-changing verbs: e→ie, o→ue

ANTE TODO Stem-changing verbs deviate from the normal pattern of regular verbs. When stem-changing verbs are conjugated, they have a vowel change in the last syllable of the stem.

CONSULTA

To review the present tense of regular **-ar** verbs, see **Estructura 2.1**, p. 50.

• • •

To review the present tense of regular **-er** and **-ir** verbs, see **Estructura 3.3**, p. 96.

INFINITIVE		VERB STEM		STEM CHANGE		CONJUGATED FORM
empezar	▶	empez-	▶	empiez-	▶	empiezo
volver		volv-		vuelv-		vuelvo

▶ In many verbs, such as **empezar** (*to begin*), the stem vowel changes from **e** to **ie**. Note that the **nosotros/as** and **vosotros/as** forms don't have a stem change.

The verb empezar (e:ie) (*to begin*)

Singular forms		Plural forms	
yo	empiezo	nosotros/as	empezamos
tú	empiezas	vosotros/as	empezáis
Ud./él/ella	empieza	Uds./ellos/ellas	empiezan

Los chicos empiezan a hablar de su visita al cenote.

Ellos vuelven a comer en el restaurante.

▶ In many other verbs, such as **volver** (*to return*), the stem vowel changes from **o** to **ue**. The **nosotros/as** and **vosotros/as** forms have no stem change.

The verb volver (o:ue) (*to return*)

Singular forms		Plural forms	
yo	vuelvo	nosotros/as	volvemos
tú	vuelves	vosotros/as	volvéis
Ud./él/ella	vuelve	Uds./ellos/ellas	vuelven

▶ To help you identify stem-changing verbs, they will appear as follows throughout the text:

empezar (e:ie), volver (o:ue)

Common stem-changing verbs

e:ie	
cerrar	to close
comenzar (a + *inf.*)	to begin
empezar (a + *inf.*)	to begin
entender	to understand
pensar	to think
perder	to lose; to miss
preferir (+ *inf.*)	to prefer
querer (+ *inf.*)	to want; to love

o:ue	
almorzar	to have lunch
contar	to count; to tell
dormir	to sleep
encontrar	to find
mostrar	to show
poder (+ *inf.*)	to be able to; can
recordar	to remember
volver	to return

¡LENGUA VIVA!

The verb **perder** can mean *to lose* or *to miss*, in the sense of "to miss a train."

Siempre pierdo mis llaves.
I always lose my keys.

Es importante no perder el autobús.
It's important not to miss the bus.

▶ **Jugar** (*to play a sport or a game*) is the only Spanish verb that has a **u:ue** stem change. **Jugar** is followed by **a** + [*definite article*] when the name of a sport or game is mentioned.

Ella juega al tenis y al golf.

Los chicos juegan al fútbol.

▶ **Comenzar** and **empezar** require the preposition **a** when they are followed by an infinitive.

Comienzan a jugar a las siete.
They begin playing at seven.

Ana **empieza a** escribir una postal.
Ana is starting to write a postcard.

▶ **Pensar** + [*infinitive*] means *to plan* or *to intend to do something.* **Pensar en** means *to think about someone* or *something.*

¿Piensan ir al gimnasio?
Are you planning to go to the gym?

¿En qué **piensas**?
What are you thinking about?

¡INTÉNTALO! Provide the present tense forms of these verbs.

cerrar (e:ie)

1. Ustedes ___cierran___.
2. Tú _____.
3. Nosotras _____.
4. Mi hermano _____.
5. Yo _____.
6. Usted _____.
7. Los chicos _____.
8. Ella _____.

dormir (o:ue)

1. Mi abuela no ___duerme___.
2. Yo no _____.
3. Tú no _____.
4. Mis hijos no _____.
5. Usted no _____.
6. Nosotros no _____.
7. Él no _____.
8. Ustedes no _____.

Práctica

1 **Completar** Complete this conversation with the appropriate forms of the verbs.

PABLO Óscar, voy al centro ahora.

ÓSCAR ¿A qué hora (1)_____ (pensar) volver? El partido de fútbol
        (2)_____ (empezar) a las dos.

PABLO (3)_____ (Volver) a la una. (4)_____ (Querer) ver el partido.

ÓSCAR (5)¿_____ (Recordar) que (*that*) nuestro equipo es muy bueno?
        (6)¡ _____ (Poder) ganar!

PABLO No, (7)_____ (pensar) que va a (8)_____ (perder). Los jugadores de
        Guadalajara son salvajes (*wild*) cuando (9)_____ (jugar).

2 **Preferencias** Indicate what these people want to do, using the cues provided.

> **modelo**
> Guillermo: estudiar / pasear en bicicleta
> *Guillermo no quiere estudiar. Prefiere pasear
> en bicicleta.*

1. tú: trabajar / dormir

▶ 2. ustedes: mirar la televisión / jugar al dominó

3. tus amigos: ir de excursión / descansar

4. tú: comer en la cafetería / ir a un restaurante

5. Elisa: ver una película / leer una revista

6. María y su hermana: tomar el sol / practicar el esquí acuático

3 **Describir** Use a verb from the list to describe what these people are doing.

almorzar	cerrar	contar	dormir	encontrar	mostrar

1. las niñas

2. yo

3. nosotros

4. tú

5. Pedro

6. Teresa

Comunicación

4 **Frecuencia** Use the verbs from the list and other stem-changing verbs you know to explain which activities you do daily (**todos los días**), which you do once a month (**una vez al mes**), and which you do once a year (**una vez al año**).

> *modelo*
> Yo recuerdo a mi familia todos los días. Yo pierdo uno de mis libros una vez al año...

cerrar	encontrar	poder	recordar
dormir	jugar	preferir	¿?
empezar	perder	querer	

5 **En la televisión** Read the television listings for Saturday. With a partner, role-play a conversation between two siblings arguing about what to watch.

> *modelo*
> **Hermano:** Podemos ver la Copa Mundial.
> **Hermana:** ¡No, no quiero ver la Copa Mundial! Prefiero ver...

	13:00	14:00	15:00	16:00	17:00	18:00	19:00	20:00	21:00	22:00	23:00
7	Copa Mundial (*World Cup*) de fútbol			República Deportiva		Campeonato (*Championship*) Mundial de Vóleibol: México-Argentina				Torneo de Natación	
8	Abierto (*Open*) Mexicano de Tenis: Santiago González (México) vs. Nicolás Almagro (España). Semifinales			Campeonato de baloncesto: Los Correcaminos de Tampico vs. los Santos de San Luis				Aficionados al buceo		Cozumel: Aventuras	
12	Yo soy Betty, la fea		Héroes		Hermanos y hermanas			Película: **Sin nombre**		Película: **El coronel no tiene quien le escriba**	
13	El padrastro			60 Minutos				El esquí acuático		Patinaje artístico	
17	Biografías: La artista Frida Kahlo			Música de la semana			Entrevista del día: Iker Casillas y su pasión por el fútbol			Cine de la noche: **Elsa y Fred**	

> **NOTA CULTURAL**
> **Iker Casillas Fernández** is a famous goalkeeper for **Real Madrid**. A native of Madrid, he is among the best goalkeepers of his generation.

Síntesis

6 **Deportes** Write a paragraph about your favorite sport. Mention why you like it, and whether you practice it or watch it on TV. Include some facts you know about the sport. Use at least three stem-changing verbs.

> *modelo*
> Mi deporte favorito es el béisbol porque es un deporte interesante. Esta noche pienso ver el partido de los Padres en la televisión. Empieza a las siete...

4.3 Stem-changing verbs: e→i

ANTE TODO You've already seen that many verbs in Spanish change their stem vowel when conjugated. There is a third kind of stem-vowel change in some verbs, such as **pedir** (*to ask for; to request*). In these verbs, the stressed vowel in the stem changes from **e** to **i**, as shown in the diagram.

INFINITIVE	VERB STEM	STEM CHANGE	CONJUGATED FORM
pedir	p**e**d-	p**i**d-	p**i**do

▶ As with other stem-changing verbs you have learned, there is no stem change in the **nosotros/as** or **vosotros/as** forms in the present tense.

The verb pedir (e:i) (*to ask for; to request*)

Singular forms		Plural forms	
yo	p**i**do	nosotros/as	pedimos
tú	p**i**des	vosotros/as	pedís
Ud./él/ella	p**i**de	Uds./ellos/ellas	p**i**den

¡LENGUA VIVA!

As you learned in **Lección 2, preguntar** means *to ask a question*. **Pedir**, however, means *to ask for something*:

Ella me pregunta cuántos años tengo.
She asks me how old I am.

Él me pide ayuda.
He asks me for help.

▶ To help you identify verbs with the **e:i** stem change, they will appear as follows throughout the text:

pedir (e:i)

▶ These are the most common **e:i** stem-changing verbs:

conseguir	**decir**	**repetir**	**seguir**
to get; to obtain	*to say; to tell*	*to repeat*	*to follow; to continue; to keep (doing something)*

Pido favores cuando es necesario.
I ask for favors when it's necessary.

Javier **dice** la verdad.
Javier is telling the truth.

Sigue con su tarea.
He continues with his homework.

Consiguen ver buenas películas.
They get to see good movies.

▶ **¡Atención!** The verb **decir** is irregular in its **yo** form: **yo digo**.

▶ The **yo** forms of **seguir** and **conseguir** have a spelling change in addition to the stem change **e:i**.

Sigo su plan.
I'm following their plan.

Consigo novelas en la librería.
I get novels at the bookstore.

¡INTÉNTALO! Provide the correct forms of the verbs.

repetir (e:i)	decir (e:i)	seguir (e:i)
1. Arturo y Eva _repiten_.	1. Yo _digo_.	1. Yo _sigo_.
2. Yo _____.	2. Él _____.	2. Nosotros _____.
3. Nosotros _____.	3. Tú _____.	3. Tú _____.
4. Julia _____.	4. Usted _____.	4. Los chicos _____.
5. Sofía y yo _____.	5. Ellas _____.	5. Usted _____.

Práctica

1 | **Completar** Complete these sentences with the correct form of the verb provided.

1. Cuando mi familia pasea por la ciudad, mi madre siempre (*always*) va a un café y _____ (pedir) una soda.
2. Pero mi padre _____ (decir) que perdemos mucho tiempo. Tiene prisa por llegar al Bosque de Chapultepec.
3. Mi padre tiene suerte, porque él siempre _____ (conseguir) lo que (*that which*) desea.
4. Cuando llegamos al parque, mis hermanos y yo _____ (seguir) conversando (*talking*) con nuestros padres.
5. Mis padres siempre _____ (repetir) la misma cosa: "Nosotros tomamos el sol aquí sin ustedes".
6. Yo siempre _____ (pedir) permiso para volver a casa un poco más tarde porque me gusta mucho el parque.

2 | **Combinar** Combine words from the two columns to create sentences about yourself and people you know.

A	B
yo	(no) pedir muchos favores
mi madre	nunca (*never*) pedir perdón
mi mejor (*best*) amigo/a	nunca seguir las instrucciones
mi familia	siempre seguir las instrucciones
mis amigos/as	conseguir libros en Internet
mis amigos/as y yo	repetir el vocabulario
mis padres	poder hablar dos lenguas
mi hermano/a	dormir hasta el mediodía
mi profesor(a) de español	siempre perder sus libros

3 | **¿Sí o no?** Indicate whether you do the following.

modelo

pedir consejos con frecuencia
Pido consejos con frecuencia./No pido consejos con frecuencia.

1. conseguir libros en la librería
2. almorzar en casa
3. perder cosas con frecuencia
4. pedir favores
5. seguir las instrucciones de un manual
6. volver tarde a casa
7. dormir mucho
8. jugar al tenis

Comunicación

4

Una entrevista Read this interview with actress Andrea de la Palma. Then indicate whether the following conclusions are **lógico** or **ilógico**, based on what you read.

MANUEL Andrea, ¿qué tipo de persona eres?

ANDREA Creo que soy una persona introvertida. No les pido demasiados favores a mis amigos. En general, pienso que soy una buena amiga; siempre digo la verdad.

MANUEL ¿Qué pides en un restaurante?

ANDREA Siempre (*Always*) pido comida (*food*) vegetariana. Hay un restaurante español muy bueno. Siempre pido tortilla española (*potato omelet*) y ¡siempre repito!

MANUEL ¿Qué deportes sigues?

ANDREA Sigo el béisbol, pero no consigo entender bien los partidos.

MANUEL Sí, ¡pueden ser muy complicados! Andrea, muchas gracias por la entrevista y por ser tan buena actriz. Siempre veo tus películas.

ANDREA El gusto es mío. ¡Muchas gracias!

	Lógico	Ilógico
1. Andrea es honesta.	O	O
2. Andrea siempre come en casa.	O	O
3. Andrea pide pollo (*chicken*) en los restaurantes.	O	O
4. A Manuel le gustan las películas.	O	O
5. Manuel sigue la carrera de Andrea.	O	O

5

Las películas Answer your partner's questions.

1. ¿Prefieres las películas románticas, las películas de acción o las películas de terror? ¿Por qué?

2. ¿Dónde consigues información sobre (*about*) cine y televisión?

3. ¿Dónde consigues las entradas (*tickets*) para el cine?

4. Para decidir qué películas vas a ver, ¿sigues las recomendaciones de los críticos de cine? ¿Qué dicen los críticos en general?

5. ¿Qué cines de tu comunidad muestran las mejores (*best*) películas?

6. ¿Vas a ver una película esta semana? ¿A qué hora empieza la película?

6

El cine With a partner, discuss good and bad movies you have seen. Use stem-changing verbs in your conversation.

> **modelo**
>
> **Estudiante 1:** Pienso que *Gravedad* es una película muy buena. Los efectos especiales son excelentes.
>
> **Estudiante 2:** Sí. Digo que Sandra Bullock es la mejor actriz...

Síntesis

7

Mi película favorita Write a paragraph about your favorite movie. Use stem-changing verbs in your description.

4.4   Verbs with irregular **yo** forms

ANTE TODO   In Spanish, several verbs have irregular **yo** forms in the present tense. You have already seen three verbs with the **-go** ending in the **yo** form: decir → **digo**, tener → **tengo**, and venir → **vengo**.

▶ Here are some common expressions with **decir**.

decir la verdad
to tell the truth

decir mentiras
to tell lies

decir que
to say that

decir la respuesta
to say the answer

▶ The verb **hacer** is often used to ask questions about what someone does. Note that when answering, **hacer** is frequently replaced with another, more specific action verb.

Verbs with irregular yo forms

	hacer *(to do;* *to make)*	**poner** *(to put;* *to place)*	**salir** *(to leave)*	**suponer** *(to suppose)*	**traer** *(to bring)*
SINGULAR FORMS	**hago** haces hace	**pongo** pones pone	**salgo** sales sale	**supongo** supones supone	**traigo** traes trae
PLURAL FORMS	hacemos hacéis hacen	ponemos ponéis ponen	salimos salís salen	suponemos suponéis suponen	traemos traéis traen

Salgo mucho los fines de semana.

Yo no salgo, yo hago la tarea y veo películas en la televisión.

▶ **Poner** can also mean to *turn on* a household appliance.

Carlos **pone** la radio.
Carlos turns on the radio.

María **pone** la televisión.
María turns on the television.

▶ **Salir de** is used to indicate that someone is leaving a particular place.

Hoy **salgo del** hospital.
Today I leave the hospital.

Sale de la clase a las cuatro.
He leaves class at four.

▶ **Salir para** is used to indicate someone's destination.

> Mañana **salgo para** México.   Hoy **salen para** España.
> *Tomorrow I leave for Mexico.*   *Today they leave for Spain.*

▶ **Salir con** means *to leave with someone* or *something*, or *to date someone*.

> Alberto **sale con** su mochila.   Margarita **sale con** Guillermo.
> *Alberto is leaving with his backpack.*   *Margarita is going out with Guillermo.*

The verbs ver and oír

▶ The verb **ver** (*to see*) has an irregular **yo** form. The other forms of **ver** are regular.

The verb ver (*to see*)			
Singular forms		**Plural forms**	
yo	**veo**	nosotros/as	vemos
tú	ves	vosotros/as	veis
Ud./él/ella	ve	Uds./ellos/ellas	ven

▶ The verb **oír** (*to hear*) has an irregular **yo** form and the spelling change **i:y** in the **tú**, **usted/él/ella**, and **ustedes/ellos/ellas** forms. The **nosotros/as** and **vosotros/as** forms have an accent mark.

The verb oír (*to hear*)			
Singular forms		**Plural forms**	
yo	**oigo**	nosotros/as	oímos
tú	oyes	vosotros/as	oís
Ud./él/ella	oye	Uds./ellos/ellas	oyen

▶ While most commonly translated as *to hear*, **oír** is also used in contexts where the verb *to listen* would be used in English.

> **Oigo** a unas personas en la otra sala.   ¿**Oyes** la radio por la mañana?
> *I hear some people in the other room.*   *Do you listen to the radio in the morning?*

¡INTÉNTALO! Provide the appropriate forms of these verbs.

1. salir   Isabel _____sale_____.   Nosotros _____.   Yo _____.
2. ver   Yo _____.   Uds. _____.   Tú _____.
3. poner   Rita y yo _____.   Yo _____.   Los niños _____.
4. hacer   Yo _____.   Tú _____.   Ud. _____.
5. oír   Él _____.   Nosotros _____.   Yo _____.
6. traer   Ellas _____.   Yo _____.   Tú _____.
7. suponer   Yo _____.   Mi amigo _____.   Nosotras _____.

Práctica

1 **Completar** Complete this conversation with the appropriate forms of the verbs.

ERNESTO David, ¿qué (1)_____ (hacer) hoy?

DAVID Ahora estudio biología, pero esta noche (2)_____ (salir) con Luisa.
Vamos al cine. Los críticos (3)_____ (decir) que la nueva (*new*) película
de Almodóvar es buena.

ERNESTO ¿Y Diana? ¿Qué (4)_____ (hacer) ella?

DAVID (5)_____ (Salir) a comer con sus padres.

ERNESTO ¿Qué (6)_____ (hacer) Andrés y Javier?

DAVID Tienen que (7)_____ (hacer) las maletas. (8)_____ (Salir) para
Monterrey mañana.

ERNESTO Pues, ¿qué (9)_____ (hacer) yo?

DAVID Yo (10)_____ (suponer) que puedes estudiar o (11)_____ (ver) la televisión.

ERNESTO No quiero estudiar. Mejor (12)_____ (poner) la televisión. Mi programa
favorito empieza en unos minutos.

2 **Oraciones** Form sentences using the cues provided and verbs from **Estructura 4.4**.

> **modelo**
>
> tú / _____ / cosas / en / su lugar / antes de (*before*) / salir
> *Tú pones las cosas en su lugar antes de salir.*

1. mis amigos / _____ / conmigo / centro
2. tú / _____ / mentiras / pero / yo _____ / verdad
3. Alberto / _____ / música del café Pasatiempos
4. yo / no / _____ / muchas películas
5. domingo / nosotros / _____ / mucha / tarea
6. si / yo / _____ / que / yo / querer / ir / cine / mis amigos / ir / también

3 **Describir** Use the verbs from **Estructura 4.4** to describe what these people are doing.

1. Fernán

2. los aficionados

3. yo

4. nosotros

5. la señora Vargas

6. el estudiante

Comunicación

4

El día de Francisco Listen to Francisco's description of his day. Then indicate whether the following conclusions are **lógico** or **ilógico**, based on what you heard.

	Lógico	Ilógico
1. Francisco duerme hasta (*until*) el mediodía.	O	O
2. A Francisco no le gustan los deportes.	O	O
3. Francisco almuerza en casa.	O	O
4. A Francisco le gustan los números.	O	O
5. Francisco sale para la casa a las tres.	O	O

5

Tu rutina Answer your partner's questions.

1. ¿Siempre (*Always*) pones tus cosas en su lugar?
2. ¿Qué prefieres hacer, oír la radio o ver la televisión?
3. ¿Oyes música cuando estudias?
4. ¿Ves películas en casa o prefieres ir al cine?
5. ¿Haces mucha tarea los fines de semana?
6. ¿Sales con tus amigos los fines de semana? ¿A qué hora? ¿Qué hacen?

6

Un día típico Write a short paragraph about what you do on a typical day. Use at least six of the verbs you have learned in this lesson.

> *modelo*
>
> Hola, me llamo Julia y vivo en Vancouver, Canadá. Por la mañana, yo...

Síntesis

7

Situación Imagine that you are speaking with your roommate. With a partner, prepare a conversation using these cues.

Estudiante 1	Estudiante 2
Ask your partner what he or she is doing.	Tell your partner that you are watching TV.
Say what you suppose he or she is watching.	Say that you like the show _____. Ask if he or she wants to watch.
Say no, because you are going out with friends, and tell where you are going.	Say you think it's a good idea, and ask what your partner and his or her friends are doing there.
Say what you are going to do, and ask your partner whether he or she wants to come along.	Say no and tell your partner what you prefer to do.

Recapitulación

SUBJECT
Javier

CONJUGATED FORM
empiezo

Main clause

Dudan

Review the grammar concepts you have learned in this lesson by completing these activities.

1   Completar Complete the chart with the correct verb forms. **30 pts.**

Infinitive	yo	nosotros/as	ellos/as
	vuelvo		
comenzar		comenzamos	
		hacemos	hacen
ir			
	juego		
repetir			repiten

2   Un día típico Complete the paragraph with the appropriate forms of the verbs in the word list. Not all verbs will be used. Some may be used more than once. **30 pts.**

almorzar	ir	salir
cerrar	jugar	seguir
empezar	mostrar	ver
hacer	querer	volver

¡Hola! Me llamo Cecilia y vivo en Puerto Vallarta, México. ¿Cómo es un día típico en mi vida (*life*)? Por la mañana bebo café con mis padres y juntos (*together*) (1) _____ las noticias (*news*) en la televisión. A las siete y media, (*yo*) (2) _____ de mi casa y tomo el autobús. Me gusta llegar temprano (*early*) a la universidad porque siempre (*always*) (3) _____ a mis amigos en la cafetería. Tomamos café y planeamos lo que (4) _____ hacer cada (*each*) día. A las ocho y cuarto, mi amiga Sandra y yo (5) _____ al laboratorio de lenguas. La clase de francés (6) _____ a las ocho y media. ¡Es mi clase favorita! A las doce y media (*yo*) (7) _____ en la cafetería con mis amigos. Después (*Afterwards*), yo (8) _____ con mis clases. Por las tardes, mis amigos (9) _____ a sus casas, pero yo (10) _____ al vóleibol con mi amigo Tomás.

RESUMEN GRAMATICAL

4.1   Present tense of *ir*   *p. 126*

yo	voy	nos.	vamos
tú	vas	vos.	vais
él	va	ellas	van

► ir a + [*infinitive*] = *to be going* + [*infinitive*]
► a + el = al
► vamos a + [*infinitive*] = *let's* (*do something*)

4.2   Stem-changing verbs e:ie, o:ue, u:ue   *pp. 129–130*

	empezar	volver	jugar
yo	empiezo	vuelvo	juego
tú	empiezas	vuelves	juegas
él	empieza	vuelve	juega
nos.	empezamos	volvemos	jugamos
vos.	empezáis	volvéis	jugáis
ellas	empiezan	vuelven	juegan

► Other e:ie verbs: cerrar, comenzar, entender, pensar, perder, preferir, querer
► Other o:ue verbs: almorzar, contar, dormir, encontrar, mostrar, poder, recordar

4.3   Stem-changing verbs e:i   *p. 133*

		pedir		
yo	pido	nos.	pedimos
tú	pides	vos.	pedís
él	pide	ellas	piden

► Other e:i verbs: conseguir, decir, repetir, seguir

4.4   Verbs with irregular yo forms   *pp. 136–137*

hacer	poner	salir	suponer	traer
hago	pongo	salgo	supongo	traigo

► ver: veo, ves, ve, vemos, veis, ven
► oír: oigo, oyes, oye, oímos, oís, oyen

3 **Oraciones** Arrange the cues provided in the correct order to form complete sentences. Make all necessary changes. **36 pts.**

1. tarea / los / hacer / sábados / nosotros / la

   _____

2. en / pizza / Andrés / una / restaurante / el / pedir

   _____

3. a / ? / museo / ir / ¿ / el / (tú)

   _____

4. de / oír / amigos / bien / los / no / Elena

   _____

5. libros / traer / yo / clase / mis / a

   _____

6. película / ver / en / Jorge y Carlos / pensar / cine / una / el

   _____

7. unos / escribir / Mariana / electrónicos / querer / mensajes

   _____

8. centro / conseguir / en / nosotros / el / videojuegos

   _____

9. tú / favores / el / pedir / tiempo / todo

   _____

4 **Rima** Complete the rhyme with the appropriate forms of the correct verbs from the list. **4 pts.**

contar	poder
oír	suponer

“Si no _____ dormir
y el sueño deseas,
lo vas a conseguir
si _____ ovejas°.”

ovejas *sheep*

Lectura

Antes de leer

Estrategia

Predicting content from visuals

When you are reading in Spanish, be sure to look for visual clues that will orient you as to the content and purpose of what you are reading. Photos and illustrations, for example, will often give you a good idea of the main points that the reading covers. You may also encounter very helpful visuals that are used to summarize large amounts of data in a way that is easy to comprehend; these include bar graphs, pie charts, flow charts, lists of percentages, and other sorts of diagrams.

Examinar el texto

Take a quick look at the visual elements of the magazine article in order to generate a list of ideas about its content.

Contestar

Read the list of ideas you wrote in **Examinar el texto**, and look again at the visual elements of the magazine article. Then answer these questions:

1. Who is the woman in the photo, and what is her role?
2. What is the article about?
3. What is the subject of the pie chart?
4. What is the subject of the bar graph?

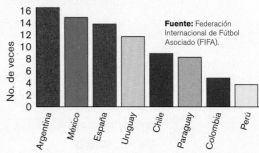

por María Úrsula Echevarría

El fútbol es el deporte más popular en el mundo° hispano, según° una encuesta° reciente realizada entre jóvenes universitarios. Mucha gente practica este deporte y tiene un equipo de fútbol favorito. Cada cuatro años se realiza la Copa Mundial°. Argentina y Uruguay han ganado° este campeonato° más de una vez°. Los aficionados siguen los partidos de fútbol en casa por tele y en muchos otros lugares como bares, restaurantes, estadios y clubes deportivos. Los jóvenes juegan al fútbol con sus amigos en parques y gimnasios.

Países hispanos en campeonatos mundiales de fútbol (1930–2014)

Bar graph — y-axis: No. de veces (0 to 16). Categories: Argentina, México, España, Uruguay, Chile, Paraguay, Colombia, Perú.

Fuente: Federación Internacional de Fútbol Asociado (FIFA).

Pero, por supuesto°, en los países de habla hispana también hay otros deportes populares. ¿Qué deporte sigue al fútbol en estos países? Bueno, ¡depende del país y de otros factores!

Después de leer

Evaluación y predicción

Which of the following sporting events would be most popular among the college students surveyed? Rate them from one (most popular) to five (least popular). Which would be the most popular at your college or university?

_____ 1. la Copa Mundial de Fútbol
_____ 2. los Juegos Olímpicos
_____ 3. el Campeonato de Wimbledon
_____ 4. la Serie Mundial de Béisbol
_____ 5. el Tour de Francia

No sólo el fútbol

En Colombia, el béisbol también es muy popular después del fútbol, aunque° esto varía según la región del país. En la costa del norte de Colombia, el béisbol es una pasión. Y el ciclismo también es un deporte que los colombianos siguen con mucho interés.

Donde el béisbol es más popular

En los países del Caribe, el béisbol es el deporte predominante. Éste es el caso en Puerto Rico, Cuba y la República Dominicana. Los niños empiezan a jugar cuando son muy pequeños. En Puerto Rico y la República Dominicana, la gente también quiere participar en otros deportes, como el baloncesto, o ver los partidos en la tele. Y para los espectadores aficionados del Caribe, el boxeo es número dos.

Donde el fútbol es más popular

En México, el béisbol es el segundo° deporte más popular después° del fútbol. Pero en Argentina, después del fútbol, el rugby tiene mucha importancia. En Perú a la gente le gusta mucho ver partidos de vóleibol. ¿Y en España? Muchas personas prefieren el baloncesto, el tenis y el ciclismo.

Deportes más populares

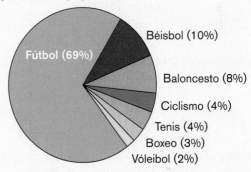

Fútbol (69%)
Béisbol (10%)
Baloncesto (8%)
Ciclismo (4%)
Tenis (4%)
Boxeo (3%)
Vóleibol (2%)

---

mundo *world* según *according to* encuesta *survey* se realiza la Copa Mundial *the World Cup is held* han ganado *have won* campeonato *championship* más de una vez *more than once* por supuesto *of course* segundo *second* después *after* aunque *although*

¿Cierto o falso?

Indicate whether each sentence is **cierto** or **falso**, then correct the false statements.

	Cierto	Falso
1. El vóleibol es el segundo deporte más popular en México.	○	○
2. En España a la gente le gustan varios deportes como el baloncesto y el ciclismo.	○	○
3. En la costa del norte de Colombia, el tenis es una pasión.	○	○
4. En el Caribe, el deporte más popular es el béisbol.	○	○

Preguntas

Answer these questions in Spanish.

1. ¿Dónde ven el fútbol los aficionados? Y tú, ¿cómo ves tus deportes favoritos?
2. ¿Te gusta el fútbol? ¿Por qué?
3. ¿Miras la Copa Mundial en la televisión?
4. ¿Qué deportes miras en la televisión?
5. En tu opinión, ¿cuáles son los tres deportes más populares en tu universidad? ¿En tu comunidad? ¿En tu país?
6. ¿Practicas deportes en tus ratos libres?

Escritura

Estrategia
Using a dictionary

A common mistake made by beginning language learners is to embrace the dictionary as the ultimate resource for reading, writing, and speaking. While it is true that the dictionary is a useful tool that can provide valuable information about vocabulary, using the dictionary correctly requires that you understand the elements of each entry.

If you glance at a Spanish-English dictionary, you will notice that its format is similar to that of an English dictionary. The word is listed first, usually followed by its pronunciation. Then come the definitions, organized by parts of speech. Sometimes the most frequently used definitions are listed first.

To find the best word for your needs, you should refer to the abbreviations and the explanatory notes that appear next to the entries. For example, imagine that you are writing about your pastimes. You want to write, "I want to buy a new racket for my match tomorrow," but you don't know the Spanish word for "racket." In the dictionary, you may find an entry like this:

> **racket** *s* **1**. alboroto; **2**. raqueta (*dep.*)

The abbreviation key at the front of the dictionary says that *s* corresponds to **sustantivo** (*noun*). Then, the first word you see is **alboroto**. The definition of **alboroto** is *noise* or *racket*, so **alboroto** is probably not the word you're looking for. The second word is **raqueta**, followed by the abbreviation *dep.*, which stands for **deportes**. This indicates that the word **raqueta** is the best choice for your needs.

Tema
Escribir un folleto

Choose one topic to write a brochure.

1. You are the head of the Homecoming Committee at your school this year. Create a pamphlet that lists events for Friday night, Saturday, and Sunday. Include a brief description of each event and its time and location. Include activities for different age groups, since some alumni will bring their families.

2. You are on the Freshman Student Orientation Committee and are in charge of creating a pamphlet for new students that describes the sports offered at your school. Write the flyer and include activities for both men and women.

3. You work for the Chamber of Commerce in your community. It is your job to market your community to potential residents. Write a brief pamphlet that describes the recreational opportunities your community provides, the areas where the activities take place, and the costs, if any. Be sure to include activities that will appeal to singles as well as couples and families; you should include activities for all age groups and for both men and women.

Escuchar

Estrategia

Listening for the gist

Listening for the general idea, or gist, can help you follow what someone is saying even if you can't hear or understand some of the words. When you listen for the gist, you simply try to capture the essence of what you hear without focusing on individual words.

 To help you practice this strategy, you will listen to a paragraph made up of three sentences. Jot down a brief summary of what you hear.

Preparación

Based on the photo, what do you think Anabela is like? Do you and Anabela have similar interests?

Ahora escucha

You will hear first José talking, then Anabela. As you listen, check off each person's favorite activities.

Pasatiempos favoritos de José

1. _____ leer el correo electrónico
2. _____ jugar al béisbol
3. _____ ver películas de acción
4. _____ ir al café
5. _____ ir a partidos de béisbol
6. _____ ver películas románticas
7. _____ dormir la siesta
8. _____ escribir mensajes electrónicos

Pasatiempos favoritos de Anabela

9. _____ esquiar
10. _____ nadar
11. _____ practicar el ciclismo
12. _____ jugar al golf
13. _____ jugar al baloncesto
14. _____ ir a ver partidos de tenis
15. _____ escalar montañas
16. _____ ver televisión

Comprensión

Preguntas

Answer these questions about José's and Anabela's pastimes.

1. ¿Quién practica más deportes?
2. ¿Quién piensa que es importante descansar?
3. ¿A qué deporte es aficionado José?
4. ¿Por qué Anabela no practica el baloncesto?
5. ¿Qué películas le gustan a la novia de José?
6. ¿Cuál es el deporte favorito de Anabela?

Seleccionar

Which person do these statements best describe?

1. Le gusta practicar deportes.
2. Prefiere las películas de acción.
3. Le gustan las computadoras.
4. Le gusta nadar.
5. Siempre (*Always*) duerme una siesta por la tarde.
6. Quiere ir de vacaciones a las montañas.

En pantalla

In many Spanish-speaking countries, soccer isn't just a game; it's a way of life. Many countries have professional and amateur leagues, and soccer is even played in the streets. Every four years, during the World Cup, even those who aren't big fans of the sport find it impossible not to get swept up in "soccer fever." During the month-long Cup, passions only increase with each of the sixty-four matches played. Companies also get caught up in the soccer craze, running ad campaigns and offering promotions with prizes ranging from commemorative glasses to all-expenses-paid trips to the World Cup venue.

Vocabulario útil	
cracks	stars, aces (sports)
lo tuvo a Pelé de hijo	he was a better player than Pelé (coll. expr. Peru)
Dios me hizo	God made me
patito feo	ugly duckling
plata	money (S. America)
jugando	playing

Comprensión

Indicate whether each statement is **cierto** or **falso**.

	Cierto	Falso
1. La familia juega al baloncesto.	O	O
2. No hay mujeres en el anuncio (*ad*).	O	O
3. La pareja tiene cinco hijos.	O	O
4. El narrador es un mariachi.	O	O

Preguntas

Answer these questions in Spanish.

1. En el anuncio hay varios elementos culturales representativos de la cultura de los países hispanos. ¿Cuáles son?

2. ¿Qué otros elementos culturales de los países hispanos conoces (*do you know*)?

jugaba *used to play* cuna *crib* barriga *womb* Por eso *That's why*
esperaban que yo fuera *they expected that I would be*
el mejor de todos *the best of all*

Anuncio de Totofútbol

Mi hermano mayor jugaba° desde la cuna°.

Mi segundo hermano, desde la barriga°.

Por eso° esperaban que yo fuera° el mejor de todos°.

The rivalry between the teams **Real Madrid** and **FC Barcelona** is perhaps the fiercest in all of soccer—just imagine if they occupied the same city! Well, each team also has competing clubs within its respective city: Spain's capital has the **Club Atlético de Madrid**, and Barcelona is home to **Espanyol**. In fact, across the Spanish-speaking world, it is common for a city to have more than one professional team, often with strikingly dissimilar origins, identity, and fan base. For example, in Bogotá, the **Millonarios** were so named for the large sums spent on players, while the **Santa Fe** team is one of the most traditional in Colombian soccer. **River Plate** and **Boca Juniors**, who enjoy a famous rivalry, are just two of twenty-four clubs in Buenos Aires—the city with the most professional soccer teams in the world.

Vocabulario útil

afición	*fans*
celebran	*they celebrate*
preferido/a	*favorite*
rivalidad	*rivalry*
se junta con	*it's tied up with*

Preparación

What is the most popular sport at your school? What teams are your rivals? How do students celebrate a win?

Escoger

Select the correct answer.

1. Un partido entre el Barça y el Real Madrid es un _____ (deporte/evento) importante en toda España.

2. Los aficionados _____ (miran/celebran) las victorias de sus equipos en las calles (*streets*).

3. La rivalidad entre el Real Madrid y el Barça está relacionada con la _____ (religión/política).

¡Fútbol en España!

(Hay mucha afición al fútbol en España.)

¿Y cuál es vuestro jugador favorito?

—¿Y quién va a ganar?
—El Real Madrid.

México

El país en cifras

▶ **Área:** 1.972.550 km²
(761.603 millas²), *casi° tres veces°*
el área de Texas

La situación geográfica de México,
al sur° de los Estados Unidos, ha
influido en° la economía y la sociedad de los dos
países. Una de las consecuencias es la emigración
de la población mexicana al país vecino°. Hoy día,
más de 33 millones de personas de ascendencia
mexicana viven en los Estados Unidos.

▶ **Población:** 118.818.000
▶ **Capital:** México, D.F. (y su área
metropolitana)—19.319.000
▶ **Ciudades principales:** Guadalajara
—4.338.000, Monterrey—3.838.000,
Puebla—2.278.000,
Ciudad Juárez—1.321.000
▶ **Moneda:** peso mexicano
▶ **Idiomas:** español (oficial), náhuatl,
otras lenguas indígenas

Bandera de México

Mexicanos célebres

▶ **Benito Juárez,** héroe nacional (1806–1872)
▶ **Octavio Paz,** poeta (1914–1998)
▶ **Elena Poniatowska,** periodista y escritora
(1932–)
▶ **Mario Molina,** Premio Nobel de Química, 1995;
químico (1943–)
▶ **Paulina Rubio,** cantante (1971–)

casi *almost* veces *times* sur *south* ha influido en *has influenced*
vecino *neighboring* se llenan de luz *get filled with light* flores *flowers*
Muertos *Dead* se ríen *laugh* muerte *death* lo cual se refleja *which is*
reflected calaveras de azúcar *sugar skulls* pan *bread* huesos *bones*

Cabo San Lucas

ESTADOS UNIDOS

Autorretrato con mono
(*Self-portrait with monkey*),
1938, Frida Kahlo

Ciudad Juárez
Golfo de California
Baja California
Río Grande
Río Bravo del Norte
Sierra Madre Oriental
Sierra Madre Occidental
Monterrey

ESTADOS UNIDOS
MÉXICO
OCÉANO PACÍFICO
OCÉANO ATLÁNTICO
AMÉRICA DEL SUR

Océano Pacífico
Ciudad de México
Puerto Vallarta
Guadalajara
Puebla
Acapulco

Artesanías
en Taxco, Guerrero

Pirámide de Kukulcán
en Chichén Itzá

¡Increíble pero cierto!

Cada dos de noviembre los cementerios de
México se llenan de luz°, música y flores°. El Día
de Muertos° no es un evento triste; es una fiesta
en honor a las personas muertas. En ese día,
los mexicanos se ríen° de la muerte°, lo cual se
refleja° en detalles como las calaveras de azúcar°
y el pan° de muerto —pan en forma de huesos°.

Ciudades • México, D.F.

La Ciudad de México, fundada° en 1525, también se llama el D.F. o Distrito Federal. Muchos turistas e inmigrantes vienen a la ciudad porque es el centro cultural y económico del país. El crecimiento° de la población es de los más altos° del mundo. El D.F. tiene una población mayor que las de Nueva York, Madrid o París.

Artes • Diego Rivera y Frida Kahlo

Frida Kahlo y Diego Rivera eran° artistas mexicanos muy famosos. Se casaron° en 1929. Los dos se interesaron° en las condiciones sociales de la gente indígena de su país. Puedes ver algunas° de sus obras° en el Museo de Arte Moderno de la Ciudad de México.

Golfo
de México

Península
de Yucatán

Bahía de
Campeche

Mérida

Cancún

Veracruz

Istmo de
Tehuantepec

BELICE

GUATEMALA

Historia • Los aztecas

Los aztecas dominaron° en México del siglo° XIV al siglo XVI. Sus canales, puentes° y pirámides con templos religiosos eran muy importantes.
El fin del imperio azteca comenzó° con la llegada° de los españoles en 1519, pero la presencia azteca sigue hoy. La Ciudad de México está situada en la capital azteca de Tenochtitlán, y muchos turistas van a visitar sus ruinas.

Economía • La plata

México es el mayor productor de plata° del mundo°. Estados como Zacatecas y Durango tienen ciudades fundadas cerca de los más grandes yacimientos° de plata del país. Estas ciudades fueron° en la época colonial unas de las más ricas e importantes. Hoy en día, aún° conservan mucho de su encanto° y esplendor.

¿Qué aprendiste? Responde a cada pregunta con una oración completa.

1. ¿Qué lenguas hablan los mexicanos?

2. ¿Cómo es la población del D.F. en comparación con la de otras ciudades?

3. ¿En qué se interesaron Frida Kahlo y Diego Rivera?

4. Nombra algunas de las estructuras de la arquitectura azteca.

5. ¿Dónde está situada la capital de México?

6. ¿Qué estados de México tienen los mayores yacimientos de plata?

Conexión Internet Investiga estos temas en Internet.

1. Busca información sobre dos lugares de México. ¿Te gustaría (*Would you like*) vivir allí? ¿Por qué?

2. Busca información sobre dos artistas mexicanos. ¿Cómo se llaman sus obras más famosas?

....

fundada *founded* **crecimiento** *growth* **más altos** *highest* **eran** *were* **Se casaron** *They got married* **se interesaron** *were interested* **algunas** *some* **obras** *works* **dominaron** *dominated* **siglo** *century* **puentes** *bridges* **comenzó** *started* **llegada** *arrival* **plata** *silver* **mundo** *world* **yacimientos** *deposits* **fueron** *were* **aún** *still* **encanto** *charm*

Pasatiempos

andar en patineta	to skateboard
bucear	to scuba dive
escalar montañas (f., pl.)	to climb mountains
escribir una carta	to write a letter
escribir un mensaje electrónico	to write an e-mail
esquiar	to ski
ganar	to win
ir de excursión	to go on a hike
leer el correo electrónico	to read e-mail
leer un periódico	to read a newspaper
leer una revista	to read a magazine
nadar	to swim
pasear	to take a walk
pasear en bicicleta	to ride a bicycle
patinar (en línea)	to (inline) skate
practicar deportes (m., pl.)	to play sports
tomar el sol	to sunbathe
ver películas (f., pl.)	to watch movies
visitar monumentos (m., pl.)	to visit monuments
la diversión	fun activity; entertainment; recreation
el fin de semana	weekend
el pasatiempo	pastime; hobby
los ratos libres	spare (free) time
el videojuego	video game

Deportes

el baloncesto	basketball
el béisbol	baseball
el ciclismo	cycling
el equipo	team
el esquí (acuático)	(water) skiing
el fútbol	soccer
el fútbol americano	football
el golf	golf
el hockey	hockey
el/la jugador(a)	player
la natación	swimming
el partido	game; match
la pelota	ball
el tenis	tennis
el vóleibol	volleyball

Adjetivos

deportivo/a	sports-related
favorito/a	favorite

Lugares

el café	café
el centro	downtown
el cine	movie theater
el gimnasio	gymnasium
la iglesia	church
el lugar	place
el museo	museum
el parque	park
la piscina	swimming pool
la plaza	city or town square
el restaurante	restaurant

Verbos

almorzar (o:ue)	to have lunch
cerrar (e:ie)	to close
comenzar (e:ie)	to begin
conseguir (e:i)	to get; to obtain
contar (o:ue)	to count; to tell
decir (e:i)	to say; to tell
dormir (o:ue)	to sleep
empezar (e:ie)	to begin
encontrar (o:ue)	to find
entender (e:ie)	to understand
hacer	to do; to make
ir	to go
jugar (u:ue)	to play (a sport or a game)
mostrar (o:ue)	to show
oír	to hear
pedir (e:i)	to ask for; to request
pensar (e:ie)	to think
pensar (+ inf.)	to intend
pensar en	to think about
perder (e:ie)	to lose; to miss
poder (o:ue)	to be able to; can
poner	to put; to place
preferir (e:ie)	to prefer
querer (e:ie)	to want; to love
recordar (o:ue)	to remember
repetir (e:i)	to repeat
salir	to leave
seguir (e:i)	to follow; to continue
suponer	to suppose
traer	to bring
ver	to see
volver (o:ue)	to return

Decir expressions	See page 136.
Expresiones útiles	See page 121.

Las vacaciones

5

A PRIMERA VISTA
- ¿Están ellos en una montaña o en un museo?
- ¿Son viejos o jóvenes?
- ¿Pasean o ven una película? ¿Andan en patineta o van de excursión?
- ¿Es posible esquiar en este lugar?

Las vacaciones

Más vocabulario

la cama	*bed*
la habitación individual, doble	*single, double room*
el piso	*floor (of a building)*
la planta baja	*ground floor*
el campo	*countryside*
el paisaje	*landscape*
el equipaje	*luggage*
la estación de autobuses, del metro, de tren	*bus, subway, train station*
la llegada	*arrival*
el pasaje (de ida y vuelta)	*(round-trip) ticket*
la salida	*departure; exit*
la tabla de (wind)surf	*surfboard/sailboard*
acampar	*to camp*
estar de vacaciones	*to be on vacation*
hacer las maletas	*to pack (one's suitcases)*
hacer un viaje	*to take a trip*
hacer (wind)surf	*to (wind)surf*
ir de compras	*to go shopping*
ir de vacaciones	*to go on vacation*
ir en autobús (m.), auto(móvil) (m.), motocicleta (f.), taxi (m.)	*to go by bus, car, motorcycle, taxi*

Variación léxica

automóvil ⟷ coche (*Esp.*), carro (*Amér. L.*)

autobús ⟷ camión (*Méx.*), guagua (*Caribe*)

motocicleta ⟷ moto (*coloquial*)

la agente de viajes

el pasaporte

Confirma una reservación. (confirmar)

En la agencia de viajes

la habitación

el ascensor

el empleado

la llave

la huésped

el huésped

En el hotel

Saca/Toma fotos.
(sacar, tomar)

BIENVENIDOS

el avión

el viajero

la inspectora
de aduanas

En el aeropuerto

Pesca.
(pescar)

Monta a caballo.
(montar)

Va en barco.
(ir)

Juegan a las
cartas. (jugar)

el mar

la playa

En la playa

Práctica

1 Escuchar Indicate who would probably make each statement you hear. Each answer is used twice.

a. el agente de viajes
b. el inspector de aduanas
c. un empleado del hotel

1. _____   4. _____
2. _____   5. _____
3. _____   6. _____

2 ¿Cierto o falso? Mario and his wife, Natalia, are planning their next vacation with a travel agent. Indicate whether each statement is **cierto** or **falso** according to what you hear in the conversation.

	Cierto	Falso
1. Mario y Natalia están en Puerto Rico.	○	○
2. Ellos quieren hacer un viaje a Puerto Rico.	○	○
3. Natalia prefiere ir a la montaña.	○	○
4. Mario quiere pescar en Puerto Rico.	○	○
5. La agente de viajes va a confirmar la reservación.	○	○

3 Escoger Choose the best answer for each sentence.

1. Un huésped es una persona que _____.
   a. toma fotos   b. está en un hotel   c. pesca en el mar
2. Abrimos la puerta con _____.
   a. una llave   b. un caballo   c. una llegada
3. Enrique tiene _____ porque va a viajar a otro (*another*) país.
   a. un pasaporte   b. una foto   c. una llegada
4. Antes de (*Before*) ir de vacaciones, hay que _____.
   a. pescar   b. ir en tren   c. hacer las maletas
5. Nosotros vamos en _____ al aeropuerto.
   a. autobús   b. pasaje   c. viajero
6. Me gusta mucho ir al campo. El _____ es increíble.
   a. paisaje   b. pasaje   c. equipaje

4 Analogías Complete the analogies using the words below. Two words will not be used.

auto	huésped	mar	sacar
empleado	llegada	pasaporte	tren

1. acampar ⟶ campo ⊜ pescar ⟶
2. agencia de viajes ⟶ agente ⊜ hotel ⟶
3. llave ⟶ habitación ⊜ pasaje ⟶
4. estudiante ⟶ libro ⊜ turista ⟶
5. aeropuerto ⟶ viajero ⊜ hotel ⟶
6. maleta ⟶ hacer ⊜ foto ⟶

Las estaciones y los meses del año

el invierno: **diciembre, enero, febrero**

la primavera: **marzo, abril, mayo**

el verano: **junio, julio, agosto**

el otoño: **septiembre, octubre, noviembre**

—**¿Cuál es la fecha de hoy?**   *What is today's date?*
—**Es el primero de octubre.**   *It's the first of October.*
—**Es el dos de marzo.**   *It's March 2nd.*
—**Es el diez de noviembre.**   *It's November 10th.*

El tiempo

—**¿Qué tiempo hace?**   *How's the weather?*
—**Hace buen/mal tiempo.**   *The weather is good/bad.*

Hace (mucho) calor.
It's (very) hot.

Hace (mucho) frío.
It's (very) cold.

Llueve. (llover o:ue)
It's raining.

Está lloviendo.
It's raining.

Nieva. (nevar e:ie)
It's snowing.

Está nevando.
It's snowing.

Más vocabulario

Está (muy) nublado.	*It's (very) cloudy.*
Hace fresco.	*It's cool.*
Hace (mucho) sol.	*It's (very) sunny.*
Hace (mucho) viento.	*It's (very) windy.*

5 **El Hotel Regis** Label the floors of the hotel.

Números ordinales	
primer (before a masculine singular noun), **primero/a**	first
segundo/a	second
tercer (before a masculine singular noun), **tercero/a**	third
cuarto/a	fourth
quinto/a	fifth
sexto/a	sixth
séptimo/a	seventh
octavo/a	eighth
noveno/a	ninth
décimo/a	tenth

a. _____ piso
b. _____ piso
c. _____ piso
d. _____ piso
e. _____ piso
f. _____ piso
g. _____ piso
h. _____ baja

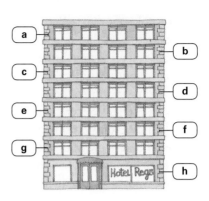

6 **Contestar** Look at the illustrations of the months and seasons on the previous page. Then answer these questions.

> **modelo**
>
> **Estudiante 1:** ¿Cuál es el primer mes de la primavera?
> **Estudiante 2:** marzo

1. ¿Cuál es el primer mes del invierno?
2. ¿Cuál es el segundo mes de la primavera?
3. ¿Cuál es el tercer mes del otoño?
4. ¿Cuál es el primer mes del año?
5. ¿Cuál es el quinto mes del año?
6. ¿Cuál es el octavo mes del año?
7. ¿Cuál es el décimo mes del año?
8. ¿Cuál es el segundo mes del verano?
9. ¿Cuál es el tercer mes del invierno?
10. ¿Cuál es el sexto mes del año?

7 **Las estaciones** Name the season that applies to the description.

1. Las clases terminan.
2. Vamos a la playa.
3. Acampamos.
4. Nieva mucho.
5. Las clases empiezan.
6. Hace mucho calor.
7. Llueve mucho.
8. Esquiamos.
9. el entrenamiento (*training*) de béisbol
10. el Día de Acción de Gracias (*Thanksgiving*)

8 **¿Cuál es la fecha?** Give the dates for these holidays.

> **modelo**
>
> el día de San Valentín   14 de febrero

1. el día de San Patricio
2. el día de Halloween
3. el primer día de verano
4. el Año Nuevo
5. mi cumpleaños (*birthday*)
6. mi día de fiesta favorito

9

Seleccionar Paco is talking about his family and friends. Choose the word or phrase that best completes each sentence.

1. A mis padres les gusta ir a Yucatán porque (hace sol, nieva).
2. Mi primo de Kansas dice que durante (*during*) un tornado, hace mucho (sol, viento).
3. Mis amigos van a esquiar si (nieva, está nublado).
4. Tomo el sol cuando (hace calor, llueve).
5. Nosotros vamos a ver una película si hace (buen, mal) tiempo.
6. Mi hermana prefiere correr cuando (hace mucho calor, hace fresco).
7. Mis tíos van de excursión si hace (buen, mal) tiempo.
8. Mi padre no quiere jugar al golf si (hace fresco, llueve).
9. Cuando hace mucho (sol, frío) no salgo de casa y tomo chocolate caliente (*hot*).
10. Hoy mi sobrino va al parque porque (está lloviendo, hace buen tiempo).

10

El clima With a partner, take turns asking and answering questions about the weather and temperatures in these cities. Use the model as a guide.

> **modelo**
>
> **Estudiante 1:** ¿Qué tiempo hace hoy en Nueva York?
> **Estudiante 2:** Hace frío y hace viento.
> **Estudiante 1:** ¿Cuál es la temperatura máxima?
> **Estudiante 2:** Treinta y un grados (*degrees*).
> **Estudiante 1:** ¿Y la temperatura mínima?
> **Estudiante 2:** Diez grados.

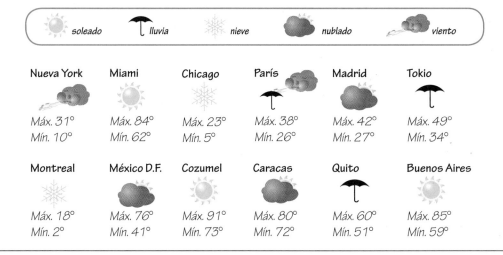

soleado   lluvia   nieve   nublado   viento

Nueva York	Miami	Chicago	París	Madrid	Tokio
Máx. 31°	Máx. 84°	Máx. 23°	Máx. 38°	Máx. 42°	Máx. 49°
Mín. 10°	Mín. 62°	Mín. 5°	Mín. 26°	Mín. 27°	Mín. 34°

Montreal	México D.F.	Cozumel	Caracas	Quito	Buenos Aires
Máx. 18°	Máx. 76°	Máx. 91°	Máx. 80°	Máx. 60°	Máx. 85°
Mín. 2°	Mín. 41°	Mín. 73°	Mín. 72°	Mín. 51°	Mín. 59°

11

Completar Complete these sentences with your own ideas.

1. Cuando hace sol, yo...
2. Cuando llueve, mis amigos y yo...
3. Cuando hace calor, mi familia...
4. Cuando hace viento, la gente...
5. Cuando hace frío, yo...
6. Cuando hace mal tiempo, mis amigos...
7. Cuando nieva, muchas personas...
8. Cuando está nublado, mis amigos y yo...
9. Cuando hace fresco, mis padres...
10. Cuando hace buen tiempo, mis amigos...

NOTA CULTURAL

In most Spanish-speaking countries, temperatures are given in degrees Celsius. Use these formulas to convert between **grados centígrados** and **grados Fahrenheit**.

degrees C. × 9 ÷ 5 + 32 = degrees F.

degrees F. - 32 × 5 ÷ 9 = degrees C.

CONSULTA

Calor and **frío** can apply to both weather and people. Use **hacer** to describe weather conditions or climate.

(**Hace frío en Santiago**. *It's cold in Santiago*.)

Use **tener** to refer to people.

(**El viajero tiene frío**. *The traveler is cold*.)

See **Estructura 3.4**, p. 101.

Comunicación

12

En la agencia de viajes Listen to the conversation between Mr. Vega and a travel agent. Then indicate whether the following conclusions are **lógico** or **ilógico**, based on what you heard.

	Lógico	Ilógico
1. El señor Vega quiere visitar la Antártida.	○	○
2. Hace calor en Puerto Rico.	○	○
3. El señor Vega va a ver el mar en Puerto Rico.	○	○
4. El señor Vega va a comprar un pasaje de ida y vuelta.	○	○
5. El señor Vega viaja con su familia.	○	○

13

Preguntas personales Answer your partner's questions.

1. ¿Cuál es la fecha de hoy? ¿Qué estación es?
2. ¿Te gusta esta estación? ¿Por qué?
3. ¿Qué estación prefieres? ¿Por qué?
4. ¿Prefieres el mar o las montañas? ¿La playa o el campo? ¿Por qué?
5. Cuando haces un viaje, ¿qué te gusta hacer y ver?
6. ¿Piensas ir de vacaciones este verano? ¿Adónde quieres ir? ¿Por qué?
7. ¿Qué deseas ver y qué lugares quieres visitar?
8. ¿Cómo te gusta viajar? ¿En avión? ¿En motocicleta...?

14

Itinerario Create a trip itinerary for a friend, a relative, or someone famous. First, choose a destination. Include information about transportation and accommodations, as well as a section for each day with activities.

- fechas
- lugar
- transporte
- hotel
- actividades

Síntesis

15

Un viaje With a partner, role-play a conversation between a travel agent and a client planning a trip. Discuss destinations, dates, transportation, hotel accommodations, and activities for the trip.

¡Vamos a la playa!

Los seis amigos hacen un viaje a la playa.

PERSONAJES

 FELIPE

 JUAN CARLOS

1

TÍA ANA MARÍA ¿Están listos para su viaje a la playa?

TODOS Sí.

TÍA ANA MARÍA Excelente... ¡A la estación de autobuses!

MARU ¿Dónde está Miguel?

FELIPE Yo lo traigo.

2

(*se escucha un grito de Miguel*)

FELIPE Ya está listo. Y tal vez enojado. Ahorita vamos.

EMPLEADO Bienvenidas. ¿En qué puedo servirles?

MARU Hola. Tenemos una reservación para seis personas para esta noche.

EMPLEADO ¿A nombre de quién?

JIMENA ¿Díaz? ¿López? No estoy segura.

3

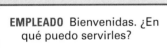

EMPLEADO No encuentro su nombre. Ah, no, ahora sí lo veo, aquí está. Díaz. Dos habitaciones en el primer piso para seis huéspedes.

4

FELIPE No está nada mal el hotel, ¿verdad? Limpio, cómodo... ¡Oye, Miguel! ¿Todavía estás enojado conmigo? (*a Juan Carlos*) Miguel está de mal humor. No me habla.

JUAN CARLOS ¿Todavía?

5

6

EMPLEADO Aquí están las llaves de sus habitaciones.

MARU Gracias. Una cosa más. Mi novio y yo queremos hacer windsurf, pero no tenemos tablas.

EMPLEADO El botones las puede conseguir para ustedes.

MARISSA   **JIMENA**   **MARU**   **MIGUEL**   **MAITE FUENTES**   **ANA MARÍA**   **EMPLEADO**

7

JUAN CARLOS ¿Qué hace este libro aquí? ¿Estás estudiando en la playa?

JIMENA Sí, es que tengo un examen la próxima semana.

8

JUAN CARLOS Ay, Jimena. ¡No! ¿Vamos a nadar?

JIMENA Bueno, como estudiar es tan aburrido y el tiempo está tan bonito...

MARISSA Yo estoy un poco cansada. ¿Y tú? ¿Por qué no estás nadando?

FELIPE Es por causa de Miguel.

9

10

MARISSA Hmm, estoy confundida.

FELIPE Esta mañana. ¡Sigue enojado conmigo!

MARISSA No puede seguir enojado tanto tiempo.

Expresiones útiles

Talking with hotel personnel

¿En qué puedo servirles?
How can I help you?
Tenemos una reservación.
We have a reservation.
¿A nombre de quién?
In whose name?
¿Quizás López? ¿Tal vez Díaz?
Maybe López? Maybe Díaz?
Ahora lo veo, aquí está. Díaz.
Now I see it. Here it is. Díaz.
Dos habitaciones en el primer piso para seis huéspedes.
Two rooms on the first floor for six guests.
Aquí están las llaves.
Here are the keys.

Describing a hotel

No está nada mal el hotel.
The hotel isn't bad at all.
Todo está tan limpio y cómodo.
Everything is so clean and comfortable.
Es excelente/estupendo/fabuloso/ fenomenal/increíble/magnífico/ maravilloso/perfecto.
It's excellent/stupendous/fabulous/ phenomenal/incredible/magnificent/ marvelous/perfect.

Talking about how you feel

Yo estoy un poco cansado/a.
I am a little tired.
Estoy confundido/a. *I'm confused.*
Todavía estoy/Sigo enojado/a contigo.
I'm still angry with you.

Additional vocabulary

afuera *outside*
amable *nice; friendly*
el balde *bucket*
el/la botones *bellhop*
la crema de afeitar
shaving cream
el frente (frío) *(cold) front*
el grito *scream*
la temporada *period of time*
entonces *so, then*
es igual *it's the same*

¿Qué pasó?

1 **Completar** Complete these sentences with the correct term from the word bank.

aburrido	botones	la llave
el aeropuerto	la estación de autobuses	montar a caballo
amable	habitaciones	reservación

1. Los amigos van a _____ para ir a la playa.
2. La _____ del hotel está a nombre de los Díaz.
3. Los amigos tienen dos _____ para seis personas.
4. El _____ puede conseguir tablas de windsurf para Maru.
5. Jimena dice que estudiar en vacaciones es muy _____.

CONSULTA

The meaning of some adjectives, such as **aburrido**, changes depending on whether they are used with **ser** or **estar**. See **Estructura 5.3**, pp. 170–171.

2 **Identificar** Identify the person who would make each statement.

     EMPLEADO   **MARU**   **TÍA ANA MARÍA**   **FELIPE**   **JUAN CARLOS**

1. No lo encuentro, ¿a nombre de quién está su reservación?
2. ¿Por qué estás estudiando en la playa? ¡Mejor vamos a nadar!
3. Nuestra reservación es para seis personas en dos habitaciones.
4. El hotel es limpio y cómodo, pero estoy triste porque Miguel no me habla.
5. Suban al autobús y ¡buen viaje a la playa!

3 **Ordenar** Place these events in the correct order.

_____ a. El empleado busca la reservación.
_____ b. Marissa dice que está confundida.
_____ c. Los amigos están listos para ir a la playa.
_____ d. El empleado da (*gives*) las llaves de las habitaciones a las chicas.
_____ e. Miguel grita (*screams*).

4 **Conversar** With a partner, use these cues to create a conversation between a hotel employee and a guest in Mexico.

Huésped	**Empleado/a**
Say hi to the employee and ask for your reservation.	→ Tell the guest that you can't find his/her reservation.
Tell the employee that the reservation is in your name.	→ Tell him/her that you found the reservation and that it's for a double room.
Tell the employee that the hotel is very clean and comfortable.	→ Say that you agree with the guest, welcome him/her, and give him/her the keys.
Ask the employee to call the bellhop to help you with your luggage.	→ Call the bellhop to help the guest with his/her luggage.

Pronunciación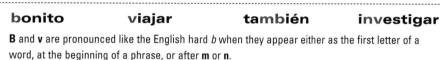
Spanish b and v

bueno   vóleibol   biblioteca   vivir

There is no difference in pronunciation between the Spanish letters **b** and **v**. However, each letter can be pronounced two different ways, depending on which letters appear next to them.

bonito   viajar   también   investigar

B and **v** are pronounced like the English hard *b* when they appear either as the first letter of a word, at the beginning of a phrase, or after **m** or **n**.

deber   novio   abril   cerveza

In all other positions, **b** and **v** have a softer pronunciation, which has no equivalent in English. Unlike the hard **b**, which is produced by tightly closing the lips and stopping the flow of air, the soft **b** is produced by keeping the lips slightly open.

bola   vela   Caribe   declive

In both pronunciations, there is no difference in sound between **b** and **v**. The English *v* sound, produced by friction between the upper teeth and lower lip, does not exist in Spanish. Instead, the soft **b** comes from friction between the two lips.

Verónica y su esposo cantan boleros.

When **b** or **v** begins a word, its pronunciation depends on the previous word. At the beginning of a phrase or after a word that ends in **m** or **n**, it is pronounced as a hard **b**.

Benito   es de Boquerón pero vive   en Victoria.

Words that begin with **b** or **v** are pronounced with a soft **b** if they appear immediately after a word that ends in a vowel or any consonant other than **m** or **n**.

Práctica Read these words aloud to practice the **b** and the **v**.

1. hablamos
2. trabajar
3. botones
4. van
5. contabilidad
6. bien
7. doble
8. novia
9. béisbol
10. nublado
11. llave
12. invierno

Oraciones Read these sentences aloud to practice the **b** and the **v**.

1. Vamos a Guaynabo en autobús.
2. Voy de vacaciones a la Isla Culebra.
3. Tengo una habitación individual en el octavo piso.
4. Víctor y Eva van en avión al Caribe.
5. La planta baja es bonita también.
6. ¿Qué vamos a ver en Bayamón?
7. Beatriz, la novia de Víctor, es de Arecibo, Puerto Rico.

Refranes Read these sayings aloud to practice the **b** and the **v**.

No hay mal que por bien no venga.[1]

Hombre prevenido vale por dos.[2]

1 Every cloud has a silver lining.
2 An ounce of prevention equals a pound of cure.

Las cataratas
del Iguazú

Imagine the impressive and majestic Niagara Falls, the most powerful waterfall in North America. Now, if you can, imagine a waterfall four times as wide and almost twice as tall that caused Eleanor Roosevelt to exclaim "Poor Niagara!" upon seeing it for the first time. Welcome to **las cataratas del Iguazú!**

Garganta del Diablo
Isla San Martín

Iguazú is located in Iguazú National Park, an area of subtropical jungle where Argentina meets Brazil. Its name comes from the indigenous Guaraní word for "great water." A UNESCO World Heritage Site, **las cataratas del Iguazú** span three kilometers and comprise 275 cascades split into two main sections by San Martín Island. Most of the falls are about 82 meters (270 feet) high. The horseshoe-shaped cataract **Garganta del Diablo** (Devil's Throat) has the greatest water flow and is considered to be the most impressive; it also marks the border between Argentina and Brazil.

Each country offers different views and tourist options. Most visitors opt to use the numerous catwalks that are available on both sides; however, from the Argentinean side, tourists can get very close to the falls, whereas Brazil provides more panoramic views. If you don't mind getting wet, a jet boat tour is a good choice; those looking for wildlife—such as toucans, ocelots, butterflies, and jaguars—should head for San Martín Island. Brazil boasts less conventional ways to view the falls, such as helicopter rides and rappelling, while Argentina focuses on sustainability with its **Tren Ecológico de la Selva** (*Ecological Jungle Train*), an environmentally friendly way to reach the walkways.

No matter which way you choose to enjoy the falls, you are certain to be captivated.

Más cascadas° en Latinoamérica

Nombre	País	Altura°	Datos
Salto Ángel	Venezuela	979 metros	la más alta° del mundo°
Catarata del Gocta	Perú	771 metros	descubierta° en 2006
Piedra Volada	México	453 metros	la más alta de México

cascadas *waterfalls* Altura *Height* más alta *tallest* mundo *world*
descubierta *discovered*

1 **¿Cierto o falso?** Indicate whether these statements are **cierto** or **falso**. Correct the false statements.

1. Iguazú Falls is located on the border of Argentina and Brazil.

2. Niagara Falls is four times as wide as Iguazú Falls.

3. Iguazú Falls has a few cascades, each about 82 meters.

4. Tourists visiting Iguazú can see exotic wildlife.

5. *Iguazú* is the Guaraní word for "blue water."

6. You can access the walkways by taking the **Garganta del Diablo**.

7. It is possible for tourists to visit Iguazú Falls by air.

8. **Salto Ángel** is the tallest waterfall in the world.

9. There are no waterfalls in Mexico.

10. For the best views of Iguazú Falls, tourists should visit the Brazilian side.

Viajes y turismo

el asiento del medio, del pasillo, de la ventanilla	*center, aisle, window seat*
el itinerario	*itinerary*
media pensión	*breakfast and one meal included*
el ómnibus (Perú)	**el autobús**
pensión completa	*all meals included*
el puente	*long weekend (lit., bridge)*

Destinos populares

- **Las playas del Parque Nacional Manuel Antonio** (Costa Rica) ofrecen° la oportunidad de nadar y luego caminar por el bosque tropical°.

- **Teotihuacán** (México) Desde antes de la época° de los aztecas, aquí se celebra el equinoccio de primavera en la Pirámide del Sol.

- **Puerto Chicama** (Perú), con sus olas° de cuatro kilómetros de largo°, es un destino para surfistas expertos.

- **Tikal** (Guatemala) Aquí puedes ver las maravillas de la selva° y ruinas de la civilización maya.

- **Las playas de Rincón** (Puerto Rico) Son ideales para descansar y observar ballenas°.

ofrecen *offer* bosque tropical *rainforest*
Desde antes de la época *Since before the time* olas *waves*
de largo *in length* selva *jungle* ballenas *whales*

Punta del Este

One of South America's largest and most fashionable beach resort towns is Uruguay's **Punta del Este**, a narrow strip of land containing twenty miles of pristine beaches. Its peninsular shape gives it two very different seascapes. **La Playa Mansa**, facing the bay and therefore the more protected side, has calm waters. Here, people practice water sports like swimming, water skiing, windsurfing, and diving. **La Playa Brava**, facing the east, receives the Atlantic Ocean's powerful, wave-producing winds, making it popular for surfing, body boarding, and kite surfing. Besides the beaches, posh shopping, and world-famous nightlife, **Punta** offers its 600,000 yearly visitors yacht and fishing clubs, golf courses, and excursions to observe sea lions at the **Isla de Lobos** nature reserve.

¿Cuáles son los sitios más populares para el turismo en Puerto Rico? | Use the Web to find more cultural information related to this **Cultura** section.

2 **Comprensión** Complete the sentences.

1. En las playas de Rincón puedes ver _____.
2. Cerca de 600.000 turistas visitan _____ cada año.
3. En el avión pides un _____ si te gusta ver el paisaje.
4. En Punta del Este, la gente prefiere nadar en la Playa _____.
5. El _____ es un medio de transporte en Perú.

3 **De vacaciones** Spring break is coming up, and you want to go on a short vacation with a friend. Decide which of the locations featured on these pages best suits your likes and interests. Come to an agreement about how you will get there, where you prefer to stay and for how long, and what each of you will do during your free time.

5.1 Estar with conditions and emotions

ANTE TODO As you learned in **Lecciones 1** and **2**, the verb **estar** is used to talk about how you feel and to say where people, places, and things are located. **Estar** is also used with adjectives to talk about certain emotional and physical conditions.

CONSULTA

To review the present tense of **estar**, see **Estructura 2.3**, p. 59.

• • •

To review the present tense of **ser**, see **Estructura 1.3**, p. 20.

▶ Use **estar** with adjectives to describe the physical condition of places and things.

La habitación **está** sucia.
The room is dirty.

La puerta **está** cerrada.
The door is closed.

▶ Use **estar** with adjectives to describe how people feel, both mentally and physically.

Yo estoy cansada.

¿Están listos para su viaje?

▶ **¡Atención!** Two important expressions with **estar** that you can use to talk about conditions and emotions are **estar de buen humor** (*to be in a good mood*) and **estar de mal humor** (*to be in a bad mood*).

Adjectives that describe emotions and conditions

abierto/a	open	**contento/a**	content	**listo/a**	ready
aburrido/a	bored	**desordenado/a**	disorderly	**nervioso/a**	nervous
alegre	happy	**enamorado/a (de)**	in love (with)	**ocupado/a**	busy
avergonzado/a	embarrassed			**ordenado/a**	orderly
cansado/a	tired	**enojado/a**	angry	**preocupado/a (por)**	worried (about)
cerrado/a	closed	**equivocado/a**	wrong		
cómodo/a	comfortable	**feliz**	happy	**seguro/a**	sure
confundido/a	confused	**limpio/a**	clean	**sucio/a**	dirty
				triste	sad

¡INTÉNTALO! Provide the present tense forms of **estar**, and choose which adjective best completes the sentence.

1. La biblioteca ___*está*___ (cerrada / nerviosa) los domingos por la noche. cerrada
2. Nosotros _____ muy (ocupados / equivocados) todos los lunes.
3. Ellas _____ (alegres / confundidas) porque tienen vacaciones.
4. Javier _____ (enamorado / ordenado) de Maribel.
5. Diana _____ (enojada / limpia) con su novio.
6. Yo _____ (nerviosa / abierta) por el viaje.
7. La habitación siempre _____ (ordenada / segura) cuando vienen sus padres.
8. Ustedes no comprenden; _____ (equivocados / tristes).

Práctica y Comunicación

1 **¿Cómo están?** Complete Martín's statements about how he and other people are feeling. In the first blank, fill in the correct form of **estar**. In the second blank, fill in the adjective that best fits the context.

1. Yo _____ un poco _____ porque tengo un examen mañana.
2. Mi hermana Patricia _____ muy _____ porque mañana va a hacer una excursión al campo.
3. Mis hermanos Juan y José salen de la casa a las cinco de la mañana. Por la noche, siempre _____ muy _____.
4. Mi amigo Ramiro _____ _____; su novia se llama Adela.
5. Mi papá y sus colegas _____ muy _____ hoy. ¡Hay mucho trabajo!
6. Patricia y yo _____ un poco _____ por ellos porque trabajan mucho.
7. Mi amiga Mónica _____ un poco _____ porque su novio no puede salir esta noche.
8. Esta clase no es muy interesante. ¿Tú _____ _____ también?

2 **Describir** Describe these people and places.

1. Anabela

2. Juan y Luisa

3. la habitación de Teresa

4. la habitación de César

3 **Situaciones** With a partner, use **estar** to talk about how you feel in these situations.

1. Cuando hace sol...
2. Cuando tomas un examen...
3. Cuando viajas en avión...
4. Cuando llueve...
5. Cuando ves una película con tu actor/actriz favorito/a...

4 **Emociones** Write an e-mail to a friend explaining what you do when you feel a certain way. Use five adjectives of emotion.

> **modelo**
> Cuando estoy preocupado, hablo por teléfono con mi madre.
> Cuando estoy aburrido, miro la televisión...

5.2 The present progressive

ANTE TODO   Both Spanish and English use the present progressive, which consists of the present tense of the verb *to be* and the present participle of another verb (the *-ing* form in English).

Las chicas están hablando con el empleado del hotel.

¿Estás estudiando en la playa?

▶ Form the present progressive with the present tense of **estar** and a present participle.

FORM OF **ESTAR** + PRESENT PARTICIPLE		FORM OF **ESTAR** + PRESENT PARTICIPLE	
Estoy	**pescando.**	**Estamos**	**comiendo.**
I am	*fishing.*	*We are*	*eating.*

▶ The present participle of regular **-ar**, **-er**, and **-ir** verbs is formed as follows:

INFINITIVE	STEM	ENDING	PRESENT PARTICIPLE
hablar	habl-	**-ando**	habl**ando**
comer	com-	**-iendo**	com**iendo**
escribir	escrib-	**-iendo**	escrib**iendo**

▶ **¡Atención!** When the stem of an **-er** or **-ir** verb ends in a vowel, the present participle ends in **-yendo**.

INFINITIVE	STEM	ENDING	PRESENT PARTICIPLE
leer	le-	**-yendo**	le**yendo**
oír	o-	**-yendo**	o**yendo**
traer	tra-	**-yendo**	tra**yendo**

▶ **Ir**, **poder**, and **venir** have irregular present participles (**yendo, pudiendo, viniendo**). Several other verbs have irregular present participles that you will need to learn.

▶ **-Ir** stem-changing verbs have a stem change in the present participle.

-ir stem-changing verbs

e:ie in the present tense	e → i in the present participle
preferir	prefir**i**endo

e:i in the present tense	e → i in the present participle
conseguir	consigu**i**endo

o:ue in the present tense	o → u in the present participle
dormir	d**u**rmiendo

The use of the present progressive is much more restricted in Spanish than in English. In Spanish, the present progressive is mainly used to emphasize that an action is in progress at the time of speaking.

Maru **está escuchando** música latina **ahora mismo**.
Maru is listening to Latin music right now.

Felipe y su amigo **todavía están jugando** al fútbol.
Felipe and his friend are still playing soccer.

In English, the present progressive is often used to talk about situations and actions that occur over an extended period of time or in the future. In Spanish, the simple present tense is often used instead.

Xavier **estudia** computación este semestre.
Xavier is studying computer science this semester.

Marissa **sale** mañana para los Estados Unidos.
Marissa is leaving tomorrow for the United States.

¿Está pensando en su futuro?
Nosotros, sí.

🏛 BANCO 🏛
CONGRESO

Preparándolo para el mañana

¡INTÉNTALO! Create complete sentences by putting the verbs in the present progressive.

1. mis amigos / descansar en la playa *Mis amigos están descansando en la playa.*
2. nosotros / practicar deportes _____
3. Carmen / comer en casa _____
4. nuestro equipo / ganar el partido _____
5. yo / leer el periódico _____
6. él / pensar comprar una bicicleta _____
7. ustedes / jugar a las cartas _____
8. José y Francisco / dormir _____
9. Marisa / leer correo electrónico _____
10. yo / preparar sándwiches _____
11. Carlos / tomar fotos _____
12. ¿dormir / tú? _____

Práctica

1 **Completar** Alfredo's Spanish class is preparing to travel to Puerto Rico. Use the present progressive of the verb in parentheses to complete Alfredo's description of what everyone is doing.

1. Yo _____ (investigar) la situación política de la isla (*island*).
2. La esposa del profesor _____ (hacer) las maletas.
3. Marta y José Luis _____ (buscar) información sobre San Juan en Internet.
4. Enrique y yo _____ (leer) un correo electrónico de nuestro amigo puertorriqueño.
5. Javier _____ (aprender) mucho sobre la cultura puertorriqueña.
6. Y tú _____ (practicar) el español, ¿verdad?

2 **¿Qué están haciendo?** María and her friends are vacationing at a resort in San Juan, Puerto Rico. Complete her description of what everyone is doing right now.

CONSULTA

For more information about Puerto Rico, see **Panorama**, pp. 186–187.

1. Yo

2. Javier

3. Alejandro y Rebeca

4. Celia y yo

5. Samuel

6. Lorenzo

3 **Personajes famosos** Say what these celebrities are doing right now, using the cues provided.

> **modelo**
>
> Shakira
>
> Shakira está cantando una canción ahora mismo.

A		B	
Isabel Allende	Nelly Furtado	bailar	hacer
Rachael Ray	Dwight Howard	cantar	jugar
James Cameron	Las Rockettes de	correr	preparar
Venus y Serena	Nueva York	escribir	¿?
Williams	¿?	hablar	¿?
Joey Votto	¿?		

AYUDA

Isabel Allende: **novelas**
Rachael Ray: **televisión, negocios** (*business*)
James Cameron: **cine**
Venus y Serena Williams: **tenis**
Joey Votto: **béisbol**
Nelly Furtado: **canciones**
Dwight Howard: **baloncesto**
Las Rockettes de Nueva York: **baile**

Comunicación

4 **Las vacaciones** Read Elena's description of her family vacation. Then indicate whether these conclusions are **lógico** or **ilógico**, based on what you read.

> Está lloviendo. Mis tres hermanos están jugando a las cartas. Mi hermana está leyendo una revista. Mi madre está buscando la llave de la habitación. Mi padre está durmiendo. ¿Y yo? Estoy escribiendo este mensaje electrónico...

	Lógico	Ilógico
1. Hace mal tiempo.	○	○
2. La familia es pequeña.	○	○
3. La madre está contenta.	○	○
4. El padre está en la cama.	○	○
5. La familia está en un hotel.	○	○

5 **Preguntar** Answer your partner's questions about what you are doing at these times.

> **modelo**
>
> 8:00 a.m.
> **Estudiante 1:** Son las ocho de la mañana. ¿Qué estás haciendo?
> **Estudiante 2:** Estoy desayunando.

1. 5:00 a.m.	3. 11:00 a.m.	5. 2:00 p.m.	7. 9:00 p.m.
2. 9:30 a.m.	4. 12:00 p.m.	6. 5:00 p.m.	8. 11:30 p.m.

6 **Describir** Use the present progressive to write a description of what is happening in this Spanish beach scene.

NOTA CULTURAL

Nearly 60 million tourists travel to Spain every year, many of them drawn by the warm climate and beautiful coasts. Tourists wanting a beach vacation go mostly to the **Costa del Sol** or the Balearic Islands, in the Mediterranean.

Síntesis

7 **¿Qué están haciendo?** With a partner, take turns asking each other what people are doing right now. You could ask about other students, professors, or even celebrities.

bailar	comer	escribir	estudiar	leer
cantar	enseñar	escuchar	jugar	mirar

5.3 Ser and estar

ANTE TODO You have already learned that **ser** and **estar** both mean *to be* but are used for different purposes. These charts summarize the key differences in usage between **ser** and **estar**.

¡ATENCIÓN!

Ser de expresses not only origin (**Es de Buenos Aires.**) and possession (**Es la pluma de Maru.**), but also what material something is made of (**La bicicleta es de metal.**).

Uses of ser

1. **Nationality and place of origin** . . . .
Juan Carlos **es** argentino.
Es de Buenos Aires.

2. **Profession or occupation** . . . .
Adela **es** agente de viajes.
Francisco **es** médico.

3. **Characteristics of people and things** . . .
José y Clara **son** simpáticos.
El clima de Puerto Rico **es** agradable.

4. **Generalizations** . . . .
¡**Es** fabuloso viajar!
Es difícil estudiar a la una de la mañana.

5. **Possession** . . . .
Es la pluma de Jimena.
Son las llaves del señor Díaz.

6. **What something is made of** . . . .
La bicicleta **es** de metal.
Los pasajes **son** de papel.

7. **Time and date** . . . .
Hoy **es** martes. **Son** las dos.
Hoy **es** el primero de julio.

8. **Where or when an event takes place** . . .
El partido **es** en el estadio Santa Fe.
La conferencia **es** a las siete.

Ellos son mis amigos.

Miguel está enojado conmigo.

Uses of estar

1. **Location or spatial relationships** . . . . .
El aeropuerto **está** lejos de la ciudad.
Tu habitación **está** en el tercer piso.

2. **Health** . . . .
¿Cómo **estás**?
Estoy bien, gracias.

3. **Physical states and conditions** . . . .
El profesor **está** ocupado.
Las ventanas **están** abiertas.

4. **Emotional states** . . . .
Marissa **está** feliz hoy.
Estoy muy enojado con Maru.

5. **Certain weather expressions** . . . .
Está lloviendo.
Está nublado.

6. **Ongoing actions (progressive tenses)** . .
Estamos estudiando para un examen.
Ana **está** leyendo una novela.

Ser and estar with adjectives

▶ With many descriptive adjectives, **ser** and **estar** can both be used, but the meaning will change.

Juan **es** delgado.
Juan is thin.

Juan **está** más delgado hoy.
Juan looks thinner today.

Ana **es** nerviosa.
Ana is a nervous person.

Ana **está** nerviosa por el examen.
Ana is nervous because of the exam.

▶ In the examples above, the statements with **ser** are general observations about the inherent qualities of Juan and Ana. The statements with **estar** describe conditions that are variable.

▶ Here are some adjectives that change in meaning when used with **ser** and **estar**.

With ser	With estar
El chico **es listo**. *The boy is smart.*	El chico **está listo**. *The boy is ready.*
La profesora **es mala**. *The professor is bad.*	La profesora **está mala**. *The professor is sick.*
Jaime **es aburrido**. *Jaime is boring.*	Jaime **está aburrido**. *Jaime is bored.*
Las peras **son verdes**. *Pears are green.*	Las peras **están verdes**. *The pears are not ripe.*
El gato **es muy vivo**. *The cat is very clever.*	El gato **está vivo**. *The cat is alive.*
Iván **es un hombre seguro**. *Iván is a confident man.*	Iván no **está seguro**. *Iván is not sure.*

¡ATENCIÓN!

When referring to objects, **ser seguro/a** means *to be safe*.
El puente es seguro.
The bridge is safe.

¡INTÉNTALO! Form complete sentences by using the correct form of **ser** or **estar** and making any other necessary changes.

1. Alejandra / cansado
   Alejandra está cansada.
2. ellos / pelirrojo
3. Carmen / alto
4. yo / la clase de español
5. película / a las once
6. hoy / viernes
7. nosotras / enojado
8. Antonio / médico
9. Romeo y Julieta / enamorado
10. libros / de Ana
11. Marisa y Juan / estudiando
12. partido de baloncesto / gimnasio

Práctica

1 **¿Ser o estar?** Indicate whether each adjective takes **ser** or **estar**. **¡Ojo!**
Three of them can take both verbs.

	ser	estar			ser	estar
1. delgada	○	○	5. seguro	○	○
2. canadiense	○	○	6. enojada	○	○
3. enamorado	○	○	7. importante	○	○
4. lista	○	○	8. avergonzada	○	○

2 **Completar** Complete this conversation with the appropriate forms of **ser** and **estar**.

EDUARDO ¡Hola, Ceci! ¿Cómo (1)_____?

CECILIA Hola, Eduardo. Bien, gracias. ¡Qué guapo (2)_____ hoy!

EDUARDO Gracias. (3)_____ muy amable. Oye, ¿qué (4)_____ haciendo?
(5)¿_____ ocupada?

CECILIA No, sólo le (6)_____ escribiendo una carta a mi prima Pilar.

EDUARDO ¿De dónde (7)_____ ella?

CECILIA Pilar (8)_____ de Ecuador. Su papá (9)_____ médico en Quito. Pero
ahora Pilar y su familia (10)_____ de vacaciones en Ponce, Puerto Rico.

EDUARDO Y... ¿cómo (11)_____ Pilar?

CECILIA (12)_____ muy lista. Y también (13)_____ alta, rubia y muy bonita.

3 **En el parque** Describe the people in the drawing. Your descriptions should answer
the questions provided.

1. ¿Quiénes son?
2. ¿Dónde están?
3. ¿Cómo son?
4. ¿Cómo están?
5. ¿Qué están haciendo?
6. ¿Qué estación es?
7. ¿Qué tiempo hace?
8. ¿Quiénes están de vacaciones?

Comunicación

4 **Ponce** Listen to Carolina's description of her vacation. Then indicate whether the following conclusions are **lógico** or **ilógico**, based on what you heard.

	Lógico	Ilógico
1. Carolina es una turista.	○	○
2. Carolina prefiere acampar.	○	○
3. A Carolina no le gusta ir a la playa.	○	○
4. Carolina vive en Ponce.	○	○
5. A Carolina le gustan los museos.	○	○

5 **Una persona famosa** Describe a celebrity using these items as a guide.

- descripción física
- cómo está ahora
- origen
- dónde está ahora
- qué está haciendo ahora
- profesión u ocupación

6 **En el aeropuerto** With a partner, take turns assuming the identity of a character from this drawing. Your partner will ask you questions using **ser** and **estar** to figure out who you are.

modelo

> **Estudiante 2:** ¿Dónde estás?
> **Estudiante 1:** Estoy cerca de la puerta.
> **Estudiante 2:** ¿Qué estás haciendo?
> **Estudiante 1:** Estoy escuchando a otra persona.
> **Estudiante 2:** ¿Eres uno de los pasajeros?
> **Estudiante 1:** No, soy empleado del aeropuerto.
> **Estudiante 2:** ¿Eres Camilo?

Síntesis

7 **Un hotel magnífico** Write a radio ad for a vacation resort somewhere in the Spanish-speaking world. Use **ser** and **estar** in as many different ways as you can.

5.4 Direct object nouns and pronouns

SUBJECT	VERB	DIRECT OBJECT NOUN
Juan Carlos y Jimena	están tomando	fotos.
Juan Carlos and Jimena	*are taking*	*photos.*

▶ A direct object noun receives the action of the verb directly and generally follows the verb. In the example above, the direct object noun answers the question *What are Juan Carlos and Jimena taking?*

▶ When a direct object noun in Spanish is a person or a pet, it is preceded by the word **a**. This is called the personal **a**; there is no English equivalent for this construction.

Mariela mira **a** Carlos.
Mariela is watching Carlos.

Mariela mira televisión.
Mariela is watching TV.

▶ In the first sentence above, the personal **a** is required because the direct object is a person. In the second sentence, the personal **a** is not required because the direct object is a thing, not a person.

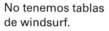
No tenemos tablas de windsurf.

Miguel no me perdona.

El botones las puede conseguir para ustedes.

▶ Direct object pronouns are words that replace direct object nouns. Like English, Spanish uses a direct object pronoun to avoid repeating a noun already mentioned.

	DIRECT OBJECT			DIRECT OBJECT PRONOUN	
Maribel hace	las maletas.		Maribel	las	hace.
Felipe compra	el sombrero.		Felipe	lo	compra.
Vicky tiene	la llave.		Vicky	la	tiene.

Direct object pronouns

SINGULAR		PLURAL	
me	*me*	**nos**	*us*
te	*you* (fam.)	**os**	*you* (fam.)
lo	*you* (m., form.)	**los**	*you* (m.)
	him; it (m.)		*them* (m.)
la	*you* (f., form.)	**las**	*you* (f.)
	her; it (f.)		*them* (f.)

▶ In affirmative sentences, direct object pronouns generally appear before the conjugated verb. In negative sentences, the pronoun is placed between the word **no** and the verb.

Adela practica **el tenis.**
Adela **lo** practica.

Carmen compra **los pasajes.**
Carmen **los** compra.

Gabriela no tiene **las llaves.**
Gabriela **no las** tiene.

Diego no hace **las maletas.**
Diego **no las** hace.

▶ When the verb is an infinitive construction, such as **ir a** + [*infinitive*], the direct object pronoun can be placed before the conjugated form or attached to the infinitive.

Ellos van a escribir **unas postales.**
Ellos **las** van a escribir.
Ellos van a escribir**las.**

Lidia quiere ver **una película.**
Lidia **la** quiere ver.
Lidia quiere ver**la.**

▶ When the verb is in the present progressive, the direct object pronoun can be placed before the conjugated form or attached to the present participle. **¡Atención!** When a direct object pronoun is attached to the present participle, an accent mark is added to maintain the proper stress.

Gerardo está leyendo **la lección.**
Gerardo **la** está leyendo.
Gerardo está leyéndo**la.**

Toni está mirando **el partido.**
Toni **lo** está mirando.
Toni está mirándo**lo.**

CONSULTA

To learn more about accents, see **Lección 4, Pronunciación**, p. 123, **Lección 10, Ortografía**, p. 339, and **Lección 11, Ortografía**, p. 375.

¡INTÉNTALO! Choose the correct direct object pronoun for each sentence.

1. Tienes el libro de español. *c*
   a. La tienes. b. Los tienes. c. Lo tienes.
2. Voy a ver el partido de baloncesto.
   a. Voy a verlo. b. Voy a verte. c. Voy a vernos.
3. El artista quiere dibujar a Luisa y a su mamá.
   a. Quiere dibujarme. b. Quiere dibujarla. c. Quiere dibujarlas.
4. Marcos busca la llave.
   a. Me busca. b. La busca. c. Las busca.
5. Rita me lleva al aeropuerto y también lleva a Tomás.
   a. Nos lleva. b. Las lleva. c. Te lleva.
6. Puedo oír a Gerardo y a Miguel.
   a. Puedo oírte. b. Puedo oírlos. c. Puedo oírlo.
7. Quieren estudiar la gramática.
   a. Quieren estudiarnos. b. Quieren estudiarlo. c. Quieren estudiarla.
8. ¿Practicas los verbos irregulares?
   a. ¿Los practicas? b. ¿Las practicas? c. ¿Lo practicas?
9. Ignacio ve la película.
   a. La ve. b. Lo ve. c. Las ve.
10. Sandra va a invitar a Mario a la excursión. También me va a invitar a mí.
    a. Los va a invitar. b. Lo va a invitar. c. Nos va a invitar.

Práctica

1 **Simplificar** Professor Vega's class is planning a trip to Costa Rica. Describe their preparations by changing the direct object nouns into direct object pronouns.

> **modelo**
> La profesora Vega tiene su pasaporte.
> *La profesora Vega lo tiene.*

1. Gustavo y Héctor confirman las reservaciones.
2. Nosotros leemos los folletos (*brochures*).
3. Ana María estudia el mapa.
4. Yo aprendo los nombres de los monumentos de San José.
5. Alicia escucha a la profesora.
6. Miguel escribe las instrucciones para ir al hotel.
7. Esteban busca el pasaje.
8. Nosotros planeamos una excursión.

¡LENGUA VIVA! There are many Spanish words that correspond to *ticket*. **Billete** and **pasaje** usually refer to a ticket for travel, such as an airplane ticket. **Entrada** refers to a ticket to an event, such as a concert or a movie. **Boleto** can be used in either case.

2 **Vacaciones** Ramón is going to San Juan, Puerto Rico, with his friends, Javier and Marcos. Express his thoughts more succinctly using direct object pronouns.

> **modelo**
> Quiero hacer una excursión.
> *Quiero hacerla./La quiero hacer.*

1. Voy a hacer mi maleta.
2. Necesitamos llevar los pasaportes.
3. Marcos está pidiendo el folleto turístico.
4. Javier debe llamar a sus padres.
5. Ellos desean visitar el Viejo San Juan.
6. Puedo llamar a Javier por la mañana.
7. Prefiero llevar mi cámara.
8. No queremos perder nuestras reservaciones de hotel.

NOTA CULTURAL Puerto Rico is a U.S. territory, so people do not need travel documents when traveling to and from Puerto Rico from the U.S. mainland. However, everyone must meet all requirements for entering the U.S. when traveling directly to Puerto Rico from abroad.

3 **¿Quién?** The Garza family is preparing to go on a vacation to Puerto Rico. Based on the clues, answer the questions. Use direct object pronouns in your answers.

> **modelo**
> ¿Quién hace las reservaciones para el hotel? (el Sr. Garza)
> *El Sr. Garza las hace.*

1. ¿Quién compra los pasajes para el vuelo (*flight*)? (la Sra. Garza)
2. ¿Quién tiene que hacer las maletas de los niños? (María)
3. ¿Quiénes buscan los pasaportes? (Antonio y María)
4. ¿Quién va a confirmar las reservaciones de hotel? (la Sra. Garza)
5. ¿Quién busca la cámara? (María)
6. ¿Quién compra un mapa de Puerto Rico? (Antonio)

Comunicación

4

Escuchar Listen to Mercedes and Gabriel, two students in Chicago, talk about their winter break. Then indicate whether the following conclusions are **lógico** or **ilógico**, based on what you heard.

	Lógico	Ilógico
1. Gabriel va a la playa.	○	○
2. Gabriel está listo para salir.	○	○
3. Va a hacer frío en Chicago.	○	○
4. Gabriel viaja a España.	○	○
5. Mercedes va a viajar también.	○	○

5

Entrevista Answer your partner's questions. Use direct object pronouns.

1. ¿Ves mucho la televisión?
2. ¿Cuándo vas a ver tu programa favorito?
3. ¿Quién prepara la comida (*food*) en tu casa?
4. ¿Te visita mucho tu familia?
5. ¿Visitas mucho a tus abuelos?
6. ¿Nos entienden nuestros padres a nosotros?
7. ¿Cuándo ves a tus amigos/as?
8. ¿Cuándo te llaman tus amigos/as?

6

De mal humor The weather has ruined your plans to go to the beach. Using words from the list, your partner offers some suggestions to cheer you up. Use direct object pronouns in your responses.

> **modelo**
> **Estudiante 1:** ¿Quieres ver la película de Ryan Gosling?
> **Estudiante 2:** No la quiero ver.

computadora	fotos	libro
película	revista	videojuegos

Síntesis

7

Adivinanzas Write five riddles with descriptions of people, places, or things. Follow the model. Then see whether your instructor can solve your riddles.

> **modelo**
> Lo uso para (*I use it to*) escribir en mi cuaderno.
> No es muy grande y tiene borrador. ¿Qué es?

Recapitulación

SUBJECT   CONJUGATED FORM   Main clause
Javier   empiezo
dudan

Review the grammar concepts you have learned in this lesson by completing these activities.

1   **Completar** Complete the chart with the correct present participle of these verbs. **16 pts.**

Infinitive	Present participle	Infinitive	Present participle
hacer		estar	
acampar		ser	
tener		vivir	
venir		estudiar	

2   **Vacaciones en París** Complete this paragraph about Julia's trip to Paris with the correct form of **ser** or **estar**. **24 pts.**

Hoy (1) _____ (es/está) el 3 de julio y voy a París por tres semanas. (Yo) (2) _____ (Soy/Estoy) muy feliz porque voy a ver a mi mejor amiga. Ella (3) _____ (es/está) de Puerto Rico, pero ahora (4) _____ (es/está) viviendo en París. También (yo) (5) _____ (soy/estoy) un poco nerviosa porque (6) _____ (es/está) mi primer viaje a Francia. El vuelo (*flight*) (7) _____ (es/está) hoy por la tarde, pero ahora (8) _____ (es/está) lloviendo. Por eso (9) _____ (somos/estamos) preocupadas, porque probablemente el avión va a salir tarde. Mi equipaje ya (10) _____ (es/está) listo. (11) _____ (Es/Está) tarde y me tengo que ir. ¡Va a (12) _____ (ser/estar) un viaje fenomenal!

3   **¿Qué hacen?** Respond to these questions by indicating what people do with the items mentioned. Use direct object pronouns. **20 pts.**

> **modelo**
> ¿Qué hacen ellos con la película? (ver)
> La ven.

1. ¿Qué haces tú con el libro de viajes? (leer) _____
2. ¿Qué hacen los turistas en la ciudad? (explorar) _____
3. ¿Qué hace el botones con el equipaje? (llevar) _____
4. ¿Qué hace la agente con las reservaciones? (confirmar) _____
5. ¿Qué hacen ustedes con los pasaportes? (mostrar) _____

RESUMEN GRAMATICAL

5.1   **Estar with conditions and emotions**   *p. 164*

▶ Yo **est**oy aburrido/a, feliz, nervioso/a.

▶ El cuarto **est**á desordenado, limpio, ordenado.

▶ Estos libros **est**án abiertos, cerrados, sucios.

5.2   **The present progressive**   *pp. 166–167*

▶ The present progressive is formed with the present tense of estar plus the present participle.

Forming the present participle

infinitive	stem	ending	present participle
hablar	habl-	-ando	habl**ando**
comer	com-	-iendo	com**iendo**
escribir	escrib-	-iendo	escrib**iendo**

-ir stem-changing verbs

	infinitive	present participle
e:ie	preferir	pref**i**riendo
e:i	conseguir	cons**i**guiendo
o:ue	dormir	d**u**rmiendo

▶ Irregular present participles: **yendo (ir), pudiendo (poder), viniendo (venir)**

5.3   **Ser and estar**   *pp. 170–171*

▶ Uses of ser: nationality, origin, profession or occupation, characteristics, generalizations, possession, what something is made of, time and date, time and place of events

▶ Uses of estar: location, health, physical states and conditions, emotional states, weather expressions, ongoing actions

▶ Many adjectives can be used with both **ser** and **estar**, but the meaning of the adjectives will change.

Juan **es** delgado.   Juan **está** más delgado hoy.
Juan is thin.   *Juan looks thinner today.*

4 **Opuestos** Complete these sentences with the appropriate form of the verb **estar** and an antonym for the underlined adjective. `20 pts.`

> **modelo**
>
> Mis respuestas están <u>bien</u>, pero las de Susana *están mal*.

1. Las tiendas están <u>abiertas</u>, pero la agencia de viajes _____ _____.
2. No me gustan las habitaciones <u>desordenadas</u>. Incluso (*Even*) mi habitación de hotel _____ _____.
3. Nosotras estamos <u>tristes</u> cuando trabajamos. Hoy comienzan las vacaciones y _____ _____.
4. En esta ciudad los autobuses están <u>sucios</u>, pero los taxis _____ _____.
5. —El avión sale a las 5:30, ¿verdad? —No, estás <u>confundida</u>. Yo _____ _____ de que el avión sale a las 5:00.

5.4 **Direct object nouns and pronouns**   *pp. 174–175*

Direct object pronouns

Singular		Plural	
me	lo	nos	los
te	la	os	las

In affirmative sentences:
Adela practica el tenis. → Adela lo practica.

In negative sentences: Adela **no** lo practica.

With an infinitive:
Adela lo va a practicar./Adela va a practicarlo.

With the present progressive:
Adela lo está practicando./Adela está practicándolo.

---

5 **En la playa** Describe what these people are doing. Complete the sentences using the present progressive tense. `16 pts.`

1. El Sr. Camacho _____.
2. Felicia _____.
3. Leo _____.
4. Nosotros _____.

6 **Refrán** Complete this Spanish saying by filling in the missing present participles. Refer to the translation and the drawing. `4 pts.`

¡LA CIUDAD ESTÁ MUY SUCIA!

❝ Se consigue más _____ que _____. ❞

(You can accomplish more by doing than by saying.)

Lectura

Antes de leer

Estrategia
Scanning

Scanning involves glancing over a document in search of specific information. For example, you can scan a document to identify its format, to find cognates, to locate visual clues about the document's content, or to find specific facts. Scanning allows you to learn a great deal about a text without having to read it word for word.

Examinar el texto

Scan the reading selection for cognates and write down a few of them.

1. _____   4. _____
2. _____   5. _____
3. _____   6. _____

Based on the cognates you found, what do you think this document is about?

_____

Preguntas

Read these questions. Then scan the document again to look for answers.

1. What is the format of the reading selection?
   _____

2. Which place is the document about?
   _____

3. What are some of the visual cues this document provides? What do they tell you about the content of the document?
   _____

4. Who produced the document, and what do you think it is for?
   _____

Turismo ecológico en Puerto Rico

Hotel Vistahermosa
~ Lajas, Puerto Rico ~

- 40 habitaciones individuales
- 15 habitaciones dobles
- Teléfono/TV por cable/Internet

- Aire acondicionado
- Restaurante (Bar)
- Piscina
- Área de juegos
- Cajero automático°

El hotel está situado en Playa Grande, un pequeño pueblo de pescadores del mar Caribe. Es el lugar perfecto para el viajero que viene de vacaciones. Las playas son seguras y limpias, ideales para tomar el sol, descansar, tomar fotografías y nadar. Está abierto los 365 días del año. Hay una rebaja° especial para estudiantes universitarios.

DIRECCIÓN: Playa Grande 406, Lajas, PR 00667, cerca del Parque Nacional Foresta.

Cajero automático *ATM* rebaja *discount*

Atracciones cercanas

Playa Grande ¿Busca la playa perfecta? Playa Grande es la playa que está buscando. Usted puede pescar, sacar fotos, nadar y pasear en bicicleta. Playa Grande es un paraíso para el turista que quiere practicar deportes acuáticos. El lugar es bonito e interesante y usted va a tener muchas oportunidades para descansar y disfrutar en familia.

Valle Niebla Ir de excursión, tomar café, montar a caballo, caminar, hacer picnics. Más de cien lugares para acampar.

Bahía Fosforescente Sacar fotos, salidas de noche, excursión en barco. Una maravillosa experiencia llena de luz°.

Arrecifes de Coral Sacar fotos, bucear, explorar. Es un lugar único en el Caribe.

Playa Vieja Tomar el sol, pasear en bicicleta, jugar a las cartas, escuchar música. Ideal para la familia.

Parque Nacional Foresta Sacar fotos, visitar el Museo de Arte Nativo. Reserva Mundial de la Biosfera.

Santuario de las Aves Sacar fotos, observar aves°, seguir rutas de excursión.

llena de luz *full of light* **aves** *birds*

Después de leer

Listas
Which amenities of Hotel Vistahermosa would most interest these potential guests? Explain your choices.

1. dos padres con un hijo de seis años y una hija de ocho años

   _____

2. un hombre y una mujer en su luna de miel (*honeymoon*)

   _____

3. una persona en un viaje de negocios (*business trip*)

   _____

Conversaciones
Answer your partner's questions.

1. ¿Quieres visitar el Hotel Vistahermosa? ¿Por qué?
2. Tienes tiempo de visitar sólo tres de las atracciones turísticas que están cerca del hotel. ¿Cuáles vas a visitar? ¿Por qué?
3. ¿Qué prefieres hacer en Valle Niebla? ¿En Playa Vieja? ¿En el Parque Nacional Foresta?

Situaciones
You have just arrived at Hotel Vistahermosa. Your partner is the concierge. Use the phrases below to express your interests and ask for suggestions about where to go.

1. montar a caballo
2. bucear
3. pasear en bicicleta
4. pescar
5. observar aves

Contestar
Answer these questions.

1. ¿Quieres visitar Puerto Rico? Explica tu respuesta.

   _____

2. ¿Adónde quieres ir de vacaciones el verano que viene? Explica tu respuesta.

   _____

Escritura

Estrategia
Making an outline

When we write to share information, an outline can serve to separate topics and subtopics, providing a framework for the presentation of data. Consider the following excerpt from an outline of the tourist brochure on pages 180–181.

IV. Descripción del sitio (con foto)
   A. Playa Grande
      1. Playas seguras y limpias
      2. Ideal para tomar el sol, descansar, tomar fotografías, nadar
   B. El hotel
      1. Abierto los 365 días del año
      2. Rebaja para estudiantes universitarios

Mapa de ideas

Idea maps can be used to create outlines. The major sections of an idea map correspond to the Roman numerals in an outline. The minor idea map sections correspond to the outline's capital letters, and so on. Examine the idea map that led to the outline above.

Tema

Escribir un folleto

Write a tourist brochure for a hotel or resort you have visited. If you wish, you may write about an imaginary location. You may want to include some of this information in your brochure:

▶ the name of the hotel or resort
▶ phone and fax numbers that tourists can use to make contact
▶ the hotel website that tourists can consult
▶ an e-mail address that tourists can use to request information
▶ a description of the exterior of the hotel or resort
▶ a description of the interior of the hotel or resort, including facilities and amenities
▶ a description of the surrounding area, including its climate
▶ a listing of nearby scenic natural attractions
▶ a listing of nearby cultural attractions
▶ a listing of recreational activities that tourists can pursue in the vicinity of the hotel or resort

Escuchar

Estrategia
Listening for key words

By listening for key words or phrases, you can identify the subject and main ideas of what you hear, as well as some of the details.

 To practice this strategy, you will now listen to a short paragraph. As you listen, jot down the key words that help you identify the subject of the paragraph and its main ideas.

Preparación

Based on the illustration, who do you think Hernán Jiménez is, and what is he doing? What key words might you listen for to help you understand what he is saying?

Ahora escucha

Now you are going to listen to a weather report by Hernán Jiménez. Note which phrases are correct according to the key words and phrases you hear.

Santo Domingo

1. hace sol
2. va a hacer frío
3. una mañana de mal tiempo
4. va a estar nublado
5. buena tarde para tomar el sol
6. buena mañana para la playa

San Francisco de Macorís

1. hace frío
2. hace sol
3. va a nevar
4. va a llover
5. hace calor
6. mal día para excursiones

Comprensión

¿Cierto o falso?
Indicate whether each statement is **cierto** or **falso**, based on the weather report. Correct the false statements.

1. Según el meteorólogo, la temperatura en Santo Domingo es de 26 grados.

   _____

2. La temperatura máxima en Santo Domingo hoy va a ser de 30 grados.

   _____

3. Está lloviendo ahora en Santo Domingo.

   _____

4. En San Francisco de Macorís la temperatura mínima de hoy va a ser de 20 grados.

   _____

5. Va a llover mucho hoy en San Francisco de Macorís.

   _____

Preguntas
Answer these questions about the weather report.

1. ¿Hace viento en Santo Domingo ahora?
2. ¿Está nublado en Santo Domingo ahora?
3. ¿Está nevando ahora en San Francisco de Macorís?
4. ¿Qué tiempo hace en San Francisco de Macorís?

En pantalla

If you like adventure or extreme sports, Latin America might be a good destination for you. The area of Patagonia, located in Chile and Argentina, offers both breath-taking scenery and an adrenaline rush. Here, one can enjoy a variety of sports, including whitewater rafting, kayaking, trekking, and skiing. One weeklong itinerary in Argentina might include camping, hiking the granite rock of Mount Fitz Roy, and trekking across the deep blue Perito Moreno Glacier, a massive 18-mile-long sheet of ice and one of the world's few advancing glaciers.

Now, hold on to your helmets as we travel to Mexico to see what sort of adventure you can experience there.

Vocabulario útil	
callejones	*alleyways, narrow streets*
calles	*streets*
carrera de bicicleta	*bicycle race*
descender (escaleras)	*to descend (stairs)*
reto, desafío	*challenge*

Preparación

Some areas attract tourists because of their unusual sports and activities. Do you know of any such destinations? Where?

Preguntas

Answer these questions in complete sentences.

1. ¿Por qué viajan ciclistas (*cyclists*) a Taxco?

2. ¿Es Taxco una ciudad turística moderna o colonial?

3. ¿Hay competidores de otros (*other*) países en la carrera de bicicleta?

4. ¿Cómo está el reportero (*reporter*) después (*after*) de descender las escaleras, aburrido o cansado?

Deportes extremos

In pairs, discuss these questions: **¿Cómo son las personas que hacen deportes extremos? ¿Por qué crees que los practican? ¿Viajarías (***Would you travel***) a algún destino para practicarlos?**

Reportaje sobre Down Taxco

El reto es descender en el menor° tiempo posible...

... desde lo más alto° de la ciudad hasta° la plaza central.

El principal desafío es el diseño° de la ciudad...

menor *least* lo más alto *the highest point* hasta *to* diseño *design*

Between 1438 and 1533, when the vast and powerful Incan Empire was at its height, the Incas built an elaborate network of **caminos** (*trails*) that traversed the Andes Mountains and converged on the empire's capital, Cuzco. Today, hundreds of thousands of tourists come to Peru annually to walk the surviving trails and enjoy the spectacular scenery. The most popular trail, **el Camino Inca**, leads from Cuzco to **Intipunku** (*Sun Gate*), the entrance to the ancient mountain city of Machu Picchu.

Vocabulario útil	
ciudadela	*citadel*
de cultivo	*farming*
el/la guía	*guide*
maravilla	*wonder*
quechua	*Quechua (indigenous Peruvian)*
sector (urbano)	*(urban) sector*

Preparación

Have you ever visited an archeological or historic site? Where? Why did you go there?

Completar

Complete these sentences. Make the necessary changes.

1. Las ruinas de Machu Picchu son una antigua _____ inca.

2. La ciudadela estaba (*was*) dividida en tres sectores: _____ , religioso y de cultivo.

3. Cada año los _____ reciben a cientos (*hundreds*) de turistas de diferentes países.

4. Hoy en día, la cultura _____ está presente en las comunidades andinas (*Andean*) de Perú.

¡Vacaciones en Perú!

Machu Picchu [...] se encuentra aislada sobre° esta montaña...

... siempre he querido° venir [...] Me encantan° las civilizaciones antiguas°.

Somos una familia francesa [...] Perú es un país muy, muy bonito de verdad.

se encuentra aislada sobre *it is isolated on* siempre he querido *I have always wanted* Me encantan *I love* antiguas *ancient*

Puerto Rico

El país en cifras

▶ **Área:** 8.959 km² (3.459 millas²)
  menor° que el área de Connecticut
▶ **Población:** 3.667.084
Puerto Rico es una de las islas más densamente pobladas° del mundo. Más de la mitad de la población vive en San Juan, la capital.
▶ **Capital:** San Juan—2.730.000
▶ **Ciudades principales:** Arecibo, Bayamón, Fajardo, Mayagüez, Ponce
▶ **Moneda:** dólar estadounidense
▶ **Idiomas:** español (oficial); inglés (oficial)
Aproximadamente la cuarta parte de la población puertorriqueña habla inglés, pero en las zonas turísticas este porcentaje es mucho más alto. El uso del inglés es obligatorio para documentos federales.

Bandera
de Puerto Rico

Puertorriqueños célebres

▶ **Raúl Juliá,** actor (1940–1994)
▶ **Roberto Clemente,** beisbolista (1934–1972)
▶ **Julia de Burgos,** escritora (1914–1953)
▶ **Benicio del Toro,** actor y productor (1967–)
▶ **Rosie Pérez,** actriz y bailarina (1964–)
▶ **José Rivera,** dramaturgo y guionista (1955–)

menor *less* pobladas *populated* río subterráneo *underground river* más largo *longest* cuevas *caves* bóveda *vault* fortaleza *fort* caber *fit*

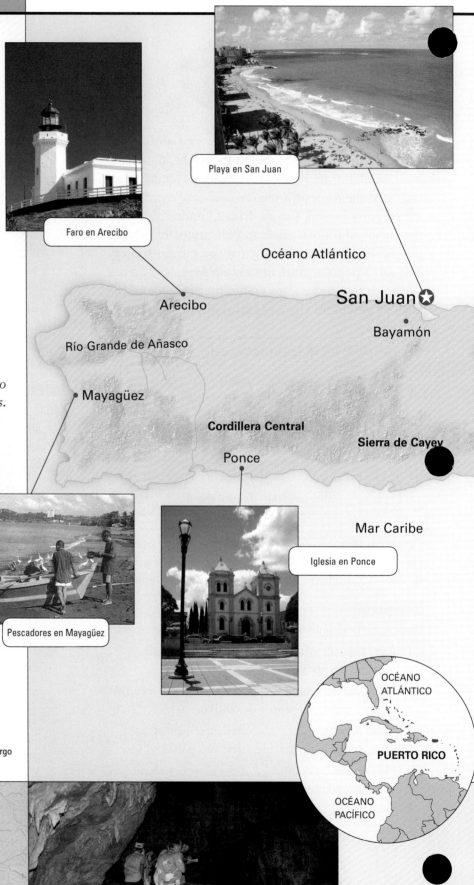

Faro en Arecibo

Playa en San Juan

Océano Atlántico

San Juan ✪

Arecibo

Bayamón

Río Grande de Añasco

Mayagüez

Cordillera Central

Sierra de Cayey

Ponce

Mar Caribe

Iglesia en Ponce

Pescadores en Mayagüez

OCÉANO
ATLÁNTICO

PUERTO RICO

OCÉANO
PACÍFICO

¡Increíble pero cierto!

El río Camuy es el tercer río subterráneo° más largo° del mundo y tiene el sistema de cuevas° más grande del hemisferio occidental.
La Cueva de los Tres Pueblos es una gigantesca bóveda°, tan grande que toda la fortaleza° del Morro puede caber° en su interior.

Lugares • **El Morro**

El Morro es una fortaleza que se construyó para proteger° la bahía° de San Juan desde principios del siglo° XVI hasta principios del siglo XX. Hoy día muchos turistas visitan este lugar, convertido en un museo. Es el sitio más fotografiado de Puerto Rico. La arquitectura de la fortaleza es impresionante. Tiene misteriosos túneles, oscuras mazmorras° y vistas fabulosas de la bahía.

Artes • **Salsa**

La salsa, un estilo musical de origen puertorriqueño y cubano, nació° en el barrio latino de la ciudad de Nueva York. Dos de los músicos de salsa más famosos son Tito Puente y Willie Colón, los dos de Nueva York. Las estrellas° de la salsa en Puerto Rico son Felipe Rodríguez y Héctor Lavoe. Hoy en día, Puerto Rico es el centro internacional de este estilo musical. El Gran Combo de Puerto Rico es una de las orquestas de salsa más famosas del mundo°.

Río Loíza — Fajardo — Isla de Culebra — Isla de Vieques

Ciencias • **El Observatorio de Arecibo**

El Observatorio de Arecibo tiene uno de los radiotelescopios más grandes del mundo. Gracias a este telescopio, los científicos° pueden estudiar las propiedades de la Tierra°, la Luna° y otros cuerpos celestes. También pueden analizar fenómenos celestiales como los quasares y pulsares, y detectar emisiones de radio de otras galaxias, en busca de inteligencia extraterrestre.

Historia • **Relación con los Estados Unidos**

Puerto Rico pasó a ser° parte de los Estados Unidos después de° la guerra° de 1898 y se hizo° un estado libre asociado en 1952. Los puertorriqueños, ciudadanos° estadounidenses desde° 1917, tienen representación política en el Congreso, pero no votan en las elecciones presidenciales y no pagan impuestos° federales. Hay un debate entre los puertorriqueños: ¿debe la isla seguir como estado libre asociado, hacerse un estado como los otros° o volverse° independiente?

¿Qué aprendiste? Contesta las preguntas con una oración completa.
1. ¿Cuál es la moneda de Puerto Rico?
2. ¿Qué idiomas se hablan (are spoken) en Puerto Rico?
3. ¿Cuál es el sitio más fotografiado de Puerto Rico?
4. ¿Qué es el Gran Combo?
5. ¿Qué hacen los científicos en el Observatorio de Arecibo?

Conexión Internet Investiga estos temas en Internet.
1. Describe a dos puertorriqueños famosos. ¿Cómo son? ¿Qué hacen? ¿Dónde viven? ¿Por qué son célebres?
2. Busca información sobre lugares en los que se puede hacer ecoturismo en Puerto Rico.

proteger *protect* bahía *bay* siglo *century* mazmorras *dungeons* nació *was born* estrellas *stars* mundo *world* científicos *scientists* Tierra *Earth* Luna *Moon* pasó a ser *became* después de *after* guerra *war* se hizo *became* ciudadanos *citizens* desde *since* pagan impuestos *pay taxes* otros *others* volverse *to become*

Los viajes y las vacaciones

acampar	to camp
confirmar una reservación	to confirm a reservation
estar de vacaciones (*f. pl.*)	to be on vacation
hacer las maletas	to pack (one's suitcases)
hacer un viaje	to take a trip
hacer (wind)surf	to (wind)surf
ir de compras (*f. pl.*)	to go shopping
ir de vacaciones	to go on vacation
ir en autobús (*m.*), auto(móvil) (*m.*), avión (*m.*), barco (*m.*), moto(cicleta) (*f.*), taxi (*m.*)	to go by bus, car, plane, boat, motorcycle, taxi
jugar a las cartas	to play cards
montar a caballo (*m.*)	to ride a horse
pescar	to fish
sacar/tomar fotos (*f. pl.*)	to take photos
el/la agente de viajes	travel agent
el/la inspector(a) de aduanas	customs inspector
el/la viajero/a	traveler
el aeropuerto	airport
la agencia de viajes	travel agency
el campo	countryside
el equipaje	luggage
la estación de autobuses, del metro, de tren	bus, subway, train station
la llegada	arrival
el mar	sea
el paisaje	landscape
el pasaje (de ida y vuelta)	(round-trip) ticket
el pasaporte	passport
la playa	beach
la salida	departure; exit
la tabla de (wind)surf	surfboard/sailboard

El hotel

el ascensor	elevator
la cama	bed
el/la empleado/a	employee
la habitación individual, doble	single, double room
el hotel	hotel
el/la huésped	guest
la llave	key
el piso	floor (of a building)
la planta baja	ground floor

Adjetivos

abierto/a	open
aburrido/a	bored; boring
alegre	happy
amable	nice; friendly
avergonzado/a	embarrassed
cansado/a	tired
cerrado/a	closed
cómodo/a	comfortable
confundido/a	confused
contento/a	content
desordenado/a	disorderly
enamorado/a (de)	in love (with)
enojado/a	angry
equivocado/a	wrong
feliz	happy
limpio/a	clean
listo/a	ready; smart
nervioso/a	nervous
ocupado/a	busy
ordenado/a	orderly
preocupado/a (por)	worried (about)
seguro/a	sure; safe; confident
sucio/a	dirty
triste	sad

Los números ordinales

primer, primero/a	first
segundo/a	second
tercer, tercero/a	third
cuarto/a	fourth
quinto/a	fifth
sexto/a	sixth
séptimo/a	seventh
octavo/a	eighth
noveno/a	ninth
décimo/a	tenth

Palabras adicionales

ahora mismo	right now
el año	year
¿Cuál es la fecha (de hoy)?	What is the date (today)?
de buen/mal humor	in a good/bad mood
la estación	season
el mes	month
todavía	yet; still

Seasons, months, and dates	See page 154.
Weather expressions	See page 154.
Direct object pronouns	See page 174.
Expresiones útiles	See page 159.

¡De compras!

A PRIMERA VISTA
- ¿Está comprando algo la chica?
- ¿Crees que busca una maleta o una blusa?
- ¿Está contenta o enojada?
- ¿Cómo es la chica?

¡De compras!

Más vocabulario

el abrigo	*coat*
los calcetines (el calcetín)	*sock(s)*
el cinturón	*belt*
las gafas (de sol)	*(sun)glasses*
los guantes	*gloves*
el impermeable	*raincoat*
la ropa	*clothes*
la ropa interior	*underwear*
las sandalias	*sandals*
el traje	*suit*
el vestido	*dress*
los zapatos de tenis	*sneakers*
el regalo	*gift*
el almacén	*department store*
el centro comercial	*shopping mall*
el mercado (al aire libre)	*(open-air) market*
el precio (fijo)	*(fixed; set) price*
la rebaja	*sale*
la tienda	*store*
costar (o:ue)	*to cost*
gastar	*to spend (money)*
pagar	*to pay*
regatear	*to bargain*
vender	*to sell*
hacer juego (con)	*to match (with)*
llevar	*to wear; to take*
usar	*to wear; to use*

Variación léxica

calcetines	⟷	medias (*Amér. L.*)
cinturón	⟷	correa (*Col., Venez.*)
gafas/lentes	⟷	espejuelos (*Cuba, P.R.*), anteojos (*Arg., Chile*)
zapatos de tenis	⟷	zapatillas de deporte (*Esp.*), zapatillas (*Arg., Perú*)

el sombrero

un par de zapatos

los zapatos

la chaqueta

la caja

la cartera

la dependienta/la vendedora

la corbata

la tarjeta de crédito

los (blue)jeans

la bota

Práctica

1 **Escuchar** 🎧 Listen to Juanita and Vicente talk about what they're packing for their vacations. Indicate who is packing each item. If both are packing an item, write both names. If neither is packing an item, write an **X**.

1. abrigo _____
2. zapatos de tenis _____
3. impermeable _____
4. chaqueta _____
5. sandalias _____
6. bluejeans _____
7. gafas de sol _____
8. camisetas _____
9. traje de baño _____
10. botas _____
11. pantalones cortos _____
12. suéter _____

2 **¿Lógico o ilógico?** 🎧 Listen to Guillermo and Ana talk about vacation destinations. Indicate whether each statement is **lógico** or **ilógico**.

1. _____   3. _____
2. _____   4. _____

3 **Completar** Anita is talking about going shopping. Complete each sentence with the correct word(s), adding definite or indefinite articles when necessary.

caja	medias	tarjeta de crédito
centro comercial	par	traje de baño
dependientas	ropa	vendedores

1. Hoy voy a ir de compras al _____.
2. Voy a ir a la tienda de ropa para mujeres. Siempre hay muchas rebajas y las _____ son muy simpáticas.
3. Necesito comprar _____ de zapatos.
4. Y tengo que comprar _____ porque el sábado voy a la playa con mis amigos.
5. También voy a comprar unas _____ para mi mamá.
6. Voy a pagar todo (*everything*) en _____.
7. Pero hoy no tengo dinero. Voy a tener que usar mi _____.
8. Mañana voy al mercado al aire libre. Me gusta regatear con los _____.

4 **Escoger** Choose the item in each group that does not belong.

1. almacén • centro comercial • mercado • sombrero
2. camisa • camiseta • blusa • botas
3. jeans • bolsa • falda • pantalones
4. abrigo • suéter • corbata • chaqueta
5. mercado • tienda • almacén • cartera
6. pagar • llevar • hacer juego (con) • usar
7. botas • sandalias • zapatos • traje
8. vender • regatear • ropa interior • gastar

Los colores

amarillo/a	anaranjado/a	azul

blanco/a	gris	marrón, café	morado/a	negro/a

rojo/a	rosado/a	verde

¡LENGUA VIVA!

The names of colors vary throughout the Spanish-speaking world. For example, in some countries, **anaranjado/a** may be referred to as **naranja**, **morado/a** as **púrpura**, and **rojo/a** as **colorado/a**.

Other terms that will prove helpful include **claro** (*light*) and **oscuro** (*dark*): **azul claro, azul oscuro**.

Adjetivos

barato/a	cheap
bueno/a	good
cada	each
caro/a	expensive
corto/a	short (in length)
elegante	elegant
hermoso/a	beautiful
largo/a	long
loco/a	crazy
nuevo/a	new
otro/a	other; another
pobre	poor
rico/a	rich

5

Contrastes Complete each phrase with the opposite of the underlined word.

1. una corbata <u>barata</u> • unas camisas…
2. unas vendedoras <u>malas</u> • unos dependientes…
3. un vestido <u>corto</u> • una falda…
4. un hombre muy <u>pobre</u> • una mujer muy…
5. una cartera <u>nueva</u> • un cinturón…
6. unos trajes <u>hermosos</u> • unos jeans…
7. un impermeable <u>caro</u> • unos suéteres…
8. unos calcetines <u>blancos</u> • unas medias…

6

Preguntas Answer these questions.

1. ¿De qué color es la rosa de Texas?
2. ¿De qué color es la bandera (*flag*) de Canadá?
3. ¿De qué color es la casa donde vive el presidente de los EE.UU.?
4. ¿De qué color es el océano Atlántico?
5. ¿De qué color es la nieve?
6. ¿De qué color es el café?
7. ¿De qué color es el dólar de los EE.UU.?
8. ¿De qué color es la cebra (*zebra*)?

CONSULTA

Like other adjectives you have seen, colors must agree in gender and number with the nouns they modify.

Ex: **las camisas verdes, el vestido amarillo**.

For a review of descriptive adjectives, see **Estructura 3.1**, pp. 88–89.

Comunicación

7

Los regalos Listen to the conversation between Victoria and her friend Juan Manuel. Then indicate whether the following conclusions are **lógico** or **ilógico**, based on what you heard.

	Lógico	Ilógico
1. Juan Manuel quiere ir de compras.	○	○
2. A la mamá de Victoria le gusta nadar.	○	○
3. El papá de Victoria usa camisas.	○	○
4. Victoria va a regatear.	○	○
5. Victoria le va a comprar a su hermano unas botas.	○	○

8

Preferencias Answer your partner's questions.

1. ¿Adónde vas a comprar ropa? ¿Por qué?
2. ¿Qué tipo de ropa prefieres? ¿Por qué?
3. ¿Cuáles son tus colores favoritos?
4. En tu opinión, ¿es importante comprar ropa nueva frecuentemente? ¿Por qué?
5. ¿Gastas mucho dinero en ropa cada mes? ¿Buscas rebajas?
6. ¿Regateas cuando compras ropa? ¿Usas tarjetas de crédito?

9

El viaje Write an e-mail to a relative about a trip you are taking with your friends this summer. Include where you are going, what the weather is going to be like, what activities you are going to do, and what clothes you are taking.

10

Las maletas With a partner, take turns asking questions about the drawings. Include the topics from the list to talk about Carmela's vacation and Pepe's trip to Bariloche.

- ropa
- color
- lugar
- tiempo
- actividades

NOTA CULTURAL

Bariloche is a popular resort for skiing in South America. Located in Argentina's Patagonia region, the town is also known for its chocolate factories and its beautiful lakes, mountains, and forests.

CONSULTA

To review weather, see **Lección 5, Contextos,** p. 154.

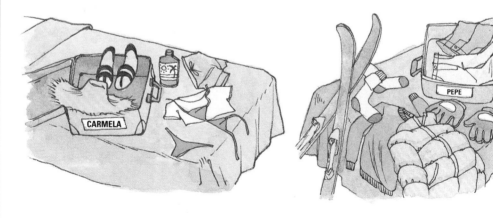

En el mercado

Los chicos van de compras al mercado. ¿Quién hizo la mejor compra?

MARISSA Oigan, vamos al mercado.

JUAN CARLOS ¡Sí! Los chicos en un equipo y las chicas en otro.

FELIPE Tenemos dos horas para ir de compras.

MARU Y don Guillermo decide quién gana.

JIMENA Esta falda azul es muy elegante.

MARISSA ¡Sí! Además, este color está de moda.

MARU Éste rojo es de algodón.

(*Las chicas encuentran unas bolsas.*)

VENDEDOR Ésta de rayas cuesta 190 pesos, ésta 120 pesos y ésta 220 pesos.

MARISSA ¿Me das aquella blusa rosada? Me parece que hace juego con esta falda, ¿no? ¿No tienen otras tallas?

JIMENA Sí, aquí. ¿Qué talla usas?

MARISSA Uso talla 4.

JIMENA La encontré. ¡Qué ropa más bonita!

(*En otra parte del mercado*)

FELIPE Juan Carlos compró una camisa de muy buena calidad.

MIGUEL (*a la vendedora*) ¿Puedo ver ésos, por favor?

VENDEDORA Sí, señor. Le doy un muy buen precio.

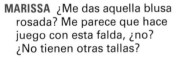

VENDEDOR Son 530 por las tres bolsas. Pero como ustedes son tan bonitas, son 500 pesos.

MARU Señor, no somos turistas ricas. Somos estudiantes pobres.

VENDEDOR Bueno, son 480 pesos.

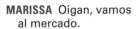

MARISSA **JIMENA** **MARU** **MIGUEL** **DON GUILLERMO** **VENDEDORA** **VENDEDOR**

JUAN CARLOS Miren, mi nueva camisa. Elegante, ¿verdad?

FELIPE A ver, Juan Carlos... te queda bien.

MARU ¿Qué compraste?

MIGUEL Sólo esto.

MARU ¡Qué bonitos aretes! Gracias, mi amor.

JUAN CARLOS Y ustedes, ¿qué compraron?

JIMENA Bolsas.

MARU Acabamos de comprar tres bolsas por sólo 480 pesos. ¡Una ganga!

FELIPE Don Guillermo, usted tiene que decidir quién gana. ¿Los chicos o las chicas?

DON GUILLERMO El ganador es... Miguel. ¡Porque no compró nada para él, sino para su novia!

Expresiones útiles

Talking about clothing

¡Qué ropa más bonita!
What nice clothing!
Esta falda azul es muy elegante.
This blue skirt is very elegant.
Está de moda.
It's in style.
Éste rojo es de algodón/lana.
This red one is cotton/wool.
Ésta de rayas/lunares/cuadros es de seda.
This striped / polka-dotted / plaid one is silk.
Es de muy buena calidad.
It's very good quality.
¿Qué talla usas/llevas?
What size do you wear?
Uso/Llevo talla 4.
I wear a size 4.
¿Qué número calza?
What size shoe do you wear?
Yo calzo siete.
I wear a size seven.

Negotiating a price

¿Cuánto cuesta?
How much does it cost?
Demasiado caro/a.
Too expensive.
Es una ganga.
It's a bargain.

Saying what you bought

¿Qué compraste?/¿Qué compró usted?
What did you buy?
Sólo compré esto.
I only bought this.
¡Qué bonitos aretes!
What beautiful earrings!
Y ustedes, ¿qué compraron?
And you guys, what did you buy?

Additional vocabulary

híjole *wow*

¿Qué pasó?

1

¿Cierto o falso? Indicate whether each sentence is **cierto** or **falso**. Correct the false statements.

	Cierto	Falso
1. Jimena dice que la falda azul no es elegante.	○	○
2. Juan Carlos compra una camisa.	○	○
3. Marissa dice que el azul es un color que está de moda.	○	○
4. Miguel compra unas sandalias para Maru.	○	○

NOTA CULTURAL

Las guayaberas are a popular men's shirt worn in hot climates. They are usually made of cotton, linen, or silk and decorated with pleats, pockets, and sometimes embroidery. They can be worn instead of a jacket to formal occasions or as everyday clothing.

2

Identificar Provide the first initial of the person who would make each statement.

____ 1. ¿Te gusta cómo se me ven mis nuevos aretes?
____ 2. Juan Carlos compró una camisa de muy buena calidad.
____ 3. No podemos pagar 500, señor, eso es muy caro.
____ 4. Aquí tienen ropa de muchas tallas.
____ 5. Esta falda me gusta mucho, el color azul es muy elegante.
____ 6. Hay que darnos prisa, sólo tenemos dos horas para ir de compras.

MARU

FELIPE

JIMENA

3

Completar Answer the questions using the information in the **Fotonovela**.

1. ¿Qué talla es Marissa?
2. ¿Cuánto les pide el vendedor por las tres bolsas?
3. ¿Cuál es el precio que pagan las tres amigas por las bolsas?
4. ¿Qué dice Juan Carlos sobre su nueva camisa?
5. ¿Quién ganó al hacer las compras? ¿Por qué?

AYUDA

When discussing prices, it's important to keep in mind singular and plural forms of verbs.

La **camisa cuesta** diez dólares.

Las **botas cuestan** sesenta dólares.

El **precio** de las botas **es** sesenta dólares.

Los **precios** de la ropa **son** altos.

4

Conversar With a partner, role-play a conversation between a customer and a salesperson in an open-air market. Use these expressions and also look at **Expresiones útiles** on the previous page.

¿Qué desea?	Estoy buscando...	Prefiero el/la rojo/a.
What would you like?	*I'm looking for...*	*I prefer the red one.*

Cliente/a	**Vendedor(a)**
Say good afternoon.	→ Greet the customer and ask what he/she would like.
Explain that you are looking for a particular item of clothing.	→ Show him/her some items and ask what he/she prefers.
Discuss colors and sizes.	→ Discuss colors and sizes.
Ask for the price and begin bargaining.	→ Tell him/her a price. Negotiate a price.
Settle on a price and purchase the item.	→ Accept a price and say thank you.

Pronunciación 🎧
The consonants **d** and **t**

¿Dónde?	**vender**	**nadar**	**verdad**

Like **b** and **v**, the Spanish **d** can have a hard sound or a soft sound, depending on which letters appear next to it.

Don	**dinero**	**tienda**	**falda**

At the beginning of a phrase and after **n** or **l**, the letter **d** is pronounced with a hard sound. This sound is similar to the English *d* in *dog*, but a little softer and duller. The tongue should touch the back of the upper teeth, not the roof of the mouth.

medias	**verde**	**vestido**	**huésped**

In all other positions, **d** has a soft sound. It is similar to the English *th* in *there*, but a little softer.

Don Diego no tiene el diccionario

When **d** begins a word, its pronunciation depends on the previous word. At the beginning of a phrase or after a word that ends in **n** or **l**, it is pronounced as a hard **d**.

Doña Dolores es de la capital

Words that begin with **d** are pronounced with a soft **d** if they appear immediately after a word that ends in a vowel or any consonant other than **n** or **l**.

traje	**pantalones**	**tarjeta**	**tienda**

When pronouncing the Spanish **t**, the tongue should touch the back of the upper teeth, not the roof of the mouth. Unlike the English *t*, no air is expelled from the mouth.

Práctica   Read these phrases aloud to practice the **d** and the **t**.

1. Hasta pronto.
2. De nada.
3. Mucho gusto.
4. Lo siento.
5. No hay de qué.
6. ¿De dónde es usted?
7. ¡Todos a bordo!
8. No puedo.
9. Es estupendo.
10. No tengo computadora.
11. ¿Cuándo vienen?
12. Son las tres y media.

Oraciones   Read these sentences aloud to practice the **d** and the **t**.

1. Don Teodoro tiene una tienda en un almacén en La Habana.
2. Don Teodoro vende muchos trajes, vestidos y zapatos todos los días.
3. Un día un turista, Federico Machado, entra en la tienda para comprar un par de botas.
4. Federico regatea con don Teodoro y compra las botas y también un par de sandalias.

Refranes   Read these sayings aloud to practice the **d** and the **t**.

En la variedad está el gusto.[1]

Aunque la mona se vista de seda, mona se queda.[2]

1 *Variety is the spice of life.*
2 *You can't make a silk purse out of a sow's ear.*

Los mercados al aire libre

Mercados al aire libre are an integral part of commerce and culture in the Spanish-speaking world. Whether they take place daily or weekly, these markets are an important forum where tourists, locals, and vendors interact. People come to the marketplace to shop, socialize, taste local foods, and watch street performers. Wandering from one **puesto** (*stand*) to the next, one can browse for fresh fruits and vegetables, clothing, CDs and DVDs, and **artesanías** (*crafts*). Some markets offer a mix of products, while others specialize in food, fashion, or used merchandise, such as antiques and books.

When shoppers see an item they like, they can bargain with the vendor. Friendly bargaining is an expected ritual and may result in a significantly lower price. When selling food, vendors may give the customer a little extra of what they purchase; this free addition is known as **la ñapa**.

Many open-air markets are also tourist attractions. The market in Otavalo, Ecuador, is world-famous and has taken place every Saturday since pre-Incan times. This market is well-known for the colorful textiles woven by the **otavaleños**, the indigenous people of the area. One can also find leather goods and wood carvings from nearby towns. Another popular market is **El Rastro**, held every Sunday in Madrid, Spain. Sellers set up **puestos** along the streets to display their wares, which range from local artwork and antiques to inexpensive clothing and electronics.

Mercado de Otavalo

mariscos *seafood* pescado *fish* verduras *vegetables* flores *flowers*

Otros mercados famosos

Mercado	Lugar	Productos
Feria Artesanal de Recoleta	Buenos Aires, Argentina	artesanías
Mercado Central	Santiago, Chile	mariscos°, pescado°, frutas, verduras°
Tianguis Cultural del Chopo	Ciudad de México, México	ropa, música, revistas, libros, arte, artesanías
El mercado de Chichicastenango	Chichicastenango, Guatemala	frutas y verduras, flores°, cerámica, textiles

1 **¿Cierto o falso?** Indicate whether these statements are **cierto** or **falso**. Correct the false statements.

1. Generally, open-air markets specialize in one type of goods.

2. Bargaining is commonplace at outdoor markets.

3. Only new goods can be found at open-air markets.

4. A Spaniard in search of antiques could search at **El Rastro**.

5. If you are in Guatemala and want to buy ceramics, you can go to Chichicastenango.

6. A **ñapa** is a tax on open-air market goods.

7. The **otavaleños** weave colorful textiles to sell on Saturdays.

8. Santiago's **Mercado Central** is known for books and music.

ASÍ SE DICE

La ropa

la chamarra (Méx.)	la chaqueta
de manga corta/larga	*short/long-sleeved*
los mahones (P. Rico); el pantalón de mezclilla (Méx.); los tejanos (Esp.); los vaqueros (Arg., Cuba, Esp., Uru.)	los bluejeans
la marca	*brand*
la playera (Méx.); la remera (Arg.)	la camiseta

EL MUNDO HISPANO

Diseñadores de moda

• **Adolfo Domínguez** (España) Su ropa tiene un estilo minimalista y práctico. Usa telas° naturales y cómodas en sus diseños.

• **Silvia Tcherassi** (Colombia) Los colores vivos y las líneas asimétricas de sus vestidos y trajes muestran influencias tropicales.

• **Óscar de la Renta** (República Dominicana) Diseñó ropa opulenta para la mujer clásica.

• **Narciso Rodríguez** (EE.UU.) En sus diseños delicados y finos predominan los colores blanco y negro. Hizo° el vestido de boda° de Carolyn Bessette Kennedy. También diseñó varios vestidos para Michelle Obama.

telas *fabrics* Hizo *He made* de boda *wedding*

PERFIL

Carolina Herrera

In 1980, at the urging of some friends, **Carolina Herrera** created a fashion collection as a "test." The Venezuelan designer received such a favorable response that within one year she moved her family from Caracas to New York City and created her own label, Carolina Herrera, Ltd.

"I love elegance and intricacy, but whether it is in a piece of clothing or a fragrance, the intricacy must appear as simplicity," Herrera once stated. She quickly found that many sophisticated women agreed; from the start, her sleek and glamorous designs have been in constant demand. Over the years, Herrera has grown her brand into a veritable fashion empire that encompasses her fashion and bridal collections, cosmetics, perfume, and accessories that are sold around the globe.

Conexión Internet

¿Qué marcas de ropa son populares en el mundo hispano?

Use the Web to find more cultural information related to this **Cultura** section.

ACTIVIDADES

2 **Comprensión** Complete these sentences.

1. Adolfo Domínguez usa telas _____ y _____ en su ropa.

2. Si hace fresco en el D.F., puedes llevar una _____.

3. La diseñadora _____ hace ropa, perfumes y más.

4. La ropa de _____ muestra influencias tropicales.

5. Los _____ son una ropa casual en Puerto Rico.

3 **Mi ropa favorita** Write a brief description of your favorite article of clothing. Mention what store it is from, the brand, colors, fabric, style, and any other information.

6.1 Saber and conocer

ANTE TODO Spanish has two verbs that mean *to know*: **saber** and **conocer**. They cannot be used interchangeably. Note the irregular **yo** forms.

The verbs **saber** and **conocer**		
	saber *(to know)*	**conocer** *(to know)*
SINGULAR FORMS		
yo	**sé**	**conozco**
tú	**sabes**	**conoces**
Ud./él/ella	**sabe**	**conoce**
PLURAL FORMS		
nosotros/as	**sabemos**	**conocemos**
vosotros/as	**sabéis**	**conocéis**
Uds./ellos/ellas	**saben**	**conocen**

▶ **Saber** means *to know a fact or piece(s) of information* or *to know how to do something.*

No **sé** tu número de teléfono.
I don't know your telephone number.

Mi hermana **sabe** hablar francés.
My sister knows how to speak French.

▶ **Conocer** means *to know* or *be familiar/acquainted* with a person, place, or thing.

¿**Conoces** la ciudad de Nueva York?
Do you know New York City?

No **conozco** a tu amigo Esteban.
I don't know your friend Esteban.

▶ When the direct object of **conocer** is a person or pet, the personal **a** is used.

¿Conoces La Habana?
Do you know Havana?

but

¿Conoces **a** Celia Cruz?
Do you know Celia Cruz?

▶ **¡Atención!** **Parecer** (*to seem*) and **ofrecer** (*to offer*) are conjugated like **conocer**.

▶ **¡Atención!** **Conducir** (*to drive*) and **traducir** (*to translate*) also have an irregular **yo** form, but since they are **-ir** verbs, they are conjugated differently from **conocer**.

conducir	**conduzco, conduces, conduce, conducimos, conducís, conducen**
traducir	**traduzco, traduces, traduce, traducimos, traducís, traducen**

NOTA CULTURAL

Cuban singer **Celia Cruz** (1925–2003), known as the "Queen of Salsa," recorded many albums over her long career. Adored by her fans, she was famous for her colorful and lively on-stage performances.

¡INTÉNTALO! Provide the appropriate forms of these verbs.

saber

1. José no ___sabe___ la hora.
2. Sara y yo _____ jugar al tenis.
3. ¿Por qué no _____ tú estos verbos?
4. Mis padres _____ hablar japonés.
5. Yo _____ a qué hora es la clase.
6. Usted no _____ dónde vivo.
7. Mi hermano no _____ nadar.
8. Nosotros _____ muchas cosas.

conocer

1. Usted y yo ___conocemos___ bien Miami.
2. ¿Tú _____ a mi amigo Manuel?
3. Sergio y Taydé _____ mi pueblo.
4. Emiliano _____ a mis padres.
5. Yo _____ muy bien el centro.
6. ¿Ustedes _____ la tienda Gigante?
7. Nosotras _____ una playa hermosa.
8. ¿Usted _____ a mi profesora?

Práctica y Comunicación

1

Completar Indicate the correct verb for each sentence.

1. Mis hermanos (conocen/saben) conducir, pero yo no (sé/conozco).
2. —¿(Conocen/Saben) ustedes dónde está el estadio? —No, no lo (conocemos/sabemos).
3. —¿(Conoces/Sabes) a Lady Gaga? —Bueno, (sé/conozco) quién es, pero no la (conozco/sé).
4. Mi profesora (sabe/conoce) Cuba y también (conoce/sabe) bailar salsa.

2

Combinar Combine elements from each column to create sentences.

A	B	C
Shakira	(no) conocer	Jimmy Fallon
los Yankees	(no) saber	cantar y bailar
el primer ministro		La Habana Vieja
de Canadá		muchas personas importantes
mis amigos y yo		hablar dos lenguas extranjeras
tú		jugar al béisbol

3

Mi compañera de cuarto Listen as Jennifer describes her roommate. Then indicate whether the following conclusions are **lógico** or **ilógico**, based on what you heard.

	Lógico	Ilógico
1. Jennifer y Laura son amigas.	O	O
2. Laura es antipática.	O	O
3. A Laura le gustan las lenguas extranjeras.	O	O
4. Laura prefiere comprar ropa cara.	O	O
5. Laura no tiene pasatiempos.	O	O
6. Laura conoce a muchas personas.	O	O

4

Preguntas Answer your partner's questions. Use complete sentences.

1. ¿Conoces a un(a) cantante famoso/a? ¿Te gusta cómo canta?
2. En tu familia, ¿quién sabe cantar bien? ¿Tu opinión es objetiva?
3. Y tú, ¿conduces bien o mal? ¿Y tus amigos?
4. Si un(a) amigo/a no conduce muy bien, ¿le ofreces crítica constructiva?
5. ¿Cómo parecen estar tus amigos hoy?

5

Conocimientos Tell about three things you know how to do, three places you are familiar with, and three people you know.

6

Anuncio Write an advertisement using two examples each of **saber** and **conocer**.

6.2 Indirect object pronouns

ANTE TODO   In **Lección 5**, you learned that a direct object receives the action of the verb directly. In contrast, an indirect object receives the action of the verb indirectly.

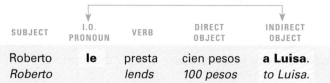

SUBJECT	I.O. PRONOUN	VERB	DIRECT OBJECT	INDIRECT OBJECT
Roberto	**le**	presta	cien pesos	**a Luisa**.
Roberto		*lends*	*100 pesos*	*to Luisa.*

An indirect object is a noun or pronoun that answers the question *to whom* or *for whom* an action is done. In the preceding example, the indirect object answers this question: **¿A quién le presta Roberto cien pesos?** *To whom does Roberto lend 100 pesos?*

Indirect object pronouns

Singular forms		Plural forms	
me	(to, for) *me*	**nos**	(to, for) *us*
te	(to, for) *you* (fam.)	**os**	(to, for) *you* (fam.)
le	(to, for) *you* (form.)	**les**	(to, for) *you*
	(to, for) *him; her*		(to, for) *them*

▶ **¡Atención!** The forms of indirect object pronouns for the first and second persons (**me**, **te**, **nos**, **os**) are the same as the direct object pronouns. Indirect object pronouns agree in number with the corresponding nouns, but not in gender.

Acabo de mostrarles que sí sabemos regatear.

Bueno, le doy un descuento.

Using indirect object pronouns

▶ Spanish speakers commonly use both an indirect object pronoun and the noun to which it refers in the same sentence. This is done to emphasize and clarify to whom the pronoun refers.

I.O. PRONOUN		INDIRECT OBJECT		I.O. PRONOUN		INDIRECT OBJECT

Ella **le** vende la ropa **a Elena**.   **Les** prestamos el dinero **a Inés y a Álex**.

▶ Indirect object pronouns are also used without the indirect object noun when the person for whom the action is being done is known.

Ana **le** presta la falda **a Elena**.   También **le** presta unos jeans.
Ana lends her skirt to Elena.   *She also lends her a pair of jeans.*

▶ Indirect object pronouns are usually placed before the conjugated form of the verb. In negative sentences the pronoun is placed between **no** and the conjugated verb.

CONSULTA

For more information on accents, see **Lección 4, Pronunciación**, p. 123, **Lección 10, Ortografía**, p. 339, and **Lección 11, Ortografía**, p. 375.

Martín **me** compra un regalo.	Eva **no me** escribe cartas.
Martín is buying me a gift.	*Eva doesn't write me letters.*

▶ When a conjugated verb is followed by an infinitive or the present progressive, the indirect object pronoun may be placed before the conjugated verb or attached to the infinitive or present participle. **¡Atención!** When an indirect object pronoun is attached to a present participle, an accent mark is added to maintain the proper stress.

Él no quiere **pagarte**./	Él está **escribiéndole** una postal a ella./
Él no **te** quiere pagar.	Él **le** está escribiendo una postal a ella.
He does not want to pay you.	*He is writing a postcard to her.*

▶ Because the indirect object pronouns **le** and **les** have multiple meanings, Spanish speakers often clarify to whom the pronouns refer with the preposition **a** + [*pronoun*] or **a** + [*noun*].

UNCLARIFIED STATEMENTS	CLARIFIED STATEMENTS
Yo **le** compro un abrigo.	Yo **le** compro un abrigo **a usted/él/ella**.
Ella **le** describe un libro.	Ella **le** describe un libro **a Juan**.

UNCLARIFIED STATEMENTS	CLARIFIED STATEMENTS
Él **les** vende unos sombreros.	Él **les** vende unos sombreros **a ustedes/ellos/ellas**.
Ellos **les** hablan muy claro.	Ellos **les** hablan muy claro **a los clientes**.

▶ The irregular verbs **dar** (*to give*) and **decir** (*to say; to tell*) are often used with indirect object pronouns.

The verbs dar and decir

	Singular forms				Plural forms		
		dar	decir			dar	decir
yo		**doy**	**digo**	nosotros/as		**damos**	**decimos**
tú		**das**	**dices**	vosotros/as		**dais**	**decís**
Ud./él/ella		**da**	**dice**	Uds./ellos/ellas		**dan**	**dicen**

Me dan una fiesta cada año.	**Te digo** la verdad.
They give (throw) me a party every year.	*I'm telling you the truth.*
Voy a **darle** consejos.	No **les digo** mentiras a mis padres.
I'm going to give her advice.	*I don't tell lies to my parents.*

¡INTÉNTALO! Use the cues in parentheses to provide the correct indirect object pronoun for each sentence.

1. Juan ___le___ quiere dar un regalo. (*to Elena*)
2. María _____ prepara un café. (*for us*)
3. Beatriz y Felipe _____ escriben desde (*from*) Cuba. (*to me*)
4. Marta y yo _____ compramos unos guantes. (*for them*)
5. Los vendedores _____ venden ropa. (*to you, fam. sing.*)
6. La dependienta _____ muestra los guantes. (*to us*)

Práctica

1 **Completar** Fill in the blanks with the correct pronouns to complete Mónica's description of her family's holiday shopping.

1. Juan y yo _____ damos una blusa a nuestra hermana Gisela.
2. Mi tía _____ da a nosotros una mesa para la casa.
3. Gisela _____ da dos corbatas a su novio.
4. A mi mamá yo _____ doy un par de guantes negros.
5. A mi profesora _____ doy dos libros de José Martí.
6. Juan _____ da un regalo a mis padres.
7. Mis padres _____ dan un traje nuevo a mí.
8. Y a ti, yo _____ doy un regalo también. ¿Quieres verlo?

2 **En La Habana** Describe what happens on Pascual's trip to Cuba based on the cues provided.

1. ellos / cantar / canción / (mí)

2. él / comprar / libros / (sus hijos) / Plaza de Armas

3. yo / preparar el almuerzo (*lunch*) / (ti)

4. él / explicar cómo llegar / (conductor)

5. mi novia / sacar / foto / (nosotros)

6. el guía (*guide*) / mostrar / catedral de San Cristóbal / (ustedes)

3 **Combinar** Use an item from each column and an indirect object pronoun to create logical sentences.

> **modelo**
>
> Mis padres les dan regalos a mis primos.

A	B	C	D
yo	comprar	mensajes electrónicos	mí
el dependiente	dar	corbata	ustedes
el profesor Arce	decir	dinero en efectivo	clienta
la vendedora	escribir	tarea	novia
mis padres	explicar	problemas	primos
tú	pagar	regalos	ti
nosotros/as	prestar	ropa	nosotros
¿?	vender	¿?	¿?

Comunicación

4 **Días locos** Gabriela is e-mailing her friend Sandra about her semester. Indicate whether the following conclusions are **lógico** or **ilógico**, based on what you read.

De:	Gabriela
Para:	Sandra
Asunto:	Días locos

Los profesores nos dan mucha tarea. ¡Vivo en la biblioteca! Mi mamá me escribe mensajes electrónicos cada dos horas. Obviamente, yo no tengo tiempo de contestarle, pero ¡ella no me entiende! Rodrigo, el hermano menor de Ana, viene a visitarme todo el tiempo y me da regalos. ¡También me canta! Le tengo que decir la verdad: ¡No quiero su atención!

	Lógico	Ilógico
1. Gabriela tiene muchos ratos libres.	O	O
2. La mamá de Gabriela está enojada con ella.	O	O
3. Rodrigo está enamorado de Gabriela.	O	O
4. Gabriela está enamorada de Rodrigo.	O	O
5. Rodrigo le debe dar más regalos a Gabriela.	O	O

5 **Entrevista** Answer your partner's questions.

1. ¿Qué tiendas, almacenes o centros comerciales prefieres?
2. ¿A quién le compras regalos cuando hay rebajas?
3. ¿A quién le prestas dinero cuando lo necesita?
4. ¿Me explicas cómo regatear?
5. ¿Te dan tus padres su tarjeta de crédito cuando vas de compras?

6 **¡Somos ricos!** You and another student chipped in on a lottery ticket and you won! Now you want to spend money on your loved ones. Write a paragraph telling what you plan to buy for your family and your friends.

> **modelo**
> *Quiero comprarle un vestido de Carolina Herrera a mi madre...*

Síntesis

7 **Minidrama** With a partner, role-play a conversation between a customer and a clerk in a clothing store. The customer should talk about the clothes he/she is looking for and for whom he/she is buying the clothes. The clerk should recommend different items based on the customer's descriptions. Use these expressions and also look at **Expresiones útiles** on page 195.

Me queda grande/pequeño. *It's big/small on me.*	**¿Está en rebaja?** *Is it on sale?*
¿Tiene otro color? *Do you have another color?*	**También estoy buscando...** *I'm also looking for...*

6.3 Preterite tense of regular verbs

ANTE TODO   In order to talk about events in the past, Spanish uses two simple tenses: the preterite and the imperfect. In this lesson, you will learn how to form the preterite tense, which is used to express actions or states completed in the past.

Preterite of regular -ar, -er, and -ir verbs

		-ar verbs **comprar**	-er verbs **vender**	-ir verbs **escribir**
SINGULAR FORMS	yo	compr**é** *I bought*	vend**í** *I sold*	escrib**í** *I wrote*
	tú	compr**aste**	vend**iste**	escrib**iste**
	Ud./él/ella	compr**ó**	vend**ió**	escrib**ió**
PLURAL FORMS	nosotros/as	compr**amos**	vend**imos**	escrib**imos**
	vosotros/as	compr**asteis**	vend**isteis**	escrib**isteis**
	Uds./ellos/ellas	compr**aron**	vend**ieron**	escrib**ieron**

▶ **¡Atención!** The **yo** and **Ud./él/ella** forms of all three conjugations have written accents on the last syllable to show that it is stressed.

▶ As the chart shows, the endings for regular **-er** and **-ir** verbs are identical in the preterite.

¿Qué compraste?

Compré estos aretes.

▶ Note that the **nosotros/as** forms of regular **-ar** and **-ir** verbs in the preterite are identical to the present tense forms. Context will help you determine which tense is being used.

En invierno **compramos** ropa.
In the winter, we buy clothes.

Anoche **compramos** unos zapatos.
Last night we bought some shoes.

▶ **-Ar** and **-er** verbs that have a stem change in the present tense are regular in the preterite. They do *not* have a stem change.

	PRESENT	PRETERITE
cerrar (e:ie)	La tienda **cierra** a las seis.	La tienda **cerró** a las seis.
volver (o:ue)	Carlitos **vuelve** tarde.	Carlitos **volvió** tarde.
jugar (u:ue)	Él **juega** al fútbol.	Él **jugó** al fútbol.

▶ **¡Atención!** **-Ir** verbs that have a stem change in the present tense also have a stem change in the preterite.

CONSULTA

There are a few high-frequency irregular verbs in the preterite. You will learn more about them in **Estructura 9.1**, p. 310.

CONSULTA

You will learn about the preterite of **-ir** stem-changing verbs in **Estructura 8.1**, p. 274.

▶ Verbs that end in **-car**, **-gar**, and **-zar** have a spelling change in the first person singular (**yo** form) in the preterite.

bus**car**	▶	bus**c-**	▶	**qu-**	▶	yo bus**qu**é
lle**gar**		lle**g-**		**gu-**		yo lle**gu**é
empe**zar**		empe**z-**		**c-**		yo empe**c**é

▶ Except for the **yo** form, all other forms of **-car**, **-gar**, and **-zar** verbs are regular in the preterite.

▶ Three other verbs—**creer**, **leer**, and **oír**—have spelling changes in the preterite. The **i** of the verb endings of **creer**, **leer**, and **oír** carries an accent in the **yo**, **tú**, **nosotros/as**, and **vosotros/as** forms, and changes to **y** in the **Ud./él/ella** and **Uds./ellos/ellas forms**.

creer	▶	cre-	▶	cre**í**, cre**í**ste, cre**y**ó, cre**í**mos, cre**í**steis, cre**y**eron
leer		le-		le**í**, le**í**ste, le**y**ó, le**í**mos, le**í**steis, le**y**eron
oír		o-		o**í**, o**í**ste, o**y**ó, o**í**mos, o**í**steis, o**y**eron

▶ **Ver** is regular in the preterite, but none of its forms has an accent.

ver ⟶ vi, viste, vio, vimos, visteis, vieron

Words commonly used with the preterite

anoche	last night		pasado/a (*adj.*)	last; past
anteayer	the day before yesterday		el año pasado	last year
			la semana pasada	last week
ayer	yesterday		una vez	once
de repente	suddenly		dos veces	twice
desde... hasta...	from... until...		ya	already

Ayer llegué a Santiago de Cuba.
Yesterday I arrived in Santiago de Cuba.

Anoche oí un ruido extraño.
Last night I heard a strange noise.

▶ **Acabar de** + [*infinitive*] is used to say that something has just occurred. Note that **acabar** is in the present tense in this construction.

Acabo de comprar una falda.
I just bought a skirt.

Acabas de ir de compras.
You just went shopping.

¡INTÉNTALO! Provide the appropriate preterite forms of the verbs.

	comer	salir	comenzar	leer
1. ellas	comieron	salieron	comenzaron	leyeron
2. tú	_____	_____	_____	_____
3. usted	_____	_____	_____	_____
4. nosotros	_____	_____	_____	_____
5. yo	_____	_____	_____	_____

Práctica

1

Completar Andrea is talking about what happened last weekend. Complete each sentence by choosing the correct verb and putting it in the preterite.

1. El viernes a las cuatro de la tarde, la profesora Mora _____ (asistir, costar, usar) a una reunión (*meeting*) de profesores.
2. A la una, yo _____ (llegar, bucear, llevar) a la tienda con mis amigos.
3. Mis amigos y yo _____ (comprar, regatear, gastar) dos o tres cosas.
4. Yo _____ (costar, comprar, escribir) unos pantalones negros y mi amigo Mateo _____ (gastar, pasear, comprar) una camisa azul.
5. Después, nosotros _____ (llevar, vivir, comer) cerca de un mercado.
6. A las tres, Pepe _____ (hablar, pasear, nadar) con su novia por teléfono.
7. El sábado por la tarde, mi mamá _____ (escribir, beber, vivir) una carta.
8. El domingo mi tía _____ (decidir, salir, escribir) comprarme un traje.
9. A las cuatro de la tarde, mi tía _____ (beber, salir, encontrar) el traje y después nosotras _____ (acabar, ver, salir) una película.

2

Preguntas Imagine that you have a pesky friend who keeps asking you questions. Respond that you already did or have just done what he/she asks. Make sure you and your partner take turns playing the role of the pesky friend and responding to his/her questions.

> **modelo**
>
> leer la lección
> **Estudiante 1:** ¿Leíste la lección?
> **Estudiante 2:** Sí, ya la leí./Sí, acabo de leerla.

1. escribir el mensaje electrónico
2. lavar (*to wash*) la ropa
3. oír las noticias (*news*)
4. comprar pantalones cortos
5. practicar los verbos
6. pagar la cuenta (*bill*)
7. empezar la composición
8. ver la película *Diarios de motocicleta*

3

¿Cuándo? Use the time expressions from the word bank to talk about when you and others did the activities listed.

| anoche | anteayer | el mes pasado | una vez |
| ayer | la semana pasada | el año pasado | dos veces |

1. mi compañero/a de cuarto: llegar tarde a clase
2. mi mejor (*best*) amigo/a: salir con un(a) chico/a guapo/a
3. mis padres: ver una película
4. yo: llevar un traje/vestido
5. el presidente/primer ministro de mi país: asistir a una conferencia internacional
6. mis amigos y yo: comer en un restaurante
7. ¿?: comprar algo (*something*) bueno, bonito y barato

Comunicación

4 **¿Estás listo?** Listen to the conversation between Matilde and Hernán. Then indicate whether the following conclusions are **lógico** or **ilógico**, based on what you heard.

	Lógico	Ilógico
1. Hernán compró un pasaje de ida y vuelta.	○	○
2. Matilde va a viajar con Hernán.	○	○
3. Hernán buscó su pasaporte.	○	○
4. Los documentos personales de Hernán están en su mochila.	○	○
5. Hernán tiene mucho equipaje.	○	○

5 **Ayer** Tell your partner at what time you did these activities yesterday.

1. desayunar
2. salir de la casa
3. almorzar
4. ver a un(a) amigo/a
5. volver a la casa
6. cenar

6 **Las vacaciones** Imagine that you took these photos on a vacation with friends. Use the pictures to describe the trip.

7 **Mi última compra** Write a short paragraph describing the last time you went shopping. Use at least four verbs in the preterite tense.

Síntesis

8 **Conversación** With a partner, talk about what you did last week. Don't forget to include school activities, shopping, and pastimes.

6.4 Demonstrative adjectives and pronouns

Demonstrative adjectives

ANTE TODO   In Spanish, as in English, demonstrative adjectives are words that "demonstrate" or "point out" nouns. Demonstrative adjectives precede the nouns they modify and, like other Spanish adjectives you have studied, agree with them in gender and number. Observe these examples and then study the chart below.

esta camisa	**ese** vendedor	**aquellos** zapatos
this shirt	*that salesman*	*those shoes (over there)*

Demonstrative adjectives				
Singular		**Plural**		
MASCULINE	FEMININE	MASCULINE	FEMININE	
este	**esta**	**estos**	**estas**	*this; these*
ese	**esa**	**esos**	**esas**	*that; those*
aquel	**aquella**	**aquellos**	**aquellas**	*that; those (over there)*

▶ There are three sets of demonstrative adjectives. To determine which one to use, you must establish the relationship between the speaker and the noun(s) being pointed out.

▶ The demonstrative adjectives **este**, **esta**, **estos**, and **estas** are used to point out things that are close to the speaker and the listener.

Me gustan estos zapatos.

▶ The demonstrative adjectives **ese**, **esa**, **esos**, and **esas** are used to point out things that are not close in space and time to the speaker. They may, however, be close to the listener.

Prefiero esos zapatos.

The demonstrative adjectives **aquel**, **aquella**, **aquellos**, and **aquellas** are used to point out things that are far away from the speaker and the listener.

Aquel auto es de mi hermana.

Demonstrative pronouns

Demonstrative pronouns are identical to their corresponding demonstrative adjectives, with the exception that they traditionally carry an accent mark on the stressed vowel. The **Real Academia** no longer requires this accent, but it is still commonly used.

Demonstrative pronouns

Singular		Plural	
MASCULINE	FEMININE	MASCULINE	FEMININE
éste	**ésta**	**éstos**	**éstas**
ése	**ésa**	**ésos**	**ésas**
aquél	**aquélla**	**aquéllos**	**aquéllas**

—¿Quieres comprar **este suéter**?
Do you want to buy this sweater?

—No, no quiero **éste**. Quiero **ése**.
No, I don't want this one. I want that one.

—¿Vas a leer **estas revistas**?
Are you going to read these magazines?

—Sí, voy a leer **éstas**. También voy a leer **aquéllas**.
Yes, I'm going to read these. I'll also read those (over there).

¡Atención! Like demonstrative adjectives, demonstrative pronouns agree in gender and number with the corresponding noun.

Este libro es de Pablito.   **Éstos** son de Juana.

There are three neuter demonstrative pronouns: **esto**, **eso**, and **aquello**. These forms refer to unidentified or unspecified things, situations, ideas, and concepts. They do not change in gender or number and never carry an accent mark.

—¿Qué es **esto**?
What's this?

—**Eso** es interesante.
That's interesting.

—**Aquello** es bonito.
That's pretty.

¡INTÉNTALO!   Provide the correct form of the demonstrative adjective for these nouns.

1. la falda / este _____ *esta falda* _____
2. los estudiantes / este _____
3. los países / aquel _____
4. la ventana / ese _____

5. los periodistas / ese _____
6. el chico / aquel _____
7. las sandalias / este _____
8. las chicas / aquel _____

Práctica

1 **Cambiar** Make the singular sentences plural and the plural sentences singular.

> **modelo**
>
> **Estas camisas son blancas.**
> Esta camisa es blanca.

1. Aquellos sombreros son muy elegantes.
2. Ese abrigo es muy caro.
3. Estos cinturones son hermosos.
4. Esos precios son muy buenos.
5. Estas faldas son muy cortas.
6. ¿Quieres ir a aquel almacén?
7. Esas blusas son baratas.
8. Esta corbata hace juego con mi traje.

2 **Completar** Here are some things people might say while shopping. Complete the sentences with the correct demonstrative pronouns.

1. No me gustan esos zapatos. Voy a comprar _____. (*these*)
2. ¿Vas a comprar ese traje o _____? (*this one*)
3. Esta guayabera es bonita, pero prefiero _____. (*that one*)
4. Estas corbatas rojas son muy bonitas, pero _____ son fabulosas. (*those*)
5. Estos cinturones cuestan demasiado. Prefiero _____. (*those over there*)
6. ¿Te gustan esas botas o _____? (*these*)
7. Esa bolsa roja es bonita, pero prefiero _____. (*that one over there*)
8. No voy a comprar estas botas; voy a comprar _____. (*those over there*)
9. ¿Prefieres estos pantalones o _____? (*those*)
10. Me gusta este vestido, pero voy a comprar _____. (*that one*)
11. Me gusta ese almacén, pero _____ es mejor (*better*). (*that one over there*)
12. Esa blusa es bonita, pero cuesta demasiado. Voy a comprar _____. (*this one*)

3 **Describir** Look for two items that are one of these colors: **amarillo**, **azul**, **blanco**, **marrón**, **negro**, **verde**, **rojo**. Point them out, first using demonstrative adjectives, and then demonstrative pronouns.

> **modelo**
>
> **azul**
> Esta silla es azul. Aquella mochila es azul.
> Ésta es azul. Aquélla es azul.

Comunicación

4

🎧

De compras Listen to the conversation between Alejandra and a clerk. Then indicate whether the following conclusions are **lógico** or **ilógico**, based on what you heard.

	Lógico	Ilógico
1. A Alejandra no le gusta llevar faldas.	○	○
2. Alejandra va a comprar la blusa blanca.	○	○
3. La dependienta trabaja en un almacén.	○	○
4. A Alejandra le gustan los colores azul y gris.	○	○
5. El cinturón negro es muy caro.	○	○
6. Alejandra va a comprar una cartera también.	○	○

5

En una tienda Imagine that you and a partner are in Madrid shopping at Zara. Study the floor plan, then have a conversation about your surroundings. Use demonstrative adjectives and pronouns.

NOTA CULTURAL

Zara is an international clothing company based in Spain. Its innovative processes take a product from the design room to the manufacturing shelves in less than a month. This means that the merchandise is constantly changing to keep up with the most current trends.

> **modelo**
>
> **Estudiante 1:** Me gusta este suéter azul.
> **Estudiante 2:** Yo prefiero aquella chaqueta.

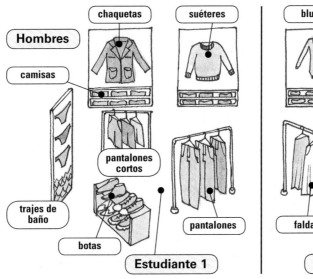

Síntesis

6

En el café Write a conversation between two people sitting at a busy sidewalk café. Use as many demonstrative adjectives and pronouns as possible to describe the people and things around them.

> **modelo**
>
> Carmen: Esa corbata es fea, ¿no?
> Susana: Sí. No me gustan las corbatas rosadas y verdes. Y ese traje...

Recapitulación

Review the grammar concepts you have learned in this lesson by completing these activities.

1   Completar Complete the chart with the correct preterite or infinitive form of the verbs. **30 pts.**

Infinitive	yo	ella	ellos
			tomaron
		abrió	
comprender			
	leí		
pagar			

2   En la tienda Look at the drawing and complete the conversation with demonstrative adjectives and pronouns. **14 pts.**

CLIENTE Buenos días, señorita. Deseo comprar (1) _____ corbata.

VENDEDORA Muy bien, señor. ¿No le interesa mirar (2) _____ trajes que están allá? Hay unos que hacen juego con la corbata.

CLIENTE (3) _____ de allá son de lana, ¿no? Prefiero ver (4) _____ traje marrón que está detrás de usted.

VENDEDORA Estupendo. Como puede ver, es de seda. Cuesta seiscientos cincuenta dólares.

CLIENTE Ah… eh… no, creo que sólo voy a comprar la corbata, gracias.

VENDEDORA Bueno… si busca algo más económico, hay rebaja en (5) _____ sombreros. Cuestan sólo treinta dólares.

CLIENTE ¡Magnífico! Me gusta (6) _____, el blanco que está hasta arriba (*at the top*). Y quiero pagar todo con (7) _____ tarjeta.

VENDEDORA Sí, señor. Ahora mismo le traigo el sombrero.

RESUMEN GRAMATICAL

6.1 Saber and conocer   *p. 200*

saber	conocer
sé	conozco
sabes	conoces
sabe	conoce
sabemos	conocemos
sabéis	conocéis
saben	conocen

► **saber** = to know facts/how to do something
► **conocer** = to know a person, place, or thing

6.2 Indirect object pronouns   *pp. 202–203*

Indirect object pronouns

Singular	Plural
me	nos
te	os
le	les

► **dar** = doy, das, da, damos, dais, dan
► **decir (e:i)** = digo, dices, dice, decimos, decís, dicen

6.3 Preterite tense of regular verbs   *pp. 206–207*

comprar	vender	escribir
compré	vendí	escribí
compraste	vendiste	escribiste
compró	vendió	escribió
compramos	vendimos	escribimos
comprasteis	vendisteis	escribisteis
compraron	vendieron	escribieron

Verbs with spelling changes in the preterite

► **-car:** buscar → yo busqué
► **-gar:** llegar → yo llegué
► **-zar:** empezar → yo empecé
► **creer:** creí, creíste, creyó, creímos, creísteis, creyeron
► **leer:** leí, leíste, leyó, leímos, leísteis, leyeron
► **oír:** oí, oíste, oyó, oímos, oísteis, oyeron
► **ver:** vi, viste, vio, vimos, visteis, vieron

3 **¿Saber o conocer?** Complete each dialogue with the correct form of **saber** or **conocer**. **20 pts.**

1. —¿Qué _____ hacer tú?
   —(Yo) _____ jugar al fútbol.
2. —¿_____ tú esta tienda de ropa?
   —No, (yo) no la _____. ¿Es buena?
3. —¿Tus padres no _____ a tu novio?
   —No, ¡ellos no _____ que tengo novio!
4. —Mi compañero de cuarto todavía no me
   _____ bien.
   —Y tú, ¿lo quieres _____ a él?
5. —¿_____ ustedes dónde está el mercado?
   —No, nosotros no _____ bien esta ciudad.

4 **Oraciones** Form complete sentences using the information provided. Use indirect object pronouns and the present tense of the verbs. **32 pts.**

1. Javier / prestar / el abrigo / a Maripili
   _____

2. nosotros / vender / ropa / a los clientes
   _____

3. el vendedor / traer / las camisetas / a mis amigos y a mí
   _____

4. yo / querer dar / consejos / a ti
   _____

5. ¿tú / ir a comprar / un regalo / a mí?
   _____

6. el dependiente / mostrar / las corbatas / a Santiago
   _____

7. los hijos / pedir / dinero / a sus padres
   _____

8. la profesora / escribir / mensajes electrónicos / a nosotros
   _____

5 **Poema** Write the missing words to complete the excerpt from the poem *Romance sonámbulo* by Federico García Lorca. **4 pts.**

6.4 **Demonstrative adjectives and pronouns** *pp. 210–211*

Demonstrative adjectives

Singular		Plural	
Masc.	**Fem.**	**Masc.**	**Fem.**
este	esta	estos	estas
ese	esa	esos	esas
aquel	aquella	aquellos	aquellas

Demonstrative pronouns

Singular		Plural	
Masc.	**Fem.**	**Masc.**	**Fem.**
éste	ésta	éstos	éstas
ése	ésa	ésos	ésas
aquél	aquélla	aquéllos	aquéllas

❝Verde que _____ quiero verde.
Verde viento. Verdes ramas°.
El barco sobre la mar
y el caballo en la montaña, [...]
Verde que te quiero _____ (*green*).**❞**

ramas *branches*

Lectura

Antes de leer

Estrategia

Skimming

Skimming involves quickly reading through a document to absorb its general meaning. This allows you to understand the main ideas without having to read word for word. When you skim a text, you might want to look at its title and subtitles. You might also want to read the first sentence of each paragraph.

Examinar el texto

Look at the format of the reading selection. How is it organized? What does the organization of the document tell you about its content?

Buscar cognados

Scan the reading selection to locate at least five cognates. Based on the cognates, what do you think the reading selection is about?

1. _____   4. _____
2. _____   5. _____
3. _____

The reading selection is about _____.

Impresiones generales

Now skim the reading selection to understand its general meaning. Jot down your impressions. What new information did you learn about the document by skimming it? Based on all the information you now have, answer these questions in Spanish.

1. Who created this document?
2. What is its purpose?
3. Who is its intended audience?

Corona

http://corona.cl

¡Corona tiene las ofertas más locas del verano!

La tienda más elegante de la ciudad con precios increíbles

niños | **mujeres** | casa | baño | equipaje

Faldas largas
ROPA BONITA
Algodón. De distintos colores
Talla mediana
Precio especial: 8.000 pesos

Blusas de seda
BAMBÚ
De cuadros y de lunares
Ahora: 21.000 pesos
40% de rebaja

Vestido de algodón
PANAMÁ
Colores blanco, azul y verde
Ahora: 18.000 pesos
30% de rebaja

Accesorios
BELLEZA
Cinturones, gafas de sol, sombreros, medias
Diversos estilos
Todos con un 40% de rebaja

Carteras
ELEGANCIA
Colores anaranjado, blanco, rosado y amarillo
Ahora: 15.000 pesos
50% de rebaja

Sandalias de playa
GINO
Números del 35 al 38
A sólo 12.000 pesos
50% de descuento

Lunes a sábado de 9 a 21 horas.
Domingo de 10 a 14 horas.

Real° Liquidación °¡Grandes rebajas!

¡La rebaja está de moda en Corona!

y con la tarjeta de crédito más conveniente del mercado.

bebé | **hombres** | jardín | joyas | electrónica

**Chaquetas
CASINO**
Microfibra. Colores negro, café y gris
Tallas: P, M, G, XG
Ahora: 22.500 pesos

**Traje inglés
GALES**
Modelos originales
Ahora: 105.000 pesos
30% de rebaja

**Pantalones
OCÉANO**
Colores negro, gris y café
Ahora: 11.500 pesos
30% de rebaja

**Accesorios
GUAPO**
Gafas de sol, corbatas, cinturones, calcetines
Diversos estilos
Todos con un 40% de rebaja

**Zapatos
COLOR**
Italianos y franceses
Números del 40 al 45
A sólo 20.000 pesos

**Ropa interior
ATLÁNTICO**
Tallas: P, M, G
Colores blanco, negro y gris
40% de rebaja

Real *Royal* Liquidación *Clearance sale*

Por la compra de 40.000 pesos, puede llevar un regalo gratis.
- Un hermoso cinturón de mujer
- Un par de calcetines
- Una corbata de seda
- Una bolsa para la playa
- Una mochila
- Unas medias

Después de leer

Completar

Complete this paragraph about the reading selection with the correct forms of the words from the word bank.

almacén	hacer juego	tarjeta de crédito
caro	increíble	tienda
dinero	pantalones	verano
falda	rebaja	zapato

En este anuncio, el _____ Corona anuncia la liquidación de _____ con grandes _____. Con muy poco _____ usted puede conseguir ropa fina y elegante. Si no tiene dinero en efectivo, puede utilizar su _____ y pagar luego. Para el caballero con gustos refinados, hay _____ importados de París y Roma.
La señora elegante puede encontrar blusas de seda que _____ con todo tipo de _____ o _____. Los precios de esta liquidación son realmente _____.

¿Cierto o falso?

Indicate whether each statement is **cierto** or **falso**. Correct the false statements.

1. Hay sandalias de playa.
2. Las corbatas tienen una rebaja del 30%.
3. El almacén Corona tiene un departamento de zapatos.
4. Normalmente las sandalias cuestan 22.000 pesos.
5. Cuando gastas 30.000 pesos en la tienda, llevas un regalo gratis.
6. Tienen carteras amarillas.

Preguntas

Answer these questions.

1. Imagina que vas a ir a la tienda Corona. ¿Qué departamentos vas a visitar? ¿El departamento de ropa para señoras, el departamento de ropa para caballeros…?
2. ¿Qué vas a buscar en Corona?
3. ¿Hay tiendas similares a la tienda Corona en tu pueblo o ciudad? ¿Cómo se llaman? ¿Tienen muchas gangas?

Escritura

Estrategia

How to report an interview

There are several ways to prepare a written report about an interview. For example, you can transcribe the interview verbatim, you can simply summarize it, or you can summarize it but quote the speakers occasionally. In any event, the report should begin with an interesting title and a brief introduction, which may include the five Ws (*what, where, when, who, why*) and the H (*how*) of the interview. The report should end with an interesting conclusion. Note that when you transcribe dialogue in Spanish, you should pay careful attention to format and punctuation.

Writing dialogue in Spanish

- If you need to transcribe an interview verbatim, you can use speakers' names to indicate a change of speaker.

CARMELA	¿Qué compraste? ¿Encontraste muchas gangas?
ROBERTO	Sí, muchas. Compré un suéter, una camisa y dos corbatas. Y tú, ¿qué compraste?
CARMELA	Una blusa y una falda muy bonitas. ¿Cuánto costó tu camisa?
ROBERTO	Sólo diez dólares. ¿Cuánto costó tu blusa?
CARMELA	Veinte dólares.

- You can also use a dash (*raya*) to mark the beginning of each speaker's words.

  —¿Qué compraste?

  —Un suéter y una camisa muy bonitos. Y tú, ¿encontraste muchas gangas?

  —Sí... compré dos blusas, tres camisetas y un par de zapatos.

  —¡A ver!

Tema

Escribe un informe

Write a report for the school newspaper about an interview you conducted with a student about his or her shopping habits and clothing preferences. First, brainstorm a list of interview questions. Then conduct the interview using the questions below as a guide, but feel free to ask other questions as they occur to you.

Examples of questions:

▶ ¿Cuándo vas de compras?

▶ ¿Adónde vas de compras?

▶ ¿Con quién vas de compras?

▶ ¿Qué tiendas, almacenes o centros comerciales prefieres?

▶ ¿Compras ropa de catálogos o por Internet?

▶ ¿Prefieres comprar ropa cara o barata? ¿Por qué? ¿Te gusta buscar gangas?

▶ ¿Qué ropa llevas cuando vas a clase?

▶ ¿Qué ropa llevas cuando sales a bailar?

▶ ¿Qué ropa llevas cuando practicas un deporte?

▶ ¿Cuáles son tus colores favoritos? ¿Compras mucha ropa de esos colores?

▶ ¿Les das ropa a tu familia o a tus amigos/as?

Escuchar

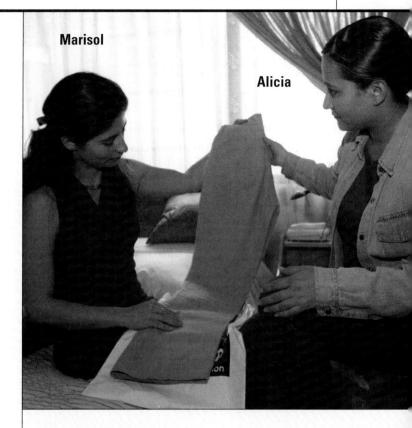

Marisol

Alicia

Estrategia

Listening for linguistic cues

You can enhance your listening comprehension by listening for specific linguistic cues. For example, if you listen for the endings of conjugated verbs, or for familiar constructions, such as **acabar de** + [*infinitive*] or **ir a** + [*infinitive*], you can find out whether an event already took place, is taking place now, or will take place in the future. Verb endings also give clues about who is participating in the action.

 To practice listening for linguistic cues, you will now listen to four sentences. As you listen, note whether each sentence refers to a past, present, or future action. Also jot down the subject of each sentence.

Preparación

Based on the photograph, what do you think Marisol has recently done? What do you think Marisol and Alicia are talking about? What else can you guess about their conversation from the visual clues in the photograph?

Ahora escucha

Now you are going to hear Marisol and Alicia's conversation. Make a list of the clothing items that each person mentions. Then put a check mark after the item if the person actually purchased it.

Marisol	Alicia
1. _____	1. _____
2. _____	2. _____
3. _____	3. _____
4. _____	4. _____

Comprensión

¿Cierto o falso?

Indicate whether each statement is **cierto** or **falso.** Then correct the false statements.

1. Marisol y Alicia acaban de ir de compras juntas (*together*).
2. Marisol va a comprar unos pantalones y una blusa mañana.
3. Marisol compró una blusa de cuadros.
4. Alicia compró unos zapatos nuevos hoy.
5. Alicia y Marisol van a ir al café.
6. Marisol gastó todo el dinero de la semana en ropa nueva.

Preguntas

Answer the following questions. Be sure to explain your answers.

1. ¿Crees que Alicia y Marisol son buenas amigas? ¿Por qué?
2. ¿Cuál de las dos estudiantes es más ahorradora (*frugal*)? ¿Por qué?
3. ¿Crees que a Alicia le gusta la ropa que Marisol compró?
4. ¿Crees que la moda es importante para Alicia? ¿Para Marisol? ¿Por qué?
5. ¿Es importante para ti estar a la moda? ¿Por qué?

En pantalla

Grocery stores in Mexico make one-stop shopping easy! Similar to the concept of a *Super-Walmart* in the U.S., most **supermercados°** in Mexico sell appliances, clothing, medicine, gardening supplies, electronics, and toys in addition to groceries. Large chains, like **Comercial Mexicana,** and smaller grocery stores alike typically sell a variety of products, allowing customers to satisfy all of their routine weekly shopping needs in one trip. Watch the **En pantalla** videoclip to see how one customer takes advantage of one-stop shopping at his local supermarket.

Vocabulario útil	
con lo que ahorré	*with what I saved*
corazón	*sweetheart*
de peluche	*stuffed (toy)*
dragón	*dragon*
¿Me lo compras?	*Would you buy it for me?*

Comprensión

Indicate whether each statement is **cierto** or **falso**.

	Cierto	Falso
1. El niño quiere un elefante de peluche.	○	○
2. La señora usa zapatos negros.	○	○
3. El niño sigue a la señora hasta la caja.	○	○
4. La señora no es la mamá del niño.	○	○

Conversar

With a partner, have a conversation in Spanish between two friends at a clothing store.

Estudiante 1: Would you buy me a(n)...?
Estudiante 2: No, because it costs...
Estudiante 1: Please! I always (**siempre**) buy you...
Estudiante 2: OK, I will buy you this... How much does it cost?
Estudiante 1: It's on sale! It only costs....

Anuncio de Comercial Mexicana

¿Me lo compras?

No, corazón.

¿Me lo compras, me lo compras, me lo compras?

In the Spanish-speaking world, most city dwellers shop at large supermarkets and little stores that specialize in just one item, such as a butcher shop (**carnicería**), vegetable market (**verdulería**), perfume shop (**perfumería**), or hat shop (**sombrerería**). In small towns where supermarkets are less common, many people rely exclusively on specialty shops. This requires shopping more frequently—often every day or every other day for perishable items—but also means that the foods they consume are fresher and the goods are usually locally produced. Each neighborhood generally has its own shops, so people don't have to walk far to find fresh bread (at a **panadería**) for the midday meal.

Comprar en los mercados

Trescientos colones.

Vocabulario útil

colones (pl.)	*currency from Costa Rica*
¿Cuánto vale?	*¿Cuánto cuesta?*
descuento	*discount*
disculpe	*excuse me*
¿Dónde queda...?	*Where is... located?*
los helados	*ice cream*
el regateo	*bargaining*

... pero me hace un buen descuento.

Preparación

Have you ever been to an open-air market? What did you buy? Have you ever negotiated a price? What did you say?

Comprensión

Select the option that best summarizes this episode.

a. Randy Cruz va al mercado al aire libre para comprar papayas. Luego va al Mercado Central. Él les pregunta a varios clientes qué compran, prueba (*tastes*) platos típicos y busca la heladería.

b. Randy Cruz va al mercado al aire libre para comprar papayas y pedir un descuento. Luego va al Mercado Central para preguntarles a los clientes qué compran en los mercados.

¿Qué compran en el Mercado Central?

Cuba

El país en cifras

▶ **Área:** 110.860 km² (42.803 millas²), *aproximadamente el área de Pensilvania*
▶ **Población:** 11.061.886
▶ **Capital:** La Habana—2.116.000

La Habana Vieja fue declarada° Patrimonio° Cultural de la Humanidad por la UNESCO en 1982. Este distrito es uno de los lugares más fascinantes de Cuba. En La Plaza de Armas, se puede visitar el majestuoso Palacio de Capitanes Generales, que ahora es un museo. En la calle° Obispo, frecuentada por el autor Ernest Hemingway, hay hermosos cafés, clubes nocturnos y tiendas elegantes.

▶ **Ciudades principales:** Santiago de Cuba; Camagüey; Holguín; Guantánamo
▶ **Moneda:** peso cubano
▶ **Idiomas:** español (oficial)

Bandera de Cuba

Cubanos célebres

▶ **Carlos Finlay,** doctor y científico (1833–1915)
▶ **José Martí,** político y poeta (1853–1895)
▶ **Fidel Castro,** ex primer ministro, ex comandante en jefe° de las fuerzas armadas (1926–2016)
▶ **Zoé Valdés,** escritora (1959–)
▶ **Ibrahim Ferrer,** músico (1927–2005)
▶ **Carlos Acosta,** bailarín (1973–)

fue declarada *was declared* Patrimonio *Heritage* calle *street*
comandante en jefe *commander in chief* liviano *light*
colibrí abeja *bee hummingbird* ave *bird* mundo *world*
miden *measure* pesan *weigh*

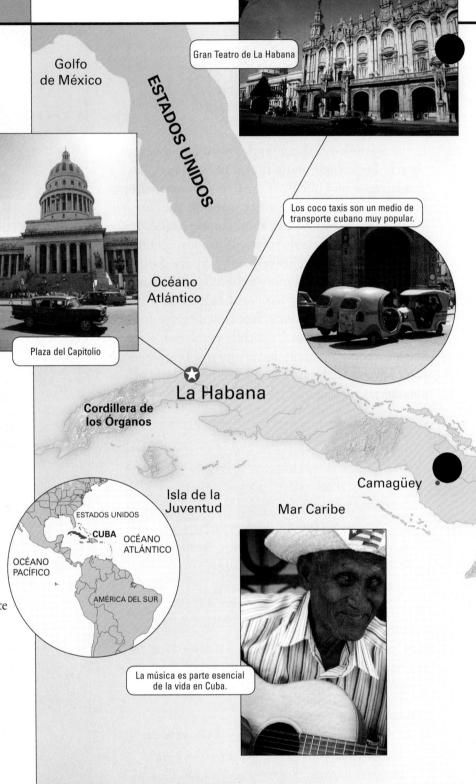

Gran Teatro de La Habana

Golfo de México

ESTADOS UNIDOS

Océano Atlántico

Los coco taxis son un medio de transporte cubano muy popular.

Plaza del Capitolio

La Habana

Cordillera de los Órganos

ESTADOS UNIDOS

CUBA

OCÉANO ATLÁNTICO

OCÉANO PACÍFICO

AMÉRICA DEL SUR

Isla de la Juventud

Mar Caribe

Camagüey

La música es parte esencial de la vida en Cuba.

¡Increíble pero cierto!

Pequeño y liviano°, el colibrí abeja° de Cuba es una de las más de 320 especies de colibrí y es también el ave° más pequeña del mundo°. Menores que muchos insectos, estas aves minúsculas miden° 5 centímetros y pesan° sólo 1,95 gramos.

Baile • Ballet Nacional de Cuba

La bailarina Alicia Alonso fundó el Ballet Nacional de Cuba en 1948, después de° convertirse en una estrella° internacional en el Ballet de Nueva York y en Broadway. El Ballet Nacional de Cuba es famoso en todo el mundo por su creatividad y perfección técnica.

Economía • La caña de azúcar y el tabaco

La caña de azúcar° es el producto agrícola° que más se cultiva en la isla y su exportación es muy importante para la economía del país. El tabaco, que se usa para fabricar los famosos puros° cubanos, es otro cultivo° de mucha importancia.

Gente • Población

La población cubana tiene raíces° muy heterogéneas. La inmigración a la isla fue determinante° desde la colonia hasta mediados° del siglo° XX. Los cubanos de hoy son descendientes de africanos, europeos, chinos y antillanos, entre otros.

Música • Buena Vista Social Club

En 1997 nace° el fenómeno musical conocido como *Buena Vista Social Club*. Este proyecto reúne° a un grupo de importantes músicos de Cuba, la mayoría ya mayores, con una larga trayectoria interpretando canciones clásicas del son° cubano. Ese mismo año ganaron un *Grammy*. Hoy en día estos músicos son conocidos en todo el mundo, y personas de todas las edades bailan al ritmo° de su música.

Holguín

Santiago de Cuba
Guantánamo

Sierra Maestra

¿Qué aprendiste? Responde a las preguntas con una oración completa.
1. ¿Qué autor está asociado con la Habana Vieja?
2. ¿Por qué es famoso el Ballet Nacional de Cuba?
3. ¿Cuáles son los dos cultivos más importantes para la economía cubana?
4. ¿Qué fabrican los cubanos con la planta del tabaco?
5. ¿De dónde son muchos de los inmigrantes que llegaron a Cuba?
6. ¿En qué año ganó un *Grammy* el disco *Buena Vista Social Club*?

Conexión Internet Investiga estos temas en Internet.
1. Busca información sobre un(a) cubano/a célebre. ¿Por qué es célebre? ¿Qué hace? ¿Todavía vive en Cuba?
2. Busca información sobre una de las ciudades principales de Cuba. ¿Qué atracciones hay en esta ciudad?

....

después de *after* estrella *star* caña de azúcar *sugar cane* agrícola *farming* puros *cigars* cultivo *crop* raíces *roots* determinante *deciding* mediados *halfway through* siglo *century* nace *is born* reúne *gets together* son *Cuban musical genre* ritmo *rhythm*

La ropa

el abrigo	coat
los (blue)jeans	jeans
la blusa	blouse
la bolsa	purse; bag
la bota	boot
los calcetines (el calcetín)	sock(s)
la camisa	shirt
la camiseta	t-shirt
la cartera	wallet
la chaqueta	jacket
el cinturón	belt
la corbata	tie
la falda	skirt
las gafas (de sol)	(sun)glasses
los guantes	gloves
el impermeable	raincoat
las medias	pantyhose; stockings
los pantalones	pants
los pantalones cortos	shorts
la ropa	clothes
la ropa interior	underwear
las sandalias	sandals
el sombrero	hat
el suéter	sweater
el traje	suit
el traje de baño	bathing suit
el vestido	dress
los zapatos de tenis	sneakers

Verbos

conducir	to drive
conocer	to know; to be acquainted with
dar	to give
ofrecer	to offer
parecer	to seem
saber	to know; to know how
traducir	to translate

Ir de compras

el almacén	department store
la caja	cash register
el centro comercial	shopping mall
el/la cliente/a	customer
el/la dependiente/a	clerk
el dinero	money
(en) efectivo	cash
el mercado (al aire libre)	(open-air) market
un par (de zapatos)	a pair (of shoes)
el precio (fijo)	(fixed; set) price
la rebaja	sale
el regalo	gift
la tarjeta de crédito	credit card
la tienda	store
el/la vendedor(a)	salesperson
costar (o:ue)	to cost
gastar	to spend (money)
hacer juego (con)	to match (with)
llevar	to wear; to take
pagar	to pay
regatear	to bargain
usar	to wear; to use
vender	to sell

Adjetivos

barato/a	cheap
bueno/a	good
cada	each
caro/a	expensive
corto/a	short (in length)
elegante	elegant
hermoso/a	beautiful
largo/a	long
loco/a	crazy
nuevo/a	new
otro/a	other; another
pobre	poor
rico/a	rich

Los colores

el color	color
amarillo/a	yellow
anaranjado/a	orange
azul	blue
blanco/a	white
gris	gray
marrón, café	brown
morado/a	purple
negro/a	black
rojo/a	red
rosado/a	pink
verde	green

Palabras adicionales

acabar de (+ inf.)	to have just done something
anoche	last night
anteayer	the day before yesterday
ayer	yesterday
de repente	suddenly
desde	from
dos veces	twice
hasta	until
pasado/a (adj.)	last; past
el año pasado	last year
la semana pasada	last week
prestar	to lend; to loan
una vez	once
ya	already

Indirect object pronouns	See page 202.
Demonstrative adjectives and pronouns	See page 210.
Expresiones útiles	See page 195.

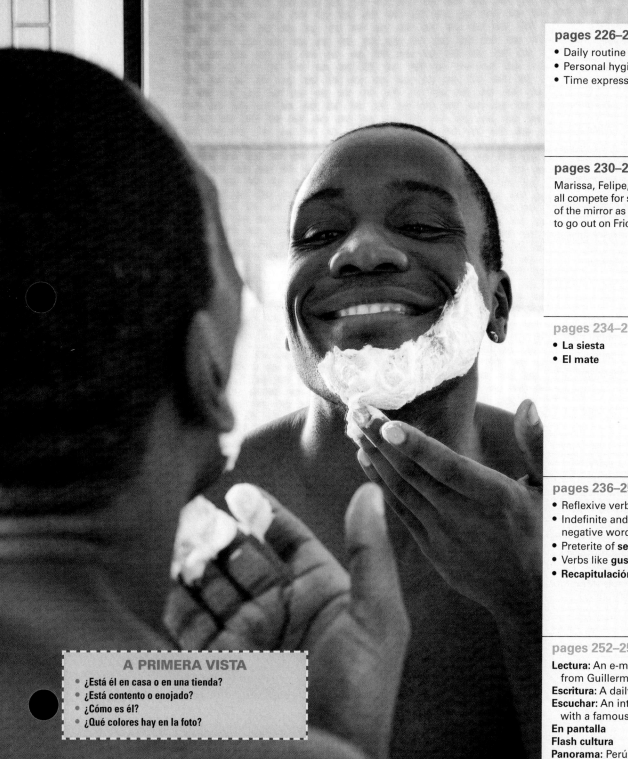

La rutina diaria

Communicative Goals

You will learn how to:
- **Describe your daily routine**
- **Talk about personal hygiene**
- **Reassure someone**

7

A PRIMERA VISTA
- **¿Está él en casa o en una tienda?**
- **¿Está contento o enojado?**
- **¿Cómo es él?**
- **¿Qué colores hay en la foto?**

La rutina diaria

En la habitación por la mañana

En el baño por la mañana

Se peina.
(peinarse)

Se acuesta.
(acostarse)

En la habitación por la noche

Se lava las manos.
(lavarse las manos)

Se cepilla los dientes.
(cepillarse los dientes)

la toalla

las pantuflas

la pasta de
dientes

En el baño por la noche

Práctica

1 **Escuchar** Escucha las oraciones e indica si cada oración es **cierta** o **falsa**, según el dibujo.

1. _____   6. _____
2. _____   7. _____
3. _____   8. _____
4. _____   9. _____
5. _____   10. _____

2 **Ordenar** Escucha la rutina diaria de Marta. Después ordena los verbos según lo que escuchaste.

____ a. almorzar   ____ e. desayunar
____ b. ducharse   ____ f. dormirse
____ c. peinarse   ____ g. despertarse
____ d. ver la televisión ____ h. estudiar en la biblioteca

3 **Seleccionar** Selecciona la palabra que no está relacionada con cada grupo.

1. lavabo • toalla • despertador • jabón _____
2. manos • antes de • después de • por último _____
3. acostarse • jabón • despertarse • dormirse _____
4. espejo • lavabo • despertador • entonces _____
5. dormirse • toalla • vestirse • levantarse _____
6. pelo • cara • manos • inodoro _____
7. espejo • champú • jabón • pasta de dientes _____
8. maquillarse • vestirse • peinarse • dientes _____
9. baño • dormirse • despertador • acostarse _____
10. ducharse • luego • bañarse • lavarse _____

4 **Identificar** Identifica las cosas que cada persona necesita. Sigue el modelo.

modelo
Jorge / lavarse la cara
Jorge necesita jabón y una toalla para lavarse la cara.

1. Mariana / maquillarse
2. Gerardo / despertarse
3. Celia / bañarse
4. Gabriel / ducharse
5. Roberto / afeitarse
6. Sonia / lavarse el pelo
7. Vanesa / lavarse las manos
8. Manuel / vestirse
9. Simón / acostarse
10. Daniela / cepillarse los dientes

5 **La rutina de Andrés** Ordena esta rutina de una manera lógica.

a. Se afeita después de cepillarse los dientes. _____

b. Se acuesta a las once y media de la noche. _____

c. Por último, se duerme. _____

d. Después de afeitarse, sale para las clases. _____

e. Asiste a todas sus clases y vuelve a su casa. _____

f. Andrés se despierta a las seis y media de la mañana. _____

g. Después de volver a casa, come un poco. Luego estudia en su habitación. _____

h. Se viste y entonces se cepilla los dientes. _____

i. Se cepilla los dientes antes de acostarse. _____

j. Se ducha antes de vestirse. _____

6 **La rutina diaria** Mira los dibujos y describe lo que hacen Ángel y Lupita.

1.

2.

3.

4.

5.

6.

7.

8.

Comunicación

7

La farmacia Lee el anuncio y luego indica si las conclusiones son **lógicas** o **ilógicas**.

LA FARMACIA NUEVO SOL tiene todo
lo que necesitas para la vida diaria.

Esta semana tenemos grandes rebajas.

Con poco dinero puedes comprar lo que necesitas para el cuarto de baño ideal.

Para los hombres ofrecemos…
Excelentes cremas de afeitar de Guapo y Máximo

Para las mujeres ofrecemos…
Nuevo maquillaje de Marisol y jabones de baño Ilusiones y Belleza

Y para todos tenemos los mejores jabones, pastas de dientes y cepillos de dientes.

¡Visita **LA FARMACIA NUEVO SOL!**
Tenemos los mejores precios. Visita nuestra tienda muy cerca de tu casa.

	Lógico	Ilógico
1. Pedro está en la farmacia porque necesita un producto para lavarse la cara.	○	○
2. Gabriela está en la farmacia porque quiere comprar un producto de Marisol.	○	○
3. Raúl está en la farmacia porque necesita un abrigo.	○	○
4. Luis Alberto está en la farmacia porque quiere comprar un producto de Máximo.	○	○
5. Mariana va a volver la semana que viene a la farmacia para comprar jabones, maquillaje y un cepillo de dientes.	○	○

8

Rutinas diarias Escribe una descripción de la rutina diaria de tres de estas personas. Usa palabras de la lista.

antes (de)	entonces	primero
después (de)	luego	tarde
durante el día	por último	temprano

- un(a) profesor(a) de la universidad
- un(a) turista
- un hombre o una mujer de negocios (*businessman/woman*)
- un vigilante nocturno (*night watchman*)
- un(a) jubilado/a (*retired person*)
- el presidente/primer ministro de tu país
- un niño de cuatro años
- Daniel Espinosa

¡Necesito arreglarme!

Es viernes por la tarde y Marissa, Jimena y Felipe se preparan para salir.

1

MARISSA ¿Hola? ¿Está ocupado?

JIMENA Sí. Me estoy lavando la cara.

MARISSA Necesito usar el baño.

MARISSA Tengo que terminar de arreglarme. Voy al cine esta noche.

JIMENA Yo también tengo que salir. ¿Te importa si me maquillo primero? Me voy a encontrar con mi amiga Elena en una hora.

JIMENA No te preocupes, Marissa. Llegaste primero. Entonces, te arreglas el pelo y después me maquillo.

FELIPE ¿Y yo? Tengo crema de afeitar en la cara. No me voy a ir. Estoy aquí y aquí me quedo.

JIMENA ¡Felipe! ¿Qué estás haciendo?

FELIPE Me estoy afeitando. ¿Hay algún problema?

JIMENA ¡Siempre haces lo mismo!

FELIPE Pues, yo no vi a nadie aquí.

JIMENA ¿Por qué no te afeitaste por la mañana?

FELIPE Porque cada vez que quiero usar el baño, una de ustedes está aquí. O bañándose o maquillándose.

MARISSA Tú ganas. ¿Adónde vas a ir esta noche, Felipe?

FELIPE Juan Carlos y yo vamos a ir a un café en el centro. Siempre hay música en vivo. (*Sale.*) Me siento guapísimo. Todavía me falta cambiarme la camisa.

FELIPE

MARISSA ¿Adónde vas esta noche?

JIMENA A la biblioteca.

MARISSA ¡Es viernes! ¡Nadie debe estudiar los viernes! Voy a ver una película de Pedro Almodóvar con unas amigas.

MARISSA ¿Por qué no vienen tú y Elena al cine con nosotras? Después, podemos ir a ese café y molestar a Felipe.

JIMENA No sé.

MARISSA ¿Cuándo fue la última vez que viste a Juan Carlos?

JIMENA Cuando fuimos a Mérida.

MARISSA A ti te gusta ese chico.

JIMENA No tengo idea de qué estás hablando. Si no te importa, nos vemos en el cine.

Expresiones útiles

Talking about getting ready

Necesito arreglarme.
I need to get ready.
Me estoy lavando la cara.
I'm washing my face.
¿Te importa si me maquillo primero?
Is it OK with you if I put on my makeup first?
Tú te arreglas el pelo y después yo me maquillo.
You fix your hair and then I'll put on my makeup.
Todavía me falta cambiarme la camisa.
I still have to change my shirt.

Reassuring someone

Tranquilo/a.
Relax.
No te preocupes.
Don't worry.

Talking about past actions

¿Cuándo fue la última vez que viste a Juan Carlos?
When was the last time you saw Juan Carlos?
Cuando fuimos a Mérida.
When we went to Mérida.

Talking about likes and dislikes

Me fascinan las películas de Almodóvar.
I love Almodóvar's movies.
Me encanta la música en vivo.
I love live music.
Me molesta compartir el baño.
It bothers me to share the bathroom.

Additional vocabulary

encontrarse con *to meet up with*
molestar *to bother*
nadie *no one*

¿Qué pasó?

1 **¿Cierto o falso?** Indica si lo que dicen estas oraciones es **cierto** o **falso**. Corrige las oraciones falsas.

1. Marissa va a ver una película de Pedro Almodóvar con unas amigas.

2. Jimena se va a encontrar con Elena en dos horas.

3. Felipe se siente muy feo después de afeitarse.

4. Jimena quiere maquillarse.

5. Marissa quiere ir al café para molestar a Juan Carlos.

2 **Identificar** Identifica quién puede decir estas oraciones. Puedes usar cada nombre más de una vez.

1. No puedo usar el baño porque siempre están aquí, o bañándose o maquillándose. _____
2. Quiero arreglarme el pelo porque voy al cine esta noche. _____
3. Hoy voy a ir a la biblioteca. _____
4. ¡Necesito arreglarme! _____
5. Te gusta Juan Carlos. _____
6. ¿Por qué quieres afeitarte cuando estamos en el baño? _____

MARISSA

FELIPE

JIMENA

3 **Ordenar** Ordena correctamente los planes que tiene Marissa.

_____ a. Voy al café.
_____ b. Me arreglo el pelo.
_____ c. Molesto a Felipe.
_____ d. Me encuentro con unas amigas.
_____ e. Entro al baño.
_____ f. Voy al cine.

4 **En el baño** Trabajen en parejas para representar los papeles de dos compañeros/as de cuarto que deben usar el baño al mismo tiempo para hacer su rutina diaria. Usen las instrucciones como guía.

Estudiante 1	Estudiante 2
Di (*Say*) que quieres arreglarte porque vas a ir al cine.	Di (*Say*) que necesitas arreglarte porque te vas a encontrar con tus amigos/as.
Pregunta si puedes secarte (*dry*) el pelo.	Responde que no porque necesitas lavarte la cara.
Di que puede lavarse la cara, pero que después necesitas secarte el pelo.	Di que puede secarse el pelo, pero que después necesitas peinarte.

Pronunciación 🎧

The consonant r

ropa	**rutina**	**rico**	**Ramón**

In Spanish, **r** has a strong trilled sound at the beginning of a word. No English words have a trill, but English speakers often produce a trill when they imitate the sound of a motor.

gustar	**durante**	**primero**	**crema**

In any other position, **r** has a weak sound similar to the English *tt* in *better* or the English *dd* in *ladder*. In contrast to English, the tongue touches the roof of the mouth behind the teeth.

pizarra	**corro**	**marrón**	**aburrido**

The letter combination **rr**, which only appears between vowels, always has a strong trilled sound.

caro	**carro**	**pero**	**perro**

Between vowels, the difference between the strong trilled **rr** and the weak **r** is very important, as a mispronunciation could lead to confusion between two different words.

Práctica Lee las palabras en voz alta, prestando (*paying*) atención a la pronunciación de la **r** y la **rr.**

1. Perú	4. madre	7. rubio	10. tarde
2. Rosa	5. comprar	8. reloj	11. cerrar
3. borrador	6. favor	9. Arequipa	12. despertador

Oraciones Lee las oraciones en voz alta, prestando atención a la pronunciación de la **r** y la **rr.**

1. Ramón Robles Ruiz es programador. Su esposa Rosaura es artista.
2. A Rosaura Robles le encanta regatear en el mercado.
3. Ramón nunca regatea… le aburre regatear.
4. Rosaura siempre compra cosas baratas.
5. Ramón no es rico, pero prefiere comprar cosas muy caras.
6. ¡El martes Ramón compró un carro nuevo!

Refranes Lee en voz alta los refranes, prestando atención a la **r** y a la **rr.**

Perro que ladra no muerde.[1]

No se ganó Zamora en una hora.[2]

1 A dog's bark is worse than its bite.
2 Rome wasn't built in a day.

La siesta

¿Sientes cansancio° después de comer? ¿Te cuesta° volver al trabajo° o a clase después del almuerzo? Estas sensaciones son normales. A muchas personas les gusta relajarse° después de almorzar. Este momento de descanso es **la siesta**. La siesta es popular en los países hispanos y viene de una antigua costumbre° del área del Mediterráneo. La palabra *siesta* viene del latín, es una forma corta de decir "sexta hora". La sexta hora del día es después del mediodía, el momento de más calor. Debido al° calor y al cansancio, los habitantes de España, Italia, Grecia y Portugal tienen la costumbre de dormir la siesta desde hace° más de° dos mil años. Los españoles y los portugueses llevaron la costumbre a los países americanos.

Aunque° hoy día esta costumbre está desapareciendo° en las grandes ciudades, la siesta todavía es importante en la cultura hispana. En pueblos pequeños, por ejemplo, muchas oficinas° y tiendas tienen la costumbre de cerrar por dos o tres horas después del mediodía. Los empleados van a su casa, almuerzan con sus familias, duermen la siesta o hacen actividades, como ir al gimnasio, y luego regresan al trabajo entre las 2:30 y las 4:30 de la tarde.

Los estudios científicos explican que una siesta corta después de almorzar ayuda° a trabajar más y mejor° durante la tarde. Pero ¡cuidado! Esta siesta debe durar° sólo entre veinte y cuarenta minutos. Si dormimos más, entramos en la fase de sueño profundo y es difícil despertarse.

Hoy, algunas empresas° de los EE.UU., Canadá, Japón, Inglaterra y Alemania tienen salas° especiales donde los empleados pueden dormir la siesta.

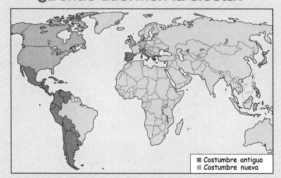

¿Dónde duermen la siesta?

■ Costumbre antigua
□ Costumbre nueva

En los lugares donde la siesta es una costumbre antigua, las personas la duermen en su casa. En los países donde la siesta es una costumbre nueva, la gente duerme en sus lugares de trabajo o en centros de siesta.

Sientes cansancio *Do you feel tired* Te cuesta *Is it hard for you* trabajo *work* relajarse *to relax* antigua costumbre *old custom* Debido al *Because (of)* desde hace *for* más de *more than* Aunque *Although* está desapareciendo *is disappearing* oficinas *offices* ayuda *helps* mejor *better* durar *last* algunas empresas *some businesses* salas *rooms*

1 **¿Cierto o falso?** Indica si lo que dicen las oraciones es **cierto** o **falso**. Corrige la información falsa.

1. La costumbre de la siesta empezó en Asia.
2. La palabra *siesta* está relacionada con la sexta hora del día.
3. Los españoles y los portugueses llevaron la costumbre de la siesta a Latinoamérica.
4. La siesta ayuda a trabajar más y mejor durante la tarde.
5. Los horarios de trabajo de las grandes ciudades hispanas son los mismos que los pueblos pequeños.
6. Una siesta larga siempre es mejor que una siesta corta.
7. En los Estados Unidos, los empleados de algunas empresas pueden dormir la siesta en el trabajo.
8. Es fácil despertar de un sueño profundo.

ASÍ SE DICE

El cuidado personal

el aseo; el excusado; el servicio; el váter (Esp.)	el baño
el cortaúñas	*nail clippers*
el desodorante	*deodorant*
el enjuague bucal	*mouthwash*
el hilo dental/ la seda dental	*dental floss*
la máquina de afeitar/ de rasurar (Méx.)	*electric razor*

EL MUNDO HISPANO

Costumbres especiales

- **México y El Salvador** Los vendedores pasan por las calles anunciando a gritos° su mercancía°: tanques de gas y flores° en México; pan y tortillas en El Salvador.

- **Costa Rica** Para encontrar las direcciones°, los costarricenses usan referencias a anécdotas, lugares o características geográficas. Por ejemplo: *200 metros norte de la iglesia Católica, frente al° supermercado Mi Mega.*

- **Argentina** En Tigre, una ciudad junto al Río° de la Plata, la gente usa barcos particulares°, barcos colectivos y barcos-taxi para ir de una isla a otra. Todas las mañanas, un barco colectivo recoge° a los niños y los lleva a la escuela.

gritos *shouts* mercancía *merchandise* flores *flowers* direcciones *addresses* frente al *opposite* Río *River* particulares *private* recoge *picks up*

PERFIL

El mate

El mate es una parte muy importante de la rutina diaria en muchos países. Es una bebida° muy similar al té que se consume en Argentina, Uruguay y Paraguay. Tradicionalmente se bebe caliente° con una *bombilla*° y en un recipiente° que también se llama *mate.* Por ser amarga°, algunos le agregan° azúcar para suavizar su sabor°. El mate se puede tomar a cualquier° hora y en cualquier lugar, aunque en Argentina las personas prefieren sentarse en círculo e ir pasando el mate de mano en mano mientras° conversan. Los uruguayos, por otra parte, acostumbran llevar el agua° caliente para el mate en un termo°

bajo el brazo° y lo beben mientras caminan. Si ves a una persona con un termo bajo el brazo y un mate en la mano, ¡es casi seguro que es de Uruguay!

bebida *drink* caliente *hot* bombilla *straw (in Argentina)* recipiente *container* amarga *bitter* agregan *add* suavizar su sabor *soften its flavor* cualquier *any* mientras *while* agua *water* termo *thermos* bajo el brazo *under their arm*

Conexión Internet

¿Qué costumbres son populares en los países hispanos?	Use the Web to find more cultural information related to this **Cultura** section.

ACTIVIDADES

2 **Comprensión** Completa las oraciones.

1. Uso _____ para limpiar (*to clean*) entre los dientes.
2. En _____ las personas compran pan y tortillas a los vendedores que pasan por la calle.
3. El _____ es una bebida similar al té.
4. Los uruguayos beben mate mientras _____.

3 **¿Qué costumbres tienes?** Escribe cuatro oraciones sobre una costumbre que compartes con tus amigos o con tu familia (por ejemplo: ir al cine, ir a eventos deportivos, leer, comer juntos, etc.). Explica qué haces, cuándo lo haces y con quién.

7.1

Reflexive verbs

ANTE TODO   A reflexive verb is used to indicate that the subject does something to or for himself or herself. In other words, it "reflects" the action of the verb back to the subject. Reflexive verbs always use reflexive pronouns.

SUBJECT	REFLEXIVE VERB
Joaquín	**se ducha** por la mañana.

The verb **lavarse** (*to wash oneself*)

SINGULAR FORMS			
	yo	**me lavo**	*I wash (myself)*
	tú	**te lavas**	*you wash (yourself)*
	Ud.	**se lava**	*you wash (yourself)*
	él/ella	**se lava**	*he/she washes (himself/herself)*

PLURAL FORMS			
	nosotros/as	**nos lavamos**	*we wash (ourselves)*
	vosotros/as	**os laváis**	*you wash (yourselves)*
	Uds.	**se lavan**	*you wash (yourselves)*
	ellos/ellas	**se lavan**	*they wash (themselves)*

▶ The pronoun **se** attached to an infinitive identifies the verb as reflexive: **lavarse.**

▶ When a reflexive verb is conjugated, the reflexive pronoun agrees with the subject.

Me afeito.   **Te despiertas** a las siete.

¿Te importa si me maquillo primero?

A las chicas les encanta maquillarse durante horas y horas.

▶ Like object pronouns, reflexive pronouns generally appear before a conjugated verb. With infinitives and present participles, they may be placed before the conjugated verb or attached to the infinitive or present participle.

Ellos **se** van a vestir.   **Nos** estamos lavando las manos.
Ellos van a vestir**se.**   Estamos lavándo**nos** las manos.
They are going to get dressed.   *We are washing our hands.*

▶ **¡Atención!** When a reflexive pronoun is attached to a present participle, an accent mark is added to maintain the original stress.

bañando ⟶ bañ**á**ndo**se**   durmiendo ⟶ durmi**é**ndo**se**

You have already learned several adjectives that can be used with **ponerse** when it means *to become*:

alegre, cómodo/a, contento/a, elegante, guapo/a, nervioso/a, rojo/a, and **triste**.

Common reflexive verbs

acordarse (de) (o:ue)	*to remember*	**llamarse**	*to be called; to be named*
acostarse (o:ue)	*to go to bed*		
afeitarse	*to shave*	**maquillarse**	*to put on makeup*
bañarse	*to take a bath*	**peinarse**	*to comb one's hair*
cepillarse	*to brush*	**ponerse**	*to put on*
despertarse (e:ie)	*to wake up*	**ponerse (+ adj.)**	*to become (+ adj.)*
dormirse (o:ue)	*to go to sleep; to fall asleep*	**preocuparse (por)**	*to worry (about)*
		probarse (o:ue)	*to try on*
ducharse	*to take a shower*	**quedarse**	*to stay*
enojarse (con)	*to get angry (with)*	**quitarse**	*to take off*
irse	*to go away; to leave*	**secarse**	*to dry (oneself)*
lavarse	*to wash (oneself)*	**sentarse** (e:ie)	*to sit down*
levantarse	*to get up*	**sentirse** (e:ie)	*to feel*
		vestirse (e:i)	*to get dressed*

COMPARE & CONTRAST

Unlike English, a number of verbs in Spanish can be reflexive or non-reflexive. If the verb acts upon the subject, the reflexive form is used. If the verb acts upon something other than the subject, the non-reflexive form is used. Compare these sentences.

Lola **lava** los platos.

Lola **se lava** la cara.

As the preceding sentences show, reflexive verbs sometimes have different meanings than their non-reflexive counterparts. For example, **lavar** means *to wash*, while **lavarse** means *to wash oneself, to wash up*.

▶ **¡Atención!** Parts of the body or clothing are generally not referred to with possessives, but with articles.

La niña se quitó **un** zapato.   Necesito cepillarme **los** dientes.

¡INTÉNTALO!   Indica el presente de estos verbos reflexivos.

despertarse	**ponerse**
1. Mis hermanos _se despiertan_ tarde.	1. Él _se pone_ una chaqueta.
2. Tú _____ tarde.	2. Yo _____ una chaqueta.
3. Nosotros _____ tarde.	3. Usted _____ una chaqueta.
4. Benito _____ tarde.	4. Nosotras _____ una chaqueta.
5. Yo _____ tarde.	5. Las niñas _____ una chaqueta.

Práctica

1

Nuestra rutina La familia de Blanca sigue la misma rutina todos los días. Según Blanca, ¿qué hacen ellos?

> **modelo**
>
> mamá / despertarse a las 5:00
>
> *Mamá se despierta a las cinco.*

1. Roberto y yo / levantarse a las 7:00
2. papá / ducharse primero y / luego afeitarse
3. yo / lavarse la cara y / vestirse antes de tomar café
4. mamá / peinarse y / luego maquillarse
5. todos (nosotros) / sentarse a la mesa para comer
6. Roberto / cepillarse los dientes después de comer
7. yo / ponerse el abrigo antes de salir
8. nosotros / irse

2

La fiesta elegante Selecciona el verbo apropiado y completa las oraciones con la forma correcta.

1. Tú _____ (lavar / lavarse) el auto antes de ir a la fiesta.
2. Nosotros _____ (bañar / bañarse) antes de ir a la fiesta.
3. Para llegar a tiempo, Raúl y Marta _____ (acostar / acostarse) a los niños antes de salir.
4. Cecilia _____ (maquillar / maquillarse) antes de salir.
5. Mis amigos siempre _____ (vestir / vestirse) con ropa muy elegante.
6. Julia y Ana _____ (poner / ponerse) los vestidos nuevos.
7. Usted _____ (ir / irse) a llegar antes que (*before*) los demás invitados, ¿no?
8. En general, _____ (afeitar / afeitarse) yo mismo, pero hoy es un día especial y el barbero (*barber*) me _____ (afeitar / afeitarse). ¡Será una fiesta inolvidable!

3

Describir Mira los dibujos y describe lo que estas personas hacen.

1. el joven

2. Carmen

3. Juan

4. los pasajeros

5. Estrella

6. Toni

Comunicación

4

¡Esto fue el colmo! Escucha lo que ocurrió ayer en la residencia estudiantil donde vive Julia. Luego, indica si las conclusiones son **lógicas** o **ilógicas**, según lo que escuchaste.

	Lógico	Ilógico
1. En la residencia estudiantil de Julia cada habitación tiene un cuarto de baño.	○	○
2. Las estudiantes siguen un horario para usar el cuarto de baño.	○	○
3. Normalmente, las estudiantes no se quedan mucho tiempo en el cuarto de baño.	○	○
4. A Julia le gusta tener prisa.	○	○
5. La chica nueva va a quedarse en el cuarto de baño por menos tiempo mañana.	○	○

5

Preguntas personales Contesta las preguntas de tu compañero/a.

1. ¿A qué hora te levantas durante la semana?
2. ¿A qué hora te levantas los fines de semana?
3. ¿Usas un despertador para levantarte?
4. ¿Te enojas frecuentemente con tus amigos?
5. ¿Te preocupas fácilmente? ¿Qué te preocupa?
6. ¿Qué haces cuando te sientes triste?
7. ¿Y cuando te sientes alegre?
8. ¿A qué hora te acuestas los fines de semana?

6

Debate ¿Quiénes necesitan más tiempo para arreglarse antes de salir: los hombres o las mujeres? En parejas, discutan este tema y defiendan sus ideas con ejemplos.

Síntesis

7

Mi rutina diaria Quieres contarle a un(a) amigo/a lo que haces durante la semana. Escríbele un mensaje electrónico en el que describas tu rutina diaria. Incluye las horas.

7.2 | Indefinite and negative words

ANTE TODO Indefinite words refer to people and things that are not specific, for example, *someone* or *something*. Negative words deny the existence of people and things or contradict statements, for instance, *no one* or *nothing*. Spanish indefinite words have corresponding negative words, which are opposite in meaning.

Indefinite and negative words

Indefinite words		Negative words	
algo	*something; anything*	**nada**	*nothing; not anything*
alguien	*someone; somebody; anyone*	**nadie**	*no one; nobody; not anyone*
alguno/a(s), algún	*some; any*	**ninguno/a, ningún**	*no; none; not any*
o... o	*either... or*	**ni... ni**	*neither... nor*
siempre	*always*	**nunca, jamás**	*never, not ever*
también	*also; too*	**tampoco**	*neither; not either*

▶ There are two ways to form negative sentences in Spanish. You can place the negative word before the verb, or you can place **no** before the verb and the negative word after.

Nadie se levanta temprano.
No one gets up early.

No se levanta nadie temprano.
No one gets up early.

Ellos **nunca gritan**.
They never shout.

Ellos **no gritan nunca**.
They never shout.

¿Hay algún problema?

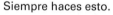
Siempre haces esto.

▶ Because they refer to people, **alguien** and **nadie** are often used with the personal **a**. The personal **a** is also used before **alguno/a, algunos/as,** and **ninguno/a** when these words refer to people and they are the direct object of the verb.

—Perdón, señor, ¿busca usted
a alguien?
—No, gracias, señorita, no busco
a nadie.

—Tomás, ¿buscas **a alguno** de
tus hermanos?
—No, mamá, no busco **a ninguno**.

▶ **¡Atención!** Before a masculine singular noun, **alguno** and **ninguno** are shortened to **algún** and **ningún**.

—¿Tienen ustedes **algún**
amigo peruano?

—No, no tenemos **ningún**
amigo peruano.

AYUDA

Alguno/a, algunos/as are not always used in the same way English uses *some* or *any*. Often, **algún** is used where *a* would be used in English.

¿Tienes algún libro que hable de los incas?
Do you have a book that talks about the Incas?

Note that **ninguno/a** is rarely used in the plural.

—**¿Visitaste algunos museos?**
—**No, no visité ninguno.**

COMPARE & CONTRAST

In English, it is incorrect to use more than one negative word in a sentence. In Spanish, however, sentences frequently contain two or more negative words. Compare these Spanish and English sentences.

Nunca le escribo a **nadie**.
I never write to anyone.

No me preocupo **nunca** por **nada**.
I do not ever worry about anything.

As the preceding sentences show, once an English sentence contains one negative word (for example, *not* or *never*), no other negative word may be used. Instead, indefinite (or affirmative) words are used. In Spanish, however, once a sentence is negative, no other affirmative (that is, indefinite) word may be used. Instead, all indefinite ideas must be expressed in the negative.

▶ **Pero** is used to mean *but*. The meaning of **sino** is *but rather* or *on the contrary*. It is used when the first part of the sentence is negative and the second part contradicts it.

Los estudiantes no se acuestan temprano **sino** tarde.
The students don't go to bed early, but rather late.

Esas gafas son caras, **pero** bonitas.
Those glasses are expensive, but pretty.

María no habla francés **sino** español.
María doesn't speak French, but rather Spanish.

José es inteligente, **pero** no saca buenas notas.
José is intelligent but doesn't get good grades.

¡INTÉNTALO! Cambia las oraciones para que sean negativas.

1. Siempre se viste bien.
   ___Nunca___ se viste bien.
   ___No___ se viste bien ___nunca___.

2. Alguien se ducha.
   _____ se ducha.
   _____ se ducha _____.

3. Ellas van también.
   Ellas _____ van.
   Ellas _____ van _____.

4. Alguien se pone nervioso.
   _____ se pone nervioso.
   _____ se pone nervioso _____.

5. Tú siempre te lavas las manos.
   Tú _____ te lavas las manos.
   Tú ___ te lavas las manos _____.

6. Voy a traer algo.
   _____ voy a traer _____.

7. Juan se afeita también.
   Juan _____ se afeita.
   Juan _____ se afeita _____.

8. Mis amigos viven en una residencia o en casa.
   Mis amigos _____ viven _____ en una residencia _____ en casa.

9. La profesora hace algo en su escritorio.
   La profesora _____ hace _____ en su escritorio.

10. Tú y yo vamos al mercado.
    _____ tú _____ yo vamos al mercado.

11. Tienen un espejo en su casa.
    _____ tienen _____ espejo en su casa.

12. Algunos niños se ponen los abrigos.
    _____ niño se pone el abrigo.

Práctica

1 **¿Pero o sino?** Forma oraciones sobre estas personas usando **pero** o **sino**.

> **modelo**
>
> muchos estudiantes viven en residencias estudiantiles / muchos de
> ellos quieren vivir fuera del (*off*) campus
> *Muchos estudiantes viven en residencias estudiantiles, pero muchos
> de ellos quieren vivir fuera del campus.*

1. Marcos nunca se despierta temprano / siempre llega puntual a clase
2. Lisa y Katarina no se acuestan temprano / muy tarde
3. Alfonso es inteligente / algunas veces es antipático
4. los directores de la residencia no son ecuatorianos / peruanos
5. no nos acordamos de comprar champú / compramos jabón
6. Emilia no es estudiante / profesora
7. no quiero levantarme / tengo que ir a clase
8. Miguel no se afeita por la mañana / por la noche

2 **Completar** Completa esta conversación. Usa expresiones negativas en tus respuestas.

AURELIO	Ana María, ¿encontraste algún regalo para Eliana?
ANA MARÍA	(1)_____
AURELIO	¿Viste a alguna amiga en el centro comercial?
ANA MARÍA	(2)_____
AURELIO	¿Me llamó alguien?
ANA MARÍA	(3)_____
AURELIO	¿Quieres ir al teatro o al cine esta noche?
ANA MARÍA	(4)_____
AURELIO	¿No quieres salir a comer?
ANA MARÍA	(5)_____
AURELIO	¿Hay algo interesante en la televisión esta noche?
ANA MARÍA	(6)_____
AURELIO	¿Tienes algún problema?
ANA MARÍA	(7)_____

Comunicación

3 **Entre amigos** Escucha la conversación entre Felipe y Mercedes. Luego, indica si las conclusiones son **lógicas** o **ilógicas**, según lo que escuchaste.

	Lógico	Ilógico
1. El novelista peruano está en la residencia estudiantil.	○	○
2. Mercedes ni conoce Perú ni sabe quién es el novelista.	○	○
3. El amigo peruano de Mercedes vive en Cuzco.	○	○
4. Felipe quiere viajar.	○	○
5. Mercedes va a ir al centro estudiantil.	○	○

4 **Entrevista** Contesta las preguntas de tu compañero/a. Usa oraciones completas y las expresiones **siempre**, **algunas veces** y **nunca**.

1. ¿Te levantas antes de la siete de la mañana?
2. ¿Te duchas por la mañana?
3. ¿Te secas el pelo después de ducharte?
4. ¿Ves la televisión antes de acostarte?
5. ¿Te cepillas los dientes después de comer?
6. ¿Te bañas por la noche?

5 **La universidad** En parejas, háganse preguntas sobre qué hay en su universidad: residencias bonitas, departamento de ingeniería, cines, librerías baratas, equipo de fútbol, playa, clases fáciles, museo, profesores/as estrictos/as. Sigan el modelo.

> **modelo**
>
> **Estudiante 1:** ¿Hay algunas residencias bonitas?
> **Estudiante 2:** Sí, hay una/algunas. Está(n) detrás del estadio.
> **Estudiante 1:** ¿Hay algún museo?
> **Estudiante 2:** No, no hay ninguno.

Síntesis

6 **Anuncio** Escribe un anuncio para un producto o una tienda. Usa expresiones indefinidas y negativas.

¿Buscas algún producto especial?

¡Siempre hay algo para todos en las tiendas García!

7.3 Preterite of **ser** and **ir**

ANTE TODO

In **Lección 6**, you learned how to form the preterite tense of regular -ar, -er, and -ir verbs. The following chart contains the preterite forms of **ser** (*to be*) and **ir** (*to go*). Since these forms are irregular, you will need to memorize them.

		Preterite of ser and ir	
		ser *(to be)*	**ir** *(to go)*
SINGULAR FORMS	yo	**fui**	**fui**
	tú	**fuiste**	**fuiste**
	Ud./él/ella	**fue**	**fue**
PLURAL FORMS	nosotros/as	**fuimos**	**fuimos**
	vosotros/as	**fuisteis**	**fuisteis**
	Uds./ellos/ellas	**fueron**	**fueron**

AYUDA

Note that, whereas regular -er and -ir verbs have accent marks in the **yo** and **Ud./él/ella** forms of the preterite, **ser** and **ir** do not.

▶ Since the preterite forms of **ser** and **ir** are identical, context clarifies which of the two verbs is being used.

Él **fue** a comprar champú y jabón.
He went to buy shampoo and soap.

¿Cómo **fue** la película anoche?
How was the movie last night?

¿Cuándo fue la última vez que viste a Juan Carlos?

Cuando fuimos a Mérida.

¡INTÉNTALO! Completa las oraciones usando el pretérito de **ser** e **ir**.

ir

1. Los viajeros _____fueron_____ a Perú.
2. Patricia _____ a Cuzco.
3. Tú _____ a Iquitos.
4. Gregorio y yo _____ a Lima.
5. Yo _____ a Trujillo.
6. Ustedes _____ a Arequipa.
7. Mi padre _____ a Lima.
8. Nosotras _____ a Cuzco.
9. Él _____ a Machu Picchu.
10. Usted _____ a Nazca.

ser

1. Usted _____fue_____ muy amable.
2. Yo _____ muy cordial.
3. Ellos _____ simpáticos.
4. Nosotros _____ muy tontos.
5. Ella _____ antipática.
6. Tú _____ muy generoso.
7. Ustedes _____ cordiales.
8. La gente _____ amable.
9. Tomás y yo _____ muy felices.
10. Los profesores _____ buenos.

Práctica y Comunicación

1

Completar Completa estas conversaciones con la forma correcta del pretérito de **ser** o **ir**. Indica el infinitivo de cada forma verbal.

Conversación 1

		ser	ir
RAÚL	¿Adónde (1)_____ ustedes de vacaciones?	○	○
PILAR	(2)_____ a Perú.	○	○
RAÚL	¿Cómo (3)_____ el viaje?	○	○
▶PILAR	¡(4)_____ estupendo! Machu Picchu y El Callao son increíbles.	○	○
RAÚL	¿(5)_____ caro el viaje?	○	○
PILAR	No, el precio (6)_____ muy bajo. Sólo costó tres mil dólares.	○	○

Conversación 2

		ser	ir
ISABEL	Tina y Vicente (7)_____ novios, ¿no?	○	○
LUCÍA	Sí, pero ahora no. Anoche Tina (8)_____ a comer con Gregorio	○	○
	y la semana pasada ellos (9)_____ al partido de fútbol.	○	○
ISABEL	¿Ah sí? Javier y yo (10)_____ al partido y no los vimos.	○	○

NOTA CULTURAL

La ciudad peruana de **El Callao**, fundada en 1537, fue por muchos años el puerto (*port*) más activo de la costa del Pacífico en Suramérica. En el siglo XVIII, se construyó (*was built*) una fortaleza allí para proteger (*protect*) la ciudad de los ataques de piratas y bucaneros.

2

Descripciones Forma oraciones con estos elementos. Usa el pretérito.

A	B	C	D
yo	(no) ir	a un restaurante	ayer
tú	(no) ser	en autobús	anoche
mi mejor amigo/a		estudiante	anteayer
nosotros		muy simpático/a	la semana pasada
mis amigos		a la playa	año pasado
ustedes		dependiente/a en una tienda	

3

Preguntas Contesta las preguntas de tu compañero/a.

1. ¿Cuándo fuiste al cine por última vez?
2. ¿Con quién fuiste?
3. ¿Fuiste en auto, en autobús o en metro?
4. En tu opinión, ¿fue una buena película o no? ¿Por qué?
5. ¿Adónde fuiste/fueron después?
6. ¿Fue buena idea ir al cine?

4

El viaje Acabas de regresar de viaje. Escríbeles un mensaje electrónico a tus padres contándoles detalles de tu viaje. Usa el pretérito de **ir** y **ser**.

modelo
El viaje fue maravilloso/horrible...

7.4 Verbs like **gustar**

 ANTE TODO In **Lección 2**, you learned how to express preferences with **gustar**. You will now learn more about the verb **gustar** and other similar verbs. Observe these examples.

Me gusta ese champú.

> ENGLISH EQUIVALENT
> *I like that shampoo.*
> LITERAL MEANING
> *That shampoo is pleasing to me.*

¿**Te gustaron** las clases?

> ENGLISH EQUIVALENT
> *Did you like the classes?*
> LITERAL MEANING
> *Were the classes pleasing to you?*

▶ As the examples show, constructions with **gustar** do not have a direct equivalent in English. The literal meaning of this construction is *to be pleasing to* (*someone*), and it requires the use of an indirect object pronoun.

INDIRECT OBJECT PRONOUN	VERB	SUBJECT		SUBJECT	VERB	DIRECT OBJECT
Me	**gusta**	ese champú.		I	like	that shampoo.

▶ In the diagram above, observe how in the Spanish sentence the object being liked **(ese champú)** is really the subject of the sentence. The person who likes the object, in turn, is an indirect object because it answers the question: *To whom is the shampoo pleasing?*

¿Te gusta Juan Carlos?

Me gustan los cafés que tienen música en vivo.

▶ Other verbs in Spanish are used in the same way as **gustar**. Here is a list of the most common ones.

Verbs like **gustar**

aburrir	to bore	**importar**	to be important to; to matter
encantar	to like very much; to love (inanimate objects)	**interesar**	to be interesting to; to interest
faltar	to lack; to need	**molestar**	to bother; to annoy
fascinar	to fascinate; to like very much	**quedar**	to be left over; to fit (clothing)

▶ The most commonly used verb forms of **gustar** and similar verbs are the third person (singular and plural). When the object or person being liked is singular, the singular form (**gusta**) is used. When two or more objects or persons are being liked, the plural form (**gustan**) is used. Observe the following diagram:

| me, te, le, nos, os, les | SINGULAR | encanta
interesó | ▶ | la película
el concierto |
| | PLURAL | importan
fascinaron | ▶ | las vacaciones
los museos de Lima |

▶ To express what someone likes or does not like to do, use an appropriate verb followed by an infinitive. The singular form is used even if there is more than one infinitive.

> **Nos molesta comer** a las nueve.
> *It bothers us to eat at nine o'clock.*

> **Les encanta bailar** y **cantar** en las fiestas.
> *They love to dance and sing at parties.*

▶ As you learned in **Lección 2**, the construction **a** + [*pronoun*] (**a mí, a ti, a usted, a él,** etc.) is used to clarify or to emphasize who is pleased, bored, etc. The construction **a** + [*noun*] can also be used before the indirect object pronoun to clarify or to emphasize who is pleased.

> **A los turistas** les gustó mucho Machu Picchu.
> *The tourists liked Machu Picchu a lot.*

> **A ti** te gusta cenar en casa, pero **a mí** me aburre.
> *You like eating dinner at home, but I get bored.*

▶ **¡Atención! Mí** (*me*) has an accent mark to distinguish it from the possessive adjective **mi** (*my*).

AYUDA

Note that the **a** must be repeated if there is more than one person.
A Armando y **a Carmen** les molesta levantarse temprano.

¡INTÉNTALO! Indica el pronombre de objeto indirecto y la forma del tiempo presente adecuados en cada oración.

fascinar

1. A él _le fascina_ viajar.
2. A mí _____ bailar.
3. A nosotras _____ cantar.
4. A ustedes _____ leer.
5. A ti _____ correr y patinar.
6. A ellos _____ los aviones.
7. A mis padres _____ caminar.
8. A usted _____ jugar al tenis.
9. A mi esposo y a mí _____ dormir.
10. A Alberto _____ dibujar y pintar.
11. A todos _____ opinar.
12. A Pili _____ los sombreros.

aburrir

1. A ellos _les aburren_ los deportes.
2. A ti _____ las películas.
3. A usted _____ los viajes.
4. A mí _____ las revistas.
5. A Jorge y a Luis _____ los perros.
6. A nosotros _____ las vacaciones.
7. A ustedes _____ el béisbol.
8. A Marcela _____ los libros.
9. A mis amigos _____ los museos.
10. A ella _____ el ciclismo.
11. A Omar _____ ir de compras.
12. A ti y a mí _____ el baile.

Práctica

1

Completar Completa las oraciones con todos los elementos necesarios.

1. _____ Adela _____ (encantar) la música de Tito "El Bambino".
2. A _____ me _____ (interesar) la música de otros países.
3. A mis amigos _____ (encantar) las canciones (*songs*) de Calle 13.
4. A Juan y _____ Rafael no les _____ (molestar) la música alta (*loud*).
5. _____ nosotros _____ (fascinar) los grupos de pop latino.
6. _____ señor Ruiz _____ (interesar) más la música clásica.
7. A _____ me _____ (aburrir) la música clásica.
8. ¿A _____ te _____ (faltar) dinero para el concierto de Carlos Santana?
9. No. Ya compré el boleto y _____ (quedar) cinco dólares.
10. ¿Cuánto dinero te _____ (quedar) a _____?

NOTA CULTURAL

Hoy día, la música latina es popular en los EE.UU. gracias a artistas como **Shakira**, de nacionalidad colombiana, y **Tito "El Bambino"**, puertorriqueño. Otros artistas, como **Carlos Santana** y **Gloria Estefan**, difundieron (*spread*) la música latina en los años 60, 70, 80 y 90.

2

Describir Mira los dibujos y describe lo que está pasando. Usa los verbos de la lista.

aburrir	faltar	molestar
encantar	interesar	quedar

1. a Ramón   2. a nosotros

3. a ti   4. a Sara

3

Gustos Forma oraciones con los elementos de las columnas.

> **modelo**
>
> A ti te interesan las ruinas de Machu Picchu.

A	B	C
yo	aburrir	despertarse temprano
tú	encantar	mirarse en el espejo
mi mejor amigo/a	faltar	la música rock
mis amigos y yo	fascinar	las pantuflas rosadas
Bart y Homero Simpson	interesar	la pasta de dientes con menta (*mint*)
Shakira	molestar	las ruinas de Machu Picchu
Antonio Banderas		los zapatos caros

Comunicación

4

Preferencias Escucha la conversación entre Beatriz, Eduardo y Anabel. Luego, indica si las conclusiones son **lógicas** o **ilógicas**, según lo que escuchaste.

	Lógico	Ilógico
1. En sus ratos libres, Eduardo toma el sol.	○	○
2. A Eduardo le encanta ir de excursión.	○	○
3. A una de las chicas le gusta ir de compras.	○	○
4. A Eduardo le gustan las películas.	○	○
5. A Beatriz, a Eduardo y a Anabel les interesan las mismas cosas.	○	○
6. Beatriz, Eduardo y Anabel van a ir al cine hoy.	○	○

5

Preguntas Contesta las preguntas de tu compañero/a.

1. ¿Te gusta levantarte temprano o tarde? ¿Por qué?
2. ¿Te gusta acostarte temprano o tarde?
3. ¿Te gusta dormir la siesta?
4. ¿Te encanta acampar o prefieres quedarte en un hotel cuando estás de vacaciones?
5. ¿Qué te gusta hacer en el verano?
6. ¿Qué te fascina de tu universidad? ¿Qué te molesta?
7. ¿Te interesan más las ciencias o las humanidades? ¿Por qué?
8. ¿Qué cosas te aburren?

6

Gustos Describe las cosas que les gustan o no les gustan a las personas de tu generación: ¿qué les interesa?, ¿qué les molesta?, ¿qué les aburre?, ¿qué les fascina?, ¿qué les falta?

Síntesis

7

Situación Trabajen en parejas para representar los papeles de un(a) cliente/a y un(a) dependiente/a en una tienda de ropa. Usen las instrucciones como guía.

Dependiente/a

Saluda al/a la cliente/a y pregúntale en qué le puedes servir.

Pregúntale si le interesan los estilos modernos y empieza a mostrarle la ropa.

Habla de los gustos del/de la cliente/a.

Da opiniones favorables al/a la cliente/a (las botas le quedan fantásticas...).

Cliente/a

Saluda al/a la dependiente/a y dile (*tell him/her*) qué quieres comprar y qué colores prefieres.

Explícale que los estilos modernos te interesan. Selecciona las cosas que te interesan.

Habla de la ropa (me queda(n) bien/mal, me encanta(n)...).

Decide cuáles son las cosas que te gustan y qué vas a comprar.

Recapitulación

Completa estas actividades para repasar los conceptos de gramática que aprendiste en esta lección.

1 **Completar** Completa la tabla con la forma correcta de los verbos. **24 pts.**

yo	tú	nosotros	ellas
me levanto			
	te afeitas		
		nos vestimos	
			se secan

2 **Hoy y ayer** Cambia los verbos del presente al pretérito. **10 pts.**

1. Vamos de compras hoy. _____ de compras hoy.
2. Por último, voy a poner el despertador. Por último, _____ a poner el despertador.
3. Lalo es el primero en levantarse. Lalo _____ el primero en levantarse.
4. ¿Vas a tu habitación? ¿ _____ a tu habitación?
5. ¿Ustedes son profesores. Ustedes _____ profesores.

3 **Reflexivos** Completa cada conversación con la forma correcta de los verbos reflexivos. **22 pts.**

TOMÁS Yo siempre (1) _____ (bañarse) antes de (2) _____ (acostarse). Esto me relaja porque no (3) _____ (dormirse) fácilmente. Y así puedo (4) _____ (levantarse) más tarde. Y tú, ¿cuándo (5) _____ (ducharse)?

LETI Pues por la mañana, para poder (6) _____ (despertarse).

DAVID ¿Cómo (7) _____ (sentirse) Pepa hoy?

MARÍA Todavía está enojada.

DAVID ¿De verdad? Ella nunca (8) _____ (enojarse) con nadie.

BETO ¿(Nosotros) (9) _____ (Irse) de esta tienda? Estoy cansado.

SARA Pero antes vamos a (10) _____ (probarse) estos sombreros. Si quieres, después (nosotros) (11) _____ (sentarse) un rato.

RESUMEN GRAMATICAL

7.1 Reflexive verbs *pp. 236–237*

lavarse	
me lavo	nos lavamos
te lavas	os laváis
se lava	se lavan

7.2 Indefinite and negative words *pp. 240–241*

Indefinite words	Negative words
algo	nada
alguien	nadie
alguno/a(s), algún	ninguno/a, ningún
o... o	ni... ni
siempre	nunca, jamás
también	tampoco

7.3 Preterite of ser and ir *p. 244*

► The preterite of **ser** and **ir** are identical. Context will determine the meaning.

ser and ir	
fui	fuimos
fuiste	fuisteis
fue	fueron

7.4 Verbs like gustar *pp. 246–247*

aburrir	importar
encantar	interesar
faltar	molestar
fascinar	quedar

me, te, le, nos, os, les

SINGULAR
encanta / interesó → la película / el concierto

PLURAL
importan / fascinaron → las vacaciones / los museos

► Use the construction **a** + [*noun/pronoun*] to clarify the person in question.

A mí me encanta ver películas, ¿y a ti?

4 **Conversaciones** Completa cada conversación de manera lógica con palabras de la lista. No tienes que usar todas las palabras. **18 pts.**

algo	nada	ningún	siempre
alguien	nadie	nunca	también
algún	ni... ni	o... o	tampoco

1. —¿Tienes _____ plan para esta noche?

   —No, prefiero quedarme en casa. Hoy no quiero ver a _____.

   —Yo _____ me quedo. Estoy muy cansado.

2. —¿Puedo entrar? ¿Hay _____ en el cuarto de baño?

   —Sí. ¡Un momento! Ahora mismo salgo.

3. —¿Puedes prestarme _____ para peinarme? No encuentro _____ mi cepillo _____ mi peine.

   —Lo siento, yo _____ encuentro los míos (*mine*).

4. —¿Me prestas tu maquillaje?

   —Lo siento, no tengo. _____ me maquillo.

5 **Oraciones** Forma oraciones completas con los elementos dados (*given*). Usa el presente de los verbos. **24 pts.**

1. David y Juan / molestar / levantarse temprano
2. Lucía / encantar / las películas de terror
3. todos (nosotros) / importar / la educación
4. tú / aburrir / ver / la televisión
5. yo / faltar / las pantuflas
6. ustedes / quedar / diez dólares
7. él / fascinar / regatear
8. tú y yo / interesar / los museos

6 **Adivinanza** Completa la adivinanza con las palabras que faltan y adivina la respuesta. **2 pts.**

"Cuanto más° _____ (*it dries you*), más se moja°.**"**

¿Qué es?_____

Cuanto más *The more* se moja *it gets wet*

Lectura

Antes de leer

Estrategia
Predicting content from the title

Prediction is an invaluable strategy in reading for comprehension. For example, we can usually predict the content of a newspaper article from its headline. We often decide whether to read the article based on its headline. Predicting content from the title will help you increase your reading comprehension in Spanish.

Examinar el texto

Lee el título de la lectura y haz tres predicciones sobre el contenido. Escribe tus predicciones en una hoja de papel.

Cognados

Haz una lista de seis cognados que encuentres en la lectura.

1. _____
2. _____
3. _____
4. _____
5. _____
6. _____

¿Qué te dicen los cognados sobre el tema de la lectura?

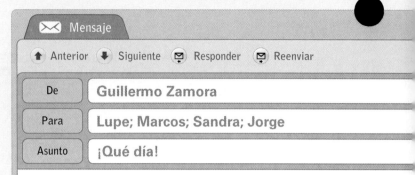

⬆ Anterior	⬇ Siguiente	✉ Responder	✉ Reenviar

De	Guillermo Zamora
Para	Lupe; Marcos; Sandra; Jorge
Asunto	¡Qué día!

Hola, chicos:

La semana pasada me di cuenta° de que necesito organizar mejor° mi rutina... pero especialmente debo prepararme mejor para los exámenes. Me falta disciplina, me molesta no tener control de mi tiempo y nunca deseo repetir los eventos de la semana pasada. ☹

El miércoles pasé todo el día y 😳 toda la noche estudiando para el examen de biología del jueves por la mañana. Me aburre la biología y no empecé a estudiar hasta el día antes del examen. El jueves a las 8, después de no dormir en toda la noche, fui exhausto al examen. Fue difícil, pero afortunadamente° me acordé de todo el material. Esa noche me acosté temprano y dormí mucho. 😴

Me desperté a las 7, y fue extraño° ver a mi compañero de cuarto, Andrés, preparándose para ir a dormir. Como° siempre se enferma°, tiene problemas para dormir y no hablamos mucho, no le comenté nada. Fui al baño a cepillarme los dientes para ir a clase. ¿Y Andrés? Él se acostó. "Debe estar enfermo°, ¡otra vez!", pensé. 😮

Marcar Imprimir Redactar Bandeja entrada

Enviar

Mi clase es a las 8, y fue necesario hacer las cosas rápido. Todo empezó a ir mal... eso pasa siempre cuando uno tiene prisa. Cuando busqué mis cosas para el baño, no las encontré. Entonces me duché sin jabón, me cepillé los dientes sin cepillo de dientes y me peiné con las manos. Tampoco encontré ropa limpia y usé la sucia. Rápido, tomé mis libros. ¿Y Andrés? Roncando°... ¡a las 7:50!

Cuando salí corriendo para la clase, la prisa no me permitió ver el campus desierto. Cuando llegué a la clase, no vi a nadie. No vi al profesor ni a los estudiantes. Por último miré mi reloj, y vi la hora. Las 8 en punto... ¡de la noche!

¡Dormí 24 horas!

Guillermo

me di cuenta *I realized* **mejor** *better* **afortunadamente** *fortunately* **extraño** *strange* **Como** *Since* **se enferma** *he gets sick* **enfermo** *sick* **Roncando** *Snoring*

Después de leer

Seleccionar
Selecciona la respuesta correcta.
1. ¿Quién es el/la narrador(a)?
   a. Andrés
   b. una profesora
   c. Guillermo
2. ¿Qué le molesta al narrador?
   a. Le molestan los exámenes de biología.
   b. Le molesta no tener control de su tiempo.
   c. Le molesta mucho organizar su rutina.
3. ¿Por qué está exhausto?
   a. Porque fue a una fiesta la noche anterior.
   b. Porque no le gusta la biología.
   c. Porque pasó la noche anterior estudiando.
4. ¿Por qué no hay nadie en clase?
   a. Porque es de noche.
   b. Porque todos están de vacaciones.
   c. Porque el profesor canceló la clase.
5. ¿Cómo es la relación de Guillermo y Andrés?
   a. Son buenos amigos.
   b. No hablan mucho.
   c. Tienen una buena relación.

Ordenar
Ordena los sucesos de la narración. Utiliza los números del 1 al 9.
   a. Toma el examen de biología. ____
   b. No encuentra sus cosas para el baño. ____
   c. Andrés se duerme. ____
   d. Pasa todo el día y toda la noche estudiando para un examen. ____
   e. Se ducha sin jabón. ____
   f. Se acuesta temprano. ____
   g. Vuelve a su cuarto después de las 8 de la noche. ____
   h. Se despierta a las 7 y su compañero de cuarto se prepara para dormir. ____
   i. Va a clase y no hay nadie. ____

Contestar
Contesta estas preguntas.
1. ¿Cómo es tu rutina diaria? ¿Muy organizada?
2. ¿Cuándo empiezas a estudiar para los exámenes?
3. Para comunicarte con tus amigos/as, ¿prefieres el teléfono o el correo electrónico? ¿Por qué?

Escritura

Estrategia
Sequencing events

Paying strict attention to sequencing in a narrative will ensure that your writing flows logically from one part to the next.

Every composition should have an introduction, a body, and a conclusion. The introduction presents the subject, the setting, the situation, and the people involved. The main part, or the body, describes the events and people's reactions to these events. The conclusion brings the narrative to a close.

Adverbs and adverbial phrases are sometimes used as transitions between the introduction, the body, and the conclusion. Here is a list of commonly used adverbs in Spanish:

Adverbios	
además; también	in addition; also
al principio; en un principio	at first
antes (de)	before
después	then
después (de)	after
entonces; luego	then
más tarde	later (on)
primero	first
pronto	soon
por fin; finalmente	finally
al final	finally

Tema
Escribe tu rutina

Imagina tu rutina diaria en uno de estos lugares:

- una isla desierta
- el Polo Norte
- un crucero° transatlántico
- un desierto

Escribe una composición en la que describes tu rutina diaria en uno de estos lugares o en algún otro lugar interesante que imagines°. Mientras planeas tu composición, considera cómo cambian algunos de los elementos más básicos de tu rutina diaria en el lugar que escogiste°. Por ejemplo, ¿dónde te acuestas en el Polo Norte? ¿Cómo te duchas en el desierto?

Usa el presente de los verbos reflexivos que conoces e incluye algunos de los adverbios de esta página para organizar la secuencia de tus actividades. Piensa también en la información que debes incluir en cada sección de la narración. Por ejemplo, en la introducción puedes hacer una descripción del lugar y de las personas que están allí, y en la conclusión puedes dar tus opiniones acerca del° lugar y de tu vida diaria allí.

crucero *cruise ship* que imagines *that you dream up* escogiste *you chose*
acerca del *about the*

Escuchar

Estrategia

Using background information

Once you discern the topic of a conversation, take a minute to think about what you already know about the subject. Using this background information will help you guess the meaning of unknown words or linguistic structures.

 To help you practice this strategy, you will now listen to a short paragraph. Jot down the subject of the paragraph, and then use your knowledge of the subject to listen for and write down the paragraph's main points.

Preparación

Según la foto, ¿dónde están Carolina y Julián? Piensa en lo que sabes de este tipo de situación. ¿De qué van a hablar?

Ahora escucha

Ahora escucha la entrevista entre Carolina y Julián, teniendo en cuenta (*taking into account*) lo que sabes sobre este tipo de situación. Elige la información que completa correctamente cada oración.

1. Julián es ____.
   a. político
   b. deportista profesional
   c. artista de cine
2. El público de Julián quiere saber de ____.
   a. sus películas
   b. su vida
   c. su novia
3. Julián habla de ____.
   a. sus viajes y sus rutinas
   b. sus parientes y amigos
   c. sus comidas favoritas
4. Julián ____.
   a. se levanta y se acuesta a diferentes horas todos los días
   b. tiene una rutina diaria
   c. no quiere hablar de su vida

Comprensión

¿Cierto o falso?

Indica si las oraciones son **ciertas** o **falsas** según la información que Julián da en la entrevista.

1. Es difícil despertarme; generalmente duermo hasta las diez.
2. Pienso que mi vida no es más interesante que las vidas de ustedes.
3. Me gusta tener tiempo para pensar y meditar.
4. Nunca hago mucho ejercicio; no soy una persona activa.
5. Me fascinan las actividades tranquilas, como escribir y escuchar música clásica.
6. Los viajes me parecen aburridos.

Preguntas?

1. ¿Qué tiene Julián en común con otras personas de su misma profesión?
2. ¿Te parece que Julián siempre fue rico? ¿Por qué?
3. ¿Qué piensas de Julián como persona?

En pantalla

La fiesta de quince años se celebra en algunos países de Latinoamérica cuando las chicas cumplen° quince años. Los quince años representan la transición de niña a mujer. Los orígenes de esta ceremonia son mayas y aztecas, pero también tiene influencias del catolicismo. La celebración varía según el país, pero es común en todas la importancia del vestido de la quinceañera°, la elaboración de las invitaciones, el baile de la quinceañera con su padre y con otros familiares° y, por último, el banquete para los invitados°.

Vocabulario útil

cubren	*cover*
granos	*zits, pimples*
hice	*I did*
peor	*worse*
tapar	*to cover*
tenía	*I had*

Escoger

Escoge la opción correcta para cada oración.
1. La chica se levantó ___ el día de las fotos.
   a. con granos   b. muy tarde
2. Después de levantarse, la chica ___.
   a. se bañó   b. se maquilló
3. Para las fotos, la chica tapó los granos con ___.
   a. la flora y la fauna   b. maquillaje Asepxia
4. Ahora la chica ___.
   a. tiene muchos granos   b. usa maquillaje Asepxia

Una fiesta

Describe la última fiesta a la que fuiste. Puedes usar estas preguntas como guía.
▶ ¿Qué te gustó más? ¿Te aburrió algo?
▶ ¿Cuántas personas fueron?
▶ ¿Cómo te preparaste para la fiesta? ¿Te duchaste antes de ir a la fiesta? ¿Te maquillaste? ¿Te afeitaste?

Anuncio de Asepxia

Me levanté con una invasión de granos.

Tuve que° taparlos con lo que pude°...

Ahora Florencia usa maquillajes Asepxia.

cumplen *turn* quinceañera *young woman celebrating her fifteenth birthday*
familiares *family members* invitados *guests* Tuve que *I had to* lo que pude
what I could

En este episodio de *Flash cultura* vas a conocer unos entremeses° españoles llamados **tapas**. Hay varias teorías sobre el origen de su nombre. Una dice que viene de la costumbre antigua° de **tapar**° los vasos de vino para evitar° que insectos o polvo entren en° ellos. Otra teoría cuenta que el rey Alfonso X debía° beber un poco de vino por indicación médica y decidió acompañarlo° con algunos bocados° para tapar los efectos del alcohol. Cuando estuvo° mejor, ordenó que siempre en Castilla se sirviera° algo de comer con las bebidas° alcohólicas.

Vocabulario útil

económicas	*inexpensive*
montaditos	*bread slices with assorted toppings*
pagar propinas	*to tip*
tapar el hambre	*to take the edge off (lit. putting the lid on one's hunger)*

Preparación

En el área donde vives, ¿qué hacen las personas normalmente después del trabajo (*work*)? ¿Van a sus casas? ¿Salen con amigos? ¿Comen?

Ordenar

Ordena estos sucesos de manera lógica.

_____ a. El empleado cuenta los palillos (*counts the toothpicks*) de los montaditos que Mari Carmen comió.

_____ b. Mari Carmen va al barrio de la Ribera.

_____ c. Un hombre en un bar explica cuándo sale a tomar tapas.

_____ d. Un hombre explica la tradición de los montaditos o pinchos.

_____ e. Carmen le pregunta a la chica si los montaditos son buenos para la salud.

Tapas para todos los días

1

Estamos en la Plaza Cataluña, el puro centro de Barcelona.

2

—¿Cuándo sueles° venir a tomar tapas?
—Generalmente después del trabajo.

3

Éstos son los montaditos, o también llamados pinchos. ¿Te gustan?

entremeses *appetizers* antigua *ancient* tapar *cover* evitar *avoid* entren en *would get in* debía *should* acompañarlo *accompany it* bocados *snacks* estuvo *he was* se sirviera *they should serve* bebidas *drinks* sueles *do you tend*

Perú

El país en cifras

▶ **Área:** 1.285.220 km² (496.224 millas²),
un poco menos que el área de Alaska
▶ **Población:** 30.147.000
▶ **Capital:** Lima —8.769.000
▶ **Ciudades principales:** Arequipa —778.000,
Trujillo, Chiclayo, Callao, Iquitos
*Iquitos es un puerto muy importante en el río
Amazonas. Desde Iquitos se envían° muchos
productos a otros lugares, incluyendo goma°,
nueces°, madera°, arroz°, café y tabaco. Iquitos
es también un destino popular para
los ecoturistas que visitan la selva°.*
▶ **Moneda:** nuevo sol
▶ **Idiomas:** español (oficial);
quechua, aimara y otras
lenguas indígenas (oficiales
en los territorios donde se usan)

Bandera de Perú

Peruanos célebres

▶ **Clorinda Matto de Turner,** escritora (1854–1909)
▶ **César Vallejo,** poeta (1892–1938)
▶ **Javier Pérez de Cuéllar,** diplomático (1920–)
▶ **Juan Diego Flórez,** cantante de ópera (1973–)
▶ **Mario Vargas Llosa,** escritor (1936–)

Mario Vargas Llosa, Premio
Nobel de Literatura 2010

se envían *are shipped* goma *rubber* nueces *nuts* madera *timber*
arroz *rice* selva *jungle* Hace más de *More than... ago*
grabó *engraved* tamaño *size*

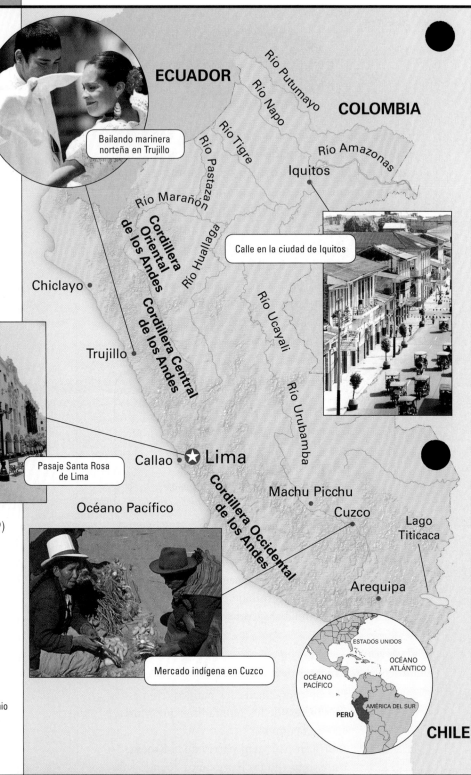

Bailando marinera norteña en Trujillo

ECUADOR

Río Putumayo

Río Napo

COLOMBIA

Río Tigre

Río Pastazan

Río Amazonas

Iquitos

Río Marañón

Cordillera Oriental de los Andes

Río Huallaga

Calle en la ciudad de Iquitos

Chiclayo

Cordillera Central de los Andes

Río Ucayali

Trujillo

Río Urubamba

Callao ⭐ Lima

Pasaje Santa Rosa de Lima

Océano Pacífico

Cordillera Occidental de los Andes

Machu Picchu

Cuzco

Lago Titicaca

Arequipa

Mercado indígena en Cuzco

ESTADOS UNIDOS

OCÉANO ATLÁNTICO

OCÉANO PACÍFICO

AMÉRICA DEL SUR

PERÚ

CHILE

¡Increíble pero cierto!

Hace más de° dos mil años la civilización nazca
de Perú grabó° más de dos mil kilómetros
de líneas en el desierto. Los dibujos sólo son
descifrables desde el aire. Uno de ellos es un
cóndor del tamaño° de un estadio. Las Líneas
de Nazca son uno de los grandes misterios de
la humanidad.

Lugares • Lima

Lima es una ciudad moderna y antigua° a la vez°. La Iglesia de San Francisco es notable por su arquitectura barroca colonial. También son fascinantes las exhibiciones sobre los incas en el Museo Oro del Perú y en el Museo Nacional de Antropología y Arqueología. Barranco, el barrio° bohemio de la ciudad, es famoso por su ambiente cultural y sus bares y restaurantes.

BRASIL

Historia • Machu Picchu

A 80 kilómetros al noroeste de Cuzco está Machu Picchu, una ciudad antigua del Imperio inca. Está a una altitud de 2.350 metros (7.710 pies), entre dos cimas° de los Andes. Cuando los españoles llegaron a Perú y recorrieron la región, nunca encontraron Machu Picchu. En 1911, el arqueólogo estadounidense Hiram Bingham la redescubrió. Todavía no se sabe ni cómo se construyó° una ciudad a esa altura, ni por qué los incas la abandonaron. Sin embargo°, esta ciudad situada en desniveles° naturales es el ejemplo más conocido de la arquitectura inca.

Artes • La música andina

Machu Picchu aún no existía° cuando se originó la música cautivadora° de las culturas indígenas de los Andes. Los ritmos actuales de la música andina tienen influencias españolas y africanas. Varios tipos de flauta°, entre ellos la quena y la zampoña, caracterizan esta música. En las décadas de los sesenta y los setenta se popularizó un movimiento para preservar la música andina, y hasta° Simon y Garfunkel incorporaron a su repertorio la canción *El cóndor pasa.*

Economía • Llamas y alpacas

Perú se conoce por sus llamas, alpacas, guanacos y vicuñas, todos ellos animales mamíferos° parientes del camello. Estos animales todavía tienen una enorme importancia en la economía del país. Dan lana para exportar a otros países y para hacer ropa, mantas°, bolsas y otros artículos artesanales. La llama se usa también para la carga y el transporte.

BOLIVIA

¿Qué aprendiste? Contesta las preguntas con una oración completa.
1. ¿Qué productos envía Iquitos a otros lugares?
2. ¿Cuáles son las lenguas oficiales de Perú?
3. ¿Por qué es notable la Iglesia de San Francisco en Lima?
4. ¿Qué información sobre Machu Picchu no se sabe todavía?
5. ¿Qué son la quena y la zampoña?
6. ¿Qué hacen los peruanos con la lana de sus llamas y alpacas?

Conexión Internet Investiga estos temas en Internet.

1. Investiga la cultura incaica. ¿Cuáles son algunos de los aspectos interesantes de su cultura?
2. Busca información sobre dos artistas, escritores o músicos peruanos.

antigua *old* a la vez *at the same time* barrio *neighborhood* cimas *summits* se construyó *was built* Sin embargo *However*
desniveles *uneven pieces of land* aún no existía *didn't exist yet* cautivadora *captivating* flauta *flute* hasta *even*
mamíferos *mammalian* mantas *blankets*

Los verbos reflexivos

acordarse (de) (o:ue)	to remember
acostarse (o:ue)	to go to bed
afeitarse	to shave
bañarse	to take a bath
cepillarse el pelo	to brush one's hair
cepillarse los dientes	to brush one's teeth
despertarse (e:ie)	to wake up
dormirse (o:ue)	to go to sleep; to fall asleep
ducharse	to take a shower
enojarse (con)	to get angry (with)
irse	to go away; to leave
lavarse la cara	to wash one's face
lavarse las manos	to wash one's hands
levantarse	to get up
llamarse	to be called; to be named
maquillarse	to put on makeup
peinarse	to comb one's hair
ponerse	to put on
ponerse (+ *adj.*)	to become (+ adj.)
preocuparse (por)	to worry (about)
probarse (o:ue)	to try on
quedarse	to stay
quitarse	to take off
secarse	to dry (oneself)
sentarse (e:ie)	to sit down
sentirse (e:ie)	to feel
vestirse (e:i)	to get dressed

Palabras de secuencia

antes (de)	before
después	afterwards; then
después (de)	after
durante	during
entonces	then
luego	then
más tarde	later (on)
por último	finally

Palabras indefinidas y negativas

algo	something; anything
alguien	someone; somebody; anyone
alguno/a(s), algún	some; any
jamás	never; not ever
nada	nothing; not anything
nadie	no one; nobody; not anyone
ni… ni	neither… nor
ninguno/a, ningún	no; none; not any
nunca	never; not ever
o… o	either… or
siempre	always
también	also; too
tampoco	neither; not either

En el baño

el baño, el cuarto de baño	bathroom
el champú	shampoo
la crema de afeitar	shaving cream
la ducha	shower
el espejo	mirror
el inodoro	toilet
el jabón	soap
el lavabo	sink
el maquillaje	makeup
la pasta de dientes	toothpaste
la toalla	towel

Verbos similares a *gustar*

aburrir	to bore
encantar	to like very much; to love (inanimate objects)
faltar	to lack; to need
fascinar	to fascinate; to like very much
importar	to be important to; to matter
interesar	to be interesting to; to interest
molestar	to bother; to annoy
quedar	to be left over; to fit (clothing)

Palabras adicionales

el despertador	alarm clock
las pantuflas	slippers
la rutina diaria	daily routine
por la mañana	in the morning
por la noche	at night
por la tarde	in the afternoon; in the evening

Expresiones útiles	See page 231.

La comida

Communicative Goals

You will learn how to:
- **Order food in a restaurant**
- **Talk about and describe food**

contextos | fotonovela | cultura | estructura | adelante

A PRIMERA VISTA
- ¿Dónde está ella?
- ¿Qué hace?
- ¿Es parte de su rutina diaria?
- ¿Qué colores hay en la foto?

La comida

Más vocabulario

el/la camarero/a	*waiter/waitress*
la comida	*food; meal*
la cuenta	*bill*
el/la dueño/a	*owner*
los entremeses	*appetizers*
el menú	*menu*
el plato (principal)	*(main) dish*
la propina	*tip*
la sección de (no) fumar	*(non) smoking section*
el agua (mineral)	*(mineral) water*
la bebida	*drink*
la cerveza	*beer*
la leche	*milk*
el refresco	*soft drink*
el ajo	*garlic*
las arvejas	*peas*
los cereales	*cereal; grains*
los frijoles	*beans*
el melocotón	*peach*
el pollo (asado)	*(roast) chicken*
el queso	*cheese*
el sándwich	*sandwich*
el yogur	*yogurt*
el aceite	*oil*
la margarina	*margarine*
la mayonesa	*mayonnaise*
el vinagre	*vinegar*
delicioso/a	*delicious*
sabroso/a	*tasty; delicious*
saber (a)	*to taste (like)*

Variación léxica

camarones ⟷ gambas (*Esp.*)

camarero ⟷ mesero (*Amér. L.*), mesonero (*Ven.*), mozo (*Arg., Chile, Urug., Perú*)

refresco ⟷ gaseosa (*Amér. C., Amér. S.*)

Práctica

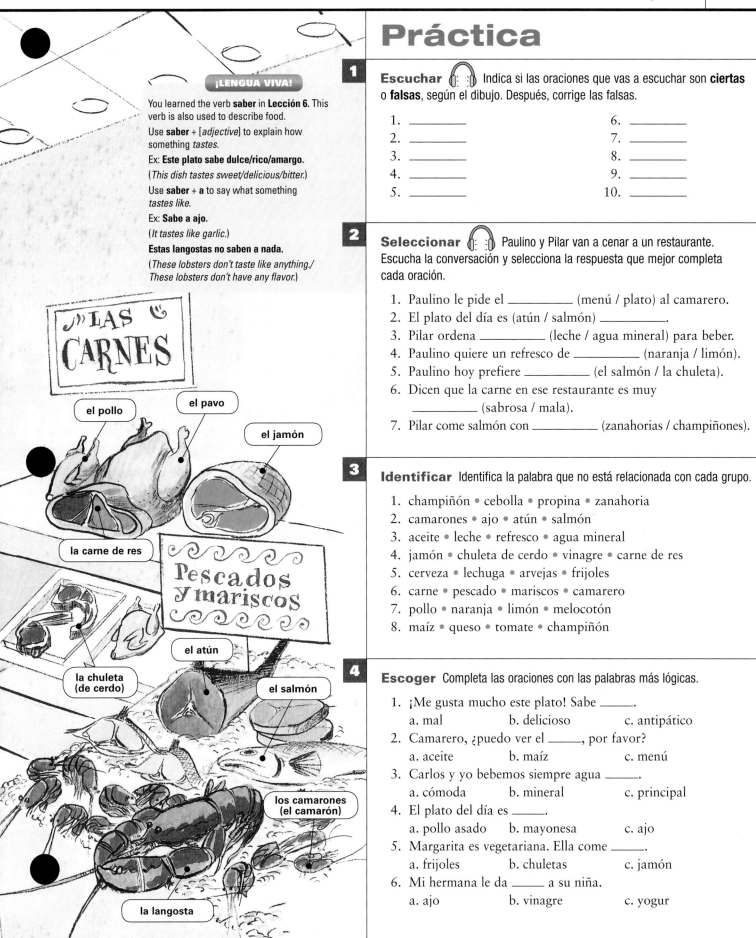

¡LENGUA VIVA!

You learned the verb **saber** in **Lección 6**. This verb is also used to describe food.

Use **saber** + [*adjective*] to explain how something *tastes*.

Ex: **Este plato sabe dulce/rico/amargo.**

(*This dish tastes sweet/delicious/bitter.*)

Use **saber** + **a** to say what something *tastes like*.

Ex: **Sabe a ajo.**

(*It tastes like garlic.*)

Estas langostas no saben a nada.

(*These lobsters don't taste like anything./ These lobsters don't have any flavor.*)

LAS CARNES

el pollo
el pavo
el jamón
la carne de res

Pescados y mariscos

la chuleta (de cerdo)
el atún
el salmón
los camarones (el camarón)
la langosta

---

1 **Escuchar** Indica si las oraciones que vas a escuchar son **ciertas** o **falsas**, según el dibujo. Después, corrige las falsas.

1. _____   6. _____
2. _____   7. _____
3. _____   8. _____
4. _____   9. _____
5. _____   10. _____

2 **Seleccionar** Paulino y Pilar van a cenar a un restaurante. Escucha la conversación y selecciona la respuesta que mejor completa cada oración.

1. Paulino le pide el _____ (menú / plato) al camarero.
2. El plato del día es (atún / salmón) _____.
3. Pilar ordena _____ (leche / agua mineral) para beber.
4. Paulino quiere un refresco de _____ (naranja / limón).
5. Paulino hoy prefiere _____ (el salmón / la chuleta).
6. Dicen que la carne en ese restaurante es muy _____ (sabrosa / mala).
7. Pilar come salmón con _____ (zanahorias / champiñones).

3 **Identificar** Identifica la palabra que no está relacionada con cada grupo.

1. champiñón • cebolla • propina • zanahoria
2. camarones • ajo • atún • salmón
3. aceite • leche • refresco • agua mineral
4. jamón • chuleta de cerdo • vinagre • carne de res
5. cerveza • lechuga • arvejas • frijoles
6. carne • pescado • mariscos • camarero
7. pollo • naranja • limón • melocotón
8. maíz • queso • tomate • champiñón

4 **Escoger** Completa las oraciones con las palabras más lógicas.

1. ¡Me gusta mucho este plato! Sabe _____.
   a. mal   b. delicioso   c. antipático
2. Camarero, ¿puedo ver el _____, por favor?
   a. aceite   b. maíz   c. menú
3. Carlos y yo bebemos siempre agua _____.
   a. cómoda   b. mineral   c. principal
4. El plato del día es _____.
   a. pollo asado   b. mayonesa   c. ajo
5. Margarita es vegetariana. Ella come _____.
   a. frijoles   b. chuletas   c. jamón
6. Mi hermana le da _____ a su niña.
   a. ajo   b. vinagre   c. yogur

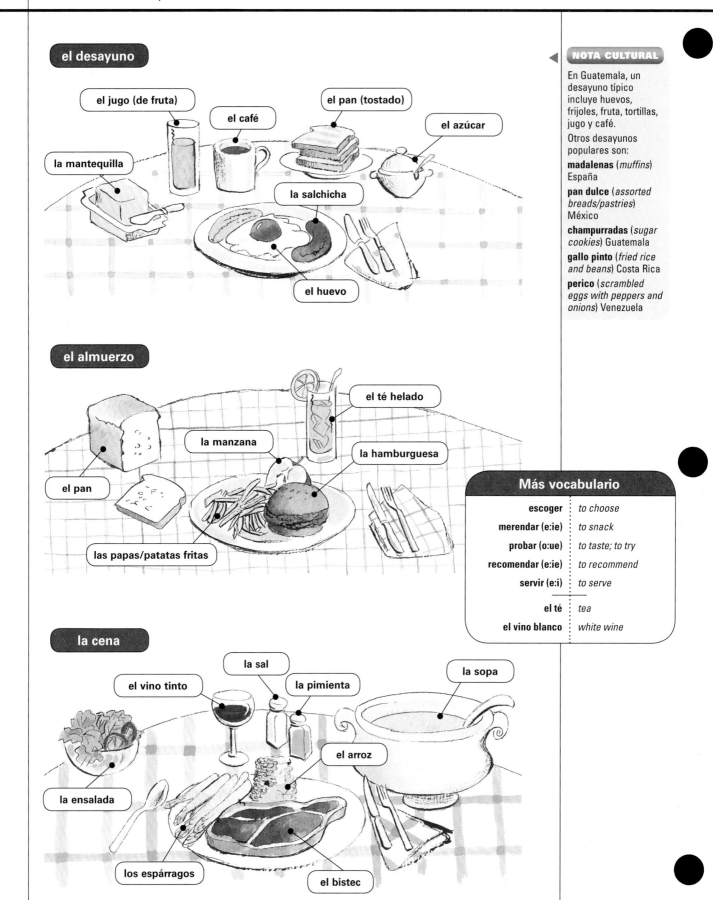

el desayuno

el jugo (de fruta)

el café

el pan (tostado)

el azúcar

la mantequilla

la salchicha

el huevo

el almuerzo

el té helado

la manzana

la hamburguesa

el pan

las papas/patatas fritas

la cena

la sal

el vino tinto

la pimienta

la sopa

el arroz

la ensalada

los espárragos

el bistec

NOTA CULTURAL

En Guatemala, un desayuno típico incluye huevos, frijoles, fruta, tortillas, jugo y café.

Otros desayunos populares son:

madalenas (*muffins*) España

pan dulce (*assorted breads/pastries*) México

champurradas (*sugar cookies*) Guatemala

gallo pinto (*fried rice and beans*) Costa Rica

perico (*scrambled eggs with peppers and onions*) Venezuela

Más vocabulario

escoger	*to choose*
merendar (e:ie)	*to snack*
probar (o:ue)	*to taste; to try*
recomendar (e:ie)	*to recommend*
servir (e:i)	*to serve*
el té	*tea*
el vino blanco	*white wine*

5 **Completar** Relaciona cada producto con el grupo alimenticio (*food group*) correcto.

> *modelo*
> ___La carne___ es del grupo uno.

el aceite	las bananas	los cereales	la leche
el arroz	el café	los espárragos	el pescado
el azúcar	la carne	los frijoles	el vino

1. _____ y el queso son del grupo cuatro.
2. _____ son del grupo ocho.
3. _____ y el pollo son del grupo tres.
4. _____ es del grupo cinco.
5. _____ es del grupo dos.
6. Las manzanas y _____ son del grupo siete.
7. _____ es del grupo seis.
8. _____ son del grupo diez.
9. _____ y los tomates son del grupo nueve.
10. El pan y _____ son del grupo diez.

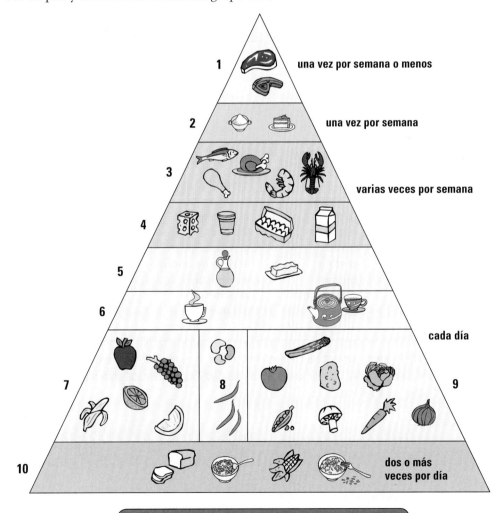

La Pirámide Alimenticia Latinoamericana

6 **¿Cierto o falso?** Consulta la Pirámide Alimenticia Latinoamericana de la página 265 e indica si lo que dice cada oración es **cierto** o **falso**. Si la oración es falsa, escribe las comidas que sí están en el grupo indicado.

> **modelo**
>
> El queso está en el grupo diez.
> *Falso. En ese grupo están el maíz, el pan, los cereales y el arroz.*

1. La manzana, la banana, el limón y las arvejas están en el grupo siete.

2. En el grupo cuatro están los huevos, la leche y el aceite.

3. El azúcar está en el grupo dos.

4. En el grupo diez están el pan, el arroz y el maíz.

5. El pollo está en el grupo uno.

6. En el grupo nueve están la lechuga, el tomate, las arvejas, la naranja, la papa, los espárragos y la cebolla.

7. El café y el té están en el mismo grupo.

8. En el grupo cinco está el arroz.

9. El pescado, el yogur y el bistec están en el grupo tres.

7 **Combinar** Combina palabras de cada columna, en cualquier (*any*) orden, para formar diez oraciones lógicas sobre las comidas. Añade otras palabras si es necesario.

> **modelo**
>
> *La camarera nos sirve la ensalada.*

A	B	C
el/la camarero/a	almorzar	la sección de no fumar
el/la dueño/a	escoger	el desayuno
mi familia	gustar	la ensalada
mi novio/a	merendar	las uvas
mis amigos y yo	pedir	el restaurante
mis padres	preferir	el jugo de naranja
mi hermano/a	probar	el refresco
el/la médico/a	recomendar	el plato
yo	servir	el arroz

8 **Un menú** Usa la Pirámide Alimenticia Latinoamericana de la página 265 para crear un menú para una cena especial. Incluye alimentos de los diez grupos para los entremeses, los platos principales y las bebidas.

> **modelo**
>
> *La cena especial que voy a preparar es deliciosa.*
> *Primero, hay dos entremeses: ensalada César y sopa*
> *de langosta. El plato principal es salmón con salsa de*
> *ajo y espárragos. También voy a servir arroz...*

Comunicación

9

En el restaurante Escucha la conversación entre Andrea, Julio y un camarero. Luego, indica si las conclusiones son **lógicas** o **ilógicas**, según lo que escuchaste.

	Lógico	Ilógico
1. Andrea y Julio están almorzando.	○	○
2. Andrea no come carne.	○	○
3. Julio no sabe qué pedir.	○	○
4. Andrea y Julio piden entremeses y platos principales.	○	○
5. El restaurante sirve bebidas alcohólicas.	○	○
6. Después de comer, Andrea y Julio van a ir al cine.	○	○

10

Conversación Contesta las preguntas de tu compañero/a.

1. ¿Qué te gusta cenar?
2. ¿A qué hora, dónde y con quién almuerzas?
3. ¿Qué almuerzas normalmente?
4. ¿Desayunas? ¿Qué comes y bebes por la mañana?
5. ¿Qué comida te gusta más?
6. ¿Te gusta probar comidas diferentes?
7. ¿Preparas comida en casa? ¿Qué preparas?
8. ¿Eres vegetariano/a? ¿Crees que ser vegetariano/a es buena idea? ¿Por qué?
9. ¿Qué tipo de comida sirve tu restaurante favorito?

11

Describir Describe lo que ocurre en las fotos. Incluye en tu descripción las respuestas a estas preguntas.

▶ ¿Quiénes están en las fotos?

▶ ¿Dónde están?

▶ ¿Qué hora es?

▶ ¿Qué comen y qué beben?

Una cena... romántica

Maru y Miguel quieren tener una cena romántica, pero les espera una sorpresa.

PERSONAJES   MARU   MIGUEL

MARU No sé qué pedir. ¿Qué me recomiendas?

MIGUEL No estoy seguro. Las chuletas de cerdo se ven muy buenas.

MARU ¿Vas a pedirlas?

MIGUEL No sé.

MIGUEL ¡Qué bonitos! ¿Quién te los dio?

MARU Me los compró un chico muy guapo e inteligente.

MIGUEL ¿Es tan guapo como yo?

MARU Sí, como tú, guapísimo.

MIGUEL Por nosotros.

MARU Dos años.

(*El camarero llega a la mesa.*)

CAMARERO ¿Les gustaría saber nuestras especialidades del día?

MARU Sí, por favor.

CAMARERO Para el entremés, tenemos ceviche de camarón. De plato principal ofrecemos bistec con verduras a la plancha.

MARU Voy a probar el jamón.

CAMARERO Perfecto. ¿Y para usted, caballero?

MIGUEL Pollo asado con champiñones y papas, por favor.

CAMARERO Excelente.

(*en otra parte del restaurante*)

JUAN CARLOS Disculpe. ¿Qué me puede contar del pollo? ¿Dónde lo consiguió el chef?

CAMARERO ¡Oiga! ¿Qué está haciendo?

CAMARERO **JUAN CARLOS** **FELIPE** **GERENTE**

FELIPE Los espárragos están sabrosísimos esta noche. Usted pidió el pollo, señor. Estos champiñones saben a mantequilla.

GERENTE ¿Qué pasa aquí, Esteban?

CAMARERO Lo siento, señor. Me quitaron la comida.

GERENTE (*a Felipe*) Señor, ¿quién es usted? ¿Qué cree que está haciendo?

JUAN CARLOS Felipe y yo les servimos la comida a nuestros amigos. Pero desafortunadamente, salió todo mal.

FELIPE Soy el peor camarero del mundo. ¡Lo siento! Nosotros vamos a pagar la comida.

JUAN CARLOS ¿Nosotros?

FELIPE Todo esto fue idea tuya, Juan Carlos.

JUAN CARLOS ¿Mi idea? ¡Felipe! (*al gerente*) Señor, él es más responsable que yo.

GERENTE Tú y tú, vamos.

Expresiones útiles

Ordering food

¿Qué me recomiendas?
What do you recommend?
Las chuletas de cerdo se ven muy buenas.
The pork chops look good.
¿Les gustaría saber nuestras especialidades del día?
Would you like to hear our specials?
Para el entremés, tenemos ceviche de camarón.
For an appetizer, we have shrimp ceviche.
De plato principal ofrecemos bistec con verduras a la plancha.
For a main course, we have beef with grilled vegetables.
Voy a probar el jamón.
I am going to try the ham.

Describing people and things

¡Qué bonitos! ¿Quién te los dio?
How pretty! Who gave them to you?
Me los compró un chico muy guapo e inteligente.
A really handsome, intelligent guy bought them for me.
¿Es tan guapo como yo?
Is he as handsome as I am?
Sí, como tú, guapísimo.
Yes, like you, gorgeous.
Soy el peor camarero del mundo.
I am the worst waiter in the world.
Él es más responsable que yo.
He is more responsible than I am.

Additional vocabulary

el/la gerente *manager*
caballero *gentleman, sir*

¿Qué pasó?

1 **Escoger** Escoge la respuesta que completa mejor cada oración.

1. Miguel lleva a Maru a un restaurante para _____.
   a. almorzar   b. desayunar   c. cenar
2. El camarero les ofrece _____ como plato principal.
   a. ceviche de camarón   b. bistec con verduras a la plancha
   c. pescado, arroz y ensalada
3. Miguel va a pedir _____.
   a. pollo asado con champiñones y papas
   b. langosta al horno   c. pescado con verduras a la mantequilla
4. Felipe les lleva la comida a sus amigos y prueba _____.
   a. el jamón y los vinos   b. el atún y la lechuga
   c. los espárragos y los champiñones

NOTA CULTURAL

El **ceviche** es un plato típico de varios países hispanos como México, Perú y Costa Rica. En México, se prepara con pescado o mariscos frescos, jugo de limón, jitomate, cebolla, chile y cilantro. Se puede comer como plato fuerte, pero también como entremés o botana (*snack*). Casi siempre se sirve con tostadas (*fried tortillas*) o galletas saladas (*crackers*).

2 **Identificar** Indica quién puede decir estas oraciones.

1. ¡Qué desastre! Soy un camarero muy malo.
2. Les recomiendo el bistec con verduras a la plancha.
3. Tal vez escoja las chuletas de cerdo, creo que son muy sabrosas.
4. ¿Qué pasa aquí?
5. Dígame las especialidades del día, por favor.
6. No fue mi idea. Felipe es más responsable que yo.

FELIPE   MARU   JUAN CARLOS

CAMARERO   MIGUEL   GERENTE

3 **Preguntas** Contesta estas preguntas sobre la **Fotonovela**.

1. ¿Por qué fueron Maru y Miguel a un restaurante?
2. ¿Qué entremés es una de las especialidades del día?
3. ¿Qué pidió Maru?
4. ¿Quiénes van a pagar la cuenta?

4 **En el restaurante**

1. Prepara con un(a) compañero/a una conversación en la que le preguntas si conoce algún buen restaurante en tu comunidad. Tu compañero/a responde que él/ella sí conoce un restaurante que sirve una comida deliciosa. Lo/La invitas a cenar y tu compañero/a acepta. Determinan la hora para verse en el restaurante.

2. Trabaja con un(a) compañero/a para representar los papeles de un(a) cliente/a y un(a) camarero/a en un restaurante. El/La camarero/a te pregunta qué te puede servir y tú preguntas cuál es la especialidad de la casa. El/La camarero/a te dice cuál es la especialidad y te recomienda algunos platos del menú. Tú pides entremeses, un plato principal y escoges una bebida. El/La camarero/a te sirve la comida y tú le das las gracias.

CONSULTA

To review indefinite words like **algún**, see **Estructura 7.2**, p. 240.

Pronunciación 🎧

ll, ñ, c, and z

pollo	llave	ella	cebolla

Most Spanish speakers pronounce **ll** like the *y* in *yes*.

mañana	señor	baño	niña

The letter **ñ** is pronounced much like the *ny* in *canyon*.

café	colombiano	cuando	rico

Before **a**, **o**, or **u**, the Spanish **c** is pronounced like the *c* in *car*.

cereales	delicioso	conducir	conocer

Before **e** or **i**, the Spanish **c** is pronounced like the *s* in *sit*. (In parts of Spain, **c** before **e** or **i** is pronounced like the *th* in *think*.)

zeta	zanahoria	almuerzo	cerveza

The Spanish **z** is pronounced like the *s* in *sit*. (In parts of Spain, **z** is pronounced like the *th* in *think*.)

Práctica Lee las palabras en voz alta.

1. mantequilla	5. español	9. quince
2. cuñado	6. cepillo	10. compañera
3. aceite	7. zapato	11. almorzar
4. manzana	8. azúcar	12. calle

Oraciones Lee las oraciones en voz alta.

1. Mi compañero de cuarto se llama Toño Núñez. Su familia es de la Ciudad de Guatemala y de Quetzaltenango.
2. Dice que la comida de su mamá es deliciosa, especialmente su pollo al champiñón y sus tortillas de maíz.
3. Creo que Toño tiene razón porque hoy cené en su casa y quiero volver mañana para cenar allí otra vez.

Refranes Lee los refranes en voz alta.

> Panza llena, corazón contento.[2]

> Las apariencias engañan.[1]

1 Looks can be deceiving.
2 A full belly makes a happy heart.

EN DETALLE

Frutas y verduras
de América

Imagínate una pizza sin salsa° de tomate o una hamburguesa sin papas fritas. Ahora piensa que quieres ver una película, pero las palomitas de maíz° y el chocolate no existen. ¡Qué mundo° tan insípido°! Muchas de las comidas más populares del mundo tienen ingredientes esenciales que son originarios del continente llamado Nuevo Mundo. Estas frutas y verduras no fueron introducidas en Europa sino hasta° el siglo° XVI.

El tomate, por ejemplo, era° usado como planta ornamental cuando llegó por primera vez a Europa porque pensaron que era venenoso°. El maíz, por su parte, era ya la base de la comida de muchos países latinoamericanos muchos siglos antes de la llegada de los españoles.

La papa fue un alimento° básico para los incas. Incluso consiguieron deshidratarla para almacenarla° por largos períodos de tiempo. El cacao (planta con la que se hace el chocolate) fue muy importante para los aztecas y los mayas. Ellos usaban sus semillas° como moneda° y como ingrediente de diversas salsas. También las molían° para preparar una bebida, mezclándolas° con agua ¡y con chile!

El aguacate°, la guayaba°, la papaya, la piña y el maracuyá (o fruta de la pasión) son otros ejemplos de frutas originarias de América que son hoy día conocidas en todo el mundo.

Mole

¿En qué alimentos encontramos estas frutas y verduras?

Tomate: pizza, ketchup, salsa de tomate, sopa de tomate

Maíz: palomitas de maíz, tamales, tortillas, arepas (Colombia y Venezuela), pan

Papa: papas fritas, frituras de papa°, puré de papas°, sopa de papas, tortilla de patatas (España)

Cacao: mole (México), chocolatinas°, cereales, helados°, tartas°

Aguacate: guacamole (México), coctel de camarones, sopa de aguacate, nachos, enchiladas hondureñas

---

salsa *sauce* palomitas de maíz *popcorn* mundo *world* insípido *flavorless* hasta *until* siglo *century* era *was* venenoso *poisonous* alimento *food* almacenarla *to store it* semillas *seeds* moneda *currency* las molían *they used to grind them* mezclándolas *mixing them* aguacate *avocado* guayaba *guava* frituras de papa *chips* puré de papas *mashed potatoes* chocolatinas *chocolate bars* helados *ice cream* tartas *cakes*

ACTIVIDADES

1 **¿Cierto o falso?** Indica si lo que dicen las oraciones es **cierto** o **falso. Corrige la información falsa.**

1. El tomate se introdujo a Europa como planta ornamental.

2. Los incas sólo consiguieron almacenar las papas por poco tiempo.

3. Los aztecas y los mayas usaron las papas como moneda.

4. El maíz era una comida poco popular en Latinoamérica.

5. El aguacate era el alimento básico de los incas.

6. En México se hace una salsa con chocolate.

7. El aguacate, la guayaba, la papaya, la piña y el maracuyá son originarios de América.

8. Las arepas se hacen con cacao.

9. El aguacate es un ingrediente del cóctel de camarones.

10. En España hacen una tortilla con papas.

ASÍ SE DICE

La comida

el banano (Col.), el cambur (Ven.), el guineo (Nic.), el plátano (Amér. L., Esp.)	la banana
el choclo (Amér. S.), el elote (Méx.), el jojoto (Ven.), la mazorca (Esp.)	*corncob*
las caraotas (Ven.), los porotos (Amér. S.), las habichuelas (P. R.)	los frijoles
el durazno (Méx.)	el melocotón
el jitomate (Méx.)	el tomate

EL MUNDO HISPANO

Algunos platos típicos

- **Ceviche peruano:** Es un plato de pescado crudo que se marina° en jugo de limón, con sal, pimienta, cebolla y ají°. Se sirve con lechuga, maíz, camote° y papa amarilla.

- **Gazpacho andaluz:** Es una sopa fría típica del sur de España. Se hace con verduras crudas y molidas°: tomate, ají, pepino° y ajo. También lleva pan, sal, aceite y vinagre.

- **Sancocho colombiano:** Es una sopa de pollo, pescado o carne con plátano, maíz, zanahoria, yuca, papas, cebolla, cilantro y ajo. Se sirve con arroz blanco.

se marina *gets marinated* ají *pepper*
camote *sweet potato* molidas *mashed* pepino *cucumber*

PERFIL

Ferran Adrià: arte en la cocina°

¿Qué haces si un amigo te invita a comer croquetas líquidas o paella de *Kellogg's*? ¿Piensas que es una broma°? ¡Cuidado! Puedes estar perdiendo la oportunidad de probar los platos de uno de los chefs más innovadores del mundo°: **Ferran Adrià.**

Este artista de la cocina basa su éxito° en la creatividad y en la química. Adrià modifica combinaciones de ingredientes y juega con contrastes de gustos y sensaciones: frío-caliente, crudo°-cocido°,

Aire de zanahorias

dulce°-salado°... A partir de nuevas técnicas, altera la textura de los alimentos sin alterar su sabor°. Sus platos sorprendentes° y divertidos atraen a muchos nuevos chefs a su academia de cocina experimental. Quizás un día compraremos° en el supermercado té esférico°, carne líquida y espuma° de tomate.

cocina *kitchen* broma *joke* mundo *world* éxito *success* crudo *raw*
cocido *cooked* dulce *sweet* salado *savory* sabor *taste* sorprendentes
surprising compraremos *we will buy* esférico *spheric* espuma *foam*

Conexión Internet

¿Qué platos comen los hispanos en los Estados Unidos?	Use the Web to find more cultural information related to this Cultura section.

ACTIVIDADES

2 **Comprensión** Empareja cada palabra con su definición.

1. fruta amarilla
2. sopa típica de Colombia
3. ingrediente del ceviche
4. chef español

a. gazpacho
b. Ferran Adrià
c. sancocho
d. guineo
e. pescado

3 **¿Qué plato especial hay en tu región?** Escribe cuatro oraciones sobre un plato típico de tu región. Explica los ingredientes que contiene y cómo se sirve.

8.1 Preterite of stem-changing verbs

ANTE TODO As you learned in **Lección 6**, **–ar** and **–er** stem-changing verbs have no stem change in the preterite. **–Ir** stem-changing verbs, however, do have a stem change. Study the following chart and observe where the stem changes occur.

CONSULTA

There are a few high-frequency irregular verbs in the preterite. You will learn more about them in **Estructura 9.1**, p. 310.

Preterite of –ir stem-changing verbs		
	servir (to serve)	**dormir** (to sleep)
SINGULAR FORMS		
yo	serví	dormí
tú	serviste	dormiste
Ud./él/ella	si**r**vió	d**u**rmió
PLURAL FORMS		
nosotros/as	servimos	dormimos
vosotros/as	servisteis	dormisteis
Uds./ellos/ellas	si**r**vieron	d**u**rmieron

▶ Stem-changing **–ir** verbs, in the preterite only, have a stem change in the third-person singular and plural forms. The stem change consists of either **e** to **i** or **o** to **u**.

(e → i) pedir: **pi**dió, **pi**dieron   (o → u) morir (*to die*): **mu**rió, **mu**rieron

¿Quién pidió el jamón?

Yo lo pedí.

¡INTÉNTALO! Cambia cada infinitivo al pretérito.

1. Yo ___serví, dormí, pedí...___. (servir, dormir, pedir, preferir, repetir, seguir)

2. Usted _____. (morir, conseguir, pedir, sentirse, servir, vestirse)

3. Tú _____. (conseguir, servir, morir, pedir, dormir, repetir)

4. Ellas _____. (repetir, dormir, seguir, preferir, morir, servir)

5. Nosotros _____. (seguir, preferir, servir, vestirse, pedir, dormirse)

6. Ustedes _____. (sentirse, vestirse, conseguir, pedir, repetir, dormirse)

7. Él _____. (dormir, morir, preferir, repetir, seguir, pedir)

Práctica

1

Completar Completa estas oraciones para describir lo que pasó anoche en el restaurante El Famoso.

▶ 1. Paula y Humberto Suárez llegaron al restaurante El Famoso a las ocho y _____ (seguir) al camarero a una mesa en la sección de no fumar.
2. El señor Suárez _____ (pedir) una chuleta de cerdo.
3. La señora Suárez _____ (preferir) probar los camarones.
4. De tomar, los dos _____ (pedir) vino tinto.
5. El camarero _____ (repetir) el pedido (*the order*) para confirmarlo.
6. La comida tardó mucho (*took a long time*) en llegar y los señores Suárez _____ (dormirse) esperando la comida.
7. A las nueve y media el camarero les _____ (servir) la comida.
8. Después de comer la chuleta, el señor Suárez _____ (sentirse) muy mal.
9. Pobre señor Suárez… ¿por qué no _____ (pedir) los camarones?

2

El camarero loco En el restaurante La Hermosa trabaja un camarero muy distraído que siempre comete muchos errores. Indica lo que los clientes pidieron y lo que el camarero les sirvió.

modelo

Armando / papas fritas
Armando pidió papas fritas, pero el camarero le sirvió maíz.

1. nosotros / jugo de naranja   2. Beatriz / queso   3. tú / arroz

4. Elena y Alejandro / atún   5. usted / agua mineral   6. yo / hamburguesa

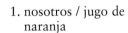

Comunicación

3

El crítico Lee lo que escribió un crítico sobre el restaurante Las Delicias. Luego, indica si las conclusiones son **lógicas** o **ilógicas**, según lo que leíste.

> Llegué al restaurante Las Delicias a las 7:30 p.m., hora de mi reservación. Después de esperar una hora, finalmente me llevaron a mi mesa. ¡Les digo la verdad! Pedí una ensalada de verduras y atún como entremés y el camarero me recomendó el pollo a la naranja como plato principal. Después de quince minutos, el camarero me ofreció pan, pero no se acordó de traer la mantequilla. A las nueve llegó mi ensalada. Después de tres minutos, me levanté de la mesa para ir al baño ¡y el camarero se llevó mi plato! A las 9:45 llegó mi plato principal. ¡Encontré un pelo en el plato! Preferí no pedir nada más. Nunca voy a volver a ese restaurante.

	Lógico	Ilógico
1. La cena empieza a las ocho y media en el restaurante Las Delicias.	○	○
2. El crítico no puede comer productos derivados de la leche.	○	○
3. El camarero piensa que el pollo a la naranja del restaurante sabe bien.	○	○
4. El crítico no consiguió terminar ninguno de sus platos.	○	○
5. El crítico se sintió enojado al salir del restaurante.	○	○

4

Entrevista Contesta las preguntas de tu compañero/a.

1. ¿Te acostaste tarde o temprano anoche? ¿A qué hora te dormiste? ¿Dormiste bien?
2. ¿A qué hora te despertaste esta mañana? Y, ¿a qué hora te levantaste?
3. ¿A qué hora vas a acostarte esta noche?
4. ¿Qué almorzaste ayer? ¿Quién te sirvió el almuerzo?
5. ¿Qué cenaste ayer?
6. ¿Cenaste en un restaurante recientemente? ¿Con quién(es)?
7. ¿Qué pediste en el restaurante? ¿Qué pidieron los demás?

Síntesis

5

Describir Estudia la foto y las preguntas. Luego, escribe una descripción de la primera (¿y la última?) cita de César y Libertad.

▶ ¿Adónde salieron a cenar?

▶ ¿Qué pidieron?

▶ ¿Les gustó la comida?

▶ ¿Quién prefirió una cena vegetariana? ¿Por qué?

▶ ¿Cómo se vistieron?

▶ ¿De qué hablaron? ¿Les gustó la conversación?

▶ ¿Van a volver a verse? ¿Por qué?

CONSULTA

To review words commonly associated with the preterite, such as **anoche**, see **Estructura 6.3**, p. 207.

8.2   Double object pronouns

ANTE TODO   In **Lecciones 5** and **6**, you learned that direct and indirect object pronouns replace nouns and that they often refer to nouns that have already been referenced. You will now learn how to use direct and indirect object pronouns together. Observe the following diagram.

Indirect Object Pronouns			Direct Object Pronouns	
me	nos		lo	los
te	os	**+**	la	las
le (se)	les (se)			

▶ When direct and indirect object pronouns are used together, the indirect object pronoun always precedes the direct object pronoun.

    I.O.   D.O.   DOUBLE OBJECT PRONOUNS

La camarera **me** muestra **el menú**.   ⟶   La camarera **me lo** muestra.
The waitress shows me the menu.   *The waitress shows it to me.*

    I.O.   D.O.   DOUBLE OBJECT PRONOUNS

Nos sirven **los platos**.   ⟶   **Nos los** sirven.
They serve us the dishes.   *They serve them to us.*

    I.O.   D.O.   DOUBLE OBJECT PRONOUNS

Maribel **te** pidió **una hamburguesa**.   ⟶   Maribel **te la** pidió.
Maribel ordered a hamburger for you.   *Maribel ordered it for you.*

¿Quién te los dio?

Me los compró un chico muy guapo.

▶ In Spanish, two pronouns that begin with the letter **l** cannot be used together. Therefore, the indirect object pronouns **le** and **les** always change to **se** when they are used with **lo, los, la,** and **las**.

    I.O.   D.O.   DOUBLE OBJECT PRONOUNS

Le escribí **la carta**.   ⟶   **Se la** escribí.
I wrote him the letter.   *I wrote it to him.*

    I.O.   D.O.   DOUBLE OBJECT PRONOUNS

Les sirvió **los sándwiches**.   ⟶   **Se los** sirvió.
He served them the sandwiches.   *He served them to them.*

▶ Because **se** has multiple meanings, Spanish speakers often clarify to whom the pronoun refers by adding **a usted, a él, a ella, a ustedes, a ellos,** or **a ellas**.

¿El sombrero? Carlos **se** lo
    vendió **a ella**.
The hat? Carlos sold it to her.

¿Las verduras? Ellos **se** las
    compran **a usted**.
The vegetables? They are buying them for you.

▶ Double object pronouns are placed before a conjugated verb. With infinitives and present participles, they may be placed before the conjugated verb or attached to the end of the infinitive or present participle.

DOUBLE OBJECT
PRONOUNS
Te lo voy a mostrar.

DOUBLE OBJECT
PRONOUNS
Voy a mostrár**telo**.

DOUBLE OBJECT
PRONOUNS
Nos las están comprando.

DOUBLE OBJECT
PRONOUNS
Están comprándo**noslas**.

Mi abuelo **me lo** está leyendo.
Mi abuelo está leyéndo**melo**.

El camarero **se los** va a servir.
El camarero va a servír**selos**.

▶ As you can see above, when double object pronouns are attached to an infinitive or a present participle, an accent mark is added to maintain the original stress.

¡INTÉNTALO!   Escribe el pronombre de objeto directo o indirecto que falta en cada oración.

Objeto directo

1. ¿La ensalada? El camarero nos ____la____ sirvió.
2. ¿El salmón? La dueña me _____ recomienda.
3. ¿La comida? Voy a prepárarte_____.
4. ¿Las bebidas? Estamos pidiéndose_____.
5. ¿Los refrescos? Te _____ puedo traer ahora.
6. ¿Los platos de arroz? Van a servírnos_____ después.

Objeto indirecto

1. ¿Puedes traerme tu plato? No, no ____te____ lo puedo traer.
2. ¿Quieres mostrarle la carta? Sí, voy a mostrár_____la ahora.
3. ¿Les serviste la carne? No, no _____ la serví.
4. ¿Vas a leerle el menú? No, no _____ lo voy a leer.
5. ¿Me recomiendas la langosta? Sí, _____ la recomiendo.
6. ¿Cuándo vas a prepararnos la cena? _____ la voy a preparar en una hora.

Práctica

1 **Responder** Imagínate que trabajas de camarero/a en un restaurante. Responde a los pedidos (*requests*) de estos clientes usando pronombres.

> **modelo**
>
> Sra. Gómez: Una ensalada, por favor.
>
> *Sí, señora. Enseguida (Right away) se la traigo.*

1. Sres. López: La mantequilla, por favor.
2. Srta. Rivas: Los camarones, por favor.
3. Sra. Lugones: El pollo asado, por favor.
4. Tus amigos: Café, por favor.
5. Tu profesor(a) de español: Papas fritas, por favor.
6. Dra. González: La chuleta de cerdo, por favor.
7. Tu padre: Los champiñones, por favor.
8. Dr. Torres: La cuenta, por favor.

2 **¿Quién?** La señora Cevallos está planeando una cena. Se pregunta cómo va a resolver ciertas situaciones. Indica lo que ella está pensando. Cambia los sustantivos subrayados por pronombres de objeto directo y haz los otros cambios necesarios.

> **modelo**
>
> ¡No tengo carne! ¿Quién va a traerme la carne del supermercado? (mi esposo)
>
> *Mi esposo va a traérmela./Mi esposo me la va a traer.*

1. ¡Las invitaciones! ¿Quién les manda las invitaciones a los invitados (*guests*)? (mi hija)
2. No tengo tiempo de ir a la bodega. ¿Quién me puede comprar el vino? (mi hijo)
3. ¡Ay! No tengo suficientes platos (*plates*). ¿Quién puede prestarme los platos que necesito? (mi mamá)
4. Nos falta mantequilla. ¿Quién nos trae la mantequilla? (mi cuñada)
5. ¡Los entremeses! ¿Quién está preparándonos los entremeses? (Silvia y Renata)
6. No hay suficientes sillas. ¿Quién nos trae las sillas que faltan? (Héctor y Lorena)
7. No tengo tiempo de pedirle el aceite a Mónica. ¿Quién puede pedirle el aceite? (mi hijo)
8. ¿Quién va a servirles la cena a los invitados? (mis hijos)
9. Quiero poner buena música de fondo (*background*). ¿Quién me va a recomendar la música? (mi esposo)
10. ¡Los postres! ¿Quién va a preparar los postres para los invitados? (Sra. Villalba)

Comunicación

3

Una fiesta Escucha la conversación entre Eva y Marcela. Luego, indica si las conclusiones son **lógicas** o **ilógicas**, según lo que escuchaste.

	Lógico	Ilógico
1. Sebastián no es vegetariano.	○	○
2. A una de las chicas no le gustan las verduras.	○	○
3. Las dos chicas van a prepararle platos diferentes a Sebastián.	○	○
4. A Sebastián le encanta el vino blanco.	○	○
5. La fiesta de Sebastián se va a celebrar en un restaurante de mariscos.	○	○

4

Preguntas Contesta las preguntas de tu compañero/a.

> **modelo**
>
> **Estudiante 1:** ¿Les prestas tu casa a tus amigos? ¿Por qué?
> **Estudiante 2:** No, no se la presto a mis amigos porque no son muy responsables.

1. ¿Quién te presta dinero cuando lo necesitas?
2. ¿Les prestas dinero a tus amigos cuando lo necesitan? ¿Por qué?
3. ¿Les escribes mensajes electrónicos a tus amigos? ¿Y a tu familia?
4. ¿Les das regalos a tus amigos? ¿Cuándo?
5. ¿Quién te va a preparar la cena esta noche?
6. ¿Quién te va a preparar el desayuno mañana?

5

Contestar Trabajen en parejas. Túrnense para hacer preguntas, usando las palabras interrogativas **¿quién?** o **¿cuándo?**, y para contestarlas. Sigan el modelo.

> **modelo**
>
> nos enseña español
> **Estudiante 1:** ¿Quién nos enseña español?
> **Estudiante 2:** La profesora Camacho nos lo enseña.

1. te puede explicar la tarea cuando no la entiendes
2. les vende el almuerzo a los estudiantes
3. va a prepararles una cena a tus amigos
4. te escribe mensajes de texto
5. te prepara comida
6. me vas a recomendar un libro
7. te compró tu computadora
8. nos va a dar la tarea

Síntesis

6

Regalos Recibiste muchos regalos de cumpleaños. Escríbele un mensaje electrónico a un(a) amigo/a contándole sobre los regalos que recibiste y quiénes te los compraron.

 # Comparisons

ANTE TODO Both Spanish and English use comparisons to indicate which of two
people or things has a lesser, equal, or greater degree of a quality.

> (Comparisons)
>
> **menos interesante**   **más grande**   **tan sabroso como**
> *less interesting*   *bigger*   *as delicious as*

Comparisons of inequality

▶ Comparisons of inequality are formed by placing **más** (*more*) or **menos** (*less*) before
adjectives, adverbs, and nouns and **que** (*than*) after them.

$$\textbf{más/menos} + \begin{bmatrix} \textit{adjective} \\ \textit{adverb} \\ \textit{noun} \end{bmatrix} + \textbf{que}$$

▶ **¡Atención!** Note that while English has a comparative form for short adjectives
(*tall**er***), such forms do not exist in Spanish (**más** alto).

(adjectives)

Los bistecs son **más caros que** el pollo. | Estas uvas son **menos ricas que** esa pera.
Steaks are more expensive than chicken. | *These grapes are less tasty than that pear.*

(adverbs)

Me acuesto **más tarde que** tú. | Luis se despierta **menos temprano que** yo.
I go to bed later than you (do). | *Luis wakes up less early than I (do).*

(nouns)

Juan prepara **más platos que** José. | Susana come **menos carne que** Enrique.
Juan prepares more dishes than José (does). | *Susana eats less meat than Enrique (does).*

> La ensalada es menos
> cara que la sopa.

> ¿El pollo es más rico
> que el jamón?

▶ When the comparison involves a numerical expression, **de** is used before the number
instead of **que**.

Hay más **de** cincuenta naranjas. | Llego en menos **de** diez minutos.
There are more than fifty oranges. | *I'll be there in less than ten minutes.*

▶ With verbs, this construction is used to make comparisons of inequality.

$$\begin{bmatrix} \textit{verb} \end{bmatrix} + \textbf{más/menos que}$$

Mis hermanos **comen más que** yo. | Arturo **duerme menos que** su padre.
My brothers eat more than I (do). | *Arturo sleeps less than his father (does).*

Comparisons of equality

▶ This construction is used to make comparisons of equality.

> **tan** + [*adjective* / *adverb*] + **como**   **tanto/a(s)** + [*singular noun* / *plural noun*] + **como**

> ¿Es tan guapo como yo?

> ¿Aquí vienen tantos mexicanos como extranjeros?

▶ **¡Atención!** Note that unlike **tan**, **tanto** acts as an adjective and therefore agrees in number and gender with the noun it modifies.

> Estas uvas son **tan ricas como** aquéllas.
> *These grapes are as tasty as those ones (are).*

> Yo probé **tantos platos como** él.
> *I tried as many dishes as he did.*

▶ **Tan** and **tanto** can also be used for emphasis, rather than to compare, with these meanings: **tan** *so*, **tanto** *so much*, **tantos/as** *so many*.

> ¡Tu almuerzo es **tan** grande!
> *Your lunch is so big!*

> ¡Comes **tantas** manzanas!
> *You eat so many apples!*

> ¡Comes **tanto**!
> *You eat so much!*

> ¡Preparan **tantos** platos!
> *They prepare so many dishes!*

▶ Comparisons of equality with verbs are formed by placing **tanto como** after the verb. Note that in this construction **tanto** does not change in number or gender.

> [*verb*] + **tanto como**

> Tú viajas **tanto como** mi tía.
> *You travel as much as my aunt (does).*

> Ellos hablan **tanto como** mis hermanas.
> *They talk as much as my sisters.*

Sabemos **tanto como** ustedes.
We know as much as you (do).

No estudio **tanto como** Felipe.
I don't study as much as Felipe (does).

Irregular comparisons

▶ Some adjectives have irregular comparative forms.

Irregular comparative forms			
Adjective		**Comparative form**	
bueno/a	good	**mejor**	better
malo/a	bad	**peor**	worse
grande	grown, adult	**mayor**	older
pequeño/a	young	**menor**	younger
joven	young	**menor**	younger
viejo/a	old	**mayor**	older

CONSULTA

To review how descriptive adjectives like **bueno**, **malo**, and **grande** are shortened before nouns, see **Estructura 3.1**, p. 90.

▶ When **grande** and **pequeño/a** refer to age, the irregular comparative forms, **mayor** and **menor**, are used. However, when these adjectives refer to size, the regular forms, **más grande** and **más pequeño/a**, are used.

Yo soy **menor** que tú.
I'm younger than you.

Pedí un plato **más pequeño**.
I ordered a smaller dish.

Nuestro hijo es **mayor** que
el hijo de los Andrade.
Our son is older than the Andrades' son.

La ensalada de Isabel es **más grande**
que ésa.
Isabel's salad is bigger than that one.

▶ The adverbs **bien** and **mal** have the same irregular comparative forms as the adjectives **bueno/a** and **malo/a**.

Julio nada **mejor** que los otros chicos.
Julio swims better than the other boys.

Ellas cantan **peor** que las otras chicas.
They sing worse than the other girls.

 **¡INTÉNTALO!**   Escribe el equivalente de las palabras en inglés.

1. Ernesto mira más televisión ___que___ (*than*) Alberto.
2. Tú eres _____ (*less*) simpático que Federico.
3. La camarera sirve _____ (*as much*) carne como pescado.
4. Recibo _____ (*more*) propinas que tú.
5. No estudio _____ (*as much as*) tú.
6. ¿Sabes jugar al tenis tan bien _____ (*as*) tu hermana?
7. ¿Puedes beber _____ (*as many*) refrescos como yo?
8. Mis amigos parecen _____ (*as*) simpáticos como ustedes.

Práctica

1 **Escoger** Escoge la palabra correcta para comparar a dos hermanas muy diferentes. Haz los cambios necesarios.

1. Lucila es más alta y más bonita _____ Tita. (de, más, menos, que)
2. Tita es más delgada porque come _____ verduras que su hermana. (de, más, menos, que)
3. Lucila es más _____ que Tita porque es alegre. (listo, simpático, bajo)
4. A Tita le gusta comer en casa. Va a _____ restaurantes que su hermana. (más, menos, que) Es tímida, pero activa. Hace _____ ejercicio (*exercise*) que su hermana. (más, tanto, menos) Todos los días toma más _____ cinco vasos (*glasses*) de agua mineral. (que, tan, de)
5. Lucila come muchas papas fritas y se preocupa _____ que Tita por comer frutas. (de, más, menos) ¡Son _____ diferentes! Pero se llevan (*they get along*) muy bien. (como, tan, tanto)

2 **Emparejar** Compara a Mario y a Luis, los novios de Lucila y Tita, completando las oraciones de la columna A con las palabras o frases de la columna B.

A
1. Mario es _____ como Luis.
2. Mario viaja tanto _____ Luis.
3. Luis toma _____ clases de cocina (*cooking*) como Mario.
4. Luis habla _____ tan bien como Mario.
5. Mario tiene tantos _____ como Luis.
6. ¡Qué casualidad (*coincidence*)! Mario y Luis también son hermanos, pero no hay tanta _____ entre ellos como entre Lucila y Tita.

B
tantas
diferencia
tan interesante
amigos extranjeros
como
francés

3 **Oraciones** Combina elementos de las columnas A, B y C para hacer comparaciones. Escribe oraciones completas.

modelo
Chris Hemsworth tiene tantos autos como Jennifer Aniston.
Jennifer Aniston es menos musculosa que Chris Hemsworth.

A	B	C
la comida japonesa	costar	la gente de Montreal
el fútbol	saber	la música *country*
Chris Hemsworth	ser	el brócoli
el pollo	tener	el presidente de los EE.UU.
la gente de Vancouver	¿?	la comida italiana
la primera dama (*lady*) de los EE.UU.		el hockey
las universidades privadas		Jennifer Aniston
las espinacas		las universidades públicas
la música rap		la carne de res

Comunicación

4 **La cena de aniversario** Lucía y Andrés quieren celebrar el aniversario de sus padres en un restaurante. Lee el mensaje de Lucía a Andrés. Luego, indica si las conclusiones son **lógicas** o **ilógicas**, según lo que leíste.

De:	Lucía
Para:	Andrés
Asunto:	Aniversario

¿Conoces los restaurantes Pomodoro y Chez Lucien? Bueno, Pomodoro sirve comida italiana y Chez Lucien sirve comida francesa. En primer lugar, la comida de Pomodoro es tan buena como la comida de Chez Lucien. Los entremeses de Pomodoro me gustaron más que los de Chez Lucien, pero los platos principales de Chez Lucien, en mi opinión, son mejores. En Pomodoro hay más opciones para escoger: su menú tiene más de veinte platos. Pero Chez Lucien tiene más de cien vinos diferentes, y a papá le encantan los vinos. Por otro lado, los camareros de Chez Lucien no son tan amables como los camareros de Pomodoro. Tú sabes que a mamá le importa el servicio de un restaurante más que su comida. Pero Pomodoro no acepta reservaciones, y a mí me molesta mucho esperar. ¿Qué piensas? ¿Adónde vamos?

	Lógico	Ilógico
1. Lucía probó entremeses y platos principales en los dos restaurantes.	○	○
2. Al papá de Andrés y de Lucía le va a gustar Chez Lucien más que Pomodoro.	○	○
3. A la mamá de Andrés y de Lucía le va a gustar Chez Lucien más que Pomodoro.	○	○
4. Lucía va a preferir ir a Pomodoro.	○	○
5. El menú de Chez Lucien tiene más de veinte platos.	○	○

5 **Comparaciones** Haz comparaciones entre tú y una persona de cada una de las siguientes categorías.

▶ una persona de tu familia

▶ un(a) amigo/a especial

▶ una persona famosa

6 **Intercambiar** En parejas, hagan comparaciones sobre diferentes cosas: restaurantes, comidas, tiendas, profesores, libros, películas, etc.

Síntesis

7 **La familia López** Escribe comparaciones entre Sara, Sabrina, Cristina, Ricardo y David.

8.4 Superlatives

 **ANTE TODO**   Both English and Spanish use superlatives to express the highest or lowest degree of a quality.

el/la mejor	**el/la peor**	**el/la más alto/a**
the best	*the worst*	*the tallest*

▶ This construction is used to form superlatives. Note that the noun is always preceded by a definite article and that **de** is equivalent to the English *in* or *of*.

$$\text{el/la/los/las} + \boxed{noun} + \text{más/menos} + \boxed{adjective} + \text{de}$$

▶ The noun can be omitted if the person, place, or thing referred to is clear.

¿El restaurante Las Delicias?   Recomiendo el pollo asado.
Es **el más elegante** de la ciudad.   Es **el más sabroso** del menú.
The restaurant Las Delicias?   *I recommend the roast chicken.*
It's the most elegant (one) in the city.   *It's the most delicious on the menu.*

▶ Here are some irregular superlative forms.

Irregular superlatives

Adjective		Superlative form	
bueno/a	*good*	**el/la mejor**	*(the) best*
malo/a	*bad*	**el/la peor**	*(the) worst*
grande	*grown, adult*	**el/la mayor**	*(the) oldest*
pequeño/a	*young*	**el/la menor**	*(the) youngest*
joven	*young*	**el/la menor**	*(the) youngest*
viejo/a	*old*	**el/la mayor**	*(the) oldest*

▶ The absolute superlative is equivalent to *extremely*, *super*, or *very*. To form the absolute superlative of most adjectives and adverbs, drop the final vowel, if there is one, and add **-ísimo/a(s)**.

malo ⟶ mal- ⟶ **malísimo**   mucho ⟶ much- ⟶ **muchísimo**

¡El bistec está **malísimo**!   Comes **muchísimo**.

▶ Note these spelling changes.

rico ⟶ **riquísimo**   largo ⟶ **larguísimo**   feliz ⟶ **felicísimo**

fácil ⟶ **facilísimo**   joven ⟶ **jovencísimo**   trabajador ⟶ **trabajadorcísimo**

¡ATENCIÓN!

While **más** alone means *more*, after **el**, **la**, **los**, or **las**, it means *most*. Likewise, **menos** can mean *less* or *least*.

Es **el café más rico del** país.

It's the most delicious coffee in the country.

Es **el menú menos caro de** todos éstos.

It is the least expensive menu of all of these.

CONSULTA

The rule you learned in **Estructura 8.3** (p. 283) regarding the use of **mayor/menor** with age, but not with size, is also true with superlative forms.

¡INTÉNTALO!   Escribe el equivalente de las palabras en inglés.

1. Marisa es <u>la más inteligente</u> (*the most intelligent*) de todas.
2. Ricardo y Tomás son _____ (*the least boring*) de la fiesta.
3. Miguel y Antonio son _____ (*the worst*) estudiantes de la clase.
4. Mi profesor de biología es _____ (*the oldest*) de la universidad.

Práctica y Comunicación

1

El más... Contesta las preguntas afirmativamente. Usa las palabras entre paréntesis.

> **modelo**
>
> El cuarto está sucísimo, ¿no? (residencia)
> Sí, es el más sucio de la residencia.

1. El almacén Velasco es buenísimo, ¿no? (centro comercial)
2. La silla de tu madre es comodísima, ¿no? (casa)
3. Ángela y Julia están nerviosísimas por el examen, ¿no? (clase)
4. Jorge es jovencísimo, ¿no? (mis amigos)

2

Las cafeterías Lee la carta de Martín al periódico de la universidad en la que describe las diferentes cafeterías. Luego, indica si las conclusiones son **lógicas** o **ilógicas**, según lo que leíste.

> Las cafeterías son muy diferentes entre ellas. Unas sirven comida buenísima y otras sirven comida malísima. La cafetería Asturias tiene la mejor comida. El problema es que también es la cafetería menos ordenada. Muchísimos estudiantes van a esa cafetería y las mesas siempre están sucísimas. Las sillas son las menos cómodas de la universidad y nunca están en su lugar. Cuando no voy con mis amigos a comer allí, prefiero llevar la comida a mi cuarto. La cafetería Mérida es la más cómoda: hay muchísimas sillas y mesas, y siempre está limpísima... pero la comida es la peor. Siempre veo a los estudiantes más inteligentes de mis clases en esa cafetería... ¡estudiando!

	Lógico	Ilógico
1. Los estudiantes prefieren la comida de la cafetería Asturias.	○	○
2. Las cafeterías de la universidad tienen las mismas sillas.	○	○
3. Es difícil encontrar una mesa libre en la cafetería Mérida.	○	○
4. Algunos estudiantes van a la cafetería Mérida pero no comen allí.	○	○

3

Superlativos Trabajen en parejas para hacer comparaciones. Usen los superlativos.

> **modelo**
>
> Angelina Jolie, Bill Gates, Jimmy Carter
> **Estudiante 1:** Bill Gates es el más rico de los tres.
> **Estudiante 2:** Sí, ¡es riquísimo! Y Jimmy Carter es el mayor de los tres.

1. Guatemala, Argentina, España
2. Jaguar, Prius, Smart
3. la comida mexicana, la comida francesa, la comida árabe
4. Amy Adams, Meryl Streep, Jennifer Lawrence
5. Ciudad de México, Buenos Aires, Nueva York
6. *Don Quijote de la Mancha*, *Cien años de soledad*, *Como agua para chocolate*
7. el fútbol americano, el golf, el béisbol
8. las películas románticas, las películas de acción, las películas cómicas

4

Dos restaurantes ¿Cuál es el mejor restaurante que conoces? ¿Y el peor? Escribe un párrafo de por lo menos (*at least*) seis oraciones donde expliques por qué piensas así. Puedes hablar de la calidad de la comida, del ambiente, de los precios, del servicio, etc.

SUBJECT
Javier
CONJUGATED FORM
empiezo
Main clause
Dudan

Recapitulación

Completa estas actividades para repasar los conceptos de gramática que aprendiste en esta lección.

1 **Completar** Completa la tabla con la forma correcta del pretérito. **27 pts.**

Infinitive	yo	usted	ellos
dormir			
servir			
vestirse			

2 **La cena** Completa la conversación con el pretérito de los verbos. **21 pts.**

PAULA ¡Hola, Daniel! ¿Qué tal el fin de semana?

DANIEL Muy bien. Marta y yo (1) _____ (conseguir) hacer muchas cosas, pero lo mejor fue la cena del sábado.

PAULA Ah, ¿sí? ¿Adónde fueron?

DANIEL Al restaurante Vistahermosa. Es elegante, así que (nosotros) (2) _____ (vestirse) bien.

PAULA Y, ¿qué platos (3) _____ (pedir, ustedes)?

DANIEL Yo (4) _____ (pedir) camarones y Marta (5) _____ (preferir) el pollo. Y al final, el camarero nos (6) _____ (servir) flan.

PAULA ¡Qué rico!

DANIEL Sí. Pero después de la cena Marta no (7) _____ (sentirse) bien.

3 **Camareros** Genaro y Úrsula son camareros en un restaurante. Completa la conversación que tienen con su jefe usando pronombres. **12 pts.**

JEFE Úrsula, ¿le ofreciste agua fría al cliente de la mesa 22?

ÚRSULA Sí, (1) _____ de inmediato.

JEFE Genaro, ¿los clientes de la mesa 5 te pidieron ensaladas?

GENARO Sí, (2) _____.

ÚRSULA Genaro, ¿recuerdas si ya me mostraste los vinos nuevos?

GENARO Sí, ya (3) _____.

JEFE Genaro, ¿van a pagarte la cuenta los clientes de la mesa 5?

GENARO Sí, (4) _____ ahora mismo.

RESUMEN GRAMATICAL

8.1 **Preterite of stem-changing verbs** *p. 274*

servir	dormir
serví	dormí
serviste	dormiste
sirvió	durmió
servimos	dormimos
servisteis	dormisteis
sirvieron	durmieron

8.2 **Double object pronouns** *pp. 277–278*

Indirect Object Pronouns: me, te, le (se), nos, os, les (se)

Direct Object Pronouns: lo, la, los, las

Le escribí la carta. → Se la escribí.
Nos van a servir los platos. → Nos los van a servir./
Van a servírnoslos.

8.3 **Comparisons** *pp. 281–283*

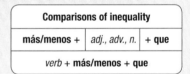

Comparisons of inequality		
más/menos +	adj., adv., n.	+ que
verb + más/menos + que		

Comparisons of equality		
tan +	adj., adv.,	+ como
tanto/a(s) +	noun	+ como
verb + tanto como		

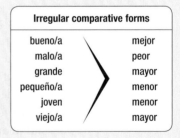

Irregular comparative forms	
bueno/a	mejor
malo/a	peor
grande	mayor
pequeño/a	menor
joven	menor
viejo/a	mayor

8.4 **Superlatives**   *p. 286*

el/la/ los/las +	noun	+ más/ menos +	adjective	+ de

▶ Irregular superlatives follow the same pattern as irregular comparatives.

4 **El menú** Observa el menú y sus características. Completa las oraciones basándote en los elementos dados. Usa comparativos y superlativos.   **36 pts.**

Ensaladas	*Precio*	*Calorías*
Ensalada de tomates	$9.00	170
Ensalada de mariscos	$12.99	325
Ensalada de zanahorias	$9.00	200

Platos principales		
Pollo con champiñones	$13.00	495
Cerdo con papas	$10.50	725
Atún con espárragos	$18.95	495

1. ensalada de mariscos / otras ensaladas / costar
   La ensalada de mariscos _____ las otras ensaladas.
2. pollo con champiñones / cerdo con papas / calorías
   El pollo con champiñones tiene _____ el cerdo con papas.
3. atún con espárragos / pollo con champiñones / calorías
   El atún con espárragos tiene _____ el pollo con champiñones.
4. ensalada de tomates / ensalada de zanahorias / caro
   La ensalada de tomates es _____ la ensalada de zanahorias.
5. cerdo con papas / platos principales / caro
   El cerdo con papas es _____ los platos principales.
6. ensalada de zanahorias / ensalada de tomates / costar
   La ensalada de zanahorias _____ la ensalada de tomates.
7. ensalada de mariscos / ensaladas / caro
   La ensalada de mariscos es _____ las ensaladas.
8. ensalada de zanahorias / ensalada de tomates / calorías
   La ensalada de zanahorias tiene _____ la ensalada de tomates.
9. atún con espárragos / platos principales / barato
   El atún con espárragos es _____ los platos principales.

5 **Adivinanza** Completa la adivinanza y adivina la respuesta.   **4 pts.**

“ En el campo yo nací°,
mis hermanos son
los _____ (*garlic, pl.*),
y aquél que llora° por mí
me está partiendo°
en pedazos°. ”
¿Quién soy? _____

nací *was born* llora *cries* partiendo *cutting* pedazos *pieces*

Lectura

Antes de leer

Estrategia

Reading for the main idea

As you know, you can learn a great deal about a reading selection by looking at the format and looking for cognates, titles, and subtitles. You can skim to get the gist of the reading selection and scan it for specific information. Reading for the main idea is another useful strategy; it involves locating the topic sentences of each paragraph to determine the author's purpose for writing a particular piece. Topic sentences can provide clues about the content of each paragraph, as well as the general organization of the reading. Your choice of which reading strategies to use will depend on the style and format of each reading selection.

Examinar el texto

En esta sección tenemos dos textos diferentes. ¿Qué estrategias puedes usar para leer la crítica culinaria°? ¿Cuáles son las apropiadas para familiarizarte con el menú? Utiliza las estrategias más eficaces° para cada texto. ¿Qué tienen en común? ¿Qué tipo de comida sirven en el restaurante?

Identificar la idea principal

Lee la primera oración de cada párrafo de la crítica culinaria del restaurante **La feria del maíz.** Apunta° el tema principal de cada párrafo. Luego lee todo el primer párrafo. ¿Crees que el restaurante le gustó al autor de la crítica culinaria? ¿Por qué? Ahora lee la crítica entera. En tu opinión, ¿cuál es la idea principal de la crítica? ¿Por qué la escribió el autor?

MENÚ

Entremeses

Tortilla servida con
- Ajiaceite (chile, aceite) • Ajicomino (chile, comino)

Pan tostado servido con
- Queso frito a la pimienta • Salsa de ajo y mayonesa

Sopas

- Tomate • Cebolla • Verduras • Pollo y huevo
- Carne de res • Mariscos

Entradas

Tomaticán
(tomate, papas, maíz, chile, arvejas y zanahorias)

Tamales
(maíz, azúcar, ajo, cebolla)

Frijoles enchilados
(frijoles negros, carne de cerdo o de res, arroz, chile)

Chilaquil
(tortilla de maíz, queso, hierbas y chile)

Tacos
(tortillas, pollo, verduras y salsa)

Cóctel de mariscos
(camarones, langosta, vinagre, sal, pimienta, aceite)

Postres°

- Plátanos caribeños • Cóctel de frutas al ron°
- Uvate (uvas, azúcar de caña y ron) • Flan napolitano
- Helado° de piña y naranja • Pastel° de yogur

Después de leer

Preguntas

Contesta estas preguntas sobre la crítica culinaria de **La feria del maíz.**

1. ¿Quién es el dueño y chef de **La feria del maíz**?

2. ¿Qué tipo de comida se sirve en el restaurante?

3. ¿Cuál es el problema con el servicio?

4. ¿Cómo es el ambiente del restaurante?

5. ¿Qué comidas probó el autor?

6. ¿Quieres ir al restaurante **La feria del maíz**? ¿Por qué?

---

crítica culinaria *restaurant review* eficaces *effective*
Apunta *Jot down*

23F

Gastronomía

Por Eduardo Fernández

La feria del maíz

Sobresaliente°. En el nuevo restaurante **La feria del maíz** va a encontrar la perfecta combinación entre la comida tradicional y el encanto° de la vieja ciudad de Antigua. Ernesto Sandoval, antiguo jefe de cocina° del famoso restaurante **El fogón**, está teniendo mucho éxito° en su nueva aventura culinaria.

El gerente°, el experimentado José Sierra, controla a la perfección la calidad del servicio. El camarero que me atendió esa noche fue muy amable en todo momento. Sólo hay que comentar que,

**La feria del maíz
13 calle 4-41 Zona 1
La Antigua, Guatemala
2329912**

*lunes a sábado
10:30am-11:30pm
domingo 10:00am-10:00pm*

Comida ♈♈♈♈♈

Servicio ♈♈♈

Ambiente ♈♈♈♈

Precio ♈♈♈

debido al éxito inmediato de **La feria del maíz**, se necesitan más camareros para atender a los clientes de una forma más eficaz. En esta ocasión, el mesero se

tomó unos veinte minutos en traerme la bebida.

Afortunadamente, no me importó mucho la espera entre plato y plato, pues el ambiente es tan agradable que me sentí como en casa. El restaurante mantiene el estilo colonial de Antigua. Por dentro°, es elegante y rústico a la vez. Cuando el tiempo lo permite, se puede comer también en el patio, donde hay muchas flores.

El servicio de camareros y el ambiente agradable del local pasan a un segundo plano cuando llega la comida, de una calidad extraordinaria. Las tortillas de casa se sirven con un ajiaceite delicioso. La sopa

de mariscos es excelente y los tamales, pues, tengo que confesar que son mejores que los de mi abuelita. También recomiendo los tacos de pollo, servidos con un mole buenísimo. De postre, don Ernesto me preparó su especialidad, unos plátanos caribeños sabrosísimos.

Los precios pueden parecer altos° para una comida tradicional, pero la calidad de los productos con que se cocinan los platos y el exquisito ambiente de **La feria del maíz** garantizan° una experiencia inolvidable°.

Bebidas

- Cerveza negra • Chilate (bebida de maíz, chile y cacao)
- Jugos de fruta • Agua mineral • Té helado
- Vino tinto/blanco • Ron

Postres *Desserts* ron *rum* Helado *Ice cream* Pastel *Cake* Sobresaliente *Outstanding* encanto *charm* jefe de cocina *head chef* éxito *success* gerente *manager* Por dentro *Inside* altos *high* garantizan *guarantee* inolvidable *unforgettable*

Un(a) guía turístico/a

Tú eres un(a) guía turístico/a en Guatemala. Estás en el restaurante **La feria del maíz** con un grupo de turistas norteamericanos. Ellos no hablan español y quieren pedir de comer, pero necesitan tu ayuda. Lee nuevamente el menú e indica qué error comete cada turista.

1. La señora Johnson es diabética y no puede comer azúcar. Pide sopa de verduras y tamales. No pide nada de postre.

2. Los señores Petit son vegetarianos y piden sopa de tomate, frijoles enchilados y plátanos caribeños.

3. El señor Smith, que es alérgico al chocolate, pide tortilla servida con ajiaceite, chilaquil y chilate para beber.

4. La adorable hija del señor Smith tiene sólo cuatro años y le gustan mucho las verduras y las frutas naturales. Su papá le pide tomaticán y un cóctel de frutas.

5. La señorita Jackson está a dieta y pide uvate, flan napolitano y helado.

Escritura

Estrategia

Expressing and supporting opinions

Written reviews are just one of the many kinds of writing which require you to state your opinions. In order to convince your reader to take your opinions seriously, it is important to support them as thoroughly as possible. Details, facts, examples, and other forms of evidence are necessary. In a restaurant review, for example, it is not enough just to rate the food, service, and atmosphere. Readers will want details about the dishes you ordered, the kind of service you received, and the type of atmosphere you encountered. If you were writing a concert or album review, what kinds of details might your readers expect to find?

It is easier to include details that support your opinions if you plan ahead. Before going to a place or event that you are planning to review, write a list of questions that your readers might ask. Decide which aspects of the experience you are going to rate and list the details that will help you decide upon a rating. You can then organize these lists into a questionnaire and a rating sheet. Bring these forms with you to help you make your opinions and to remind you of the kinds of information you need to gather in order to support those opinions. Later, these forms will help you organize your review into logical categories. They can also provide the details and other evidence you need to convince your readers of your opinions.

Tema

Escribir una crítica

Escribe una crítica culinaria° sobre un restaurante local para el periódico de la universidad. Clasifica el restaurante dándole de una a cinco estrellas° y anota tus recomendaciones para futuros clientes del restaurante. Incluye tus opiniones acerca de°:

▶ La comida

    ¿Qué tipo de comida es? ¿Qué tipo de ingredientes usan? ¿Es de buena calidad? ¿Cuál es el mejor plato? ¿Y el peor? ¿Quién es el/la chef?

▶ El servicio

    ¿Es necesario esperar mucho para conseguir una mesa? ¿Tienen los camareros un buen conocimiento del menú? ¿Atienden a los clientes con rapidez° y cortesía?

▶ El ambiente

    ¿Cómo es la decoración del restaurante? ¿Es el ambiente informal o elegante? ¿Hay música o algún tipo de entretenimiento°? ¿Hay un bar? ¿Un patio?

▶ Información práctica

    ¿Cómo son los precios? ¿Se aceptan tarjetas de crédito? ¿Cuál es la dirección° y el número de teléfono? ¿Quién es el/la dueño/a? ¿El/La gerente?

crítica culinaria *restaurant review* estrellas *stars* acerca de *about*
rapidez *speed* entretenimiento *entertainment* dirección *address*

Escuchar

Estrategia

Jotting down notes as you listen

Jotting down notes while you listen to a conversation in Spanish can help you keep track of the important points or details. It will help you to focus actively on comprehension rather than on remembering what you have heard.

 To practice this strategy, you will now listen to a paragraph. Jot down the main points you hear.

Preparación

Mira la foto. ¿Dónde están estas personas y qué hacen? ¿Sobre qué crees que están hablando?

Ahora escucha 🎧

Rosa y Roberto están en un restaurante. Escucha la conversación entre ellos y la camarera y toma nota de cuáles son los especiales del día, qué pidieron y qué bebidas se mencionan.

> **Especiales del día**

Entremeses

_____

Plato principal

_____

_____

_____

> **¿Qué pidieron?**

Roberto

_____

Rosa

_____

> **Bebidas**

_____

_____

Comprensión

Seleccionar

Usa tus notas para seleccionar la opción correcta para completar cada oración.

1. Dos de los mejores platos del restaurante son _____.
   a. los entremeses del día y el cerdo
   b. el salmón y el arroz con pollo
   c. la carne y el arroz con pollo

2. La camarera _____.
   a. los lleva a su mesa, les muestra el menú y les sirve el postre
   b. les habla de los especiales del día, les recomienda unos platos y ellos deciden qué van a comer
   c. les lleva unas bebidas, les recomienda unos platos y les sirve pan

3. Roberto va a comer _____ Rosa.
   a. tantos platos como
   b. más platos que
   c. menos platos que

Preguntas

Contesta las preguntas: ¿Conoces los platos que Rosa y Roberto pidieron? ¿Conoces platos con los mismos ingredientes? ¿En qué son diferentes o similares? ¿Cuál te gusta más? ¿Por qué?

En pantalla

La sopa es un plato muy importante en las cocinas°
del mundo hispano. Se pueden tomar° frías, como
el famoso gazpacho español, a base de tomate y
otras verduras y servida totalmente líquida. La
mayoría se sirven calientes, como el pozole de
México, un plato precolombino preparado con
nixtamal°, cerdo, chiles y otras especias°. Otra
sopa de origen indígena es la changua, de la
región andina central de Colombia. Aunque° las
sopas normalmente forman parte del almuerzo,
la changua siempre se toma en el desayuno: se
hace con agua, leche, huevo y cilantro.

Vocabulario útil	
bajar	*to descend*
la escalera	*staircase*
lo que yo quiera	*whatever I want*
sabor marinero	*seafood flavor*

Ordenar

Ordena cronológicamente estas oraciones.

_____ a. El niño abre la puerta.

_____ b. El niño decide almorzar.

_____ c. El niño baja la escalera con una maleta.

_____ d. El niño se va a lavar las manos.

_____ e. La madre dice que la sopa está servida.

Sopas

Describe tu sopa favorita. ¿Cuál es tu sopa favorita?
¿Quién la prepara o dónde la compras? ¿Qué
ingredientes tiene? ¿Con qué se sirve? ¿Cómo la
prefieres, caliente o fría? ¿La tomas en el almuerzo
o en la cena? ¿En invierno o en verano?

Anuncio de Sopas Roa

Me voy de esta casa.

Ya está servida° la sopa...

... y lavarme las manos.

cocinas *cuisines* tomar *to eat (soup)* nixtamal *hominy* especias *spices*
Aunque *Although* está servida *it is served*

España y la mayoría de los países de Latinoamérica tienen una producción muy abundante de frutas y verduras. Es por esto que en los hogares° hispanos se acostumbra° cocinar° con productos frescos° más que con alimentos° que vienen en latas° o frascos°. Las salsas mexicanas, el gazpacho español y el sancocho colombiano, por ejemplo, deben prepararse con ingredientes frescos para que mantengan° su sabor° auténtico. Actualmente, en los Estados Unidos está creciendo el interés en cocinar con productos frescos y orgánicos. Cada vez hay más mercados donde los agricultores° pueden vender sus frutas y verduras directamente° al público. Además, las personas prefieren consumir productos locales de temporada°. En este episodio de *Flash cultura* vas a ver algunas de las frutas y verduras típicas de la comida hispana.

Vocabulario útil	
blanda	*soft*
cocinar	*to cook*
dura	*hard*
¿Está lista para ordenar?	*Are you ready to order?*
pruébala	*try it, taste it*
las ventas	*sales*

Preparación

¿Probaste alguna vez comida latina? ¿La compraste en un supermercado o fuiste a un restaurante? ¿Qué plato(s) probaste? ¿Te gustó?

¿Cierto o falso?

Indica si cada oración es **cierta** o **falsa**.

1. En Los Ángeles hay comida de países latinoamericanos y de España.
2. Leticia explica que la tortilla del taco americano es blanda y la del taco mexicano es dura.
3. Las ventas de salsa son bajas en los Estados Unidos.
4. Leticia fue a un restaurante ecuatoriano.
5. Leticia probó Inca Kola en un supermercado.

hogares *homes* se acostumbra *they are used* cocinar *to cook* frescos *fresh* alimentos *foods* latas *cans* frascos *jars* para que mantengan *so that they keep* sabor *flavor* agricultores *farmers* directamente *directly* de temporada *seasonal* mostrará *will show*

La comida latina

La mejor comida latina no sólo se encuentra en los grandes restaurantes.

Marta nos mostrará° algunos de los platos de la comida mexicana.

... hay más lugares donde podemos comprar productos hispanos.

Guatemala

El país en cifras

- ▶ **Área:** 108.890 km² (42.042 millas²), *un poco más pequeño que Tennessee*
- ▶ **Población:** 14.647.000
- ▶ **Capital:** Ciudad de Guatemala—1.075.000
- ▶ **Ciudades principales:** Quetzaltenango, Escuintla, Mazatenango, Puerto Barrios
- ▶ **Moneda:** quetzal
- ▶ **Idiomas:** español (oficial), lenguas mayas, xinca, garífuna

El español es la lengua de un 60 por ciento° de la población; el otro 40 por ciento tiene como lengua materna el xinca, el garífuna o, en su mayoría°, una de las lenguas mayas (cakchiquel, quiché y kekchícomo, entre otras). Una palabra que las lenguas mayas tienen en común es ixim, que significa 'maíz', un cultivo° de mucha importancia en estas culturas.

Bandera de Guatemala

Guatemaltecos célebres

- ▶ **Carlos Mérida,** pintor (1891–1984)
- ▶ **Miguel Ángel Asturias,** escritor (1899–1974)
- ▶ **Margarita Carrera,** poeta y ensayista (1929–)
- ▶ **Rigoberta Menchú Tum,** activista (1959–), Premio Nobel de la Paz° en 1992
- ▶ **Jaime Viñals Massanet,** montañista (1966–)

por ciento *percent* en su mayoría *most of them* cultivo *crop*
Paz *Peace* telas *fabrics* tinte *dye* aplastados *crushed*
hace... destiñan *keeps the colors from running*

ESTADOS UNIDOS
OCÉANO ATLÁNTICO
GUATEMALA
OCÉANO PACÍFICO
AMÉRICA DEL SUR

Palacio Nacional de la Cultura en la Ciudad de Guatemala

MÉXICO

Sierra de Lacandón

Río Usumacinta

Lago Petén Itzá

Río de la Pasión

BELICE

Mujeres indígenas limpiando cebollas

Lago de Izabal

Quetzaltenango

Sierra de las Minas

Sierra Madre

Lago de Atitlán

Río Motagua

★Guatemala

Antigua Guatemala

Mazatenango

Escuintla

Iglesia de la Merced en Antigua Guatemala

EL SALVADOR

Océano Pacífico

¡Increíble pero cierto!

¿Qué "ingrediente" secreto se encuentra en las telas° tradicionales de Guatemala? ¡El mosquito! El excepcional tinte° de estas telas es producto de una combinación de flores y de mosquitos aplastados°. El insecto hace que los colores no se destiñan°. Quizás es por esto que los artesanos representan la figura del mosquito en muchas de sus telas.

Ciudades • **Antigua Guatemala**

Antigua Guatemala fue fundada en 1543. Fue una capital de gran importancia hasta 1773, cuando un terremoto° la destruyó. Sin embargo, conserva el carácter original de su arquitectura y hoy es uno de los centros turísticos del país. Su celebración de la Semana Santa° es, para muchas personas, la más importante del hemisferio.

Naturaleza • **El quetzal**

El quetzal simbolizó la libertad para los antiguos° mayas porque creían° que este pájaro° no podía° vivir en cautiverio°. Hoy el quetzal es el símbolo nacional. El pájaro da su nombre a la moneda nacional y aparece también en los billetes° del país. Desafortunadamente, está en peligro° de extinción. Para su protección, el gobierno mantiene una reserva ecológica especial.

Mar Caribe

Golfo de Honduras

Historia • **Los mayas**

Desde 1500 a.C. hasta 900 d.C., los mayas habitaron gran parte de lo que ahora es Guatemala. Su civilización fue muy avanzada. Los mayas fueron arquitectos y constructores de pirámides, templos y observatorios. También descubrieron° y usaron el cero antes que los europeos, e inventaron un calendario complejo° y preciso.

• Puerto Barríos

Artesanía • **La ropa tradicional**

La ropa tradicional de los guatemaltecos se llama *huipil* y muestra el amor° de la cultura maya por la naturaleza. Ellos se inspiran en las flores°, plantas y animales para crear sus diseños° de colores vivos° y formas geométricas. El diseño y los colores de cada *huipil* indican el pueblo de origen y a veces también el sexo y la edad° de la persona que lo lleva.

HONDURAS

¿Qué aprendiste? Contesta cada pregunta con una oración completa.

1. ¿Qué significa la palabra *ixim*?

2. ¿Quién es Rigoberta Menchú?

3. ¿Qué pájaro representa a Guatemala?

4. ¿Qué simbolizó el quetzal para los mayas?

5. ¿Cuál es la moneda nacional de Guatemala?

6. ¿De qué fueron arquitectos los mayas?

7. ¿Qué celebración de la Antigua Guatemala es la más importante del hemisferio para muchas personas?

8. ¿Qué descubrieron los mayas antes que los europeos?

9. ¿Qué muestra la ropa tradicional de los guatemaltecos?

10. ¿Qué indica un *huipil* con su diseño y sus colores?

Conexión Internet Investiga estos temas en Internet.

1. Busca información sobre Rigoberta Menchú. ¿De dónde es? ¿Qué libros publicó? ¿Por qué es famosa?

2. Estudia un sitio arqueológico de Guatemala para aprender más sobre los mayas.

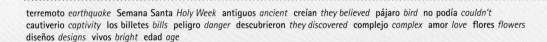

terremoto *earthquake* Semana Santa *Holy Week* antiguos *ancient* creían *they believed* pájaro *bird* no podía *couldn't* cautiverio *captivity* los billetes *bills* peligro *danger* descubrieron *they discovered* complejo *complex* amor *love* flores *flowers* diseños *designs* vivos *bright* edad *age*

Las comidas

el/la camarero/a	waiter/waitress
la comida	food; meal
la cuenta	bill
el/la dueño/a	owner
el menú	menu
la propina	tip
la sección de (no) fumar	(non) smoking section
el almuerzo	lunch
la cena	dinner
el desayuno	breakfast
los entremeses	appetizers
el plato (principal)	(main) dish
delicioso/a	delicious
rico/a	tasty; delicious
sabroso/a	tasty; delicious

Las frutas

la banana	banana
las frutas	fruits
el limón	lemon
la manzana	apple
el melocotón	peach
la naranja	orange
la pera	pear
la uva	grape

Las verduras

las arvejas	peas
la cebolla	onion
el champiñón	mushroom
la ensalada	salad
los espárragos	asparagus
los frijoles	beans
la lechuga	lettuce
el maíz	corn
las papas/patatas (fritas)	(fried) potatoes; French fries
el tomate	tomato
las verduras	vegetables
la zanahoria	carrot

La carne y el pescado

el atún	tuna
el bistec	steak
los camarones	shrimp
la carne	meat
la carne de res	beef
la chuleta (de cerdo)	(pork) chop
la hamburguesa	hamburger
el jamón	ham
la langosta	lobster
los mariscos	shellfish
el pavo	turkey
el pescado	fish
el pollo (asado)	(roast) chicken
la salchicha	sausage
el salmón	salmon

Otras comidas

el aceite	oil
el ajo	garlic
el arroz	rice
el azúcar	sugar
los cereales	cereal; grains
el huevo	egg
la mantequilla	butter
la margarina	margarine
la mayonesa	mayonnaise
el pan (tostado)	(toasted) bread
la pimienta	black pepper
el queso	cheese
la sal	salt
el sándwich	sandwich
la sopa	soup
el vinagre	vinegar
el yogur	yogurt

Las bebidas

el agua (mineral)	(mineral) water
la bebida	drink
el café	coffee
la cerveza	beer
el jugo (de fruta)	(fruit) juice
la leche	milk
el refresco	soft drink
el té (helado)	(iced) tea
el vino (blanco/ tinto)	(white/red) wine

Verbos

escoger	to choose
merendar (e:ie)	to snack
morir (o:ue)	to die
pedir (e:i)	to order (food)
probar (o:ue)	to taste; to try
recomendar (e:ie)	to recommend
saber (a)	to taste (like)
servir (e:i)	to serve

Las comparaciones

como	like; as
más de (+ number)	more than
más... que	more... than
menos de (+ number)	fewer than
menos... que	less... than
tan... como	as... as
tantos/as... como	as many... as
tanto... como	as much... as
el/la mayor	the oldest
el/la mejor	the best
el/la menor	the youngest
el/la peor	the worst
mejor	better
peor	worse

Expresiones útiles	See page 269.

Las fiestas

Communicative Goals

You will learn how to:

- **Express congratulations**
- **Express gratitude**
- **Ask for and pay the bill at a restaurant**

A PRIMERA VISTA

- ¿Se conocen ellos?
- ¿Cómo se sienten, alegres o tristes?
- ¿Está el hombre más contento que la mujer?
- ¿De qué color es su ropa?

Las fiestas

Más vocabulario

la alegría	happiness
la amistad	friendship
el amor	love
el beso	kiss
la sorpresa	surprise
el aniversario (de bodas)	(wedding) anniversary
la boda	wedding
el cumpleaños	birthday
el día de fiesta	holiday
el divorcio	divorce
el matrimonio	marriage
la Navidad	Christmas
la quinceañera	young woman celebrating her fifteenth birthday
el/la recién casado/a	newlywed
cambiar (de)	to change
celebrar	to celebrate
divertirse (e:ie)	to have fun
graduarse (de/en)	to graduate (from/in)
invitar	to invite
jubilarse	to retire (from work)
nacer	to be born
odiar	to hate
pasarlo bien/mal	to have a good/bad time
reírse (e:i)	to laugh
relajarse	to relax
sonreír (e:i)	to smile
sorprender	to surprise
juntos/as	together
¡Felicidades!/ ¡Felicitaciones!	Congratulations!

Variación léxica

pastel ⟷ torta (Arg., Col., Venez.)
comprometerse ⟷ prometerse (Esp.)

la pareja

la botella de vino

el pastel (de chocolate)

el flan de caramelo

las galletas

los postres

el champán

los dulces

FELIZ CUMPLEAÑOS

brindar

el invitado

regalar

el helado

Relaciones personales

casarse (con)	*to get married (to)*
comprometerse (con)	*to get engaged (to)*
divorciarse (de)	*to get divorced (from)*
enamorarse (de)	*to fall in love (with)*
llevarse bien/mal (con)	*to get along well/ badly (with)*
romper (con)	*to break up (with)*
salir (con)	*to go out (with); to date*
separarse (de)	*to separate (from)*
tener una cita	*to have a date; to have an appointment*

Práctica

1 **Escuchar** 🎧 Escucha la conversación e indica si las oraciones son **ciertas** o **falsas**.

1. A Silvia no le gusta mucho el chocolate.
2. Silvia sabe que sus amigos le van a hacer una fiesta.
3. Los amigos de Silvia le compraron un pastel de chocolate.
4. Los amigos brindan por Silvia con refrescos.
5. Silvia y sus amigos van a comer helado.
6. Los amigos de Silvia le van a servir flan y galletas.

2 **Ordenar** 🎧 Escucha la narración y ordena las oraciones de acuerdo con los eventos de la vida de Beatriz.

_____ a. Beatriz se compromete con Roberto.

_____ b. Beatriz se gradúa.

_____ c. Beatriz sale con Emilio.

_____ d. Sus padres le hacen una gran fiesta.

_____ e. La pareja se casa.

_____ f. Beatriz nace en Montevideo.

3 **Emparejar** Indica la letra de la frase que mejor completa cada oración.

a. **cambió de**	d. **nos divertimos**	g. **se llevan bien**
b. **lo pasaron mal**	e. **se casaron**	h. **sonrió**
c. **nació**	f. **se jubiló**	i. **tenemos una cita**

1. María y sus compañeras de cuarto _____. Son buenas amigas.
2. Pablo y yo _____ en la fiesta. Bailamos y comimos mucho.
3. Manuel y Felipe _____ en el cine. La película fue muy mala.
4. ¡Tengo una nueva sobrina! Ella _____ ayer por la mañana.
5. Mi madre _____ profesión. Ahora es artista.
6. Mi padre _____ el año pasado. Ahora no trabaja.
7. Jorge y yo _____ esta noche. Vamos a ir a un restaurante muy elegante.
8. Jaime y Laura _____ el septiembre pasado. La boda fue maravillosa.

4 **Definiciones** Define las palabras y escribe una oración para cada ejemplo.

> **modelo**
>
> **romper (con)** *una pareja termina la relación*
> *Marta rompió con su novio.*

1. regalar
2. helado
3. pareja
4. invitado
5. casarse
6. pasarlo bien
7. sorpresa
8. amistad

Las etapas de la vida de Sergio

el nacimiento

la niñez

la adolescencia

la juventud

la madurez

la vejez

Más vocabulario	
la edad	*age*
el estado civil	*marital status*
las etapas de la vida	*the stages of life*
la muerte	*death*
casado/a	*married*
divorciado/a	*divorced*
separado/a	*separated*
soltero/a	*single*
viudo/a	*widower/widow*

NOTA CULTURAL

Viña del Mar es una ciudad en la costa de Chile, situada al oeste de Santiago. Tiene playas hermosas, excelentes hoteles, casinos y buenos restaurantes. El poeta Pablo Neruda pasó muchos años allí.

5   **Las etapas de la vida** Identifica las etapas de la vida que se describen en estas oraciones.

1. Mi abuela se jubiló y se mudó (*moved*) a Viña del Mar.
2. Mi padre trabaja para una compañía grande en Santiago.
3. ¿Viste a mi nuevo sobrino en el hospital? Es precioso y ¡tan pequeño!
4. Mi abuelo murió este año.
5. Mi hermana celebró su fiesta de quince años.
6. Mi hermana pequeña juega con muñecas (*dolls*).

¡LENGUA VIVA!

The term **quinceañera** refers to a girl who is celebrating her 15th birthday. The party is called **la fiesta de quince años**.

6   **Cambiar** Imagina que eres el/la hermano/a mayor. Cada vez que tu hermana menor dice algo, se equivoca. Corrígela (*Correct her*), cambiando las expresiones subrayadas (*underlined*).

> **modelo**
>
> La <u>niñez</u> es cuando trabajamos mucho.
> *No, te equivocas (you're wrong). La madurez es cuando trabajamos mucho.*

1. <u>El nacimiento</u> es el fin de la vida.
2. <u>La juventud</u> es la etapa cuando nos jubilamos.
3. A los sesenta y cinco años, muchas personas <u>comienzan a trabajar.</u>
4. Julián y nuestra prima <u>se divorcian</u> mañana.
5. Mamá <u>odia</u> a su hermana.
6. El abuelo murió, por eso la abuela es <u>separada</u>.
7. Cuando te gradúas de la universidad, estás en la etapa de <u>la adolescencia</u>.
8. Mi tío nunca se casó; es <u>viudo</u>.

AYUDA

Other ways to contradict someone:
No es verdad.
It's not true.
Creo que no.
I don't think so.
¡Claro que no!
Of course not!
¡Qué va!
No way!

Comunicación

7 **La invitación** Lee el mensaje electrónico de Marcela a su amigo Adrián. Luego, indica si las conclusiones son **lógicas** o **ilógicas**, según lo que leíste.

De:	Marcela
Para:	Adrián
Asunto:	Fiesta

Adrián, te quiero invitar a la fiesta que vamos a hacerle a mi bisabuelo Alfonso por su cumpleaños. ¡Cumple cien años! Queremos celebrar su larga y extraordinaria vida a lo grande: va a haber deliciosos entremeses, riquísimos dulces y mucho champán. También vamos a tener tu postre favorito, pastel de chocolate. Tienes que venir a la fiesta. Te vas a relajar mucho y no vas a pensar en los exámenes finales que tenemos el próximo mes. ¡Vas a bailar toda la noche! También vamos a darle una sorpresa a mi bisabuelo: su mejor amigo de la niñez, Roberto, va a venir desde Santiago. ¡Ellos se vieron por última vez en 1940! Te espero entonces este sábado a las 7:30 p.m. en la casa de mis padres.

	Lógico	Ilógico
1. Marcela y Adrián van a la misma universidad.	○	○
2. La fiesta es una cena formal.	○	○
3. A Adrián no le gustan los postres.	○	○
4. Alfonso conoce a Roberto desde la muerte de su esposa.	○	○
5. En la fiesta van a brindar por Alfonso.	○	○

8 **Preguntas** Contesta las preguntas de tu compañero/a.

1. ¿Te importa la amistad? ¿Por qué?
2. ¿Es mejor tener un(a) buen(a) amigo/a o muchos/as amigos/as?
3. ¿Cuáles son las características que buscas en tus amigos/as?
4. ¿Tienes novio/a? ¿A qué edad es posible enamorarse?
5. ¿Deben las parejas hacer todo juntos? ¿Deben tener las mismas opiniones? ¿Por qué?

¡LENGUA VIVA!
While a **buen(a) amigo/a** is a *good friend*, the term **amigo/a íntimo/a** refers to a *close friend*, or a very good friend, without any romantic overtones.

9 **Una fiesta** Trabaja con un(a) compañero/a para planear una fiesta. Recuerda incluir la siguiente información.

- tipo de fiesta
- lugar
- fecha
- invitados
- comida
- bebidas
- música

El Día de Muertos

La familia Díaz conmemora el Día de Muertos.

PERSONAJES

 MARISSA

 JIMENA

 FELIPE

 JUAN CARLOS

MAITE FUENTES El Día de Muertos se celebra en México el primero y el segundo de noviembre. Como pueden ver, hay calaveras de azúcar, flores, música y comida por todas partes. Ésta es una fiesta única que todos deben ver por lo menos una vez en la vida.

MARISSA *Holy moley!* ¡Está delicioso!

TÍA ANA MARÍA Mi mamá me enseñó a prepararlo. El mole siempre fue el plato favorito de mi papá. Mi hijo Eduardo nació el día de su cumpleaños. Por eso le pusimos su nombre.

MARISSA ¿Cómo se conocieron?

TÍA ANA MARÍA En la fiesta de un amigo. Fue amor a primera vista.

MARISSA (*Señala la foto.*) La voy a llevar al altar.

TÍO RAMÓN ¿Dónde están mis hermanos?

JIMENA Mi papá y Felipe están en el otro cuarto. Esos dos antipáticos no quieren decirnos qué están haciendo. Y la tía Ana María...

TÍO RAMÓN ... está en la cocina.

TÍA ANA MARÍA Marissa, ¿le puedes llevar esa foto que está ahí a Carolina? La necesita para el altar.

MARISSA Sí. ¿Son sus padres?

TÍA ANA MARÍA Sí, el día de su boda.

TÍA ANA MARÍA Ramón, ¿cómo estás?

TÍO RAMÓN Bien, gracias. ¿Y Mateo? ¿No vino contigo?

TÍA ANA MARÍA No. Ya sabes que me casé con un doctor y, pues, trabaja muchísimo.

SRA. DÍAZ

SR. DÍAZ

TÍA ANA MARÍA

TÍO RAMÓN

TÍA NAYELI

DON DIEGO

MARTA

VALENTINA

MAITE FUENTES

SR. DÍAZ Familia Díaz, deben prepararse...

FELIPE ... ¡para la sorpresa de sus vidas!

JUAN CARLOS Gracias por invitarme.

SR. DÍAZ Juan Carlos, como eres nuestro amigo, ya eres parte de la familia.

(En el cementerio)

JIMENA Yo hice las galletas y el pastel. ¿Dónde los puse?

MARTA Postres... ¿Cuál prefiero? ¿Galletas? ¿Pastel? ¡Dulces!

VALENTINA Me gustan las galletas.

SR. DÍAZ Brindamos por ustedes, mamá y papá.

TÍO RAMÓN Todas las otras noches estamos separados. Pero esta noche estamos juntos.

TÍA ANA MARÍA Con gratitud y amor.

Expresiones útiles

Discussing family history

El mole siempre fue el plato favorito de mi papá.
Mole was always my dad's favorite dish.
Mi hijo Eduardo nació el día de su cumpleaños.
My son Eduardo was born on his birthday.
Por eso le pusimos su nombre.
That's why we named him after him (after my father).
¿Cómo se conocieron sus padres?
How did your parents meet?
En la fiesta de un amigo. Fue amor a primera vista.
At a friend's party. It was love at first sight.

Talking about a party/celebration

Ésta es una fiesta única que todos deben ver por lo menos una vez.
This is a unique celebration that everyone should see at least once.
Gracias por invitarme.
Thanks for inviting me.
Brindamos por ustedes.
A toast to you.

Additional vocabulary

alma *soul*
altar *altar*
ángel *angel*
calavera de azúcar
skull made out of sugar
cementerio *cemetery*
cocina *kitchen*
disfraz *costume*

¿Qué pasó?

1 Completar Completa las oraciones con la información correcta, según la **Fotonovela**.

1. El Día de Muertos es una _____ única que todos deben ver.
2. La tía Ana María preparó _____ para celebrar.
3. Marissa lleva la _____ al altar.
4. Jimena hizo las _____ y el _____.
5. Marta no sabe qué _____ prefiere.

2 Identificar Identifica quién puede decir estas oraciones. Vas a usar un nombre dos veces.

1. Mis padres se conocieron en la fiesta de un amigo.
2. El Día de Muertos se celebra con flores, calaveras de azúcar, música y comida.
3. Gracias por invitarme a celebrar este Día de Muertos.
4. Los de la foto son mis padres el día de su boda.
5. A mí me gustan mucho las galletas.
6. ¡Qué bueno que estás aquí, Juan Carlos! Eres uno más de la familia.

 SR. DÍAZ
 MAITE FUENTES
 JUAN CARLOS
 VALENTINA
 TÍA ANA MARÍA

3 Seleccionar Selecciona algunas de las opciones de la lista para completar las oraciones.

amor	días de fiesta	pasarlo bien	salieron
el champán	divorciarse	postres	se enamoraron
cumpleaños	flan	la quinceañera	una sorpresa

1. El Sr. Díaz y Felipe prepararon _____ para la familia.
2. Los _____, como el Día de Muertos, se celebran con la familia.
3. Eduardo, el hijo de Ana María, nació el día del _____ de su abuelo.
4. La tía Ana María siente gratitud y _____ hacia (*toward*) sus padres.
5. Los días de fiesta también son para _____ con los amigos.
6. El Día de Muertos se hacen muchos _____.
7. Los padres de la tía Ana María _____ a primera vista.

4 Una cena Trabajen en parejas para representar una conversación en una cena de Año Nuevo.

- Una persona brinda por el año que está por comenzar y por estar con su familia y amigos.
- Cada persona habla de cuál es su comida favorita en año nuevo.
- Después de la cena, una persona dice que es hora de (*it's time to*) comer las uvas.
- Cada persona dice qué desea para el año que empieza.
- Después, cada persona debe desear Feliz Año Nuevo a las demás.

NOTA CULTURAL
Comer doce uvas a las doce de la noche del 31 de diciembre de cada año es una costumbre que nació en España y que también se observa en varios países de Latinoamérica. Se debe comer una uva por cada una de las 12 campanadas (*strokes*) del reloj y se cree que (*it's believed that*) quien lo hace va a tener un año próspero.

Pronunciación 🎧
The letters h, j, and g

helado	hombre	hola	hermosa

The Spanish **h** is always silent.

José	jubilarse	dejar	pareja

The letter **j** is pronounced much like the English *h* in *his*.

agencia	general	Gil	Gisela

The letter **g** can be pronounced three different ways. Before **e** or **i**, the letter **g** is pronounced much like the English *h*.

Gustavo, gracias por llamar el domingo.

At the beginning of a phrase or after the letter **n**, the Spanish **g** is pronounced like the English *g* in *girl*.

Me gradué en agosto.

In any other position, the Spanish **g** has a somewhat softer sound.

Guerra	conseguir	guantes	agua

In the combinations **gue** and **gui**, the **g** has a hard sound and the **u** is silent. In the combination **gua**, the **g** has a hard sound and the **u** is pronounced like the English *w*.

Práctica Lee las palabras en voz alta, prestando atención a la **h**, la **j** y la **g**.

1. hamburguesa
2. jugar
3. oreja
4. guapa
5. geografía
6. magnífico
7. espejo
8. hago
9. seguir
10. gracias
11. hijo
12. galleta
13. Jorge
14. tengo
15. ahora
16. guantes

Oraciones Lee las oraciones en voz alta, prestando atención a la **h**, la **j** y la **g**.

1. Hola. Me llamo Gustavo Hinojosa Lugones y vivo en Santiago de Chile.
2. Tengo una familia grande; somos tres hermanos y tres hermanas.
3. Voy a graduarme en mayo.
4. Para celebrar mi graduación, mis padres van a regalarme un viaje a Egipto.
5. ¡Qué generosos son!

Refranes Lee los refranes en voz alta, prestando atención a la **h**, la **j** y la **g**.

A la larga, lo más dulce amarga.[1]

El hábito no hace al monje.[2]

1 Too much of a good thing.
2 The clothes don't make the man.

Semana Santa: vacaciones y tradición

¿Te imaginas pasar veinticuatro horas tocando un tambor° entre miles de personas? Así es como mucha gente celebra el Viernes Santo° en el pequeño pueblo de **Calanda**, España.

De todas las celebraciones hispanas, la Semana Santa° es una de las más espectaculares y únicas.

Procesión en Sevilla, España

Semana Santa es la semana antes de Pascua°, una celebración religiosa que conmemora la Pasión de Jesucristo. Generalmente, la gente tiene unos días de vacaciones en esta semana. Algunas personas aprovechan° estos días para viajar, pero otras prefieren participar en las tradicionales celebraciones religiosas en las calles. En **Antigua**, Guatemala, hacen alfombras° de flores° y altares; también organizan Vía Crucis° y danzas. En las famosas procesiones y desfiles° religiosos de **Sevilla**, España, los fieles°

sacan a las calles imágenes religiosas. Las imágenes van encima de plataformas ricamente decoradas con abundantes flores y velas°. En la procesión, los penitentes llevan túnicas y unos sombreros cónicos que les cubren° la cara°. En sus manos llevan faroles° o velas encendidas.

Si visitas algún país hispano durante la Semana Santa, debes asistir a un desfile. Las playas y las discotecas pueden esperar hasta la semana siguiente.

Alfombra de flores en Antigua, Guatemala

Otras celebraciones famosas

Ayacucho, Perú: Además de alfombras de flores y procesiones, aquí hay una antigua tradición llamada "quema de la chamiza"°.

Iztapalapa, Ciudad de México: Es famoso el Vía Crucis del cerro° de la Estrella. Es una representación del recorrido° de Jesucristo con la cruz°.

Popayán, Colombia: En las procesiones "chiquitas" los niños llevan imágenes que son copias pequeñas de las que llevan los mayores.

tocando un tambor *playing a drum* Viernes Santo *Good Friday* Semana Santa *Holy Week* Pascua *Easter Sunday* aprovechan *take advantage of* alfombras *carpets* flores *flowers* Vía Crucis *Stations of the Cross* desfiles *parades* fieles *faithful* velas *candles* cubren *cover* cara *face* faroles *lamps* quema de la chamiza *burning of brushwood* cerro *hill* recorrido *route* cruz *cross*

ACTIVIDADES

1 **¿Cierto o falso?** Indica si lo que dicen las oraciones sobre Semana Santa en países hispanos es **cierto** o **falso**. Corrige las falsas.

1. La Semana Santa se celebra después de Pascua.

2. Las personas tienen días libres durante la Semana Santa.

3. Todas las personas asisten a las celebraciones religiosas.

4. En los países hispanos, las celebraciones se hacen en las calles.

5. En Antigua y en Ayacucho es típico hacer alfombras de flores.

6. En Sevilla, sacan imágenes religiosas a las calles.

7. En Sevilla, las túnicas cubren la cara.

8. En la procesión en Sevilla algunas personas llevan flores en sus manos.

9. El Vía Crucis de Iztapalapa es en el interior de una iglesia.

10. Las procesiones "chiquitas" son famosas en Sevilla, España.

Fiestas y celebraciones

la despedida de soltero/a	bachelor(ette) party
el día feriado/festivo	el día de fiesta
disfrutar	to enjoy
festejar	celebrar
los fuegos artificiales	fireworks
pasarlo en grande	divertirse mucho
la vela	candle

EL MUNDO HISPANO

Celebraciones latinoamericanas

- **Oruro, Bolivia** Durante el carnaval de Oruro se realiza la famosa Diablada, una antigua danza° que muestra la lucha° entre el Bien y el Mal: ángeles contra° demonios.

- **Panchimalco, El Salvador** La primera semana de mayo, Panchimalco se cubre de flores y de color. También hacen el Desfile de las palmas° y bailan danzas antiguas.

- **Quito, Ecuador** El mes de agosto es el Mes de las Artes. Danza, teatro, música, cine, artesanías° y otros eventos culturales inundan la ciudad.

- **San Pedro Sula, Honduras** En junio se celebra la Feria Juniana. Hay comida típica, bailes, desfiles, conciertos, rodeos, exposiciones ganaderas° y eventos deportivos y culturales.

danza *dance* lucha *fight* contra *versus* palmas *palm leaves* artesanías *handcrafts* exposiciones ganaderas *cattle shows*

PERFIL

Festival de Viña del Mar

En 1959 unos estudiantes de **Viña del Mar**, Chile, celebraron una fiesta en una casa de campo conocida como la Quinta Vergara donde hubo° un espectáculo° musical. En 1960 repitieron el evento. Asistió tanta gente que muchos vieron el espectáculo parados° o sentados en el suelo°. Algunos se subieron a los árboles°.

Años después, se convirtió en el **Festival Internacional de la Canción**. Este evento se celebra en febrero, en el mismo lugar donde empezó. ¡Pero ahora nadie necesita subirse a un árbol para verlo! Hay un anfiteatro con capacidad para quince mil personas.

En el festival hay concursos° musicales y conciertos de artistas famosos como Calle 13 y Nelly Furtado.

Nelly Furtado

hubo *there was* espectáculo *show* parados *standing* suelo *floor* se subieron a los árboles *climbed trees* concursos *competitions*

Conexión Internet

¿Qué celebraciones hispanas hay en los Estados Unidos y Canadá?

Use the Web to find more cultural information related to this **Cultura** section.

ACTIVIDADES

2 Comprensión Contesta las preguntas.
1. ¿Cuántas personas por día pueden asistir al Festival de Viña del Mar?
2. ¿Qué es la Diablada?
3. ¿Qué celebran en Quito en agosto?
4. Nombra dos atracciones en la Feria Juniana de San Pedro Sula.
5. ¿Qué es la Quinta Vergara?

3 ¿Cuál es tu celebración favorita? Escribe un pequeño párrafo sobre la celebración que más te gusta de tu comunidad. Explica cómo se llama, cuándo ocurre y cómo es.

9.1 Irregular preterites

ANTE TODO You already know that the verbs **ir** and **ser** are irregular in the preterite. You will now learn other verbs whose preterite forms are also irregular.

Preterite of tener, venir, and decir

		tener (u-stem)	venir (i-stem)	decir (j-stem)
SINGULAR FORMS	yo	tuve	vine	dije
	tú	tuviste	viniste	dijiste
	Ud./él/ella	tuvo	vino	dijo
PLURAL FORMS	nosotros/as	tuvimos	vinimos	dijimos
	vosotros/as	tuvisteis	vinisteis	dijisteis
	Uds./ellos/ellas	tuvieron	vinieron	dijeron

▶ **¡Atención!** The endings of these verbs are the regular preterite endings of **-er/-ir** verbs, except for the **yo** and **usted/él/ella** forms. Note that these two endings are unaccented.

▶ These verbs observe similar stem changes to **tener, venir,** and **decir.**

INFINITIVE	U-STEM	PRETERITE FORMS
poder	pud-	pude, pudiste, pudo, pudimos, pudisteis, pudieron
poner	pus-	puse, pusiste, puso, pusimos, pusisteis, pusieron
saber	sup-	supe, supiste, supo, supimos, supisteis, supieron
estar	estuv-	estuve, estuviste, estuvo, estuvimos, estuvisteis, estuvieron

INFINITIVE	I-STEM	PRETERITE FORMS
querer	quis-	quise, quisiste, quiso, quisimos, quisisteis, quisieron
hacer	hic-	hice, hiciste, hizo, hicimos, hicisteis, hicieron

INFINITIVE	J-STEM	PRETERITE FORMS
traer	traj-	traje, trajiste, trajo, trajimos, trajisteis, trajeron
conducir	conduj-	conduje, condujiste, condujo, condujimos, condujisteis, condujeron
traducir	traduj-	traduje, tradujiste, tradujo, tradujimos, tradujisteis, tradujeron

¡ATENCIÓN!
Note the **c → z** spelling change in the third-person singular form of **hacer: hizo.**

▶ **¡Atención!** Most verbs that end in **-cir** are **j**-stem verbs in the preterite. For example, **producir → produje, produjiste,** etc.

> **Produjimos** un documental sobre los accidentes en la casa.
> *We produced a documentary about accidents in the home.*

▶ Notice that the preterites with **j**-stems omit the letter **i** in the **ustedes/ellos/ellas** form.

> Mis amigos **trajeron** comida a la fiesta.
> *My friends brought food to the party.*

> Ellos **dijeron** la verdad.
> *They told the truth.*

The preterite of dar

yo	d**i**		nosotros/as	d**imos**
tú	d**iste**		vosotros/as	d**isteis**
Ud./él/ella	d**io**		Uds./ellos/ellas	d**ieron**

SINGULAR FORMS   PLURAL FORMS

▶ The endings for **dar** are the same as the regular preterite endings for **-er** and **-ir** verbs, except that there are no accent marks.

La camarera me **dio** el menú.
The waitress gave me the menu.

Le **di** a Juan algunos consejos.
I gave Juan some advice.

Los invitados le **dieron** un regalo.
The guests gave him/her a gift.

Nosotros **dimos** una gran fiesta.
We gave a great party.

▶ The preterite of **hay** (*inf.* **haber**) is **hubo** (*there was; there were*).

CONSULTA

Note that there are other ways to say *there was* or *there were* in Spanish. See **Estructura 10.1**, p. 342.

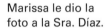

Marissa le dio la foto a la Sra. Díaz.

Hubo una celebración en casa de los Díaz.

¡INTÉNTALO! Escribe la forma correcta del pretérito de cada verbo que está entre paréntesis.

1. (querer) tú _quisiste_
2. (decir) usted _____
3. (hacer) nosotras _____
4. (traer) yo _____
5. (conducir) ellas _____
6. (estar) ella _____
7. (tener) tú _____
8. (dar) ella y yo _____
9. (traducir) yo _____
10. (haber) ayer _____
11. (saber) usted _____
12. (poner) ellos _____
13. (venir) yo _____
14. (poder) tú _____
15. (querer) ustedes _____
16. (estar) nosotros _____
17. (decir) tú _____
18. (saber) ellos _____
19. (hacer) él _____
20. (poner) yo _____
21. (traer) nosotras _____
22. (tener) yo _____
23. (dar) tú _____
24. (poder) ustedes _____

Práctica

1 **Completar** Completa estas oraciones con el pretérito de los verbos entre paréntesis.

1. El sábado _____ (haber) una fiesta sorpresa para Elsa en mi casa.
2. Sofía _____ (hacer) un pastel para la fiesta y Miguel _____ (traer) un flan.
3. Los amigos y parientes de Elsa _____ (venir) y _____ (traer) regalos.
4. El hermano de Elsa no _____ (venir) porque _____ (tener) que trabajar.
5. Su tía María Dolores tampoco _____ (poder) venir.
6. Cuando Elsa abrió la puerta, todos gritaron: "¡Feliz cumpleaños!" y su esposo le _____ (dar) un beso.
7. Elsa no _____ (saber) cómo reaccionar (*react*). _____ (Estar) un poco nerviosa al principio, pero pronto sus amigos _____ (poner) música y ella _____ (poder) relajarse bailando con su esposo.
8. Al final de la noche, todos _____ (decir) que se divirtieron mucho.

NOTA CULTURAL

El **flan** es un postre muy popular en los países de habla hispana. Se prepara con huevos, leche y azúcar y se sirve con salsa de caramelo. Existen variedades deliciosas como el flan de chocolate o el flan de coco.

2 **Describir** Usa verbos de la lista para describir lo que estas personas hicieron. Debes dar por lo menos dos oraciones por cada dibujo.

dar	hacer	tener	traer
estar	poner	traducir	venir

1. el señor López

2. Norma

3. anoche nosotros

4. Roberto y Elena

Comunicación

3

La petición de mano Lee el mensaje electrónico de Marta a su amiga Victoria. Luego, indica si las conclusiones son **lógicas** o **ilógicas**, según lo que leíste.

De:	Marta
Para:	Victoria
Asunto:	David

¡Me acabo de comprometer con David! Estoy muy feliz. Es muy inteligente y simpático. ¡Y guapo también! Como David es muy tradicional, habló con mi papá primero. Condujo tres horas para ir a la casa de mis padres. David no habla bien el español; tradujo varias frases en Internet y se las aprendió de memoria para decírselas a mi papá. ¡Pobre! La comunicación no fue ideal, pero a mi papá le gustó el gesto (*gesture*) de David. ¿Y la petición de mano? Bueno, ese día David hizo una reservación en mi restaurante favorito. La cena estuvo deliciosa y nos divertimos mucho como siempre. Después de cenar, David dijo algo, pero yo no oí bien lo que dijo. Luego vi el hermoso anillo (*ring*) de diamantes: ¡qué sorpresa! David preguntó otra vez: "¿Quieres casarte conmigo?" Hubo un silencio muy largo. Cuando yo pude hablar, le dije: "¡Sí!".

	Lógico	Ilógico
1. Marta está enamorada de David.	○	○
2. A David no le importa la opinión del padre de Marta.	○	○
3. David y el padre de Marta tuvieron una conversación muy larga e interesante.	○	○
4. Los padres de Marta viven en la misma ciudad que David y Marta.	○	○
5. David trajo el anillo al restaurante.	○	○

4

Preguntas Contesta las preguntas de tu compañero/a.

1. ¿Fuiste a una fiesta de cumpleaños el año pasado? ¿De quién?
2. ¿Quiénes fueron a la fiesta?
3. ¿Cómo estuvo el ambiente de la fiesta?
4. ¿Quién llevó regalos, bebidas o comida? ¿Llevaste algo especial?
5. ¿Hubo comida? ¿Quién la hizo?
6. ¿Qué regalos trajeron los invitados?
7. ¿Cuántos invitados hubo en la fiesta?
8. ¿Qué tipo de música hubo?

5

Una fiesta Describe una fiesta a la que fuiste. Incluye en tu descripción cuál fue la ocasión, quién dio la fiesta, quiénes estuvieron allí, qué trajeron los invitados y qué hicieron los invitados.

Síntesis

6

Conversación En parejas, preparen una conversación en la que uno/a de ustedes va a visitar a su hermano/a para explicarle por qué no fue a su fiesta de graduación y para saber cómo estuvo la fiesta. Incluyan esta información en la conversación:

- cuál fue el menú
- quiénes vinieron a la fiesta y quiénes no pudieron venir
- quiénes prepararon la comida o trajeron algo
- si él/ella tuvo que preparar algo
- lo que la gente hizo antes y después de comer
- cómo lo pasaron, bien o mal

9.2 # Verbs that change meaning in the preterite

ANTE TODO   The verbs **conocer**, **saber**, **poder**, and **querer** change meanings when used in the preterite. Because of this, each of them corresponds to more than one verb in English, depending on its tense.

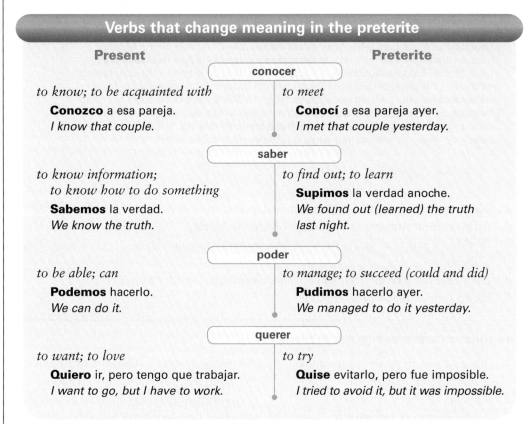

Present	Preterite
conocer	
to know; to be acquainted with	*to meet*
Conozco a esa pareja.	**Conocí** a esa pareja ayer.
I know that couple.	*I met that couple yesterday.*
saber	
to know information; *to know how to do something*	*to find out; to learn*
Sabemos la verdad.	**Supimos** la verdad anoche.
We know the truth.	*We found out (learned) the truth last night.*
poder	
to be able; can	*to manage; to succeed (could and did)*
Podemos hacerlo.	**Pudimos** hacerlo ayer.
We can do it.	*We managed to do it yesterday.*
querer	
to want; to love	*to try*
Quiero ir, pero tengo que trabajar.	**Quise** evitarlo, pero fue imposible.
I want to go, but I have to work.	*I tried to avoid it, but it was impossible.*

> **¡ATENCIÓN!**
> In the preterite, the verbs **poder** and **querer** have different meanings, depending on whether they are used in affirmative or negative sentences.
> **pude** *I succeeded*
> **no pude** *I failed (to)*
> **quise** *I tried (to)*
> **no quise** *I refused (to)*

¡INTÉNTALO!   Elige la respuesta más lógica.

1. Yo no hice lo que me pidieron mis padres. ¡Tengo mis principios!
   a. No quise hacerlo.   b. No supe hacerlo.

2. Hablamos por primera vez con Nuria y Ana en la boda.
   a. Las conocimos en la boda.   b. Les dijimos en la boda.

3. Por fin hablé con mi hermano después de llamarlo siete veces.
   a. No quise hablar con él.   b. Pude hablar con él.

4. Josefina se acostó para relajarse. Se durmió inmediatamente.
   a. Pudo relajarse.   b. No pudo relajarse.

5. Después de mucho buscar, encontraste la definición en el diccionario.
   a. No supiste la respuesta.   b. Supiste la respuesta.

6. Las chicas fueron a la fiesta. Cantaron y bailaron mucho.
   a. Ellas pudieron divertirse.   b. Ellas no supieron divertirse.

Práctica y Comunicación

1 **Carlos y Eva** Forma oraciones con los siguientes elementos. Usa el pretérito y haz todos los cambios necesarios. Al final, inventa la razón del divorcio de Carlos y Eva.

1. anoche / mi esposa y yo / saber / que / Carlos y Eva / divorciarse

2. los / conocer / viaje / isla de Pascua

3. no / poder / hablar / mucho / con / ellos / ese día

4. pero / ellos / ser / simpático / y / nosotros / hacer planes / vernos / con más / frecuencia

5. yo / poder / encontrar / su / número / teléfono / páginas / amarillo

6. (yo) querer / llamar / los / ese día / pero / no / tener / tiempo

7. cuando / los / llamar / nosotros / poder / hablar / Eva

8. nosotros / saber / razón / divorcio / después / hablar / ella

9. _____

NOTA CULTURAL

La isla de Pascua es un remoto territorio chileno situado en el océano Pacífico Sur. Sus inmensas estatuas son uno de los mayores misterios del mundo: nadie sabe cómo o por qué se crearon. Para más información, véase **Panorama**, p. 329.

2 **Completar** En parejas, túrnense para completar estas frases de una manera lógica.

1. Ayer mi compañero/a de cuarto supo…
2. Esta mañana no pude…
3. Conocí a mi mejor amigo/a en…
4. Mis padres no quisieron…
5. Mi mejor amigo/a no pudo…
6. Mi novio/a y yo nos conocimos en…
7. La semana pasada supe…
8. Ayer mis amigos quisieron…

3 **Telenovela** Escribe el diálogo para una escena de una telenovela (*soap opera*). La escena trata de una situación amorosa entre tres personas: Mirta, Daniel y Raúl. Usa el pretérito de **conocer, poder, querer** y **saber** en tu diálogo.

PASIÓN — AVENTURA
SUSPENSO — VENGANZA
LA MUJER DOBLE

Síntesis

4 **Conversación** En una hoja de papel, escribe dos listas: las cosas que hiciste durante el fin de semana y las cosas que quisiste hacer, pero no pudiste. Luego, compara tu lista con la de un(a) compañero/a, y expliquen ambos por qué no pudieron hacer esas cosas.

9.3 ¿Qué? and ¿cuál?

ANTE TODO You've already learned how to use interrogative words and phrases. As you know, **¿qué?** and **¿cuál?** or **¿cuáles?** mean *what?* or *which?* However, they are not interchangeable.

▶ **¿Qué?** is used to ask for a definition or an explanation.

¿Qué es el flan?
What is flan?

¿Qué estudias?
What do you study?

▶ **¿Cuál(es)?** is used when there is more than one possibility to choose from.

¿Cuál de los dos prefieres,
el vino o el champán?
*Which of these (two) do you prefer,
wine or champagne?*

¿Cuáles son tus medias,
las negras o las blancas?
*Which ones are your socks,
the black ones or the white ones?*

▶ **¿Cuál?** should not be used before a noun; in this case, **¿qué?** is used.

¿Qué sorpresa te dieron tus amigos?
What surprise did your friends give you?

¿Qué colores te gustan?
What colors do you like?

▶ **¿Qué?** used before a noun has the same meaning as **¿cuál?**

¿Qué regalo te gusta?
What (Which) gift do you like?

¿Qué dulces quieren ustedes?
What (Which) sweets do you want?

Review of interrogative words and phrases

¿a qué hora?	at what time?	¿cuántos/as?	how many?
¿adónde?	(to) where?	¿de dónde?	from where?
¿cómo?	how?	¿dónde?	where?
¿cuál(es)?	what?; which?	¿por qué?	why?
¿cuándo?	when?	¿qué?	what?; which?
¿cuánto/a?	how much?	¿quién(es)?	who?

¡INTÉNTALO! Completa las preguntas con **¿qué?** o **¿cuál(es)?**, según el contexto.

1. ¿ _Cuál_ de los dos te gusta más?
2. ¿ _____ es tu teléfono?
3. ¿ _____ tipo de pastel pediste?
4. ¿ _____ es una galleta?
5. ¿ _____ haces ahora?
6. ¿ _____ son tus platos favoritos?
7. ¿ _____ bebidas te gustan más?
8. ¿ _____ es esto?
9. ¿ _____ es el mejor?
10. ¿ _____ es tu opinión?
11. ¿ _____ fiestas celebras tú?
12. ¿ _____ botella de vino prefieres?
13. ¿ _____ es tu helado favorito?
14. ¿ _____ pones en la mesa?
15. ¿ _____ restaurante prefieres?
16. ¿ _____ estudiantes estudian más?
17. ¿ _____ quieres comer esta noche?
18. ¿ _____ es la sorpresa mañana?
19. ¿ _____ postre prefieres?
20. ¿ _____ opinas?

Práctica y Comunicación

1

Completar Tu clase de español va a crear un sitio web. Completa estas preguntas con alguna(s) palabra(s) interrogativa(s). Luego, contesta las preguntas.

1. ¿_____ es la fecha de tu cumpleaños?
2. ¿_____ naciste?
3. ¿_____ es tu estado civil?
4. ¿_____ te relajas?
5. ¿_____ es tu mejor amigo/a?
6. ¿_____ cosas te hacen reír?
7. ¿_____ postres te gustan? ¿_____ te gusta más?
8. ¿_____ problemas tuviste en la primera cita con alguien?

2

El aniversario Escucha la conversación entre Silvia y su prima Gisela. Luego, indica si las conclusiones siguientes son **lógicas** o **ilógicas**, según lo que escuchaste.

	Lógico	Ilógico
1. Silvia y Gisela llegaron juntas a la fiesta.	○	○
2. Silvia comió antes que Gisela en la fiesta.	○	○
3. A Gisela no le gustan las verduras.	○	○
4. Silvia probó cada uno de los postres.	○	○
5. Gisela va a comer flan.	○	○

3

Una invitación En parejas, lean esta invitación. Luego, túrnense para hacer y contestar preguntas con **qué** y **cuál** basadas en la información de la invitación.

modelo

Estudiante 1: ¿Cuál es el nombre del padre de la novia?
Estudiante 2: Su nombre es Fernando Sandoval Valera.

> Fernando Sandoval Valera   Lorenzo Vásquez Amaral
> Isabel Arzipe de Sandoval   Elena Soto de Vásquez
>
> tienen el agrado de invitarlos
> a la boda de sus hijos
>
> María Luisa y José Antonio
>
> La ceremonia religiosa tendrá lugar
> el sábado 10 de junio a las dos de la tarde
> en el Templo de Santo Domingo
> (Calle Santo Domingo, 961).
>
> Después de la ceremonia, sírvanse pasar a la recepción en el salón
> de baile del Hotel Metrópoli (Sotero del Río, 465).

¡LENGUA VIVA!

The word **invitar** is not always used exactly like *invite*. Sometimes, if you say **Te invito un café**, it means that you are offering to buy that person a coffee.

9.4 Pronouns after prepositions

ANTE TODO In Spanish, as in English, the object of a preposition is the noun or pronoun that follows a preposition. Observe the following diagram.

PREPOSITION	NOUN	PREPOSITION	PRONOUN
La sopa es para	Alicia	y para	él.

Prepositional pronouns

	Singular		Plural	
	mí	me	**nosotros/as**	us
	ti	you (fam.)	**vosotros/as**	you (fam.)
preposition +	**Ud.**	you (form.)	**Uds.**	you
	él	him	**ellos**	them (m.)
	ella	her	**ellas**	them (f.)

▶ Note that, except for **mí** and **ti,** these pronouns are the same as the subject pronouns. **¡Atención! Mí** (*me*) has an accent mark to distinguish it from the possessive adjective **mi** (*my*).

▶ The preposition **con** combines with **mí** and **ti** to form **conmigo** and **contigo**, respectively.

—¿Quieres venir **conmigo** a Concepción?   —Sí, gracias, me gustaría ir **contigo**.
Do you want to come with me to Concepción?   *Yes, thanks, I would like to go with you.*

▶ The preposition **entre** is followed by **tú** and **yo** instead of **ti** and **mí**.

Papá va a sentarse **entre tú y yo**.
Dad is going to sit between you and me.

CONSULTA

For more prepositions, refer to **Estructura 2.3,** p. 60.

¡INTÉNTALO! Completa estas oraciones con las preposiciones y los pronombres apropiados.

1. (*with him*) No quiero ir ___con él___.
2. (*for her*) Las galletas son _____.
3. (*for me*) Los mariscos son _____.
4. (*with you*, pl.) Preferimos estar _____.
5. (*with you*, sing. fam.) Me gusta salir _____.
6. (*with me*) ¿Por qué no quieres tener una cita _____?
7. (*for her*) La cuenta es _____.
8. (*for them*, m.) La habitación es muy pequeña _____.
9. (*with them*, f.) Anoche celebré la Navidad _____.
10. (*for you*, sing. fam.) Este beso es _____.
11. (*with you*, sing. fam.) Nunca me aburro _____.
12. (*with you*, pl.) ¡Qué bien que vamos _____!
13. (*for you*, sing. fam.) _____ la vida es muy fácil.
14. (*for them*, f.) _____ no hay sorpresas.

Práctica y Comunicación

1 **Completar** David sale con sus amigos a comer. Para saber quién come qué, lee el mensaje electrónico que David le envió (*sent*) a Cecilia dos días después y completa el diálogo en el restaurante con los pronombres apropiados.

> **modelo**
>
> **Camarero:** Los camarones en salsa verde, ¿para quién son?
> **David:** Son para _____*ella*_____.

Para: Cecilia	Asunto: El menú

Hola, Cecilia:

¿Recuerdas la comida del viernes? Quiero repetir el menú en mi casa el miércoles. Ahora voy a escribir lo que comimos, luego me dices si falta algún plato. Yo pedí el filete de pescado y Maribel camarones en salsa verde. Tatiana pidió un plato grandísimo de machas a la parmesana. Diana y Silvia pidieron langostas, ¿te acuerdas? Y tú, ¿qué pediste? Ah, sí, un bistec grande con papas. Héctor también pidió un bistec, pero más pequeño. Miguel pidió pollo y vino tinto para todos. Y la profesora comió ensalada verde porque está a dieta. ¿Falta algo? Espero tu mensaje. Hasta pronto. David.

CAMARERO	El filete de pescado, ¿para quién es?
DAVID	Es para (1)_____.
CAMARERO	Aquí está. ¿Y las machas a la parmesana y las langostas?
DAVID	Las machas son para (2)_____.
SILVIA Y DIANA	Las langostas son para (3)_____.
CAMARERO	Tengo un bistec grande…
DAVID	Cecilia, es para (4)_____, ¿no es cierto? Y el bistec más pequeño es para (5)_____.
CAMARERO	¿Y la botella de vino?
MIGUEL	Es para todos (6)_____, y el pollo es para (7)_____.
CAMARERO	(*a la profesora*) Entonces la ensalada verde es para (8)_____.

2 **Preguntas** En parejas, túrnense para hacerse preguntas tomando las frases de la lista. Usen los pronombres apropiados en sus respuestas.

> **modelo**
>
> tú / acordarte de tus amigos de la infancia
> **Estudiante 1:** ¿Te acuerdas de tus amigos de la infancia?
> **Estudiante 2:** No, no me acuerdo de ellos.

tu familia / vivir contigo	tú / querer practicar el español conmigo
tú / preocuparte por tus padres	tus padres / preocuparse mucho por ti
yo / poder estudiar contigo	tú / comprar regalos para tus amigos
tú / llevarte bien con tus parientes	tus amigos / sacar muchas fotos de ti

3 **Feliz cumpleaños** Escribe un párrafo de cinco oraciones que describa cómo celebraste tu último cumpleaños. Usa el pretérito y los pronombres que acabas de aprender.

SUBJECT
Javier

CONJUGATED FORM
empiezo

Main clause

Dudan

Recapitulación

Completa estas actividades para repasar los conceptos de gramática que aprendiste en esta lección.

1 **Completar** Completa la tabla con el pretérito de los verbos. **18 pts.**

Infinitive	yo	ella	nosotros
conducir			
hacer			
saber			

2 **Mi fiesta** Completa este mensaje electrónico con el pretérito de los verbos de la lista. Vas a usar cada verbo sólo una vez. **30 pts.**

dar	haber	tener
decir	hacer	traer
estar	poder	venir
	poner	

Hola, Omar:

Como tú no (1) _____ venir a mi fiesta de cumpleaños, quiero contarte cómo fue. El día de mi cumpleaños, muy temprano por la mañana, mis hermanos me (2) _____ una gran sorpresa: ellos (3) _____ un regalo delante de la puerta de mi habitación: ¡una bicicleta roja preciosa! Mi madre nos preparó un desayuno riquísimo. Después de desayunar, mis hermanos y yo (4) _____ que limpiar toda la casa, así que (*therefore*) no (5) _____ más celebración hasta la tarde. A las seis y media (nosotros) (6) _____ una barbacoa en el patio de la casa. Todos los invitados (7) _____ bebidas y regalos. (8) _____ todos mis amigos, excepto tú, ¡qué pena! :-(
La fiesta (9) _____ muy animada hasta las diez de la noche, cuando mis padres (10) _____ que los vecinos (*neighbors*) iban a (*were going to*) protestar y entonces todos se fueron a sus casas.

RESUMEN GRAMATICAL

9.1 **Irregular preterites** *pp. 310–311*

u-stem	estar poder poner saber tener	estuv- pud- pus- sup- tuv-	
i-stem	hacer querer venir	hic- quis- vin-	-e, -iste, -o, -imos, -isteis, -(i)eron
j-stem	conducir decir traducir traer	conduj- dij- traduj- traj-	

▶ Preterite of **dar**: **di, diste, dio, dimos, disteis, dieron**

▶ Preterite of **hay** (*inf.* **haber**): **hubo**

9.2 **Verbs that change meaning in the preterite** *p. 314*

Present	Preterite
conocer	
to know; to be acquainted with	to meet
saber	
to know info.; to know how to do something	to find out; to learn
poder	
to be able; can	to manage; to succeed
querer	
to want; to love	to try

9.3 **¿Qué? and ¿cuál?** *p. 316*

▶ Use **¿qué?** to ask for a definition or an explanation.

▶ Use **¿cuál(es)?** when there is more than one possibility to choose from.

▶ **¿Cuál?** should not be used before a noun; use **¿qué?** instead.

▶ **¿Qué?** used before a noun has the same meaning as **¿cuál?**

3   **¿Presente o pretérito?** Escoge la forma correcta de los verbos en paréntesis. **18 pts.**

1. Después de muchos intentos (*tries*), (podemos/ pudimos) hacer una piñata.
2. —¿Conoces a Pepe?
   —Sí, lo (conozco/ conocí) en tu fiesta.
3. Como no es de aquí, Cristina no (sabe/supo) mucho de las celebraciones locales.
4. Yo no (quiero/quise) ir a un restaurante grande, pero tú decides.
5. Ellos (quieren/quisieron) darme una sorpresa, pero Nina me lo dijo todo.
6. Mañana se terminan las vacaciones; por fin (podemos/pudimos) volver a la escuela.

| **9.4** | **Pronouns after prepositions** | *p. 318* |

Prepositional pronouns

	Singular	Plural
	mí	nosotros/as
	ti	vosotros/as
Preposition +	Ud.	Uds.
	él	ellos
	ella	ellas

▶ Exceptions: **conmigo, contigo, entre tú y yo**

4   **Preguntas** Escribe una pregunta para cada respuesta con los elementos dados. Empieza con **qué, cuál** o **cuáles** de acuerdo con el contexto y haz los cambios necesarios. **16 pts.**

1. —¿? / pastel / querer —Quiero el pastel de chocolate.
2. —¿? / ser / sangría —La sangría es una bebida típica española.
3. —¿? / ser / restaurante favorito —Mis restaurantes favoritos son Dalí y Jaleo.
4. —¿? / ser / dirección electrónica —Mi dirección electrónica es paco@email.com.

5   **¿Dónde me siento?** Completa la conversación con los pronombres apropiados. **14 pts.**

JUAN A ver, te voy a decir dónde te vas a sentar. Manuel, ¿ves esa silla? Es para _____. Y esa otra silla es para tu novia, que todavía no está aquí.

MANUEL Muy bien, yo la reservo para _____.

HUGO ¿Y esta silla es para _____ (*me*)?

JUAN No, Hugo. No es para _____. Es para Carmina, que viene con Julio.

HUGO No, Carmina y Julio no pueden venir. Hablé con _____ y me avisaron.

JUAN Pues ellos se lo pierden (*it's their loss*). ¡Más comida para _____ (*us*)!

CAMARERO Aquí tienen el menú. Les doy un minuto y enseguida estoy con _____.

6   **Poema** Completa este fragmento del poema *Elegía nocturna* de Carlos Pellicer con el pretérito de los verbos entre paréntesis. **4 pts.**

" Ay de mi corazón° que nadie _____ (querer) tomar de entre mis manos desoladas. Tú _____ (venir) a mirar sus llamaradas° y le miraste arder° claro° y sereno. "

corazón *heart* llamaradas *flames* arder *to burn* claro *clear*

Lectura

Antes de leer

Estrategia
Recognizing word families

Recognizing root words can help you guess the meaning of words in context, ensuring better comprehension of a reading selection. Using this strategy will enrich your Spanish vocabulary as you will see below.

Examinar el texto

Familiarízate con el texto usando las estrategias de lectura más efectivas para ti. ¿Qué tipo de documento es? ¿De qué tratan° las cuatro secciones del documento? Explica tus respuestas.

Raíces°

Completa el siguiente cuadro° para ampliar tu vocabulario. Usa palabras de la lectura de esta lección y vocabulario de las lecciones anteriores. ¿Qué significan las palabras que escribiste en el cuadro?

Verbos	Sustantivos	Otras formas
1. agradecer *to thank, to be grateful for*	*agradecimiento/ gracias gratitude/thanks*	*agradecido grateful, thankful*
2. estudiar	_____	_____
3. _____	_____	celebrado
4. _____	baile	_____
5. bautizar	_____	_____

¿De qué tratan...? *What are... about?* Raíces *Roots* cuadro *chart*

Vida social

Matrimonio
Espinoza Álvarez-
Reyes Salazar

El día sábado 17 de junio a las 19 horas, se celebró el matrimonio de Silvia Reyes y Carlos Espinoza en la catedral de Santiago. La ceremonia fue oficiada por el pastor Federico Salas y participaron los padres de los novios, el señor Jorge Espinoza y señora y el señor José Alfredo Reyes y señora. Después de la ceremonia, los padres de los recién casados ofrecieron una fiesta bailable en el restaurante La Misión.

Bautismo
José María recibió el bautismo el 26 de junio.

Sus padres, don Roberto Lagos Moreno y doña María Angélica Sánchez, compartieron la alegría de la fiesta con todos sus parientes y amigos. La ceremonia religiosa tuvo lugar° en la catedral de Aguas Blancas. Después de la ceremonia, padres, parientes y amigos celebraron una fiesta en la residencia de la familia Lagos.

32B

Fiesta de quince años

El doctor don Amador Larenas Fernández y la señora Felisa Vera de Larenas celebraron los quince años de su hija Ana Ester junto a sus parientes y amigos. La quinceañera reside en la ciudad de Valparaíso y es estudiante del Colegio Francés. La fiesta de presentación en sociedad de la señorita Ana Ester fue el día viernes 2 de mayo a las 19 horas en el Club Español. Entre los invitados especiales asistieron el alcalde° de la ciudad, don Pedro Castedo, y su esposa. La música estuvo a cargo de la Orquesta Americana. ¡Feliz cumpleaños, le deseamos a la señorita Ana Ester en su fiesta bailable!

Expresión de gracias
Carmen Godoy Tapia

Agradecemos° sinceramente a todas las personas que nos acompañaron en el último adiós a nuestra apreciada esposa, madre, abuela y tía, la señora Carmen Godoy Tapia. El funeral tuvo lugar el día 28 de junio en la ciudad de Viña del Mar. La vida de Carmen Godoy fue un ejemplo de trabajo, amistad, alegría y amor para todos nosotros. Su esposo, hijos y familia agradecen de todo corazón° su asistencia° al funeral a todos los parientes y amigos.

tuvo lugar *took place* alcalde *mayor* Agradecemos *We thank*
de todo corazón *sincerely* asistencia *attendance*

Después de leer

Corregir
Escribe estos comentarios otra vez para corregir la información errónea.

1. El alcalde y su esposa asistieron a la boda de Silvia y Carlos.

2. Todos los anuncios (*announcements*) describen eventos felices.

3. Felisa Vera de Larenas cumple quince años.

4. Roberto Lagos y María Angélica Sánchez son hermanos.

5. Carmen Godoy Tapia les dio las gracias a las personas que asistieron al funeral.

Identificar
Escribe el nombre de la(s) persona(s) descrita(s) (*described*).

1. Dejó viudo a su esposo el 28 de junio.

2. Sus padres y todos los invitados brindaron por él, pero él no entendió por qué.

3. El Club Español les presentó una cuenta considerable.

4. Unió a los novios en santo matrimonio.

5. Su fiesta de cumpleaños se celebró en Valparaíso.

Un anuncio
Inventa un anuncio breve sobre una celebración importante. Puede ser una graduación, un matrimonio o una gran fiesta en la que participas. Incluye la siguiente información.

1. nombres de los participantes

2. la fecha, la hora y el lugar

3. qué se celebra

4. otros detalles de interés

Escritura

Estrategia

Planning and writing a comparative analysis

Writing any kind of comparative analysis requires careful planning. Venn diagrams are useful for organizing your ideas visually before comparing and contrasting people, places, objects, events, or issues. To create a Venn diagram, draw two circles that overlap one another and label the top of each circle. List the differences between the two elements in the outer rings of the two circles, then list their similarities where the two circles overlap. Review the following example.

Diferencias y similitudes

Boda de Silvia Reyes y Carlos Espinoza

Fiesta de quince años de Ana Ester Larenas Vera

Diferencias:
1. Primero hay una celebración religiosa.
2. Se celebra en un restaurante.

Similitudes:
1. Las dos fiestas se celebran por la noche.
2. Las dos fiestas son bailables.

Diferencias:
1. Se celebra en un club.
2. Vienen invitados especiales.

La lista de palabras y expresiones a la derecha puede ayudarte a escribir este tipo de ensayo (essay).

Tema

Escribir una composición

Compara una celebración familiar (como una boda, una fiesta de cumpleaños o una graduación) a la que tú asististe recientemente con otro tipo de celebración. Utiliza palabras y expresiones de esta lista.

Para expresar similitudes

además; también	*in addition; also*
al igual que	*the same as*
como	*as; like*
de la misma manera	*in the same manner (way)*
del mismo modo	*in the same manner (way)*
tan + [adjetivo] + como	*as + [adjective] + as*
tanto/a(s) + [sustantivo] + como	*as many/much + [noun] + as*

Para expresar diferencias

a diferencia de	*unlike*
a pesar de	*in spite of*
aunque	*although*
en cambio	*on the other hand*
más/menos... que	*more/less . . . than*
no obstante	*nevertheless; however*
por el contrario	*on the contrary*
por otro lado	*on the other hand*
sin embargo	*nevertheless; however*

Escuchar

Estrategia

Guessing the meaning of words through context

When you hear an unfamiliar word, you can often guess its meaning by listening to the words and phrases around it.

 To practice this strategy, you will now listen to a paragraph. Jot down the unfamiliar words that you hear. Then listen to the paragraph again and jot down the word or words that give the most useful clues to the meaning of each unfamiliar word.

Preparación

Lee la invitación. ¿De qué crees que van a hablar Rosa y Josefina?

Ahora escucha

Ahora escucha la conversación entre Josefina y Rosa. Cuando oigas una de las palabras de la columna A, usa el contexto para identificar el sinónimo o la definición en la columna B.

A	B
_____ 1. festejar	a. conmemoración religiosa de una muerte
_____ 2. dicha	b. tolera
_____ 3. bien parecido	c. suerte
_____ 4. finge (fingir)	d. celebrar
_____ 5. soporta (soportar)	e. me divertí
_____ 6. yo lo disfruté (disfrutar)	f. horror
	g. crea una ficción
	h. guapo

Margarita Robles de García
y Roberto García Olmos

Piden su presencia en la celebración
del décimo aniversario de bodas
el día 13 de marzo
con una misa en la Iglesia Virgen del Coromoto
a las 6:30

seguida por cena y baile
en el restaurante El Campanero,
Calle Principal, Las Mercedes
a las 8:30

Comprensión

¿Cierto o falso?

Lee cada oración e indica si lo que dice es **cierto** o **falso**. Corrige las oraciones falsas.

1. No invitaron a mucha gente a la fiesta de Margarita y Roberto porque ellos no conocen a muchas personas.

2. Algunos fueron a la fiesta con pareja y otros fueron sin compañero/a.

3. Margarita y Roberto decidieron celebrar el décimo aniversario porque no hicieron una fiesta el día de su boda.

4. Rafael les parece interesante a Rosa y a Josefina.

5. Josefina se divirtió mucho en la fiesta porque bailó toda la noche con Rafael.

Preguntas

Contesta estas preguntas con oraciones completas.

1. ¿Son solteras Rosa y Josefina? ¿Cómo lo sabes?

2. ¿Tienen las chicas una amistad de mucho tiempo con la pareja que celebra su aniversario? ¿Cómo lo sabes?

En pantalla

Desfiles°, música, asados°, fuegos artificiales° y baile son los elementos de una buena fiesta. ¿Celebrar durante toda una semana? ¡Eso sí que es una fiesta espectacular! El 18 de septiembre Chile conmemora su independencia de España y los chilenos demuestran su orgullo° nacional durante una semana llena de celebraciones. Durante las Fiestas Patrias° casi todas las oficinas° y escuelas se cierran para que la gente se reúna° a festejar. Desfiles y rodeos representan la tradición de los vaqueros° del país, y la gente baila cueca, el baile nacional. Las familias y los amigos se reúnen para preparar y comer platos tradicionales como las empanadas y asados. Otra de las tradiciones de estas fiestas es hacer volar cometas°, llamadas volantines. Mira el video para descubrir cómo se celebran otras fiestas en Chile.

Vocabulario útil

conejo	*bunny*
disfraces	*costumes*
mariscal	*traditional Chilean soup with raw seafood*
sustos	*frights*
vieja (Chi.)	*mother*

Seleccionar

Selecciona la palabra que no está relacionada con cada grupo.
1. disfraces • noviembre • arbolito • sustos
2. volantines • arbolito • regalos • diciembre
3. conejo • enero • huevitos • chocolates
4. septiembre • volantines • disfraces • asado

Fiesta

Imagina que vas a organizar una fiesta para celebrar el 4 de julio. Escribe una invitación electrónica para invitar a tus parientes y amigos a la fiesta. Describe los planes que tienes para la fiesta y diles a tus amigos qué tiene que traer cada uno.

Fiestas patrias: Chilevisión

Noviembre: disfraces, dulces...

Mayo: besito, tarjeta, tecito con la mamá...

Septiembre... Septiembre: familia, parada militar...

Desfiles/Paradas *Parades* asados *barbecues* fuegos artificiales *fireworks* orgullo *pride* Fiestas Patrias *Independence Day celebrations* oficinas *offices* se reúna *would get together* vaqueros *cowboys* cometas/volantines *kites*

Flash CULTURA

El Día de los Reyes Magos* es una celebración muy popular en muchos países hispanos. No sólo es el día en que los reyes les traen regalos a los niños, también es una fiesta llena° de tradiciones. La tarde del 5 de enero, en muchas ciudades como Barcelona, España, se hace un desfile° en que los reyes regalan dulces a los niños y reciben sus cartas con peticiones. Esa noche, antes de irse a dormir, los niños deben dejar un zapato junto a la ventana y un bocado° para los reyes. En Puerto Rico, por ejemplo, los niños ponen una caja con hierba° bajo su cama para alimentar a los camellos° de los reyes.

Vocabulario útil

los cabezudos	carnival figures with large heads
los carteles	posters
fiesta de pueblo	popular celebration
santos de palo	wooden saints

Preparación

¿Se celebra la Navidad en tu país? ¿Qué otras fiestas importantes se celebran? En cada caso, ¿cuántos días dura la fiesta? ¿Cuáles son las tradiciones y actividades típicas? ¿Hay alguna comida típica en esa celebración?

Elegir

Indica cuál de las dos opciones resume mejor este episodio.

a. Las Navidades puertorriqueñas son las más largas y terminan después de las fiestas de la calle San Sebastián. Esta fiesta de pueblo se celebra con baile, música y distintas expresiones artísticas típicas.

b. En la celebración de las Navidades puertorriqueñas, los cabezudos son una tradición de España y son el elemento más importante de la fiesta. A la gente le gusta bailar y hacer procesiones por la noche.

* According to the Christian tradition, the Three Wise Men were the three kings that traveled to Bethlehem after the birth of Baby Jesus, carrying with them gifts of gold, frankincense, and myrrh to pay him homage.

llena *full* desfile *parade* bocado *snack* hierba *grass* alimentar los camellos *feed the camels*

Las fiestas

Los cabezudos son una tradición [...] de España.

Hay mucha gente y mucho arte.

Es una fiesta de pueblo... una tradición. Vengo todos los años.

Chile

El país en cifras

- ▶ **Área:** 756.950 km² (292.259 millas²), *dos veces el área de Montana*
- ▶ **Población:** 17.363.000
  Aproximadamente el 80 por ciento de la población del país es urbana.
- ▶ **Capital:** Santiago de Chile—6.034.000
- ▶ **Ciudades principales:** Valparaíso—865.000, Concepción, Viña del Mar, Temuco
- ▶ **Moneda:** peso chileno
- ▶ **Idiomas:** español (oficial), mapuche

Bandera de Chile

Chilenos célebres

- ▶ **Bernardo O'Higgins,** militar° y héroe nacional (1778–1842)
- ▶ **Gabriela Mistral,** Premio Nobel de Literatura, 1945; poeta y diplomática (1889–1957)
- ▶ **Pablo Neruda,** Premio Nobel de Literatura, 1971; poeta (1904–1973)
- ▶ **Isabel Allende,** novelista (1942–)
- ▶ **Ana Tijoux,** cantante (1977–)

Pablo Neruda

militar *soldier* desierto *desert* el más seco *the driest* mundo *world* han tenido *have had* ha sido usado *has been used* Marte *Mars*

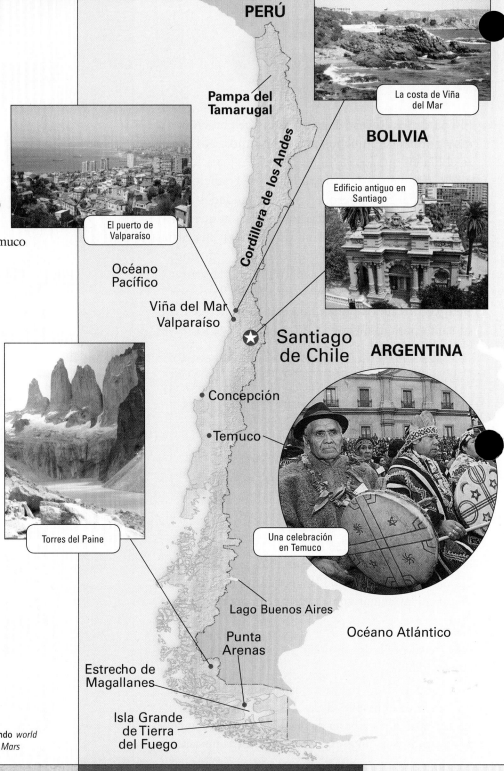

PERÚ

La costa de Viña del Mar

Pampa del Tamarugal

BOLIVIA

Cordillera de los Andes

El puerto de Valparaíso

Océano Pacífico

Edificio antiguo en Santiago

Viña del Mar
Valparaíso

Santiago de Chile

ARGENTINA

Concepción

Temuco

Torres del Paine

Una celebración en Temuco

Lago Buenos Aires

Océano Atlántico

Punta Arenas

Estrecho de Magallanes

Isla Grande de Tierra del Fuego

¡Increíble pero cierto!

El desierto° de Atacama, en el norte de Chile, es el más seco° del mundo°. Con más de cien mil km² de superficie, algunas zonas de este desierto nunca han tenido° lluvia. Atacama ha sido usado° como escenario para representar a Marte° en películas y series de televisión.

Lugares • **La isla de Pascua**

La isla de Pascua° recibió ese nombre porque los exploradores holandeses° llegaron a la isla por primera vez el día de Pascua de 1722. Ahora es parte del territorio de Chile. La isla de Pascua es famosa por los *moái*, estatuas enormes que representan personas con rasgos° muy exagerados. Estas estatuas las construyeron los *rapa nui*, los antiguos habitantes de la zona. Todavía no se sabe mucho sobre los *rapa nui*, ni tampoco se sabe por qué decidieron abandonar la isla.

Deportes • **Los deportes de invierno**

Hay muchos lugares para practicar deportes de invierno en Chile porque las montañas nevadas de los Andes ocupan gran parte del país. El Parque Nacional Villarrica, por ejemplo, situado al pie de un volcán y junto a° un lago, es un sitio popular para el esquí y el *snowboard*. Para los que prefieren deportes más extremos, el centro de esquí Valle Nevado organiza excursiones para practicar heliesquí.

Ciencias • **Astronomía**

Los observatorios chilenos, situados en los Andes, son lugares excelentes para las observaciones astronómicas. Científicos° de todo el mundo van a Chile para estudiar las estrellas° y otros cuerpos celestes. Hoy día Chile está construyendo nuevos observatorios y telescopios para mejorar las imágenes del universo.

Economía • **El vino**

La producción de vino comenzó en Chile en el siglo° XVI. Ahora la industria del vino constituye una parte importante de la actividad agrícola del país y la exportación de sus productos está aumentando° cada vez más. Los vinos chilenos son muy apreciados internacionalmente por su gran variedad, sus ricos y complejos sabores° y su precio moderado. Los más conocidos son los vinos de Aconcagua y del valle del Maipo.

¿Qué aprendiste? Contesta cada pregunta con una oración completa.

1. ¿Qué porcentaje (*percentage*) de la población chilena es urbana?

2. ¿Qué son los *moái*? ¿Dónde están?

3. ¿Qué deporte extremo ofrece el centro de esquí Valle Nevado?

4. ¿Por qué van a Chile científicos de todo el mundo?

5. ¿Cuándo comenzó la producción de vino en Chile?

6. ¿Por qué son apreciados internacionalmente los vinos chilenos?

Conexión Internet Investiga estos temas en Internet.

1. Busca información sobre Pablo Neruda e Isabel Allende. ¿Dónde y cuándo nacieron? ¿Cuáles son algunas de sus obras (*works*)? ¿Cuáles son algunos de los temas de sus obras?

2. Busca información sobre sitios donde los chilenos y los turistas practican deportes de invierno en Chile. Selecciona un sitio y descríbelo.

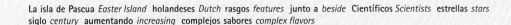

La isla de Pascua *Easter Island* holandeses *Dutch* rasgos *features* junto a *beside* Científicos *Scientists* estrellas *stars* siglo *century* aumentando *increasing* complejos sabores *complex flavors*

Las celebraciones

el aniversario (de bodas)	(wedding) anniversary
la boda	wedding
el cumpleaños	birthday
el día de fiesta	holiday
la fiesta	party
el/la invitado/a	guest
la Navidad	Christmas
la quinceañera	young woman celebrating her fifteenth birthday
la sorpresa	surprise
brindar	to toast (drink)
celebrar	to celebrate
divertirse (e:ie)	to have fun
invitar	to invite
pasarlo bien/mal	to have a good/bad time
regalar	to give (a gift)
reírse (e:i)	to laugh
relajarse	to relax
sonreír (e:i)	to smile
sorprender	to surprise

Los postres y otras comidas

la botella (de vino)	bottle (of wine)
el champán	champagne
los dulces	sweets; candy
el flan (de caramelo)	baked (caramel) custard
la galleta	cookie
el helado	ice cream
el pastel (de chocolate)	(chocolate) cake; pie
el postre	dessert

Las relaciones personales

la amistad	friendship
el amor	love
el divorcio	divorce
el estado civil	marital status
el matrimonio	marriage
la pareja	(married) couple; partner
el/la recién casado/a	newlywed
casarse (con)	to get married (to)
comprometerse (con)	to get engaged (to)
divorciarse (de)	to get divorced (from)
enamorarse (de)	to fall in love (with)
llevarse bien/mal (con)	to get along well/ badly (with)
odiar	to hate
romper (con)	to break up (with)
salir (con)	to go out (with); to date
separarse (de)	to separate (from)
tener una cita	to have a date; to have an appointment
casado/a	married
divorciado/a	divorced
juntos/as	together
separado/a	separated
soltero/a	single
viudo/a	widower/widow

Las etapas de la vida

la adolescencia	adolescence
la edad	age
las etapas de la vida	the stages of life
la juventud	youth
la madurez	maturity; middle age
la muerte	death
el nacimiento	birth
la niñez	childhood
la vejez	old age
cambiar (de)	to change
graduarse (de/en)	to graduate (from/in)
jubilarse	to retire (from work)
nacer	to be born

Palabras adicionales

la alegría	happiness
el beso	kiss
conmigo	with me
contigo	with you
¡Felicidades!/ ¡Felicitaciones!	Congratulations!
¡Feliz cumpleaños!	Happy birthday!

Expresiones útiles	See page 305.

En el consultorio

10

Communicative Goals

You will learn how to:

- **Describe how you feel physically**
- **Talk about health and medical conditions**

contextos

fotonovela

cultura

estructura

adelante

A PRIMERA VISTA

- ¿Están en una farmacia o en un hospital?
- ¿La mujer es médica o dentista?
- ¿Qué hace ella, una operación o un examen médico?
- ¿Crees que la paciente está nerviosa?

En el consultorio

Más vocabulario

la clínica	clinic
el consultorio	doctor's office
el/la dentista	dentist
el examen médico	physical exam
la farmacia	pharmacy
el hospital	hospital
la operación	operation
la sala de emergencia(s)	emergency room
el cuerpo	body
el oído	(sense of) hearing; inner ear
el accidente	accident
la salud	health
el síntoma	symptom
caerse	to fall (down)
darse con	to bump into; to run into
doler (o:ue)	to hurt
enfermarse	to get sick
estar enfermo/a	to be sick
lastimarse (el pie)	to injure (one's foot)
poner una inyección	to give an injection
recetar	to prescribe
romperse (la pierna)	to break (one's leg)
sacar(se) un diente	to have a tooth removed
sufrir una enfermedad	to suffer an illness
torcerse (o:ue) (el tobillo)	to sprain (one's ankle)
toser	to cough

Variación léxica

gripe	⟷	gripa (Col., Gua., Méx.)
resfriado	⟷	catarro (Cuba, Esp., Gua.)
sala de emergencia(s)	⟷	sala de urgencias (Arg., Col., Esp., Méx.)
romperse	⟷	quebrarse (Arg., Gua.)

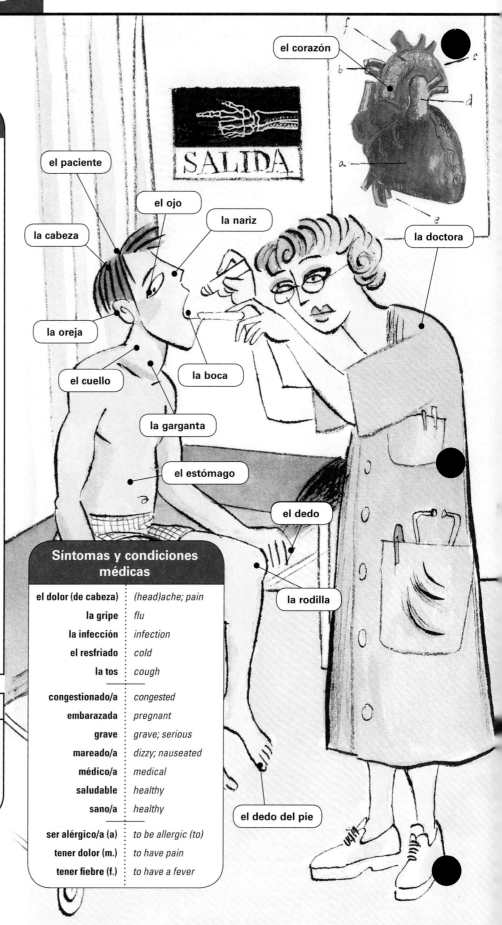

el corazón

el paciente

el ojo

la nariz

la cabeza

SALIDA

la doctora

la oreja

el cuello

la boca

la garganta

el estómago

el dedo

la rodilla

el dedo del pie

Síntomas y condiciones médicas

el dolor (de cabeza)	(head)ache; pain
la gripe	flu
la infección	infection
el resfriado	cold
la tos	cough
congestionado/a	congested
embarazada	pregnant
grave	grave; serious
mareado/a	dizzy; nauseated
médico/a	medical
saludable	healthy
sano/a	healthy
ser alérgico/a (a)	to be allergic (to)
tener dolor (m.)	to have pain
tener fiebre (f.)	to have a fever

Práctica

1 **Escuchar** 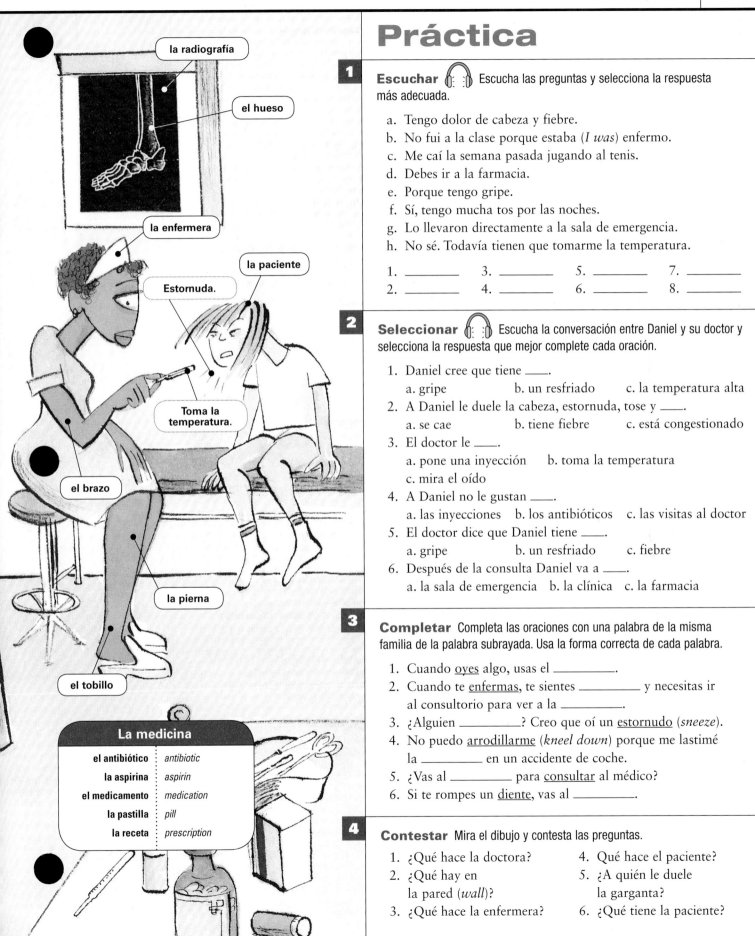 Escucha las preguntas y selecciona la respuesta más adecuada.

a. Tengo dolor de cabeza y fiebre.
b. No fui a la clase porque estaba (*I was*) enfermo.
c. Me caí la semana pasada jugando al tenis.
d. Debes ir a la farmacia.
e. Porque tengo gripe.
f. Sí, tengo mucha tos por las noches.
g. Lo llevaron directamente a la sala de emergencia.
h. No sé. Todavía tienen que tomarme la temperatura.

1. _____ 3. _____ 5. _____ 7. _____
2. _____ 4. _____ 6. _____ 8. _____

2 **Seleccionar** Escucha la conversación entre Daniel y su doctor y selecciona la respuesta que mejor complete cada oración.

1. Daniel cree que tiene ____.
   a. gripe   b. un resfriado   c. la temperatura alta
2. A Daniel le duele la cabeza, estornuda, tose y ____.
   a. se cae   b. tiene fiebre   c. está congestionado
3. El doctor le ____.
   a. pone una inyección   b. toma la temperatura
   c. mira el oído
4. A Daniel no le gustan ____.
   a. las inyecciones   b. los antibióticos   c. las visitas al doctor
5. El doctor dice que Daniel tiene ____.
   a. gripe   b. un resfriado   c. fiebre
6. Después de la consulta Daniel va a ____.
   a. la sala de emergencia   b. la clínica   c. la farmacia

3 **Completar** Completa las oraciones con una palabra de la misma familia de la palabra subrayada. Usa la forma correcta de cada palabra.

1. Cuando oyes algo, usas el _____.
2. Cuando te enfermas, te sientes _____ y necesitas ir al consultorio para ver a la _____.
3. ¿Alguien _____? Creo que oí un estornudo (*sneeze*).
4. No puedo arrodillarme (*kneel down*) porque me lastimé la _____ en un accidente de coche.
5. ¿Vas al _____ para consultar al médico?
6. Si te rompes un diente, vas al _____.

4 **Contestar** Mira el dibujo y contesta las preguntas.

1. ¿Qué hace la doctora?
2. ¿Qué hay en la pared (*wall*)?
3. ¿Qué hace la enfermera?
4. ¿Qué hace el paciente?
5. ¿A quién le duele la garganta?
6. ¿Qué tiene la paciente?

la radiografía

el hueso

la enfermera

la paciente

Estornuda.

Toma la temperatura.

el brazo

la pierna

el tobillo

La medicina

el antibiótico	*antibiotic*
la aspirina	*aspirin*
el medicamento	*medication*
la pastilla	*pill*
la receta	*prescription*

5 **Asociaciones** Identifica las partes del cuerpo que asocias con estas actividades.

> *modelo*
> nadar
> *Usamos los brazos y las piernas para nadar.*

1. hablar por teléfono
2. tocar el piano
3. correr en el parque
4. escuchar música
5. ver una película

6. toser
7. llevar zapatos
8. comprar perfume
9. estudiar biología
10. comer pollo asado

AYUDA

Remember that in Spanish, parts of the body are usually referred to with an article and not a possessive adjective: **Me duelen los pies.** The indirect object pronoun **me** is used to express the concept of *my*.

6 **Cuestionario** Contesta el cuestionario seleccionando las respuestas que reflejen mejor tus experiencias. Suma (*Add*) los puntos de cada respuesta y anota el resultado.

¿Tienes buena salud?

27–30 puntos	Salud y hábitos excelentes
23–26 puntos	Salud y hábitos buenos
22 puntos o menos	Salud y hábitos problemáticos

1. **¿Con qué frecuencia te enfermas? (resfriados, gripe, etc.)**
   Cuatro veces por año o más. (1 punto)
   Dos o tres veces por año. (2 puntos)
   Casi nunca. (3 puntos)

2. **¿Con qué frecuencia tienes dolores de estómago o problemas digestivos?**
   Con mucha frecuencia. (1 punto)
   A veces. (2 puntos)
   Casi nunca. (3 puntos)

3. **¿Con qué frecuencia sufres de dolores de cabeza?**
   Frecuentemente. (1 punto)
   A veces. (2 puntos)
   Casi nunca. (3 puntos)

4. **¿Comes verduras y frutas?**
   No, casi nunca como verduras ni frutas. (1 punto)
   Sí, a veces. (2 puntos)
   Sí, todos los días. (3 puntos)

5. **¿Eres alérgico/a a algo?**
   Sí, a muchas cosas. (1 punto)
   Sí, a algunas cosas. (2 puntos)
   No. (3 puntos)

6. **¿Haces ejercicios aeróbicos?**
   No, casi nunca hago ejercicios aeróbicos. (1 punto)
   Sí, a veces. (2 puntos)
   Sí, con frecuencia. (3 puntos)

7. **¿Con qué frecuencia te haces un examen médico?**
   Nunca o casi nunca. (1 punto)
   Cada dos años. (2 puntos)
   Cada año y/o antes de empezar a practicar un deporte. (3 puntos)

8. **¿Con qué frecuencia vas al dentista?**
   Nunca voy al dentista. (1 punto)
   Sólo cuando me duele un diente. (2 puntos)
   Por lo menos una vez por año. (3 puntos)

9. **¿Qué comes normalmente por la mañana?**
   No como nada por la mañana. (1 punto)
   Tomo una bebida dietética. (2 puntos)
   Como cereal y fruta. (3 puntos)

10. **¿Con qué frecuencia te sientes mareado/a?**
    Frecuentemente. (1 punto)
    A veces. (2 puntos)
    Casi nunca. (3 puntos)

Comunicación

7

En el hospital Escucha la conversación entre Javier, Victoria y una doctora. Luego, indica si las conclusiones son **lógicas** o **ilógicas**, según lo que escuchaste.

	Lógico	Ilógico
1. Un pasatiempo de Javier es practicar deportes.	○	○
2. La situación de Javier es grave.	○	○
3. Es necesario esperar mucho en ese hospital para ver un doctor.	○	○
4. Javier no está contento con el diagnóstico de la doctora.	○	○
5. Javier es un mal paciente.	○	○

8

¿Qué les pasó? Describe qué les pasó y cómo se sienten estas personas.

1. Adela

2. Francisco

3. Pilar

4. Pedro

5. Cristina

6. Félix

9

Un accidente Escribe un párrafo sobre un accidente o una enfermedad que tuviste. Incluye información relacionada con estas preguntas.

✔ ¿Qué ocurrió?
✔ ¿Dónde ocurrió?
✔ ¿Cuándo ocurrió?
✔ ¿Cómo ocurrió?
✔ ¿Quién te ayudó y cómo?
✔ ¿Tuviste algún problema después del accidente o después de la enfermedad?
✔ ¿Cuánto tiempo tuviste el problema?

10

No me siento bien En parejas, representen una situación entre un(a) paciente y un(a) enfermero/a. Incluyan en la conversación los síntomas del/de la paciente, dónde tiene dolor, la medicina que debe tomar y lo que debe hacer para sentirse mejor.

¡Qué dolor!

Jimena no se siente bien y tiene que ir al doctor.

PERSONAJES   ELENA   JIMENA

ELENA ¿Cómo te sientes?

JIMENA Me duele un poco la garganta. Pero no tengo fiebre.

ELENA Creo que tienes un resfriado. Te voy a llevar a casa.

JIMENA Hola, don Diego. Gracias por venir.

DON DIEGO Fui a la farmacia. Aquí están las pastillas para el resfriado. Se debe tomar una cada seis horas con las comidas. Y no se deben tomar más de seis pastillas al día.

ELENA ¿Don Diego ya fue a la farmacia? ¿Cuánto tiempo hace que lo llamaste?

JIMENA Hace media hora. Ay, qué cosas, de niña apenas me enfermaba. No perdí ni un solo día de clases.

ELENA Yo tampoco.

ELENA Nunca tenía resfriados, pero me rompí el brazo dos veces. Mi hermana y yo estábamos paseando en bicicleta y casi me di con un señor que caminaba por la calle. Me caí y me rompí el brazo.

JIMENA ¿Qué es esto?

ELENA Es té de jengibre. Cuando me dolía el estómago, mi mamá siempre me hacía tomarlo. Se dice que es bueno para el dolor de estómago.

JIMENA Pero no me duele el estómago.

(*La Sra. Díaz llama a Jimena.*)

JIMENA Hola, mamá. Don Diego me trajo los medicamentos... ¿Al doctor? ¿Estás segura? Allá nos vemos. (*A Elena*) Mi mamá ya hizo una cita para mí con el Dr. Meléndez.

DON DIEGO

SRA. DÍAZ

DR. MELÉNDEZ

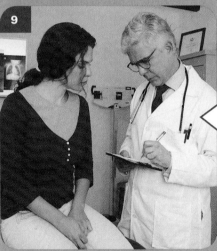

SRA. DÍAZ ¿Te pusiste un suéter anoche?

JIMENA No, mamá. Se me olvidó.

SRA. DÍAZ Doctor, esta jovencita salió anoche, se le olvidó ponerse un suéter y parece que le dio un resfriado.

DR. MELÉNDEZ Jimena, ¿cuáles son tus síntomas?

JIMENA Toso con frecuencia y me duele la garganta.

DR. MELÉNDEZ ¿Cuánto tiempo hace que tienes estos síntomas?

JIMENA Hace dos días que me duele la garganta.

DR. MELÉNDEZ Muy bien. Aquí no tienes infección. No tienes fiebre. Te voy a mandar algo para la garganta. Puedes ir por los medicamentos inmediatamente a la farmacia.

SRA. DÍAZ Doctor, ¿cómo está? ¿Es grave?

DR. MELÉNDEZ No, no es nada grave. Jimena, la próxima vez, escucha a tu mamá. ¡Tienes que usar suéter!

Expresiones útiles

Discussing medical conditions

¿Cómo te sientes?
How do you feel?
Me duele un poco la garganta.
My throat hurts a little.
No me duele el estómago.
My stomach doesn't hurt.
De niño/a apenas me enfermaba.
As a child, I rarely got sick.
¡Soy alérgico/a a chile!
I'm allergic to chili powder!

Discussing remedies

Se dice que el té de jengibre es bueno para el dolor de estómago.
They say ginger tea is good for stomachaches.
Aquí están las pastillas para el resfriado.
Here are the pills for your cold.
Se debe tomar una cada seis horas.
You should take one every six hours.

Expressions with **hacer**

Hace + [*period of time*] **que** + [*present /preterite*]
¿Cuánto tiempo hace que tienes estos síntomas?
How long have you had these symptoms?
Hace dos días que me duele la garganta.
My throat has been hurting for two days.
¿Cuánto tiempo hace que lo llamaste?
How long has it been since you called him?
Hace media hora.
It's been a half hour (since I called).

Additional vocabulary

canela *cinnamon*
miel *honey*
terco *stubborn*

¿Qué pasó?

1 **¿Cierto o falso?** Decide si lo que dicen estas oraciones sobre Jimena es **cierto** o **falso**. Corrige las oraciones falsas.

	Cierto	Falso
1. Dice que de niña apenas se enfermaba.	○	○
2. Tiene dolor de garganta y fiebre.	○	○
3. Olvidó ponerse un suéter anoche.	○	○
4. Hace tres días que le duele la garganta.	○	○
5. El doctor le dice que tiene una infección.	○	○

2 **Identificar** Identifica quién puede decir estas oraciones.

1. Como dice tu mamá, tienes que usar suéter.
2. Por pasear en bicicleta me rompí el brazo dos veces.
3. ¿Cuánto tiempo hace que toses y te duele la garganta?
4. Tengo cita con el Dr. Meléndez.
5. Dicen que el té de jengibre es muy bueno para los dolores de estómago.
6. Nunca perdí un día de clases porque apenas me enfermaba.

DR. MELÉNDEZ

ELENA

JIMENA

3 **Ordenar** Pon estos sucesos en el orden correcto.

a. Jimena va a ver al doctor. _____
b. El doctor le dice a la Sra. Díaz que no es nada serio. _____
c. Elena le habla a Jimena de cuando se rompió el brazo. _____
d. El doctor le receta medicamentos. _____
e. Jimena le dice a Elena que le duele la garganta. _____
f. Don Diego le trae a Jimena las pastillas para el resfriado. _____

4 **En el consultorio** Trabajen en parejas para representar los papeles de un(a) médico/a y su paciente. Usen las instrucciones como guía.

El/La médico/a

Pregúntale al / a la paciente qué le pasó.

Pregúntale cuánto tiempo hace que se cayó.

Mira el dedo. Debes recomendar un tratamiento (*treatment*) al / a la paciente.

El/La paciente

→ Dile que te caíste en casa. Describe tu dolor.

→ Describe la situación. Piensas que te rompiste el dedo.

→ Debes hacer preguntas al / a la médico/a sobre el tratamiento (*treatment*).

AYUDA

Here are some useful expressions:
¿Cómo se lastimó...?
¿Qué le pasó?
¿Cuánto tiempo hace que...?
Tengo...
Estoy...
¿Es usted alérgico/a a algún medicamento?
Usted debe...

Ortografía
El acento y las sílabas fuertes

In Spanish, written accent marks are used on many words. Here is a review of some of the principles governing word stress and the use of written accents.

as-pi-ri-na   gri-pe   to-man   an-tes

In Spanish, when a word ends in a vowel, **-n**, or **-s**, the spoken stress usually falls on the next-to-last syllable. Words of this type are very common and do not need a written accent.

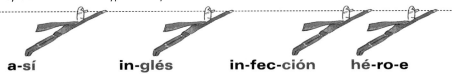

a-sí   in-glés   in-fec-ción   hé-ro-e

When a word ends in a vowel, **-n**, or **-s**, and the spoken stress does *not* fall on the next-to-last syllable, then a written accent is needed.

hos-pi-tal   na-riz   re-ce-tar   to-ser

When a word ends in any consonant *other* than **-n** or **-s**, the spoken stress usually falls on the last syllable. Words of this type are very common and do not need a written accent.

lá-piz   fút-bol   hués-ped   sué-ter

When a word ends in any consonant *other* than **-n** or **-s** and the spoken stress does *not* fall on the last syllable, then a written accent is needed.

far-ma-cia   bio-lo-gí-a   su-cio   frí-o

Diphthongs (two weak vowels or a strong and weak vowel together) are normally pronounced as a single syllable. A written accent is needed when a diphthong is broken into two syllables.

sol   pan   mar   tos

Spanish words of only one syllable do not usually carry a written accent (unless it is to distinguish meaning: **se** and **sé**).

CONSULTA

In Spanish, **a**, **e**, and **o** are considered strong vowels while **i** and **u** are weak vowels. To review this concept, see **Lección 3**, **Pronunciación**, p. 85.

Práctica Busca las palabras que necesitan acento escrito y escribe su forma correcta.

1. sal-mon
2. ins-pec-tor
3. nu-me-ro
4. fa-cil
5. ju-go
6. a-bri-go
7. ra-pi-do
8. sa-ba-do
9. vez
10. me-nu
11. o-pe-ra-cion
12. im-per-me-a-ble
13. a-de-mas
14. re-ga-te-ar
15. an-ti-pa-ti-co
16. far-ma-cia
17. es-qui
18. pen-sion
19. pa-is
20. per-don

El ahorcado Juega al ahorcado (*hangman*) para adivinar las palabras.

1. __ l __ __ __ __ __ a   Vas allí cuando estás enfermo.
2. __ __ __ __ e __ c __ __ n   Se usa para poner una vacuna (*vaccination*).
3. __ __ d __ o __ __ __ __ __ a   Permite ver los huesos.
4. __ __ __ __ i __ o   Trabaja en un hospital.
5. a __ __ __ b __ __ __ __ __ __   Es una medicina.

EN DETALLE

Servicios de salud

¿Sabías que en los países hispanos no necesitas pagar por los servicios de salud? Ésta es una de las diferencias que hay entre países como los Estados Unidos y los países hispanos.

En la mayor parte de estos países, el gobierno ofrece servicios médicos muy baratos o gratuitos° a sus ciudadanos°. Los turistas y extranjeros también pueden tener acceso a los servicios médicos a bajo° costo. La Seguridad Social y organizaciones similares son las responsables de gestionar° estos servicios.

Naturalmente, esto no funciona igual° en todos los países. En Ecuador, México y Perú, la situación varía según las regiones. Los habitantes de las ciudades y pueblos grandes tienen acceso a más servicios médicos, mientras que quienes viven en pueblos remotos sólo cuentan con° pequeñas clínicas.

Por su parte, Costa Rica, Colombia, Cuba y España tienen sistemas de salud muy desarrollados°.

Cruz verde de farmacia en Madrid, España

Las farmacias

Farmacia de guardia: Las farmacias generalmente tienen un horario comercial. Sin embargo°, en cada barrio° hay una farmacia de guardia que abre las veinticuatro horas del día.

Productos farmacéuticos: Todavía hay muchas farmacias tradicionales que están más especializadas en medicinas y productos farmacéuticos. No venden una gran variedad de productos.

Recetas: Muchos medicamentos se venden sin receta médica. Los farmacéuticos aconsejan° a las personas sobre problemas de salud y les dan las medicinas.

Cruz° verde: En muchos países, las farmacias tienen como símbolo una cruz verde. Cuando la cruz verde está encendida°, la farmacia está abierta.

En España, por ejemplo, la mayoría de la gente tiene acceso a ellos y en muchos casos son completamente gratuitos. Según un informe de la Organización Mundial de la Salud, el sistema de salud español ocupa uno de los primeros diez lugares del mundo. Esto se debe no sólo al buen funcionamiento° del sistema, sino también al nivel de salud general de la población. Impresionante, ¿no?

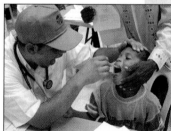
Consulta médica en la República Dominicana

gratuitos *free (of charge)* ciudadanos *citizens* bajo *low*
gestionar *to manage* igual *in the same way* cuentan con *have*
desarrollados *developed* funcionamiento *operation*
Sin embargo *However* barrio *neighborhood* aconsejan *advise*
Cruz *Cross* encendida *lit (up)*

ACTIVIDADES

1 **¿Cierto o falso?** Indica si lo que dicen las oraciones es cierto o falso. Corrige la información falsa.

1. En los países hispanos los gobiernos ofrecen servicios de salud accesibles a sus ciudadanos.

2. En los países hispanos los extranjeros tienen que pagar mucho dinero por los servicios médicos.

3. El sistema de salud español es uno de los mejores del mundo.

4. Las farmacias de guardia abren sólo los sábados y domingos.

5. En los países hispanos las farmacias venden una gran variedad de productos.

6. Los farmacéuticos de los países hispanos aconsejan a los enfermos y venden algunas medicinas sin necesidad de receta.

7. En México y otros países, los pueblos remotos cuentan con grandes centros médicos.

8. Muchas farmacias usan una cruz verde como símbolo.

ASÍ SE DICE

La salud

el chequeo (Esp., Méx.)	el examen médico
la droguería (Col.)	la farmacia
la herida	*injury; wound*
la píldora	la pastilla
los primeros auxilios	*first aid*
la sangre	*blood*

EL MUNDO HISPANO

Remedios caseros° y plantas medicinales

- **Achiote°** En Suramérica se usa para curar inflamaciones de garganta. Las hojas° de achiote se cuecen° en agua, se cuelan° y se hacen gárgaras° con esa agua.

- **Ají** En Perú se usan cataplasmas° de las semillas° de ají para aliviar los dolores reumáticos y la tortícolis°.

- **Azúcar** En Nicaragua y otros países centroamericanos se usa el azúcar para detener° la sangre en pequeñas heridas.

- **Sábila (aloe vera)** En Latinoamérica, el jugo de las hojas de sábila se usa para reducir cicatrices°. Se recomienda aplicarlo sobre la cicatriz dos veces al día, durante varios meses.

Remedios caseros *Home remedies* Achiote *Annatto* hojas *leaves* se cuecen *are cooked* se cuelan *they are drained* gárgaras *gargles* cataplasmas *pastes* semillas *seeds* tortícolis *stiff neck* detener *to stop* cicatrices *scars*

PERFILES

Curanderos° y chamanes

¿Quieres ser doctor(a), juez(a)°, político/a o psicólogo/a? En algunas sociedades de las Américas **los curanderos** y **los chamanes** no tienen que escoger entre estas profesiones porque ellos son mediadores de conflictos y dan consejos a la comunidad. Su opinión es muy respetada.

Códice Florentino, México, siglo XVI

Desde las culturas antiguas° de las Américas muchas personas piensan que la salud del cuerpo y de la mente sólo puede existir si hay un equilibrio entre el ser humano y la naturaleza. Los curanderos y los chamanes son quienes cuidan este equilibrio.

Los curanderos se especializan más en enfermedades físicas, mientras que los chamanes están más

Cuzco, Perú

relacionados con los males° de la mente y el alma°. Ambos° usan plantas, masajes y rituales y sus conocimientos se basan en la tradición, la experiencia, la observación y la intuición.

Curanderos *Healers* juez(a) *judge* antiguas *ancient* males *illnesses* alma *soul* Ambos *Both*

Conexión Internet

¿Cuáles son algunos hospitales importantes del mundo hispano?

Use the Web to find more cultural information related to this **Cultura** section.

ACTIVIDADES

2 **Comprensión** Contesta las preguntas.
1. ¿Cómo se les llama a las farmacias en Colombia?
2. ¿Qué parte del achiote se usa para curar la garganta?
3. ¿Cómo se aplica la sábila para reducir cicatrices?
4. En algunas partes de las Américas, ¿quiénes mantienen el equilibrio entre el ser humano y la naturaleza?
5. ¿Qué usan los curanderos y chamanes para curar?

3 **¿Qué haces cuando tienes gripe?** Escribe cuatro oraciones sobre las cosas que haces cuando tienes gripe. Explica si vas al médico, si tomas medicamentos o si sigues alguna dieta especial.

10.1 The imperfect tense

ANTE TODO In **Lecciones 6–9,** you learned the preterite tense. You will now learn the imperfect, which describes past activities in a different way.

The imperfect of regular verbs

		cantar	beber	escribir
SINGULAR FORMS	yo	cant**aba**	beb**ía**	escrib**ía**
	tú	cant**abas**	beb**ías**	escrib**ías**
	Ud./él/ella	cant**aba**	beb**ía**	escrib**ía**
PLURAL FORMS	nosotros/as	cant**ábamos**	beb**íamos**	escrib**íamos**
	vosotros/as	cant**abais**	beb**íais**	escrib**íais**
	Uds./ellos/ellas	cant**aban**	beb**ían**	escrib**ían**

De niña apenas me enfermaba.

Cuando me dolía el estómago, mi mamá me daba té de jengibre.

▶ There are no stem changes in the imperfect.

entender (e:ie)   **Entendíamos** japonés.
We used to understand Japanese.

servir (e:i)   El camarero les **servía** el café.
The waiter was serving them coffee.

doler (o:ue)   A Javier le **dolía** el tobillo.
Javier's ankle was hurting.

▶ The imperfect form of **hay** is **había** *(there was; there were; there used to be).*

▶ **¡Atención!** **Ir, ser,** and **ver** are the only verbs that are irregular in the imperfect.

The imperfect of irregular verbs

		ir	ser	ver
SINGULAR FORMS	yo	**iba**	**era**	**veía**
	tú	**ibas**	**eras**	**veías**
	Ud./él/ella	**iba**	**era**	**veía**
PLURAL FORMS	nosotros/as	**íbamos**	**éramos**	**veíamos**
	vosotros/as	**ibais**	**erais**	**veíais**
	Uds./ellos/ellas	**iban**	**eran**	**veían**

CONSULTA

You will learn more about the contrast between the preterite and the imperfect in **Estructura 10.2**, pp. 346–347.

Uses of the imperfect

▶ As a general rule, the imperfect is used to describe actions that are seen by the speaker as incomplete or "continuing," while the preterite is used to describe actions that have been completed. The imperfect expresses what was happening at a certain time or how things used to be. The preterite, in contrast, expresses a completed action.

—¿Qué te **pasó**?
What happened to you?

—Me **torcí** el tobillo.
I sprained my ankle.

—¿Dónde **vivías** de niño?
Where did you live as a child?

—**Vivía** en San José.
I lived in San José.

▶ These expressions are often used with the imperfect because they express habitual or repeated actions: **de niño/a** (*as a child*), **todos los días** (*every day*), **mientras** (*while*).

Uses of the imperfect

1. **Habitual or repeated actions** . . . .
Íbamos al parque los domingos.
We used to go to the park on Sundays.

2. **Events or actions that were in progress**
Yo **leía** mientras él **estudiaba**.
I was reading while he was studying.

3. **Physical characteristics** . . . .
Era alto y guapo.
He was tall and handsome.

4. **Mental or emotional states** . . . .
Quería mucho a su familia.
He loved his family very much.

5. **Telling time** . . . .
Eran las tres y media.
It was 3:30.

6. **Age** . . . .
Los niños **tenían** seis años.
The children were six years old.

¡INTÉNTALO!   Indica la forma correcta de cada verbo en el imperfecto.

1. Mis hermanos _____veían_____ (ver) televisión todas las tardes.
2. Yo _____ (viajar) en el tren de las 3:30.
3. ¿Dónde _____ (vivir) Samuel de niño?
4. Tú _____ (hablar) con Javier.
5. Leonardo y yo _____ (correr) por el parque.
6. Ustedes _____ (ir) a la clínica.
7. Nadia _____ (bailar) merengue.
8. ¿Cuándo _____ (asistir) tú a clase de español?
9. Yo _____ (ser) muy feliz.
10. Nosotras _____ (comprender) las preguntas.

Práctica

1 **Completar** Primero, completa las oraciones con el imperfecto de los verbos. Luego, pon las oraciones en orden lógico.

a. El doctor dijo que no _____ (ser) nada grave. _____

b. El doctor _____ (querer) ver la nariz del niño. _____

c. Su mamá _____ (estar) dibujando cuando Miguelito entró llorando. _____

d. Miguelito _____ (tener) la nariz hinchada (*swollen*). Fueron al hospital. _____

e. Miguelito no _____ (ir) a jugar más. Ahora quería ir a casa a descansar. _____

f. Miguelito y sus amigos _____ (jugar) al béisbol en el patio. _____

g. _____ (Ser) las dos de la tarde. _____

h. Miguelito le dijo a la enfermera que _____ (dolerle) la nariz. _____

2 **Transformar** Forma oraciones completas para describir lo que hacían Julieta y César. Usa las formas correctas del imperfecto y añade todas las palabras necesarias.

1. Julieta y César / ser / paramédicos

2. trabajar / juntos y / llevarse / muy bien

3. cuando / haber / accidente, / siempre / analizar / situación / con cuidado

4. preocuparse / mucho / por / pacientes

5. si / paciente / tener / mucho / dolor, / ponerle / inyección

3 **En la escuela de medicina** Usa los verbos de la lista para completar las oraciones con las formas correctas del imperfecto. Algunos verbos se usan más de una vez.

caerse	enfermarse	ir	querer	tener
comprender	estornudar	pensar	sentirse	tomar
doler	hacer	poder	ser	toser

1. Cuando Javier y Victoria _____ estudiantes de medicina, siempre _____ que ir al médico.

2. Cada vez que él _____ un examen, a Javier le _____ mucho la cabeza.

3. Cuando Victoria _____ ejercicios aeróbicos, siempre _____ mareada.

4. Todas las primaveras, Javier _____ mucho porque es alérgico al polen.

5. Victoria también _____ de su bicicleta camino a la escuela.

6. Después de comer en la cafetería, a Victoria siempre le _____ el estómago.

7. Javier _____ ser médico para ayudar a los demás.

8. Pero no _____ por qué él _____ con tanta frecuencia.

9. Cuando Victoria _____ fiebre, no _____ ni leer el termómetro.

10. A Javier _____ los dientes, pero nunca _____ ir al dentista.

11. Victoria _____ mucho cuando _____ congestionada.

12. Javier y Victoria _____ que nunca _____ a graduarse.

Comunicación

4 **El paciente de Daniel** Lee el mensaje electrónico de Daniel a su mamá. Luego, indica si las conclusiones son **lógicas** o **ilógicas**, según lo que leíste.

De:	Daniel
Para:	Mamá
Asunto:	Hospital

Me encanta mi nuevo trabajo en el hospital. Veo a muchos pacientes y aprendo algo nuevo todos los días. Te cuento que había un hombre viejo que venía al hospital todos los miércoles. Les decía a los enfermeros que estaba enfermo o que tenía algún dolor: una semana era un dolor de cabeza, otra semana era un dolor de oído, en fin… siempre tenía algo. Cuando yo lo examinaba, no veía ningún problema serio y, por el contrario, él no parecía sentirse muy mal porque hablaba mucho: me contaba historias de su juventud. Sólo quería conversar conmigo y siempre preguntaba por mí. No quería a otro doctor. Cuando yo estaba ocupado con otros pacientes, él me esperaba. Me gusta hablar con él, pero estoy muy ocupado en el hospital. Ahora nos vemos en un café todos los miércoles cuando termina mi turno (*shift*) en el hospital.
Daniel

	Lógico	Ilógico
1. Daniel es enfermero.	○	○
2. Daniel veía a este mismo paciente una vez por semana.	○	○
3. Este paciente sufría una enfermedad grave.	○	○
4. Cuando Daniel no podía ver a este paciente, el paciente buscaba a otro doctor.	○	○
5. Daniel no le recetaba nada a este paciente cuando lo veía.	○	○

5 **Entrevista** Contesta las preguntas de tu compañero/a.

1. Cuando eras estudiante de primaria, ¿te gustaban tus profesores/as?
2. ¿Veías mucha televisión cuando eras niño/a?
3. Cuando tenías diez años, ¿cuál era tu programa de televisión favorito?
4. Cuando eras niño/a, ¿qué hacía tu familia durante las vacaciones?
5. ¿Cuántos años tenías en 2010?
6. Cuando estabas en el quinto año escolar, ¿qué hacías con tus amigos/as?
7. Cuando tenías once años, ¿cuál era tu grupo musical favorito?
8. Antes de tomar esta clase, ¿sabías hablar español?

6 **Describir** Describe en un párrafo cómo era tu niñez. Puedes usar las sugerencias de la lista.

- las vacaciones
- ocasiones especiales
- qué hacías durante el verano
- celebraciones con tu familia
- cómo era tu escuela
- cómo eran tus amigos/as
- a qué jugabas
- qué hacías cuando te sentías enfermo/a

Síntesis

7 **En la escuela primaria** En parejas, túrnense para hacerse preguntas sobre cómo era su vida durante la escuela primaria. Pueden usar las sugerencias de la lista u otras ideas.

| comer comida saludable | lastimarse con frecuencia |
| enfermarse mucho | ser alérgico/a a algo |

The preterite and the imperfect

10.2

ANTE TODO Now that you have learned the forms of the preterite and the imperfect, you will learn more about how they are used. The preterite and the imperfect are not interchangeable. In Spanish, the choice between these two tenses depends on the context and on the point of view of the speaker.

Me rompí el brazo cuando estaba paseando en bicicleta.

Tenía dolor de cabeza, pero me tomé una aspirina y se me fue.

COMPARE & CONTRAST

Use the preterite to...

1. Express actions that are viewed by the speaker as completed

Sandra **se rompió** la pierna.
Sandra broke her leg.

Fueron a Buenos Aires ayer.
They went to Buenos Aires yesterday.

2. Express the beginning or end of a past action

La película **empezó** a las nueve.
The movie began at nine o'clock.

Ayer **terminé** el proyecto para la clase de química.
Yesterday I finished the project for chemistry class.

3. Narrate a series of past actions or events

La doctora me **miró** los oídos, me **hizo** unas preguntas y **escribió** la receta.
The doctor looked in my ears, asked me some questions, and wrote the prescription.

Me di con la mesa, **me caí** y **me lastimé** el pie.
I bumped into the table, I fell, and I injured my foot.

Use the imperfect to...

1. Describe an ongoing past action with no reference to its beginning or end

Sandra **esperaba** al doctor.
Sandra was waiting for the doctor.

El médico **se preocupaba** por sus pacientes.
The doctor worried about his patients.

2. Express habitual past actions and events

Cuando **era** joven, **jugaba** al tenis.
When I was young, I used to play tennis.

De niño, Eduardo **se enfermaba** con mucha frecuencia.
As a child, Eduardo used to get sick very frequently.

3. Describe physical and emotional states or characteristics

La chica **quería** descansar. **Se sentía** mal y **tenía** dolor de cabeza.
The girl wanted to rest. She felt ill and had a headache.

Ellos **eran** altos y **tenían** ojos verdes.
They were tall and had green eyes.

Estábamos felices de ver a la familia.
We were happy to see our family.

AYUDA

These words and expressions, as well as similar ones, commonly occur with the preterite: **ayer, anteayer, una vez, dos veces, tres veces, el año pasado, de repente.** They usually imply that an action has happened at a specific point in time. For a review, see **Estructura 6.3**, p. 207.

AYUDA

These words and expressions, as well as similar ones, commonly occur with the imperfect: **de niño/a, todos los días, mientras, siempre, con frecuencia, todas las semanas.** They usually express habitual or repeated actions in the past.

▶ The preterite and the imperfect often appear in the same sentence. In such cases, the imperfect describes what *was happening*, while the preterite describes the action that "interrupted" the ongoing activity.

> **Miraba** la tele cuando **sonó** el teléfono.
> *I was watching TV when the phone rang.*

> Felicia **leía** el periódico cuando **llegó** Ramiro.
> *Felicia was reading the newspaper when Ramiro arrived.*

▶ You will also see the preterite and the imperfect together in narratives such as fiction, news, and the retelling of events. The imperfect provides background information, such as time, weather, and location, while the preterite indicates the specific events that occurred.

> **Eran** las dos de la mañana y el detective ya no **podía** mantenerse despierto. **Se bajó** lentamente del coche, **estiró** las piernas y **levantó** los brazos hacia el cielo oscuro.
> *It was two in the morning, and the detective could no longer stay awake. He slowly stepped out of the car, stretched his legs, and raised his arms toward the dark sky.*

> La luna **estaba** llena y no **había** en el cielo ni una sola nube. De repente, el detective **escuchó** un grito espeluznante proveniente del parque.
> *The moon was full and there wasn't a single cloud in the sky. Suddenly, the detective heard a piercing scream coming from the park.*

Un médico colombiano desarrolló una vacuna contra la malaria

En 1986, el doctor colombiano Manuel Elkin Patarroyo creó la primera vacuna sintética para combatir la malaria. Esta enfermedad parecía haberse erradicado hacía décadas en muchas partes del mundo. Sin embargo, justo cuando Patarroyo terminó de elaborar la inmunización, los casos de malaria empezaban a aumentar de nuevo. En mayo de 1993, el doctor colombiano cedió la patente de la vacuna a la Organización Mundial de la Salud en nombre de Colombia. Los grandes laboratorios farmacéuticos presionaron a la OMS porque querían la vacuna. Las presiones no tuvieron éxito y, en 1995, el doctor Patarroyo y la OMS pactaron continuar con el acuerdo inicial: la vacuna seguía siendo propiedad de la OMS.

¡INTÉNTALO! Elige el pretérito o el imperfecto para completar la historia. Explica por qué se usa ese tiempo verbal en cada ocasión.

1. ____Eran____ (Fueron/Eran) las doce.
2. _____ (Hubo/Había) mucha gente en la calle.
3. A las doce y media, Tomás y yo _____ (entramos/entrábamos) en el restaurante Tárcoles.
4. Todos los días yo _____ (almorcé/almorzaba) con Tomás al mediodía.
5. El camarero _____ (llegó/llegaba) inmediatamente con el menú.
6. Nosotros _____ (empezamos/empezábamos) a leerlo.
7. Yo _____ (pedí/pedía) el pescado.
8. De repente, el camarero _____ (volvió/volvía) a nuestra mesa.
9. Y nos _____ (dio/daba) una mala noticia.
10. Desafortunadamente, no _____ (tuvieron/tenían) más pescado.
11. Por eso Tomás y yo _____ (decidimos/decidíamos) comer en otro lugar.
12. _____ (Llovió/Llovía) mucho cuando _____ (salimos/salíamos) del restaurante.
13. Así que _____ (regresamos/regresábamos) al restaurante Tárcoles.
14. Esta vez, _____ (pedí/pedía) arroz con pollo.

Práctica

1

En el periódico Completa esta noticia con las formas correctas del pretérito o el imperfecto.

Un accidente trágico

Ayer temprano por la mañana (1)_____ (haber) un trágico accidente en el centro de San José cuando el conductor de un autobús no (2)_____ (ver) venir un carro. La mujer que (3)_____ (manejar) el carro (4)_____ (morir) al instante y los paramédicos (5)_____ (tener) que llevar al pasajero al hospital porque (6)_____ (sufrir) varias fracturas. El conductor del autobús (7)_____ (decir) que no (8)_____ (ver) el carro hasta el último momento porque (9)_____ (estar) muy nublado y (10)_____ (llover). Él (11)_____ (intentar) (*to attempt*) dar un viraje brusco (*to swerve*), pero (12)_____ (perder) el control del autobús y no (13)_____ (poder) evitar (*to avoid*) el accidente. Según nos informaron, no (14)_____ (lastimarse) ningún pasajero del autobús.

> **AYUDA**
>
> Reading Spanish-language newspapers is a good way to practice verb tenses. You will find that both the imperfect and the preterite occur with great regularity. Many newsstands carry international papers, and many Spanish-language newspapers (such as Spain's *El País*, Mexico's *Reforma*, and Argentina's *Clarín*) are on the Web.

2

Seleccionar Utiliza el tiempo verbal adecuado, según el contexto.

1. La semana pasada, Manolo y Aurora _____ (querer) dar una fiesta. _____ (Decidir) invitar a seis amigos y servirles mucha comida.
2. Manolo y Aurora _____ (estar) preparando la comida cuando Elena _____ (llamar). Como siempre, _____ (tener) que estudiar para un examen.
3. A las seis, _____ (volver) a sonar el teléfono. Su amigo Francisco tampoco _____ (poder) ir a la fiesta, porque _____ (tener) fiebre. Manolo y Aurora _____ (sentirse) muy tristes, pero _____ (tener) que preparar la comida.
4. Después de otros quince minutos, _____ (sonar) el teléfono. Sus amigos, los señores Vega, _____ (estar) en camino (*en route*) al hospital: a su hijo le _____ (doler) mucho el estómago. Sólo dos de los amigos _____ (poder) ir a la cena.
5. Por supuesto, _____ (ir) a tener demasiada comida. Finalmente, cinco minutos antes de las ocho, _____ (llamar) Ramón y Javier. Ellos _____ (pensar) que la fiesta _____ (ser) la próxima semana.
6. Tristes, Manolo y Aurora _____ (sentarse) a comer solos. Mientras _____ (comer), pronto _____ (llegar) a la conclusión de que _____ (ser) mejor estar solos: ¡La comida _____ (estar) malísima!

3

Completar Completa las frases de una manera lógica. Usa el pretérito o el imperfecto.

1. De niño/a, yo...
2. Yo conducía el auto mientras...
3. Anoche mi novio/a...
4. Ayer el/la profesor(a)...
5. La semana pasada un(a) amigo/a...
6. Con frecuencia mis padres...
7. Esta mañana en la cafetería...
8. Hablábamos con el doctor cuando...

Comunicación

4

¡Qué nervios! Escucha lo que le cuenta Sandra a su amiga sobre su día. Luego, indica si las conclusiones son **lógicas** o **ilógicas**, según lo que escuchaste.

	Lógico	Ilógico
1. Sandra trabaja en un hospital o una clínica.	O	O
2. La enfermera es antipática.	O	O
3. Sandra no tiene mucha experiencia profesional.	O	O
4. El paciente trabaja como enfermero.	O	O
5. Cuando era joven, el paciente tuvo una experiencia similar a la experiencia de Sandra.	O	O

5

Entrevista Contesta las preguntas de tu compañero/a.

1. ¿Quién era tu mejor amigo/a en la escuela secundaria?
2. ¿Cuántos años tenías cuando lo/la conociste?
3. ¿Cómo era él/ella?
4. ¿Qué le gustaba hacer? ¿Tenían ustedes los mismos pasatiempos?
5. ¿Adónde iban los fines de semana?
6. ¿Cuándo fue la última vez que lo/la viste?

6

La sala de emergencias Mira la lista de pacientes e inventa una historia para cada uno de ellos para explicar por qué están en la sala de emergencias.

> **modelo**
>
> Eran las tres de la tarde. Como todos los días, Pablo jugaba al fútbol con sus amigos. Estaba muy contento. De repente, se cayó y se rompió el brazo. Entonces fue a la sala de emergencias.

Paciente	Edad	Hora	Estado
1. Pablo Romero	9 años	15:20	hueso roto (el brazo)
2. Estela Rodríguez	45 años	15:25	tobillo torcido
3. Lupe Quintana	29 años	15:37	embarazada, dolores
4. Manuel López	52 años	15:45	infección de garganta
5. Marta Díaz	3 años	16:00	congestión, fiebre
6. Roberto Salazar	32 años	16:06	dolor de oído
7. Marco Brito	18 años	16:18	daño en el cuello, posible fractura
8. Ana María Ortiz	66 años	16:29	reacción alérgica a un medicamento

Síntesis

7

La primera vez Escribe un párrafo sobre la primera vez que te rompiste un hueso, pasaste la noche en un hospital, fuiste a la sala de emergencias, etc. Incluye en tu párrafo qué edad tenías, qué pasó y cómo te sentías.

10.3 Constructions with se

ANTE TODO   In **Lección 7,** you learned how to use **se** as the third person reflexive pronoun (**Él <u>se</u> despierta. Ellos <u>se</u> visten. Ella <u>se</u> baña.**). **Se** can also be used to form constructions in which the person performing the action is not expressed or is de-emphasized.

Impersonal constructions with se

▶ In Spanish, verbs that are not reflexive can be used with **se** to form impersonal constructions. These are statements in which the person performing the action is not defined.

Se habla español en Costa Rica.
Spanish is spoken in Costa Rica.

Se hacen operaciones aquí.
They perform operations here.

Se puede leer en la sala de espera.
You can read in the waiting room.

Se necesitan medicinas enseguida.
They need medicine right away.

▶ **¡Atención!** Note that the third person singular verb form is used with singular nouns and the third person plural form is used with plural nouns.

Se vende ropa.

Se venden camisas.

▶ You often see the impersonal **se** in signs, advertisements, and directions.

SE PROHÍBE
NADAR

Se necesitan
programadores
Grupo Tecno
Tel. 778-34-34

ENTRADA

Se entra por la
izquierda

Se for unplanned events

¿Te pusiste un suéter anoche?

No, mamá.
Se me olvidó.

▶ **Se** also describes accidental or unplanned events. In this construction, the person who performs the action is de-emphasized, implying that the accident or unplanned event is not his or her direct responsibility. Note this construction.

se + [INDIRECT OBJECT PRONOUN] + [VERB] + [SUBJECT]

Se   me   cayó   la pluma.

▶ In this type of construction, what would normally be the direct object of the sentence becomes the subject, and it agrees with the verb, not with the indirect object pronoun.

I.O. PRONOUN	VERB		SUBJECT
Se	me, te, le, nos, os, les	quedó cayó dañó **SINGULAR**	la receta. la taza. el radio.
		rompieron olvidaron perdieron **PLURAL**	las botellas. las pastillas. las llaves.

▶ These verbs are the ones most frequently used with **se** to describe unplanned events.

Verbs commonly used with se

caer	*to fall; to drop*	**perder (e:ie)**	*to lose*
dañar	*to damage; to break down*	**quedar**	*to be left behind*
olvidar	*to forget*	**romper**	*to break*

Se me perdió el teléfono de la farmacia.
I lost the pharmacy's phone number.

Se nos olvidaron los pasajes.
We forgot the tickets.

▶ **¡Atención!** While Spanish has a verb for *to fall* (**caer**), there is no direct translation for *to drop.* **Dejar caer** (*To let fall*) or a **se** construction is often used to mean *to drop.*

El médico **dejó caer** la aspirina.
The doctor dropped the aspirin.

A mí **se me cayeron** los cuadernos.
I dropped the notebooks.

CONSULTA

For an explanation of prepositional pronouns, refer to **Estructura 9.4,** p. 318.

▶ To clarify or emphasize who the person involved in the action is, this construction commonly begins with the preposition **a** + [*noun*] or **a** + [*prepositional pronoun*].

Al paciente se le perdió la receta.
The patient lost his prescription.

A ustedes se les quedaron los libros en casa.
You left the books at home.

¡INTÉNTALO!   Completa las oraciones con **se** impersonal y los verbos en presente.

A

1. <u>Se enseñan</u> (enseñar) cinco lenguas en esta universidad.
2. _____ (comer) muy bien en Las Delicias.
3. _____ (vender) muchas camisetas allí.
4. _____ (servir) platos exquisitos cada noche.

Completa las oraciones con **se** y los verbos en pretérito.

B

1. <u>Se me rompieron</u> (*I broke*) las gafas.
2. _____ (*You* (fam., sing.) *dropped*) las pastillas.
3. _____ (*They lost*) la receta.
4. _____ (*You* (form., sing.) *left*) aquí la radiografía.

Práctica

1 **¿Cierto o falso?** Lee estas oraciones sobre la vida en 1901. Indica si lo que dice cada oración es **cierto** o **falso**. Luego corrige las oraciones falsas.

1. Se veía mucha televisión.
2. Se escribían muchos libros.
3. Se viajaba mucho en tren.
4. Se montaba a caballo.
5. Se mandaba correo electrónico.
6. Se preparaban comidas en casa.
7. Se llevaban minifaldas.
8. Se pasaba mucho tiempo con la familia.

2 **Traducir** Traduce estos letreros (*signs*) y anuncios al español.

1. Nurses needed
2. Eating and drinking prohibited
3. Programmers sought
4. English is spoken
5. Computers sold
6. No talking
7. Teacher needed
8. Books sold
9. Do not enter
10. Spanish is spoken

3 **¿Qué pasó?** Mira los dibujos e indica lo que pasó en cada uno.

1. camarero / pastel

2. Sr. Álvarez / espejo

3. Arturo / tarea

4. Sra. Domínguez / llaves

5. Carla y Lupe / botellas de vino

6. Juana / platos

Comunicación

4

Se necesitan voluntarios Lee la carta de Mauricio que apareció en el periódico de la universidad. Luego, indica si las conclusiones son **lógicas** o **ilógicas**, según lo que leíste.

> La semana pasada leí un artículo en el periódico de la universidad: se necesitaban voluntarios para llevar medicamentos a una zona muy pobre de la ciudad. El evento era un sábado y yo no tengo clases ese día, así que me inscribí (*so I signed up*). La mañana del sábado tenía mucha prisa. Salí corriendo y me di con la puerta en la cara: se me rompieron las gafas. No podía conducir porque no veía bien y tuve que tomar el autobús. Llegué tarde al lugar del evento. El encargado (*person in charge*) me dijo: "¿Se le perdió el reloj? La cita era a las nueve de la mañana. Son las diez… Bueno, se nos quedaron medicamentos en el camión (*truck*). ¿Puede ayudar?" Yo contesté que sí. Trabajé cinco horas, y al final del día estaba muy cansado. No pensé que ése iba a ser mi trabajo cuando leí el artículo, pero ayudamos a muchas personas que no tienen dinero para pagar por medicamentos.
> Mauricio Romero

	Lógico	Ilógico
1. Mauricio es dentista.	○	○
2. Mauricio se rompió la nariz cuando se dio con la puerta.	○	○
3. En el evento del sábado se regalaron medicamentos.	○	○
4. Mauricio no necesita gafas para conducir.	○	○
5. El encargado del evento se enojó con Mauricio cuando llegó tarde.	○	○

5

¿Distraído/a yo? Contesta las preguntas de tu compañero/a.

¿Alguna vez…
1. se te olvidó invitar a alguien a una fiesta o comida? ¿A quién?
2. se te quedó algo importante en la casa? ¿Qué?
3. se te perdió algo importante durante un viaje? ¿Qué?
4. se te rompió algo muy caro? ¿Qué?

¿Sabes…
5. si en el supermercado se aceptan cheques?
6. dónde se arreglan zapatos y botas?

6

Opiniones En parejas, terminen cada oración con ideas originales.

1. No se tiene que dejar propina cuando…
2. Antes de viajar, se debe…
3. Si se come bien, …
4. Para tener una vida sana, se debe…
5. Se sirve la mejor comida en…
6. Se hablan muchas lenguas en…

Síntesis

7

Anuncio Prepara el guión (*script*) para un anuncio de televisión de un producto. En el guión usa el imperfecto y por lo menos (*at least*) dos construcciones con **se**.

> **modelo**
>
> Se me cayeron unos libros en el pie y me dolía mucho. Pero ahora no, gracias a SuperAspirina 500. ¡Dos pastillas y se me fue el dolor! Se puede comprar SuperAspirina 500 en todas las farmacias Recetamax.

10.4 Adverbs

ANTE TODO   Adverbs are words that describe how, when, and where actions take place. They can modify verbs, adjectives, and even other adverbs. In previous lessons, you have already learned many Spanish adverbs, such as the ones below.

aquí	hoy	nunca
ayer	mal	siempre
bien	muy	temprano

▶ The most common adverbs end in **-mente**, equivalent to the English ending *-ly*.

verdaderamente *truly, really*   **generalmente** *generally*   **simplemente** *simply*

▶ To form these adverbs, add **-mente** to the feminine form of the adjective. If the adjective does not have a special feminine form, just add **-mente** to the standard form. **¡Atención!** Adjectives do not lose their accents when adding **-mente**.

ADJECTIVE	FEMININE FORM	SUFFIX	ADVERB
seguro	segura	-mente	seguramente
fabuloso	fabulosa	-mente	fabulosamente
enorme		-mente	enormemente
fácil		-mente	fácilmente

▶ Adverbs that end in **-mente** generally follow the verb, while adverbs that modify an adjective or another adverb precede the word they modify.

Maira dibuja **maravillosamente**.   Sergio está **casi siempre** ocupado.
Maira draws wonderfully.   *Sergio is almost always busy.*

Common adverbs and adverbial expressions

a menudo	*often*	**así**	*like this; so*	**menos**	*less*
a tiempo	*on time*	**bastante**	*enough; rather*	**muchas veces**	*a lot; many times*
a veces	*sometimes*	**casi**	*almost*		
además (de)	*furthermore; besides*	**con frecuencia**	*frequently*	**poco**	*little*
				por lo menos	*at least*
apenas	*hardly; scarcely*	**de vez en cuando**	*from time to time*		
				pronto	*soon*
		despacio	*slowly*	**rápido**	*quickly*

¡ATENCIÓN!

When a sentence contains two or more adverbs in sequence, the suffix **-mente** is dropped from all but the last adverb.
Ex: **El médico nos habló simple y abiertamente.** *The doctor spoke to us simply and openly.*

¡ATENCIÓN!

Rápido functions as an adjective (**Ella tiene una computadora rápida.**) as well as an adverb (**Ellas corren rápido.**). Note that as an adverb, **rápido** does not need to agree with any other word in the sentence. You can also use the adverb **rápidamente** (**Ella corre rápidamente.**).

¡INTÉNTALO!   Transforma los adjetivos en adverbios.

1. alegre _alegremente_
2. constante _____
3. gradual _____
4. perfecto _____

5. real _____
6. frecuente _____
7. tranquilo _____
8. regular _____

9. maravilloso _____
10. normal _____
11. básico _____
12. afortunado _____

Práctica

1

Escoger Completa la historia con los adverbios adecuados.

1. La cita era a las dos, pero llegamos _____. (menos, nunca, tarde)
2. El problema fue que _____ se nos dañó el despertador. (aquí, ayer, despacio)
3. La recepcionista no se enojó porque sabe que normalmente llego _____. (a veces, a tiempo, poco)
4. _____ el doctor estaba listo. (Por lo menos, Muchas veces, Casi)
5. _____ tuvimos que esperar cinco minutos. (Así, Además, Apenas)
6. El doctor dijo que nuestra hija Irene necesitaba cambiar su rutina diaria _____. (temprano, menos, inmediatamente)
7. El doctor nos explicó _____ las recomendaciones del Cirujano General (*Surgeon General*) sobre la salud de los jóvenes. (de vez en cuando, bien, apenas)
8. _____ nos dijo que Irene estaba bien, pero tenía que hacer más ejercicio y comer mejor. (Bastante, Afortunadamente, A menudo)

NOTA CULTURAL

La doctora Antonia Novello, de Puerto Rico, fue la primera mujer y la primera hispana en tomar el cargo de **Cirujana General** de los Estados Unidos (1990–1993).

Comunicación

2

Medicina natural Escucha el programa de radio *Medicina Natural* de esta semana en el que hablan sobre los remedios caseros (*home remedies*). Luego, indica si las conclusiones son **lógicas** o **ilógicas**, según lo que escuchaste.

	Lógico	Ilógico
1. La doctora Martínez es una invitada del programa *Medicina Natural*.	○	○
2. Guillermo es un niño.	○	○
3. Se toma el remedio de la abuela cuando se siente mareado.	○	○
4. El remedio de la abuela de Guillermo es delicioso.	○	○
5. Guillermo toma este remedio de vez en cuando.	○	○

3

¿Con qué frecuencia? En parejas, túrnense para hacerse preguntas sobre la frecuencia con la que hacen varias actividades. Pueden usar las sugerencias de la lista u otras ideas.

modelo

ir al doctor
Estudiante 1: *¿Con qué frecuencia vas al doctor?*
Estudiante 2: *Voy al doctor por lo menos una vez al año para hacerme un examen médico.*

estar enfermo/a	jugar a las cartas	tener dolor de cabeza
hacer un viaje	leer el correo electrónico	ver una película en el cine
ir al dentista	practicar deportes	

Recapitulación

Completa estas actividades para repasar los conceptos de gramática que aprendiste en esta lección.

1 Completar Completa el cuadro con la forma correcta del imperfecto. **24 pts.**

yo/Ud./él/ella	tú	nosotros	Uds./ellos/ellas
era			
	cantabas		
		veníamos	
			querían

2 Adverbios Escoge el adverbio correcto de la lista para completar estas oraciones. Lee con cuidado las oraciones; los adverbios sólo se usan una vez. No vas a usar uno de los adverbios. **24 pts.**

a menudo	apenas	fácilmente
a tiempo	casi	maravillosamente
además	despacio	por lo menos

1. Pablito se cae _____; un promedio (*average*) de cuatro veces por semana.
2. No me duele nada y no sufro de ninguna enfermedad; me siento _____ bien.
3. —Doctor, ¿cómo supo que tuve una operación de garganta? —Muy _____, lo leí en su historial médico (*medical history*).
4. ¿Le duele mucho la espalda (*back*)? Entonces tiene que levantarse _____.
5. Ya te sientes mucho mejor, ¿verdad? Mañana puedes volver al trabajo; tu temperatura es _____ normal.
6. Es importante hacer ejercicio con regularidad, _____ tres veces a la semana.
7. El examen médico no comenzó ni tarde ni temprano. Comenzó _____, a las tres de la tarde.
8. Parece que ya te estás curando del resfriado. _____ estás congestionada.

RESUMEN GRAMATICAL

10.1 The imperfect tense *pp. 342–343*

The imperfect of regular verbs

cantar	beber	escribir
cantaba	bebía	escribía
cantabas	bebías	escribías
cantaba	bebía	escribía
cantábamos	bebíamos	escribíamos
cantabais	bebíais	escribíais
cantaban	bebían	escribían

► There are no stem changes in the imperfect: entender (e:ie) → entendía; servir (e:i) → servía; doler (o:ue) → dolía
► The imperfect of **hay** is **había**.
► Only three verbs are irregular in the imperfect.
ir: iba, ibas, iba, íbamos, ibais, iban
ser: era, eras, era, éramos, erais, eran
ver: veía, veías, veía, veíamos, veíais, veían

10.2 The preterite and the imperfect *pp. 346–347*

Preterite	Imperfect
1. Completed actions Fueron a Buenos Aires ayer.	1. Ongoing past action Usted miraba el fútbol.
2. Beginning or end of past action La película empezó a las nueve.	2. Habitual past actions Todos los domingos yo visitaba a mi abuela.
3. Series of past actions or events Me caí y me lastimé el pie.	3. Description of states or characteristics Ella era alta. Quería descansar.

10.3 Constructions with se *pp. 350–351*

Impersonal constructions with **se**

Se	prohíbe fumar.
	habla español.
	hablan varios idiomas.

3 **Un accidente** Escoge el imperfecto o el pretérito según el contexto para completar esta conversación. **30 pts.**

NURIA Hola, Felipe. ¿Estás bien? ¿Qué es eso? ¿(1) (Te lastimaste/Te lastimabas) el pie?

FELIPE Ayer (2) (tuve/tenía) un pequeño accidente.

NURIA Cuéntame. ¿Cómo (3) (pasó/pasaba)?

FELIPE Bueno, (4) (fueron/eran) las cinco de la tarde y (5) (llovió/llovía) mucho cuando (6) (salí/salía) de la casa en mi bicicleta. No (7) (vi/veía) a una chica que (8) (caminó/caminaba) en mi dirección, y los dos (9) (nos caímos/nos caíamos) al suelo (*ground*).

NURIA Y la chica, ¿está bien ella?

FELIPE Sí. Cuando llegamos al hospital, ella sólo (10) (tuvo/tenía) dolor de cabeza.

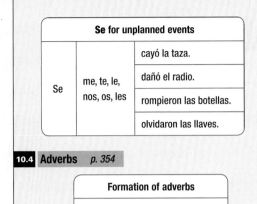

Se for unplanned events		
Se	me, te, le, nos, os, les	cayó la taza.
		dañó el radio.
		rompieron las botellas.
		olvidaron las llaves.

10.4 **Adverbs** *p. 354*

Formation of adverbs
fácil → fácilmente
seguro → seguramente
verdadero → verdaderamente

4 **Oraciones** Escribe oraciones con **se** a partir de los elementos dados (*given*). Usa el tiempo especificado entre paréntesis y añade pronombres cuando sea necesario. **18 pts.**

> **modelo**
> Carlos / quedar / la tarea en casa (pretérito)
> A Carlos se le quedó la tarea en casa.

1. en la farmacia / vender / medicamentos (presente)
2. ¿(tú) / olvidar / las llaves / otra vez? (pretérito)
3. (yo) / dañar / la computadora (pretérito)
4. en esta clase / prohibir / hablar inglés (presente)
5. ellos / romper / las gafas / en el accidente (pretérito)
6. (nosotros) / perder / el dinero (pretérito)

5 **Refrán** Completa el refrán con las palabras que faltan. **4 pts.**

 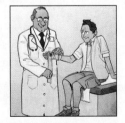 

❝Lo que _____ (*well*) se aprende,
nunca _____ pierde.❞

Lectura

Antes de leer

Estrategia

Activating background knowledge

Using what you already know about a particular subject will often help you better understand a reading selection. For example, if you read an article about a recent medical discovery, you might think about what you already know about health in order to understand unfamiliar words or concepts.

Examinar el texto

Utiliza las estrategias de lectura que tú consideras más efectivas para hacer algunas observaciones preliminares acerca del texto. Luego contesta estas preguntas:

- Analiza el formato del texto: ¿Qué tipo de texto es? ¿Dónde crees que se publicó este artículo?
- ¿Quiénes son Carla Baron y Tomás Monterrey?
- Mira la foto del libro. ¿Qué sugiere el título del libro sobre su contenido?

Conocimiento previo

Ahora piensa en tu conocimiento previo° sobre el cuidado de la salud en los viajes. Considera estas preguntas:

- ¿Viajaste alguna vez a otro estado o a otro país?
- ¿Tuviste problemas durante tus viajes con el agua, la comida o el clima del lugar?
- ¿Olvidaste poner en tu maleta algún medicamento que después necesitaste?
- Imagina que un(a) amigo/a se va de viaje. Indica por lo menos cinco cosas que debe hacer para prevenir cualquier problema de salud.

conocimiento previo *background knowledge*

Libro de la semana

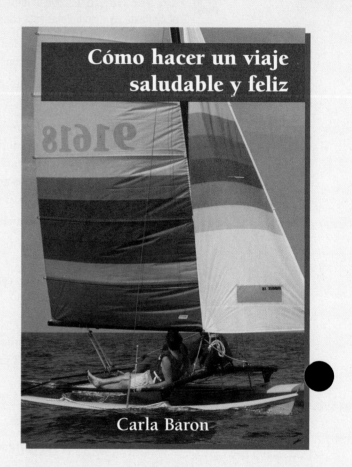

Cómo hacer un viaje saludable y feliz

Carla Baron

Después de leer

Correspondencias

Busca las correspondencias entre los problemas y las recomendaciones.

Problemas

1. el agua _____
2. el sol _____
3. la comida _____
4. la identificación _____
5. el clima _____

Recomendaciones

a. Hay que adaptarse a los ingredientes desconocidos (*unknown*).
b. Toma sólo productos purificados (*purified*).
c. Es importante llevar ropa adecuada cuando viajas.
d. Lleva loción o crema con alta protección solar.
e. Lleva tu pasaporte.

Entrevista a Carla Baron
por Tomás Monterrey

Tomás: ¿Por qué escribió su libro *Cómo hacer un viaje saludable y feliz?*

Carla: Me encanta viajar, conocer otras culturas y escribir. Mi primer viaje lo hice cuando era estudiante universitaria. Todavía recuerdo el día en que llegamos a San Juan, Puerto Rico. Era el panorama ideal para unas vacaciones maravillosas, pero al llegar a la habitación del hotel, bebí mucha agua de la llave° y luego pedí un jugo de frutas con mucho hielo°. El clima en San Juan es tropical y yo tenía mucha sed y calor. Los síntomas llegaron en menos de media hora: pasé dos días con dolor de estómago y corriendo al cuarto de baño cada diez minutos. Desde entonces, siempre que viajo sólo bebo agua mineral y llevo un pequeño bolso con medicinas necesarias, como pastillas para el dolor y también bloqueador solar, una crema repelente de mosquitos y un desinfectante.

Tomás: ¿Son reales° las situaciones que se narran en su libro?

Carla: Sí, son reales y son mis propias° historias°. A menudo los autores crean caricaturas divertidas de un turista en dificultades. ¡En mi libro la turista en dificultades soy yo!

Tomás: ¿Qué recomendaciones puede encontrar el lector en su libro?

Carla: Bueno, mi libro es anecdótico y humorístico, pero el tema de la salud se trata° de manera seria. En general, se dan recomendaciones sobre ropa adecuada para cada sitio, consejos para protegerse del sol, y comidas y bebidas adecuadas para el turista que viaja al Caribe o Suramérica.

Tomás: ¿Tiene algún consejo para las personas que se enferman cuando viajan?

Carla: Muchas veces los turistas toman el avión sin saber nada acerca del país que van a visitar. Ponen toda su ropa en la maleta, toman el pasaporte, la cámara fotográfica y ¡a volar°! Es necesario tomar precauciones porque nuestro cuerpo necesita adaptarse al clima, al sol, a la humedad, al agua y a la comida. Se trata de° viajar, admirar las maravillas del mundo y regresar a casa con hermosos recuerdos. En resumen, el secreto es "prevenir en vez de° curar".

llave *faucet* hielo *ice* reales *true* propias *own* historias *stories*
se trata *is treated* ¡a volar! *Off they go!* Se trata de *It's a question of*
en vez de *instead of*

Seleccionar

Selecciona la respuesta correcta.

1. El tema principal de este libro es _____.
   a. Puerto Rico b. la salud y el agua c. otras culturas
   d. el cuidado de la salud en los viajes
2. Las situaciones narradas en el libro son _____.
   a. autobiográficas b. inventadas c. ficticias
   d. imaginarias
3. ¿Qué recomendaciones no vas a encontrar en este libro? _____
   a. cómo vestirse adecuadamente
   b. cómo prevenir las quemaduras solares
   c. consejos sobre la comida y la bebida
   d. cómo dar propina en los países del Caribe o de Suramérica
4. En opinión de la señorita Baron, _____.
   a. es bueno tomar agua de la llave y beber jugo de frutas con mucho hielo
   b. es mejor tomar solamente agua embotellada (*bottled*)
   c. los minerales son buenos para el dolor abdominal
   d. es importante visitar el cuarto de baño cada diez minutos
5. ¿Cuál de estos productos no lleva la autora cuando viaja a otros países? _____
   a. desinfectante
   b. crema repelente
   c. detergente
   d. pastillas medicinales

Escritura

Estrategia

Mastering the simple past tenses

In Spanish, when you write about events that occurred in the past you will need to know when to use the preterite and when to use the imperfect tense. A good understanding of the uses of each tense will make it much easier to determine which one to use as you write.

Look at the summary of the uses of the preterite and the imperfect and write your own example sentence for each of the rules described.

Preterite vs. imperfect

Preterite

1. Completed actions

   _____

   _____

2. Beginning or end of past actions

   _____

   _____

3. Series of past actions

   _____

   _____

Imperfect

1. Ongoing past actions

   _____

   _____

2. Habitual past actions

   _____

   _____

3. Mental, physical, and emotional states and characteristics in the past

   _____

   _____

Use your example sentences and the chart as a guide to help you decide which tense to use as you are writing a story or other type of narration about the past.

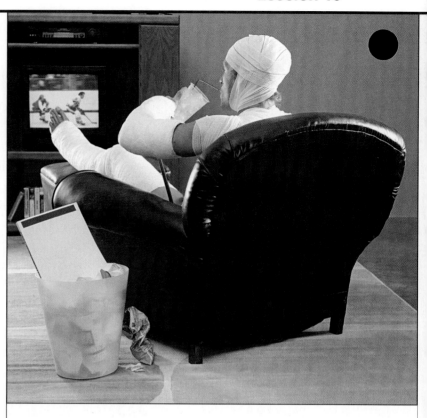

Tema

Escribir una historia

Escribe una historia acerca de una experiencia tuya° (o de otra persona) con una enfermedad, accidente o problema médico. Tu historia puede ser real o imaginaria y puede tratarse de un incidente divertido, humorístico o desastroso. Incluye todos los detalles relevantes. Consulta la lista de sugerencias° con detalles que puedes incluir.

▶ Descripción del/de la paciente
   nombre y apellidos
   edad
   características físicas
   historial médico°

▶ Descripción de los síntomas
   enfermedades
   accidente
   problemas médicos

▶ Descripción del tratamiento°
   tratamientos
   recetas
   operaciones

tuya *of yours* **sugerencias** *suggestions* **historial médico** *medical history*
tratamiento *treatment*

Escuchar

Estrategia

Listening for specific information

You can listen for specific information effectively once you identify the subject of a conversation and use your background knowledge to predict what kinds of information you might hear.

 To practice this strategy, you will listen to a paragraph from a letter Marta wrote to a friend about her fifteenth birthday celebration. Before you listen to the paragraph, use what you know about this type of party to predict the content of the letter. What kinds of details might Marta include in her description of the celebration? Now listen to the paragraph and jot down the specific information Marta relates. Then compare these details to the predictions you made about the letter.

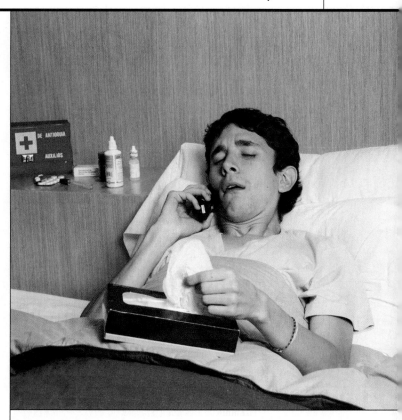

Preparación

Mira la foto. ¿Con quién crees que está conversando Carlos Peña? ¿De qué están hablando?

Ahora escucha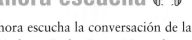

Ahora escucha la conversación de la señorita Méndez y Carlos Peña. Marca las oraciones donde se mencionan los síntomas de Carlos.

1. ____ Tiene infección en los ojos.
2. ____ Se lastimó el dedo.
3. ____ No puede dormir.
4. ____ Siente dolor en los huesos.
5. ____ Está mareado.
6. ____ Está congestionado.
7. ____ Le duele el estómago.
8. ____ Le duele la cabeza.
9. ____ Es alérgico a la aspirina.
10. ____ Tiene tos.
11. ____ Le duele la garganta.
12. ____ Se rompió la pierna.
13. ____ Tiene dolor de oído.
14. ____ Tiene frío.

Comprensión

Preguntas

1. ¿Tiene fiebre Carlos?

2. ¿Cuánto tiempo hace que le duele la garganta a Carlos?

3. ¿Qué tiene que hacer el médico antes de recetarle algo a Carlos?

4. ¿A qué hora es su cita con el médico?

5. Después de darle una cita con el médico, ¿qué otra información le pide a Carlos la señorita del consultorio?

6. En tu opinión, ¿qué tiene Carlos? ¿Gripe? ¿Un resfriado? ¿Alergias? Explica tu opinión.

Diálogo

Escribe el diálogo entre el Dr. Aguilar y Carlos Peña en el consultorio del médico. Usa la información del diálogo telefónico para pensar en lo que dice el médico mientras examina a Carlos. Imagina cómo responde Carlos y qué preguntas le hace al médico. ¿Cuál es el diagnóstico del médico?

En pantalla

El objetivo de esta original y divertida campaña es informar y sensibilizar° a la sociedad sobre la enfermedad del Parkinson y el sufrimiento que ocasiona° a los que la padecen°. Además de darse a conocer° y enfrentarse a° la indiferencia, con esta campaña también se pretende° recaudar fondos°, ya que la Asociación Parkinson Alicante se ha visto afectada por la crisis económica española, disminuyendo así el número de ayudas recibidas.

Vocabulario útil	
aullar	to howl
hombre lobo	werewolf
lucha	fight, battle
manada	pack (of wolves)
subvenciones	subsidies
tiembla	trembles, shakes

Preparación

¿Conoces alguna ONG (organización no gubernamental)? ¿Cuál? ¿Qué cosas se hacen en esa organización para ayudar a los demás? Utiliza construcciones con **se**.

Escoger

Elige la opción correcta.

1. Las _____ a la asociación estaban fallando.
   a. subvenciones   b. peticiones
2. La asociación decidió inventar una _____ para el Parkinson.
   a. pastilla   b. causa
3. Michael J. Fox hizo el papel de un _____ y tiene Parkinson.
   a. hombre lobo   b. hombre araña
4. La forma para llegar a todo el mundo es _____ lo más fuerte (*loud*) posible.
   a. cantar   b. aullar

Una campaña

Crea una campaña para transformar una organización, real o ficticia. Utiliza el imperfecto y construcciones con **se**.

Asociación Parkinson Alicante

Hemos decidido inventarnos una causa para el Parkinson.

Tal vez la gente pueda creerse que ser hombre lobo provoque Parkinson.

Queremos que la gente conozca la asociación y nos ayude en esta lucha.

sensibilizar *to raise awareness* ocasiona *causes* la padecen *suffer from it* darse a conocer *spreading the word* enfrentarse a *to fight against* se pretende *the hope is to* recaudar fondos *to raise money*

Argentina tiene una gran tradición médica influenciada desde el siglo XIX por la medicina francesa. Tres de los cinco premios Nobel de esta nación están relacionados con investigaciones médicas que han hecho° grandes aportes° al avance de las ciencias de la salud. Además, existen otros adelantos° de médicos argentinos que han hecho historia. Entre ellos se cuentan el *bypass* coronario, desarrollado° por el cirujano° René Favaloro en 1967, y la técnica de cirugía cardiovascular sin circulación extracorpórea° desarrollada en 1978 por Federico Benetti, quien es considerado uno de los padres de la cirugía cardíaca moderna.

Vocabulario útil

la cita previa	*previous appointment*
la guardia	*emergency room*
Me di un golpe.	*I got hit.*
la práctica	*rotation (hands-on medical experience)*

Preparación

¿Qué haces si tienes un pequeño accidente o quieres hacer una consulta? ¿Visitas a tu médico general o vas al hospital? ¿Debes pedir un turno (*appointment*)?

¿Cierto o falso?

Indica si las oraciones son **ciertas** o **falsas**.

1. Silvina tuvo un accidente en su automóvil.
2. Silvina fue a la guardia del hospital.
3. La guardia del hospital está abierta sólo durante el día y es necesario tener cita previa.
4. Los entrevistados (*interviewees*) tienen enfermedades graves.
5. En Argentina, los médicos reciben la certificación cuando terminan la práctica.

La salud

¿Le podría° pedir que me explique qué es la guardia?

Nuestro hospital público es gratuito para todas las personas.

... la carrera de medicina comienza con el primer año de la universidad.

han hecho *have done* aportes *contributions* adelantos *advances* desarrollado *developed* cirujano *surgeon* extracorpórea *out-of-body* podría *could*

Costa Rica

El país en cifras

▶ **Área:** 51.100 km² (19.730 millas²), *aproximadamente el área de Virginia Occidental°*

▶ **Población:** 4.755.000

Costa Rica es el país de Centroamérica con la población más homogénea. El 94% de sus habitantes es blanco y mestizo°. Más del 50% de la población es de ascendencia° española y un alto porcentaje tiene sus orígenes en otros países europeos.

▶ **Capital:** San José —1.515.000

▶ **Ciudades principales:** Alajuela, Cartago, Puntarenas, Heredia

▶ **Moneda:** colón costarricense

▶ **Idioma:** español (oficial)

Bandera de Costa Rica

Costarricenses célebres

▶ **Carmen Lyra,** escritora (1888–1949)

▶ **Chavela Vargas,** cantante (1919–2012)

▶ **Óscar Arias Sánchez,** ex presidente de Costa Rica (1941–)

▶ **Laura Chinchilla Miranda,** ex presidenta de Costa Rica (1959–)

▶ **Claudia Poll,** nadadora° olímpica (1972–)

Óscar Arias recibió el Premio Nobel de la Paz en 1987.

Virginia Occidental *West Virginia* mestizo *of indigenous and white parentage* ascendencia *descent* nadadora *swimmer* ejército *army* gastos *expenditures* invertir *to invest* cuartel *barracks*

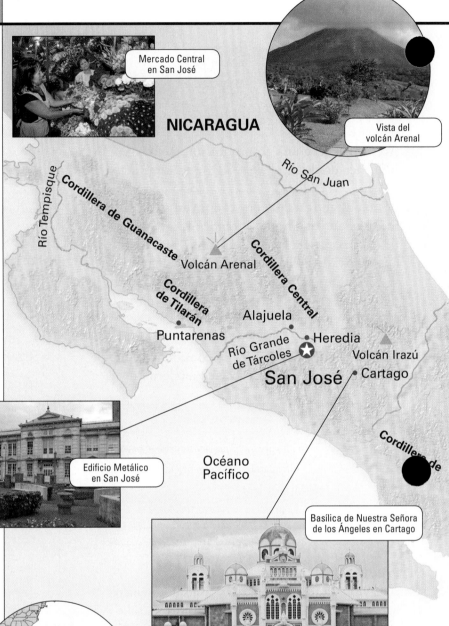

Mercado Central en San José

NICARAGUA

Vista del volcán Arenal

Río San Juan

Río Tempisque

Cordillera de Guanacaste

Cordillera Central

Volcán Arenal

Cordillera de Tilarán

Alajuela

Puntarenas

Río Grande de Tárcoles

Heredia

Volcán Irazú

San José

Cartago

Cordillera de

Océano Pacífico

Edificio Metálico en San José

Basílica de Nuestra Señora de los Ángeles en Cartago

ESTADOS UNIDOS

OCÉANO ATLÁNTICO

COSTA RICA

OCÉANO PACÍFICO

AMÉRICA DEL SUR

¡Increíble pero cierto!

Costa Rica no tiene ejército°. Sin gastos° militares, el gobierno puede invertir° más dinero en la educación y las artes. En la foto aparece el Museo Nacional de Costa Rica, antiguo cuartel° del ejército.

MUSEO NACIONAL DE C

Lugares • Los parques nacionales

El sistema de parques nacionales de Costa Rica ocupa aproximadamente el 12% de su territorio y fue establecido° para la protección de su biodiversidad. En los parques, los ecoturistas pueden admirar montañas, cataratas° y una gran variedad de plantas exóticas. Algunos ofrecen también la oportunidad de ver quetzales°, monos°, jaguares, armadillos y mariposas° en su hábitat natural.

Economía • Las plantaciones de café

Costa Rica fue el primer país centroamericano en desarrollar° la industria del café. En el siglo° XIX, los costarricenses empezaron a exportar esta semilla a Inglaterra°, lo que significó una contribución importante a la economía de la nación. Actualmente, más de 50.000 costarricenses trabajan en el cultivo del café. Este producto representa cerca del 15% de sus exportaciones anuales.

Mar Caribe

• Limón

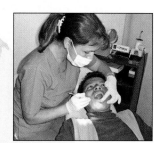

Sociedad • Una nación progresista

Costa Rica es un país progresista. Tiene un nivel de alfabetización° del 96%, uno de los más altos de Latinoamérica. En 1871, esta nación centroamericana abolió la pena de muerte° y en 1948 eliminó el ejército e hizo obligatoria y gratuita° la educación para todos sus ciudadanos.

Talamanca

PANAMÁ

Parque Morazán en San José

¿Qué aprendiste? Contesta las preguntas con oraciones completas.

1. ¿Cómo se llama la capital de Costa Rica?

2. ¿Quién es Claudia Poll?

3. ¿Qué porcentaje del territorio de Costa Rica ocupan los parques nacionales?

4. ¿Para qué se establecieron los parques nacionales?

5. ¿Qué pueden ver los turistas en los parques nacionales?

6. ¿Cuántos costarricenses trabajan en las plantaciones de café hoy día?

7. ¿Cuándo eliminó Costa Rica la pena de muerte?

Conexión Internet Investiga estos temas en Internet.

1. Busca información sobre Óscar Arias Sánchez. ¿Quién es? ¿Por qué se le considera (*is he considered*) un costarricense célebre?

2. Busca información sobre los artistas de Costa Rica. ¿Qué artista, escritor o cantante te interesa más? ¿Por qué?

....

establecido *established* **cataratas** *waterfalls* **quetzales** *type of tropical bird* **monos** *monkeys* **mariposas** *butterflies* **en desarrollar** *to develop* **siglo** *century* **Inglaterra** *England* **nivel de alfabetización** *literacy rate* **pena de muerte** *death penalty* **gratuita** *free*

El cuerpo

la boca	mouth
el brazo	arm
la cabeza	head
el corazón	heart
el cuello	neck
el cuerpo	body
el dedo	finger
el dedo del pie	toe
el estómago	stomach
la garganta	throat
el hueso	bone
la nariz	nose
el oído	(sense of) hearing; inner ear
el ojo	eye
la oreja	(outer) ear
el pie	foot
la pierna	leg
la rodilla	knee
el tobillo	ankle

La salud

el accidente	accident
el antibiótico	antibiotic
la aspirina	aspirin
la clínica	clinic
el consultorio	doctor's office
el/la dentista	dentist
el/la doctor(a)	doctor
el dolor (de cabeza)	(head)ache; pain
el/la enfermero/a	nurse
el examen médico	physical exam
la farmacia	pharmacy
la gripe	flu
el hospital	hospital
la infección	infection
el medicamento	medication
la medicina	medicine
la operación	operation
el/la paciente	patient
la pastilla	pill
la radiografía	X-ray
la receta	prescription
el resfriado	cold (illness)
la sala de emergencia(s)	emergency room
la salud	health
el síntoma	symptom
la tos	cough

Verbos

caerse	to fall (down)
dañar	to damage; to break down
darse con	to bump into; to run into
doler (o:ue)	to hurt
enfermarse	to get sick
estar enfermo/a	to be sick
estornudar	to sneeze
lastimarse (el pie)	to injure (one's foot)
olvidar	to forget
poner una inyección	to give an injection
prohibir	to prohibit
recetar	to prescribe
romper	to break
romperse (la pierna)	to break (one's leg)
sacar(se) un diente	to have a tooth removed
ser alérgico/a (a)	to be allergic (to)
sufrir una enfermedad	to suffer an illness
tener dolor (m.)	to have pain
tener fiebre (f.)	to have a fever
tomar la temperatura	to take someone's temperature
torcerse (o:ue) (el tobillo)	to sprain (one's ankle)
toser	to cough

Adjetivos

congestionado/a	congested
embarazada	pregnant
grave	grave; serious
mareado/a	dizzy; nauseated
médico/a	medical
saludable	healthy
sano/a	healthy

Adverbios

a menudo	often
a tiempo	on time
a veces	sometimes
además (de)	furthermore; besides
apenas	hardly; scarcely
así	like this; so
bastante	enough; rather
casi	almost
con frecuencia	frequently
de niño/a	as a child
de vez en cuando	from time to time
despacio	slowly
menos	less
muchas veces	a lot; many times
poco	little
por lo menos	at least
pronto	soon
rápido	quickly
todos los días	every day

Conjunción

mientras	while

Expresiones útiles	See page 337.

La tecnología

11

Communicative Goals

You will learn how to:

- Talk about using technology and electronics
- Use common expressions on the telephone
- Talk about car trouble

A PRIMERA VISTA
- ¿Qué hacen las chicas?
- ¿Crees que usan sus teléfonos con frecuencia?
- ¿Son unas chicas saludables?
- ¿Qué partes del cuerpo se ven en la foto?

La tecnología

Más vocabulario

la cámara digital/de video	*digital/video camera*
el canal	*(TV) channel*
el cargador	*charger*
el correo de voz	*voice mail*
el estéreo	*stereo*
el reproductor de CD	*CD player*
la aplicación	*app*
el archivo	*file*
la arroba	*@ symbol*
el blog	*blog*
el buscador	*browser*
la conexión inalámbrica	*wireless connection*
la dirección electrónica	*e-mail address*
Internet	*Internet*
el mensaje de texto	*text message*
la página principal	*home page*
el programa de computación	*software*
la red	*network; Web*
el sitio web	*website*
apagar	*to turn off*
borrar	*to erase*
chatear	*to chat*
descargar	*to download*
escanear	*to scan*
funcionar	*to work*
grabar	*to record*
guardar	*to save*
imprimir	*to print*
llamar	*to call*
navegar (en Internet)	*to surf (the Internet)*
poner, prender	*to turn on*
sonar (o:ue)	*to ring*
descompuesto/a	*not working; out of order*
lento/a	*slow*
lleno/a	*full*

Variación léxica

computadora ←→ ordenador (*Esp.*), computador (*Col.*)

descargar ←→ bajar (*Arg., Col., Esp., Ven.*)

Práctica

el control remoto

el reproductor de MP3

el disco compacto

1 **Escuchar** 🎧 Escucha la conversación entre dos amigas. Después completa las oraciones.

1. María y Ana están en _____.
   a. una tienda   b. un cibercafé   c. un restaurante
2. A María le encantan _____.
   a. los celulares   b. las cámaras digitales   c. los cibercafés
3. Ana y María _____ las fotos.
   a. escanean   b. borran   c. imprimen
4. María quiere tomar un café y _____.
   a. poner la computadora   b. sacar fotos digitales
   c. navegar en Internet
5. Ana paga por el café y _____.
   a. el uso de Internet   b. la impresora   c. la cámara

2 **¿Cierto o falso?** 🎧 Escucha las oraciones e indica si lo que dice cada una es **cierto** o **falso**, según el dibujo.

1. _____   5. _____
2. _____   6. _____
3. _____   7. _____
4. _____   8. _____

3 **Oraciones** Escribe oraciones usando estos elementos. Usa el pretérito y añade las palabras necesarias.

1. yo / descargar / fotos / Internet

2. tú / apagar / televisor / diez / noche

3. Daniel y su esposa / comprar / computadora portátil / ayer

4. Sara y yo / ir / cibercafé / para / navegar en Internet

5. Jaime / decidir / comprar / reproductor de MP3

6. teléfono celular / sonar / pero / yo / no contestar

4 **Preguntas** Mira el dibujo y contesta las preguntas.

1. ¿Qué tipo de café es?
2. ¿Cuántas impresoras hay? ¿Cuántos ratones?
3. ¿Por qué vinieron estas personas al café?
4. ¿Qué hace el camarero?
5. ¿Qué hace la mujer en la computadora? ¿Y el hombre?
6. ¿Qué máquinas están cerca del televisor?
7. ¿Dónde hay un cibercafé en tu comunidad?
8. ¿Por qué puedes tú necesitar un cibercafé?

el capó, el cofre

Revisa el aceite. (revisar)

el carro, el coche

el parabrisas

Llena el tanque. (llenar)

el radio

la gasolina

el navegador GPS

el baúl

el volante

la llanta

En la gasolinera

Más vocabulario

la autopista	highway
la calle	street
la carretera	highway; (main) road
la circulación, el tráfico	traffic
el garaje, el taller (mecánico)	garage; (mechanic's) repair shop
la licencia de conducir	driver's license
el/la mecánico/a	mechanic
la policía	police (force)
la velocidad máxima	speed limit
arrancar	to start
arreglar	to fix; to arrange
bajar(se) de	to get off of/out of (a vehicle)
conducir, manejar	to drive
estacionar	to park
parar	to stop
subir(se) a	to get on/into (a vehicle)

5 **Completar** Completa estas oraciones con las palabras correctas.

1. Para poder conducir legalmente, necesitas…
2. Puedes poner las maletas en…
3. Si tu carro no funciona, debes llevarlo a…
4. Para llenar el tanque de tu coche, necesitas ir a…
5. Antes de un viaje largo, es importante revisar…
6. Otra palabra para autopista es…
7. Mientras hablas por teléfono celular, no es buena idea…
8. Otra palabra para coche es…

¡LENGUA VIVA!

Aunque **carro** es el término que se usa en la mayoría de países hispanos, no es el único. En España, por ejemplo, se dice **coche**, y en Argentina, Chile y Uruguay se dice **auto**.

6 **Conversación** Completa la conversación con las palabras de la lista.

el aceite	la gasolina	llenar	el parabrisas	el taller
el baúl	las llantas	manejar	revisar	el volante

EMPLEADO Bienvenido al (1) _____ mecánico Óscar. ¿En qué le puedo servir?

JUAN Buenos días. Quiero (2) _____ el tanque y revisar (3) _____, por favor.

EMPLEADO Con mucho gusto. Si quiere, también le limpio (4) _____.

JUAN Sí, gracias. Está un poquito sucio. La próxima semana tengo que (5) _____ hasta Buenos Aires. ¿Puede cambiar (6) _____? Están gastadas (*worn*).

EMPLEADO Claro que sí, pero voy a tardar (*it will take me*) un par de horas.

JUAN Mejor regreso mañana. Ahora no tengo tiempo. ¿Cuánto le debo por (7) _____?

EMPLEADO Sesenta pesos. Y veinticinco por (8) _____ y cambiar el aceite.

CONSULTA

For more information about **Buenos Aires**, see **Panorama**, p. 400.

Comunicación

7

Postal Lee la tarjeta postal que encontraste. Luego, indica si las conclusiones son **lógicas** o **ilógicas**, según lo que leíste.

19 julio de 1979

Hola, Paco:

¡Saludos! Estamos de viaje por unas semanas. La Costa del Sol es muy bonita. No hemos encontrado (we haven't found) a tus amigos porque nunca están en casa cuando llamamos. El teléfono suena y suena y nadie contesta. Vamos a seguir llamando.

Sacamos muchas fotos muy divertidas. Cuando regresemos y las revelemos (get them developed), te las voy a enseñar. Las playas son preciosas. Hasta ahora el único problema fue que la oficina en la cual reservamos un carro perdió nuestros papeles y tuvimos que esperar mucho tiempo.

También tuvimos un pequeño problema con el hotel. La agencia de viajes nos reservó una habitación en un hotel que está muy lejos de todo. No podemos cambiarla, pero no me importa mucho. A pesar de eso, estamos contentos.

Tu hermana, Gabriela

EUROPA 12ᵖᵗˢ
ESPAÑA

Francisco Jiménez
San Lorenzo 3250
Rosario, Argentina 2000

	Lógico	Ilógico
1. Paco y Francisco son la misma persona.	○	○
2. Los amigos de Paco tenían correo de voz.	○	○
3. Gabriela y Francisco viajaron juntos a la Costa del Sol.	○	○
4. Gabriela tenía una cámara digital.	○	○
5. Gabriela se divirtió en su viaje.	○	○

8

Preguntas Contesta las preguntas de tu compañero/a.

1. a. ¿Tienes un teléfono celular? ¿Para qué lo usas?

   b. ¿Qué utilizas más para comunicarte: el teléfono o el correo electrónico? ¿Por qué?

2. a. ¿Con qué frecuencia usas la computadora?

   b. ¿Para qué usas Internet?

   c. ¿Qué sitios web visitas a menudo?

3. a. ¿Miras la televisión con frecuencia? ¿Qué programas ves?

   b. ¿Dónde miras tus programas favoritos, en la tele o en la computadora?

   c. ¿Qué prefieres usar para escuchar música: la radio, tu teléfono o tu computadora?

9

Ayer y hoy ¿Cómo era la tecnología en los años setenta y ochenta? ¿Cómo es la tecnología hoy? Haz una comparación entre ellas.

En el taller

El coche de Miguel está descompuesto y Maru tiene problemas con su computadora.

 MIGUEL

 JORGE

1

MIGUEL ¿Cómo lo ves?

JORGE Creo que puedo arreglarlo. ¿Me pasas la llave?

2

JORGE ¿Y dónde está Maru?

MIGUEL Acaba de enviarme un mensaje de texto: "Última noticia sobre la computadora portátil: todavía está descompuesta. Moni intenta arreglarla. Voy para allá".

JORGE ¿Está descompuesta tu computadora?

MIGUEL No, la mía no, la suya. Una amiga la está ayudando.

JORGE Un mal día para la tecnología, ¿no?

MIGUEL Ella está preparando un proyecto para ver si puede hacer sus prácticas profesionales en el Museo de Antropología.

JORGE ¿Y todo está en la computadora?

MIGUEL Y claro.

3

4

MARU Buenos días, Jorge.

JORGE ¡Qué gusto verte, Maru! ¿Cómo está la computadora?

MARU Mi amiga Mónica recuperó muchos archivos, pero muchos otros se borraron.

5

6

MARU Estamos en una triste situación. Yo necesito una computadora nueva, y Miguel necesita otro coche.

JORGE Y un televisor nuevo para mí, por favor.

MARU

MARU ¿Qué vamos a hacer, Miguel?

MIGUEL Tranquila, cariño. Por eso tenemos amigos como Jorge y Mónica. Nos ayudamos los unos a los otros.

JORGE ¿No te sientes afortunada, Maru? No te preocupes. Sube.

MIGUEL ¡Por fin!

MARU Gracias, Jorge. Eres el mejor mecánico de la ciudad.

MIGUEL ¿Cuánto te debo por el trabajo?

JORGE Hombre, no es nada. Guárdalo para el coche nuevo. Eso sí, recomiéndame con tus amigos.

MIGUEL Gracias, Jorge.

JORGE No manejes en carretera. Revisa el aceite cada 1.500 kilómetros y asegúrate de llenarle el tanque... No manejes con el cofre abierto. Nos vemos.

Expresiones útiles

Giving instructions to a friend

¿Me pasas la llave?
Can you pass me the wrench?
No lo manejes en carretera.
Don't drive it on the highway.
Revisa el aceite cada 1.500 kilómetros.
Check the oil every 1,500 kilometers.
Asegúrate de llenar el tanque.
Make sure to fill up the tank.
No manejes con el cofre abierto.
Don't drive with the hood open.
Recomiéndame con tus amigos.
Recommend me to your friends.

Taking a phone call

Aló./Bueno./Diga.
Hello.
¿Quién habla?/¿De parte de quién?
Who is speaking/calling?
Con él/ella habla.
Speaking.
¿Puedo dejar un recado?
May I leave a message?

Reassuring someone

Tranquilo/a, cariño.
Relax, sweetie.
Nos ayudamos los unos a los otros.
We help each other out.
No te preocupes.
Don't worry.

Additional vocabulary

entregar *to hand in*
el intento *attempt*
la noticia *news*
el proyecto *project*
recuperar *to recover*

¿Qué pasó?

1 **Seleccionar** Selecciona las respuestas que completan correctamente estas oraciones.

1. Jorge intenta arreglar _____.
   a. la computadora de Maru   b. el coche de Miguel   c. el teléfono celular de Felipe
2. Maru dice que se borraron muchos _____ de su computadora.
   a. archivos   b. sitios web   c. mensajes de texto
3. Jorge dice que necesita un _____.
   a. navegador GPS   b. reproductor de DVD   c. televisor
4. Maru dice que Jorge es el mejor _____.
   a. mecánico de la ciudad   b. amigo del mundo   c. compañero de la clase
5. Jorge le dice a Miguel que no maneje su coche en _____.
   a. el tráfico   b. el centro de la ciudad   c. la carretera

2 **Identificar** Identifica quién puede decir estas oraciones.

1. Cómprate un coche nuevo y recomiéndame con tus amigos.
2. El mensaje de texto de Maru dice que su computadora todavía está descompuesta.
3. Mi amiga Mónica me ayudó a recuperar muchos archivos, pero necesito una computadora nueva.
4. No conduzcas con el cofre abierto y recuerda que el tanque debe estar lleno.
5. Muchos de los archivos de mi computadora se borraron.

MARU

MIGUEL

JORGE

3 **Problema mecánico** Trabajen en parejas para representar los papeles de un(a) mecánico/a y un(a) cliente/a que está llamando al taller porque su carro está descompuesto. Usen las instrucciones como guía.

Mecánico/a	Cliente/a
Contesta el teléfono con un saludo y el nombre del taller.	Saluda y explica que tu carro está descompuesto.
Pregunta qué tipo de problema tiene exactamente.	Explica que tu carro no arranca cuando hace frío.
Di que debe traer el carro al taller.	Pregunta cuándo puedes llevarlo.
Ofrece una hora para revisar el carro.	Acepta la hora que ofrece el/la mecánico/a.

Ahora cambien los papeles y representen otra conversación. Ustedes son un(a) técnico/a y un(a) cliente/a. Usen estas ideas:

el celular no guarda mensajes   la impresora imprime muy lentamente
la computadora no descarga fotos   el reproductor de DVD está descompuesto

Ortografía
La acentuación de palabras similares
Although accent marks usually indicate which syllable in a word is stressed, they are also used to distinguish between words that have the same or similar spellings.

Él maneja el coche.   **Sí, voy si quieres.**

Although one-syllable words do not usually carry written accents, some *do* have accent marks to distinguish them from words that have the same spelling but different meanings.

Sé cocinar.   **Se baña.**   **¿Tomas té?**   **Te duermes.**

Sé (*I know*) and **té** (*tea*) have accent marks to distinguish them from the pronouns **se** and **te**.

---

 para mí   **mi cámara**   **Tú lees.**   **tu estéreo**

Mí (*Me*) and **tú** (*you*) have accent marks to distinguish them from the possessive adjectives **mi** and **tu**.

¿Por qué vas?   **Voy porque quiero.**

Several words of more than one syllable also have accent marks to distinguish them from words that have the same or similar spellings.

Éste es rápido.   **Este tren es rápido.**

Demonstrative pronouns may have accent marks to distinguish them from demonstrative adjectives.

¿Cuándo fuiste?   **Fui cuando me llamó.**
¿Dónde trabajas?   **Voy al taller donde trabajo.**

Adverbs have accent marks when they are used to convey a question.

Práctica Marca los acentos en las palabras que los necesitan.

ANA Alo, soy Ana. ¿Que tal?
JUAN Hola, pero… ¿por que me llamas tan tarde?
ANA Porque mañana tienes que llevarme a la universidad. Mi auto esta dañado.
JUAN ¿Como se daño?
ANA Se daño el sabado. Un vecino (*neighbor*) choco con (*crashed into*) el.

Crucigrama Utiliza las siguientes pistas (*clues*) para completar el crucigrama. ¡Ojo con los acentos!

Horizontales
1. Él _____ levanta.
4. No voy _____ no puedo.
7. Tú _____ acuestas.
9. ¿ _____ es el examen?
10. Quiero este video y _____.

Verticales
2. ¿Cómo _____ usted?
3. Eres _____ mi hermano.
5. ¿ _____ tal?
6. Me gusta _____ suéter.
8. Navego _____ la red.

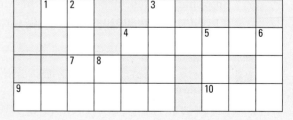

EN DETALLE

Las redes
sociales

¿Cómo te comunicas con tu familia y con tus amigos? Al igual que° en los Estados Unidos, en los países hispanohablantes las redes sociales han tenido° un gran impacto en los últimos años. Los usos básicos de los teléfonos celulares ya no son las llamadas° y los mensajes de texto, sino el contacto entre amigos y familiares por medio de° redes sociales y de aplicaciones como Facebook, Twitter, Tuenti o Instagram.

La mayoría de los hispanos tiene un perfil° en Facebook o en Twitter, pero el método de comunicación más popular en los países hispanohablantes es Whatsapp. Por medio de esta aplicación de mensajería los usuarios° pueden crear grupos y enviarse° un número ilimitado de imágenes, videos y mensajes de texto y de audio. Su popularidad se debe a que es una forma rápida y prácticamente gratuita° de comunicarse.

Hoy en día, los teléfonos inteligentes y los contratos telefónicos son más asequibles°, por lo que la mayoría de los hispanos disfruta de estos celulares y de sus ventajas tecnológicas. Gracias a las redes sociales y a las aplicaciones, las personas pueden estar en constante comunicación con sus seres queridos° más lejanos°. La inevitable pregunta es: ¿Qué ocurre con los seres queridos que están cerca? La influencia que tienen las redes sociales en las relaciones humanas es cada vez un tema más polémico.

El español en las redes sociales

- El español es la tercera lengua más utilizada en las redes sociales.
- El español es la segunda lengua más usada en Twitter, con un crecimiento° de más de 800% en los últimos diez años.
- Facebook tiene 80 millones de usuarios hispanohablantes.
- Sólo en España, Whatsapp tiene 20 millones de usuarios que usan la aplicación un promedio° de 150 veces al día.

Al igual que *Like* han tenido *have had* llamadas *calls* por medio de *through* perfil *profile* usuarios *users* enviarse *send each other* gratuita *free* asequibles *affordable* seres queridos *loved ones* lejanos *distant* crecimiento *growth* promedio *average*

ACTIVIDADES

1 **¿Cierto o falso?** Indica si lo que dicen estas oraciones es **cierto** o **falso**. Corrige la información falsa.

1. Los hispanos prefieren las llamadas para comunicarse con sus familias y con sus amigos.
2. Twitter no se usa en Latinoamérica.
3. Whatsapp es un método de comunicación muy común en los países hispanos.
4. Whatsapp permite enviar fotos a los contactos del celular.
5. Pocos hispanos pueden comprar un teléfono inteligente.
6. Una ventaja de las redes sociales es el contacto con las personas que están lejos.
7. El español es la segunda lengua más utilizada en las redes sociales.
8. Los españoles visitan constantemente la aplicación de Whatsapp.

La tecnología

los audífonos (Méx., Col.), los auriculares (Arg.), los cascos (Esp.)	headset; earphones
el móvil (Esp.)	el celular
el manos libres (Amér. S.)	hands-free system
la memoria	memory
mensajear (Méx.)	enviar y recibir mensajes de texto

EL MUNDO HISPANO

Las bicimotos

- **Argentina** El *ciclomotor* se usa mayormente° para repartir a domicilio° comidas y medicinas.

- **Perú** La *motito* se usa mucho para el reparto a domicilio de pan fresco todos los días.

- **México** La *Vespa* se usa para evitar° el tráfico en grandes ciudades.

- **España** La población usa el *Vespino* para ir y volver al trabajo cada día.

- **Puerto Rico** Una *scooter* es el medio de transporte favorito en las zonas rurales.

- **República Dominicana** Las *moto-taxis* son el medio de transporte más económico, ¡pero no olvides el casco°!

mayormente *mainly* repartir a domicilio *home delivery of* evitar *to avoid* casco *helmet*

PERFIL

Los mensajes de texto

¿Qué tienen en común un **mensaje de texto** y un telegrama?: la necesidad de decir lo máximo en el menor espacio posible —y rápidamente—. Así como los abuelos se las arreglaron° para hacer más baratos sus telegramas, que se cobraban° por número de palabras, ahora los jóvenes buscan ahorrar° espacio, tiempo y dinero, en sus mensajes de texto. Esta economía del lenguaje dio origen al **lenguaje chat**, una forma de escritura muy creativa y compacta. Olvídate de la gramática, la puntuación y la ortografía: es tan flexible que evoluciona° todos los días con el uso que cada quien° le da, aunque° hay muchas palabras y expresiones ya establecidas°. Fácilmente encontrarás° abreviaturas (**xq?**, "¿Por qué?"; **tkm**, "Te quiero mucho."), sustitución de sonidos por números (**a2**, "Adiós."; **5mntrios**, "Sin comentarios."), símbolos (**ad+**, "además") y omisión de vocales y acentos (**tb**, "también"; **k tl?**, "¿Qué tal?"). Ahora que lo sabes, si un amigo te envía: **cont xfa, m dbs $!**°, puedes responderle: **ntp, ns vms + trd**°.

se las arreglaron *they managed to* se cobraban *were charged* ahorrar *to save* evoluciona *evolves* cada quien *each person* aunque *although* establecidas *fixed* encontrarás *you will find* cont xfa, m dbs $! Contesta, por favor, ¡me debes dinero! ntp, ns vms +trd No te preocupes, nos vemos más tarde.

Conexión Internet

¿Qué sitios web son populares entre los jóvenes hispanos? | Use the Web to find more cultural information related to this Cultura section.

ACTIVIDADES

2 **Comprensión** Contesta las preguntas.
1. ¿Cuáles son tres formas de decir *headset*?
2. ¿Para qué se usan las bicimotos en Argentina?
3. ¿Qué dio origen al "lenguaje chat"?
4. ¿Es importante escribir los acentos en los mensajes de texto?

3 **¿Cómo te comunicas?** Escribe un párrafo breve en donde expliques qué utilizas para comunicarte con tus amigos/as (correo electrónico, redes sociales, teléfono, etc.) y de qué hablan cuando se llaman por teléfono.

11.1 | Familiar commands

ANTE TODO In Spanish, the command forms are used to give orders or advice. You use **tú** commands (**mandatos familiares**) when you want to give an order or advice to someone you normally address with the familiar **tú**.

Infinitive	Present tense él/ella form	Affirmative tú command
hablar	habla	**habla** (tú)
guardar	guarda	**guarda** (tú)
prender	prende	**prende** (tú)
volver	vuelve	**vuelve** (tú)
pedir	pide	**pide** (tú)
imprimir	imprime	**imprime** (tú)

▶ Affirmative **tú** commands usually have the same form as the **él/ella** form of the present indicative.

Guarda el documento antes de cerrarlo.
Save the document before closing it.

Imprime tu tarea para la clase de inglés.
Print your homework for English class.

▶ The following verbs have irregular affirmative **tú** commands.

Irregular affirmative tú commands

decir	**di**	salir	**sal**
hacer	**haz**	ser	**sé**
ir	**ve**	tener	**ten**
poner	**pon**	venir	**ven**

¡Sal ahora mismo!
Leave at once!

Haz los ejercicios.
Do the exercises.

▶ Since **ir** and **ver** have the same **tú** command (**ve**), context will determine the meaning.

Ve al cibercafé con Yolanda.
Go to the cybercafé with Yolanda.

Ve ese programa... es muy interesante.
See that program... it's very interesting.

Súbete al coche y préndelo.

No lo manejes en la carretera.

▶ The negative **tú** commands are formed by dropping the final **-o** of the **yo** form of the present tense. For **-ar** verbs, add **-es**. For **-er** and **-ir** verbs, add **-as**.

Negative tú commands

Infinitive	Present tense yo form	Negative tú command
hablar	hablo	**no hables** (tú)
guardar	guardo	**no guardes** (tú)
prender	prendo	**no prendas** (tú)
volver	vuelvo	**no vuelvas** (tú)
pedir	pido	**no pidas** (tú)

Héctor, **no pares** el carro aquí.   **No prendas** la computadora todavía.
Héctor, don't stop the car here.   *Don't turn on the computer yet.*

▶ Verbs with irregular **yo** forms maintain the same irregularity in their negative **tú** commands. These verbs include **conducir, conocer, decir, hacer, ofrecer, oír, poner, salir, tener, traducir, traer, venir,** and **ver**.

No pongas el disco en la computadora.   **No conduzcas** tan rápido.
Don't put the disk in the computer.   *Don't drive so fast.*

▶ Note also that stem-changing verbs keep their stem changes in negative **tú** commands.

No p**ie**rdas tu celular.   No v**ue**lvas a esa gasolinera.   No rep**i**tas las instrucciones.
Don't lose your cell phone.   *Don't go back to that gas station.*   *Don't repeat the instructions.*

▶ Verbs ending in **-car**, **-gar**, and **-zar** have a spelling change in the negative **tú** commands.

sa**car**	c → **qu**	no sa**qu**es
apa**gar**	g → **gu**	no apa**gu**es
almor**zar**	z → **c**	no almuer**c**es

▶ The following verbs have irregular negative **tú** commands.

Irregular negative tú commands

dar	**no des**
estar	**no estés**
ir	**no vayas**
saber	**no sepas**
ser	**no seas**

¡ATENCIÓN!

In affirmative commands, reflexive, indirect, and direct object pronouns are always attached to the end of the verb. In negative commands, these pronouns always precede the verb.

Bórralos./No los borres.

Escríbeles un mensaje electrónico./**No les escribas** un mensaje electrónico.

• • •

When a pronoun is attached to an affirmative command that has two or more syllables, an accent mark is added to maintain the original stress:

borra → **bórralos**

prende → **préndela**

imprime → **imprímelo**

¡INTÉNTALO!   Indica los mandatos familiares afirmativos y negativos de estos verbos.

1. correr   ____*Corre*____ más rápido.   No ____*corras*____ más rápido.
2. llenar   _____ el tanque.   No _____ el tanque.
3. salir   _____ ahora.   No _____ ahora.
4. descargar   _____ ese documento.   No _____ ese documento.
5. levantarse   _____ temprano.   No _____ temprano.
6. hacerlo   _____ ya.   No _____ ahora.

Práctica

1 **Completar** Tu mejor amigo no entiende nada de tecnología y te pide ayuda. Completa los comentarios de tu amigo con el mandato de cada verbo.

1. No _____ en una hora. _____ ahora mismo. (venir)
2. _____ tu tarea después. No la _____ ahora. (hacer)
3. No _____ a la tienda a comprar papel para la impresora. _____ a la cafetería a comprarme algo de comer. (ir)
4. No _____ que no puedes abrir un archivo. _____ que el programa de computación funciona sin problemas. (decirme)
5. _____ generoso con tu tiempo y no _____ antipático si no entiendo fácilmente. (ser)
6. _____ mucha paciencia y no _____ prisa. (tener)
7. _____ tu teléfono celular, pero no _____ la computadora. (apagar)

2 **Cambiar** Pedro y Marina no pueden ponerse de acuerdo (*agree*) cuando viajan en su carro. Cuando Pedro dice que algo es necesario, Marina expresa una opinión diferente. Usa la información entre paréntesis para formar las órdenes que Marina le da a Pedro.

> **modelo**
>
> **Pedro:** Necesito revisar el aceite del carro. (seguir hasta el próximo pueblo)
> **Marina:** *No revises el aceite del carro. Sigue hasta el próximo pueblo.*

1. Necesito conducir más rápido. (parar el carro)
2. Necesito poner el radio. (hablarme)
3. Necesito almorzar ahora. (comer más tarde)
4. Necesito sacar los discos compactos. (manejar con cuidado)
5. Necesito estacionar el carro en esta calle. (pensar en otra opción)
6. Necesito volver a esa gasolinera. (arreglar el carro en un taller)
7. Necesito leer el mapa. (pedirle ayuda a aquella señora)
8. Necesito dormir en el carro. (acostarse en una cama)

3 **Problemas** Tú trabajas en el centro de computadoras de la universidad. Muchos estudiantes están llamando con problemas. Dales órdenes para ayudarlos a resolverlos.

> **modelo**
>
> **Problema:** *No veo nada en la pantalla.*
> **Tu respuesta:** *Prende la pantalla de tu computadora.*

apagar...	descargar...	grabar...	imprimir...	prender...
borrar...	funcionar...	guardar...	navegar...	volver...

1. No me gusta este programa de computación.
2. Tengo miedo de perder mi documento.
3. Prefiero leer este sitio web en papel.
4. Mi correo electrónico funciona muy lentamente.
5. Busco información sobre los gauchos de Argentina.
6. Tengo demasiados archivos en mi computadora.
7. Mi computadora se congeló (*froze*).
8. Quiero ver las fotos del cumpleaños de mi hermana.

NOTA CULTURAL

Los gauchos (*nomadic cowboys*), conocidos por su habilidad (*skill*) para montar a caballo y utilizar el lazo, viven en la Región Pampeana, una llanura muy extensa ubicada en el centro de Argentina y dedicada a la agricultura (*agriculture*).

Comunicación

4

El carro de Cristina Lee el mensaje de Joaquín a su hermana Cristina. Luego, indica si las conclusiones son **lógicas** o **ilógicas**, según lo que leíste.

De:	Joaquín
Para:	Cristina
Asunto:	Carro

¿Cómo te fue con el carro esta primera semana? ¿Ya te familiarizaste con él? Voy a extrañarlo (*to miss it*). Fue mi primer carro: desde el último año de la escuela secundaria hasta terminar la universidad. ¡Pero ahora es tu carro, hermanita! Recuerda que tienes que comprar llantas nuevas antes del invierno. Esas llantas están muy viejas para usarlas en la nieve. El próximo mes, lleva el carro al taller para su mantenimiento. Revisa el aceite y arregla el navegador GPS. Si (*If*) quieres, lleva el carro al taller que está en la calle Independencia. Yo lo llevaba allí y el mecánico me conoce. Dile que eres mi hermana y te va a hacer un descuento. Por último, conduce siempre con cuidado. ¡NUNCA escribas mensajes de texto mientras conduces! ¿Vienes este fin de semana a visitarme? Dejé unos discos compactos en el baúl; tráelos, por favor.

	Lógico	Ilógico
1. Joaquín le regaló su carro a Cristina.	O	O
2. Joaquín llevó el carro al taller la semana pasada.	O	O
3. Cristina tiene un teléfono celular.	O	O
4. Joaquín se preocupa por Cristina.	O	O
5. Joaquín le prestó unos discos compactos a Cristina.	O	O

5

La tecnología Escribe por lo menos seis oraciones en las que le digas a un(a) amigo/a qué hacer para tener "una buena relación" con la tecnología. Usa mandatos familiares afirmativos y negativos.

Síntesis

6

¿Qué hago? En parejas, túrnense para darse consejos (*advice*) usando mandatos familiares afirmativos o negativos. Pueden usar las sugerencias de la lista o inventar sus propias situaciones.

> **modelo**
>
> tener un resfriado
> **Estudiante 1:** Tengo un resfriado.
> **Estudiante 2:** Toma medicina./No te levantes hoy.

estar aburrido/a	tener un carro que no	que no funciona bien
conducir mal	arranca	olvidar el cumpleaños
gastar mucho dinero	perder la licencia de	de alguien
tener dolor de cabeza	conducir	tener un teléfono celular
estar cansado/a	tener una computadora	que está descompuesto

11.2 **Por** and **para**

ANTE TODO Unlike English, Spanish has two words that mean *for*: **por** and **para**. These two prepositions are not interchangeable. Study the following charts to see how they are used.

▶ **Por** and **para** are most commonly used to describe aspects of movement, time, and action, but in different circumstances.

Por	Para
Movement	
Through or by a place	**Toward a destination**
La excursión nos llevó **por** el centro.	Mis amigos van **para** el estadio.
The tour took us through downtown.	*My friends are going to the stadium.*
Time	
Duration of an event	**Action deadline**
Ana navegó la red **por** dos horas.	Tengo que escribir un ensayo **para** mañana.
Ana surfed the net for two hours.	*I have to write an essay by tomorrow.*
Action	
Reason or motive for an action or circumstance	**Indication of for whom something is intended or done**
Llegué a casa tarde **por** el tráfico.	Estoy preparando una sorpresa **para** Eduardo.
I got home late because of the traffic.	*I'm preparing a surprise for Eduardo.*

▶ Here is a list of the uses of **por** and **para**.

Por is used to indicate...

1. **Movement: Motion or a general location..**
   (around, through, along, by)
   Pasamos **por** el parque y **por** el río.
   We passed by the park and along the river.

2. **Time: Duration of an action ....**
   (for, during, in)
   Estuve en la Patagonia **por** un mes.
   I was in Patagonia for a month.

3. **Action: Reason or motive for an action..**
   (because of, on account of, on behalf of)
   Lo hizo **por** su familia.
   She did it on behalf of her family.

4. **Object of a search ....**
   (for, in search of)
   Vengo **por** ti a las ocho.
   I'm coming for you at eight.
   Manuel fue **por** su cámara digital.
   Manuel went in search of his digital camera.

5. **Means by which something is done ...**
   (by, by way of, by means of)
   Ellos viajan **por** la autopista.
   They travel by (by way of) the highway.

6. **Exchange or substitution ....**
   (for, in exchange for)
   Le di dinero **por** el reproductor de MP3.
   I gave him money for the MP3 player.

7. **Unit of measure....................**
   (per, by)
   José manejaba a 120 kilómetros **por** hora.
   José was driving 120 kilometers per hour.

¡ATENCIÓN!

Por is also used in several idiomatic expressions, including:
por aquí *around here*
por ejemplo *for example*
por eso *that's why; therefore*
por fin *finally*

AYUDA

Remember that when giving an exact time, **de** is used instead of **por** before **la mañana**, **la tarde**, or **la noche**.
La clase empieza a las nueve **de** la mañana.

•••

In addition to **por**, **durante** is also commonly used to mean *for* when referring to time.
Esperé al mecánico **durante** cincuenta minutos.

> (**Para is used to indicate...**)

1. **Movement: Destination** . . . . (*toward, in the direction of*)	Salimos **para** Córdoba el sábado. *We are leaving for Córdoba on Saturday.*
2. **Time: Deadline or a specific time in the future** . . . . (*by, for*)	Él va a arreglar el carro **para** el viernes. *He will fix the car by Friday.*
3. **Action: Purpose or goal** + [*infinitive*] . . . . (*in order to*)	Juan estudia **para** (ser) mecánico. *Juan is studying to be a mechanic.*
4. **Purpose** + [*noun*] . . . . (*for, used for*)	Es una llanta **para** el carro. *It's a tire for the car.*
5. **The recipient of something** . . . . (*for*)	Compré una impresora **para** mi hijo. *I bought a printer for my son.*
6. **Comparison with others or an opinion** . . (*for, considering*)	**Para** un joven, es demasiado serio. *For a young person, he is too serious.* **Para** mí, esta lección no es difícil. *For me, this lesson isn't difficult.*
7. **In the employment of** . . . . (*for*)	Sara trabaja **para** Telecom Argentina. *Sara works for Telecom Argentina.*

▶ In many cases it is grammatically correct to use either **por** or **para** in a sentence. The meaning of the sentence is different, however, depending on which preposition is used.

Caminé **por** el parque.
I walked through the park.

Caminé **para** el parque.
I walked to (toward) the park.

Trabajó **por** su padre.
He worked for (in place of) his father.

Trabajó **para** su padre.
He worked for his father('s company).

(**¡INTÉNTALO!**)   Completa estas oraciones con las preposiciones **por** o **para**.

1. Fuimos al cibercafé __por__ la tarde.
2. Necesitas un navegador GPS _____ encontrar la casa de Luis.
3. Entraron _____ la puerta.
4. Quiero un pasaje _____ Buenos Aires.
5. _____ arrancar el carro, necesito la llave.
6. Arreglé el televisor _____ mi amigo.
7. Estuvieron nerviosos _____ el examen.
8. ¿No hay una gasolinera _____ aquí?
9. El reproductor de MP3 es _____ usted.
10. Juan está enfermo. Tengo que trabajar _____ él.
11. Estuvimos en Canadá _____ dos meses.
12. _____ mí, el español es fácil.
13. Tengo que estudiar la lección _____ el lunes.
14. Voy a ir _____ la carretera.
15. Compré dulces _____ mi novia.
16. Compramos el auto _____ un buen precio.

Práctica

1 **Completar** Completa este párrafo con las preposiciones **por** o **para**.

El mes pasado mi esposo y yo hicimos un viaje a Buenos Aires y sólo pagamos dos mil dólares (1)_____ los pasajes. Estuvimos en Buenos Aires (2)_____ una semana y paseamos por toda la ciudad. Durante el día caminamos (3)_____ la plaza San Martín, el microcentro y el barrio de La Boca, donde viven muchos artistas. (4)_____ la noche fuimos a una tanguería, que es una especie de teatro, (5)_____ mirar a la gente bailar tango. Dos días después decidimos hacer una excursión (6)_____ las pampas (7)_____ ver el paisaje y un rodeo con gauchos. Alquilamos (*We rented*) un carro y manejamos (8)_____ todas partes y pasamos unos días muy agradables. El último día que estuvimos en Buenos Aires fuimos a Galerías Pacífico (9)_____ comprar recuerdos (*souvenirs*) (10)_____ nuestros hijos y nietos. Compramos tantos regalos que tuvimos que pagar impuestos (*duties*) en la aduana al regresar.

2 **Oraciones** Crea oraciones originales con los elementos de las columnas. Une los elementos usando **por** o **para**.

> **modelo**
> Fuimos a Mar del Plata por razones de salud para visitar a un especialista.

(no) fue al mercado	por/para	comprar frutas	por/para	¿?
(no) fuimos a las montañas	por/para	tres días	por/para	¿?
(no) fuiste a Mar del Plata	por/para	razones de salud	por/para	¿?
(no) fueron a Buenos Aires	por/para	tomar el sol	por/para	¿?

3 **Describir** Usa **por** o **para** y el tiempo presente para describir estos dibujos.

1. _____   2. _____   3. _____

4. _____   5. _____   6. _____

Comunicación

4 **Los planes** Escucha la conversación telefónica entre Antonio y Sonia. Luego, indica si las conclusiones son **lógicas** o **ilógicas**, según lo que escuchaste.

	Lógico	Ilógico
1. En junio hace frío en Bariloche.	○	○
2. Sonia va a viajar por las carreteras.	○	○
3. Sonia vive en Santiago de Chile.	○	○
4. Antonio vive en Buenos Aires.	○	○
5. Sonia va al centro por una bolsa.	○	○
6. Sonia no sabe esquiar.	○	○

5 **Descripciones** En parejas, usen **por** o **para** y completen estas frases de manera lógica.

1. En casa, hablo con mis amigos…
2. Mi padre/madre trabaja…
3. A veces voy a la biblioteca…
4. Esta noche tengo que estudiar…
5. Compré un regalo…
6. Necesito hacer la tarea…

6 **Situación** En parejas, dramaticen esta situación. Utilicen muchos ejemplos de **por** y **para.**

Hijo/a

Pídele dinero a tu padre/madre.

Dile que quieres comprar un carro.

Explica tres razones por las que necesitas un carro.

Dile que por no tener un carro tu vida es muy difícil.

Padre/Madre

→ Pregúntale a tu hijo/a para qué lo necesita.

→ Pregúntale por qué necesita un carro.

→ Explica por qué sus razones son buenas o malas.

→ Decide si vas a darle el dinero y explica por qué.

Síntesis

7 **La tecnología y tú** Escribe un párrafo sobre cómo usas los diferentes tipos de tecnología y aparatos (*devices*) electrónicos en tu vida diaria: para qué tareas (*tasks*), en qué momento del día, por cuánto tiempo, etc.

11.3 Reciprocal reflexives

ANTE TODO In **Lección 7**, you learned that reflexive verbs indicate that the subject of a sentence does the action to itself. Reciprocal reflexives, on the other hand, express a shared or reciprocal action between two or more people or things. In this context, the pronoun means *(to) each other* or *(to) one another*.

Luis y Marta **se** miran en el espejo.
Luis and Marta look at themselves in the mirror.

Luis y Marta **se** miran.
Luis and Marta look at each other.

▶ Only the plural forms of the reflexive pronouns (**nos, os, se**) are used to express reciprocal actions because the action must involve more than one person or thing.

Cuando **nos vimos** en la calle, **nos abrazamos**.
When we saw each other on the street, we hugged (one another).

Ustedes **se** van a **encontrar** en el cibercafé, ¿no?
You are meeting (each other) at the cybercafé, right?

Nos ayudamos cuando usamos la computadora.
We help each other when we use the computer.

Las amigas **se saludaron** y **se besaron**.
The friends greeted each other and kissed (one another).

¡ATENCIÓN!

Here is a list of common verbs that can express reciprocal actions:

abrazar(se) *to hug; to embrace (each other)*
ayudar(se) *to help (each other)*
besar(se) *to kiss (each other)*
encontrar(se) *to meet (each other); to run into (each other)*
saludar(se) *to greet (each other)*

¡INTÉNTALO! Indica el reflexivo recíproco adecuado de estos verbos en el presente o el pretérito.

presente

1. (escribir) Los novios _se escriben_.
   Nosotros _____.
   Ana y Ernesto _____.
2. (escuchar) Mis tíos _____.
   Nosotros _____.
   Ellos _____.
3. (ver) Nosotros _____.
   Fernando y Tomás _____.
   Ustedes _____.
4. (llamar) Ellas _____.
   Mis hermanos _____.
   Pepa y yo _____.

pretérito

1. (saludar) Nicolás y tú _se saludaron_.
   Nuestros vecinos _____.
   Nosotros _____.
2. (hablar) Los amigos _____.
   Elena y yo _____.
   Ustedes _____.
3. (conocer) Alberto y yo _____.
   Ustedes _____.
   Ellos _____.
4. (encontrar) Ana y Javier _____.
   Los primos _____.
   Mi hermana y yo _____.

Práctica y Comunicación

1 **Un amor recíproco** Describe a Laura y a Elián usando los verbos recíprocos.

> **modelo**
> Laura veía a Elián todos los días. Elián veía a Laura todos los días.
> *Laura y Elián se veían todos los días.*

1. Laura conocía bien a Elián. Elián conocía bien a Laura.

2. Laura miraba a Elián con amor. Elián la miraba con amor también.

3. Laura entendía bien a Elián. Elián entendía bien a Laura.

4. Laura hablaba con Elián todas las noches por teléfono. Elián hablaba con Laura todas las noches por teléfono.

5. Laura ayudaba a Elián con sus problemas. Elián la ayudaba también con sus problemas.

2 **Describir** Mira los dibujos y describe lo que estas personas hicieron.

1. Las hermanas _____.

2. Ellos _____.

3. Gilberto y Mercedes _____ / _____ / _____.

4. Tú y yo _____ / _____.

3 **Preguntas** Contesta las preguntas de tu compañero/a.

1. ¿Se vieron tú y tu mejor amigo/a ayer? ¿Cuándo se ven ustedes normalmente?
2. ¿Dónde y cuándo se encuentran tú y tus amigos?
3. ¿Se ayudan tú y tu mejor amigo/a con sus problemas?
4. ¿Se entienden bien tú y tus amigos?
5. ¿Dónde se conocieron tú y tu mejor amigo/a?
6. ¿Cuándo se dan regalos tú y tu novio/a?
7. ¿Se escriben tú y tus amigos mensajes de texto o prefieren llamarse por teléfono?
8. ¿Siempre se llevan bien tú y tu mejor amigo/a? Explica tu respuesta.

Stressed possessive adjectives and pronouns

ANTE TODO   Spanish has two types of possessive adjectives: the unstressed (or short) forms you learned in **Lección 3** and the stressed (or long) forms. The stressed forms are used for emphasis or to express *of mine, of yours,* and so on.

Stressed possessive adjectives

Masculine singular	Feminine singular	Masculine plural	Feminine plural	
mío	**mía**	**míos**	**mías**	*my; (of) mine*
tuyo	**tuya**	**tuyos**	**tuyas**	*your; (of) yours* (fam.)
suyo	**suya**	**suyos**	**suyas**	*your; (of) yours* (form.)*; his; (of) his; her; (of) hers; its*
nuestro	**nuestra**	**nuestros**	**nuestras**	*our; (of) ours*
vuestro	**vuestra**	**vuestros**	**vuestras**	*your; (of) yours* (fam.)
suyo	**suya**	**suyos**	**suyas**	*your; (of) yours; their; (of) theirs*

▶ **¡Atención!** Used with **un/una**, these possessives are similar in meaning to the English expression *of mine/yours/etc.*

>   Juancho es **un** amigo **mío**.   Ella es **una** compañera **nuestra**.
>   *Juancho is a friend of mine.*   *She is a classmate of ours.*

▶ Stressed possessive adjectives agree in gender and number with the nouns they modify. While unstressed possessive adjectives are placed before the noun, stressed possessive adjectives are placed after the noun they modify.

>   **su** impresora   la impresora **suya**
>   *her printer*   *her printer*
>
>   **nuestros** televisores   los televisores **nuestros**
>   *our television sets*   *our television sets*

▶ A definite article, an indefinite article, or a demonstrative adjective usually precedes a noun modified by a stressed possessive adjective.

>   ⎧ **unos** discos compactos **tuyos**.   *I love some of your CDs.*
>   Me encantan   ⎨ **los** discos compactos **tuyos**.   *I love your CDs.*
>   ⎩ **estos** discos compactos **tuyos**. *I love these CDs of yours.*

▶ Since **suyo, suya, suyos,** and **suyas** have more than one meaning, you can avoid confusion by using the construction: [*article*] + [*noun*] + **de** + [*subject pronoun*].

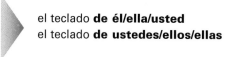

>   **el** teclado **suyo**   el teclado **de él/ella/usted**
>   el teclado **de ustedes/ellos/ellas**

CONSULTA

This is the same construction you learned in **Lección 3** for clarifying **su** and **sus**. To review unstressed possessive adjectives, see **Estructura 3.2**, p. 93.

Possessive pronouns

▶ Possessive pronouns are used to replace a noun + [*possessive adjective*]. In Spanish, the possessive pronouns have the same forms as the stressed possessive adjectives, but they are preceded by a definite article.

la cámara **nuestra**	**la nuestra**
el navegador GPS **tuyo**	**el tuyo**
los archivos **suyos**	**los suyos**

▶ A possessive pronoun agrees in number and gender with the noun it replaces.

—Aquí está **mi coche**. ¿Dónde está **el tuyo**?
Here's my car. Where is yours?

—**El mío** está en el taller de mi hermano.
Mine is at my brother's garage.

—¿Tienes **las revistas** de Carlos?
Do you have Carlos' magazines?

—No, pero tengo **las nuestras**.
No, but I have ours.

¿También está descompuesta tu computadora?

No, la mía no, la suya.

¡INTÉNTALO! Indica las formas tónicas (*stressed*) de estos adjetivos posesivos y los pronombres posesivos correspondientes.

	adjetivos	pronombres
1. su cámara digital	la cámara digital suya	la suya
2. mi televisor		
3. nuestros discos compactos		
4. tus aplicaciones		
5. su monitor		
6. mis videos		
7. nuestra impresora		
8. tu estéreo		
9. nuestro blog		
10. mi computadora		

Práctica

1

Oraciones Forma oraciones con estas palabras. Usa el presente y haz los cambios necesarios.

1. un / amiga / suyo / vivir / Mendoza
2. ¿me / prestar / calculadora / tuyo?
3. el / coche / suyo / nunca / funcionar / bien
4. no / nos / interesar / problemas / suyo
5. yo / querer / cámara digital / mío / ahora mismo
6. un / amigos / nuestro / manejar / como / loco

2

¿Es suyo? Un policía ha capturado (*has captured*) al hombre que robó (*robbed*) en tu casa. Ahora quiere saber qué cosas son tuyas. Túrnate con un(a) compañero/a para hacer el papel del policía y usa las pistas (*clues*) para contestar las preguntas.

> **modelo**
>
> no/viejo
> **Policía:** Esta impresora, ¿es suya?
> **Estudiante:** No, no es mía. La mía era más vieja.

1. sí

2. no/pequeño

3. sí

4. sí

5. no/grande

6. no/caro

3

Conversaciones Completa estas conversaciones con las formas adecuadas de los pronombres posesivos.

1. —La casa de ellos estaba en la Avenida Alvear. ¿Dónde estaba la casa de ustedes?
   —_____ estaba en la calle Bolívar.
2. —A Carmen le encanta su monitor nuevo.
   —¿Sí? A José no le gusta _____.
3. —Puse mis discos aquí. ¿Dónde pusiste _____, Alfonso?
   —Puse _____ en el escritorio.
4. —Se me olvidó traer mis llaves. ¿Trajeron ustedes _____?
   —No, dejamos _____ en casa.
5. —Yo compré mi computadora en una tienda y Marta compró _____ en Internet. Y _____, ¿dónde la compraste?
   —_____ es de Cíbermax.

Comunicación

4

Eso es mío Escucha la conversación entre Pablo y Ana. Luego, indica si las conclusiones son **lógicas** o **ilógicas**, según lo que escuchaste.

	Lógico	Ilógico
1. Pablo y Ana acaban de romper.	○	○
2. Pablo tiene licencia de conducir.	○	○
3. Pablo es camarero.	○	○
4. Ana se va a llevar la computadora.	○	○
5. Pablo y Ana van a ver una película juntos.	○	○

5

Comparar Trabajen en parejas. Intenta (*Try to*) convencer a tu compañero/a de que algo que tú tienes es mejor que lo que él/ella tiene. Pueden hablar de sus carros, computadoras, televisores, teléfonos celulares, clases, horarios o trabajos.

> **modelo**
>
> **Estudiante 1:** Mi televisor tiene una pantalla de veinte pulgadas (*inches*). ¿Y el tuyo?
> **Estudiante 2:** El mío es mejor porque tiene una pantalla de treinta y siete pulgadas.
> **Estudiante 1:** Pues el mío...

Síntesis

6

Inventos locos Imagina que acabas de inventar un aparato (*device*) tecnológico revolucionario. Dibuja tu invento y descríbelo contestando las preguntas que siguen.

> **modelo**
>
> Este invento mío se usa para cocinar huevos y funciona de una manera muy fácil...

- ¿Para qué se usa?
- ¿Cómo es?
- ¿Cuánto cuesta?

- ¿Qué personas van a comprar este aparato?

Javier

SUBJECT

CONJUGATED FORM
empiezo

Main clause

dudan

Recapitulación

Completa estas actividades para repasar los conceptos de gramática que aprendiste en esta lección.

1 Completar Completa la tabla con las formas de los mandatos familiares. **16 pts.**

Infinitivo	Mandato	
	Afirmativo	**Negativo**
comer	come	no comas
hacer		
sacar		
venir		
ir		

2 Por y para Completa el diálogo con **por** o **para**. **20 pts.**

MARIO Hola, yo trabajo (1) _____ el periódico de la universidad. ¿Puedo hacerte unas preguntas?

INÉS Sí, claro.

MARIO ¿Navegas mucho (2) _____ la red?

INÉS Sí, todos los días me conecto a Internet (3) _____ leer mi correo y navego (4) _____ una hora. También me gusta hablar (5) _____ *Skype* con mis amigos. Es muy bueno y, (6) _____ mí, es divertido.

MARIO ¿Y qué piensas sobre hacer la tarea en la computadora?

INÉS En general, me parece bien, pero (7) _____ ejemplo, anoche hice unos ejercicios (8) _____ la clase de álgebra y al final me dolieron los ojos. (9) _____ eso a veces prefiero hacer la tarea a mano.

MARIO Muy bien. Muchas gracias (10) _____ tu tiempo.

3 Posesivos Completa las oraciones y confirma de quién son las cosas. **12 pts.**

1. —¿Éste es mi video? —Sí, es el _____ (*fam.*).
2. —¿Ésta es la cámara de tu papá? —Sí, es la _____.
3. —¿Ese teléfono es de Pilar? —Sí, es el _____.
4. —¿Éstos son los cargadores de ustedes? —No, no son _____.
5. —¿Ésta es tu computadora portátil? —No, no es _____.
6. —¿Ésas son mis fotos? —Sí, son las _____ (*form.*).

11.1 Familiar commands *pp. 378–379*

tú commands		
Infinitive	**Affirmative**	**Negative**
guardar	guard**a**	no guard**es**
volver	vuelv**e**	no vuelv**as**
imprimir	imprim**e**	no imprim**as**

▶ Irregular **tú** command forms

dar → **no des**   saber → **no sepas**

decir → **di**   salir → **sal**

estar → **no estés**   ser → **sé, no seas**

hacer → **haz**   tener → **ten**

ir → **ve, no vayas**   venir → **ven**

poner → **pon**

▶ Verbs ending in **-car, -gar, -zar** have a spelling change in the negative **tú** commands:

sa**car** → **no saques**
apa**gar** → **no apagues**
almor**zar** → **no almuerces**

11.2 Por and para *pp. 382–383*

▶ Uses of **por:**

motion or general location; duration; reason or motive; object of a search; means by which something is done; exchange or substitution; unit of measure

▶ Uses of **para:**

destination; deadline; purpose or goal; recipient of something; comparison or opinion; in the employment of

11.3 Reciprocal reflexives *p. 386*

▶ Reciprocal reflexives express a shared or reciprocal action between two or more people or things. Only the plural forms (**nos, os, se**) are used.

Cuando **nos vimos** en la calle, **nos abrazamos**.

▶ Common verbs that can express reciprocal actions:

abrazar(se), ayudar(se), besar(se), conocer(se), encontrar(se), escribir(se), escuchar(se), hablar(se), llamar(se), mirar(se), saludar(se), ver(se)

4 **Ángel y diablito** A Juan le gusta pedir consejos a su ángel y a su diablito imaginarios. Completa las respuestas con mandatos familiares desde las dos perspectivas. `24 pts.`

1. Estoy manejando. ¿Voy más rápido?
   Á No, no _____ más rápido.
   D Sí, _____ más rápido.
2. Es el reproductor de MP3 de mi hermana.
   ¿Lo pongo en mi mochila?
   Á No, no _____ en tu mochila.
   D Sí, _____ en tu mochila.
3. Necesito estirar (*to stretch*) las piernas.
   ¿Doy un paseo?
   Á Sí, _____ un paseo.
   D No, no _____ un paseo.
4. Mi amigo necesita imprimir algo. ¿Apago la impresora?
   Á No, no _____ la impresora.
   D Sí, _____ la impresora.

11.4 **Stressed possessive adjectives and pronouns**

pp. 388–389

Stressed possessive adjectives	
Masculine	**Feminine**
mío(s)	mía(s)
tuyo(s)	tuya(s)
suyo(s)	suya(s)
nuestro(s)	nuestra(s)
vuestro(s)	vuestra(s)
suyo(s)	suya(s)

la impresora **suya** → la **suya**

las llaves **mías** → las **mías**

5 **Oraciones** Forma oraciones para expresar acciones recíprocas con el tiempo indicado. `24 pts.`

> **modelo**
>
> tú y yo / conocer / bien (presente) *Tú y yo nos conocemos bien.*

1. José y Paco / llamar / una vez por semana (imperfecto)
2. mi novia y yo / ver / todos los días (presente)
3. los compañeros de clase / ayudar / con la tarea (pretérito)
4. tú y tu mamá / escribir / por correo electrónico / cada semana (imperfecto)
5. mis hermanas y yo / entender / perfectamente (presente)
6. los profesores / saludar / con mucho respeto (pretérito)

6 **Saber compartir** Completa la expresión con los dos pronombres posesivos que faltan. `4 pts.`

“ Lo que° es _____ es _____. ”

Lo que *What*

Lectura

Antes de leer

Estrategia
Recognizing borrowed words

One way languages grow is by borrowing words from each other. English words that relate to technology often are borrowed by Spanish and other languages throughout the world. Sometimes the words are modified slightly to fit the sounds of the languages that borrow them. When reading in Spanish, you can often increase your understanding by looking for words borrowed from English or other languages you know.

Examinar el texto

Observa la tira cómica°. ¿De qué trata°? ¿Cómo lo sabes?

Buscar

Esta lectura contiene una palabra tomada° del inglés. Encuéntrala.

_____

Repasa° las palabras nuevas relacionadas con la tecnología que aprendiste en **Contextos** y expande la lista de palabras tomadas del inglés.

_____   _____
_____   _____
_____   _____

Sobre el autor

Juan Matías Loiseau (1974–). Más conocido como Tute, este artista nació en Buenos Aires, Argentina. Estudió diseño gráfico, humorismo y cine. Sus tiras cómicas se publican en Estados Unidos, Francia y toda Latinoamérica.

tira cómica *comic strip* ¿De qué trata? *What is it about?*
tomada *taken* Repasa *Review*

Después de leer

Comprensión

Indica si las oraciones son **ciertas** o **falsas**. Corrige las falsas.

Cierto   Falso

_____   _____   1. Hay tres personajes en la tira cómica: un usuario de teléfono, un amigo y un empleado de la empresa (*company*) telefónica.

_____   _____   2. El nuevo servicio de teléfono incluye las llamadas telefónicas únicamente.

_____   _____   3. El empleado duerme en su casa.

_____   _____   4. El contrato de teléfono dura (*lasts*) un año.

_____   _____   5. El usuario y el amigo están trabajando (*working*).

Preguntas

Contesta estas preguntas con oraciones completas. Usa el pretérito y el imperfecto.

1. ¿Al usuario le gustaba usar el teléfono celular todo el tiempo?
   _____

2. ¿Por qué el usuario decidió tirar el teléfono al mar?
   _____

3. Según el amigo, ¿para qué tenía el usuario que tirar el teléfono celular al mar?
   _____

4. ¿Qué ocurrió cuando el usuario tiró el teléfono?
   _____

5. ¿Qué le dijo el empleado al usuario cuando salió del mar?
   _____

Contestar

Contesta las preguntas.

1. ¿Te sientes identificado/a con el usuario de teléfono de la tira cómica? ¿Por qué?

2. ¿Cuáles son los aspectos positivos y los negativos de tener teléfono celular?

3. ¿Cuál es para ti el límite que debe tener la tecnología en nuestras vidas?

te viene *comes with* tipo *guy, dude* te avisa *alerts you* escuchás *listen (Arg.)*
distraídos *careless* piso *floor* bolsa de dormir *sleeping bag* darle de baja *to suspend*
harto *fed up* revolear *throw it away with energy (S. America)* bien hecho *well done*
llamada perdida *missed call*

Escritura

Estrategia
Listing key words

Once you have determined the purpose for a piece of writing and identified your audience, it is helpful to make a list of key words you can use while writing. If you were to write a description of your campus, for example, you would probably need a list of prepositions that describe location, such as **al lado de** and **detrás de**. Likewise, a list of descriptive adjectives would be useful to you if you were writing about the people and places of your childhood.

By preparing a list of potential words ahead of time, you will find it easier to avoid using the dictionary while writing your first draft. You will probably also learn a few new words in Spanish while preparing your list of key words.

Listing useful vocabulary is also a valuable organizational strategy, since the act of brainstorming key words will help you to form ideas about your topic. In addition, a list of key words can help you avoid redundancy when you write.

If you were going to help someone write a personal ad, what words would be most helpful to you? Jot a few of them down.

1. _____
2. _____
3. _____
4. _____
5. _____
6. _____

Tema
Escribir instrucciones

Un(a) amigo/a tuyo/a quiere escribir un anuncio personal en un sitio web para citas románticas. Tú tienes experiencia con esto y vas a decirle qué debe y no debe decir en su perfil°.

Escríbele un mensaje electrónico en el que le explicas claramente° cómo hacerlo.

Cuando escribas tu mensaje, considera esta información:

▶ el nombre del sitio web

▶ mandatos afirmativos que describen en detalle lo que tu amigo/a debe escribir

▶ una descripción física, sus pasatiempos, sus actividades favoritas y otras cosas originales como el tipo de carro que tiene o su signo del zodiaco

▶ su dirección electrónica, su número de teléfono celular, etc.

▶ mandatos negativos sobre cosas que tu amigo/a no debe escribir en el anuncio

perfil *profile* **claramente** *clearly*

Escuchar

Estrategia
Recognizing the genre of spoken discourse

You will encounter many different genres of spoken discourse in Spanish. For example, you may hear a political speech, a radio interview, a commercial, a voicemail message, or a news broadcast. Try to identify the genre of what you hear so that you can activate your background knowledge about that type of discourse and identify the speakers' motives and intentions.

To practice this strategy, you will now listen to two short selections. Identify the genre of each one.

Preparación

Mira la foto de Ricardo Moreno. ¿Puedes imaginarte qué tipo de discurso vas a oír?

Ahora escucha

Mientras escuchas a Ricardo Moreno, contesta las preguntas.

1. ¿Qué tipo de discurso es?
   a. las noticias° por radio o televisión
   b. una conversación entre amigos
   c. un anuncio comercial
   d. una reseña° de una película

2. ¿De qué habla?
   a. del tiempo   c. de un producto o servicio
   b. de su vida   d. de algo que oyó o vio

3. ¿Cuál es el propósito°?
   a. informar   c. relacionarse con alguien
   b. vender   d. dar opiniones

Comprensión

Identificar
Indica si esta información está incluida en el discurso; si está incluida, escribe los detalles que escuchaste.

	Sí	No
1. El anuncio describe un servicio.	○	○
2. Explica cómo está de salud.	○	○
3. Informa sobre la variedad de productos.	○	○
4. Pide tu opinión.	○	○
5. Explica por qué es la mejor tienda.	○	○
6. Informa sobre el tiempo para mañana.	○	○
7. Informa dónde se puede conseguir el servicio.	○	○
8. Informa sobre las noticias del mundo.	○	○

Haz un anuncio
Haz un anuncio comercial de algún producto. No te olvides de dar toda la información necesaria.

noticias *news* reseña *review* propósito *purpose*

En pantalla

No sólo del fútbol y el béisbol viven los aficionados hispanos; también del automovilismo°. En Argentina es el segundo deporte más popular después del fútbol. En la Fórmula 1, la leyenda del argentino Juan Manuel Fangio aún sigue viva. España tiene circuitos importantes, como Jerez y Montmeló, y pilotos reconocidos como Fernando Alonso y Pedro de la Rosa. En México encontramos la tradicional Copa Turmex y las *NASCAR Corona Series*, y pilotos como Adrián Fernández y Esteban Gutiérrez. En NASCAR, el colombiano Juan Pablo Montoya y el cubanoamericano Aric Almirola han hecho un buen papel°.

Vocabulario útil	
¿Cómo quedó?	How does it look?
cuénteme	tell me
la llama	flame; llama (the animal)
malinterpretar	misunderstand
veamos	let's see

Preparación

¿Alguna vez le pediste a alguien que hiciera algo y te malinterpretó o se lo pediste a la persona equivocada?

Ordenar

Ordena cronológicamente estas oraciones.

a. El dueño del taller malinterpretó el pedido.

b. El cliente se sorprendió cuando lo vio y se le cayó el casco (*helmet*).

c. Pensó que el cliente no se refería a (*didn't refer to*) las llamas de fuego sino a los animales.

d. El cliente pidió que pintaran (*painted*) su carro con llamas.

e. El dueño estaba muy orgulloso (*proud*) cuando le mostró al cliente cómo quedó el carro.

¿Cómo terminó?

Imagina el final de la historia. ¿Cómo se sentían el cliente y el dueño del taller? ¿Qué ocurrió después? ¿Encontraron una solución? Usa el pretérito y el imperfecto.

automovilismo *car racing* han hecho un buen papel *have done a good job*

Anuncio de Davivienda

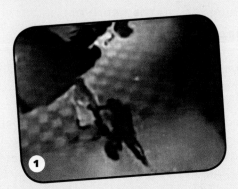

Don Álex, lo estábamos esperando.

Cuénteme. ¿Cómo quedó mi carro?

Quedó espectacular [...] Llamas por arriba, por los lados...

Hoy día, en cualquier ciudad grande latinoamericana puedes encontrar **un cibercafé**. Allí uno puede disfrutar de° un refresco o un café mientras navega en Internet, escribe mensajes electrónicos o chatea. De hecho°, el negocio° del cibercafé está mucho más desarrollado° en Latinoamérica que en los Estados Unidos. En una ciudad hispana, es común ver varios en una misma cuadra°. Los cibercafés ofrecen servicios especializados que permiten su coexistencia. Por ejemplo, mientras que el cibercafé Videomax atrae° a los niños con videojuegos, el Conécta-T ofrece servicio de chat con cámara para jóvenes, y el Mundo° Ejecutivo atrae a profesionales, todos en la misma calle.

Vocabulario útil

comunidad indígena	*indigenous community*
localizados	*located*
usuarios	*users*

Preparación

¿Con qué frecuencia navegas en Internet? ¿Dónde lo haces, en tu casa o en un lugar público?

Elegir

Indica cuál de las dos opciones resume mejor este episodio.

a. En Cuzco, Internet es un elemento importante para las comunidades indígenas que quieren vender sus productos en otros países. Con Internet inalámbrica, estas comunidades chatean con clientes en otros países.

b. En Cuzco, la comunidad y los turistas usan la tecnología de los celulares e Internet para comunicarse con sus familias o vender productos. Para navegar en Internet, se pueden visitar las cabinas de Internet o ir a la Plaza de Armas con una computadora portátil.

disfrutar de *enjoy* De hecho *In fact* negocio *business* desarrollado *developed* cuadra *(city) block* atrae *attracts* Mundo *World*

Maravillas de la tecnología

... los cibercafés se conocen comúnmente como "cabinas de Internet" y están localizados por todo el país.

... el primer *hotspot* de Cuzco [...] permite a los usuarios navegar de manera inalámbrica...

Puedo usar Internet en medio de la plaza y nadie me molesta.

Argentina

El país en cifras

▶ **Área:** 2.780.400 km² (1.074.000 millas²)
Argentina es el país de habla española más grande del mundo. Su territorio es dos veces el tamaño° de Alaska.

▶ **Población:** 43.024.000

▶ **Capital:** Buenos Aires (y su área metropolitana) —13.528.000
En el gran Buenos Aires vive más del treinta por ciento de la población total del país. La ciudad es conocida° como el "París de Suramérica" por su estilo parisino°.

Buenos Aires

▶ **Ciudades principales:**
Córdoba —1.493.000, Rosario —1.231.000, Mendoza —917.000

▶ **Moneda:** peso argentino

▶ **Idiomas:** español (oficial), lenguas indígenas

Bandera de Argentina

Argentinos célebres

▶ **Jorge Luis Borges,** escritor (1899–1986)
▶ **María Eva Duarte de Perón ("Evita"),** primera dama° (1919–1952)
▶ **Mercedes Sosa,** cantante (1935–2009)
▶ **Leandro "Gato" Barbieri,** saxofonista (1932–)
▶ **Adolfo Pérez Esquivel,** activista (1931–), Premio Nobel de la Paz en 1980

tamaño *size* conocida *known* parisino *Parisian* primera dama *First Lady*
anchas *wide* mide *it measures* campo *field*

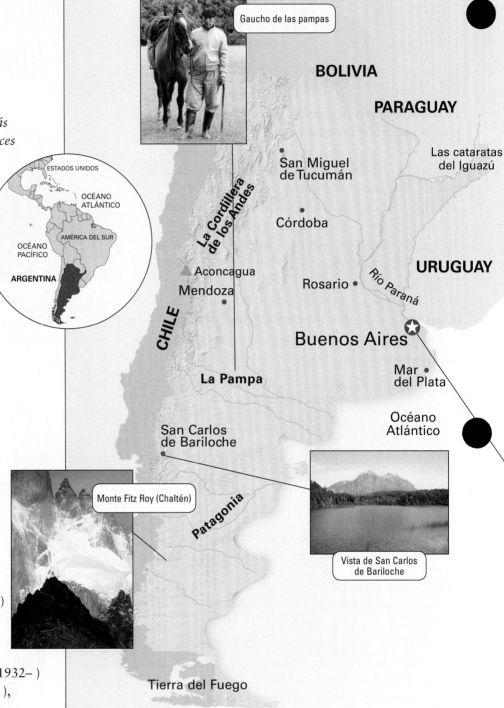

Gaucho de las pampas

BOLIVIA

PARAGUAY

Las cataratas del Iguazú

San Miguel de Tucumán

La Cordillera de los Andes

Córdoba

ESTADOS UNIDOS

OCÉANO ATLÁNTICO

OCÉANO PACÍFICO

AMÉRICA DEL SUR

ARGENTINA

▲ Aconcagua
Mendoza

CHILE

URUGUAY

Rosario

Río Paraná

Buenos Aires

Mar del Plata

La Pampa

Océano Atlántico

San Carlos de Bariloche

Monte Fitz Roy (Chaltén)

Patagonia

Vista de San Carlos de Bariloche

Tierra del Fuego

BRASIL

Historia • Inmigración europea

Se dice que Argentina es el país más "europeo" de toda Latinoamérica. Después del año 1880, inmigrantes italianos, alemanes, españoles e ingleses llegaron para establecerse en esta nación. Esta diversidad cultural ha dejado° una profunda huella° en la música, el cine y la arquitectura argentinos.

Artes • El tango

El tango es uno de los símbolos culturales más importantes de Argentina. Este género° musical es una mezcla de ritmos de origen africano, italiano y español, y se originó a finales del siglo XIX entre los porteños°. Poco después se hizo popular entre el resto de los argentinos y su fama llegó hasta París. Como baile, el tango en un principio° era provocativo y violento, pero se hizo más romántico durante los años 30. Hoy día, este estilo musical tiene adeptos° en muchas partes del mundo°.

Lugares • Las cataratas del Iguazú

Las famosas cataratas° del Iguazú se encuentran entre las fronteras de Argentina, Paraguay y Brasil, al norte de Buenos Aires. Cerca de ellas confluyen° los ríos Iguazú y Paraná. Estas extensas caídas de agua tienen hasta 80 metros (262 pies) de altura° y en época° de lluvias llegan a medir 4 kilómetros (2,5 millas) de ancho. Situadas en el Parque Nacional Iguazú, las cataratas son un destino° turístico muy visitado.

¿Qué aprendiste? Contesta cada pregunta con una oración completa.

1. ¿Qué porcentaje de la población de Argentina vive en el gran Buenos Aires?

2. ¿Quién era Mercedes Sosa?

3. Se dice que Argentina es el país más europeo de Latinoamérica. ¿Por qué?

4. ¿Qué tipo de baile es uno de los símbolos culturales más importantes de Argentina?

5. ¿Dónde y cuándo se originó el tango?

6. ¿Cómo era el baile del tango originalmente?

7. ¿En qué parque nacional están las cataratas del Iguazú?

Artesano en Buenos Aires

Conexión Internet Investiga estos temas en Internet.

1. Busca información sobre el tango. ¿Te gustan los ritmos y sonidos del tango? ¿Por qué? ¿Se baila el tango en tu comunidad?

2. ¿Quiénes fueron Juan y Eva Perón y qué importancia tienen en la historia de Argentina?

....

ha dejado *has left* **huella** *mark* **género** *genre* **porteños** *people of Buenos Aires* **en un principio** *at first* **adeptos** *followers* **mundo** *world* **cataratas** *waterfalls* **confluyen** *converge* **altura** *height* **época** *season* **destino** *destination*

La tecnología

la aplicación	app
la cámara digital/ de video	digital/video camera
el canal	(TV) channel
el cargador	charger
el cibercafé	cybercafé
el control remoto	remote control
el correo de voz	voice mail
el disco compacto	CD
el estéreo	stereo
el radio	radio (set)
el reproductor de CD	CD player
el reproductor de MP3	MP3 player
el (teléfono) celular	(cell) phone
el televisor	television set
apagar	to turn off
funcionar	to work
llamar	to call
poner, prender	to turn on
sonar (o:ue)	to ring
descompuesto/a	not working; out of order
lento/a	slow
lleno/a	full

Verbos

abrazar(se)	to hug; to embrace (each other)
ayudar(se)	to help (each other)
besar(se)	to kiss (each other)
encontrar(se) (o:ue)	to meet (each other); to run into (each other)
saludar(se)	to greet (each other)

La computadora

el archivo	file
la arroba	@ symbol
el blog	blog
el buscador	browser
la computadora (portátil)	(portable) computer; (laptop)
la conexión inalámbrica	wireless connection
la dirección electrónica	e-mail address
la impresora	printer
Internet	Internet
el mensaje de texto	text message
el monitor	(computer) monitor
la página principal	home page
la pantalla	screen
el programa de computación	software
el ratón	mouse
la red	network; Web
el reproductor de DVD	DVD player
el sitio web	website
el teclado	keyboard
borrar	to erase
chatear	to chat
descargar	to download
escanear	to scan
grabar	to record
guardar	to save
imprimir	to print
navegar (en Internet)	to surf (the Internet)

El carro

la autopista	highway
el baúl	trunk
la calle	street
la carretera	highway; (main) road
el capó, el cofre	hood
el carro, el coche	car
la circulación, el tráfico	traffic
el garaje, el taller (mecánico)	garage; (mechanic's) repair shop
la gasolina	gasoline
la gasolinera	gas station
la licencia de conducir	driver's license
la llanta	tire
el/la mecánico/a	mechanic
el navegador GPS	GPS
el parabrisas	windshield
la policía	police (force)
la velocidad máxima	speed limit
el volante	steering wheel
arrancar	to start
arreglar	to fix; to arrange
bajar(se) de	to get off of/out of (a vehicle)
conducir, manejar	to drive
estacionar	to park
llenar (el tanque)	to fill (the tank)
parar	to stop
revisar (el aceite)	to check (the oil)
subir(se) a	to get on/into (a vehicle)

Otras palabras y expresiones

por aquí	around here
por ejemplo	for example
por eso	that's why; therefore
por fin	finally

Por and para	See pages 382–383.
Stressed possessive adjectives and pronouns	See pages 388–389.
Expresiones útiles	See page 373.

La vivienda

Communicative Goals

You will learn how to:

- Welcome people to your home
- Describe your house or apartment
- Talk about household chores
- Give instructions

12

A PRIMERA VISTA

- ¿Están los chicos en casa?
- ¿Viven en una casa o en un apartamento?
- ¿Ya comieron o van a comer?
- ¿Están de buen humor o de mal humor?

La vivienda

Más vocabulario

las afueras	*suburbs; outskirts*
el alquiler	*rent (payment)*
el ama (*m., f.*) de casa	*housekeeper; caretaker*
el barrio	*neighborhood*
el edificio de apartamentos	*apartment building*
el/la vecino/a	*neighbor*
la vivienda	*housing*
el balcón	*balcony*
la entrada	*entrance*
la escalera	*stairs*
el garaje	*garage*
el jardín	*garden; yard*
el patio	*patio; yard*
el pasillo	*hallway*
el sótano	*basement*
la cafetera	*coffee maker*
el electrodoméstico	*electrical appliance*
el horno (de microondas)	*(microwave) oven*
la lavadora	*washing machine*
la luz	*light; electricity*
la secadora	*clothes dryer*
la tostadora	*toaster*
el cartel	*poster*
la mesita de noche	*night stand*
los muebles	*furniture*
alquilar	*to rent*
mudarse	*to move (from one house to another)*

Variación léxica

dormitorio	⟷	alcoba (*Arg.*); aposento (*Rep. Dom.*); recámara (*Méx.*)
apartamento	⟷	departamento (*Arg., Chile, Méx.*); piso (*Esp.*)
lavar los platos	⟷	lavar/fregar los trastes (*Amér. C., Rep. Dom.*)

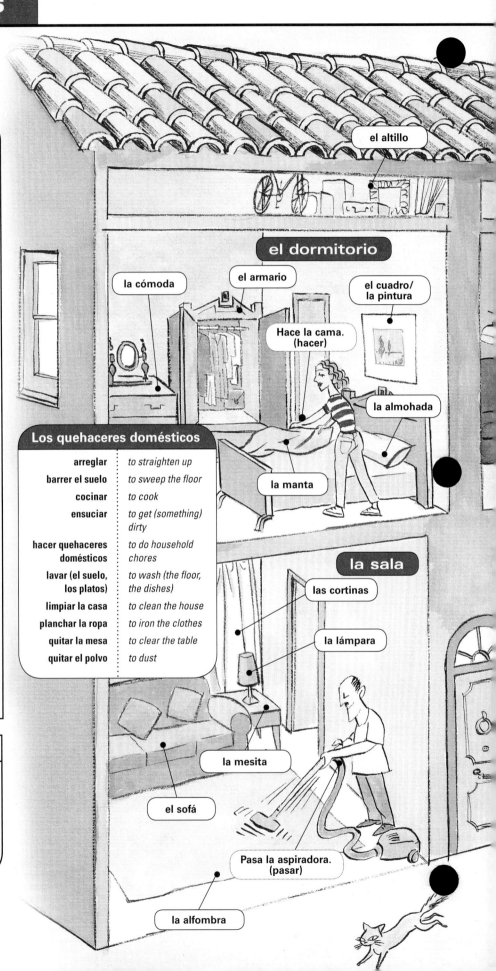

el altillo

el dormitorio

la cómoda

el armario

el cuadro/ la pintura

Hace la cama. (hacer)

la almohada

Los quehaceres domésticos

arreglar	*to straighten up*
barrer el suelo	*to sweep the floor*
cocinar	*to cook*
ensuciar	*to get (something) dirty*
hacer quehaceres domésticos	*to do household chores*
lavar (el suelo, los platos)	*to wash (the floor, the dishes)*
limpiar la casa	*to clean the house*
planchar la ropa	*to iron the clothes*
quitar la mesa	*to clear the table*
quitar el polvo	*to dust*

la manta

la sala

las cortinas

la lámpara

la mesita

el sofá

Pasa la aspiradora. (pasar)

la alfombra

la oficina

el sillón

la pared

el estante

Sacude los muebles.
(sacudir)

la cocina

el refrigerador

el congelador

la cocina, la estufa

el horno

el lavaplatos

Saca la basura.
(sacar)

Práctica

1 **Escuchar** 🎧 Escucha la conversación y completa las oraciones.

1. Pedro va a limpiar primero _____.
2. Paula va a comenzar en _____.
3. Pedro va a _____ en el sótano.
4. Pedro también va a limpiar _____.
5. Ellos están limpiando la casa porque
   _____.

2 **Respuestas** 🎧 Escucha las preguntas y selecciona la respuesta más adecuada. Una respuesta no se va a usar.

____ a. Sí, la alfombra estaba muy sucia.
____ b. No, porque todavía se están mudando.
____ c. Sí, sacudí la mesa y el estante.
____ d. Sí, puse el pollo en el horno.
____ e. Hice la cama, pero no limpié los muebles.
____ f. Sí, después de sacarla de la secadora.

3 **Escoger** Escoge la letra de la respuesta correcta.

1. Cuando quieres tener una lámpara y un despertador cerca de tu cama, puedes ponerlos en _____.
   a. el barrio   b. el cuadro   c. la mesita de noche
2. Si no quieres vivir en el centro de la ciudad, puedes mudarte _____.
   a. al alquiler   b. a las afueras   c. a la vivienda
3. Guardamos (*We keep*) los pantalones, las camisas y los zapatos en _____.
   a. la secadora   b. el armario   c. el patio
4. Para subir de la planta baja al primer piso, usas _____.
   a. la entrada   b. el cartel   c. la escalera
5. Ponemos cuadros y pinturas en _____.
   a. las paredes   b. los quehaceres   c. los jardines

4 **Definiciones** Identifica cada cosa que se describe. Luego inventa tus propias descripciones de algunas palabras y expresiones de **Contextos**.

> **modelo**
>
> Es donde pones los libros.
> *el estante*

1. Es donde pones la cabeza cuando duermes.
2. Es el quehacer doméstico que haces después de comer.
3. Algunos de ellos son las cómodas y los sillones.
4. Son las personas que viven en tu barrio.
5. _____
6. _____

la taza

el vaso

la copa

Pone la mesa.
(poner)

la cuchara

la servilleta

el plato

el tenedor

el cuchillo

el comedor

5 **Completar** Completa estas frases con las palabras más adecuadas.

1. Para tomar vino necesitas…
2. Para comer una ensalada necesitas…
3. Para tomar café necesitas…
4. Para poner la comida en la mesa necesitas…
5. Para limpiarte la boca después de comer necesitas…
6. Para cortar (*to cut*) un bistec necesitas…
7. Para tomar agua necesitas…
8. Para tomar sopa necesitas…

6 **Los quehaceres** Indica quién hace estos quehaceres domésticos en tu casa. Luego contesta las preguntas.

barrer el suelo	lavar los platos	planchar la ropa
cocinar	lavar la ropa	sacar la basura
hacer las camas	pasar la aspiradora	sacudir los muebles

modelo

pasar la aspiradora
Mi hermano y yo pasamos la aspiradora en mi casa.

1. ¿Quién hace más quehaceres, tú o tus compañeros/as?
2. ¿Quiénes hacen la mayoría de los quehaceres, los hombres o las mujeres?
3. ¿Piensas que debes hacer más quehaceres? ¿Por qué?

Comunicación

7

En la oficina de la agente inmobiliaria Escucha la conversación entre el señor Fuentes y una agente inmobiliaria (*real estate agent*). Luego, indica si las conclusiones son **lógica**s o **ilógicas**, según lo que escuchaste.

	Lógico	Ilógico
1. El señor Fuentes quiere tener un jardín grande.	○	○
2. El señor Fuentes vive en los Estados Unidos.	○	○
3. El apartamento está en un barrio ideal para familias con niños.	○	○
4. Al señor Fuentes y a su familia les encanta usar la escalera.	○	○
5. El señor Fuentes necesita comprar electrodomésticos si alquila el apartamento.	○	○

8

La vida doméstica Describe las habitaciones de estas fotos. Para cada foto, incluye por lo menos cinco muebles o adornos (*accessories*) y dos quehaceres que se pueden hacer en esa habitación.

9

Mi casa En parejas, túrnense para hacerse preguntas sobre su vivienda y los quehaceres domésticos.

> **modelo**
>
> ciudad o afueras
> **Estudiante 1:** ¿Dónde vives: en la ciudad o en las afueras?
> **Estudiante 2:** Vivo en la ciudad. ¿Y tú?
> **Estudiante 1:** Yo vivo en las afueras, a quince minutos de la ciudad.

- casa o apartamento
- número de pisos
- vecinos
- muebles

- número de habitaciones
- electrodomésticos en la cocina
- quehacer doméstico más aburrido
- quehacer doméstico menos aburrido

Los quehaceres

Jimena y Felipe deben limpiar el apartamento para poder ir de viaje con Marissa.

SR. DÍAZ Quieren ir a Yucatán con Marissa, ¿verdad?

SRA. DÍAZ Entonces, les sugiero que arreglen este apartamento. Regresamos más tarde.

SR. DÍAZ Les aconsejo que preparen la cena para las 8:30.

MARISSA ¿Qué pasa?

JIMENA Nuestros papás quieren que Felipe y yo arreglemos toda la casa.

FELIPE Y que, además, prepararemos la cena.

MARISSA ¡Pues, yo les ayudo!

(Don Diego llega a ayudar a los chicos.)

FELIPE Tenemos que limpiar la casa hoy.

JIMENA ¿Nos ayuda, don Diego?

DON DIEGO Claro. Recomiendo que se organicen en equipos para limpiar.

MARISSA Mis padres siempre quieren que mis hermanos y yo ayudemos con los quehaceres. No me molesta ayudar. Pero odio limpiar el baño.

JIMENA Lo que más odio yo es sacar la basura.

MARISSA Yo lleno el lavaplatos... después de vaciarlo.

DON DIEGO Juan Carlos, ¿por qué no terminas de pasar la aspiradora? Y Felipe, tú limpia el polvo. ¡Ya casi acaban!

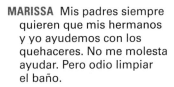

JUAN CARLOS Hola, Jimena. ¿Está Felipe? *(a Felipe)* Te olvidaste del partido de fútbol.

FELIPE Juan Carlos, ¿verdad que mi papá te considera como de la familia?

JUAN CARLOS Sí.

SRA. DÍAZ

SR. DÍAZ

MARISSA

JUAN CARLOS

DON DIEGO

7

(*Los chicos preparan la cena y ponen la mesa.*)

JUAN CARLOS ¿Dónde están los tenedores?

JIMENA Allá.

JUAN CARLOS ¿Y las servilletas?

MARISSA Aquí están.

8

FELIPE La sala está tan limpia. Le pasamos la aspiradora al sillón y a las cortinas. ¡Y también a las almohadas!

JIMENA Yucatán, ¡ya casi llegamos!

9

(*Papá y mamá regresan a casa.*)

SRA. DÍAZ ¡Qué bonita está la casa!

SR. DÍAZ Buen trabajo, muchachos. ¿Qué hay para cenar?

JIMENA Quesadillas. Vengan.

10

SRA. DÍAZ Don Diego, quédese a cenar con nosotros. Venga.

SR. DÍAZ Sí, don Diego. Pase.

DON DIEGO Gracias.

Expresiones útiles

Making recommendations

Le(s) sugiero que arregle(n) este apartamento.
I suggest you tidy up this apartment.

Le(s) aconsejo que prepare(n) la cena para las ocho y media.
I recommend that you have dinner ready for eight thirty.

Organizing work

Recomiendo que se organicen en equipos para limpiar.
I recommend that you divide yourselves into teams to clean.

Yo lleno el lavaplatos... después de vaciarlo.
I'll fill the dishwasher... after I empty it.

¿Por qué no terminas de pasar la aspiradora?
Why don't you finish vacuuming?

¡Ya casi acaban!
You're almost finished!

Felipe, tú quita el polvo.
Felipe, you dust.

Making polite requests

Don Diego, quédese a cenar con nosotros.
Don Diego, stay and have dinner with us.

Venga.
Come on.

Don Diego, pase.
Don Diego, come in.

Additional vocabulary

el plumero *duster*

¿Qué pasó?

1

¿Cierto o falso? Indica si lo que dicen estas oraciones es **cierto** o **falso**. Corrige las oraciones falsas.

	Cierto	Falso
1. Felipe y Jimena tienen que preparar el desayuno.	○	○
2. Don Diego ayuda a los chicos organizando los quehaceres domésticos.	○	○
3. Jimena le dice a Juan Carlos dónde están los tenedores.	○	○
4. A Marissa no le molesta limpiar el baño.	○	○
5. Juan Carlos termina de lavar los platos.	○	○

2

Identificar Identifica quién puede decir estas oraciones.

1. Yo les ayudo, no me molesta hacer quehaceres domésticos.
2. No me gusta sacar la basura, pero es necesario hacerlo.
3. Es importante que termines de pasar la aspiradora, Juan Carlos.
4. ¡La casa está muy limpia! ¡Qué bueno que pasamos la aspiradora!
5. ¡Buen trabajo, chicos! ¿Qué vamos a cenar?

JIMENA   DON DIEGO

FELIPE

SR. DÍAZ   MARISSA

3

Completar Los chicos y don Diego están haciendo los quehaceres. Adivina en qué cuarto está cada uno de ellos.

1. Jimena limpia el congelador. Jimena está en _____.
2. Don Diego limpia el escritorio. Don Diego está en _____.
3. Felipe pasa la aspiradora debajo de la mesa y las sillas. Felipe está en _____.
4. Juan Carlos sacude el sillón. Juan Carlos está en _____.
5. Marissa hace la cama. Marissa está en _____.

4

Mi casa En parejas, pídanse (*ask for*) ayuda para hacer dos quehaceres domésticos. Pueden usar estas frases en su conversación.

> Quiero que me ayudes a (sacar la basura).
> Por favor, ayúdame con...

Ortografía
Mayúsculas y minúsculas

Here are some of the rules that govern the use of capital letters (**mayúsculas**) and lowercase letters (**minúsculas**) in Spanish.

Los estudiantes llegaron al aeropuerto a las dos. Luego fueron al hotel.

In both Spanish and English, the first letter of every sentence is capitalized.

Rubén Blades   Panamá   Colón   los Andes

The first letter of all proper nouns (names of people, countries, cities, geographical features, etc.) is capitalized.

Cien años de soledad   Don Quijote de la Mancha
El País   Muy Interesante

The first letter of the first word in titles of books, films, and works of art is generally capitalized, as well as the first letter of any proper names. In newspaper and magazine titles, as well as other short titles, the initial letter of each word is often capitalized.

la señora Ramos   don Francisco
el presidente   Sra. Vives

Titles associated with people are *not* capitalized unless they appear as the first word in a sentence. Note, however, that the first letter of an abbreviated title is capitalized.

Último   Álex   MENÚ   PERDÓN

Accent marks should be retained on capital letters. In practice, however, this rule is often ignored.

lunes   viernes   marzo   primavera

The first letter of days, months, and seasons is <u>not</u> capitalized.

español   estadounidense   japonés   panameños

The first letter of nationalities and languages is <u>not</u> capitalized.

Profesor Herrera, ¿es cierto que somos venenosas°?

Sí, Pepito. ¿Por qué lloras?

Práctica Corrige las mayúsculas y minúsculas incorrectas.

1. soy lourdes romero. Soy Colombiana.
2. éste Es mi Hermano álex.
3. somos De panamá.
4. ¿es ud. La sra. benavides?
5. ud. Llegó el Lunes, ¿no?

Palabras desordenadas Lee el diálogo de las serpientes. Ordena las letras para saber de qué palabras se trata. Después escribe las letras indicadas para descubrir por qué llora Pepito.

m n a a P á ⌵⌵⌵⌵⌵⌵

s t e m r a ⌵⌵⌵⌵⌵⌵

i g s l é n ⌵⌵⌵⌵⌵⌵

y a U r u g u ⌵⌵⌵⌵⌵⌵⌵

r o ñ e s a ⌵⌵⌵⌵⌵⌵

¡ _orque _e acabo de morder° la _en_u_!

Respuestas: Panamá, martes, inglés, Uruguay, señora. ¡Porque me acabo de morder la lengua!

venenosas *venomous* morder *to bite*

El patio central

En las tardes cálidas° de Oaxaca, México; Córdoba, España, o Popayán, Colombia, es un placer sentarse en **el patio central** de una casa y tomar un refresco disfrutando de° una buena conversación. De influencia árabe, esta característica arquitectónica° fue traída° a las Américas por los españoles. En la época° colonial, se construyeron casas, palacios, monasterios, hospitales y escuelas con patio central. Éste es un espacio privado e íntimo en donde se puede disfrutar del sol y de la brisa° estando aislado° de la calle.

El centro del patio es un espacio abierto. Alrededor de° él, separado por columnas, hay un pasillo cubierto°. Así, en el patio hay zonas de sol y de sombra°. El patio es una parte importante de la vivienda familiar y su decoración se cuida° mucho. En el centro del patio muchas veces hay una fuente°, plantas e incluso árboles°. El agua es un elemento muy importante en la cultura islámica porque simboliza la purificación del cuerpo y del alma°. Por esta razón y para disminuir° la temperatura, el agua en estas construcciones es muy importante. El agua y la vegetación ayudan a mantener la temperatura fresca y el patio proporciona° luz y ventilación a todas las habitaciones.

La distribución

Las casas con patio central eran usualmente las viviendas de familias adineradas°. Son casas de dos o tres pisos. Los cuartos de la planta baja son las áreas comunes: cocina, comedor, sala, etc., y tienen puertas al patio. En los pisos superiores están las habitaciones privadas de la familia.

cálidas *hot* disfrutando de *enjoying* arquitectónica *architectural* traída *brought* época *era* brisa *breeze* aislado *isolated* Alrededor de *Surrounding* cubierto *covered* sombra *shade* se cuida *is looked after* fuente *fountain* árboles *trees* alma *soul* disminuir *lower* proporciona *provides* adineradas *wealthy*

ACTIVIDADES

1 **¿Cierto o falso?** Indica si lo que dicen las oraciones es **cierto** o **falso**. Corrige las falsas.

1. Los patios centrales de Latinoamérica tienen su origen en la tradición indígena.
2. Los españoles llevaron a América el concepto del patio.
3. En la época colonial las casas eran las únicas construcciones con patio central.
4. El patio es una parte importante en estas construcciones, y es por eso que se le presta atención a su decoración.
5. El patio central es un lugar de descanso que da luz y ventilación a las habitaciones.
6. Las fuentes en los patios tienen importancia por razones culturales y porque bajan la temperatura.
7. En la cultura española el agua simboliza salud y bienestar del cuerpo y del alma.
8. Las casas con patio central eran para personas adineradas.
9. Los cuartos de la planta baja son privados.
10. Los dormitorios están en los pisos superiores.

ASÍ SE DICE

La vivienda

el ático, el desván	el altillo
la cobija (Col., Méx.), la frazada (Arg., Cuba, Ven.)	la manta
el escaparate (Cuba, Ven.), el ropero (Méx.)	el armario
el fregadero	*kitchen sink*
el frigidaire (Perú); el frigorífico (Esp.), la nevera	el refrigerador
el lavavajillas (Arg., Esp., Méx.)	el lavaplatos

EL MUNDO HISPANO

Los muebles

- **Mecedora°** La mecedora es un mueble típico de Latinoamérica, especialmente de la zona del Caribe. A las personas les gusta relajarse mientras se mecen° en el patio.

- **Mesa camilla** Era un mueble popular en España hasta hace algunos años. Es una mesa con un bastidor° en la parte inferior° para poner un brasero°. En invierno, las personas se sentaban alrededor de la mesa camilla para conversar, jugar a las cartas o tomar café.

- **Hamaca** Se cree que los taínos hicieron las primeras hamacas con fibras vegetales. Su uso es muy popular en toda Latinoamérica para dormir y descansar.

Mecedora *Rocking chair* se mecen *they rock themselves* bastidor *frame* inferior *bottom* brasero *container for hot coals*

PERFIL

Las islas flotantes del lago Titicaca

Bolivia y Perú comparten el **lago Titicaca**, donde viven **los uros**, uno de los pueblos indígenas más antiguos de América. Hace muchos años, los uros fueron a vivir al lago escapando de **los incas.**

Hoy en día, siguen viviendo allí en **islas flotantes** que ellos mismos hacen con unos juncos° llamados **totora**. Primero tejen° grandes plataformas. Luego, con el mismo material, construyen sus casas sobre las plataformas. La totora es resistente, pero con el tiempo el agua la pudre°. Los habitantes de las islas necesitan renovar continuamente las plataformas y las casas. Sus muebles y sus barcos también están hechos° de juncos. Los uros viven de la pesca y del turismo; en las islas hay unas tiendas donde venden artesanías° hechas con totora.

PERÚ

Lago Titicaca → BOLIVIA

juncos *reeds* tejen *they weave* la pudre *rots it* hechos *made* artesanías *handcrafts*

Conexión Internet

¿Cómo son las casas modernas en los países hispanos?

Use the Web to find more cultural information related to this **Cultura** section.

ACTIVIDADES

2 **Comprensión** Contesta las preguntas.

1. Tu amigo mexicano te dice: "La **cobija** azul está en el **ropero**". ¿Qué quiere decir?
2. ¿Quiénes hicieron las primeras hamacas? ¿Qué material usaron?
3. ¿Qué grupo indígena vive en el lago Titicaca?
4. ¿Qué pueden comprar los turistas en las islas flotantes del lago Titicaca?

3 **Viviendas tradicionales** Escribe cuatro oraciones sobre una vivienda tradicional que conoces. Explica en qué lugar se encuentra, de qué materiales está hecha y cómo es.

12.1 | Relative pronouns

ANTE TODO In both English and Spanish, relative pronouns are used to combine two sentences or clauses that share a common element, such as a noun or pronoun. Study this diagram.

> Mis padres me regalaron **la aspiradora**.
> *My parents gave me the vacuum cleaner.*

> **La aspiradora** funciona muy bien.
> *The vacuum cleaner works really well.*

> La aspiradora **que** mis padres me regalaron funciona muy bien.
> *The vacuum cleaner that my parents gave me works really well.*

> **Lourdes** es muy inteligente.
> *Lourdes is very intelligent.*

> **Lourdes** estudia español.
> *Lourdes is studying Spanish.*

> Lourdes, **quien** estudia español, es muy inteligente.
> *Lourdes, who studies Spanish, is very intelligent.*

Eso fue todo lo que dijimos.

Mi papá se lleva bien con Juan Carlos, quien es como mi hermano.

▶ Spanish has three frequently used relative pronouns. **¡Atención!** Even though interrogative words (**qué**, **quién**, etc.) always carry an accent, relative pronouns never carry a written accent.

que	*that; which; who*
quien(es)	*who; whom; that*
lo que	*that which; what*

▶ **Que** is the most frequently used relative pronoun. It can refer to things or to people. Unlike its English counterpart, *that*, **que** is never omitted.

> ¿Dónde está la cafetera **que** compré?
> *Where is the coffee maker (that) I bought?*

> El hombre **que** limpia es Pedro.
> *The man who is cleaning is Pedro.*

▶ The relative pronoun **quien** refers only to people, and is often used after a preposition or the personal **a. Quien** has only two forms: **quien** (singular) and **quienes** (plural).

> ¿Son las chicas **de quienes** me hablaste la semana pasada?
> *Are they the girls (that) you told me about last week?*

> Eva, **a quien** conocí anoche, es mi nueva vecina.
> *Eva, whom I met last night, is my new neighbor.*

▶ **Quien(es)** is occasionally used instead of **que** in clauses set off by commas.

Lola, **quien** es cubana, es médica.
Lola, who is Cuban, is a doctor.

Su tía, **que** es alemana, ya llegó.
His aunt, who is German, already arrived.

▶ Unlike **que** and **quien(es)**, **lo que** doesn't refer to a specific noun. It refers to an idea, a situation, or a past event and means *what, that which,* or *the thing that.*

Lo que me molesta es el calor.
What bothers me is the heat.

Lo que quiero es una casa.
What I want is a house.

Este supermercado tiene todo
lo que necesito.

A Samuel no le gustó **lo que**
le dijo Violeta.

¡INTÉNTALO! Completa estas oraciones con pronombres relativos.

1. Voy a utilizar los platos ___que___ me regaló mi abuela.
2. Ana comparte un apartamento con la chica a _____ conocimos en la fiesta de Jorge.
3. Esta oficina tiene todo _____ necesitamos.
4. Puedes estudiar en el dormitorio _____ está a la derecha de la cocina.
5. Los señores _____ viven en esa casa acaban de llegar de Centroamérica.
6. Los niños a _____ viste en nuestro jardín son mis sobrinos.
7. La piscina _____ ves desde la ventana es la piscina de mis vecinos.
8. Úrsula, _____ ayudó a mamá a limpiar el refrigerador, es muy simpática.
9. El hombre de _____ hablo es mi padre.
10. _____ te dijo Pablo no es cierto.
11. Tengo que sacudir los muebles _____ están en el altillo una vez al mes.
12. No entiendo por qué no lavaste los vasos _____ te dije.
13. La mujer a _____ saludaste vive en las afueras.
14. ¿Sabes _____ necesita este dormitorio? ¡Unas cortinas!
15. No quiero volver a hacer _____ hice ayer.
16. No me gusta vivir con personas a _____ no conozco.

Práctica

1 **Combinar** Combina elementos de la columna A y la columna B para formar oraciones lógicas.

A

1. Ése es el hombre _____.
2. Rubén Blades, _____.
3. No traje _____.
4. ¿Te gusta la manta _____?
5. ¿Cómo se llama el programa _____?
6. La mujer _____.

B

a. con quien bailaba es mi vecina
b. que te compró Cecilia
c. quien es de Panamá, es un cantante muy bueno
d. que arregló mi lavadora
e. lo que necesito para la clase de matemáticas
f. que comiste en el restaurante
g. que escuchaste en la radio anoche

2 **Completar** Completa la historia sobre la casa que Jaime y Tina quieren comprar, usando los pronombres relativos **que, quien, quienes** o **lo que**.

1. Jaime y Tina son los chicos a _____ conocí la semana pasada.
2. Quieren comprar una casa _____ está en las afueras de la ciudad.
3. Es una casa _____ era de una artista famosa.
4. La artista, a _____ yo conocía, murió el año pasado y no tenía hijos.
5. Ahora se vende la casa con todos los muebles _____ ella tenía.
6. La sala tiene una alfombra _____ ella trajo de Kuwait.
7. La casa tiene muchos estantes, _____ a Tina le encanta.

3 **Oraciones** Javier y Ana acaban de casarse y han comprado (*they have bought*) una casa y muchas otras cosas. Combina sus declaraciones para formar una sola oración con los pronombres relativos **que, quien(es)** y **lo que**.

> **modelo**
>
> Vamos a usar los vasos nuevos mañana. Los pusimos en el comedor.
> *Mañana vamos a usar los vasos nuevos que pusimos en el comedor.*

1. Tenemos una cafetera nueva. Mi prima nos la regaló.

2. Tenemos una cómoda nueva. Es bueno porque no hay espacio en el armario.

3. Esos platos no nos costaron mucho. Están encima del horno.

4. Esas copas me las regaló mi amiga Amalia. Ella viene a visitarme mañana.

5. La lavadora está casi nueva. Nos la regalaron mis suegros.

6. La vecina nos dio una manta de lana. Ella la compró en México.

Comunicación

4

La mudanza Lee el mensaje electrónico de Alejandra a sus amigos. Luego, indica si las conclusiones son **lógicas** o **ilógicas**, según lo que leíste.

De:	Alejandra
Para:	Susana, Roberto, María del Carmen, José, Daniela
Asunto:	Mudanza

Como ustedes ya saben, ¡me mudo el fin de semana! Tengo algunas cosas que no pienso llevar conmigo, así que les escribo para saber si les interesa comprar o llevarse algunas de ellas. La cómoda grande que tiene un espejo está a 50 dólares. Está en muy buena condición. El sillón que está en la sala está a 25 dólares. Es muy cómodo y sólo tiene dos años. La lámpara que está cerca del balcón está a 10 dólares. Estoy regalando los cuadros y la alfombra que están en la sala. Tengo también platos, vasos, tazas y copas que son suyos si les gustan.

¡Casi estoy lista para mi nuevo apartamento! Unos amigos con quienes estudié en la escuela secundaria vinieron a ayudarme a empacar (*pack*). Todo lo que necesito ya está en mi carro. Sebastián, quien vive al lado de mi apartamento, me ayudó a limpiar el apartamento ayer. ¡Está listo! Ustedes sólo tienen que llevarse las cosas que quedan. ☺

Alejandra

	Lógico	Ilógico
1. Alejandra está vendiendo algunos de sus muebles.	○	○
2. Los amigos de Alejandra pueden ir a su apartamento y llevarse algunas de sus cosas sin pagar.	○	○
3. El viejo apartamento de Alejandra está en la planta baja.	○	○
4. Lo que Alejandra necesita es ayuda para llevar sus cosas a su nuevo apartamento.	○	○
5. El vecino de Alejandra es muy antipático.	○	○

5

Entrevista Contesta las preguntas de tu compañero/a.

1. ¿Qué es lo que más te gusta de vivir en las afueras o en la ciudad?
2. ¿Cómo son las personas que viven en tu barrio?
3. ¿Quién es la persona que hace los quehaceres domésticos en tu casa?
4. ¿Hay vecinos que te caen bien? ¿Quiénes?
5. ¿Cuál es el barrio de tu ciudad que más te gusta y por qué?
6. ¿Cuál es el lugar de la casa donde te sientes más cómodo/a? ¿Por qué?
7. ¿Qué es lo que más te gusta de tu barrio?
8. ¿Qué es lo que menos te gusta de tu barrio?

Síntesis

6

Describir Describe en un párrafo los muebles y accesorios que hay en una habitación de tu casa o apartamento, e indica lo que quieres tener en esa habitación pero todavía no tienes. Usa pronombres relativos.

> **modelo**
>
> Las cortinas que me regaló mi mamá son de color verde y están en la sala. La alfombra que compré... Lo que necesito para la sala son dos lámparas para las dos mesitas que tengo y un sofá más cómodo.

12.2   Formal (**usted/ustedes**) commands

ANTE TODO   As you learned in **Lección 11**, the command forms are used to give orders or advice. Formal commands are used with people you address as **usted** or **ustedes**. Observe these examples, then study the chart.

> **Hable** con ellos, don Francisco.
> *Talk with them, Don Francisco.*
>
> **Coma** frutas y verduras.
> *Eat fruits and vegetables.*

> **Laven** los platos ahora mismo.
> *Wash the dishes right now.*
>
> **Beban** menos té y café.
> *Drink less tea and coffee.*

AYUDA

By learning formal commands, it will be easier for you to learn the subjunctive forms that are presented in **Estructura 12.3**, p. 422.

Formal commands (Ud. and Uds.)

Infinitive	Present tense **yo** form	Ud. command	Uds. command
limpiar	limpi**o**	limpi**e**	limpi**en**
barrer	barr**o**	barr**a**	barr**an**
sacudir	sacud**o**	sacud**a**	sacud**an**
decir (e:i)	dig**o**	dig**a**	dig**an**
pensar (e:ie)	piens**o**	piens**e**	piens**en**
volver (o:ue)	vuelv**o**	vuelv**a**	vuelv**an**
servir (e:i)	sirv**o**	sirv**a**	sirv**an**

▶ The **usted** and **ustedes** commands, like the negative **tú** commands, are formed by dropping the final **-o** of the **yo** form of the present tense. For **-ar** verbs, add **-e** or **-en**. For **-er** and **-ir** verbs, add **-a** or **-an**.

Don Diego, quédese a cenar con nosotros.

No se preocupen, yo los ayudo.

▶ Verbs with irregular **yo** forms maintain the same irregularity in their formal commands. These verbs include **conducir, conocer, decir, hacer, ofrecer, oír, poner, salir, tener, traducir, traer, venir,** and **ver.**

> **Oiga,** don Manolo...
> *Listen, Don Manolo...*
>
> **¡Salga** inmediatamente!
> *Leave immediately!*

> **Ponga** la mesa, por favor.
> *Set the table, please.*
>
> **Hagan** la cama antes de salir.
> *Make the bed before leaving.*

▶ Note also that verbs maintain their stem changes in **usted** and **ustedes** commands.

e:ie	o:ue	e:i
No **pierda** la llave.	**Vuelva** temprano, joven.	**Sirva** la sopa, por favor.
Cierren la puerta.	**Duerman** bien, chicos.	**Repitan** las frases.

▶ Verbs ending in **-car**, **-gar**, and **-zar** have a spelling change in the command forms.

sa**car**	**c** ⟶ **qu**	sa**que**, sa**quen**	
ju**gar**	**g** ⟶ **gu**	jue**gue**, jue**guen**	
almor**zar**	**z** ⟶ **c**	almuer**ce**, almuer**cen**	

▶ These verbs have irregular formal commands.

Infinitive	Ud. command	Uds. command
dar	**dé**	**den**
estar	**esté**	**estén**
ir	**vaya**	**vayan**
saber	**sepa**	**sepan**
ser	**sea**	**sean**

▶ To make a formal command negative, simply place **no** before the verb.

No ponga las maletas en la cama.
Don't put the suitcases on the bed.

No ensucien los sillones.
Don't dirty the armchairs.

▶ In affirmative commands, reflexive, indirect, and direct object pronouns are always attached to the end of the verb.

Siénten**se**, por favor.
Síga**me**, Laura.

Acuésten**se** ahora.
Póngan**las** en el suelo, por favor.

▶ **¡Atención!** When a pronoun is attached to an affirmative command that has two or more syllables, an accent mark is added to maintain the original stress.

limpie ⟶ **límpielo**
diga ⟶ **dígamelo**

lean ⟶ **léanlo**
sacudan ⟶ **sacúdanlos**

▶ In negative commands, these pronouns always precede the verb.

No **se** preocupe.
No **me lo** dé.

No **los** ensucien.
No **nos las** traigan.

▶ **Usted** and **ustedes** can be used with the command forms to strike a more formal tone. In such instances, they follow the command form.

Muéstrele usted la foto a su amigo.
Show the photo to your friend.

Tomen ustedes esta mesa.
Take this table.

¡INTÉNTALO! Indica los mandatos (*commands*) afirmativos y negativos correspondientes.

1. escucharlo (Ud.) _____Escúchelo_____ . _____No lo escuche_____ .
2. decírmelo (Uds.) _____ . _____ .
3. salir (Ud.) _____ . _____ .
4. servírnoslo (Uds.) _____ . _____ .
5. barrerla (Ud.) _____ . _____ .
6. hacerlo (Ud.) _____ . _____ .

Práctica

1

Completar La señora González quiere mudarse de casa. Ayúdala a organizarse. Indica el mandato formal de cada verbo.

1. _____ los anuncios del periódico y _____. (Leer, guardarlos)
2. _____ personalmente y _____ las casas usted misma. (Ir, ver)
3. Decida qué casa quiere y _____ al agente. _____ un contrato de alquiler. (llamar, Pedirle)
4. _____ un camión (*truck*) para ese día y _____ la hora exacta de llegada. (Contratar, preguntarles)
5. El día de la mudanza (*On moving day*) _____ tranquila. _____ a revisar su lista para completar todo lo que tiene que hacer. (estar, Volver)
6. Primero, _____ a todos en casa que usted va a estar ocupada. No _____ que usted va a hacerlo todo. (decirles, decirles)
7. _____ tiempo para hacer las maletas tranquilamente. No _____ las maletas a los niños más grandes. (Sacar, hacerles)
8. No _____. _____ que todo va a salir bien. (preocuparse, Saber)

2

¿Qué dicen? Mira los dibujos y escribe un mandato lógico para cada uno. Usa palabras que aprendiste en **Contextos**.

1. _____

2. _____

3. _____

4. _____

5. _____

6. _____

Comunicación

3

La nota Juan va a alquilar su apartamento a dos estudiantes extranjeros. Lee la nota que va a dejar para ellos. Luego, indica si las conclusiones son **lógicas** o **ilógicas**, según lo que leíste.

> Enrique y Pablo:
>
> ¡Bienvenidos a Panamá! Hay jugo, pan, queso y frutas para ustedes en el refrigerador. El supermercado está a treinta minutos en carro desde el apartamento, así que les dejé algunas cosas mientras se instalan (*settle in*). No vayan al supermercado los fines de semana porque hay muchísima gente; los lunes o martes por la noche son los mejores días. No usen el horno porque está descompuesto; usen la estufa o el horno de microondas. Saquen la basura los jueves por la noche porque sólo se la llevan los viernes por la mañana. Por favor, quítense los zapatos en los dormitorios porque la alfombra es muy difícil de limpiar. Diviértanse mucho en Panamá y nos vemos la tercera semana de septiembre.
>
> Juan

	Lógico	Ilógico
1. No es muy conveniente ir al supermercado desde el apartamento de Juan.	○	○
2. Enrique y Pablo deben ir al supermercado los sábados.	○	○
3. Pablo va a hacer un pastel de chocolate durante el verano.	○	○
4. Enrique y Pablo tienen que barrer el suelo de los dormitorios.	○	○

4

Solucionar Trabajen en parejas. Un(a) estudiante presenta los problemas de la columna A y el/la otro/a los de la columna B. Usen mandatos formales y túrnense para ofrecer soluciones.

> **modelo**
>
> **Estudiante 1:** Vilma se torció un tobillo jugando al tenis. Es la tercera vez.
> **Estudiante 2:** *No juegue más al tenis. / Vaya a ver a un especialista.*

1. Se me perdió el libro de español con todas mis notas.
2. A Vicente se le cayó la botella de vino para la cena.
3. ¿Cómo? ¿Se le olvidó traer el traje de baño a la playa?

1. Mis hijas no se levantan temprano. Siempre llegan tarde a la escuela.
2. A mi abuela le robaron (*stole*) las maletas. Era su primer día de vacaciones.
3. Nuestra casa es demasiado pequeña para nuestra familia.

Síntesis

5

El anuncio Prepara el guión (*script*) para un anuncio de televisión. El anuncio debe tratar de un detergente, un electrodoméstico o una agencia inmobiliaria (*real estate agency*). Usa mandatos, los pronombres relativos (**que, quien(es)** o **lo que**) y el **se** impersonal.

> **modelo**
>
> *Compre el lavaplatos Destellos. Tiene todo lo que usted desea. Es el lavaplatos que mejor funciona. Venga a verlo ahora mismo… No pierda ni un minuto más.*

12.3 The present subjunctive

ANTE TODO With the exception of commands, all the verb forms you have been using have been in the indicative mood. The indicative is used to state facts and to express actions or states that the speaker considers to be real and definite. In contrast, the subjunctive mood expresses the speaker's attitudes toward events, as well as actions or states the speaker views as uncertain or hypothetical.

Por favor, quiten los platos de la mesa.

Les aconsejo que preparen la cena.

▶ The present subjunctive is formed very much like **usted**, **ustedes**, and *negative* **tú** commands. From the **yo** form of the present indicative, drop the **-o** ending, and replace it with the subjunctive endings.

INFINITIVE	PRESENT INDICATIVE	VERB STEM	PRESENT SUBJUNCTIVE
hablar	**hablo**	**habl-**	**hable**
comer	**como**	**com-**	**coma**
escribir	**escribo**	**escrib-**	**escriba**

▶ The present subjunctive endings are:

-ar verbs	
-e	-emos
-es	-éis
-e	-en

-er and -ir verbs	
-a	-amos
-as	-áis
-a	-an

Present subjunctive of regular verbs

		hablar	comer	escribir
SINGULAR FORMS	yo	habl**e**	com**a**	escrib**a**
	tú	habl**es**	com**as**	escrib**as**
	Ud./él/ella	habl**e**	com**a**	escrib**a**
PLURAL FORMS	nosotros/as	habl**emos**	com**amos**	escrib**amos**
	vosotros/as	habl**éis**	com**áis**	escrib**áis**
	Uds./ellos/ellas	habl**en**	com**an**	escrib**an**

AYUDA

Note that, in the present subjunctive, **-ar** verbs use endings normally associated with present tense **-er** and **-ir** verbs. Likewise, **-er** and **-ir** verbs in the present subjunctive use endings normally associated with **-ar** verbs in the present tense. Note also that, in the present subjunctive, the **yo** form is the same as the **Ud./él/ella** form.

¡LENGUA VIVA!

You may think that English has no subjunctive, but it does! While once common, it now survives mostly in set expressions such as *If I were you...* and *Be that as it may...*

▶ Verbs with irregular **yo** forms show the same irregularity in all forms of the present subjunctive.

Infinitive	Present indicative	Verb stem	Present subjunctive
conducir	conduzco	**conduzc-**	**conduzca**
conocer	conozco	**conozc-**	**conozca**
decir	digo	**dig-**	**diga**
hacer	hago	**hag-**	**haga**
ofrecer	ofrezco	**ofrezc-**	**ofrezca**
oír	oigo	**oig-**	**oiga**
parecer	parezco	**parezc-**	**parezca**
poner	pongo	**pong-**	**ponga**
tener	tengo	**teng-**	**tenga**
traducir	traduzco	**traduzc-**	**traduzca**
traer	traigo	**traig-**	**traiga**
venir	vengo	**veng-**	**venga**
ver	veo	**ve-**	**vea**

▶ To maintain the **c, g,** and **z** sounds, verbs ending in **-car, -gar,** and **-zar** have a spelling change in all forms of the present subjunctive.

sacar: sa**que**, sa**que**s, sa**que**, sa**que**mos, sa**qué**is, sa**que**n

jugar: jue**gue**, jue**gue**s, jue**gue**, ju**gue**mos, ju**gué**is, jue**gue**n

almorzar: almuer**ce**, almuer**ce**s, almuer**ce**, almor**ce**mos, almor**cé**is, almuer**ce**n

Present subjunctive of stem-changing verbs

▶ **-Ar** and **-er** stem-changing verbs have the same stem changes in the subjunctive as they do in the present indicative.

pensar (e:ie):   p**ie**nse, p**ie**nses, p**ie**nse, pensemos, penséis, p**ie**nsen

mostrar (o:ue):   m**ue**stre, m**ue**stres, m**ue**stre, mostremos, mostréis, m**ue**stren

entender (e:ie):   ent**ie**nda, ent**ie**ndas, ent**ie**nda, entendamos, entendáis, ent**ie**ndan

volver (o:ue):   v**ue**lva, v**ue**lvas, v**ue**lva, volvamos, volváis, v**ue**lvan

▶ **-Ir** stem-changing verbs have the same stem changes in the subjunctive as they do in the present indicative, but in addition, the **nosotros/as** and **vosotros/as** forms undergo a stem change. The unstressed **e** changes to **i**, while the unstressed **o** changes to **u**.

pedir (e:i):   p**i**da, p**i**das, p**i**da, p**i**damos, p**i**dáis, p**i**dan

sentir (e:ie):   s**ie**nta, s**ie**ntas, s**ie**nta, s**i**ntamos, s**i**ntáis, s**ie**ntan

dormir (o:ue):   d**ue**rma, d**ue**rmas, d**ue**rma, d**u**rmamos, d**u**rmáis, d**ue**rman

Irregular verbs in the present subjunctive

▶ These five verbs are irregular in the present subjunctive.

Irregular verbs in the present subjunctive					
	dar	**estar**	**ir**	**saber**	**ser**
SINGULAR FORMS					
yo	dé	esté	vaya	sepa	sea
tú	des	estés	vayas	sepas	seas
Ud./él/ella	dé	esté	vaya	sepa	sea
PLURAL FORMS					
nosotros/as	demos	estemos	vayamos	sepamos	seamos
vosotros/as	deis	estéis	vayáis	sepáis	seáis
Uds./ellos/ellas	den	estén	vayan	sepan	sean

▶ **¡Atención!** The subjunctive form of **hay** (*there is, there are*) is also irregular: **haya**.

General uses of the subjunctive

▶ The subjunctive is mainly used to express: 1) will and influence, 2) emotion, 3) doubt, disbelief, and denial, and 4) indefiniteness and nonexistence.

▶ The subjunctive is most often used in sentences that consist of a main clause and a subordinate clause. The main clause contains a verb or expression that triggers the use of the subjunctive. The conjunction **que** connects the subordinate clause to the main clause.

Main clause	Connector	Subordinate clause
Es muy importante	que	**vayas** al hotel ahora mismo.

▶ These impersonal expressions are always followed by clauses in the subjunctive:

Es bueno que...	**Es mejor que...**	**Es malo que...**
It's good that...	*It's better that...*	*It's bad that...*
Es importante que...	**Es necesario que...**	**Es urgente que...**
It's important that...	*It's necessary that...*	*It's urgent that...*

¡INTÉNTALO!   Indica el presente de subjuntivo de estos verbos.

1. (alquilar, beber, vivir)   que yo ___alquile, beba, viva___
2. (estudiar, aprender, asistir)   que tú _____
3. (encontrar, poder, tener)   que él _____
4. (hacer, pedir, dormir)   que nosotras _____
5. (dar, hablar, escribir)   que ellos _____
6. (pagar, empezar, buscar)   que ustedes _____
7. (ser, ir, saber)   que yo _____
8. (estar, dar, oír)   que tú _____

Práctica y Comunicación

1

Completar Completa las oraciones con el presente de subjuntivo de los verbos entre paréntesis. Luego, empareja las oraciones del primer grupo con las del segundo grupo.

A

1. Es mejor que _____ en casa. (nosotros, cenar) ____
▶ 2. Es importante que _____ las casas colgadas de Cuenca. (tú, visitar) ____
3. Señora, es urgente que le _____ el diente. Tiene una infección. (yo, sacar) ____
4. Es malo que Ana les _____ tantos dulces a los niños. (dar) ____
5. Es necesario que _____ a la una de la tarde. (ustedes, llegar) ____
6. Es importante que _____ temprano. (nosotros, acostarse) ____

B

a. Es importante que _____ más verduras. (ellos, comer)
b. No, es mejor que _____ a comer. (nosotros, salir)
c. Y yo creo que es bueno que _____ a Madrid después. (yo, ir)
d. En mi opinión, no es necesario que _____ tanto. (nosotros, dormir)
e. ¿Ah, sí? ¿Es necesario que me _____ un antibiótico también? (yo, tomar)
f. Para llegar a tiempo, es necesario que _____ temprano. (nosotros, almorzar)

2

Minidiálogos Completa los minidiálogos con expresiones impersonales de una manera lógica.

modelo

Miguelito: Mamá, no quiero arreglar mi cuarto.
Sra. Casas: Es necesario que lo arregles. Y es importante que sacudas los muebles también.

1. **MIGUELITO** Mamá, no quiero estudiar. Quiero salir a jugar con mis amigos.
   SRA. CASAS _____

2. **MIGUELITO** Mamá, es que no me gustan las verduras. Prefiero comer pasteles.
   SRA. CASAS _____

3. **MIGUELITO** ¿Tengo que poner la mesa, mamá?
   SRA. CASAS _____

4. **MIGUELITO** No me siento bien, mamá. Me duele todo el cuerpo y tengo fiebre.
   SRA. CASAS _____

3

Entrevista Contesta las preguntas de tu compañero/a. Explica tus respuestas.

1. ¿Es importante que las personas sepan una segunda lengua? ¿Por qué?
2. ¿Es urgente que los norteamericanos aprendan otras lenguas?
3. Si un(a) norteamericano/a quiere aprender francés, ¿es mejor que lo aprenda en Francia?
4. ¿Es necesario que una persona sepa decir "te amo" en la lengua nativa de su pareja?
5. ¿Es importante que un cantante de ópera entienda italiano?

Subjunctive with verbs of will and influence

ANTE TODO You will now learn how to use the subjunctive with verbs and expressions of will and influence.

Quiero que tengas dientes más blancos.

▶ Verbs of will and influence are often used when someone wants to affect the actions or behavior of other people.

Enrique **quiere** que salgamos a cenar.
Enrique wants us to go out to dinner.

Paola **prefiere** que cenemos en casa.
Paola prefers that we have dinner at home.

▶ Here is a list of widely used verbs of will and influence.

Verbs of will and influence			
aconsejar	to advise	pedir (e:i)	to ask (for)
desear	to wish; to desire	preferir (e:ie)	to prefer
importar	to be important; to matter	prohibir	to prohibit
insistir (en)	to insist (on)	querer (e:ie)	to want
mandar	to order	recomendar (e:ie)	to recommend
necesitar	to need	rogar (o:ue)	to beg
		sugerir (e:ie)	to suggest

▶ Some impersonal expressions, such as **es necesario que, es importante que, es mejor que,** and **es urgente que,** are considered expressions of will or influence.

▶ When the main clause contains an expression of will or influence, the subjunctive is required in the subordinate clause, provided that the two clauses have different subjects.

Main clause	Connector	Subordinate clause
VERB OF WILL		SUBJUNCTIVE

Mi mamá **prefiere** que yo **saque** la basura.

Les sugiero que arreglen este apartamento.

Recomiendo que se organicen en equipos.

▶ Indirect object pronouns are often used with the verbs **aconsejar, importar, mandar, pedir, prohibir, recomendar, rogar,** and **sugerir.**

Te aconsejo que estudies.
I advise you to study.

Les recomiendo que barran el suelo.
I recommend that you sweep the floor.

Le sugiero que vaya a casa.
I suggest that he go home.

Le ruego que no venga.
I'm begging you not to come.

▶ Note that all the forms of **prohibir** in the present tense carry a written accent, except for the **nosotros/as** form: **prohíbo, prohíbes, prohíbe, prohibimos, prohibís, prohíben.**

Ella les **prohíbe** que miren la televisión.
She prohibits them from watching TV.

Nos **prohíben** que nademos en la piscina.
They prohibit us from swimming in the swimming pool.

▶ The infinitive is used with words or expressions of will and influence if there is no change of subject in the sentence.

No quiero **sacudir** los muebles.
I don't want to dust the furniture.

Es importante **sacar** la basura.
It's important to take out the trash.

Paco prefiere **descansar**.
Paco prefers to rest.

No es necesario **quitar** la mesa.
It's not necessary to clear the table.

¡INTÉNTALO! Completa cada oración con la forma correcta del verbo entre paréntesis.

1. Te sugiero que ___vayas___ (ir) con ella al supermercado.
2. Él necesita que yo le _____ (prestar) dinero.
3. No queremos que tú _____ (hacer) nada especial para nosotros.
4. Mis papás quieren que yo _____ (limpiar) mi cuarto.
5. Nos piden que la _____ (ayudar) a preparar la comida.
6. Quieren que tú _____ (sacar) la basura todos los días.
7. Quiero _____ (descansar) esta noche.
8. Es importante que ustedes _____ (limpiar) los estantes.
9. Su tía les manda que _____ (poner) la mesa.
10. Te aconsejo que no _____ (salir) con él.
11. Mi tío insiste en que mi prima _____ (hacer) la cama.
12. Prefiero _____ (ir) al cine.
13. Es necesario _____ (estudiar).
14. Recomiendo que ustedes _____ (pasar) la aspiradora.

Práctica

1 **Completar** Completa el diálogo con verbos de la lista.

cocina	haga	quiere	sea
comas	ponga	saber	ser
diga	prohíbe	sé	vaya

IRENE Tengo problemas con Vilma. Sé que debo hablar con ella. ¿Qué me recomiendas que le (1)_____?

JULIA Pues, necesito (2)_____ más antes de darte consejos.

IRENE Bueno, para empezar me (3)_____ que traiga dulces a la casa.

JULIA Pero chica, tiene razón. Es mejor que tú no (4)_____ cosas dulces.

IRENE Sí, ya lo sé. Pero quiero que (5)_____ más flexible. Además, insiste en que yo (6)_____ todo en la casa.

JULIA Yo (7)_____ que Vilma (8)_____ y hace los quehaceres todos los días.

IRENE Sí, pero siempre que hay fiesta me pide que (9)_____ los cubiertos (*silverware*) y las copas en la mesa y que (10)_____ al sótano por las servilletas y los platos. ¡Es lo que más odio: ir al sótano!

JULIA Mujer, ¡Vilma sólo (11)_____ que ayudes en la casa!

2 **Aconsejar** Lee lo que dice cada persona. Luego da consejos lógicos usando verbos como **aconsejar**, **recomendar** y **prohibir**. Tus consejos deben ser diferentes de lo que la persona quiere hacer.

> **modelo**
> **Isabel:** Quiero conseguir un comedor con los muebles más caros del mundo.
> **Consejo:** *Te aconsejamos que consigas unos muebles menos caros.*

1. **DAVID**   Pienso poner el cuadro del lago de Maracaibo en la cocina.
2. **SARA**   Voy en bicicleta a comprar unas copas de cristal.
3. **SR. ALARCÓN**   Insisto en comenzar a arreglar el jardín en marzo.
4. **SRA. VILLA**   Quiero ver las tazas y los platos de la tienda El Ama de Casa Feliz.
5. **DOLORES**   Voy a poner servilletas de tela (*cloth*) para los cuarenta invitados.
6. **SR. PARDO**   Pienso poner todos mis muebles nuevos en el altillo.
7. **SRA. GONZÁLEZ** Hay una fiesta en casa esta noche, pero no quiero limpiarla.
8. **CARLITOS**   Hoy no tengo ganas de hacer las camas ni de quitar la mesa.

3 **Preguntas** Contesta las preguntas de tu compañero/a. Usa el subjuntivo.

1. ¿Te dan consejos tus amigos/as? ¿Qué te aconsejan? ¿Aceptas sus consejos? ¿Por qué?
2. ¿Qué te sugieren tus profesores que hagas antes de terminar los cursos que tomas?
3. ¿Insisten tus amigos/as en que salgas mucho con ellos?
4. ¿Qué quieres que te regalen tu familia y tus amigos/as en tu cumpleaños?
5. ¿Qué le recomiendas tú a un(a) amigo/a que no quiere salir los sábados con su novio/a?
6. ¿Qué les aconsejas a los nuevos estudiantes de tu universidad?

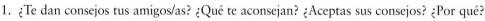

Comunicación

4

¿Qué hacemos? Escucha la conversación entre Alfredo, Juan Carlos y el señor Barriga. Luego, indica si las conclusiones son **lógicas** o **ilógicas**, según lo que escuchaste.

	Lógico	Ilógico
1. El señor Barriga es el dueño del apartamento donde viven Alfredo y Juan Carlos.	○	○
2. Alfredo y Juan Carlos necesitan conseguir dinero.	○	○
3. Es la primera vez que Alfredo y Juan Carlos están en este tipo de situación con el señor Barriga.	○	○
4. El señor Barriga está de buen humor.	○	○
5. No es urgente que Alfredo y Juan Carlos hablen con sus padres.	○	○

5

Hablar Mira la ilustración. En parejas, imaginen que Gerardo es su hermano y necesita ayuda para arreglar su casa y resolver sus problemas románticos y económicos. Usen expresiones impersonales y verbos como **aconsejar**, **sugerir** y **recomendar**.

modelo

Es mejor que arregles el apartamento más a menudo.
Te aconsejo que no dejes para mañana lo que puedes hacer hoy.

Síntesis

6

La doctora Salvamórez Trabajas como columnista del periódico *Panamá y su gente* dándole consejos a las personas con problemas en sus relaciones de pareja. Acabas de recibir un mensaje de Hernán, quien tiene problemas con su novia. Lee su mensaje y después respóndele con consejos usando el subjuntivo.

Estimada doctora Salvamórez:

Mi novia nunca quiere que yo salga de casa. No le molesta que vengan mis amigos a visitarme. Pero insiste en que nosotros sólo miremos los programas de televisión que ella quiere. Necesita saber dónde estoy en cada momento, y yo necesito que ella me dé un poco de independencia. ¿Qué hago?

Hernán

Recapitulación

Completa estas actividades para repasar los conceptos de gramática que aprendiste en esta lección.

1 **Completar** Completa el cuadro con la forma correspondiente del presente de subjuntivo. **24 pts.**

yo/él/ella	tú	nosotros/as	Uds./ellos/ellas
limpie			
	vengas		
		queramos	
			ofrezcan

2 **El apartamento ideal** Completa este folleto (*brochure*) informativo con la forma correcta del presente de subjuntivo. **16 pts.**

¿Eres joven y buscas tu primera vivienda? Te ofrezco estos consejos:

- Te sugiero que primero (tú) (1) _____ (escribir) una lista de las cosas que quieres en un apartamento.

- Quiero que después (2) _____ (pensar) muy bien cuáles son tus prioridades. Es necesario que cada persona (3) _____ (tener) sus prioridades claras, porque el hogar (*home*) perfecto no existe.

- Antes de decidir en qué área quieren vivir, les aconsejo a ti y a tu futuro/a compañero/a de apartamento que (4) _____ (salir) a ver la ciudad y que (5) _____ (conocer) los distintos barrios y las afueras.

- Pidan que el agente les (6) _____ (mostrar) todas las partes de cada casa.

- Finalmente, como consumidores, es importante que nosotros (7) _____ (saber) bien nuestros derechos (*rights*); por eso, deben insistir en que todos los puntos del contrato (8) _____ (estar) muy claros antes de firmarlo (*signing it*).

¡Buena suerte!

RESUMEN GRAMATICAL

12.1 Relative pronouns   pp. 414–415

Relative pronouns	
que	that; which; who
quien(es)	who; whom; that
lo que	that which; what

12.2 Formal commands   pp. 418–419

Formal commands (Ud. and Uds.)		
Infinitive	Present tense yo form	Ud(s). command
limpiar	limpio	limpie(n)
barrer	barro	barra(n)
sacudir	sacudo	sacuda(n)

► Verbs with stem changes or irregular **yo** forms maintain the same irregularity in the formal commands:

hacer: yo **hago** → **Hagan** la cama.

Irregular formal commands	
dar	dé (Ud.); den (Uds.)
estar	esté(n)
ir	vaya(n)
saber	sepa(n)
ser	sea(n)

12.3 The present subjunctive   pp. 422–424

Present subjunctive of regular verbs		
hablar	comer	escribir
hable	coma	escriba
hables	comas	escribas
hable	coma	escriba
hablemos	comamos	escribamos
habléis	comáis	escribáis
hablen	coman	escriban

3 **Relativos** Completa las oraciones con **lo que**, **que** o **quien**. **24 pts.**

1. Me encanta la alfombra _____ está en el comedor.
2. Mi amiga Tere, con _____ trabajo, me regaló ese cuadro.
3. Todas las cosas _____ tenemos vienen de la casa de mis abuelos.
4. Hija, no compres más cosas. _____ debes hacer ahora es organizarlo todo.
5. La agencia de decoración de _____ le hablé se llama Casabella.
6. Esas flores las dejaron en la puerta mis nuevos vecinos, a _____ aún (*yet*) no conozco.
7. Leonor no compró nada, porque _____ le gustaba era muy caro.
8. Mi amigo Aldo, a _____ visité ayer, es un cocinero excelente.

Irregular verbs in the present subjunctive		
dar		dé, des, dé, demos, deis, den
estar	est- +	-é, -és, -é, -emos, -éis, -én
ir	vay- +	
saber	sep- +	-a, -as, -a, -amos, -áis, -an
ser	se- +	

12.4 **Subjunctive with verbs of will and influence**
pp. 426–427

▶ Verbs of will and influence: **aconsejar, desear, importar, insistir (en), mandar, necesitar, pedir** (e:i), **preferir** (e:ie), **prohibir, querer** (e:ie), **recomendar** (e:ie), **rogar** (o:ue), **sugerir** (e:ie)

4 **Preparando la casa** Martín y Ángela van a hacer un curso de verano en Costa Rica y una vecina va a cuidarles (*take care of*) la casa mientras ellos no están. Completa las instrucciones de la vecina con mandatos formales. Usa cada verbo una sola vez y agrega pronombres de objeto directo o indirecto si es necesario. **30 pts.**

arreglar	dejar	hacer	pedir	sacudir
barrer	ensuciar	limpiar	poner	tener

Primero, (1) _____ ustedes las maletas. Las cosas que no se llevan a Costa Rica, (2) _____ en el altillo. Ángela, (3) _____ las habitaciones y Martín, (4) _____ usted la cocina y el baño. Después, los dos (5) _____ el suelo y (6) _____ los muebles de toda la casa. Ángela, no (7) _____ sus joyas (*jewelry*) en el apartamento. (8) _____ cuidado ¡y no (9) _____ nada antes de irse! Por último, (10) _____ a alguien que recoja (*pick up*) su correo.

5 **El circo** Completa esta famosa frase que tiene su origen en el circo (*circus*). **6 pts.**

"¡_____ (Pasar) ustedes y _____ (ver)! El espectáculo va a comenzar."

Lectura

Antes de leer

Estrategia

Locating the main parts of a sentence

Did you know that a text written in Spanish is an average of 15% longer than the same text written in English? Since the Spanish language tends to use more words to express ideas, you will often encounter long sentences when reading in Spanish. Of course, the length of sentences varies with genre and with authors' individual styles. To help you understand long sentences, identify the main parts of the sentence before trying to read it in its entirety. First locate the main verb of the sentence, along with its subject, ignoring any words or phrases set off by commas. Then reread the sentence, adding details like direct and indirect objects, transitional words, and prepositional phrases.

Examinar el texto

Mira el formato de la lectura. ¿Qué tipo de documento es? ¿Qué cognados encuentras en la lectura? ¿Qué te dicen sobre el tema de la selección?

¿Probable o improbable?

Mira brevemente el texto e indica si estas oraciones son probables o improbables.

1. Este folleto° es de interés turístico.
2. Describe un edificio moderno cubano.
3. Incluye algunas explicaciones de arquitectura.
4. Espera atraer° a visitantes al lugar.

Oraciones largas

Mira el texto y busca algunas oraciones largas. Identifica las partes principales de la oración y después examina las descripciones adicionales. ¿Qué significan las oraciones?

folleto *brochure* atraer *to attract* épocas *time periods*

Bienvenidos al Palacio de las Garzas

El palacio está abierto de martes a domingo. Para más información, llame al teléfono 507-226-7000. También puede solicitar° un folleto a la casilla° 3467, Ciudad de Panamá, Panamá.

Después de leer

Ordenar

Pon estos eventos en el orden cronológico adecuado.

_____ El palacio se convirtió en residencia presidencial.

_____ Durante diferentes épocas°, maestros, médicos y banqueros ejercieron su profesión en el palacio.

_____ El Dr. Belisario Porras ocupó el palacio por primera vez.

_____ Los españoles construyeron el palacio.

_____ Se renovó el palacio.

_____ Los turistas pueden visitar el palacio de martes a domingo.

El Palacio de las Garzas° es la residencia oficial del Presidente de Panamá desde 1903. Fue construido en 1673 para ser la casa de un gobernador español. Con el paso de los años fue almacén, escuela, hospital, aduana, banco y por último, palacio presidencial.

En la actualidad el edificio tiene tres pisos, pero los planos originales muestran una construcción de un piso con un gran patio en el centro. La restauración del palacio comenzó en el año 1922 y los trabajos fueron realizados por el arquitecto Villanueva-Meyer y el pintor Roberto Lewis. El palacio, un monumento al estilo colonial, todavía conserva su elegancia y buen gusto, y es una de las principales atracciones turísticas del barrio Casco Viejo°.

Planta baja

EL PATIO DE LAS GARZAS

Una antigua puerta de hierro° recibe a los visitantes. El patio interior todavía conserva los elementos originales de la construcción: piso de mármol°, columnas cubiertas° de nácar° y una magnífica fuente° de agua en el centro. Aquí están las nueve garzas que le dan el nombre al palacio y que representan las nueve provincias de Panamá.

Primer piso

EL SALÓN AMARILLO

Aquí el turista puede visitar una galería de cuarenta y un retratos° de gobernadores y personajes ilustres de Panamá. La principal atracción de este salón es el sillón presidencial, que se usa especialmente cuando hay cambio de presidente. Otros atractivos de esta área son el comedor Los Tamarindos, que se destaca° por la elegancia de sus muebles y sus lámparas de cristal, y el Patio Andaluz, con sus coloridos mosaicos que representan la unión de la cultura indígena y la española.

EL SALÓN DR. BELISARIO PORRAS

Este elegante y majestuoso salón es uno de los lugares más importantes del Palacio de las Garzas. Lleva su nombre en honor al Dr. Belisario Porras, quien fue tres veces presidente de Panamá (1912–1916, 1918–1920 y 1920–1924).

Segundo piso

Es el área residencial del palacio y el visitante no tiene acceso a ella. Los armarios, las cómodas y los espejos de la alcoba fueron comprados en Italia y Francia por el presidente Porras, mientras que las alfombras, cortinas y frazadas° son originarias de España.

solicitar *request* casilla *post office box* Garzas *Herons* Casco Viejo *Old Quarter* hierro *iron* mármol *marble* cubiertas *covered* nácar *mother-of-pearl* fuente *fountain* retratos *portraits* se destaca *stands out* frazadas *blankets*

Preguntas

Contesta las preguntas.

1. ¿Qué sala es notable por sus muebles elegantes y sus lámparas de cristal?

2. ¿En qué parte del palacio se encuentra la residencia del presidente?

3. ¿Dónde empiezan los turistas su visita al palacio?

4. ¿En qué lugar se representa artísticamente la rica herencia cultural de Panamá?

5. ¿Qué salón honra la memoria de un gran panameño?

6. ¿Qué partes del palacio te gustaría (*would you like*) visitar? ¿Por qué? Explica tu respuesta.

Coméntalo

Comenta sobre lo siguiente:

1. ¿Qué tiene en común el Palacio de las Garzas con otras residencias presidenciales u otras casas muy grandes?

2. ¿Te gustaría vivir en el Palacio de las Garzas? ¿Por qué?

3. Imagina que puedes diseñar tu palacio ideal. Describe los planos para cada piso del palacio.

Escritura

Estrategia
Using linking words

You can make your writing sound more sophisticated by using linking words to connect simple sentences or ideas and create more complex sentences. Consider these passages, which illustrate this effect:

Without linking words

En la actualidad el edificio tiene tres pisos. Los planos originales muestran una construcción de un piso con un gran patio en el centro. La restauración del palacio comenzó en el año 1922. Los trabajos fueron realizados por el arquitecto Villanueva-Meyer y el pintor Roberto Lewis.

With linking words

En la actualidad el edificio tiene tres pisos, pero los planos originales muestran una construcción de un piso con un gran patio en el centro. La restauración del palacio comenzó en el año 1922 y los trabajos fueron realizados por el arquitecto Villanueva-Meyer y el pintor Roberto Lewis.

Linking words

cuando	*when*
mientras	*while*
o	*or*
pero	*but*
porque	*because*
pues	*since*
que	*that; who; which*
quien(es)	*who*
sino	*but (rather)*
y	*and*

Tema
Escribir un contrato de arrendamiento°

Eres el/la administrador(a)° de un edificio de apartamentos. Prepara un contrato de arrendamiento para los nuevos inquilinos°. El contrato debe incluir estos detalles:

▶ la dirección° del apartamento y del/de la administrador(a)

▶ las fechas del contrato

▶ el precio del alquiler y el día que se debe pagar

▶ el precio del depósito

▶ información y reglas° acerca de:
     la basura
     el correo
     los animales domésticos
     el ruido°
     los servicios de electricidad y agua
     el uso de electrodomésticos

▶ otros aspectos importantes de la vida comunitaria

---

contrato de arrendamiento *lease* administrador(a) *manager* inquilinos *tenants* dirección *address* reglas *rules* ruido *noise*

Escuchar

Estrategia

Using visual cues

Visual cues like illustrations and headings provide useful clues about what you will hear.

 To practice this strategy, you will listen to a passage related to the following photo. Jot down the clues the photo gives you as you listen.

Preparación

Mira el dibujo. ¿Qué pistas te da para comprender la conversación que vas a escuchar? ¿Qué significa *bienes raíces*?

Ahora escucha

Mira los anuncios de esta página y escucha la conversación entre el señor Núñez, Adriana y Felipe. Luego indica si cada descripción se refiere a la casa ideal de Adriana y Felipe, a la casa del anuncio o al apartamento del anuncio.

Oraciones	La casa ideal	La casa del anuncio	El apartamento del anuncio
Es barato.	___	___	___
Tiene cuatro dormitorios.	___	___	___
Tiene una oficina.	___	___	___
Tiene un balcón.	___	___	___
Tiene una cocina moderna.	___	___	___
Tiene un jardín muy grande.	___	___	___
Tiene un patio.	___	___	___

18G

Bienes raíces

Se vende.
4 dormitorios,
3 baños, cocina
moderna, jardín
con árboles frutales.
B/. 225.000

Se alquila.
2 dormitorios,
1 baño.
Balcón.
Urbanización
Las Brisas. B/. 525

Comprensión

Preguntas

1. ¿Cuál es la relación entre el señor Núñez, Adriana y Felipe? ¿Cómo lo sabes?

2. ¿Qué diferencia de opinión hay entre Adriana y Felipe sobre dónde quieren vivir?

3. Usa la información de los dibujos y la conversación para entender lo que dice Adriana al final. ¿Qué significa "todo a su debido tiempo"?

Contestar

Contesta las preguntas.

1. ¿Qué tienen en común el apartamento y la casa del anuncio con el lugar donde tú vives?

2. ¿Qué piensas de la recomendación del señor Núñez?

3. ¿Qué tipo de sugerencias te da tu familia sobre dónde vivir?

4. ¿Dónde prefieres vivir tú, en un apartamento o en una casa? Explica por qué.

En pantalla

La crisis económica que vive España desde el año 2008 ha repercutido° notablemente en el estilo de vida de los españoles, y sobre todo en la cesta de la compra°, la que se ha visto reducida a productos básicos y de bajo precio. Con este anuncio, la cadena° de supermercados Carrefour promueve° que es posible ahorrar° y mantener el estilo al mismo tiempo, sin tener que prescindir de° productos de calidad a buen precio. Carrefour utiliza el humor y el optimismo ante el duro° tema de la crisis, haciendo que el cliente se sienta identificado y valorado.

Vocabulario útil	
conjunto	*outfit*
cuidar	*to take care of*
prêt-à-porter (*Fr.*)	*ready-to-wear*
suavizante	*fabric softener*

Preparación

¿Lavas tu propia ropa? ¿Tienes lavadora y secadora en casa? ¿Utilizas algún producto especial, como suavizante? ¿Qué importancia tiene para ti el cuidado de la ropa?

Ordenar

Pon en orden lo que ves en el anuncio de televisión. No vas a usar dos elementos.

_____ a. medias   _____ e. cortinas

_____ b. alfombra   _____ f. secadoras

_____ c. copas   _____ g. maquillaje

_____ d. tazas   _____ h. cuadros

Consejos

Prepara una lista de un mínimo de seis consejos para economizar en los siguientes quehaceres domésticos u otros. Utiliza el imperativo y el subjuntivo.

- lavar ropa
- cocinar
- limpiar la casa
- lavar los platos

Anuncio de Carrefour

La Asociación de mujeres que [...] quieren cuidar su ropa...

Le dicen "no" a la crisis y "sí" a Carrefour.

Porque bajamos° los precios [...], Carrefour te viene bien°.

ha repercutido *has had an effect* **cesta de la compra** *shopping basket* **cadena** *chain* **promueve** *promotes* **ahorrar** *to save (money)* **prescindir de** *to do without* **duro** *tough* **bajamos** *we lower* **viene bien** *is just right*

En el sur de la Ciudad de México hay una construcción que fusiona° el funcionalismo con elementos de la cultura mexicana. Es la casa y estudio° en que el muralista Diego Rivera y su esposa, Frida Kahlo, vivieron desde 1934. El creador fue el destacado° arquitecto y pintor mexicano Juan O'Gorman, amigo de la pareja. Como Frida y Diego necesitaban cada uno un lugar tranquilo para trabajar, O'Gorman hizo dos casas, cada una con un taller°, conectadas por un puente° en la parte superior°. En 1981, años después de la muerte de los artistas, se creó ahí el Museo Casa Estudio Diego Rivera y Frida Kahlo. Este museo busca conservar, investigar y difundir° la obra° de estos dos mexicanos, como lo hace el Museo Casa de Frida Kahlo, que vas a ver a continuación.

Vocabulario útil	
jardinero	*gardener*
muros	*walls*
la silla de ruedas	*wheelchair*
las valiosas obras	*valuable works*

Preparación

Imagina que eres un(a) artista, ¿cómo sería (*would be*) tu casa? ¿Sería muy diferente de la casa en donde vives ahora?

¿Cierto o falso?

Indica si lo que dicen estas oraciones es **cierto** o **falso**.

1. La casa de Frida Kahlo está en el centro de México, D.F.
2. La casa de Frida se transformó en un museo en los años 50.
3. Frida Kahlo vivió sola en su casa.
4. Entre las obras que se exhiben está el cuadro (*painting*) *Las dos Fridas*.
5. El jardinero actual (*current*) jamás conoció ni a Frida ni a Diego.
6. En el museo se exhiben la silla de ruedas y los aparatos ortopédicos de Frida.

fusiona *fuses* estudio *studio* destacado *prominent* taller *art studio*
puente *bridge* parte superior *top* difundir *to spread* obra *work*

La casa de Frida

①

El hogar en que nació la pintora Frida Kahlo en 1907 se caracteriza por su arquitectura típicamente mexicana...

②

Esta casa tiene varios detalles que revelan el amor de esta mexicana por la cultura de su país, por ejemplo, la cocina.

③

Uno de los espacios más atractivos de esta casa es este estudio que Diego instaló...

Panamá

El país en cifras

▶ **Área:** 75.420 km² (29.119 millas²), *aproximadamente el área de Carolina del Sur*

▶ **Población:** 3.608.000

▶ **Capital:** La Ciudad de Panamá —1.346.000

▶ **Ciudades principales:** Colón, David

▶ **Moneda:** balboa; es equivalente al dólar estadounidense.

En Panamá circulan los billetes de dólar estadounidense. El país centroamericano, sin embargo, acuña° su propia moneda. "El peso" es una moneda grande equivalente a cincuenta centavos°. La moneda de cinco centavos es llamada frecuentemente "real".

▶ **Idiomas:** español (oficial), lenguas indígenas, inglés *Muchos panameños son bilingües. La lengua materna del 14% de los panameños es el inglés.*

Bandera de Panamá

Panameños célebres

▶ **Mariano Rivera,** beisbolista (1969–)

▶ **Mireya Moscoso,** política (1946–)

▶ **Rubén Blades,** músico y político (1948–)

▶ **Danilo Pérez,** pianista (1966–)

▶ **Jorge Cham,** caricaturista (1976–)

acuña *mints* centavos *cents*
peaje *toll* promedio *average*

Un turista disfruta del bosque tropical colgado de un cable.

Mujer kuna lavando una mola

Ruinas de un fuerte panameño

Increíble pero cierto!

¿Conocías estos datos sobre el Canal de Panamá?

- Gracias al Canal de Panamá, el viaje en barco de Nueva York a Tokio es 3.000 millas más corto.
- Su construcción costó 639 millones de dólares.
- Hoy lo usan en promedio° 39 barcos al día.
- El peaje° promedio cuesta 54.000 dólares.

Lugares • El Canal de Panamá

El Canal de Panamá conecta el océano Pacífico con el océano Atlántico. La construcción de este cauce° artificial empezó en 1903 y concluyó diez años después. Es una de las principales fuentes° de ingresos° del país, gracias al dinero que aportan los más de 14.000 buques° que transitan anualmente por esta ruta y a las actividades comerciales que se han desarrollado° en torno a° ella.

Artes • La mola

La mola es una forma de arte textil de los kunas, una tribu indígena que vive principalmente en las islas San Blas. Esta pieza artesanal se confecciona con fragmentos de tela° de colores vivos. Algunos de sus diseños son abstractos, inspirados en las formas del coral, y otros son geométricos, como en las molas más tradicionales. Antiguamente, estos tejidos se usaban sólo como ropa, pero hoy día también sirven para decorar las casas.

Naturaleza • El mar

Panamá, cuyo° nombre significa "lugar de muchos peces°", es un país muy frecuentado por los aficionados del buceo y la pesca. El territorio panameño cuenta con una gran variedad de playas en los dos lados del istmo°, con el mar Caribe a un lado y el océano Pacífico al otro. Algunas zonas costeras están destinadas al turismo. Otras están protegidas por la diversidad de su fauna marina, en la que abundan los arrecifes° de coral, como el Parque Nacional Marino Isla Bastimentos.

COLOMBIA

Vista de la Ciudad de Panamá

¿Qué aprendiste? Contesta cada pregunta con una oración completa.

1. ¿Cuál es la lengua materna del catorce por ciento de los panameños?

2. ¿A qué unidad monetaria (*monetary unit*) es equivalente el balboa?

3. ¿Qué océanos une el Canal de Panamá?

4. ¿Quién es Mariano Rivera?

5. ¿Qué son las molas?

6. ¿Cómo son los diseños de las molas?

7. ¿Para qué se usan las molas?

8. ¿Cómo son las playas de Panamá?

9. ¿Qué significa "Panamá"?

Conexión Internet Investiga estos temas en Internet.

1. Investiga la historia de las relaciones entre Panamá y los Estados Unidos y la decisión de devolver (*give back*) el Canal de Panamá. ¿Estás de acuerdo con la decisión? Explica tu opinión.

2. Investiga sobre los kunas u otro grupo indígena de Panamá. ¿En qué partes del país viven? ¿Qué lenguas hablan? ¿Cómo es su cultura?

---

cauce *channel* fuentes *sources* ingresos *income* buques *ships* han desarrollado *have developed* en torno a *around* tela *fabric*
cuyo *whose* peces *fish* istmo *isthmus* arrecifes *reefs*

Las viviendas

las afueras	suburbs; outskirts
el alquiler	rent (payment)
el ama (*m., f.*) de casa	housekeeper; caretaker
el barrio	neighborhood
el edificio de apartamentos	apartment building
el/la vecino/a	neighbor
la vivienda	housing
alquilar	to rent
mudarse	to move (from one house to another)

Los cuartos y otros lugares

el altillo	attic
el balcón	balcony
la cocina	kitchen
el comedor	dining room
el dormitorio	bedroom
la entrada	entrance
la escalera	stairs
el garaje	garage
el jardín	garden; yard
la oficina	office
el pasillo	hallway
el patio	patio; yard
la sala	living room
el sótano	basement

Los muebles y otras cosas

la alfombra	carpet; rug
la almohada	pillow
el armario	closet
el cartel	poster
la cómoda	chest of drawers
las cortinas	curtains
el cuadro	picture
el estante	bookcase; bookshelves
la lámpara	lamp
la luz	light; electricity
la manta	blanket
la mesita	end table
la mesita de noche	night stand
los muebles	furniture
la pared	wall
la pintura	painting; picture
el sillón	armchair
el sofá	sofa

Los electrodomésticos

la cafetera	coffee maker
la cocina, la estufa	stove
el congelador	freezer
el electrodoméstico	electric appliance
el horno (de microondas)	(microwave) oven
la lavadora	washing machine
el lavaplatos	dishwasher
el refrigerador	refrigerator
la secadora	clothes dryer
la tostadora	toaster

La mesa

la copa	wineglass
la cuchara	(table or large) spoon
el cuchillo	knife
el plato	plate
la servilleta	napkin
la taza	cup
el tenedor	fork
el vaso	glass

Los quehaceres domésticos

arreglar	to straighten up
barrer el suelo	to sweep the floor
cocinar	to cook
ensuciar	to get (something) dirty
hacer la cama	to make the bed
hacer quehaceres domésticos	to do household chores
lavar (el suelo, los platos)	to wash (the floor, the dishes)
limpiar la casa	to clean the house
pasar la aspiradora	to vacuum
planchar la ropa	to iron the clothes
poner la mesa	to set the table
quitar la mesa	to clear the table
quitar el polvo	to dust
sacar la basura	to take out the trash
sacudir los muebles	to dust the furniture

Verbos y expresiones verbales

aconsejar	to advise
insistir (en)	to insist (on)
mandar	to order
recomendar (e:ie)	to recommend
rogar (o:ue)	to beg
sugerir (e:ie)	to suggest
Es bueno que…	It's good that…
Es importante que…	It's important that…
Es malo que…	It's bad that…
Es mejor que…	It's better that…
Es necesario que…	It's necessary that…
Es urgente que…	It's urgent that…

Relative pronouns	See page 414.
Expresiones útiles	See page 409.

La naturaleza

13

A PRIMERA VISTA
- ¿Está mareada esta mujer?
- ¿Es importante que use ropa cómoda?
- ¿Es necesario que tenga cuidado?
- ¿Le interesa la naturaleza?

La naturaleza

Más vocabulario

el bosque (tropical)	(tropical; rain) forest
el desierto	desert
la naturaleza	nature
la planta	plant
la selva, la jungla	jungle
la tierra	land; soil
el cielo	sky
la estrella	star
la luna	moon
el calentamiento global	global warming
el cambio climático	climate change
la conservación	conservation
la contaminación (del aire; del agua)	(air; water) pollution
la deforestación	deforestation
la ecología	ecology
el/la ecologista	ecologist
el ecoturismo	ecotourism
la energía (nuclear; solar)	(nuclear; solar) energy
la extinción	extinction
la fábrica	factory
el medio ambiente	environment
el peligro	danger
el recurso natural	natural resource
la solución	solution
el gobierno	government
la ley	law
la (sobre)población	(over)population
ecológico/a	ecological
puro/a	pure
renovable	renewable

Variación léxica

hierba ⟷ pasto (*Perú*); grama (*Venez., Col.*); zacate (*Méx.*)

el ave, el pájaro

el cráter

el volcán

el pez (sing.), los peces (pl.)

la vaca

el árbol

la hierba

la flor

el perro

el gato

la nube

el sol

el valle

el sendero

el lago

la piedra

el río

Más vocabulario

el animal	*animal*
la ballena	*whale*
el mono	*monkey*
la tortuga (marina)	*(sea) turtle*

Práctica

1 **Escuchar** 🎧 Mientras escuchas estas oraciones, anota los sustantivos (*nouns*) que se refieren a las plantas, los animales, la tierra y el cielo.

Plantas	Animales	Tierra	Cielo
_____	_____	_____	_____
_____	_____	_____	_____
_____	_____	_____	_____

2 **¿Cierto o falso?** 🎧 Escucha las oraciones e indica si lo que dice cada una es **cierto** o **falso**, según el dibujo.

1. _____   4. _____
2. _____   5. _____
3. _____   6. _____

3 **Seleccionar** Selecciona la palabra que no está relacionada.

1. estrella • gobierno • luna • sol
2. lago • río • mar • peligro
3. vaca • ballena • pájaro • población
4. cielo • cráter • aire • nube
5. desierto • solución • selva • bosque
6. flor • hierba • renovable • árbol

4 **Definir** Define o describe cada palabra. Sigue el modelo.

> *modelo*
>
> el cielo
>
> *El cielo está sobre la tierra y tiene nubes.*

1. la población   4. la naturaleza   7. la ecología
2. un mono   5. un desierto   8. un sendero
3. el calentamiento 6. la extinción
   global

5 **Describir** Describe estas fotos.

Recicla la lata de aluminio. (reciclar)

el envase de plástico

Recoge la botella de vidrio. (recoger)

El reciclaje

Más vocabulario	
cazar	*to hunt*
conservar	*to conserve*
contaminar	*to pollute*
controlar	*to control*
cuidar	*to take care of*
dejar de (+ *inf.*)	*to stop (doing something)*
desarrollar	*to develop*
descubrir	*to discover*
destruir	*to destroy*
estar afectado/a (por)	*to be affected (by)*
estar contaminado/a	*to be polluted*
evitar	*to avoid*
mejorar	*to improve*
proteger	*to protect*
reducir	*to reduce*
resolver (o:ue)	*to resolve; to solve*
respirar	*to breathe*

6

Completar Selecciona la palabra o la expresión adecuada para completar cada oración.

contaminar	destruyen	reciclamos
controlan	están afectadas	recoger
cuidan	mejoramos	resolver
descubrir	proteger	se desarrollaron

1. Si vemos basura en las calles, la debemos _____.
2. Los científicos trabajan para _____ nuevas soluciones.
3. Es necesario que todos trabajemos juntos para _____ los problemas del medio ambiente.
4. Debemos _____ el medio ambiente porque hoy día está en peligro.
5. Muchas leyes nuevas _____ el nivel de emisiones que producen las fábricas.
6. Las primeras civilizaciones _____ cerca de los ríos y los mares.
7. Todas las personas _____ por la contaminación.
8. Los turistas deben tener cuidado de no _____ los lugares que visitan.
9. Podemos conservar los recursos si _____ el aluminio, el vidrio y el plástico.
10. La contaminación y la deforestación _____ el medio ambiente.

Comunicación

7

¿Es importante? Lee este artículo sobre el medio ambiente. Luego, indica si las conclusiones son **lógicas** o **ilógicas**, según lo que leíste.

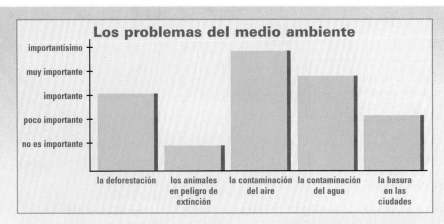

Los problemas del medio ambiente

Para celebrar El día de la Tierra, una estación de radio colombiana hizo una pequeña encuesta entre estudiantes universitarios, donde les preguntaron sobre los problemas del medio ambiente. Se les preguntó cuáles creían que eran los cinco problemas más importantes del medio ambiente. Ellos también tenían que decidir el orden de importancia de estos problemas, del uno al cinco.

Los resultados probaron (*proved*) que la mayoría de los estudiantes están preocupados por la contaminación del aire. Muchos mencionaron que no hay aire puro en las ciudades. El problema número dos para los estudiantes es que los ríos y los lagos están afectados por la contaminación. La deforestación quedó como el problema número tres, la basura en las ciudades como el número cuatro y los animales en peligro de extinción como el cinco.

		Lógico	Ilógico
1.	Expertos en el medio ambiente participaron en la encuesta.	○	○
2.	El problema que más preocupa a los estudiantes puede mejorar si más personas van al trabajo en bicicleta o en metro.	○	○
3.	Los peces están afectados por la contaminación.	○	○
4.	El reciclaje puede ayudar a reducir uno de los problemas de la encuesta.	○	○

8

Escribir una carta Escribe una carta a una fábrica (real o imaginaria) que esté contaminando el medio ambiente. Explica las consecuencias para el medio ambiente que va a tener lo que hace la fábrica, y sugiere algunas ideas para solucionar o reducir el problema. Utiliza por lo menos diez palabras de **Contextos.**

9

Situaciones En parejas, representen una de estas situaciones.

1. Un(a) representante de una agencia ambiental (*environmental*) habla con el/la presidente/a de una fábrica que está contaminando el aire o el río de la zona.

2. Un(a) guía de ecoturismo habla con un(a) turista sobre cómo disfrutar (*enjoy*) de la naturaleza y conservar el medio ambiente.

3. Un(a) representante de la universidad habla con un(a) estudiante sobre la campaña (*campaign*) ambiental de la universidad y lo/la trata de reclutar (*tries to recruit*) para un club que trabaja para la protección del medio ambiente.

Aventuras en la naturaleza

Las chicas visitan un santuario de tortugas, mientras los chicos pasean por la selva.

PERSONAJES MARISSA JIMENA

MARISSA Querida tía Ana María, lo estoy pasando muy bien. Es maravilloso que México tenga tantos programas estupendos para proteger a las tortugas. Hoy estamos en Tulum, y ¡el paisaje es espectacular! Con cariño, Marissa.

MARISSA Estoy tan feliz de que estés aquí conmigo.

JIMENA Es mucho más divertido cuando se viaja con amigos.

(Llegan Felipe y Juan Carlos)

JIMENA ¿Qué pasó?

JUAN CARLOS No lo van a creer.

FELIPE Juan Carlos encontró al grupo. ¡Yo esperaba encontrarlos también! ¡Pero nunca vinieron por mí! Yo estaba asustado. Regresé al lugar de donde salimos y esperé. Me perdí todo el recorrido.

GUÍA A menos que protejamos a los animales de la contaminación y la deforestación, muchos van a estar en peligro de extinción. Por favor, síganme y eviten pisar las plantas.

FELIPE Nos retrasamos sólo cinco minutos... Qué extraño. Estaban aquí hace unos minutos.

JUAN CARLOS ¿Adónde se fueron?

FELIPE No creo que puedan ir muy lejos.

(Se separan para buscar al grupo.)

FELIPE Decidí seguir un río y...

MARISSA No es posible que un guía continúe el recorrido cuando hay dos personas perdidas.

JIMENA Vamos a ver, chicos, ¿qué pasó? Dígannos la verdad.

JUAN CARLOS   **FELIPE**   **GUÍA**

JUAN CARLOS Felipe se cayó. Él no quería contarles.

JIMENA ¡Lo sabía!

FELIPE Y ustedes, ¿qué hicieron hoy?

JIMENA Marissa y yo fuimos al santuario de las tortugas.

MARISSA Aprendimos sobre las normas que existen para proteger a las tortugas marinas.

JIMENA Pero no cabe duda de que necesitamos aprobar más leyes para protegerlas.

MARISSA Fue muy divertido verlas tan cerca.

JUAN CARLOS Entonces se divirtieron. ¡Qué bien!

JIMENA Gracias, y tú, pobrecito, pasaste todo el día con mi hermano. Siempre te mete en problemas.

Expresiones útiles

Talking about the environment

Aprendimos sobre las normas que existen para proteger a las tortugas marinas.
We learned about the regulations that exist to protect sea turtles.

Afortunadamente, ahora la población está aumentando.
Fortunately, the population is now growing.

No cabe duda de que necesitamos aprobar más leyes para protegerlas.
There is no doubt that we need to pass more laws to protect them.

Es maravilloso que México tenga tantos programas estupendos para proteger a las tortugas.
It's marvelous that Mexico has so many wonderful programs to protect the turtles.

A menos que protejamos a los animales de la contaminación y la deforestación, muchos van a estar en peligro de extinción.
Unless we protect animals from pollution and habitat loss, many of them will become endangered.

Additional vocabulary

aumentar
to grow; to get bigger
meterse en problemas
to get into trouble
perdido/a
lost
el recorrido
tour
sobre todo
above all

¿Qué pasó?

1   **Seleccionar** Selecciona la respuesta más lógica para completar cada oración.

1. México tiene muchos programas para _____ a las tortugas.
   a. destruir   b. reciclar   c. proteger
2. Según la guía, muchos animales van a estar en peligro de _____ si no los protegemos.
   a. reciclaje   b. extinción   c. deforestación
3. La guía les pide a los visitantes que eviten pisar _____.
   a. las plantas   b. las piedras   c. la tierra
4. Felipe no quería contarles a las chicas que se _____.
   a. divirtió   b. alegró   c. cayó
5. Jimena dice que debe haber más _____ para proteger a las tortugas.
   a. playas   b. leyes   c. gobiernos

2   **Identificar** Identifica quién puede decir estas oraciones. Puedes usar algunos nombres más de una vez.

1. Fue divertido ver a las tortugas y aprender las normas para protegerlas.
2. Tenemos que evitar la contaminación y la deforestación.
3. Estoy feliz de estar aquí, Tulum es maravilloso.
4. Es una lástima que me pierda el recorrido.
5. No es posible que esa historia que nos dices sea verdad.
6. No van a creer lo que le sucedió a Felipe.
7. Tenemos que cuidar las plantas y los animales.
8. Ojalá que mi hermano no se meta en más problemas.

FELIPE   MARISSA

JIMENA

GUÍA   JUAN CARLOS

3   **Preguntas** Contesta estas preguntas usando la información de **Fotonovela**.

1. ¿Qué lugar visitan Marissa y Jimena?
2. ¿Adónde fueron Juan Carlos y Felipe?
3. Según la guía, ¿por qué muchos animales están en peligro de extinción?
4. ¿Por qué Jimena y Marissa no creen la historia de Felipe?
5. ¿Qué esperaba Felipe cuando se perdió?

4   **El medio ambiente** En parejas, discutan algunos problemas ambientales y sus posibles soluciones. Usen estas preguntas y frases en su conversación.

- ¿Hay problemas de contaminación donde vives?
- Tenemos un problema muy grave de contaminación de...
- ¿Cómo podemos resolver los problemas de la contaminación?

Ortografía
Los signos de puntuación

In Spanish, as in English, punctuation marks are important because they help you express your ideas in a clear, organized way.

> **No podía ver las llaves. Las buscó por los estantes, las mesas, las sillas, el suelo; minutos después, decidió mirar por la ventana. Allí estaban…**

The **punto y coma (;)**, **the tres puntos (…)**, and the **punto (.)** are used in very similar ways in Spanish and English.

> **Argentina, Brasil, Paraguay y Uruguay son miembros de Mercosur.**

In Spanish, the **coma (,)** is not used before **y** or **o** in a series.

> **3,5%**   **29,2%**   **3.000.000**   **$2.999,99**

In numbers, Spanish uses a **coma** where English uses a decimal point and a **punto** where English uses a comma.

 **Cómo te llamas**   **¿Dónde está?**   **¡Ven aquí!**   **Hola**

Questions in Spanish are preceded and followed by **signos de interrogación (¿ ?)**, and exclamations are preceded and followed by **signos de exclamación (¡ !)**.

Práctica   Lee el párrafo e indica los signos de puntuación necesarios.

Ayer recibí la invitación de boda de Marta mi amiga colombiana inmediatamente empecé a pensar en un posible regalo fui al almacén donde Marta y su novio tenían una lista de regalos había de todo copas cafeteras tostadoras finalmente decidí regalarles un perro ya sé que es un regalo extraño pero espero que les guste a los dos

¿Palabras de amor?   El siguiente diálogo tiene diferentes significados (*meanings*) dependiendo de los signos de puntuación que utilices y el lugar donde los pongas. Intenta encontrar los diferentes significados.

JULIÁN	me quieres
MARISOL	no puedo vivir sin ti
JULIÁN	me quieres dejar
MARISOL	no me parece mala idea
JULIÁN	no eres feliz conmigo
MARISOL	no soy feliz

EN DETALLE

¡Los Andes se mueven!

Los Andes, la cadena° de montañas más extensa de América, son conocidos como "la espina dorsal° de Suramérica". Sus 7.240 kilómetros (4.500 millas) van desde el norte° de la región entre Venezuela y Colombia, hasta el extremo sur°, entre Argentina y Chile, y pasan por casi todos los países suramericanos. La cordillera° de los Andes, formada hace 27 millones de años, es la segunda más alta del mundo, después de la del Himalaya (aunque° esta última es mucho más "joven", ya que se formó hace apenas cinco millones de años).

Para poder atravesar° de un lado a otro de los Andes, existen varios pasos o puertos° de montaña. Situados a grandes alturas°, son generalmente estrechos° y peligrosos. En algunos de ellos hay, también, vías ferroviarias°.

De acuerdo con° varias instituciones científicas, la cordillera de los Andes se eleva° y se hace más angosta° cada año. La capital de Chile se acerca° a la capital de Argentina a un ritmo° de 19,4 milímetros por año. Si ese ritmo se mantiene°, Santiago y Buenos Aires podrían unirse° en unos... 63 millones de años, ¡casi el mismo tiempo que ha transcurrido° desde la extinción de los dinosaurios!

Arequipa, Perú

Los Andes en números

3 Cordilleras que forman los Andes: Las cordilleras Central, Occidental y Oriental

900 (A.C.°) Año aproximado en que empezó el desarrollo° de la cultura chavín, en los Andes peruanos

600 Número aproximado de volcanes que hay en los Andes

6.960 Metros (22.835 pies) de altura del Aconcagua (Argentina), el pico° más alto de los Andes

cadena *range* **espina dorsal** *spine* **norte** *north* **sur** *south* **cordillera** *mountain range* **aunque** *although* **atravesar** *to cross* **puertos** *passes* **alturas** *heights* **estrechos** *narrow* **vías ferroviarias** *railroad tracks* **De acuerdo con** *According to* **se eleva** *rises* **angosta** *narrow* **se acerca** *gets closer* **ritmo** *rate* **se mantiene** *keeps going* **podrían unirse** *could join together* **ha transcurrido** *has gone by* **A.C.** *Before Christ* **desarrollo** *development* **pico** *peak*

ACTIVIDADES

1 **Escoger** Escoge la opción que completa mejor cada oración.

1. Los Andes son la cadena montañosa más extensa del…
   a. mundo.　　b. continente americano.　　c. hemisferio norte.

2. "La espina dorsal de Suramérica" es…
   a. los Andes.　　b. el Himalaya.　　c. el Aconcagua.

3. La cordillera de los Andes se extiende…
   a. de este a oeste.　　b. de sur a oeste.　　c. de norte a sur.

4. El Himalaya y los Andes tienen…
   a. diferente altura.　　b. la misma altura.　　c. el mismo color.

5. Es posible atravesar los Andes por medio de…
   a. montañas　　b. puertos　　c. metro

6. En algunos de los puertos de montaña de los Andes hay…
   a. puertas.　　b. vías ferroviarias.　　c. cordilleras.

7. En 63 millones de años, Buenos Aires y Santiago podrían…
   a. separarse.　　b. desarrollarse.　　c. unirse.

8. El Aconcagua es…
   a. una montaña.　　b. un grupo indígena.　　c. un volcán.

ASÍ SE DICE

La naturaleza

el arco iris	*rainbow*
la cascada; la catarata	*waterfall*
el cerro; la colina; la loma	*hill, hillock*
la cima; la cumbre; el tope (Col.)	*summit; mountaintop*
la maleza; los rastrojos (Col.); la yerba mala (Cuba); los hierbajos (Méx.); los yuyos (Arg.)	*weeds*
la niebla	*fog*

EL MUNDO HISPANO

Cuerpos° de agua

- **Lago de Maracaibo** es el lago natural más grande de Suramérica y tiene una conexión directa y natural con el mar.

- **Lago Titicaca** es el lago navegable más alto del mundo. Se encuentra a más de 3.800 metros de altitud.

- **Bahía Mosquito** es una bahía bioluminiscente. En sus aguas viven unos microorganismos que emiten luz° cuando sienten que algo agita° el agua.

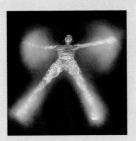

Cuerpos *Bodies* emiten luz *emit light* agita *shakes*

PERFIL

La Sierra Nevada de Santa Marta

La Sierra Nevada de Santa Marta es una cadena de montañas en la costa norte de Colombia. Se eleva abruptamente desde las costas del mar Caribe y en apenas 42 kilómetros llega a una altura de 5.775 metros

(18.947 pies) en sus picos nevados°. Tiene las montañas más altas de Colombia y es la formación montañosa costera° más alta del mundo.

Los pueblos indígenas que habitan allí lograron° mantener los frágiles ecosistemas de estas montañas a través de° un sofisticado sistema de terrazas° y senderos empedrados° que permitieron° el control de las aguas en una región de

muchas lluvias, evitando así la erosión de la tierra. La Sierra fue nombrada Reserva de la Biosfera por la UNESCO en 1979.

nevados *snowcapped* costera *coastal* lograron *managed* a través de *by means of* terrazas *terraces* empedrados *cobblestone* permitieron *allowed*

Conexión Internet

¿Dónde se puede hacer ecoturismo en Latinoamérica?	Use the Web to find more cultural information related to this **Cultura** section.

ACTIVIDADES

2 **Comprensión** Indica si lo que dice cada oración es **cierto** o **falso**. Corrige la información falsa.

1. En Colombia, *weeds* se dice **hierbajos**.
2. El lago Titicaca es el más grande del mundo.
3. La Sierra Nevada de Santa Marta es la formación montañosa costera más alta del mundo.
4. Los indígenas destruyeron el ecosistema de Santa Marta.

3 **Maravillas de la naturaleza** Escribe un párrafo breve donde describas alguna maravilla de la naturaleza que has (*you have*) visitado y que te impresionó. Puede ser cualquier (*any*) sitio natural: un río, una montaña, una selva, etc.

13.1 The subjunctive with verbs of emotion

ANTE TODO In the previous lesson, you learned how to use the subjunctive with expressions of will and influence. You will now learn how to use the subjunctive with verbs and expressions of emotion.

Main clause		Subordinate clause

Marta **espera** (que) yo **vaya** al lago este fin de semana.

▶ When the verb in the main clause of a sentence expresses an emotion or feeling, such as hope, fear, joy, pity, or surprise, the subjunctive is required in the subordinate clause.

Nos alegramos de que te **gusten** las flores.
We are happy that you like the flowers.

Siento que tú no **puedas** venir mañana.
I'm sorry that you can't come tomorrow.

Temo que Ana no **pueda** ir mañana con nosotros.
I'm afraid that Ana won't be able to go with us tomorrow.

Le **sorprende** que Juan **sea** tan joven.
It surprises him that Juan is so young.

Es una lástima que ellos no estén aquí con nosotros.

Me alegro de que te diviertas.

Common verbs and expressions of emotion

alegrarse (de)	*to be happy*	**tener miedo (de)**	*to be afraid (of)*
esperar	*to hope; to wish*	**es extraño**	*it's strange*
gustar	*to like*	**es una lástima**	*it's a shame*
molestar	*to bother*	**es ridículo**	*it's ridiculous*
sentir (e:ie)	*to be sorry; to regret*	**es terrible**	*it's terrible*
sorprender	*to surprise*	**es triste**	*it's sad*
temer	*to be afraid*	**ojalá (que)**	*I hope (that); I wish (that)*

CONSULTA

Certain verbs of emotion, like **gustar, molestar,** and **sorprender,** require indirect object pronouns. For more examples, see **Estructura 7.4,** pp. 246–247.

Me molesta que la gente no **recicle** el plástico.
It bothers me that people don't recycle plastic.

Es triste que **tengamos** problemas como el cambio climático.
It's sad that we have problems like climate change.

▶ As with expressions of will and influence, the infinitive, not the subjunctive, is used after an expression of emotion when there is no change of subject. Compare these sentences.

Temo **llegar** tarde.
I'm afraid I'll arrive late.

Temo que mi novio **llegue** tarde.
I'm afraid my boyfriend will arrive late.

▶ The expression **ojalá (que)** means *I hope* or *I wish,* and it is always followed by the subjunctive. Note that the use of **que** with this expression is optional.

Ojalá (que) se conserven nuestros recursos naturales.
I hope (that) our natural resources will be conserved.

Ojalá (que) recojan la basura hoy.
I hope (that) they collect the garbage today.

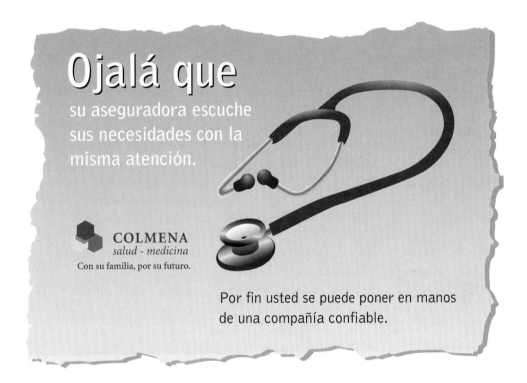

Ojalá que

su aseguradora escuche sus necesidades con la misma atención.

COLMENA
salud - medicina
Con su familia, por su futuro.

Por fin usted se puede poner en manos de una compañía confiable.

¡INTÉNTALO! Completa las oraciones con las formas correctas de los verbos.

1. Ojalá que ellos __descubran__ (descubrir) nuevas formas de energía.
2. Espero que Ana nos _____ (ayudar) a recoger la basura en la carretera.
3. Es una lástima que la gente no _____ (reciclar) más.
4. Esperamos _____ (proteger) a las tortugas marinas que llegan a esta playa.
5. Me alegro de que mis amigos _____ (querer) conservar la naturaleza.
6. Espero que tú _____ (venir) a la reunión (*meeting*) del Club de Ecología.
7. Es malo _____ (contaminar) el medio ambiente.
8. A mis padres les gusta que nosotros _____ (participar) en la reunión.
9. Es terrible que nuestras ciudades _____ (estar) afectadas por la contaminación.
10. Ojalá que yo _____ (poder) hacer algo para reducir el calentamiento global.

Práctica

1

Completar Completa el diálogo con palabras de la lista.

Bogotá, Colombia

alegro	molesta	salga
encuentren	ojalá	tengo miedo de
estén	puedan	vayan
lleguen	reduzcan	visitar

OLGA Me alegro de que Adriana y Raquel (1)_____ a Colombia. ¿Van a estudiar?

SARA Sí. Es una lástima que (2)_____ una semana tarde. Ojalá que la universidad las ayude a buscar casa. (3)_____ que no consigan dónde vivir.

OLGA Me (4)_____ que seas tan pesimista, pero sí, yo también espero que (5)_____ gente simpática y que hablen mucho español.

SARA Sí, ojalá. Van a hacer un estudio sobre la deforestación en las costas. Es triste que en tantos países los recursos naturales (6)_____ en peligro.

OLGA Pues, me (7)_____ de que no se queden mucho en la capital por la contaminación. (8)_____ tengan tiempo de viajar por el país.

SARA Sí, espero que (9)_____ ir a Medellín. Sé que también quieren (10)_____ la Catedral de Sal de Zipaquirá.

2

Transformar Transforma estos elementos en oraciones completas para formar un diálogo entre Juan y la madre de Raquel. Añade palabras si es necesario.

1. Juan, / esperar / (tú) escribirle / Raquel. / Ser / tu / novia. / Ojalá / no / sentirse / sola

2. molestarme / (usted) decirme / lo que / tener / hacer. / Ahora / mismo / le / estar / escribiendo

3. alegrarme / oírte / decir / eso. / Ser / terrible / estar / lejos / cuando / nadie / recordarte

4. señora, / ¡yo / tener / miedo de / (ella) no recordarme / mí! / Ser / triste / estar / sin / novia

5. ser / ridículo / (tú) sentirte / así. / Tú / saber / ella / querer / casarse / contigo

6. ridículo / o / no, / sorprenderme / (todos) preocuparse / ella / y / (nadie) acordarse de / mí

Comunicación

3

¿Lógico o ilógico? Lee el mensaje electrónico que Raquel le escribió a Juan. Luego, indica si las conclusiones son **lógicas** o **ilógicas**, según lo que leíste.

De:	Raquel
Para:	Juan
Asunto:	¡Hola!

Hola, Juan:

Mi amor, siento no escribirte más frecuentemente. La verdad es que estoy muy ocupada todo el tiempo. No sabes cuánto me estoy divirtiendo en Colombia. Me sorprende haber podido adaptarme tan bien. Es bueno tener tanto trabajo. Aprendo mucho más aquí que en el laboratorio de la universidad. Me encanta que me den responsabilidades y que compartan sus muchos conocimientos conmigo. Ay, pero pienso mucho en ti. Qué triste es que no podamos estar juntos por tanto tiempo. Ojalá que los días pasen rápido. Bueno, querido, es todo por ahora. Escríbeme pronto.

Te quiero y te extraño mucho,

Raquel

AYUDA

Echar de menos (a alguien) and **extrañar (a alguien)** are two ways of saying *to miss (someone)*.

	Lógico	Ilógico
1. Juan es el novio de Raquel.	○	○
2. Raquel no tiene mucho tiempo para comunicarse con Juan.	○	○
3. A Raquel le molesta tener mucho trabajo.	○	○
4. Raquel teme no ver a Juan nunca más.	○	○
5. Raquel estudió ciencias.	○	○

4

Comentar En parejas, túrnense para expresar opiniones sobre su comunidad, sus clases, su gobierno o algún otro tema, usando expresiones como **me alegro de que**, **temo que** y **es extraño que**. Luego, reaccionen a los comentarios de su compañero/a.

modelo

Estudiante 1: Me alegro de que vayan a limpiar el río.
Estudiante 2: Yo también. Me preocupa que el agua del río esté tan sucia.

Síntesis

5

Anuncio de servicio público Escribe un anuncio de servicio público sobre un problema ecológico y ofrece posible soluciones. Incluye en el anuncio verbos como **sentir**, **sorprender** y **temer**, y expresiones como **es terrible** y **ojalá**.

13.2 # The subjunctive with doubt, disbelief, and denial

 Just as the subjunctive is required with expressions of emotion, influence, and will, it is also used with expressions of doubt, disbelief, and denial.

Main clause		Subordinate clause
Dudan	que	su hijo les **diga** la verdad.

▶ The subjunctive is always used in a subordinate clause when there is a change of subject and the expression in the main clause implies negation or uncertainty.

No creo que puedan ir muy lejos.

No es posible que el guía continúe el recorrido sin ustedes.

▶ Here is a list of some common expressions of doubt, disbelief, or denial.

Expressions of doubt, disbelief, or denial

dudar	*to doubt*	**no es seguro**	*it's not certain*
negar (e:ie)	*to deny*	**no es verdad**	*it's not true*
no creer	*not to believe*	**es imposible**	*it's impossible*
no estar seguro/a (de)	*not to be sure*	**es improbable**	*it's improbable*
no es cierto	*it's not true;* *it's not certain*	**(no) es posible**	*it's (not) possible*
		(no) es probable	*it's (not) probable*

El gobierno **niega** que el agua **esté** contaminada.
The government denies that the water is contaminated.

Dudo que el gobierno **resuelva** el problema.
I doubt that the government will solve the problem.

Es probable que **haya** menos bosques y selvas en el futuro.
It's probable that there will be fewer forests and jungles in the future.

No es verdad que mi hermano **estudie** ecología.
It's not true that my brother studies ecology.

¡LENGUA VIVA!

In English, the expression *it is probable* indicates a fairly high degree of certainty. In Spanish, however, **es probable** implies uncertainty and therefore triggers the subjunctive in the subordinate clause: **Es probable que venga Elena (pero quizás no puede).**

▶ The indicative is used in a subordinate clause when there is no doubt or uncertainty in the main clause. Here is a list of some expressions of certainty.

Expressions of certainty

no dudar	*not to doubt*	**estar seguro/a (de)**	*to be sure*
no cabe duda de	*there is no doubt*	**es cierto**	*it's true; it's certain*
no hay duda de	*there is no doubt*	**es seguro**	*it's certain*
no negar (e:ie)	*not to deny*	**es verdad**	*it's true*
creer	*to believe*	**es obvio**	*it's obvious*

No negamos que **hay** demasiados carros en las carreteras.
We don't deny that there are too many cars on the highways.

No hay duda de que el Amazonas **es** uno de los ríos más largos.
There is no doubt that the Amazon is one of the longest rivers.

Es verdad que Colombia **es** un país bonito.
It's true that Colombia is a beautiful country.

Es obvio que las ballenas **están** en peligro de extinción.
It's obvious that whales are in danger of extinction.

▶ In affirmative sentences, the verb **creer** expresses belief or certainty, so it is followed by the indicative. In negative sentences, however, when doubt is implied, **creer** is followed by the subjunctive.

Creo que **debemos** usar exclusivamente la energía solar.
I believe we should use solar energy exclusively.

No creo que **haya** vida en el planeta Marte.
I don't believe that there is life on the planet Mars.

▶ The expressions **quizás** and **tal vez** are usually followed by the subjunctive because they imply doubt about something.

Quizás haga sol mañana.
Perhaps it will be sunny tomorrow.

Tal vez veamos la luna esta noche.
Perhaps we will see the moon tonight.

¡INTÉNTALO! Completa estas oraciones con la forma correcta del verbo.

1. Dudo que ellos __trabajen__ (trabajar).
2. Es cierto que él _____ (comer) mucho.
3. Es imposible que ellos _____ (salir).
4. Es probable que ustedes _____ (ganar).
5. No creo que ella _____ (volver).
6. Es posible que nosotros _____ (ir).
7. Dudamos que tú _____ (reciclar).
8. Creo que ellos _____ (jugar) al fútbol.
9. No niego que ustedes _____ (estudiar).
10. Es posible que ella no _____ (venir) a casa.
11. Es probable que Lucio y Carmen _____ (dormir).
12. Es posible que mi prima Marta _____ (llamar).
13. Tal vez Juan no nos _____ (oír).
14. No es cierto que Paco y Daniel nos _____ (ayudar).

Práctica

1 **Escoger** Escoge las respuestas correctas para completar el diálogo.

RAÚL Ustedes dudan que yo realmente (1)_____ (estudio/estudie). No niego que a veces me (2)_____ (divierto/divierta) demasiado, pero no cabe duda de que (3)_____ (tomo/tome) mis estudios en serio. Estoy seguro de que cuando me vean graduarme van a pensar de manera diferente. Creo que no (4)_____ (tienen/tengan) razón con sus críticas.

PAPÁ Es posible que tu mamá y yo no (5)_____ (tenemos/tengamos) razón. Es cierto que a veces (6)_____ (dudamos/dudemos) de ti. Pero no hay duda de que te (7)_____ (pasas/pases) toda la noche en Internet y oyendo música. No es nada seguro que (8)_____ (estás/estés) estudiando.

RAÚL Es verdad que (9)_____ (uso/use) mucho la computadora pero, ¡piensen! ¿No es posible que (10)_____ (es/sea) para buscar información para mis clases? ¡No hay duda de que Internet (11)_____ (es/sea) el mejor recurso del mundo! Es obvio que ustedes (12)_____ (piensan/piensen) que no hago nada, pero no es cierto.

PAPÁ No dudo que esta conversación nos (13)_____ (va/vaya) a ayudar. Pero tal vez esta noche (14)_____ (puedes/puedas) trabajar sin música. ¿Está bien?

2 **Dudas** Carolina es una chica que siempre miente. Expresa tus dudas sobre lo que Carolina está diciendo ahora. Usa las expresiones entre paréntesis para tus respuestas.

> **modelo**
>
> El próximo año Marta y yo vamos de vacaciones por diez meses. (dudar)
>
> *¡Ja! Dudo que vayan de vacaciones por ese tiempo. ¡Ustedes no son ricas!*

1. Estoy escribiendo una novela en español. (no creer)

2. Mi tía es la directora de PETA. (no ser verdad)

3. Dos profesores míos juegan para los Osos (*Bears*) de Chicago. (ser imposible)

4. Mi mejor amiga conoce al chef Bobby Flay. (no ser cierto)

5. Mi padre es dueño del Centro Rockefeller. (no ser posible)

6. Yo ya tengo un doctorado (*doctorate*) en lenguas. (ser improbable)

AYUDA

Here are some useful expressions to say that you don't believe someone.

¡Qué va!

¡Imposible!

¡No te creo!

¡Es mentira!

Comunicación

3

Te ruego Escucha la conversación entre un padre y su hija. Luego, indica si las conclusiones son **lógicas** o **ilógicas**, según lo que escuchaste.

	Lógico	Ilógico
1. A Juanita le interesa la ecología.	○	○
2. Juanita y su papá viven en la selva.	○	○
3. El papá de Juanita no está seguro de que ella deba ir.	○	○
4. Es improbable que Juanita se enferme de malaria.	○	○
5. Es cierto que Juanita va a llevar un abrigo, jeans y suéteres en sus maletas.	○	○

4

El futuro ¿Cómo piensas que va a ser el futuro del medio ambiente? Descríbelo usando verbos como **(no) dudar, (no) creer** y **(no) estar seguro/a de**, y expresiones como **(no) es posible** y **es obvio**.

> **modelo**
>
> Creo que los gobiernos van a crear leyes más estrictas para cuidar el medio ambiente, pero dudo que el problema del calentamiento global cambie mucho...

5

Entrevista En parejas, piensen en un problema ecológico y preparen una entrevista de un mínimo de cinco preguntas entre un(a) periodista y un(a) ecologista.

> **modelo**
>
> **Periodista:** ¿Qué piensa de la construcción de la fábrica de Química Comercial?
> **Ecologista:** No cabe duda de que los ecosistemas del lago y del parque nacional van a estar afectados por esta fábrica.
> **Periodista:** ¿Cómo van a estar afectados?
> **Ecologista:** Es posible que...

Síntesis

6

Escribir Escribe un párrafo sobre los problemas del medio ambiente en tu comunidad. Incluye tus opiniones sobre esos problemas y ofrece recomendaciones prácticas para mejorar la situación.

13.3 The subjunctive with conjunctions

ANTE TODO Conjunctions are words or phrases that connect other words and clauses in sentences. Certain conjunctions commonly introduce adverbial clauses, which describe *how, why, when,* and *where* an action takes place.

Main clause	Conjunction	Adverbial clause
Vamos a visitar a Carlos	**antes de que**	**regrese** a California.

Muchos animales van a estar en peligro de extinción, a menos que los protejamos.

Marissa habla con Jimena antes de que lleguen los chicos.

▶ With certain conjunctions, the subjunctive is used to express a hypothetical situation, uncertainty as to whether an action or event will take place, or a condition that may or may not be fulfilled.

Voy a dejar un recado **en caso de que Gustavo me llame**.
I'm going to leave a message in case Gustavo calls me.

Voy al supermercado **para que tengas** algo de comer.
I'm going to the store so that you'll have something to eat.

▶ Here is a list of the conjunctions that always require the subjunctive.

Conjunctions that require the subjunctive

a menos que	*unless*	**en caso (de) que**	*in case (that)*
antes (de) que	*before*	**para que**	*so that*
con tal (de) que	*provided that*	**sin que**	*without*

Algunos animales van a morir **a menos que** haya leyes para protegerlos.
Some animals are going to die unless there are laws to protect them.

Ellos nos llevan a la selva **para que** veamos las plantas tropicales.
They are taking us to the jungle so that we may see the tropical plants.

▶ The infinitive, not **que** + [*subjunctive*], is used after the prepositions **antes de, para,** and **sin** when there is no change of subject. **¡Atención!** While you may use a present participle with the English equivalent of these phrases, in Spanish you cannot.

Te llamamos **antes de salir** de la casa.
We will call you before leaving the house.

Te llamamos mañana **antes de que salgas**.
We will call you tomorrow before you leave.

Conjunctions with subjunctive or indicative

> Voy a formar un club de ecología tan pronto como vuelva al D.F.

> Cuando veo basura, la recojo.

Conjunctions used with subjunctive or indicative

cuando	*when*	**hasta que**	*until*
después de que	*after*	**tan pronto como**	*as soon as*
en cuanto	*as soon as*		

▶ With the conjunctions above, use the subjunctive in the subordinate clause if the main clause expresses a future action or command.

Vamos a resolver el problema **cuando desarrollemos** nuevas tecnologías.
We are going to solve the problem when we develop new technologies.

Después de que ustedes **tomen** sus refrescos, reciclen las botellas.
After you drink your soft drinks, recycle the bottles.

▶ With these conjunctions, the indicative is used in the subordinate clause if the verb in the main clause expresses an action that habitually happens, or that happened in the past.

Contaminan los ríos **cuando construyen** nuevos edificios.
They pollute the rivers when they build new buildings.

Contaminaron el río **cuando construyeron** ese edificio.
They polluted the river when they built that building.

¡INTÉNTALO!   Completa las oraciones con las formas correctas de los verbos.

1. Voy a estudiar ecología cuando ___vuelva___ (volver) a la universidad.
2. No podemos evitar el cambio climático, a menos que todos _____ (trabajar) juntos.
3. No podemos conducir sin _____ (contaminar) el aire.
4. Siempre recogemos mucha basura cuando _____ (ir) al parque.
5. Elisa habló con el presidente del Club de Ecología después de que _____ (terminar) la reunión.
6. Vamos de excursión para _____ (observar) los animales y las plantas.
7. La contaminación va a ser un problema muy serio hasta que nosotros _____ (cambiar) nuestros sistemas de producción y transporte.
8. El gobierno debe crear más parques nacionales antes de que los bosques y ríos _____ (estar) completamente contaminados.
9. La gente recicla con tal de que no _____ (ser) difícil.

Práctica

1 **Completar** La señora Montero habla de una excursión que quiere hacer con su familia. Completa las oraciones con la forma correcta de cada verbo.

1. Voy a llevar a mis hijos al parque para que _____ (aprender) sobre la naturaleza.
2. Voy a pasar todo el día allí a menos que _____ (hacer) mucho frío.
3. Podemos explorar el parque en bicicleta sin _____ (caminar) demasiado.
4. Vamos a bajar al cráter con tal de que no se _____ (prohibir).
5. Siempre llevamos al perro cuando _____ (ir) al parque.
6. No pensamos ir muy lejos en caso de que _____ (llover).
7. Vamos a almorzar a la orilla (*shore*) del río cuando nosotros _____ (terminar) de preparar la comida.
8. Mis hijos van a dejar todo limpio antes de _____ (salir) del parque.

2 **Frases** Completa estas frases de una manera lógica.

1. No podemos controlar la contaminación del aire a menos que...
2. Voy a reciclar los productos de papel y de vidrio en cuanto...
3. Debemos comprar coches eléctricos tan pronto como...
4. Protegemos los animales en peligro de extinción para que...
5. Mis amigos y yo vamos a recoger la basura de la universidad después de que...
6. No podemos desarrollar nuevas fuentes (*sources*) de energía sin...
7. Hay que eliminar la contaminación del agua para...
8. No podemos proteger la naturaleza sin que...

3 **Organizaciones colombianas** Lee las descripciones de las organizaciones de conservación. Luego expresa en tus propias (*own*) palabras las opiniones de cada organización.

Organización: Fundación Río Orinoco
Problema: La destrucción de los ríos
Solución: Programa para limpiar las orillas de los ríos y reducir la erosión y así proteger los ríos

Organización: Oficina de Turismo Internacional
Problema: Necesidad de mejorar la imagen del país en el mercado turístico internacional
Solución: Plan para promover el ecoturismo en los 54 parques nacionales, usando agencias de publicidad e implementando un plan agresivo de conservación

Organización: Asociación Nabusimake-Pico Colón
Problema: Un lugar turístico popular en la Sierra Nevada de Santa Marta necesita mejor mantenimiento
Solución: Programa de voluntarios para limpiar y mejorar los senderos

Comunicación

4   **Recomendaciones** Lee el mensaje electrónico que Juan Manuel envía a su familia y amigos. Luego, indica si las conclusiones son **lógicas** o **ilógicas**, según lo que leíste.

De:	Juan Manuel
Para:	Papá; Mamá; Marta; Ignacio; Antonio; Gabriela
Asunto:	El medio ambiente

Acabo de ver un programa de televisión muy bueno sobre el medio ambiente. Dieron recomendaciones muy simples que todos podemos seguir para ayudar un poquito a nuestro planeta. Por ejemplo, cuando cocinen poca comida (para una o dos personas), usen el horno de microondas y no el horno porque éste consume mucha más energía eléctrica. No laven la ropa con agua caliente; usen agua tibia (*warm*) o fría. Es mejor usar el lavaplatos que lavar a mano, pero no usen el lavaplatos hasta que esté completamente lleno. Después de usar la computadora por la noche, no la dejen en modo de suspensión (*sleep mode*): van a gastar menos dinero y energía si la apagan. En caso de que cambien el aceite de su auto sin ayuda de un mecánico, lleven ese aceite usado a un centro de reciclaje. Espero que puedan seguir algunas de estas recomendaciones.

Juan Manuel

	Lógico	Ilógico
1. Juan Manuel se preocupa por el medio ambiente.	○	○
2. Las personas que viven solas (*by themselves*) deben usar el horno con poca frecuencia.	○	○
3. Cuando no hay muchos platos para lavar, es mejor no usar el lavaplatos todavía.	○	○
4. Cuando una computadora está en modo de suspensión, no consume energía.	○	○
5. El aceite de auto usado se debe poner en la basura.	○	○

5   **Preguntas** En parejas, túrnense para hacerse estas preguntas.

1. ¿Qué haces cada noche antes de acostarte?
2. ¿Qué haces después de salir de casa?
3. ¿Qué vas a hacer cuando lleguen las vacaciones de verano?
4. ¿Qué piensas hacer tan pronto como te gradúes?
5. ¿Qué quieres hacer mañana, a menos que haga mal tiempo?
6. ¿Qué haces sin que tus amigos lo sepan?

6   **Predicciones** Escoge dos problemas del medio ambiente y presenta tus predicciones para cada uno. Usa expresiones como **a menos que, con tal (de) que** o **hasta que**.

> **modelo**
>
> *El problema de la deforestación es muy grave. Hasta que todos los gobiernos protejan intensamente sus bosques, el calentamiento global va a continuar y muchos animales van a estar en peligro de extinción...*

Síntesis

7   **Escribir** Escribe un diálogo de al menos siete oraciones en el que un(a) amigo/a hace comentarios pesimistas sobre la situación del medio ambiente en tu región y tú respondes con comentarios optimistas. Usa verbos y expresiones de esta lección.

Recapitulación

Completa estas actividades para repasar los conceptos de gramática que aprendiste en esta lección.

1 **Subjuntivo con conjunciones** Escoge la forma correcta del verbo para completar las oraciones. **16 pts.**

1. En cuanto (empiecen/empiezan) las vacaciones, vamos a viajar.
2. Por favor, llámeme a las siete y media en caso de que no (me despierto/me despierte).
3. Toni va a usar su bicicleta hasta que los coches híbridos (cuesten/cuestan) menos dinero.
4. Tan pronto como supe la noticia (news) (te llamé/te llame).
5. Debemos conservar el agua antes de que no (queda/quede) nada para beber.
6. ¿Siempre recoges la basura después de que (terminas/termines) de comer en un picnic?
7. Siempre quiero vender mi camioneta (SUV) cuando (yo) (piense/pienso) en la contaminación.
8. Estudiantes, pueden entrar al parque natural con tal de que no (tocan/toquen) las plantas.

2 **Creer o no creer** Completa estos diálogos con la forma correcta del presente de indicativo o de subjuntivo, según el contexto. **24 pts.**

CAROLA Creo que (1) _____ (nosotras, deber) escribir nuestra presentación sobre el reciclaje.

MÓNICA Hmm, no estoy segura de que el reciclaje (2) _____ (ser) un buen tema. No hay duda de que la gente ya (3) _____ (saber) reciclar.

CAROLA Sí, pero dudo que todos lo (4) _____ (practicar).

· · ·

PACO ¿Sabes, Néstor? El sábado voy a ir a limpiar el río con un grupo de voluntarios. ¿Quieres venir?

NÉSTOR No es seguro que (5) _____ (yo, poder) ir. El lunes hay un examen y tengo que estudiar.

PACO ¿Estás seguro de que no (6) _____ (tener) tiempo? Es imposible que (7) _____ (ir) a estudiar todo el fin de semana.

NÉSTOR Pues sí, pero es muy probable que (8) _____ (llover).

RESUMEN GRAMATICAL

13.1 The subjunctive with verbs of emotion
pp. 452–453

Verbs and expressions of emotion

alegrarse (de)	tener miedo (de)
esperar	es extraño
gustar	es una lástima
molestar	es ridículo
sentir (e:ie)	es terrible
sorprender	es triste
temer	ojalá (que)

Main clause		Subordinate clause
Marta **espera** Ojalá	que	yo **vaya** al lago mañana. **comamos** en casa.

13.2 The subjunctive with doubt, disbelief, and denial
pp. 456–457

Expressions of doubt, disbelief, or denial (used with subjunctive)

dudar	no es verdad
negar (e:ie)	es imposible
no creer	es improbable
no estar seguro/a (de)	(no) es posible
no es cierto	(no) es probable
no es seguro	

Expressions of certainty (used with indicative)

no dudar	estar seguro/a (de)
no cabe duda de	es cierto
no hay duda de	es seguro
no negar (e:ie)	es verdad
creer	es obvio

▶ The infinitive is used after these expressions when there is no change of subject.

13.3 The subjunctive with conjunctions
pp. 460–461

Conjunctions that require the subjunctive

a menos que	en caso (de) que
antes (de) que	para que
con tal (de) que	sin que

3 **Reacciones** Reacciona a estas oraciones según las pistas (*clues*). Sigue el modelo. `30 pts.`

> **modelo**
>
> Tú casi nunca reciclas nada.
> (yo, molestar)
> *A mí me molesta que tú casi nunca recicles nada.*

▶ The infinitive is used after the prepositions **antes de**, **para**, and **sin** when there is no change of subject.

Te llamamos **antes de salir** de casa.

Te llamamos mañana **antes de que salgas**.

Conjunctions used with subjunctive or indicative	
cuando	hasta que
después de que	tan pronto como
en cuanto	

1. La Ciudad de México tiene un problema grave de contaminación. (ser una lástima)

2. En ese safari permiten tocar a los animales. (ser extraño)

3. Julia y Víctor no pueden ir a las montañas. (yo, sentir)

4. El nuevo programa de reciclaje es un éxito. (nosotros, esperar)

5. A María no le gustan los perros. (ser una lástima)

6. Existen leyes ecológicas en este país. (Juan, alegrarse de)

7. El gobierno no busca soluciones. (ellos, temer)

8. La mayoría de la población no cuida el medio ambiente. (ser triste)

9. Muchas personas cazan animales en esta región. (yo, sorprender)

10. La situación mejora día a día. (ojalá que)

4 **Oraciones** Forma oraciones con estos elementos. Usa el subjuntivo cuando sea necesario. `24 pts.`

1. ser ridículo / los coches / contaminar tanto

2. no caber duda de / tú y yo / poder / hacer mucho más

3. los ecologistas / temer / no conservarse / los recursos naturales

4. yo / alegrarse de / en mi ciudad / reciclarse / el plástico, el vidrio y el aluminio

5. todos (nosotros) / ir a respirar / mejor / cuando / (nosotros) llegar / a la montaña

6. tú / negar / el gobierno / resolver / los problemas ecológicos

5 **Canción** Completa estos versos de una canción de Juan Luis Guerra. `6 pts.`

"Ojalá que _____ (llover)
café en el campo.
Pa'° que todos los niños
_____ (cantar) en el campo.**"**

Pa' *short for* Para

Lectura

Antes de leer

Estrategia
Recognizing the purpose of a text

When you are faced with an unfamiliar text, it is important to determine the writer's purpose. If you are reading an editorial in a newspaper, for example, you know that the journalist's objective is to persuade you of his or her point of view. Identifying the purpose of a text will help you better comprehend its meaning.

Examinar los textos
Primero, utiliza la estrategia de lectura para familiarizarte con los textos. Después contesta estas preguntas.

- ¿De qué tratan los textos?°
- ¿Son fábulas°, poemas, artículos de periódico…?
- ¿Cómo lo sabes?

Predicciones
Lee estas predicciones sobre la lectura e indica si estás de acuerdo° con ellas.

1. Los textos son del género° de ficción.
2. Los personajes son animales.
3. La acción de los textos tiene lugar en un zoológico.
4. Hay alguna moraleja°.

Determinar el propósito
Piensa en los posibles propósitos° de los textos. Considera estas preguntas:

- ¿Qué te dice el género de los textos sobre los posibles propósitos de los textos?
- ¿Piensas que los textos pueden tener más de un propósito? ¿Por qué?

¿De qué tratan los textos? *What are the texts about?*
fábulas *fables* **estás de acuerdo** *you agree*
género *genre* **moraleja** *moral* **propósitos** *purposes*

Sobre los autores

Félix María Samaniego (1745–1801) nació en España y escribió las *Fábulas morales* que ilustran de manera humorística el carácter humano. Los protagonistas de muchas de sus fábulas son animales que hablan.

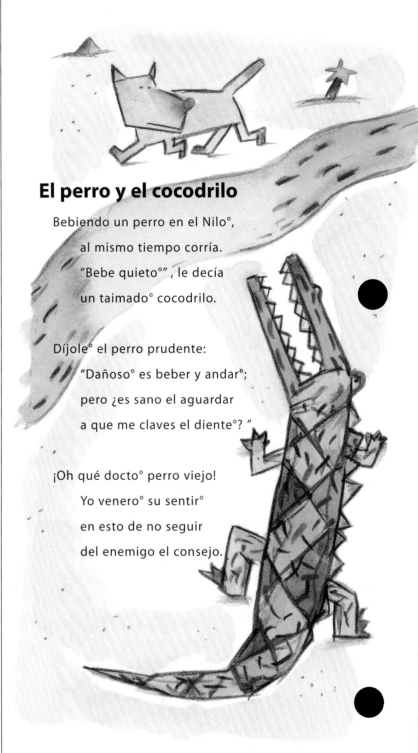

El perro y el cocodrilo

Bebiendo un perro en el Nilo°,
al mismo tiempo corría.
"Bebe quieto°", le decía
un taimado° cocodrilo.

Díjole° el perro prudente:
"Dañoso° es beber y andar°;
pero ¿es sano el aguardar
a que me claves el diente°? "

¡Oh qué docto° perro viejo!
Yo venero° su sentir°
en esto de no seguir
del enemigo el consejo.

Tomás de Iriarte (1750–1791) nació en las islas Canarias y tuvo gran éxito° con su libro *Fábulas literarias*. Su tendencia a representar la lógica a través de° símbolos de la naturaleza fue de gran influencia para muchos autores de su época°.

El pato° y la serpiente

A orillas° de un estanque°,
diciendo estaba un pato:
"¿A qué animal dio el cielo°
los dones que me ha dado°?

"Soy de agua, tierra y aire:
cuando de andar me canso°,
si se me antoja, vuelo°;
si se me antoja, nado".

Una serpiente astuta
que le estaba escuchando,
le llamó con un silbo°,
y le dijo "¡Seo° guapo!

"No hay que echar tantas plantas°;
pues ni anda como el gamo°,
ni vuela como el sacre°,
ni nada como el barbo°;

"y así tenga sabido
que lo importante y raro°
no es entender de todo,
sino ser diestro° en algo".

Nilo *Nile* quieto *in peace* taimado *sly* Díjole *Said to him* Dañoso *Harmful* andar *to walk* ¿es sano... diente? *Is it good for me to wait for you to sink your teeth into me?* docto *wise* venero *revere* sentir *wisdom* éxito *success* a través de *through* época *time* pato *duck* orillas *banks* estanque *pond* cielo *heaven* los dones... dado *the gifts that it has given me* me canso *I get tired* si se... vuelo *if I feel like it, I fly* silbo *hiss* Seo *Señor* No hay... plantas *There's no reason to boast* gamo *deer* sacre *falcon* barbo *barbel (a type of fish)* raro *rare* diestro *skillful*

Después de leer

Comprensión

Escoge la mejor opción para completar cada oración.

1. El cocodrilo _____ perro.
   a. está preocupado por el   b. quiere comerse al
   c. tiene miedo del

2. El perro _____ cocodrilo.
   a. tiene miedo del   b. es amigo del
   c. quiere quedarse con el

3. El pato cree que es un animal _____.
   a. muy famoso   b. muy hermoso
   c. de muchos talentos

4. La serpiente cree que el pato es _____.
   a. muy inteligente   b. muy tonto   c. muy feo

Preguntas

Contesta las preguntas.

1. ¿Qué representa el cocodrilo?
   _____

2. ¿Qué representa el pato?
   _____

3. ¿Cuál es la moraleja (*moral*) de "El perro y el cocodrilo"?
   _____

4. ¿Cuál es la moraleja de "El pato y la serpiente"?
   _____

Coméntalo

Contesta estas preguntas.
¿Estás de acuerdo con las moralejas de estas fábulas? ¿Por qué? ¿Cuál de estas fábulas te gusta más? ¿Por qué? ¿Conoces otras fábulas? ¿Cuál es su propósito?

Escribir

Escribe una fábula. Puedes escoger algunos animales de la lista o escoger otros. ¿Qué características deben tener estos animales?

- una abeja (*bee*)
- un gato
- un mono
- un burro
- un perro
- una tortuga
- un águila (*eagle*)
- un pavo real (*peacock*)

Escritura

Estrategia

Considering audience and purpose

Writing always has a specific purpose. During the planning stages, a writer must determine to whom he or she is addressing the piece, and what he or she wants to express to the reader. Once you have defined both your audience and your purpose, you will be able to decide which genre, vocabulary, and grammatical structures will best serve your literary composition.

Let's say you want to share your thoughts on local traffic problems. Your audience can be either the local government or the community. You could choose to write a newspaper article, a letter to the editor, or a letter to the city's governing board. But first you should ask yourself these questions:

1. Are you going to comment on traffic problems in general, or are you going to point out several specific problems?

2. Are you simply intending to register a complaint?

3. Are you simply intending to inform others and increase public awareness of the problems?

4. Are you hoping to persuade others to adopt your point of view?

5. Are you hoping to inspire others to take concrete actions?

The answers to these questions will help you establish the purpose of your writing and determine your audience. Of course, your writing can have more than one purpose. For example, you may intend for your writing to both inform others of a problem and inspire them to take action.

Tema

Escribir una carta o un artículo

Escoge uno de estos temas. Luego decide si vas a escribir una carta a un(a) amigo/a, una carta a un periódico, un artículo de periódico o de revista, etc.

1. Escribe sobre los programas que existen para proteger la naturaleza en tu comunidad. ¿Funcionan bien? ¿Participan todos los vecinos de tu comunidad en los programas? ¿Tienes dudas sobre la eficacia° de estos programas?

2. Describe uno de los atractivos naturales de tu región. ¿Te sientes optimista sobre el futuro del medio ambiente en tu región? ¿Qué están haciendo el gobierno y los ciudadanos° de tu región para proteger la naturaleza? ¿Es necesario hacer más?

3. Escribe sobre algún programa para la protección del medio ambiente a nivel° nacional. ¿Es un programa del gobierno o de una empresa° privada°? ¿Cómo funciona? ¿Quiénes participan? ¿Tienes dudas sobre el programa? ¿Crees que debe cambiarse o mejorarse? ¿Cómo?

eficacia *effectiveness* ciudadanos *citizens* nivel *level* empresa *company* privada *private*

Escuchar

Estrategia

Using background knowledge/ Guessing meaning from context

Listening for the general idea, or gist, can help you follow what someone is saying even if you can't hear or understand some of the words. When you listen for the gist, you simply try to capture the essence of what you hear without focusing on individual words.

 To practice these strategies, you will listen to a paragraph written by Jaime Urbinas, an urban planner. Before listening to the paragraph, write down what you think it will be about, based on Jaime Urbinas' profession. As you listen to the paragraph, jot down any words or expressions you don't know and use context clues to guess their meanings.

Preparación

Mira el dibujo. ¿Qué pistas° te da sobre el tema del discurso° de Soledad Morales?

Ahora escucha

Vas a escuchar un discurso de Soledad Morales, una activista preocupada por el medio ambiente. Antes de escuchar, marca las palabras y frases que tú crees que ella va a usar en su discurso. Después marca las palabras y frases que escuchaste.

Palabras	Antes de escuchar	Después de escuchar
el futuro	_____	_____
el cine	_____	_____
los recursos naturales	_____	_____
el aire	_____	_____
los ríos	_____	_____
la contaminación	_____	_____
el reciclaje	_____	_____
las diversiones	_____	_____

Comprensión

Escoger

Subraya° el equivalente correcto de cada palabra.
1. patrimonio (fatherland, heritage, acrimony)
2. ancianos (elderly, ancient, antiques)
3. entrelazadas (destined, interrupted, intertwined)
4. aguantar (to hold back, to destroy, to pollute)
5. apreciar (to value, to imitate, to consider)
6. tala (planting, cutting, watering)

Ahora tú

Escribe seis recomendaciones que crees que la señora Morales va a darle al gobierno colombiano para mejorar los problemas del medio ambiente.

1. _____
2. _____
3. _____
4. _____
5. _____
6. _____

pistas *clues* discurso *speech* Subraya *Underline*

En pantalla

La asociación sin ánimo de lucro° Ecovidrio lanza una campaña publicitaria para fomentar° el reciclaje de vidrio. La campaña se compone de° tres *spots* publicitarios protagonizados por el famoso humorista español José Mota. Ecovidrio utiliza el humor y la ironía para animar° a la sociedad a que deposite el vidrio en el contenedor verde. El objetivo es que el reciclaje se convierta en un hábito, sin excepciones, sin excusas.

Vocabulario útil	
colleja	*slap on the back of the neck*
contenedor	*container*
excusa de libro	*typical excuse*
sitio	*room; space*
tirar	*to throw away*

Preparación

¿Reciclas el vidrio? ¿Qué otros materiales reciclas? ¿Qué opinas de la gente que no recicla? ¿Crees que existen excusas válidas para no reciclar?

Escoger

Elige la opción correcta.

1. El señor tira una botella de _____ a la basura.

   a. plástico   b. vidrio

2. La excusa del hombre para no reciclar es que _____.

   a. no hay sitio   b. está muy ocupado

3. La mujer le _____ al hombre porque no recicló la botella.

   a. da una colleja   b. pide explicaciones

4. El contenedor del vidrio es _____.

   a. azul   b. verde

Reciclaje

Escribe un diálogo entre una persona que no recicla y sólo pone excusas, y otra que le explica cómo está dañando el medio ambiente al no reciclar. Usa el subjuntivo.

Anuncio de Ecovidrio

Es que no hay sitio para...

A reciclar, si hay que ir, se va.

Las excusas a la basura y el vidrio al contenedor verde.

sin ánimo de lucro *nonprofit* fomentar *to encourage*
se compone de *consists of* animar *to encourage*

Centroamérica es una región con un gran crecimiento° en el turismo, especialmente ecológico, y no por pocas razones°. Con solamente el uno por ciento° de la superficie terrestre°, esta zona tiene el ocho por ciento de las reservas naturales del planeta. Algunas de estas maravillas son la isla Coiba en Panamá, la Reserva de la Biosfera Maya en Guatemala, el volcán Mombacho en Nicaragua, el parque El Imposible en El Salvador y Pico Bonito en Honduras. En este episodio de *Flash cultura* vas a conocer más tesoros° naturales en un país ecológico por tradición: Costa Rica.

Vocabulario útil	
aguas termales	*hot springs*
hace erupción	*erupts*
los poderes curativos	*healing powers*
rocas incandescentes	*incandescent rocks*

Preparación

¿Qué sabes de los volcanes de Costa Rica? ¿Y de sus aguas termales? Si no sabes nada, escribe tres predicciones sobre cada tema.

¿Cierto o falso?

Indica si estas oraciones son **ciertas** o **falsas**.

1. Centroamérica es una zona de pocos volcanes.

2. El volcán Arenal está en un parque nacional.

3. El volcán Arenal hace erupción pocas veces.

4. Las aguas termales cerca del volcán vienen del mar.

5. Cuando Alberto sale del agua, tiene calor.

6. Se pueden ver las rocas incandescentes desde algunos hoteles.

Naturaleza en Costa Rica

Aquí existen más de cien volcanes. Hoy visitaremos el Parque Nacional Volcán Arenal.

En los alrededores del volcán [...] nacen aguas termales de origen volcánico...

Puedes escuchar cada rugido° del volcán Arenal...

crecimiento *growth* razones *reasons* por ciento *percent*
superficie terrestre *earth's surface* tesoros *treasures* rugido *roar*

Colombia

El país en cifras

▸ **Área:** 1.138.910 km² (439.734 millas²), *tres veces el área de Montana*

▸ **Población:** 46.245.000

De todos los países de habla hispana, sólo México tiene más habitantes que Colombia. Casi toda la población colombiana vive en las áreas montañosas y la costa occidental° del país. Aproximadamente el 55% de la superficie° del país está sin poblar°.

▸ **Capital:** Bogotá —8.744.000

▸ **Ciudades principales:** Medellín —3.497.000, Cali —2.352.000, Barranquilla —1.836.000, Cartagena —978.600

Medellín

▸ **Moneda:** peso colombiano

▸ **Idiomas:** español (oficial); lenguas indígenas, criollas y gitanas

Bandera de Colombia

Colombianos célebres

▸ **Edgar Negret,** escultor°, pintor (1920–2012)

▸ **Juan Pablo Montoya,** automovilista (1975–)

▸ **Fernando Botero,** pintor, escultor (1932–)

▸ **Shakira,** cantante (1977–)

▸ **Sofía Vergara,** actriz (1972–)

occidental *western* superficie *surface* sin poblar *unpopulated*
escultor *sculptor* dioses *gods* arrojaban *threw* oro *gold*
cacique *chief* llevó *led*

Palacio de
San Francisco, Bogotá

Baile típico de
Cartagena

Barranquilla

Cartagena

Mar Caribe

PANAMÁ

Sierra Nevada
de Santa Marta

VENEZUELA

Río Magdalena

ESTADOS UNIDOS

OCÉANO
ATLÁNTICO

COLOMBIA

OCÉANO
PACÍFICO

AMÉRICA DEL SUR

Cordillera Occidental de los Andes

Medellín

Cordillera Central de los Andes

Río Meta

Cali

Volcán
Nevado
del Huila

Bogotá

Océano
Pacífico

Cordillera Oriental
de los Andes

Cultivo de caña de
azúcar cerca de Cali

ECUADOR

PERÚ

¡Increíble pero cierto!

En el siglo XVI los exploradores españoles oyeron la leyenda de El Dorado. Esta leyenda cuenta que los indios, como parte de un ritual en honor a los dioses°, arrojaban° oro° a la laguna de Guatavita y el cacique° se sumergía en sus aguas cubierto de oro. Aunque esto era cierto, muy pronto la exageración llevó° al mito de una ciudad de oro.

Laguna de Guatavita

Lugares • El Museo del Oro

El famoso Museo del Oro del Banco de la República fue fundado° en Bogotá en 1939 para preservar las piezas de orfebrería° de la época precolombina. Tiene más de 30.000 piezas de oro y otros materiales; en él se pueden ver joyas°, ornamentos religiosos y figuras que representaban ídolos. El cuidado con el que se hicieron los objetos de oro refleja la creencia° de las tribus indígenas de que el oro era la expresión física de la energía creadora° de los dioses.

Literatura • Gabriel García Márquez (1927–2014)

Gabriel García Márquez, ganador del Premio Nobel de Literatura en 1982, es considerado uno de los escritores más importantes de la literatura universal. García Márquez publicó su primer cuento° en 1947, cuando era estudiante universitario. Su libro más conocido, *Cien años de soledad*, está escrito en el estilo° literario llamado "realismo mágico", un estilo que mezcla° la realidad con lo irreal y lo mítico°.

Historia • Cartagena de Indias

Los españoles fundaron la ciudad de Cartagena de Indias en 1533 y construyeron a su lado la fortaleza° más grande de las Américas, el Castillo de San Felipe de Barajas. En la ciudad de Cartagena se conservan muchos edificios de la época colonial, como iglesias, monasterios, palacios y mansiones. Cartagena es conocida también por el Festival Internacional de Música y su prestigioso Festival Internacional de Cine.

Costumbres • El Carnaval

Durante el Carnaval de Barranquilla, la ciudad vive casi exclusivamente para esta fiesta. Este festival es una fusión de las culturas que han llegado° a las costas caribeñas de Colombia y de sus grupos autóctonos°. El evento más importante es la Batalla° de Flores, un desfile° de carrozas° decoradas con flores. En 2003, la UNESCO declaró este carnaval como Patrimonio de la Humanidad°.

BRASIL

¿Qué aprendiste? Contesta cada pregunta con una oración completa.
1. ¿Cuáles son las principales ciudades de Colombia?
2. ¿Qué país de habla hispana tiene más habitantes que Colombia?
3. ¿Quién era Edgar Negret?
4. ¿Cuándo oyeron los españoles la leyenda de El Dorado?
5. ¿Para qué fue fundado el Museo del Oro?
6. ¿Quién ganó el Premio Nobel de Literatura en 1982?
7. ¿Qué construyeron los españoles al lado de la ciudad de Cartagena de Indias?
8. ¿Cuál es el evento más importante del Carnaval de Barranquilla?

Conexión Internet Investiga estos temas en Internet.
1. Busca información sobre las ciudades más grandes de Colombia. ¿Qué lugares de interés hay en estas ciudades? ¿Qué puede hacer un(a) turista en estas ciudades?
2. Busca información sobre pintores y escultores colombianos como Edgar Negret, Débora Arango o Fernando Botero. ¿Cuáles son algunas de sus obras más conocidas? ¿Cuáles son sus temas?

fundado *founded* orfebrería *goldsmithing* joyas *jewelry* creencia *belief* creadora *creative* cuento *story* estilo *style* mezcla *mixes* mítico *mythical* fortaleza *fortress* han llegado *have arrived* autóctonos *indigenous* Batalla *Battle* desfile *parade* carrozas *floats* Patrimonio de la Humanidad *World Heritage*

La naturaleza

el árbol	tree
el bosque (tropical)	(tropical; rain) forest
el cielo	sky
el cráter	crater
el desierto	desert
la estrella	star
la flor	flower
la hierba	grass
el lago	lake
la luna	moon
la naturaleza	nature
la nube	cloud
la piedra	stone
la planta	plant
el río	river
la selva, la jungla	jungle
el sendero	trail; path
el sol	sun
la tierra	land; soil
el valle	valley
el volcán	volcano

Los animales

el animal	animal
el ave, el pájaro	bird
la ballena	whale
el gato	cat
el mono	monkey
el perro	dog
el pez (sing.), los peces (pl.)	fish
la tortuga (marina)	(sea) turtle
la vaca	cow

El medio ambiente

el calentamiento global	global warming
el cambio climático	climate change
la conservación	conservation
la contaminación (del aire; del agua)	(air; water) pollution
la deforestación	deforestation
la ecología	ecology
el/la ecologista	ecologist
el ecoturismo	ecotourism
la energía (nuclear, solar)	(nuclear, solar) energy
el envase	container
la extinción	extinction
la fábrica	factory
el gobierno	government
la lata	(tin) can
la ley	law
el medio ambiente	environment
el peligro	danger
la (sobre)población	(over)population
el reciclaje	recycling
el recurso natural	natural resource
la solución	solution
cazar	to hunt
conservar	to conserve
contaminar	to pollute
controlar	to control
cuidar	to take care of
dejar de (+ *inf.*)	to stop (doing something)
desarrollar	to develop
descubrir	to discover
destruir	to destroy
estar afectado/a (por)	to be affected (by)
estar contaminado/a	to be polluted
evitar	to avoid
mejorar	to improve
proteger	to protect
reciclar	to recycle
recoger	to pick up
reducir	to reduce
resolver (o:ue)	to resolve; to solve
respirar	to breathe
de aluminio	(made) of aluminum
de plástico	(made) of plastic
de vidrio	(made) of glass
ecológico/a	ecological
puro/a	pure
renovable	renewable

Las emociones

alegrarse (de)	to be happy
esperar	to hope; to wish
sentir (e:ie)	to be sorry; to regret
temer	to be afraid
es extraño	it's strange
es una lástima	it's a shame
es ridículo	it's ridiculous
es terrible	it's terrible
es triste	it's sad
ojalá (que)	I hope (that); I wish (that)

Las dudas y certezas

(no) creer	(not) to believe
(no) dudar	(not) to doubt
(no) negar (e:ie)	(not) to deny
es imposible	it's impossible
es improbable	it's improbable
es obvio	it's obvious
no cabe duda de	there is no doubt that
no hay duda de	there is no doubt that
(no) es cierto	it's (not) certain
(no) es posible	it's (not) possible
(no) es probable	it's (not) probable
(no) es seguro	it's (not) certain
(no) es verdad	it's (not) true

Conjunciones

a menos que	unless
antes (de) que	before
con tal (de) que	provided (that)
cuando	when
después de que	after
en caso (de) que	in case (that)
en cuanto	as soon as
hasta que	until
para que	so that
sin que	without
tan pronto como	as soon as

Expresiones útiles	See page 447.

En la ciudad

14

Communicative Goals

You will learn how to:

• **Give advice to others**

• **Give and receive directions**

• **Discuss daily errands and city life**

A PRIMERA VISTA

• ¿Viven estas personas en un bosque, un pueblo o una ciudad?
• ¿Dónde están, en una calle o en un sendero?
• ¿Es posible que estén afectadas por la contaminación? ¿Por qué?
• ¿Está limpio o sucio el lugar donde están?

En la ciudad

la peluquería, el salón de belleza

el banco

el supermercado

la panadería

la joyería

el cajero automático

Indica cómo llegar. (indicar)

Está perdida. (estar)

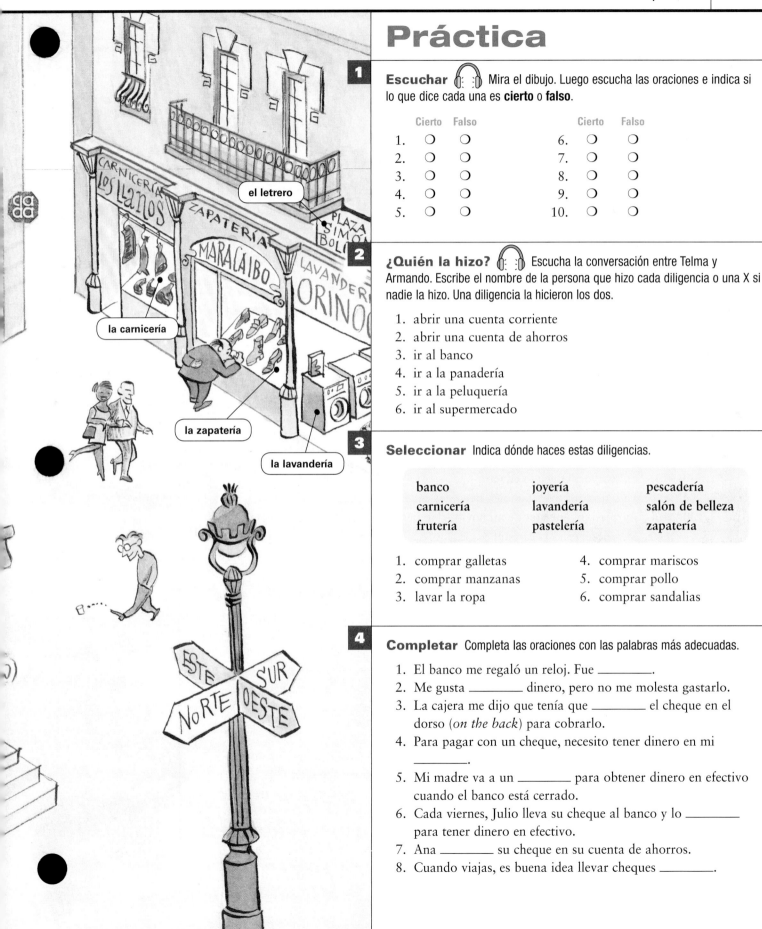

el letrero

la carnicería

la zapatería

la lavandería

Práctica

1 **Escuchar** 🎧 Mira el dibujo. Luego escucha las oraciones e indica si lo que dice cada una es **cierto** o **falso**.

	Cierto	Falso			Cierto	Falso
1.	○	○		6.	○	○
2.	○	○		7.	○	○
3.	○	○		8.	○	○
4.	○	○		9.	○	○
5.	○	○		10.	○	○

2 **¿Quién la hizo?** 🎧 Escucha la conversación entre Telma y Armando. Escribe el nombre de la persona que hizo cada diligencia o una X si nadie la hizo. Una diligencia la hicieron los dos.

1. abrir una cuenta corriente
2. abrir una cuenta de ahorros
3. ir al banco
4. ir a la panadería
5. ir a la peluquería
6. ir al supermercado

3 **Seleccionar** Indica dónde haces estas diligencias.

banco	joyería	pescadería
carnicería	lavandería	salón de belleza
frutería	pastelería	zapatería

1. comprar galletas
2. comprar manzanas
3. lavar la ropa
4. comprar mariscos
5. comprar pollo
6. comprar sandalias

4 **Completar** Completa las oraciones con las palabras más adecuadas.

1. El banco me regaló un reloj. Fue _____.
2. Me gusta _____ dinero, pero no me molesta gastarlo.
3. La cajera me dijo que tenía que _____ el cheque en el dorso (*on the back*) para cobrarlo.
4. Para pagar con un cheque, necesito tener dinero en mi _____.
5. Mi madre va a un _____ para obtener dinero en efectivo cuando el banco está cerrado.
6. Cada viernes, Julio lleva su cheque al banco y lo _____ para tener dinero en efectivo.
7. Ana _____ su cheque en su cuenta de ahorros.
8. Cuando viajas, es buena idea llevar cheques _____.

Manda/Envía un paquete.
(mandar, enviar)

la estampilla,
el sello

Hacen cola.
(hacer)

el cartero

el correo

Echa una carta al
buzón. (echar)

el sobre

En el correo

¡LENGUA VIVA!

Note that **correo** can mean either *mail* or *post office*. Other ways to say *post office* are **la oficina de correos** and **correos**.

5

Conversación Completa la conversación entre Juanita y el cartero con las palabras más adecuadas.

CARTERO   Buenas tardes, ¿es usted la señorita Ramírez? Le traigo un (1) _____.

JUANITA   Sí, soy yo. ¿Quién lo envía?

CARTERO   La señora Brito. Y también tiene dos (2) _____.

JUANITA   Ay, pero ¡ninguna es de mi novio! ¿No llegó nada de Manuel Fuentes?

CARTERO   Sí, pero él echó la carta al (3) _____ sin poner un (4) _____ en el sobre.

JUANITA   Entonces, ¿qué recomienda usted que haga?

CARTERO   Sugiero que vaya al (5) _____. Con tal de que pague el costo del sello, se le puede dar la carta sin ningún problema.

JUANITA   Uy, otra diligencia, y no tengo mucho tiempo esta tarde para (6) _____ cola en el correo, pero voy enseguida. ¡Ojalá que sea una carta de amor!

¡LENGUA VIVA!

In Spanish, **Soy yo** means *That's me* or *It's me.* **¿Eres tú?/ ¿Es usted?** means *Is that you?*

6

En el banco Tú eres un(a) empleado/a de banco y hay un(a) estudiante universitario/a que necesita abrir una cuenta corriente. Haz una lista de las palabras que pueden necesitar para la conversación. Después lee estas situaciones y modifica tu lista original según la situación.

- una pareja de recién casados quiere pedir un préstamo para comprar una casa
- una persona quiere información de los servicios que ofrece el banco
- un(a) estudiante va a estudiar al extranjero (*abroad*) y quiere saber qué tiene que hacer para llevar su dinero de una forma segura
- una persona acaba de ganar 50 millones de dólares en la lotería y quiere saber cómo invertirlos (*invest them*)

Comunicación

7

Conversación Escucha la conversación entre María y Daniel. Luego, indica a quién se refiere cada una de las afirmaciones, según lo que escuchaste.

	María	Daniel
1. Tiene que ir al banco.	○	○
2. Su carro está en el estacionamiento.	○	○
3. Cambió de pelo.	○	○
4. Va a comer algo dulce.	○	○
5. Tiene mucha ropa sucia.	○	○
6. No sabe la dirección de la otra persona.	○	○

8

El Hatillo Trabajen en parejas para representar los papeles de un(a) turista que está perdido/a en El Hatillo y de un(a) residente de la ciudad que quiere ayudarlo/la.

Plaza Bolívar
Plaza Sucre
banco
Casa de la Cultura
farmacia
iglesia
terminal
escuela
estacionamiento
joyería
zapatería
café Primavera

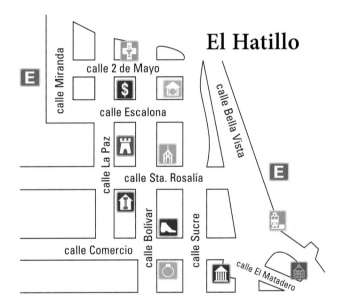

El Hatillo

modelo

Plaza Sucre, café Primavera

Estudiante 1: *Perdón, ¿por dónde queda la Plaza Sucre?*

Estudiante 2: *Del café Primavera, camine derecho por la calle Sucre hasta cruzar la calle Comercio…*

1. Plaza Bolívar, farmacia
2. Casa de la Cultura, Plaza Sucre
3. banco, terminal
4. estacionamiento (este), escuela

5. Plaza Sucre, estacionamiento (oeste)
6. joyería, banco
7. farmacia, joyería
8. zapatería, iglesia

9

Cómo llegar Escribe un minidrama en el que unos/as turistas están preguntando cómo llegar a diferentes sitios de la comunidad en la que vives.

Corriendo por la ciudad

Maru necesita entregar unos documentos en el Museo de Antropología.

MARU Miguel, ¿estás seguro de que tu coche está estacionado en la calle de Independencia? Estoy en la esquina de Zaragoza y Francisco Sosa. OK. Estoy enfrente del salón de belleza.

ADMINISTRADOR GENERAL
MUSEO DE ANTROPOLOGÍA

MIGUEL Dobla a la avenida Hidalgo. Luego cruza la calle Independencia y dobla a la derecha. El coche está enfrente de la pastelería.

MARU ¡Ahí está! Gracias, cariño. Hablamos luego.

MARU Vamos, arranca. Pensé que podías aguantar unos kilómetros más. Necesito un coche que funcione bien. (*en el teléfono*) Miguel, tu coche está descompuesto. Voy a pasar al banco porque necesito dinero, y luego me voy en taxi al museo.

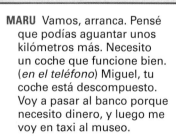

MARU Hola, Moni. Lo siento, tengo que ir a entregar un paquete y todavía tengo que ir a un cajero.

MÓNICA ¡Uf! Y la cola está súper larga.

MARU ¿Me puedes prestar algo de dinero?

MÓNICA Déjame ver cuánto tengo. Estoy haciendo diligencias, y me gasté casi todo el efectivo en la carnicería y en la panadería y en la frutería.

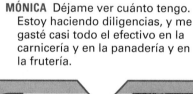

MÓNICA ¿Estás bien? Te ves pálida. Sentémonos un minuto.

MARU ¡No tengo tiempo! Tengo que llegar al Museo de Antropología. Necesito entregar...

MÓNICA ¡Ah, sí, tu proyecto!

MÓNICA

MÓNICA ¿Puedes mandarlo por correo? El correo está muy cerca de aquí.

MARU El plazo para mandarlo por correo se venció la semana pasada. Tengo que entregarlo personalmente.

MARU ¿Me podrías prestar tu coche?

MÓNICA Estás muy nerviosa para manejar con este tráfico. Te acompaño. ¡No!, mejor, yo te llevo. Mi coche está en el estacionamiento de la calle Constitución.

MARU En esta esquina dobla a la derecha. En el semáforo, a la izquierda y sigue derecho.

MÓNICA Hay demasiado tráfico. No sé si podemos...

MARU Hola, Miguel. No, no hubo más problemas. Lo entregué justo a tiempo. Nos vemos más tarde. (*a Mónica*) ¡Vamos a celebrar!

Expresiones útiles

Getting/giving directions

Estoy en la esquina de Zaragoza y Francisco Sosa.
I'm at the corner of Zaragoza and Francisco Sosa.
Dobla a la avenida Hidalgo.
Turn on Hidalgo Avenue.
Luego cruza la calle Independencia y dobla a la derecha.
Then cross Independencia Street and turn right.
El coche está enfrente de la pastelería.
The car is in front of the bakery.
En el semáforo, a la izquierda y sigue derecho.
Left at the light, then straight ahead.

Talking about errands

Voy a pasar al banco porque necesito dinero.
I'm going to the bank because I need money.
No tengo tiempo.
I don't have time.
Estoy haciendo diligencias, y me gasté casi todo el efectivo.
I'm running errands, and I spent most of my cash.

Asking for a favor

¿Me puedes prestar algo de dinero?
Could you lend me some money?
¿Me podrías prestar tu coche?
Could I borrow your car?

Talking about deadlines

Tengo que entregar mi proyecto.
I have to turn in my project.
El plazo para mandarlo por correo se venció la semana pasada.
The deadline to mail it in passed last week.

Additional vocabulary

acompañar *to accompany*
aguantar *to endure, to hold up*
ándale *come on*
pálido/a *pale*
¿Qué onda? *What's up?*

¿Qué pasó?

1 **¿Cierto o falso?** Decide si lo que dicen estas oraciones es **cierto** o **falso**. Corrige las oraciones falsas.

	Cierto	Falso
1. Miguel dice que su coche está estacionado enfrente de la carnicería.	○	○
2. Maru necesita pasar al banco porque necesita dinero.	○	○
3. Mónica gastó el efectivo en la joyería y el supermercado.	○	○
4. Maru puede mandar el paquete por correo.	○	○

2 **Ordenar** Pon los sucesos de la **Fotonovela** en el orden correcto.

a. Maru le pide dinero prestado a Mónica. _____

b. Maru entregó el paquete justo a tiempo (*just in time*). _____

c. Mónica dice que hay una cola súper larga en el banco. _____

d. Mónica lleva a Maru en su coche. _____

e. Maru dice que se va a ir en taxi al museo. _____

f. Maru le dice a Mónica que doble a la derecha en la esquina. _____

3 **Otras diligencias** Haz una lista de las diligencias que Miguel, Maru y Mónica necesitan hacer para completar estas actividades.

1. enviar un paquete por correo
2. pedir una beca (*scholarship*)
3. visitar una nueva ciudad
4. abrir una cuenta corriente
5. celebrar el cumpleaños de Mónica
6. comprar una nueva computadora portátil

MARU

MIGUEL

MÓNICA

4 **Conversación** Un(a) compañero/a y tú son vecinos/as. Uno/a de ustedes acaba de mudarse y necesita ayuda porque no conoce la ciudad. Los/Las dos tienen que hacer algunas diligencias y deciden hacerlas juntos/as. Preparen una conversación breve incluyendo planes para ir a estos lugares.

> **modelo**
>
> **Estudiante 1:** Necesito lavar mi ropa. ¿Sabes dónde queda una lavandería?
> **Estudiante 2:** Sí. Aquí a dos cuadras hay una. También tengo que lavar mi ropa. ¿Qué te parece si vamos juntos?

▶ un banco

▶ una lavandería

▶ un supermercado

▶ una heladería

▶ una panadería

AYUDA

primero *first*
luego *then*
¿Sabes dónde queda...?
Do you know where...is?
¿Qué te parece?
What do you think?
¡Cómo no!
But of course!

Ortografía

Las abreviaturas

In Spanish, as in English, abbreviations are often used in order to save space and time while writing. Here are some of the most commonly used abbreviations in Spanish.

---

usted ⟶ Ud.   ustedes ⟶ Uds.

As you have already learned, the subject pronouns **usted** and **ustedes** are often abbreviated

---

don ⟶ D.   doña ⟶ Dña.   doctor(a) ⟶ Dr(a).

señor ⟶ Sr.   señora ⟶ Sra.   señorita ⟶ Srta.

These titles are frequently abbreviated.

---

centímetro ⟶ cm   metro ⟶ m   kilómetro ⟶ km

litro ⟶ l   gramo ⟶ g, gr   kilogramo ⟶ kg

The abbreviations for these units of measurement are often used, but without periods.

---

por ejemplo ⟶ p. ej.   página(s) ⟶ pág(s).

These abbreviations are often seen in books.

---

derecha ⟶ dcha.   izquierda ⟶ izq., izqda.

código postal ⟶ C.P.   número ⟶ n.°

These abbreviations are often used in mailing addresses.

Sra. Emilia F. Bazán
Cía. Romero, S.A.
3336
Calle Lozano, n.° 37
Caracas, Venezuela

Banco ⟶ Bco.   Compañía ⟶ Cía.

cuenta corriente ⟶ c/c.   Sociedad Anónima (*Inc.*) ⟶ S.A.

These abbreviations are frequently used in the business world.

Práctica Escribe otra vez esta información usando las abreviaturas adecuadas.

1. doña María
2. señora Pérez
3. Compañía Mexicana de Inversiones
4. usted
5. Banco de Santander
6. doctor Medina
7. Código Postal 03697
8. cuenta corriente número 20-453

Emparejar En la tabla hay nueve abreviaturas. Empareja los cuadros necesarios para formarlas.

S.	c.	C.	c	co.	U
B	c/	Sr	A.	D	dc
ta.	P.	ña.	ha.	m	d.

Paseando en metro

Hoy es el primer día de Teresa en la Ciudad de México. Debe tomar el metro para ir del centro de la ciudad a Coyoacán, en el sur. Llega a la estación Zócalo y compra un pasaje por el equivalente a treinta y nueve centavos° de dólar, ¡qué ganga! Con este pasaje puede ir a cualquier° parte de la ciudad o del área metropolitana.

No sólo en México, sino también en ciudades de Venezuela, Chile, Argentina y España, hay sistemas de transporte público eficientes y muy económicos. También suele haber° varios tipos de transporte: autobús, metro, tranvía°, microbús y tren. Generalmente se pueden comprar abonos° de uno o varios días para un determinado tipo de transporte. En algunas ciudades también existen abonos de transporte

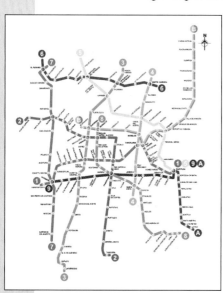

combinados que permiten usar, por ejemplo, el metro y el autobús o el autobús y el tren. En estas ciudades, los metros, autobuses y trenes pasan con mucha frecuencia. Las paradas° y estaciones están bien señalizadas°.

Vaya°, Teresa ya está llegando a Coyoacán. Con lo que ahorró en el pasaje del metro, puede comprarse un helado de mango y unos esquites° en el jardín Centenario.

El metro

El primer metro de Suramérica que se abrió al público fue el de Buenos Aires, Argentina (1913); el último, el de Lima, Perú (2011).

Ciudad	Pasajeros/Día (aprox.)
México D.F., México	5.200.000
Madrid, España	2.500.000
Santiago, Chile	2.400.000
Caracas, Venezuela	1.800.000
Buenos Aires, Argentina	1.000.000
Medellín, Colombia	770.000
Guadalajara, México	206.000

centavos *cents* cualquier *any* suele haber *there usually are* tranvía *streetcar* abonos *passes* paradas *stops* señalizadas *labeled* Vaya *Well* esquites *toasted corn kernels*

1 **¿Cierto o falso?** Indica si lo que dice cada oración es **cierto** o **falso**. Corrige la información falsa.

1. En la Ciudad de México, el pasaje de metro cuesta 39 dólares.
2. En México, un pasaje se puede usar sólo para ir al centro de la ciudad.
3. En Chile hay varios tipos de transporte público.
4. En ningún caso los abonos de transporte sirven para más de un tipo de transporte.
5. Los trenes, autobuses y metros pasan con mucha frecuencia.
6. Hay pocos letreros en las paradas y estaciones.
7. Los servicios de metro de México y España son los que mayor cantidad de viajeros transporta cada día.
8. La ciudad de Buenos Aires tiene el sistema de metro más viejo de Latinoamérica.
9. El metro que lleva menos tiempo en servicio es el de la ciudad de Medellín, Colombia.

ASÍ SE DICE

En la ciudad

el parqueadero (Col., Pan.) el parqueo (Bol., Cuba, Amér. C.)	el estacionamiento
dar un aventón (Méx.); dar botella (Cuba)	*to give (someone) a ride*
el subterráneo, el subte (Arg.)	el metro

EL MUNDO HISPANO

Apodos de ciudades

Así como Nueva York es la Gran Manzana, muchas ciudades hispanas tienen un apodo°.

- **La tacita de plata**° A Cádiz, España, se le llama así por sus edificios blancos de estilo árabe.

- **Ciudad de la eterna primavera** Arica, Chile; Cuernavaca, México, y Medellín, Colombia, llevan este sobrenombre por su clima templado° durante todo el año.

- **La docta**° Así se conoce a la ciudad argentina de Córdoba por su gran tradición universitaria.

- **La ciudad de los reyes** Así se conoce Lima, Perú, porque fue la capital del Virreinato° del Perú y allí vivían los virreyes°.

- **La arenosa** Barranquilla, Colombia, se le llama así por sus orillas del río cubiertas° de arena.

apodo *nickname* plata *silver* templado *mild* docta *erudite* Virreinato *Viceroyalty* virreyes *viceroys* cubiertas *covered*

PERFIL

Luis Barragán: arquitectura y emoción

Para el arquitecto mexicano **Luis Barragán** (1902–1988) los sentimientos° y emociones que despiertan sus diseños eran muy importantes. Afirmaba° que la arquitectura tiene una dimensión espiritual. Para él, era belleza, inspiración, magia°, serenidad, misterio, silencio, privacidad, asombro°...

Casa Barragán, Ciudad de México, 1947-1948

Las obras de Barragán muestran un suave° equilibrio entre la naturaleza y la creación humana. Su estilo también combina la arquitectura tradicional mexicana con conceptos modernos. Una característica de sus casas son las paredes envolventes° de diferentes colores con muy pocas ventanas.

En 1980, Barragán obtuvo° el Premio Pritzker, algo así como el Premio Nobel de Arquitectura. Está claro que este artista logró° que sus casas transmitieran sentimientos especiales.

sentimientos *feelings* Afirmaba *He stated* magia *magic* asombro *amazement* suave *smooth* envolventes *enveloping* obtuvo *received* logró *managed*

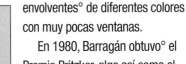

¿Qué otros arquitectos combinan las construcciones con la naturaleza? Use the Web to find more cultural information related to this **Cultura** section.

ACTIVIDADES

2 **Comprensión** Contesta las preguntas.

1. ¿En qué país estás si te dicen "Dame botella al parqueo"?
2. ¿Qué ciudades tienen clima templado todo el año?
3. ¿Qué es más importante en los diseños de Barragán: la naturaleza o la creación humana?
4. ¿Qué premio obtuvo Barragán y cuándo?

3 **¿Qué ciudad te gusta?** Escribe un párrafo breve sobre el sentimiento que despiertan las construcciones que hay en una ciudad o un pueblo que te guste mucho. Explica cómo es y cómo te sientes cuando estás allí. Inventa un apodo para este lugar.

14.1 The subjunctive in adjective clauses

ANTE TODO In **Lección 13**, you learned that the subjunctive is used in adverbial clauses after certain conjunctions. You will now learn how the subjunctive can be used in adjective clauses to express that the existence of someone or something is uncertain or indefinite.

¿Conoces una joyería que esté cerca?

No, no conozco ninguna joyería que esté cerca de aquí.

▶ The subjunctive is used in an adjective (or subordinate) clause that refers to a person, place, thing, or idea that either does not exist or whose existence is uncertain or indefinite. In the examples below, compare the differences in meaning between the statements using the indicative and those using the subjunctive.

Indicative	Subjunctive
Necesito **el libro** que **tiene** información sobre Venezuela.	Necesito **un libro** que **tenga** información sobre Venezuela.
*I need **the book** that has information about Venezuela.*	*I need **a book** that has information about Venezuela.*
Quiero vivir en **esta casa** que **tiene** jardín.	Quiero vivir en **una casa** que **tenga** jardín.
*I want to live in **this house** that has a garden.*	*I want to live in **a house** that has a garden.*
En mi barrio, hay **una heladería** que **vende** helado de mango.	En mi barrio no hay **ninguna heladería** que **venda** helado de mango.
*In my neighborhood, **there's an ice cream shop** that sells mango ice cream.*	*In my neighborhood, **there is no ice cream shop** that sells mango ice cream.*

▶ When the adjective clause refers to a person, place, thing, or idea that is clearly known, certain, or definite, the indicative is used.

Quiero ir **al supermercado** que **vende** productos venezolanos.
I want to go to the supermarket that sells Venezuelan products.

Busco **al profesor** que **enseña** japonés.
I'm looking for the professor who teaches Japanese.

Conozco **a alguien** que **va** a esa peluquería.
I know someone who goes to that beauty salon.

Tengo **un amigo** que **vive** cerca de mi casa.
I have a friend who lives near my house.

▶ The personal **a** is not used with direct objects that are hypothetical people. However, as you learned in **Lección 7**, **alguien** and **nadie** are always preceded by the personal **a** when they function as direct objects.

<table>
<tr>
<td>

Necesitamos **un empleado** que
sepa usar computadoras.
*We need an employee who knows
how to use computers.*

</td>
<td>

Necesitamos **al empleado** que
sabe usar computadoras.
*We need the employee who knows how
to use computers.*

</td>
</tr>
<tr>
<td>

Buscamos **a alguien** que
pueda cocinar.
*We're looking for someone who
can cook.*

</td>
<td>

No conocemos **a nadie** que
pueda cocinar.
*We don't know anyone who
can cook.*

</td>
</tr>
</table>

▶ The subjunctive is commonly used in questions with adjective clauses when the speaker is trying to find out information about which he or she is uncertain. However, if the person who responds to the question knows the information, the indicative is used.

—¿Hay un parque que **esté** cerca de nuestro hotel?	—Sí, hay un parque que **está** muy cerca del hotel.
Is there a park that's near our hotel?	*Yes, there's a park that's very near the hotel.*

▶ **¡Atención!** Here are some verbs that are commonly followed by adjective clauses in the subjunctive:

Verbs commonly used with subjunctive

buscar	**haber**
conocer	**necesitar**
encontrar	**querer**

SECCIÓN
AMARILLA
Busque cualquier
información que
necesite.

¡INTÉNTALO!   Escoge entre el subjuntivo y el indicativo para completar cada oración.

1. Necesito una persona que ___*pueda*___ (puede/pueda) cantar bien.
2. Buscamos a alguien que _____ (tiene/tenga) paciencia.
3. ¿Hay restaurantes aquí que _____ (sirven/sirvan) comida japonesa?
4. Tengo una amiga que _____ (saca/saque) fotografías muy bonitas.
5. Hay una carnicería que _____ (está/esté) cerca de aquí.
6. No vemos ningún apartamento que nos _____ (interesa/interese).
7. Conozco a un estudiante que _____ (come/coma) hamburguesas todos los días.
8. ¿Hay alguien que _____ (dice/diga) la verdad?

Práctica

1

Completar Completa estas oraciones con la forma correcta del indicativo o del subjuntivo de los verbos entre paréntesis.

1. Buscamos un hotel que _____ (tener) piscina.
2. ¿Sabe usted dónde _____ (quedar) el Correo Central?
3. ¿Hay algún buzón por aquí donde yo _____ (poder) echar una carta?
4. Ana quiere ir a la carnicería que _____ (estar) en la avenida Lecuna.
5. Encontramos un restaurante que _____ (servir) comida típica venezolana.
6. ¿Conoces a alguien que _____ (saber) mandar un *fax* por computadora?
7. Llamas al empleado que _____ (entender) este nuevo programa de computación.
8. No hay nada en este mundo que _____ (ser) gratis.

2

Oraciones Marta está haciendo diligencias en Caracas con una amiga. Forma oraciones con estos elementos, usando el presente de indicativo o de subjuntivo. Haz los cambios que sean necesarios.

1. yo / conocer / un / panadería / que / vender / pan / cubano

2. ¿hay / alguien / que / saber / dirección / de / un / buen / carnicería?

3. yo / querer / comprarle / mi / hija / un / zapatos / que / gustar

4. ella / no / encontrar / nada / que / gustar / en / ese / zapatería

5. ¿tener / dependientas / algo / que / ser / más / barato?

6. ¿conocer / tú / alguno / banco / que / ofrecer / cuentas / corrientes / gratis?

7. nosotras / no / conocer / nadie / que / hacer / tanto / diligencias / como / nosotras

8. nosotras / necesitar / un / línea / de / metro / que / nos / llevar / a / casa

NOTA CULTURAL

El **metro** de Caracas empezó a funcionar en 1983, después de varios años de intensa publicidad para promoverlo (*promote it*). El arte fue un recurso importante en la promoción del metro. En las estaciones se pueden admirar obras (*works*) de famosos escultores venezolanos como Carlos Cruz-Diez y Jesús Rafael Soto.

3

Anuncios clasificados Lee estos anuncios y luego describe el tipo de persona u objeto que se busca.

CLASIFICADOS

VENDEDOR(A) Se necesita persona dinámica y responsable con buena presencia. Experiencia mínima de un año. Horario de trabajo flexible. Llamar a Joyería Aurora de 10 a 13h y de 16 a 18h. Tel: 263-7553

PELUQUERÍA UNISEX Se busca persona con experiencia en peluquería y maquillaje para trabajar tiempo completo. Llamar de 9 a 13: 30h. Tel: 261-3548

COMPARTIR APARTAMENTO Se necesita compañera para compartir apartamento de 2 dormitorios en el Chaco. Alquiler $500 por mes. No fumar. Llamar al 951-3642 entre 19 y 22h.

CLASES DE INGLÉS Profesor de Inglaterra con diez años de experiencia ofrece clases para grupos o instrucción privada para individuos. Llamar al 933-4110 de 16:30 a 18:30.

SE BUSCA CONDOMINIO Se busca condominio en Sabana Grande con 3 dormitorios, 2 baños, sala, comedor y aire acondicionado. Tel: 977-2018.

EJECUTIVO DE CUENTAS Se requiere joven profesional con al menos dos años de experiencia en el sector financiero. Se ofrecen beneficios excelentes. Enviar currículum vitae al Banco Unión, Avda. Urdaneta 263, Caracas.

Comunicación

4

Un apartamento Lee la nota que Luis le escribe a un agente inmobiliario (*real estate agent*). Luego, indica si las conclusiones sobre Luis son **lógicas** o **ilógicas**, según lo que leíste.

Necesito vivir en un barrio que tenga transporte público para poder ir a la universidad, porque no tengo carro. También necesito vivir cerca de una biblioteca que tenga libros en varias lenguas. Busco un apartamento que esté cerca del supermercado y del banco. También necesito que quede cerca de la lavandería. Prefiero vivir solo, pero también puedo buscar a un estudiante que necesite un cuarto para alquilar.

Luis Herrera

		Lógico	Ilógico
1.	Quiere vivir en la ciudad.	○	○
2.	Estudia lenguas extranjeras en la universidad.	○	○
3.	Busca un edificio de apartamentos que tenga estacionamiento.	○	○
4.	Necesita un apartamento que tenga lavadora y secadora.	○	○

5

Preguntas Contesta las preguntas de tu compañero/a. Usa el presente de indicativo o de subjuntivo, según corresponda.

> **modelo**
>
> hablar ruso
> **Estudiante 1:** *¿Conoces a alguien que hable ruso?*
> **Estudiante 2:** *No, no conozco a nadie que hable ruso./Sí, conozco a alguien que habla ruso.*

1. no usar el cajero automático
2. vivir enfrente de un correo
3. ser alérgico/a a los mariscos
4. no tener cuenta de ahorros
5. casarse este año
6. levantarse a las cinco
7. saber bailar tango
8. odiar hacer cola

6

¿Compatibles? Vas a mudarte a un apartamento con dos dormitorios. Como no quieres pagar el alquiler tú solo/a, estás buscando a un(a) compañero/a para que viva contigo. Entrevista a un(a) candidato/a para ver si tiene las cuatro características que consideres importantes. Puedes usar algunas de estas opciones u otras y no olvides usar el subjuntivo.

- cocinar
- escuchar hip-hop
- gustarle la política/el arte/los deportes
- llevarse bien con los animales
- ser vegetariano/a / limpio/a / optimista
- tener paciencia

Síntesis

7

La ciudad ideal Escribe un párrafo de al menos seis oraciones en el que describas cómo es la comunidad ideal donde te gustaría (*you would like*) vivir en el futuro y compárala con la comunidad donde vives ahora. Usa cláusulas adjetivas y el vocabulario de esta lección.

14.2 Nosotros/as commands

ANTE TODO You have already learned familiar (**tú**) commands and formal (**usted/ ustedes**) commands. You will now learn **nosotros/as** commands, which are used to give orders or suggestions that include yourself and other people.

▶ **Nosotros/as** commands correspond to the English *Let's*.

▶ Both affirmative and negative **nosotros/as** commands are generally formed by using the first-person plural form of the present subjunctive.

Crucemos la calle.
Let's cross the street.

No crucemos la calle.
Let's not cross the street.

▶ The affirmative *Let's* + [*verb*] command may also be expressed with **vamos a** + [*infinitive*]. However, remember that **vamos a** + [*infinitive*] can also mean *we are going to (do something)*. Context and tone of voice determine which meaning is being expressed.

Vamos a cruzar la calle.
Let's cross the street.

Vamos a trabajar mucho.
We're going to work a lot.

▶ To express *Let's go*, the present indicative form of **ir** (**vamos**) is used, not the subjunctive. For the negative command, however, the subjunctive is used.

Vamos a la pescadería.

No **vayamos** a la pescadería.

Pensemos, ¿adónde fuiste hoy?

¡Eso es! ¡El carro de Miguel! Vamos.

▶ Object pronouns are always attached to affirmative **nosotros/as** commands. A written accent is added to maintain the original stress.

Firmemos el cheque.
Firmémoslo.

Escribamos a Ana y Raúl.
Escribámosles.

▶ Object pronouns are placed in front of negative **nosotros/as** commands.

No **les paguemos** el préstamo.

No **se lo digamos** a ellos.

CONSULTA

Remember that stem-changing **–ir** verbs have an additional stem change in the **nosotros/as** and **vosotros/as** forms of the present subjunctive. To review these forms, see **Estructura 12.3**, p. 423.

¡ATENCIÓN!

When **nos** or **se** is attached to an affirmative **nosotros/as** command, the final **–s** is dropped from the verb ending.
Sentémonos allí.
Démoselo a ella.
Mandémoselo a ellos.

• • •

The **nosotros/as** command form of **irse** is **vámonos**. Its negative form is **no nos vayamos**.

¡INTÉNTALO! Indica los mandatos afirmativos y negativos de la primera persona del plural (**nosotros/as**) de estos verbos.

1. estudiar _estudiemos, no estudiemos_
2. cenar _____
3. leer _____
4. decidir _____
5. decir _____
6. cerrar _____
7. levantarse _____
8. irse _____

Práctica

1 **Completar** Completa esta conversación con mandatos de **nosotros/as**.

MARÍA Sergio, ¿quieres hacer diligencias
ahora o por la tarde?

SERGIO No (1)_____ (dejarlas) para más
tarde. (2)_____ (Hacerlas) ahora.
¿Qué tenemos que hacer?

MARÍA Necesito comprar sellos.

SERGIO Yo también. (3)_____ (Ir)
al correo.

MARÍA Pues, antes de ir al correo, necesito
sacar dinero de mi cuenta corriente.

SERGIO Bueno, (4)_____ (buscar) un
cajero automático.

MARÍA ¿Tienes hambre?

SERGIO Sí. (5)_____ (Cruzar) la calle y
(6)_____ (entrar) en ese café.

MARÍA Buena idea.

SERGIO ¿Nos sentamos aquí?

MARÍA No, no (7)_____ (sentarse) aquí;
(8)_____ (sentarse) enfrente de la ventana.

SERGIO ¿Qué pedimos?

MARÍA (9)_____ (Pedir) café y pan dulce.

2 **Responder** Responde a cada mandato de **nosotros/as** según las indicaciones entre paréntesis.
Sustituye los sustantivos por los objetos directos e indirectos.

> **modelo**
>
> Vamos a vender el carro.
> *Sí, vendámoslo./No, no lo vendamos.*

1. Vamos a levantarnos a las seis. (sí)

2. Vamos a enviar los paquetes. (no)

3. Vamos a depositar el cheque. (sí)

4. Vamos al supermercado. (no)

5. Vamos a mandar esta postal a nuestros amigos. (no)

6. Vamos a limpiar la habitación. (sí)

7. Vamos a mirar la televisión. (no)

8. Vamos a bailar. (sí)

9. Vamos a pintar la sala. (no)

10. Vamos a comprar estampillas. (sí)

Comunicación

3

¡Quiero un celular! Escucha la conversación entre Rosa, una adolescente mimada (*spoiled*), y su madre. Luego, indica si las conclusiones son **lógicas** o **ilógicas**, según lo que escuchaste.

	Lógico	Ilógico
1. Rosa es simpática.	○	○
2. La madre de Rosa necesita hacer diligencias.	○	○
3. Rosa es una chica muy obediente.	○	○
4. El padre de Rosa es más estricto que la madre.	○	○
5. Es probable que Rosa coma pizza.	○	○

4

Preguntar Tú y tu compañero/a están de vacaciones en Caracas y se hacen sugerencias para resolver las situaciones que se presentan. Inventen mandatos afirmativos o negativos de **nosotros/as**.

> **modelo**
>
> Se nos olvidaron las tarjetas de crédito.
>
> *Paguemos en efectivo./No compremos más regalos.*

A

1. El museo está a sólo una cuadra de aquí.
2. Tenemos hambre.
3. Hay una cola larga en el cine.

B

1. Tenemos muchos cheques de viajero.
2. Tenemos prisa para llegar al cine.
3. Estamos cansados y queremos dormir.

5

Decisiones En parejas, decidan adónde quieren ir de vacaciones. Hablen de lo que quieren hacer y de lo que no quieren hacer en su viaje. Usen mandatos afirmativos y negativos de **nosotros/as**.

> **modelo**
>
> **Estudiante 1:** Visitemos la Casa Natal de Simón Bolívar en Caracas.
> **Estudiante 2:** No la visitemos. Vamos al Jardín Botánico.

Síntesis

6

Situación Tú y tu compañero/a de apartamento tienen problemas económicos. Describe los problemas y sugiere algunas soluciones. Escribe oraciones con mandatos afirmativos o negativos de **nosotros/as**.

> **modelo**
>
> Hagamos un presupuesto (*budget*).
> No gastemos tanto dinero.

14.3 Past participles used as adjectives

ANTE TODO   In **Lección 5**, you learned about present participles (**estudiando**). Both Spanish and English have past participles. The past participles of English verbs often end in **-ed** (*to turn* → *turned*), but many are also irregular (*to buy* → *bought; to drive* → *driven*).

▶ In Spanish, regular **-ar** verbs form the past participle with **-ado**. Regular **-er** and **-ir** verbs form the past participle with **-ido**.

INFINITIVE	STEM	PAST PARTICIPLE
bailar	bail-	**bailado**
comer	com-	**comido**
vivir	viv-	**vivido**

▶ **¡Atención!** The past participles of **-er** and **-ir** verbs whose stems end in **-a, -e,** or **-o** carry a written accent mark on the **i** of the **-ido** ending.

caer	**caído**	reír	**reído**
creer	**creído**	sonreír	**sonreído**
leer	**leído**	traer	**traído**
oír	**oído**		

Irregular past participles

abrir	**abierto**	morir	**muerto**
decir	**dicho**	poner	**puesto**
describir	**descrito**	resolver	**resuelto**
descubrir	**descubierto**	romper	**roto**
escribir	**escrito**	ver	**visto**
hacer	**hecho**	volver	**vuelto**

AYUDA

You already know several past participles used as adjectives: **aburrido, interesado, nublado, perdido,** etc.

• • •

Note that all irregular past participles except **dicho** and **hecho** end in **-to**.

▶ In Spanish, as in English, past participles can be used as adjectives. They are often used with the verb **estar** to describe a condition or state that results from an action. Like other Spanish adjectives, they must agree in gender and number with the nouns they modify.

En la entrada hay algunos letreros **escritos** en español.
In the entrance, there are some signs written in Spanish.

Tenemos la mesa **puesta** y la cena **hecha**.
We have the table set and dinner made.

¡INTÉNTALO!   Indica la forma correcta del participio pasado de estos verbos.

1. hablar ___hablado___
2. beber _____
3. decidir _____
4. romper _____

5. escribir _____
6. cantar _____
7. oír _____
8. traer _____

9. correr _____
10. leer _____
11. ver _____
12. hacer _____

Práctica

1 **Completar** Completa las oraciones con la forma adecuada del participio pasado del verbo que está entre paréntesis.

1. Hoy mi peluquería favorita está _____ (cerrar).
2. Por eso, voy a otro salón de belleza que está _____ (abrir) todos los días.
3. Queda en la Plaza Bolívar, una plaza muy _____ (conocer).
4. Todos los productos y servicios de esta tienda están _____ (describir) en un catálogo.
5. El nombre del salón está _____ (escribir) en el letrero y en la acera (*sidewalk*).
6. Cuando la tarea esté _____ (hacer), necesito pasar por el banco.

2 **Preparativos** Tú vas a hacer un viaje. Contesta estas preguntas sobre los preparativos (*preparations*). Responde afirmativamente y usa el participio pasado en tus respuestas.

> **modelo**
>
> ¿Firmaste el cheque de viajero?
>
> *Sí, el cheque de viajero ya está firmado.*

1. ¿Compraste los pasajes para el avión?
2. ¿Confirmaste las reservaciones para el hotel?
3. ¿Firmaste tu pasaporte?
4. ¿Lavaste la ropa?
5. ¿Resolviste el problema con el banco?
6. ¿Pagaste todas las cuentas?
7. ¿Hiciste todas las diligencias?
8. ¿Hiciste las maletas?

3 **El estudiante competitivo** Haz el papel de un(a) estudiante que es muy competitivo/a y siempre quiere ser mejor que los demás. Usa los participios pasados de los verbos subrayados.

> **modelo**
>
> A veces se me <u>daña</u> la computadora.
>
> *Yo sé mucho de computadoras. Mi computadora nunca está <u>dañada</u>.*

1. Yo no <u>hago</u> la cama todos los días.

2. Casi nunca <u>resuelvo</u> mis problemas.

3. Nunca <u>guardo</u> mis documentos importantes.

4. Es difícil para mí <u>terminar</u> mis tareas.

5. Siempre se me olvida <u>firmar</u> mis tarjetas de crédito.

6. Nunca <u>pongo</u> la mesa cuando ceno.

7. No quiero <u>escribir</u> la composición para mañana.

8. Casi nunca <u>lavo</u> mi carro.

Comunicación

4

Correo de voz Escucha este correo de voz que Camila le deja a su madre. Luego, indica si las conclusiones son **lógicas** o **ilógicas**, según lo que escuchaste.

	Lógico	Ilógico
1. Camila es irresponsable.	○	○
2. Camila vive con sus padres.	○	○
3. El papá de Camila está muerto.	○	○
4. La familia de Camila se mudó recientemente.	○	○

5

Preguntas Contesta las preguntas de tu compañero/a.

1. ¿Dejas alguna luz prendida en tu casa por la noche?
2. ¿Está ordenado tu cuarto?
3. ¿Prefieres comprar libros usados o nuevos? ¿Por qué?
4. ¿Tienes mucho dinero ahorrado?
5. ¿Necesitas pedirles dinero prestado a tus padres?
6. ¿Estás preocupado/a por el medio ambiente?
7. ¿Qué haces cuando no estás preparado/a para una clase?
8. ¿Qué haces cuando estás perdido/a en una ciudad?

6

Describir Eres agente de policía y tienes que investigar un crimen. Mira el dibujo y describe lo que encontraste en la habitación del señor Villalonga. Usa el participio pasado en la descripción.

AYUDA

You may want to use the past participles of these verbs to describe the illustration: **abrir, desordenar, hacer, poner, romper, tirar** (*to throw*).

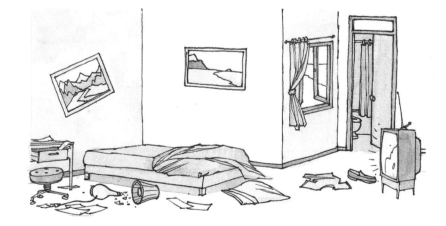

Síntesis

7

Entre líneas En parejas, representen una conversación entre un empleado de banco y una clienta. Usen las primeras dos líneas del diálogo para empezar y la última para terminar, pero inventen las líneas del medio (*middle*). Usen participios pasados.

EMPLEADO Buenos días, señora Ibáñez. ¿En qué la puedo ayudar?
CLIENTA Tengo un problema con este banco. ¡Todavía no está resuelto!
...
CLIENTA ¡No vuelvo nunca a este banco!

Recapitulación

Completa estas actividades para repasar los conceptos de gramática que aprendiste en esta lección.

1   **Completar** Completa la tabla con la forma correcta de los verbos. **16 pts.**

Infinitivo	Participio	Infinitivo	Participio
completar	completada	hacer	
corregir		pagar	pagado
creer		pedir	
decir		perder	
escribir		poner	

2   **Los novios** Completa este diálogo entre dos novios con mandatos en la forma de **nosotros/as**. **30 pts.**

SIMÓN   ¿Quieres ir al cine mañana?

CARLA   Sí, ¡qué buena idea! (1) _____ (Comprar) los boletos (*tickets*) por Internet.

SIMÓN   No, mejor (2) _____ (pedírselos) a mi prima, quien trabaja en el cine y los consigue gratis.

CARLA   ¡Fantástico!

SIMÓN   Y también quiero visitar la nueva galería de arte el fin de semana que viene.

CARLA   ¿Por qué esperar? (3) _____ (Visitarla) esta tarde.

SIMÓN   Bueno, pero primero tengo que limpiar mi apartamento.

CARLA   No hay problema. (4) _____ (Limpiarlo) juntos.

SIMÓN   Muy bien. ¿Y tú no tienes que hacer diligencias hoy? (5) _____ (Hacerlas) también.

CARLA   Sí, tengo que ir al correo y al banco. (6) _____ (Ir) al banco hoy, pero no (7) _____ (ir) al correo todavía. Antes tengo que escribir una carta.

SIMÓN   ¿Una carta misteriosa? (8) _____ (Escribirla) ahora.

CARLA   No, mejor no (9) _____ (escribirla) hasta que regresemos de la galería donde venden un papel reciclado muy lindo (*cute*).

SIMÓN   ¿Papel lindo? Pues, ¿para quién es la carta?

CARLA   No importa. (10) _____ (Empezar) a limpiar.

RESUMEN GRAMATICAL

14.1   The subjunctive in adjective clauses
pp. 486–487

▶ When adjective clauses refer to something that is known, certain, or definite, the indicative is used.

Necesito el **libro** que **tiene** fotos.

▶ When adjective clauses refer to something that is uncertain or indefinite, the subjunctive is used.

Necesito un **libro** que **tenga** fotos.

14.2   Nosotros/as commands   *p. 490*

▶ Same as **nosotros/as** form of present subjunctive.

Affirmative	Negative
Démosle un libro a Lola.	No le demos un libro a Lola.
Démoselo.	No se lo demos.

▶ While the subjunctive form of the verb **ir** is used for the negative **nosotros/as** command, the indicative is used for the affirmative command.

No **vayamos** a la plaza.   **Vamos** a la plaza.

14.3   Past participles used as adjectives   *p. 493*

Past participles		
Infinitive	Stem	Past participle
bailar	bail-	**bail**ado
comer	com-	**com**ido
vivir	viv-	**viv**ido

Irregular past participles			
abrir	**abierto**	morir	**muerto**
decir	**dicho**	poner	**puesto**
describir	**descrito**	resolver	**resuelto**
descubrir	**descubierto**	romper	**roto**
escribir	**escrito**	ver	**visto**
hacer	**hecho**	volver	**vuelto**

▶ Like common adjectives, past participles must agree with the noun they modify.

Hay unos letreros **escritos** en español.

3 **Verbos** Escribe los verbos en el presente de indicativo o de subjuntivo. `30 pts.`

1. —¿Sabes dónde hay un restaurante donde nosotros (1) _____ (poder) comer paella valenciana? —No, no conozco ninguno que (2) _____ (servir) paella, pero conozco uno que (3) _____ (especializarse) en tapas españolas.

2. Busco vendedores que (4) _____ (ser) bilingües. No estoy seguro de conocer a alguien que (5) _____ (tener) esa característica. Pero ahora que lo pienso, ¡sí! Tengo dos amigos que (6) _____ (trabajar) en el almacén Excelencia. Los voy a llamar. Debo decirles que necesitamos que (ellos) (7) _____ (saber) hablar inglés.

3. Se busca apartamento que (8) _____ (estar) bien situado, que (9) _____ (costar) menos de $800 al mes y que (10) _____ (permitir) tener perros.

4 **La mamá de Pedro** Completa las respuestas de Pedro a las preguntas de su mamá. `20 pts.`

> **modelo**
> **MAMÁ:** ¿Te ayudo a guardar la ropa?
> **PEDRO:** La ropa ya *está guardada.*

1. **MAMÁ** ¿Cuándo se van a vestir tú y tu hermano para la fiesta?
   PEDRO Nosotros ya _____.

2. **MAMÁ** Hijo, ¿puedes ordenar tu habitación?
   PEDRO La habitación ya _____ _____.

3. **MAMÁ** ¿Ya se murieron tus peces?
   PEDRO No, todavía no _____ _____.

4. **MAMÁ** ¿Te ayudo a hacer tus diligencias?
   PEDRO Gracias, mamá, pero las diligencias ya _____ _____.

5. **MAMÁ** ¿Cuándo terminas tu proyecto?
   PEDRO El proyecto ya _____ _____.

5 **Adivinanza** Completa la adivinanza y adivina la respuesta. `4 pts.`

> **" Me llegan las cartas y no sé _____ (*to read*) y, aunque° me las como, no mancho° el papel. "**
> **¿Quién soy?** _____

aunque *although* no mancho *I don't stain*

Lectura

Antes de leer

Estrategia

Identifying point of view

You can understand a narrative more completely if you identify the point of view of the narrator. You can do this by simply asking yourself from whose perspective the story is being told. Some stories are narrated in the first person. That is, the narrator is a character in the story, and everything you read is filtered through that person's thoughts, emotions, and opinions. Other stories have an omniscient narrator who is not one of the story's characters and who reports the thoughts and actions of all the characters.

Examinar el texto

Lee brevemente este cuento escrito por Marco Denevi. ¿Crees que se narra en primera persona o tiene un narrador omnisciente? ¿Cómo lo sabes?

_____

_____

Punto de vista

Éstos son fragmentos de *Esquina peligrosa* en los que se cambió el punto de vista° a primera persona. Completa cada oración de manera lógica.

1. Le _____ a mi chofer que me condujese hasta aquel barrio...

2. Al doblar la esquina _____ el almacén, el mismo viejo y sombrío almacén donde _____ había trabajado como dependiente...

3. El recuerdo de _____ niñez me puso nostálgico. Se _____ humedecieron los ojos.

4. Yo _____ la canasta de mimbre, _____ llenándola con paquetes [...] y _____ a hacer el reparto.

Marco Denevi (1922–1998) fue un escritor y dramaturgo argentino. Estudió derecho y más tarde se convirtió en escritor. Algunas de sus obras, como *Rosaura a las diez*, han sido° llevadas al cine. Denevi se caracteriza por su gran creatividad e ingenio, que jamás dejan de sorprender al lector°.

Esquina peligrosa

Marco Denevi

El señor Epidídimus, el magnate de las finanzas°, uno de los hombres más ricos del mundo, sintió un día el vehemente deseo de visitar el barrio donde había vivido cuando era niño y trabajaba como dependiente de almacén.

Le ordenó a su chofer que lo condujese hasta aquel barrio humilde° y remoto. Pero el barrio estaba tan cambiado que el señor Epidídimus no lo reconoció. En lugar de calles de tierra había bulevares asfaltados°, y las míseras casitas de antaño° habían sido reemplazadas por torres de departamentos°.

Al doblar una esquina vio el almacén, el mismo viejo y sombrío° almacén donde él había trabajado como dependiente cuando tenía doce años.

—Deténgase aquí—le dijo al chofer. Descendió del automóvil y entró en el almacén. Todo se conservaba igual que en la época de su infancia: las estanterías, la anticuada caja registradora°, la balanza de pesas° y, alrededor, el mudo asedio° de la mercadería.

El señor Epidídimus percibió el mismo olor de sesenta años atrás: un olor picante y agridulce a jabón han sido *have been* lector *reader* finanzas *finance* humilde *humble, modest* asfaltados *paved with asphalt* antaño *yesteryear* torres de departamentos *apartment buildings* sombrío *somber* anticuada caja registradora *old-fashioned cash register* balanza de pesas *scale* mudo asedio *silent siege* aserrín *sawdust* acaroína *pesticide* penumbra del fondo *half-light from the back* reparto *delivery* lodazal *bog*

amarillo, a aserrín° húmedo, a vinagre, a aceitunas, a acaroína°. El recuerdo de su niñez lo puso nostálgico. Se le humedecieron los ojos. Le pareció que retrocedía en el tiempo.

Desde la penumbra del fondo° le llegó la voz ruda del patrón:

—¿Estas son horas de venir? Te quedaste dormido, como siempre.

El señor Epidídimus tomó la canasta de mimbre, fue llenándola con paquetes de azúcar, de yerba y de fideos, y salió a hacer el reparto°.

La noche anterior había llovido y las calles de tierra estaban convertidas en un lodazal°.

(1974)

© Denevi, Marco, Cartas peligrosas y otros cuentos. Obras Completas, Tomo 5, Buenos Aires, Corregidor, 1990, págs. 192-193.

Después de leer

Comprensión

Indica si las oraciones son **ciertas** o **falsas**. Corrige las falsas.

Cierto   Falso

_____ _____ 1. El señor Epidídimus tiene una tienda con la que gana poco dinero.

_____ _____ 2. Epidídimus vivía en un barrio humilde cuando era pequeño.

_____ _____ 3. Epidídimus le ordenó al chofer que lo llevara a un barrio de gente con poco dinero.

_____ _____ 4. Cuando Epidídimus entró al almacén se acordó de experiencias pasadas.

_____ _____ 5. Epidídimus les dio órdenes a los empleados del almacén.

Interpretación

Contesta estas preguntas con oraciones completas.

1. ¿Es rico o pobre Epidídimus? ¿Cómo lo sabes?
   _____

2. ¿Por qué Epidídimus va al almacén?
   _____

3. ¿De quién es la voz "ruda" que Epidídimus escucha? ¿Qué orden crees que le dio a Epidídimus?
   _____

4. ¿Qué hace Epidídimus al final?
   _____

Coméntalo

Comenta tus impresiones y conclusiones. Toma como guía estas preguntas.

- ¿Te sorprendió el final de este cuento? ¿Por qué?
- ¿Qué va a hacer Epidídimus el resto del día?
- ¿Crees que Epidídimus niño estaba soñando o Epidídimus adulto estaba recordando?
- ¿Por qué crees que el cuento se llama *Esquina peligrosa*?

Escritura

Estrategia
Avoiding redundancies

Redundancy is the needless repetition of words or ideas. To avoid redundancy with verbs and nouns, consult a Spanish language thesaurus (**Diccionario de sinónimos**). You can also avoid redundancy by using object pronouns, possessive adjectives, demonstrative adjectives and pronouns, and relative pronouns. Remember that, in Spanish, subject pronouns are generally used only for clarification, emphasis, or contrast. Study the example below:

Redundant:

Susana quería visitar a su amiga. Susana estaba en la ciudad. Susana tomó el tren y perdió el mapa de la ciudad. Susana estaba perdida en la ciudad. Susana estaba nerviosa. Por fin, la amiga de Susana la llamó a Susana y le indicó cómo llegar.

Improved:

Susana, quien estaba en la ciudad, quería visitar a su amiga. Tomó el tren y perdió el mapa. Estaba perdida y nerviosa. Por fin, su amiga la llamó y le indicó cómo llegar.

Tema
Escribir un mensaje electrónico

Vas a visitar a un(a) amigo/a que vive en una ciudad que no conoces. Vas a pasar allí una semana y tienes que hacer también un trabajo para tu clase de literatura. Tienes planes de alquilar un carro, pero no sabes cómo llegar del aeropuerto a la casa de tu amigo/a.

Escríbele a tu amigo/a un mensaje electrónico describiendo lo que te interesa hacer allí y dale sugerencias de actividades que pueden hacer juntos/as. Menciona lo que necesitas para hacer tu trabajo. Puedes basarte en una visita real o imaginaria.

Considera esta lista de datos que puedes incluir:

▶ El nombre de la ciudad que vas a visitar

▶ Los lugares que más te interesa visitar

▶ Lo que necesitas para hacer tu trabajo:
   acceso a Internet
   saber cómo llegar a la biblioteca pública
   tiempo para estar solo/a
   libros para consultar

▶ Mandatos para las actividades que van a compartir

Escuchar

Estrategia

**Listening for specific information/
Listening for linguistic cues**

As you already know, you don't have to hear
or understand every word when listening to
Spanish. You can often get the facts you need
by listening for specific pieces of information.
You should also be aware of the linguistic
structures you hear. For example, by listening
for verb endings, you can ascertain whether
the verbs describe past, present, or future
actions, and they can also indicate who is
performing the action.

 To practice these strategies, you will listen
to a short paragraph about an environmental
issue. What environmental problem is being
discussed? What is the cause of the problem?
Has the problem been solved, or is the
solution under development?

Preparación

Describe la foto. Según la foto, ¿qué información
específica piensas que vas a oír en el diálogo?

Ahora escucha

Lee estas frases y luego escucha la conversación
entre Alberto y Eduardo. Indica si cada verbo
se refiere a algo en el pasado, en el presente o
en el futuro.

> **Acciones**

1. Demetrio / comprar en Macro _____
2. Alberto / comprar en Macro _____
3. Alberto / estudiar psicología _____
4. carro / tener frenos malos _____
5. Eduardo / comprar un anillo para
   Rebeca _____
6. Eduardo / estudiar _____

Comprensión

Descripciones

Marca las oraciones que describen correctamente a Alberto.

1. _____ Es organizado en sus estudios.
2. _____ Compró unas flores para su novia.
3. _____ No le gusta tomar el metro.
4. _____ No conoce bien la zona de Sabana
   Grande y Chacaíto.
5. _____ No tiene buen sentido de la orientación°.
6. _____ Le gusta ir a los lugares que están de moda.

Preguntas

1. ¿Por qué Alberto prefiere ir en metro a Macro?
2. ¿Crees que Alberto y Eduardo viven en una ciudad
   grande o en un pueblo? ¿Cómo lo sabes?
3. ¿Va Eduardo a acompañar a Alberto? ¿Por qué?

Conversación

En parejas, hablen de sus tiendas favoritas y de cómo llegar
a ellas. ¿En qué lugares tienen la última moda? ¿Los mejores
precios? ¿Hay buenas tiendas cerca de tu casa?

sentido de la orientación *sense of direction*

En pantalla

En algunas partes de Centroamérica, Bolivia, Chile, Colombia, Ecuador y Perú y en la mayor parte de Argentina, Uruguay y Paraguay, las personas tienen la costumbre° de usar **vos** en lugar de **tú** al hablar o escribir. Este uso es conocido como **el voseo** y se refleja también en la manera de conjugar los verbos. Por ejemplo, el presente del indicativo de los verbos regulares se conjuga con las terminaciones **-ás** (**vos hablás**), **-és** (**vos comés**) e **-ís** (**vos vivís**).

Vocabulario útil	
cargar	to carry
parecerse a	to look like
peluquero	hairdresser
ponerle	name him
segundo nombre	middle name
trato	treatment

Escoger

Elige la opción correcta.

1. El peluquero de la mamá del bebé se llama _____.

   a. José   b. Tomás

2. Al papá del bebé le gustan las películas de _____.

   a. Harry Potter   b. Sylvester Stallone

3. Tomás es el nombre del _____ de la mamá del bebé.

   a. abuelo   b. hermano

4. El regalo para el bebé está _____.

   a. en el banco   b. personalizado

En el banco

Describe cinco pasos para abrir una cuenta de ahorros conjunta (*joint*). Usa mandatos de **nosotros/as**.

¡Felicitaciones! ¿Cómo se va a llamar?

Bueno, yo le puse José.

¿Y si le ponen Tomás?

---

costumbre *custom*

En una ciudad tan grande como el D.F., la vida es más fácil gracias al Sistema de Transporte Colectivo Metro y los viajes muchas veces pueden ser interesantes: en el metro se promueve° la cultura. Allí se construyó el primer museo del mundo en un transporte colectivo. También hay programas de préstamo de libros para motivar a los usuarios a leer en el tiempo muerto° que pasan dentro° del sistema. ¿Quieres saber más? Descubre qué hace tan especial al Metro del D.F. en este episodio de *Flash cultura*.

Vocabulario útil	
concurrido	*busy, crowded*
se esconde	*is hidden*
transbordo	*transfer, change*
tranvía	*streetcar*

Preparación

Imagina que estás en México, D.F., una de las ciudades más grandes del mundo. ¿Qué transporte usas para ir de un lugar a otro? ¿Por qué?

Seleccionar

Selecciona la respuesta correcta.

1. El Bosque de Chapultepec es uno de los lugares más (solitarios/concurridos) de la ciudad.

2. En las estaciones (de transbordo/subterráneas) los pasajeros pueden cambiar de trenes para llegar fácilmente a su destino.

3. Algunas líneas del Metro no son subterráneas, sino superficiales, es decir, (paran/circulan) al nivel de la calle.

4. Dentro de algunas estaciones hay (danzas indígenas/exposiciones de arte).

El Metro del D.F.

Viajando en el Metro... puedes conocer más acerca de la cultura de este país.

Para la gente... mayor de 60 años, es el transporte totalmente gratuito.

... el Metro [...] está conectado con los demás sistemas de transporte...

se promueve *is promoted* tiempo muerto *down time* dentro *inside*

Venezuela

El país en cifras

▶ **Área:** 912.050 km² (352.144 millas²),
  aproximadamente dos veces el área de California
▶ **Población:** 28.868.000
▶ **Capital:** Caracas —3.051.000
▶ **Ciudades principales:** Maracaibo —2.153.000,
  Valencia —1.738.000, Barquisimeto
  —1.159.000, Maracay —1.040.000
▶ **Moneda:** bolívar
▶ **Idiomas:** español (oficial), lenguas
  indígenas (oficiales)

El yanomami es uno de los idiomas indígenas
que se habla en Venezuela. La cultura de los
yanomami tiene su centro en el sur de Venezuela,
en el bosque tropical. Son cazadores° y agricultores
y viven en comunidades de hasta 400 miembros.

Bandera de Venezuela

Venezolanos célebres

▶ **Teresa Carreño,** compositora y pianista
  (1853–1917)
▶ **Rómulo Gallegos,** escritor y político
  (1884–1969)
▶ **Andrés Eloy Blanco,** poeta (1896–1955)
▶ **Gustavo Dudamel,** director de orquesta (1981–)
▶ **Baruj Benacerraf,** científico (1920–2011)

En 1980, Baruj Benacerraf, junto con dos de
sus colegas, recibió el Premio Nobel por sus
investigaciones en el campo° de la inmunología y
las enfermedades autoinmunes. Nacido en Caracas,
Benacerraf también vivió en París y los
Estados Unidos.

cazadores *hunters* campo *field* caída *drop* Salto Ángel *Angel Falls*
catarata *waterfall* la dio a conocer *made it known*

Isla Margarita

Maracaibo •
Lago de Maracaibo
Valencia •
☆ Caracas
Cordillera Central de la Costa
Río Orinoco
Macizo de las Guayanas
GUYANA
Río Orinoco
BRASIL

Vista de Caracas

Una piragua

ESTADOS UNIDOS
OCÉANO ATLÁNTICO
OCÉANO PACÍFICO
VENEZUELA

¡Increíble pero cierto!

Con una caída° de 979 metros (3.212 pies)
desde la meseta de Auyan Tepuy, Salto Ángel°,
en Venezuela, es la catarata° más alta del
mundo, ¡diecisiete veces más alta que las
cataratas del Niágara! James C. Angel la dio a
conocer° en 1935. Los indígenas de la zona la
denominan "Kerepakupai Merú".

Economía • **El petróleo**

La industria petrolera° es muy importante para la economía venezolana. La mayor concentración de petróleo del país se encuentra debajo del lago Maracaibo. En 1976 se nacionalizaron las empresas° petroleras y pasaron a ser propiedad° del estado con el nombre de *Petróleos de Venezuela*. Este producto representa más del 90% de las exportaciones del país, siendo los Estados Unidos su principal comprador°.

Actualidades • **Caracas**

El *boom* petrolero de los años cincuenta transformó a Caracas en una ciudad cosmopolita. Sus rascacielos° y excelentes sistemas de transporte la hacen una de las ciudades más modernas de Latinoamérica. El metro, construido en 1983, es uno de los más modernos del mundo y sus extensas carreteras y autopistas conectan la ciudad con el interior del país. El corazón de la capital es el Parque Central, una zona de centros comerciales, tiendas, restaurantes y clubes.

Historia • **Simón Bolívar (1783–1830)**

A principios del siglo° XIX, el territorio de la actual Venezuela, al igual que gran parte de América, todavía estaba bajo el dominio de la Corona° española. El general Simón Bolívar, nacido en Caracas, es llamado "El Libertador" porque fue el líder del movimiento independentista suramericano en el área que hoy es Venezuela, Colombia, Ecuador, Perú y Bolivia.

¿Qué aprendiste? Contesta cada pregunta con una oración completa.

1. ¿Cuál es la moneda de Venezuela?
2. ¿Quién fue Rómulo Gallegos?
3. ¿Cuándo se dio a conocer el Salto Ángel?
4. ¿Cuál es el producto más exportado de Venezuela?
5. ¿Qué ocurrió en 1976 con las empresas petroleras?
6. ¿Cómo se llama la capital de Venezuela?
7. ¿Qué hay en el Parque Central de Caracas?
8. ¿Por qué es conocido Simón Bolívar como "El Libertador"?

Sombreros y hamacas
en Ciudad Bolívar

Conexión Internet Investiga estos temas en Internet.

1. Busca información sobre Simón Bolívar. ¿Cuáles son algunos de los episodios más importantes de su vida? ¿Crees que Bolívar fue un estadista (*statesman*) de primera categoría? ¿Por qué?
2. Prepara un plan para un viaje de ecoturismo por el Orinoco. ¿Qué quieres ver y hacer durante la excursión?

---

industria petrolera *oil industry* **empresas** *companies* **propiedad** *property* **comprador** *buyer* **rascacielos** *skyscrapers* **siglo** *century* **Corona** *Crown*

En la ciudad

el banco	bank
la carnicería	butcher shop
el correo	post office
el estacionamiento	parking lot
la frutería	fruit store
la heladería	ice cream shop
la joyería	jewelry store
la lavandería	laundromat
la panadería	bakery
la pastelería	pastry shop
la peluquería, el salón de belleza	beauty salon
la pescadería	fish market
el supermercado	supermarket
la zapatería	shoe store
hacer cola	to stand in line
hacer diligencias	to run errands

En el banco

el cajero automático	ATM
el cheque (de viajero)	(traveler's) check
la cuenta corriente	checking account
la cuenta de ahorros	savings account
ahorrar	to save (money)
cobrar	to cash (a check)
depositar	to deposit
firmar	to sign
llenar (un formulario)	to fill out (a form)
pagar a plazos	to pay in installments
pagar al contado/ en efectivo	to pay in cash
pedir prestado/a	to borrow
pedir un préstamo	to apply for a loan
ser gratis	to be free of charge

Cómo llegar

la cuadra	(city) block
la dirección	address
la esquina	corner
el letrero	sign
cruzar	to cross
doblar	to turn
estar perdido/a	to be lost
indicar cómo llegar	to give directions
quedar	to be located
(al) este	(to the) east
(al) norte	(to the) north
(al) oeste	(to the) west
(al) sur	(to the) south
derecho	straight (ahead)
enfrente de	opposite; facing
hacia	toward

Past participles used as adjectives	See page 493.
Expresiones útiles	See page 481.

En el correo

el cartero	mail carrier
el correo	mail; post office
la estampilla, el sello	stamp
el paquete	package
el sobre	envelope
echar (una carta) al buzón	to put (a letter) in the mailbox; to mail
enviar, mandar	to send; to mail

El bienestar

15

Communicative Goals

You will learn how to:

• Talk about health, well-being, and nutrition
• Talk about physical activities

A PRIMERA VISTA
• ¿Está la chica en un gimnasio o en un lugar al aire libre?
• ¿Practica ella deportes frecuentemente?
• ¿Es activa o sedentaria?
• ¿Es probable que le importe su salud?

El bienestar

Más vocabulario

adelgazar	*to lose weight; to slim down*
aliviar el estrés	*to reduce stress*
aliviar la tensión	*to reduce tension*
apurarse, darse prisa	*to hurry; to rush*
aumentar de peso, engordar	*to gain weight*
calentarse (e:ie)	*to warm up*
disfrutar (de)	*to enjoy; to reap the benefits (of)*
entrenarse	*to train*
estar a dieta	*to be on a diet*
estar en buena forma	*to be in good shape*
hacer gimnasia	*to work out*
llevar una vida sana	*to lead a healthy lifestyle*
mantenerse en forma	*to stay in shape*
sufrir muchas presiones	*to be under a lot of pressure*
tratar de (+ *inf.*)	*to try (to do something)*
la droga	*drug*
el/la drogadicto/a	*drug addict*
activo/a	*active*
débil	*weak*
en exceso	*in excess; too much*
flexible	*flexible*
fuerte	*strong*
sedentario/a	*sedentary*
tranquilo/a	*calm; quiet*
el bienestar	*well-being*

Variación léxica

hacer ejercicios aeróbicos ⟷ hacer aeróbic *(Esp.)*

el/la entrenador(a) ⟷ el/la monitor(a)

GIMNASIO SUCRE

el teleadicto

Hace ejercicios de estiramiento. (hacer)

la clase de ejercicios aeróbicos

Suda. (sudar)

Hace ejercicio. (hacer)

el entrenador

el músculo

SUCRE

la cinta caminadora

el masaje

No fumar.

Hacen ejercicios aeróbicos.
(hacer)

Levanta pesas.
(levantar)

Práctica

1 **Escuchar** 🎧 Mira el dibujo. Luego escucha las oraciones e indica si lo que se dice en cada oración es **cierto** o **falso**.

	Cierto	Falso			Cierto	Falso
1.	○	○		6.	○	○
2.	○	○		7.	○	○
3.	○	○		8.	○	○
4.	○	○		9.	○	○
5.	○	○		10.	○	○

2 **Seleccionar** 🎧 Escucha el anuncio del gimnasio Sucre. Marca con una **X** los servicios que se ofrecen.

_____ 1. dietas para adelgazar

_____ 2. programa para aumentar de peso

_____ 3. clases de gimnasia

_____ 4. entrenador personal

_____ 5. masajes

_____ 6. programa para dejar de fumar

3 **Identificar** Identifica el antónimo (*antonym*) de cada palabra.

apurarse	fuerte
disfrutar	mantenerse en forma
engordar	sedentario
estar enfermo	sufrir muchas presiones
flexible	tranquilo

1. activo
2. adelgazar
3. aliviar el estrés
4. débil

5. ir despacio
6. estar sano
7. nervioso
8. ser teleadicto

4 **Combinar** Combina elementos de cada columna para formar ocho oraciones lógicas sobre el bienestar.

1. David levanta pesas
2. Estás en buena forma
3. Felipe se lastimó
4. José y Rafael
5. Mi hermano
6. Sara hace ejercicios de
7. Mis primas están a dieta
8. Para llevar una vida sana,

a. aumentó de peso.
b. estiramiento.
c. porque quieren adelgazar.
d. porque haces ejercicio.
e. sudan mucho en el gimnasio.
f. un músculo de la pierna.
g. no se debe fumar.
h. y corre mucho.

Más vocabulario	
la bebida alcohólica	alcoholic beverage
la cafeína	caffeine
la caloría	calorie
la merienda	afternoon snack
la nutrición	nutrition
el/la nutricionista	nutritionist
comer una dieta equilibrada	to eat a balanced diet
consumir alcohol	to consume alcohol
descafeinado/a	decaffeinated

Labels: la proteína · la grasa · el colesterol · los minerales · las vitaminas

La nutrición

---

5   **Completar** Completa cada oración con la palabra adecuada.

1. Después de hacer ejercicio, como pollo o bistec porque contienen _____.
   a. drogas   b. proteínas   c. grasa
2. Para _____, es necesario consumir comidas de todos los grupos alimenticios (*nutrition groups*).
   a. aliviar el estrés   b. correr   c. comer una dieta equilibrada
3. Mis primas _____ una buena comida.
   a. disfrutan de   b. tratan de   c. sudan
4. Mi entrenador no come queso ni papas fritas porque contienen _____.
   a. dietas   b. vitaminas   c. mucha grasa
5. Mi padre no come mantequilla porque él necesita reducir _____.
   a. la nutrición   b. el colesterol   c. el bienestar
6. Mi novio cuenta _____ porque está a dieta.
   a. las pesas   b. los músculos   c. las calorías

CONSULTA

To review what you have learned about nutrition and food groups, see **Contextos, Lección 8**, pp. 262–265.

---

6   **La nutrición** En parejas, hablen de los tipos de comida que comen y las consecuencias que tienen para su salud.

1. ¿Cuántas comidas con mucha grasa comes regularmente? ¿Piensas que debes comer menos comidas de este tipo? ¿Por qué?
2. ¿Compras comidas con muchos minerales y vitaminas? ¿Necesitas consumir más comidas que los contienen? ¿Por qué?
3. ¿Algún miembro de tu familia tiene problemas con el colesterol? ¿Qué haces para evitar problemas con el colesterol?
4. ¿Eres vegetariano/a? ¿Conoces a alguien que sea vegetariano/a? ¿Qué piensas de la idea de no comer carne u otros productos animales? ¿Es posible comer una dieta equilibrada sin comer carne? Explica.
5. ¿Tomas cafeína en exceso? ¿Qué ventajas (*advantages*) y desventajas tiene la cafeína? Da ejemplos de productos que contienen cafeína y de productos descafeinados.
6. ¿Llevas una vida sana? ¿Y tus amigos? ¿Crees que, en general, los estudiantes llevan una vida sana? ¿Por qué?

AYUDA

Some useful words:
sano = saludable
en general = por lo general
estricto
normalmente
muchas veces
a veces
de vez en cuando

Comunicación

7 **El colesterol** Lee este párrafo sobre el colesterol. Luego, indica si las conclusiones son **lógicas** o **ilógicas**.

El colesterol es una sustancia que el cuerpo necesita para funcionar apropiadamente, pero es necesario mantener un nivel (*level*) de colesterol adecuado. El nivel deseable es menos de 200. El colesterol alto puede provocar ataques al corazón y enfermedades cardíacas, entre otras. Para evitar el colesterol alto, es importante llevar una vida sana. Es esencial comer una dieta equilibrada; los productos derivados de los animales son una buena fuente (*source*) de proteínas, pero es importante limitar su consumo si se tiene el colesterol alto. Además de cuidar la dieta, es importante mantenerse en forma. La falta de ejercicio y el exceso de peso también contribuyen a que las personas sufran de colesterol alto. Es recomendable dedicar un mínimo de 120 minutos semanales (*weekly*) al ejercicio. Por último, no se debe fumar.

	Lógico	Ilógico
1. El colesterol es necesario.	○	○
2. Se debe hacer algo si el nivel de colesterol es de 250.	○	○
3. Para evitar el colesterol alto, se debe consumir mucha carne.	○	○
4. Ser sedentario ayuda a mantener un nivel adecuado de colesterol.	○	○
5. El nivel de colesterol se puede elevar cuando se adelgaza.	○	○

8 **Recomendaciones para la salud** Imagina que estás preocupado/a por los malos hábitos de un(a) amigo/a que no está bien últimamente (*lately*). Habla de lo que está pasando en la vida de tu amigo/a y los cambios que necesita hacer para llevar una vida sana.

9 **Un anuncio** Imagina que eres dueño/a de un gimnasio con un equipo (*equipment*) moderno, entrenadores cualificados y un(a) nutricionista. Escribe un anuncio para la televisión que hable del gimnasio y atraiga (*attracts*) a una gran variedad de nuevos clientes. Incluye esta información en el anuncio.

▶ las ventajas de estar en buena forma
▶ el equipo que tienes
▶ los servicios y clases que ofreces
▶ las características únicas
▶ la dirección y el teléfono
▶ el precio para los socios (*members*)

10 **El teleadicto** Con un(a) compañero/a, representen los papeles de un(a) nutricionista y un(a) teleadicto/a. La persona sedentaria habla de sus malos hábitos para la comida y de que no hace ejercicio. También dice que toma demasiado café y que siente mucho estrés. El/La nutricionista le sugiere una dieta equilibrada con bebidas descafeinadas y una rutina para mantenerse en forma. El/La teleadicto/a le da las gracias por su ayuda.

Chichén Itzá

Los chicos exploran Chichén Itzá y se relajan en un spa.

PERSONAJES   MARISSA   FELIPE

MARISSA ¡Chichén Itzá es impresionante! Qué lástima que Maru y Miguel no hayan podido venir. Sobre todo Maru.

FELIPE Ha estado bajo mucha presión.

MARISSA ¿Ustedes ya habían venido antes?

FELIPE Sí. Nuestros papás nos trajeron cuando éramos niños.

FELIPE El otro día le gané a Juan Carlos en el parque.

JUAN CARLOS Estaba mirando hacia otro lado, cuando me di cuenta, Felipe ya había empezado a correr.

(*en otro lugar de las ruinas*)

JUAN CARLOS ¡Hace calor!

JIMENA ¡Sí! Hay que estar en buena forma para recorrer las ruinas.

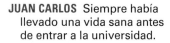

JUAN CARLOS Siempre había llevado una vida sana antes de entrar a la universidad.

JIMENA Tienes razón. La universidad hace que seamos muy sedentarios.

JUAN CARLOS ¡Busquemos a Felipe y a Marissa!

FELIPE ¡Gané!

JIMENA Qué calor. Tengo una idea. Vamos.

JUAN CARLOS   **JIMENA**   **EMPLEADA**

EMPLEADA Ofrecemos varios servicios para aliviar el estrés: masajes, saunas...

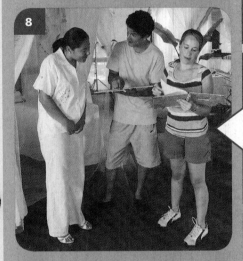

FELIPE Me gustaría un masaje.

MARISSA Yo prefiero un baño mineral.

JUAN CARLOS ¿Crees que tienes un poco de tiempo libre la semana que viene? Me gustaría invitarte a salir.

JIMENA ¿Sin Felipe?

JUAN CARLOS Sin Felipe.

EMPLEADA ¿Ya tomaron una decisión?

JIMENA Sí.

Expresiones útiles

Wishing a friend were with you

Qué lástima que no hayan podido venir.
What a shame that they were not able to come.

Sobre todo Maru.
Especially Maru.

Él/Ella ha estado bajo mucha presión.
He/She has been under a lot of pressure.

Creo que ellos ya habían venido antes.
I think they had already come (here) before.

Talking about trips

¿Ustedes ya habían venido antes?
Had you been (here) before?

Sí. He querido regresar desde que leí el Chilam Balam.
Yes. I have wanted to come back ever since I read the Chilam Balam.

¿Recuerdas cuando nos trajo papá?
Remember when Dad brought us?

Al llegar a la cima, comenzaste a llorar.
When we got to the top, you started to cry.

Talking about well-being

Siempre había llevado una vida sana antes de entrar a la universidad.
I had always maintained a healthy lifestyle before starting college.

Ofrecemos varios servicios para aliviar el estrés.
We offer many services to relieve stress.

Me gustaría un masaje.
I would like a massage.

Additional vocabulary

la cima *top, peak*
el escalón *step*
el muro *wall*
tomar una decisión *to make a decision*

¿Qué pasó?

1 **Seleccionar** Selecciona la respuesta que completa mejor cada oración.

1. Felipe y Marissa piensan que Maru _____.
   a. debe hacer ejercicio   b. aumentó de peso   c. ha estado bajo mucha presión
2. Felipe y Jimena visitaron Chichén Itzá _____.
   a. para aliviar el estrés   b. cuando eran niños   c. para llevar una vida sana
3. Jimena dice que la universidad hace a los estudiantes _____.
   a. comer una dieta equilibrada   b. ser sedentarios   c. levantar pesas
4. En el spa ofrecen servicios para _____.
   a. sudar   b. aliviar el estrés   c. ser flexibles
5. Felipe elige que le den un _____.
   a. baño mineral   b. almuerzo   c. masaje

2 **Identificar** Identifica quién puede decir estas oraciones.

1. No me di cuenta (*I didn't realize*) de que habías empezado a correr, por eso ganaste.
2. Miguel y Maru no visitaron Chichén Itzá, ¡qué lástima que no hayan podido venir!
3. Se necesita estar en buena forma para visitar este tipo de lugares.
4. Los masajes, saunas y baños minerales que ofrecemos alivian la tensión.
5. Si salimos, no invites a Felipe.
6. Yo corro más rápido que Juan Carlos.

 MARISSA   FELIPE
 JIMENA
 JUAN CARLOS   EMPLEADA

3 **Inventar** Haz descripciones de los personajes de la **Fotonovela**. Utiliza las oraciones, la lista de palabras y otras expresiones que sepan.

aliviar el estrés	hacer ejercicios de estiramiento	masaje
bienestar	llevar una vida sana	teleadicto/a
grasa	mantenerse en forma	vitamina

modelo
Marissa siempre hace ejercicios de estiramiento. Está en buena forma y lleva una vida muy sana...

1. A Juan Carlos le duelen los músculos después de hacer gimnasia.
2. Maru a veces sufre presiones y estrés en la universidad.
3. A Jimena le encanta salir con amigos o leer un buen libro.
4. Felipe trata de comer una dieta equilibrada.
5. Juan Carlos no es muy flexible.

Ortografía

Las letras **b** y **v**

Since there is no difference in pronunciation between the Spanish letters **b** and **v**, spelling words that contain these letters can be tricky. Here are some tips.

nombre	**blusa**	**absoluto**	**descubrir**

The letter **b** is always used before consonants.

bonita	**botella**	**buscar**	**bienestar**

At the beginning of words, the letter **b** is usually used when it is followed by the letter combinations **-on, -or, -ot, -u, -ur, -us, -ien,** and **-ene**.

adelgazaba	**disfrutaban**	**ibas**	**íbamos**

The letter **b** is used in the verb endings of the imperfect tense for **-ar** verbs and the verb **ir**.

voy	**vamos**	**estuvo**	**tuvieron**

The letter **v** is used in the present tense forms of **ir** and in the preterite forms of **estar** and **tener**.

octavo	**huevo**	**activa**	**grave**

The letter **v** is used in these noun and adjective endings: **-avo/a, -evo/a, -ivo/a, -ave, -eve**.

Práctica Completa las palabras con las letras **b** o **v**.

1. Una ___ez me lastimé el ___razo cuando esta___a ___uceando.
2. Manuela ol___idó sus li___ros en el auto___ús.
3. Ernesto tomó el ___orrador y se puso todo ___lanco de tiza.
4. Para tener una ___ida sana y saluda___le, necesitas tomar ___itaminas.
5. En mi pue___lo hay un ___ule___ar que tiene muchos ár___oles.

El ahorcado (*Hangman*) Juega al ahorcado para adivinar las palabras.

1. __ _u_ __ __ _s_   Están en el cielo.

2. __ _u_ __ __ _n_   Relacionado con el correo

3. __ _o_ __ _e_ __ __ _a_   Está llena de líquido.

4. __ _i_ __ _e_   Fenómeno meteorológico

5. __ _e_ __ __ __ __ _s_   Los "ojos" de la casa

Spas naturales

¿Hay algo mejor que un buen baño° para descansar y aliviar la tensión? Y si el baño se toma en una terma°, el beneficio° es mayor. Los tratamientos con agua y lodo° para mejorar la salud y el bienestar son populares en las Américas desde hace muchos siglos°. Las termas son manantiales° naturales de agua caliente. La temperatura facilita la absorción de minerales y otros elementos que contiene el agua y que son buenos para la salud. El agua de las termas se usa en piscinas, baños y duchas o en el sitio natural en el que surge°: pozas°, estanques° o cuevas°.

Ecotermales en Arenal, Costa Rica

En Baños de San Vicente, en Ecuador, son muy populares los tratamientos° con lodo volcánico.

El lodo caliente se extiende por el cuerpo; así la piel° absorbe los minerales

Volcán de lodo El Totumo, Colombia

beneficiosos para la salud; también se usa para dar masajes. La lodoterapia es útil para tratar varias enfermedades, además hace que la piel se vea radiante.

En Costa Rica, la actividad volcánica también ha dado° origen a fuentes° y pozas termales. Si te gusta cuidarte y amas la naturaleza, recuerda estos nombres: Las Hornillas y Las Pailas. Son pozas naturales de aguas termales que están cerca del volcán Rincón de la Vieja. Un baño termal en medio de un paisaje tan hermoso es una experiencia única.

baño *bath* terma *hot spring* beneficio *benefit* lodo *mud* siglos *centuries* manantiales *springs* surge *springs forth* pozas *small pools* estanques *ponds* cuevas *caves* tratamientos *treatments* piel *skin* ha dado *has given* fuentes *springs* balnearios *spas* cascadas *waterfalls* algas *seaweed* temazcales *steam and medicinal herb baths*

Otros balnearios°

Todos ofrecen piscinas, baños, pozas y duchas de aguas termales y además...

Lugar	Servicios
El Edén y Yanasara, Curgos (Perú)	cascadas° de aguas termales
Montbrió del Camp, Tarragona (España)	baños de algas°
Puyuhuapi (Chile)	duchas de agua de mar; baños de algas
Termas de Río Hondo, Santiago del Estero (Argentina)	baños de lodo
Tepoztlán, Morelos (México)	temazcales° aztecas
Uyuni, Potosí (Bolivia)	baños de sal

ACTIVIDADES

1 **¿Cierto o falso?** Indica si lo que dicen las oraciones es cierto o falso. Corrige la información falsa.

1. Las aguas termales son beneficiosas para algunas enfermedades, incluido el estrés.

2. Los tratamientos con agua y lodo se conocen sólo desde hace pocos años.

3. Las termas son manantiales naturales de agua caliente.

4. La lodoterapia es un tratamiento con barro (*mud*).

5. La temperatura de las aguas termales no afecta la absorción de los minerales.

6. Mucha gente va a Baños de San Vicente, Ecuador, por sus playas.

7. Las Hornillas son pozas de aguas termales en Costa Rica.

8. Montbrió del Camp ofrece baños de sal.

9. Es posible ver aguas termales en forma de cascadas.

10. Tepoztlán ofrece temazcales aztecas.

El ejercicio

los abdominales	sit-ups
la bicicleta estática	stationary bicycle
el calambre muscular	(muscular) cramp
el (fisi)culturismo; la musculación (Esp.)	bodybuilding
las flexiones de pecho; las lagartijas (Méx.; Col.); las planchas (Esp.)	push-ups
la cinta (trotadora) (Arg.; Chile)	la cinta caminadora

EL MUNDO HISPANO

Creencias° sobre la salud

- **Colombia** Como algunos suelos son de baldosas°, se cree que si uno anda descalzo° se enfrían° los pies y esto puede causar un resfriado o artritis.

- **Cuba** Por la mañana, muchas madres sacan a sus bebés a los patios y a las puertas de las casas. La creencia es que unos cinco minutos de sol ayudan a fijar° el calcio en los huesos y aumentan la inmunidad contra las enfermedades.

- **México** Muchas personas tienen la costumbre de tomar a diario un vaso de jugo del cactus conocido como "nopal". Se dice que es bueno para reducir el colesterol y el azúcar en la sangre y que ayuda a adelgazar.

Creencias *Beliefs* baldosas *tiles* anda descalzo *walks barefoot* se enfrían *get cold* fijar *to set*

PERFIL

La quinua

La quinua es una semilla° de gran valor° nutricional. Se produce en los Andes de Bolivia, Perú, Argentina, Colombia, Chile y Ecuador, y también en los Estados Unidos. Forma parte de la dieta básica de esos países andinos desde hace más de 5.000 años.

La quinua es rica en proteínas, hierro° y magnesio. Contiene los ocho aminoácidos básicos para el ser humano; por esto es un alimento muy completo, ideal para vegetarianos y veganos. Otra de las ventajas de la quinua es que no contiene gluten, por lo que la pueden consumir personas con alergias e intolerancia a esta proteína.

Aunque es técnicamente una semilla, la quinua es considerada un cereal por su composición y por su uso. Los granos° de la quinua pueden ser tostados para hacer harina° o se pueden cocinar de múltiples maneras. Se utiliza como reemplazo° del arroz o de la pasta, con verduras, carnes, etc.,

 en ensaladas, o como reemplazo de la avena° en el desayuno.

semilla *seed* valor *value* hierro *iron* granos *grains* harina *flour* reemplazo *replacement* avena *oats*

Conexión Internet

¿Qué sistemas de ejercicio son más populares entre los hispanos?

Use the Web to find more cultural information related to this Cultura section.

ACTIVIDADES

2 Comprensión Contesta las preguntas.
1. Una argentina te dice: "Voy a usar la cinta." ¿Qué va a hacer?
2. Según los colombianos, ¿qué efectos negativos tiene el no usar zapatos en casa?
3. ¿Qué es la quinua?
4. ¿Qué proteína no contiene la quinua?

3 **Para sentirte mejor** Entrevista a un(a) compañero/a sobre las cosas que hace todos los días y las cosas que hace al menos una o dos veces a la semana para sentirse mejor. Hablen sobre actividades deportivas, la alimentación y lo que hacen en sus ratos libres.

15.1 The present perfect

ANTE TODO In **Lección 14**, you learned how to form past participles. You will now learn how to form the present perfect indicative (**el pretérito perfecto de indicativo**), a compound tense that uses the past participle. The present perfect is used to talk about what someone *has done*. In Spanish, it is formed with the present tense of the auxiliary verb **haber** and a past participle.

Maru ha estado bajo mucha presión.

He querido regresar desde que leí el *Chilam Balam*.

Present indicative of haber

Singular forms		Plural forms	
yo	**he**	nosotros/as	**hemos**
tú	**has**	vosotros/as	**habéis**
Ud./él/ella	**ha**	Uds./ellos/ellas	**han**

Tú no **has aumentado** de peso.
You haven't gained weight.

Yo ya **he leído** esos libros.
I've already read those books.

¿**Ha asistido** Juan a la clase de yoga?
Has Juan attended the yoga class?

Hemos conocido al entrenador.
We have met the trainer.

▶ The past participle does not change in form when it is part of the present perfect tense; it only changes in form when it is used as an adjective.

Clara **ha abierto** las ventanas.
Clara has opened the windows.

Yo **he cerrado** la puerta del gimnasio.
I've closed the door to the gym.

Las ventanas están **abiertas**.
The windows are open.

La puerta del gimnasio está **cerrada**.
The door to the gym is closed.

▶ In Spanish, the present perfect indicative generally is used just as in English: to talk about what someone has done or what has occurred. It usually refers to the recent past.

He trabajado cuarenta horas esta semana.
I have worked forty hours this week.

¿Cuál es el último libro que **has leído**?
What is the last book that you have read?

▶ In English, the auxiliary verb and the past participle are often separated. In Spanish, however, these two elements—**haber** and the past participle—cannot be separated by any word.

Siempre **hemos vivido** en Bolivia.
We have always lived in Bolivia.

Usted nunca **ha venido** a mi oficina.
You have never come to my office.

¿Y Juan Carlos todavía no te ha invitado a salir?

Últimamente hemos sufrido muchas presiones en la universidad.

▶ The word **no** and any object or reflexive pronouns are placed immediately before **haber**.

Yo **no he comido** la merienda.
I haven't eaten the snack.

¿Por qué **no la has comido**?
Why haven't you eaten it?

Susana ya **se ha entrenado**.
Susana has already practiced.

Ellos **no lo han terminado**.
They haven't finished it.

▶ Note that *to have* can be either a main verb or an auxiliary verb in English. As a main verb, it corresponds to **tener,** while as an auxiliary, it corresponds to **haber**.

Tengo muchos amigos.
I have a lot of friends.

He tenido mucho éxito.
I have had a lot of success.

▶ To form the present perfect of **hay**, use the third-person singular of **haber (ha) + habido**.

Ha habido muchos problemas
con el nuevo profesor.
*There have been a lot of problems
with the new professor.*

Ha habido un accidente en
la calle Central.
*There has been an accident
on Central Street.*

¡INTÉNTALO! Indica el pretérito perfecto de indicativo de estos verbos.

1. (disfrutar, comer, vivir) yo __he disfrutado, he comido, he vivido__
2. (traer, adelgazar, compartir) tú _____
3. (venir, estar, correr) usted _____
4. (leer, resolver, poner) ella _____
5. (decir, romper, hacer) ellos _____
6. (mantenerse, dormirse) nosotros _____
7. (estar, escribir, ver) yo _____
8. (vivir, correr, morir) él _____

Práctica

1

Completar Estas oraciones describen cómo es la vida de unos estudiantes. Completa las oraciones con el pretérito perfecto de indicativo de los verbos de la lista.

adelgazar	comer	llevar
aumentar	hacer	sufrir

1. Luisa _____ muchas presiones este año.
2. Juan y Raúl _____ de peso porque no hacen ejercicio.
3. Pero María y yo _____ porque trabajamos en exceso y nos olvidamos de comer.
4. Desde siempre, yo _____ una vida muy sana.
5. Pero tú y yo no _____ gimnasia este semestre.

2

¿Qué has hecho? Indica si has hecho lo siguiente.

> **modelo**
>
> escalar una montaña
>
> *Sí, he escalado varias montañas./No, no he escalado nunca una montaña.*

1. jugar al baloncesto
2. viajar a Bolivia
3. conocer a una persona famosa
4. levantar pesas
5. comer un insecto
6. recibir un masaje
7. aprender varios idiomas
8. bailar salsa
9. ver una película en español
10. escuchar música latina
11. estar despierto/a 24 horas
12. bucear

3

La vida sana En parejas, túrnense para hacer preguntas sobre el tema de la vida sana. Sean creativos.

> **modelo**
>
> encontrar un gimnasio
>
> **Estudiante 1:** *¿Has encontrado un buen gimnasio cerca de tu casa?*
> **Estudiante 2:** *Yo no he encontrado un gimnasio, pero sé que debo buscar uno.*

1. tratar de estar en forma
2. estar a dieta los últimos dos meses
3. dejar de tomar refrescos
4. hacerse una prueba del colesterol
5. entrenarse cinco días a la semana
6. cambiar de una vida sedentaria a una vida activa
7. tomar vitaminas por las noches y por las mañanas
8. hacer ejercicio para aliviar la tensión
9. consumir mucha proteína
10. dejar de fumar

Comunicación

4

Conversación Lee la conversación entre Eva y Andrés. Luego, indica si las conclusiones son **lógicas** o **ilógicas**.

EVA   ¿Qué te pasa, Andrés? Estoy preocupada por ti. Ya nunca te veo en el gimnasio. Esta mañana, cuando nos hemos visto en clase, parecías un poco deprimido (*depressed*). ¿Qué ha pasado con ese Andrés divertido y feliz que yo conocía?

ANDRÉS He sufrido muchas presiones últimamente. He tenido mucho trabajo y mi padre ha estado un mes en el hospital. Ya se ha recuperado, pero lo hemos pasado muy mal en casa.

EVA   Lo siento muchísimo. ¿Y cómo está Marta?

ANDRÉS Ha roto conmigo, y por eso estoy tan deprimido. He comido muy mal en el último mes y he engordado también. Me siento demasiado débil para hacer ejercicio. ¿Cómo has estado tú?

EVA   Yo, bien, pero lo importante ahora es que tú te mejores. Te voy a ir a buscar a casa. ¿Has comido ya el almuerzo? Desde hoy, vas a comenzar a comer una dieta equilibrada.

	Lógico	Ilógico
1. Andrés ha cambiado.	O	O
2. Andrés vive con sus padres.	O	O
3. Marta es la ex novia de Andrés.	O	O
4. Eva lleva una vida sana.	O	O
5. Andrés está en buena forma.	O	O

5

NOTA CULTURAL

Nacido en San Diego e hijo de padres mexicanos, el actor **Mario López** se mantiene en forma haciendo ejercicio todos los días.

Describir Identifica a una persona que lleva una vida muy sana. Puede ser una persona que conoces o un personaje que aparece en una película o programa de televisión. Escribe una descripción de lo que esta persona ha hecho para llevar una vida sana.

> **modelo**
>
> Mario López siempre ha hecho todo lo posible para mantenerse en forma. Él…

Síntesis

6

Situación Trabajen en parejas para representar una conversación entre un(a) enfermero/a de la clínica de la universidad y un(a) estudiante.

- El/La estudiante no se siente nada bien.
- El/La enfermero/a debe averiguar de dónde viene el problema e investigar los hábitos del/de la estudiante.
- El/La estudiante le explica lo que ha hecho en los últimos meses y cómo se ha sentido.
- Luego el/la enfermero/a le da recomendaciones de cómo llevar una vida más sana.

15.2 The past perfect

ANTE TODO The past perfect indicative (**el pretérito pluscuamperfecto de indicativo**) is used to talk about what someone *had done* or what *had occurred* before another past action, event, or state. Like the present perfect, the past perfect uses a form of **haber**—in this case, the imperfect—plus the past participle.

Past perfect indicative			
	cerrar	**perder**	**asistir**
SINGULAR FORMS			
yo	**había** cerrado	**había** perdido	**había** asistido
tú	**habías** cerrado	**habías** perdido	**habías** asistido
Ud./él/ella	**había** cerrado	**había** perdido	**había** asistido
PLURAL FORMS			
nosotros/as	**habíamos** cerrado	**habíamos** perdido	**habíamos** asistido
vosotros/as	**habíais** cerrado	**habíais** perdido	**habíais** asistido
Uds./ellos/ellas	**habían** cerrado	**habían** perdido	**habían** asistido

Antes de 2014, **había vivido** en La Paz.
Before 2014, I had lived in La Paz.

Cuando llegamos, Luis ya **había salido**.
When we arrived, Luis had already left.

▶ The past perfect is often used with the word **ya** (*already*) to indicate that an action, event, or state had already occurred before another. Remember that, unlike its English equivalent, **ya** cannot be placed between **haber** and the past participle.

Ella **ya había salido** cuando llamaron.
She had already left when they called.

Cuando llegué, Raúl **ya se había acostado**.
When I arrived, Raúl had already gone to bed.

▶ **¡Atención!** The past perfect is often used in conjunction with **antes de** + [*noun*] or **antes de** + [*infinitive*] to describe when the action(s) occurred.

Antes de este año, nunca **había estudiado español**.
Before this year, I had never studied Spanish.

Luis **me había llamado antes de venir**.
Luis had called me before he came.

¡INTÉNTALO! Indica el pretérito pluscuamperfecto de indicativo de cada verbo.

1. Nosotros ya ___habíamos cenado___ (cenar) cuando nos llamaron.
2. Antes de tomar esta clase, yo no _____ (estudiar) nunca el español.
3. Antes de ir a México, ellos nunca _____ (ir) a otro país.
4. Eduardo nunca _____ (entrenarse) tanto en invierno.
5. Tú siempre _____ (llevar) una vida sana antes del año pasado.
6. Antes de conocerte, yo ya te _____ (ver) muchas veces.

Práctica

1

Completar Completa los minidiálogos con las formas correctas del pretérito pluscuamperfecto de indicativo.

1. **SARA** Antes de cumplir los 15 años, ¿_____ (estudiar) tú otra lengua?
    JOSÉ Sí, _____ (tomar) clases de inglés y de italiano.

▶ 2. **DOLORES** Antes de ir a Argentina, ¿_____ (probar) tú y tu familia el mate?
    TOMÁS Sí, ya _____ (tomar) mate muchas veces.

3. **ANTONIO** Antes de este año, ¿_____ (correr) usted en un maratón?
    SRA. VERA No, nunca lo _____ (hacer).

4. **SOFÍA** Antes de su enfermedad, ¿_____ (sufrir) muchas presiones tu tío?
    IRENE Sí... y él nunca _____ (mantenerse) en forma.

2

Quehaceres Indica lo que ya había hecho cada miembro de la familia antes de la llegada de la madre, la señora Ferrer.

su suegra · Teresa · el señor Ferrer · Armando · Carmen · Tomás

3

Tu vida Indica si ya habías hecho estas cosas antes de cumplir los dieciséis años.

1. hacer un viaje en avión
2. escalar una montaña
3. escribir un poema
4. filmar un video
5. enamorarte

6. tomar clases de ejercicios aeróbicos
7. montar a caballo
8. ir de pesca
9. manejar un carro
10. cantar frente a 50 o más personas

Comunicación

4 **Gimnasio Olímpico** Lee el anuncio. Luego, indica si las conclusiones son **lógicas** o **ilógicas**.

Hasta el año pasado, siempre había mirado la tele sentado en el sofá durante mis ratos libres. ¡Era sedentario y teleadicto! Jamás había practicado ningún deporte y había aumentado mucho de peso.

Este año, he empezado a comer una dieta equilibrada y voy al gimnasio todos los días. He comenzado a ser una persona muy activa y he adelgazado. Disfruto de una vida sana. ¡Me siento muy feliz!

Manténgase en forma.

¡Acabo de descubrir una nueva vida!

¡Venga al Gimnasio Olímpico hoy mismo!

	Lógico	Ilógico
1. Hasta el año pasado, el hombre del anuncio no había estado en buena forma.	○	○
2. El hombre del anuncio todavía es sedentario.	○	○
3. El hombre del anuncio come mucha grasa.	○	○
4. Ahora el hombre del anuncio mira menos la televisión.	○	○
5. El hombre del anuncio disfruta de salud física y mental.	○	○

5 **Preguntas** En parejas, túrnense para preguntarse si ya habían hecho actividades a ciertas edades: cinco, diez, quince años, etc. Pueden usar las sugerencias de la lista o incluir otras actividades.

> **modelo**
>
> levantar pesas
> **Estudiante 1:** *Cuando tenías quince años, ¿habías levantado pesas?*
> **Estudiante 2:** *No, todavía no había levantado pesas. ¿Y tú?*

- esquiar
- cocinar
- ir en barco
- probar sushi
- abrir una cuenta de ahorros
- ser paciente en un hospital

Síntesis

6 **Manteniéndote en forma** Escribe al menos cinco oraciones para describir cómo te has mantenido en forma este semestre. Di qué cosas han cambiado este semestre en relación con el año pasado.

15.3 | The present perfect subjunctive

ANTE TODO The present perfect subjunctive (**el pretérito perfecto de subjuntivo**), like the present perfect indicative, is used to talk about what *has happened*. The present perfect subjunctive is formed using the present subjunctive of the auxiliary verb **haber** and a past participle.

Present perfect indicative		Present perfect subjunctive	
PRESENT INDICATIVE OF **HABER**	PAST PARTICIPLE	PRESENT SUBJUNCTIVE OF **HABER**	PAST PARTICIPLE
yo he	hablado	yo haya	hablado

Present perfect subjunctive

		cerrar	perder	asistir
SINGULAR FORMS	yo	**haya** cerrado	**haya** perdido	**haya** asistido
	tú	**hayas** cerrado	**hayas** perdido	**hayas** asistido
	Ud./él/ella	**haya** cerrado	**haya** perdido	**haya** asistido
PLURAL FORMS	nosotros/as	**hayamos** cerrado	**hayamos** perdido	**hayamos** asistido
	vosotros/as	**hayáis** cerrado	**hayáis** perdido	**hayáis** asistido
	Uds./ellos/ellas	**hayan** cerrado	**hayan** perdido	**hayan** asistido

¡ATENCIÓN!

In Spanish the present perfect subjunctive is used to express a recent action.

No creo que lo **hayas dicho** bien.
I don't think that you have said it right.

Espero que él **haya llegado**.
I hope that he has arrived.

▶ The same conditions that trigger the use of the present subjunctive apply to the present perfect subjunctive.

Present subjunctive	Present perfect subjunctive
Espero que **duermas** bien.	Espero que **hayas dormido** bien.
I hope that you sleep well.	*I hope that you have slept well.*
No creo que **aumente** de peso.	No creo que **haya aumentado** de peso.
I don't think he will gain weight.	*I don't think he has gained weight.*

▶ The action expressed by the present perfect subjunctive is seen as occurring before the action expressed in the main clause.

Me alegro de que ustedes **se hayan reído** tanto esta tarde.
I'm glad that you have laughed so much this afternoon.

Dudo que tú **te hayas divertido** mucho con tu suegra.
I doubt that you have enjoyed yourself much with your mother-in-law.

¡INTÉNTALO! Indica el pretérito perfecto de subjuntivo de los verbos entre paréntesis.

1. Me gusta que ustedes ____hayan dicho____ (decir) la verdad.
2. No creo que tú _____ (comer) tanto.
3. Es imposible que usted _____ (poder) hacer tal (*such a*) cosa.
4. Me alegro de que tú y yo _____ (merendar) juntas.
5. Es posible que yo _____ (adelgazar) un poco esta semana.
6. Espero que ellas _____ (sentirse) mejor después de la clase.

Práctica

1 **Completar** Laura está preocupada por su familia y sus amigos/as. Completa las oraciones con la forma correcta del pretérito perfecto de subjuntivo de los verbos entre paréntesis.

1. ¡Qué lástima que Julio _____ (sentirse) tan mal en la competencia! Dudo que _____ (entrenarse) lo suficiente.

2. No creo que Lourdes y su amiga _____ (irse) de ese trabajo donde siempre tienen tantos problemas. Espero que Lourdes _____ (aprender) a aliviar el estrés.

3. Es triste que Nuria y yo _____ (perder) el partido. Esperamos que los entrenadores del gimnasio nos _____ (preparar) un buen programa para ponernos en forma.

4. No estoy segura de que Samuel _____ (llevar) una vida sana. Es bueno que él _____ (decidir) mejorar su dieta.

5. Me preocupa mucho que Ana y Rosa _____ (fumar) tanto de jóvenes. Es increíble que ellas no _____ (enfermarse).

6. Me alegro de que mi abuela _____ (disfrutar) de buena salud toda su vida. Es maravilloso que ella _____ (cumplir) noventa años.

2 **Describir** Usa el pretérito perfecto de subjuntivo para hacer dos comentarios sobre cada dibujo. Usa expresiones como **no creo que, dudo que, es probable que, me alegro de que, espero que** y **siento que**.

CONSULTA

To review verbs of will and influence, see **Estructura 12.4**, p. 426.
To review expressions of doubt, disbelief, and denial, see **Estructura 13.2**, p. 456.

> **modelo**
>
> Es probable que Javier haya levantado pesas durante muchos años.
>
> Me alegro de que Javier se haya mantenido en forma.

Javier

1. Rosa y Sandra

2. Roberto

3. Mariela

4. Lorena y su amigo

5. la señora Matos

6. Sonia y René

Comunicación

3

En el gimnasio Escucha la conversación entre Mariana y un entrenador. Luego, indica si las conclusiones son **lógicas** o **ilógicas.**

	Lógico	Ilógico
1. A Mariana no le gusta hacer ejercicio.	○	○
2. Mariana come frutas y verduras.	○	○
3. Mariana va al gimnasio porque quiere adelgazar.	○	○
4. Mariana estudia a las tres de la mañana.	○	○
5. Mariana va a sudar hoy.	○	○

4

¿Sí o no? En parejas, comenten estas afirmaciones (*statements*) usando las expresiones de la lista.

Dudo que...	Es imposible que...	Me alegro de que (no)...
Es bueno que (no)...	Espero que (no)...	No creo que...

modelo

Estudiante 1: Ya llegó el fin del año escolar.
Estudiante 2: Es imposible que haya llegado el fin del año escolar.

1. Recibí una A en la clase de español.
2. Tu mejor amigo/a aumentó de peso recientemente.
3. Beyoncé dio un concierto ayer con Jay-Z.
4. Mis padres ganaron un millón de dólares.
5. He aprendido a hablar japonés.
6. Nuestro/a profesor(a) nació en Bolivia.
7. Salí anoche con...
8. El año pasado mi familia y yo fuimos de excursión a...

5

Acontecimientos Piensa en seis acontecimientos (*events*) que hayas escuchado o leído recientemente en las noticias (*news*), o que te hayan ocurrido a ti. Describe tus opiniones e ideas acerca de cada uno de ellos. Utiliza el pretérito perfecto de subjuntivo.

modelo

Leí que la economía española mejoraba, pero dudo que haya mejorado.

6

Dieta En parejas, representen una conversación entre un(a) nutricionista y su cliente/a. El/La cliente/a explica qué ha hecho para mejorar su dieta. El/La nutricionista le expresa su opinión. Usen el pretérito perfecto de subjuntivo.

modelo

Cliente/a: He limitado mi dieta a 2000 calorías diarias.
Nutricionista: Espero que hayas llevado una vida sana y que hayas comido una dieta equilibrada. El número de calorías no es tan importante como la gente piensa...

Recapitulación

Completa estas actividades para repasar los conceptos de gramática que aprendiste en esta lección.

1 **Completar** Completa cada tabla con el pretérito pluscuamperfecto de indicativo y el pretérito perfecto de subjuntivo de los verbos. **24 pts.**

PRETÉRITO PLUSCUAMPERFECTO

Infinitivo	tú	nosotros	ustedes
disfrutar			
apurarse			

PRETÉRITO PERFECTO DE SUBJUNTIVO

Infinitivo	yo	él	ellas
tratar			
entrenarse			

2 **Preguntas** Completa las preguntas para estas respuestas usando el pretérito perfecto de indicativo. **24 pts.**

modelo
—¿Has llamado a tus padres? —Sí, los llamé ayer.

1. —¿Tú _____ ejercicio esta mañana en el gimnasio?
—No, hice ejercicio en el parque.

2. —Y ustedes, ¿_____ ya? —Sí, desayunamos en el hotel.

3. —Y Juan y Felipe, ¿adónde _____? —Fueron al cine.

4. —Paco, ¿(nosotros) _____ la cuenta del gimnasio?
—Sí, la recibimos la semana pasada.

5. —Señor Martín, ¿_____ algo ya? —Sí, pesqué uno grande. Ya me puedo ir a casa contento.

6. —Inés, ¿_____ mi pelota de fútbol? —Sí, la vi esta mañana en el coche.

7. —Yo no _____ café todavía. ¿Alguien quiere acompañarme? —No, gracias. Yo ya tomé mi café en casa.

8. —¿Ya te _____ el doctor que puedes comer chocolate?
—Sí, me lo dijo ayer.

RESUMEN GRAMATICAL

15.1 The present perfect pp. 518–519

Present indicative of **haber**	
he	hemos
has	habéis
ha	han

Present perfect: present tense of **haber** + past participle

Present perfect indicative	
he empezado	hemos empezado
has empezado	habéis empezado
ha empezado	han empezado

He empezado a ir al gimnasio con regularidad.
I have begun to go to the gym regularly.

15.2 The past perfect p. 522

Past perfect: imperfect tense of **haber** + past participle

Past perfect indicative	
había vivido	habíamos vivido
habías vivido	habíais vivido
había vivido	habían vivido

Antes de 2013, yo ya **había vivido** en tres países diferentes.
Before 2013, I had already lived in three different countries.

15.3 The present perfect subjunctive p. 525

Present perfect subjunctive: present subjunctive of **haber** + past participle

Present perfect subjunctive	
haya comido	hayamos comido
hayas comido	hayáis comido
haya comido	hayan comido

Espero que **hayas comido** bien.
I hope that you have eaten well.

3 **Oraciones** Forma oraciones completas con los elementos dados. Usa el pretérito pluscuamperfecto de indicativo y haz todos los cambios necesarios. Sigue el modelo. **24 pts.**

> **modelo**
>
> yo / ya / conocer / muchos amigos *Yo ya había conocido a muchos amigos.*

1. tú / todavía no / aprender / mantenerse en forma
2. los hermanos Falcón / todavía no / perder / partido de vóleibol
3. Elías / ya / entrenarse / para / maratón
4. nosotros / siempre / sufrir / muchas presiones
5. yo / nunca / romperse / hueso
6. la entrenadora / ya / poner / cinta caminadora

4 **Una carta** Completa esta carta con el pretérito perfecto de indicativo o de subjuntivo. **24 pts.**

Queridos papá y mamá:

¿Cómo (1) _____ (estar)? Mamá, espero que no (2) _____ (tú, enfermarse) otra vez. Yo sé que (3) _____ (tú, seguir) los consejos del doctor, pero estoy preocupada.

Y en mi vida, ¿qué (4) _____ (pasar) últimamente (lately)? Pues, nada nuevo, sólo trabajo. Los problemas en la compañía, yo los (5) _____ (resolver) casi todos. Pero estoy bien. Es verdad que (6) _____ (yo, adelgazar) un poco, pero no creo que (7) _____ (ser) a causa del estrés. Espero que no (8) _____ (ustedes, sentirse) mal porque no pude visitarlos. Es extraño que no (9) _____ (recibir) mis cartas. Tengo miedo de que (10) _____ (las cartas, perderse).

Me alegro de que papá (11) _____ (tomar) vacaciones para venir a visitarme. ¡Es increíble que nosotros no (12) _____ (verse) en casi un año!

Un abrazo y hasta muy pronto,

Belén

5 **Poema** Completa este fragmento de un poema de Nezahualcóyotl con el pretérito perfecto de indicativo de los verbos. **4 pts.**

" _____ (Llegar) aquí,
soy Yoyontzin.
Sólo busco las flores
sobre la tierra, _____ (venir)
a cortarlas. **"**

Lectura

Antes de leer

Estrategia
Making inferences

For dramatic effect and to achieve a smoother writing style, authors often do not explicitly supply the reader with all the details of a story or poem. Clues in the text can help you infer those things the writer chooses not to state in a direct manner. You simply "read between the lines" to fill in the missing information and draw conclusions. To practice making inferences, read these statements:

A Liliana le encanta ir al gimnasio. Hace años que empezó a levantar pesas.

Based on this statement alone, what inferences can you draw about Liliana?

El autor

Ve a la página 473 de tu libro y lee la biografía de Gabriel García Márquez.

El título

Sin leer el texto del cuento (*story*), lee el título. Escribe cinco oraciones que empiecen con la frase "Un día de éstos".

El cuento

Éstas son algunas palabras que vas a encontrar al leer *Un día de éstos*. Busca su significado en el diccionario. Según estas palabras, ¿de qué piensas que trata (*is about*) el cuento?

alcalde	lágrimas
dentadura postiza	muela
displicente	pañuelo
enjuto	rencor
guerrera	teniente

Un día de éstos
Gabriel García Márquez

El lunes amaneció tibio° y sin lluvia. Don Aurelio Escovar, dentista sin título y buen madrugador°, abrió su gabinete° a las seis. Sacó de la vidriera° una dentadura postiza° montada aún° en el molde de yeso° y puso sobre la mesa un puñado° de instrumentos que ordenó de mayor a menor, como en una exposición. Llevaba una camisa a rayas, sin cuello, cerrada arriba con un botón dorado°, y los pantalones sostenidos con cargadores° elásticos. Era rígido, enjuto, con una mirada que raras veces correspondía a la situación, como la mirada de los sordos°.

Cuando tuvo las cosas dispuestas sobre la mesa rodó la fresa° hacia el sillón de resortes y se sentó a pulir° la dentadura postiza. Parecía no pensar en lo que hacía, pero trabajaba con obstinación, pedaleando en la fresa incluso cuando no se servía de ella.

Después de las ocho hizo una pausa para mirar el cielo por la ventana y vio dos gallinazos° pensativos que se secaban al sol en el caballete° de la casa vecina. Siguió trabajando con la idea de que antes del almuerzo volvería a llover°. La voz destemplada° de su hijo de once años lo sacó de su abstracción.

—Papá.

—Qué.

—Dice el alcalde que si le sacas una muela.

—Dile que no estoy aquí.

Estaba puliendo un diente de oro°. Lo retiró a la distancia del brazo y lo examinó con los ojos a medio cerrar. En la salita de espera volvió a gritar su hijo.

—Dice que sí estás porque te está oyendo.

El dentista siguió examinando el diente. Sólo cuando lo puso en la mesa con los trabajos terminados, dijo:

---

amaneció tibio *dawn broke warm* madrugador *early riser* gabinete *office* vidriera *glass cabinet* dentadura postiza *dentures* montada aún *still set* yeso *plaster* puñado *handful* dorado *gold* sostenidos con cargadores *held by suspenders* sordos *deaf* rodó la fresa *he turned the drill* pulir *to polish* gallinazos *vultures* caballete *ridge* volvería a llover *it would rain again* voz destemplada *harsh voice* oro *gold* cajita de cartón *small cardboard box* puente *bridge* te pega un tiro *he will shoot you* Sin apresurarse *Without haste* gaveta *drawer* Hizo girar *He turned* apoyada *resting* umbral *threshold* mejilla *cheek* hinchada *swollen* barba *beard* marchitos *faded* hervían *were boiling* pomos de loza *china bottles* cancel de tela *cloth screen* se acercaba *was approaching* talones *heels* mandíbula *jaw* cautelosa *cautious* cacerola *saucepan* pinzas *pliers* escupidera *spittoon* aguamanil *washstand* cordal *wisdom tooth* gatillo *pliers* se aferró *clung* barras *arms* descargó *unloaded* vacío helado *icy hollowness* riñones *kidneys* no soltó un suspiro *he didn't let out a sigh* muñeca *wrist* amarga ternura *bitter tenderness* teniente *lieutenant* crujido *crunch* a través de *through* sudoroso *sweaty* jadeante *panting* se desabotonó *he unbuttoned* a tientas *blindly* bolsillo *pocket* trapo *cloth* cielorraso desfondado *ceiling with the paint sagging* telaraña polvorienta *dusty spiderweb* haga buches de *rinse your mouth out with* vaina *thing*

—Mejor.

Volvió a operar la fresa. De una cajita de cartón° donde guardaba las cosas por hacer, sacó un puente° de varias piezas y empezó a pulir el oro.

—Papá.

—Qué.

Aún no había cambiado de expresión.

—Dice que si no le sacas la muela te pega un tiro°.

Sin apresurarse°, con un movimiento extremadamente tranquilo, dejó de pedalear en la fresa, la retiró del sillón y abrió por completo la gaveta° inferior de la mesa. Allí estaba el revólver.

—Bueno —dijo—. Dile que venga a pegármelo.

Hizo girar° el sillón hasta quedar de frente a la puerta, la mano apoyada° en el borde de la gaveta. El alcalde apareció en el umbral°. Se había afeitado la mejilla° izquierda, pero en la otra, hinchada° y dolorida, tenía una barba° de cinco días. El dentista vio en sus ojos marchitos° muchas noches de desesperación. Cerró la gaveta con la punta de los dedos y dijo suavemente:

—Siéntese.

—Buenos días —dijo el alcalde.

—Buenos —dijo el dentista.

Mientras hervían° los instrumentos, el alcalde apoyó el cráneo en el cabezal de la silla y se sintió mejor. Respiraba un olor glacial. Era un gabinete pobre: una vieja silla de madera, la fresa de pedal y una vidriera con pomos de loza°. Frente a la silla, una ventana con un cancel de tela° hasta la altura de un hombre. Cuando sintió que el dentista se acercaba°, el alcalde afirmó los talones° y abrió la boca.

Don Aurelio Escovar le movió la cabeza hacia la luz. Después de observar la muela dañada, ajustó la mandíbula° con una presión cautelosa° de los dedos.

—Tiene que ser sin anestesia —dijo.

—¿Por qué?

—Porque tiene un absceso.

El alcalde lo miró en los ojos.

—Está bien —dijo, y trató de sonreír. El dentista no le correspondió. Llevó a la mesa de trabajo la cacerola° con los instrumentos hervidos y los sacó del agua con unas pinzas° frías, todavía sin apresurarse. Después rodó la escupidera° con la punta del zapato y fue a lavarse las manos en el aguamanil°. Hizo todo sin mirar al alcalde. Pero el alcalde no lo perdió de vista.

Era una cordal° inferior. El dentista abrió las piernas y apretó la muela con el gatillo° caliente. El alcalde se aferró° a las barras° de la silla, descargó° toda su fuerza en los pies y sintió un vacío helado° en los riñones°, pero no soltó un suspiro°. El dentista sólo movió la muñeca°. Sin rencor, más bien con una amarga ternura°, dijo:

—Aquí nos paga veinte muertos, teniente°.

El alcalde sintió un crujido° de huesos en la mandíbula y sus ojos se llenaron de lágrimas. Pero no suspiró hasta que no sintió salir la muela. Entonces la vio a través de° las lágrimas. Le pareció tan extraña a su dolor, que no pudo entender la tortura de sus cinco noches anteriores. Inclinado sobre la escupidera, sudoroso°, jadeante°, se desabotonó° la guerrera y buscó a tientas° el pañuelo en el bolsillo° del pantalón. El dentista le dio un trapo° limpio.

—Séquese las lágrimas —dijo.

El alcalde lo hizo. Estaba temblando. Mientras el dentista se lavaba las manos, vio el cielorraso desfondado° y una telaraña polvorienta° con huevos de araña e insectos muertos. El dentista regresó secándose. "Acuéstese —dijo— y haga buches de° agua de sal." El alcalde se puso de pie, se despidió con un displicente saludo militar, y se dirigió a la puerta estirando las piernas, sin abotonarse la guerrera.

—Me pasa la cuenta —dijo.

—¿A usted o al municipio?

El alcalde no lo miró. Cerró la puerta, y dijo, a través de la red metálica:

—Es la misma vaina°.

Después de leer

Comprensión

Completa las oraciones con la palabra o expresión correcta.

1. Don Aurelio Escovar es _____ sin título.

2. Al alcalde le duele _____.

3. Aurelio Escovar y el alcalde se llevan _____.

4. El alcalde amenaza (*threatens*) al dentista con pegarle un _____.

5. Finalmente, Aurelio Escovar _____ la muela al alcalde.

6. El alcalde llevaba varias noches sin _____.

Interpretación

Responde a estas preguntas.

1. ¿Cómo reacciona don Aurelio cuando escucha que el alcalde amenaza con pegarle un tiro? ¿Qué te dice esta actitud sobre las personalidades del dentista y del alcalde?

2. ¿Por qué crees que don Aurelio y el alcalde no se llevan bien?

3. ¿Crees que era realmente necesario no usar anestesia?

4. ¿Qué piensas que significa el comentario "aquí nos paga veinte muertos, teniente"? ¿Qué te dice esto del alcalde y su autoridad en el pueblo?

5. ¿Cómo se puede interpretar el saludo militar y la frase final del alcalde "es la misma vaina"?

Escritura

Estrategia

Organizing information logically

Many times a written piece may require you to include a great deal of information. You might want to organize your information in one of three different ways:

- ▶ chronologically (e.g., events in the history of a country)
- ▶ sequentially (e.g., steps in a recipe)
- ▶ in order of importance

Organizing your information beforehand will make both your writing and your message clearer to your readers. If you were writing a piece on weight reduction, for example, you would need to organize your ideas about two general areas: eating right and exercise. You would need to decide which of the two is more important according to your purpose in writing the piece. If your main idea is that eating right is the key to losing weight, you might want to start your piece with a discussion of good eating habits. You might want to discuss the following aspects of eating right in order of their importance:

- ▶ quantities of food
- ▶ selecting appropriate foods
- ▶ healthy recipes
- ▶ percentage of fat in each meal
- ▶ calorie count
- ▶ percentage of carbohydrates in each meal
- ▶ frequency of meals

You would then complete the piece by following the same process to discuss the various aspects of the importance of getting exercise.

Tema

Escribir un plan personal de bienestar

Desarrolla un plan personal para mejorar tu bienestar, tanto físico como emocional. Tu plan debe describir:

1. lo que has hecho para mejorar tu bienestar y llevar una vida sana
2. lo que no has podido hacer todavía
3. las actividades que debes hacer en los próximos meses

Considera también estas preguntas:

La nutrición

- ▶ ¿Comes una dieta equilibrada?
- ▶ ¿Consumes suficientes vitaminas y minerales?
- ▶ ¿Consumes demasiada grasa?
- ▶ ¿Quieres aumentar de peso o adelgazar?
- ▶ ¿Qué puedes hacer para mejorar tu dieta?

El ejercicio

- ▶ ¿Haces ejercicio? ¿Con qué frecuencia?
- ▶ ¿Vas al gimnasio? ¿Qué tipo de ejercicios haces allí?
- ▶ ¿Practicas algún deporte?
- ▶ ¿Qué puedes hacer para mejorar tu bienestar físico?

El estrés

- ▶ ¿Sufres muchas presiones?
- ▶ ¿Qué actividades o problemas te causan estrés?
- ▶ ¿Qué haces (o debes hacer) para aliviar el estrés y sentirte más tranquilo/a?
- ▶ ¿Qué puedes hacer para mejorar tu bienestar emocional?

Escuchar

Estrategia
**Listening for the gist/
Listening for cognates**

Combining these two strategies is an easy
way to get a good sense of what you hear.
When you listen for the gist, you get the
general idea of what you're hearing, which
allows you to interpret cognates and other
words in a meaningful context. Similarly,
the cognates give you information about the
details of the story that you might not have
understood when listening for the gist.

 To practice these strategies, you will listen to
a short paragraph. Write down the gist of what
you hear and jot down a few cognates. Based
on the gist and the cognates, what conclusions
can you draw about what you heard?

Preparación

Mira la foto. ¿Qué pistas° te da de lo que
vas a oír?

Ahora escucha

Escucha lo que dice Ofelia Cortez de Bauer. Anota
algunos de los cognados que escuchas y también la
idea general del discurso°.

_____
_____
_____
_____

Idea general: _____

Ahora contesta las siguientes preguntas.

1. ¿Cuál es el género° del discurso?
2. ¿Cuál es el tema?
3. ¿Cuál es el propósito°?

pistas *clues* discurso *speech* género *genre* propósito *purpose*
público *audience* debía haber incluido *should have included*

Comprensión

¿Cierto o falso?
Indica si lo que dicen estas oraciones es **cierto** o **falso**.
Corrige las oraciones falsas.

	Cierto	Falso
1. La señora Bauer habla de la importancia de estar en buena forma y de hacer ejercicio.	○	○
2. Según ella, lo más importante es que lleves el programa sugerido por los expertos.	○	○
3. La señora Bauer participa en actividades individuales y de grupo.	○	○
4. El único objetivo del tipo de programa que ella sugiere es adelgazar.	○	○

Preguntas
Responde a las preguntas.
1. Imagina que el programa de radio sigue. Según las
   pistas que ella dio, ¿qué vas a oír en la segunda parte?
2. ¿A qué tipo de público° le interesa el tema del que habla
   la señora Bauer?
3. ¿Sigues los consejos de la señora Bauer?
   Explica tu respuesta.
4. ¿Qué piensas de los consejos que ella da? ¿Hay otra
   información que ella debía haber incluido°?

En pantalla

Para Iker, cada persona se parece a un animal. Por ejemplo, su papá es un oso°. A Iker le habría gustado° ser un oso también, pero él es otro animal. Y eso es algo que nadie sabe en la escuela. Iker ha conseguido mantenerlo así gracias a algunos trucos°, pero tiene miedo de que los demás lo sepan. ¿Qué podría° pasar si° sus compañeros descubren el secreto de Iker?

Preparación

¿Cierto o falso?

Lee la lista de **Expresiones útiles** e indica si lo que dice cada oración es **cierto** o **falso**. Corrige las oraciones falsas.

_____ 1. Me prestaste tu balón (*ball*) y yo te lo tengo que devolver.

_____ 2. Si (*If*) quiero disimular algo, se lo digo a todos.

_____ 3. Es común que una hija salga igual a su madre.

_____ 4. Para hacerme un peinado especial, voy al salón de belleza.

_____ 5. Para cocinar el pan, lo meto en el congelador.

_____ 6. Si no hago ejercicios de estiramiento, me siento tieso.

Rasgos de familia

Contesta las preguntas de tu compañero/a.

1. ¿Tienes rasgos particulares? ¿Cuáles son de tu apariencia física (*physical appearance*)? ¿Cuáles son de tu personalidad?

2. ¿Cuáles de tus rasgos son buenos? ¿Cuáles son malos? ¿Cómo determinas que son buenos o malos?

3. ¿Cuáles de tus rasgos particulares, buenos y malos, te hacen una persona única?

4. ¿Es común alguno de esos rasgos en tu familia? ¿Ha pasado de generación en generación?

5. ¿Tienes compañeros que comparten tus mismos rasgos? ¿Qué tienen en común ustedes?

6. ¿Qué animal crees que serías (*you would be*) según (*according to*) tus rasgos? Explica tu respuesta.

Iker pelos tiesos

Escrito y Dirigido por:
Sandra García Velten

Expresiones útiles

devolver	*to return, to give back*
disimular	*to hide, to disguise*
me hubiera gustado	*I would have liked*
meter	*to put (something) in, to introduce*
el peinado	*hairstyle*
salir (igual) a	*to take after*
si supieran	*if they knew*
tieso/a	*stiff*

Para hablar del corto

burlarse (de)	*to make fun (of)*
esconder(se)	*to hide (onself)*
la fuerza	*strength*
orgulloso/a	*proud*
pelear(se)	*to fight (with one another)*
el rasgo	*feature, characteristic*
sentirse cohibido/a	*to feel self-conscious*

oso *bear* le habría gustado *he would have liked*
trucos *tricks* podría *could* si *if*

Escenas: Iker pelos tiesos

IKER: Tito es un mosquito; de esos que nunca dejan de molestar... ni en las noches.

IKER: Mi mamá es un perico (*parrot*), como todas las mamás.

NIÑO 3: Ey, no hay paso. (*Hey, there's no way through.*)

IKER: Pero, ¿por qué?

IKER: ... [yo] salí igual a mi abuelo... soy un puercoespín (*porcupine*).

IKER: ¿Qué me dirían si supieran mi secreto?

IKER: ¿Y por qué ese niño está pasando?

NIÑO 5: Porque éste es nuestro territorio.

Comprensión

Escoger

Escoge la opción que completa mejor cada oración.

1. Iker siempre _____ su pelo tieso.
   a. muestra
   b. corta
   c. disimula

2. En la familia de Iker, _____ el mismo rasgo.
   a. no hay dos personas con
   b. él y su abuelo comparten
   c. el abuelo y Tito tienen

3. Para Iker, su _____ es un perico.
   a. hermana
   b. mamá
   c. maestra (*teacher*)

4. Para Iker, es probable que sus compañeros _____ si saben su secreto.
   a. lo acepten
   b. se burlen de él
   c. se escondan

5. Iker se sintió _____ cuando su compañero le dijo que le gustaba su peinado.
   a. aliviado (*relieved*)
   b. cohibido
   c. enojado

6. Al final, Iker estaba _____ de mostrar su peinado natural.
   a. avergonzado
   b. nervioso
   c. orgulloso

Preguntas

Contesta estas preguntas con oraciones completas.

1. ¿En qué situaciones se le pone el pelo tieso a Iker?

2. ¿Por qué esconde Iker su peinado natural?

3. ¿Cómo se sintió Iker después de pelearse con los niños en el patio?

4. ¿Te has sentido cohibido/a alguna vez?

5. ¿Cuáles son las consecuencias positivas de presentarte ante el mundo tal y como eres?

6. ¿Crees que la percepción que tienes de ti mismo/a influye en (*influences*) la manera en que ves a los demás? Explica tu respuesta.

Superhéroes

Imagina que un día descubres que tienes un superpoder (*superpower*). Escribe un párrafo donde describas tu experiencia. No te olvides de presentar esta información:

▶ cuál es tu superpoder

▶ cómo y cuándo lo descubriste

▶ quién, además de ti, sabe que tienes ese superpoder

▶ qué características positivas y negativas implica (*involves*) tener ese superpoder

▶ cómo has usado tu superpoder para ayudar a otros

▶ si has decidido usar tu superpoder para mejorar el mundo

▶ cuál es tu nombre de superhéroe/superheroína

modelo

Puedo saltar (leap) muros de hasta cinco metros de alto. Lo supe un día que mi gato quedó atrapado en el techo de un edificio...

¿Cómo sobrevivir° en la selva de concreto de una gran ciudad hispana? Sin duda, los parques públicos son la respuesta cuando se busca un oasis. Los Bosques de Palermo en Buenos Aires, el Bosque de Chapultepec en la Ciudad de México, el Parque Quinta Vergara en Viña del Mar o la Casa de Campo en Madrid son vitales para la salud física y mental de sus habitantes. Unos tienen museos, lagos y zoológicos, otros hasta parques de diversiones° y jardines. En ellos siempre vas a ver gente haciendo ejercicio, relajándose o reunida con familiares y amigos. A continuación conocerás uno de los muchos parques de Madrid, El Retiro, y vas a ver cómo se relajan los madrileños.

Vocabulario útil	
árabe	*Moorish, Arab*
el bullicio	*hustle and bustle*
combatir el estrés	*to fight stress*
el ruido	*noise*

Preparación

¿Sufres de estrés? ¿Qué situaciones te producen estrés? ¿Qué haces para combatirlo?

¿Cierto o falso?

Indica si las oraciones son **ciertas** o **falsas**.

1. Madrid es la segunda ciudad más grande de España, después de Barcelona.

2. Madrid es una ciudad muy poco congestionada gracias a los policías de tráfico.

3. Un turista estadounidense intenta saltearse la cola (*cut the line*) para conseguir unos boletos para un espectáculo.

4. En el Parque del Retiro, puedes descansar, hacer gimnasia, etc.

5. Los baños termales Medina Mayrit son de influencia cristiana.

6. En Medina Mayrit es posible bañarse en aguas termales, tomar el té y hasta comer.

sobrevivir *to survive* parques de diversiones *amusement parks*

¿Estrés? ¿Qué estrés?

El tráfico, el ruido de las calles... Todos quieren llegar al trabajo a tiempo.

... es un lugar donde la gente viene a "retirarse", a escapar del estrés y el bullicio de la ciudad.

... en pleno centro de Madrid, encontramos los Baños Árabes [...]

Bolivia

El país en cifras

▶ **Área:** 1.098.580 km^2 (424.162 millas^2), *equivalente al área total de Francia y España*

▶ **Población:** 10.631.000

Los indígenas quechua y aimará constituyen más de la mitad° de la población de Bolivia. Estos grupos indígenas han mantenido sus culturas y lenguas tradicionales. Las personas de ascendencia° indígena y europea representan la tercera parte de la población. Los demás son de ascendencia europea nacida en Latinoamérica. Una gran mayoría de los bolivianos, más o menos el 70%, vive en el altiplano°.

▶ **Capital:** La Paz, sede° del gobierno, capital administrativa—1.715.000; Sucre, sede del Tribunal Supremo, capital constitucional y judicial

▶ **Ciudades principales:** Santa Cruz de la Sierra—1.584.000; Cochabamba, Oruro, Potosí

▶ **Moneda:** peso boliviano

▶ **Idiomas:** español (oficial), aimará (oficial), quechua (oficial)

Bandera de Bolivia

Bolivianos célebres

▶ **Jesús Lara,** escritor (1898–1980)
▶ **Víctor Paz Estenssoro,** político y presidente (1907–2001)
▶ **María Luisa Pacheco,** pintora (1919–1982)
▶ **Matilde Casazola,** poeta (1942–)
▶ **Edmundo Paz Soldán,** escritor (1967–)

mitad *half* ascendencia *descent* altiplano *high plateau* sede *seat*
paraguas *umbrella* cascada *waterfall*

Plaza 14 de Septiembre
Vista de la ciudad de Sucre
Vista de la ciudad de Oruro

PERÚ
BRASIL
Río Beni
Río Mamoré
Río Grande
Illampu
Lago Titicaca
La Paz
Tiahuanaco
Cordillera Oriental de los Andes
Oruro
Cordillera Central de los Andes
Sucre
Santa Cruz de la Sierra
Cochabamba
Lago Poopó
Potosí
Río Pilcomayo
PARAGUAY
ARGENTINA
CHILE

ESTADOS UNIDOS
OCÉANO ATLÁNTICO
OCÉANO PACÍFICO
BOLIVIA

¡Increíble pero cierto!

La Paz es la capital más alta del mundo. Su aeropuerto está situado a una altitud de 4.061 metros (13.325 pies). Ah, y si viajas en carro hasta La Paz, ¡no te olvides del paraguas°! En la carretera, que cruza 9.000 metros de densa selva, te encontrarás con una cascada°.

Lugares • El lago Titicaca

Titicaca, situado en los Andes de Bolivia y Perú, es el lago navegable más alto del mundo, a una altitud de 3.810 metros (12.500 pies). Con un área de más de 8.300 kilómetros² (3.200 millas²), también es el segundo lago más grande de Suramérica, después del lago de Maracaibo (Venezuela). La mitología inca cuenta que los hijos del dios° Sol emergieron de las profundas aguas del lago Titicaca para fundar su imperio°.

Artes • La música andina

La música andina, compartida por Bolivia, Perú, Ecuador, Chile y Argentina, es el aspecto más conocido de su folclore. Hay muchos conjuntos° profesionales que dan a conocer° esta música popular, de origen indígena, alrededor° del mundo. Algunos de los grupos más importantes y que llevan más de treinta años actuando en escenarios internacionales son Los Kjarkas (Bolivia), Inti Illimani (Chile), Los Chaskis (Argentina) e Illapu (Chile).

Historia • Tiahuanaco

Tiahuanaco, que significa "Ciudad de los dioses", es un sitio arqueológico de ruinas preincaicas situado cerca de La Paz y del lago Titicaca. Se piensa que los antepasados° de los indígenas aimará fundaron este centro ceremonial hace unos 15.000 años. En el año 1100, la ciudad tenía unos 60.000 habitantes. En este sitio se pueden ver el Templo de Kalasasaya, el Monolito Ponce, el Templete Subterráneo, la Puerta del Sol y la Puerta de la Luna. La Puerta del Sol es un impresionante monumento que tiene tres metros de alto y cuatro de ancho° y que pesa unas 10 toneladas.

¿Qué aprendiste? Contesta las preguntas con una oración completa.

1. ¿Qué idiomas se hablan en Bolivia?
2. ¿Dónde vive la mayoría de los bolivianos?
3. ¿Cuál es la capital administrativa de Bolivia?
4. Según la mitología inca, ¿qué ocurrió en el lago Titicaca?
5. ¿De qué países es la música andina?
6. ¿Qué origen tiene esta música?
7. ¿Cómo se llama el sitio arqueológico situado cerca de La Paz y el lago Titicaca?
8. ¿Qué es la Puerta del Sol?

Conexión Internet Investiga estos temas en Internet.

1. Busca información sobre un(a) boliviano/a célebre. ¿Cuáles son algunos de los episodios más importantes de su vida? ¿Qué ha hecho esta persona? ¿Por qué es célebre?
2. Busca información sobre Tiahuanaco u otro sitio arqueológico en Bolivia. ¿Qué han descubierto los arqueólogos en ese sitio?

dios *god* imperio *empire* conjuntos *groups* dan a conocer *make known* alrededor *around* antepasados *ancestors* ancho *wide*

El bienestar

el bienestar	well-being
la droga	drug
el/la drogadicto/a	drug addict
el masaje	massage
el/la teleadicto/a	couch potato
adelgazar	to lose weight; to slim down
aliviar el estrés	to reduce stress
aliviar la tensión	to reduce tension
apurarse, darse prisa	to hurry; to rush
aumentar de peso, engordar	to gain weight
disfrutar (de)	to enjoy; to reap the benefits (of)
estar a dieta	to be on a diet
(no) fumar	(not) to smoke
llevar una vida sana	to lead a healthy lifestyle
sufrir muchas presiones	to be under a lot of pressure
tratar de (+ *inf.*)	to try (to do something)
activo/a	active
débil	weak
en exceso	in excess; too much
flexible	flexible
fuerte	strong
sedentario/a	sedentary
tranquilo/a	calm; quiet

En el gimnasio

la cinta caminadora	treadmill
la clase de ejercicios aeróbicos	aerobics class
el/la entrenador(a)	trainer
el músculo	muscle
calentarse (e:ie)	to warm up
entrenarse	to train
estar en buena forma	to be in good shape
hacer ejercicio	to exercise
hacer ejercicios aeróbicos	to do aerobics
hacer ejercicios de estiramiento	to do stretching exercises
hacer gimnasia	to work out
levantar pesas	to lift weights
mantenerse en forma	to stay in shape
sudar	to sweat

La nutrición

la bebida alcohólica	alcoholic beverage
la cafeína	caffeine
la caloría	calorie
el colesterol	cholesterol
la grasa	fat
la merienda	afternoon snack
el mineral	mineral
la nutrición	nutrition
el/la nutricionista	nutritionist
la proteína	protein
la vitamina	vitamin
comer una dieta equilibrada	to eat a balanced diet
consumir alcohol	to consume alcohol
descafeinado/a	decaffeinated

Expresiones útiles	See page 513.

Communicative Goals

You will learn how to:

- Talk about your future plans
- Talk about and discuss work
- Interview for a job
- Express agreement and disagreement

A PRIMERA VISTA
- ¿Están trabajando las personas en la foto?
- ¿Dibujan algo?
- ¿Llevan ropa profesional?
- ¿Están descansando o están ocupados?

El mundo del trabajo

Más vocabulario

el/la abogado/a	*lawyer*
el actor, la actriz	*actor*
el/la consejero/a	*counselor; advisor*
el/la contador(a)	*accountant*
el/la corredor(a) de bolsa	*stockbroker*
el/la diseñador(a)	*designer*
el/la electricista	*electrician*
el/la gerente	*manager*
el hombre/la mujer de negocios	*businessperson*
el/la jefe/a	*boss*
el/la maestro/a	*teacher*
el/la político/a	*politician*
el/la psicólogo/a	*psychologist*
el/la secretario/a	*secretary*
el/la técnico/a	*technician*
el ascenso	*promotion*
el aumento de sueldo	*raise*
la carrera	*career*
la compañía, la empresa	*company; firm*
el empleo	*job; employment*
los negocios	*business; commerce*
la ocupación	*occupation*
el oficio	*trade*
la profesión	*profession*
la reunión	*meeting*
el teletrabajo	*telecommuting*
el trabajo	*job; work*
la videoconferencia	*videoconference*
dejar	*to quit; to leave behind*
despedir (e:i)	*to fire*
invertir (e:ie)	*to invest*
renunciar (a)	*to resign (from)*
tener éxito	*to be successful*
comercial	*commercial; business-related*

Variación léxica

abogado/a ⟷ licenciado/a (*Amér. C.*)

contador(a) ⟷ contable (*Esp.*)

el carpintero

el pintor

el arquitecto

el peluquero

la arqueóloga

el científico

Práctica

1 **Escuchar** 🎧 Escucha la descripción que hace Juan Figueres de su profesión y luego completa las oraciones con las palabras adecuadas.

1. Juan Figueres es _____.
   a. actor   b. hombre de negocios   c. pintor
2. El Sr. Figueres es el _____ de una compañía multinacional.
   a. secretario   b. técnico   c. gerente
3. El Sr. Figueres quería _____ en la cual pudiera (*he could*) trabajar en otros países.
   a. una carrera   b. un ascenso   c. un aumento de sueldo
4. El Sr. Figueres viaja mucho porque _____.
   a. tiene reuniones en otros países   b. es político
   c. toma muchas vacaciones

2 **¿Cierto o falso?** 🎧 Escucha las descripciones de las profesiones de Ana y Marco. Indica si lo que dice cada oración es **cierto** o **falso**.

1. Ana es maestra de inglés.
2. Ana asiste a muchas reuniones.
3. Ana recibió un aumento de sueldo.
4. Marco hace muchos viajes.
5. Marco quiere dejar su empresa.
6. El jefe de Marco es cocinero.

3 **Escoger** Escoge la ocupación que corresponda a cada descripción.

la arquitecta	el científico	la electricista
el bombero	el corredor de bolsa	el maestro
la carpintera	el diseñador	la técnica

1. Desarrolla teorías de biología, química, física, etc.
2. Nos ayuda a iluminar nuestras casas.
3. Combate los incendios (*fires*) que destruyen edificios.
4. Ayuda a la gente a invertir su dinero.
5. Enseña a los niños.
6. Diseña ropa.
7. Arregla las computadoras.
8. Diseña edificios.

4 **Asociaciones** ¿Qué profesiones asocias con estas palabras?

modelo

emociones *psicólogo/a*

1. pinturas
2. consejos
3. elecciones
4. comida
5. leyes
6. teatro
7. pirámide
8. periódico
9. pelo

el cocinero

el bombero

la reportera

5

Conversación Completa la entrevista con el nuevo vocabulario que se ofrece en la lista de la derecha.

ENTREVISTADOR	Recibí la (1) _____ que usted llenó y vi que tiene mucha experiencia.
ASPIRANTE	Por eso decidí mandar una copia de mi (2) _____ cuando vi su (3) _____ en Internet.
ENTREVISTADOR	Me alegro de que lo haya hecho. Pero dígame, ¿por qué dejó usted su (4) _____ anterior?
ASPIRANTE	Lo dejé porque quiero un mejor (5) _____.
ENTREVISTADOR	¿Y cuánto quiere (6) _____ usted?
ASPIRANTE	Pues, eso depende de los (7) _____ que me puedan ofrecer.
ENTREVISTADOR	Muy bien. Pues, creo que usted tiene la experiencia necesaria, pero tengo que (8) _____ a dos aspirantes más. Le vamos a llamar la semana que viene.
ASPIRANTE	Hasta pronto, y gracias por la (9) _____.

Más vocabulario

el anuncio	*advertisement*
el/la aspirante	*candidate; applicant*
los beneficios	*benefits*
el currículum	*résumé*
la entrevista	*interview*
el/la entrevistador(a)	*interviewer*
el puesto	*position; job*
el salario, el sueldo	*salary*
la solicitud (de trabajo)	*(job) application*
contratar	*to hire*
entrevistar	*to interview*
ganar	*to earn*
obtener	*to obtain; to get*
solicitar	*to apply (for a job)*

6

Completar Escoge la respuesta que completa cada oración.

1. Voy a _____ mi empleo.
   a. tener éxito   b. renunciar a   c. entrevistar
2. Quiero dejar mi _____ porque no me llevo bien con mi jefe.
   a. anuncio   b. gerente   c. puesto
3. Por eso, fui a una _____ con una consejera de carreras.
   a. profesión   b. reunión   c. ocupación
4. Ella me dijo que necesito revisar mi _____.
   a. currículum   b. compañía   c. aspirante
5. ¿Cuándo obtuviste _____ más reciente?, me preguntó.
   a. la reunión   b. la videoconferencia   c. el aumento de sueldo
6. Le dije que deseo trabajar en una empresa con excelentes _____.
   a. beneficios   b. entrevistas   c. solicitudes de trabajo
7. Y quiero tener la oportunidad de _____ en la nueva empresa.
   a. invertir   b. obtener   c. perder

¡LENGUA VIVA!

Trabajo, empleo, and **puesto** can all be translated as *job*, but each has additional meanings: **trabajo** means *work*, **empleo** means *employment*, and **puesto** means *position*.

7

Preguntas Contesta cada pregunta con una respuesta breve.

1. ¿Te gusta tu especialización?
2. ¿Lees los anuncios de empleo en el periódico o en Internet con regularidad?
3. ¿Piensas que una carrera que beneficia a otros es más importante que un empleo con un salario muy bueno? Explica tu respuesta.
4. ¿Obtienes siempre los puestos que quieres?
5. ¿Te preparas bien para las entrevistas?
6. ¿Crees que una persona debe renunciar a un puesto si no le ofrecen ascensos?
7. ¿Te gustaría (*Would you like*) más un teletrabajo o un trabajo tradicional en una oficina?
8. ¿Piensas que los jefes siempre tienen razón?
9. ¿Quieres crear tu propia empresa? ¿Por qué?
10. ¿Cuál es tu carrera ideal?

Comunicación

8   **Anuncio** Lee el anuncio para un puesto. Luego, indica si las conclusiones son **lógicas** o **ilógicas**.

> ### Oficina de abogados Álvarez & Asociados, en Santo Domingo, necesita SECRETARIO/A
>
> **Se requiere:**
> - Experiencia laboral en puesto similar
> - Capacidad organizativa y comunicativa
> - Nivel nativo de español e inglés
> - Dominio de programas de computación
>
> **Se ofrece:**
> - Ambiente agradable de trabajo
> - Horario de 9 de la mañana a 5 de la tarde
> - Salario competitivo
> - Seguro (*insurance*) médico y dental
> - 20 días de vacaciones anuales
>
> **Los aspirantes al puesto deben enviar su currículum por correo electrónico.**

	Lógico	Ilógico
1. Para obtener este puesto, hay que ser abogado/a.	○	○
2. Un aspirante antipático no debe solicitar este puesto.	○	○
3. Para obtener este puesto, hay que ser bilingüe.	○	○
4. El horario es flexible.	○	○
5. No se ofrecen beneficios.	○	○

9   **Currículum** Crea el currículum de una persona famosa. Incluye las siguientes categorías.

- objetivos profesionales
- experiencia laboral
- formación académica
- otros datos (*facts*) de interés

10   **Una entrevista** Trabaja con un(a) compañero/a para representar los papeles de un(a) aspirante a un puesto y un(a) entrevistador(a).

El/La entrevistador(a) debe describir...

▶ el puesto,
▶ las responsabilidades,
▶ el salario y
▶ los beneficios.

El/La aspirante debe...

▶ presentar su experiencia y
▶ obtener más información sobre el puesto.

Entonces...

▶ el/la entrevistador(a) debe decidir si va a contratar al/a la aspirante y
▶ el/la aspirante debe decidir si va a aceptar el puesto.

La entrevista de trabajo

Los chicos hablan de sus planes para el futuro. Y la Sra. Díaz prepara a Miguel para unas entrevistas de trabajo.

PERSONAJES **MARISSA** **FELIPE**

MARISSA En menos de dos meses, ya habré regresado a mi casa en Wisconsin.

FELIPE No pensé que el año terminara tan pronto.

JIMENA ¡Todavía no se ha acabado! Tengo que escribir tres ensayos.

MARISSA ¿Qué piensas hacer después de graduarte, Felipe?

JUAN CARLOS Vamos a crear una compañía de asesores de negocios.

FELIPE Les enseñaremos a las empresas a disminuir la cantidad de contaminación que producen.

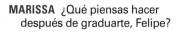

(*Mientras tanto, en la oficina de la Sra. Díaz*)

MIGUEL Gracias por recibirme hoy.

SRA. DÍAZ De nada, Miguel. Estoy muy feliz de poder ayudarte con las entrevistas de trabajo.

MARISSA Estoy segura de que tendrán mucho éxito.

FELIPE También me gustaría viajar. Me muero por ir a visitarte a los Estados Unidos.

JIMENA Pues date prisa. Pronto estará lejos trabajando como arqueóloga.

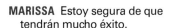

MARISSA No sé cómo vaya a ser mi vida a los 30 años. Probablemente me habré ido de Wisconsin y seré arqueóloga en un país exótico.

JUAN CARLOS (*a Jimena*) Para entonces ya serás doctora.

SRA. DÍAZ Durante la entrevista, tienes que convencer al entrevistador de que tú eres el mejor candidato. ¿Estás listo para comenzar?

MIGUEL Sí.

JIMENA

JUAN CARLOS

MIGUEL

SRA. DÍAZ

MIGUEL Mucho gusto. Soy Miguel Ángel Lagasca Martínez.

SRA. DÍAZ Encantada, Miguel. Veamos. Hábleme sobre su trabajo en el Museo Guggenheim de Bilbao.

MIGUEL Estuve allí seis meses en una práctica.

SRA. DÍAZ ¿Cuáles son sus planes para el futuro?

MIGUEL Seguir estudiando historia del arte, especialmente la española y la latinoamericana. Me encanta el arte moderno. En el futuro, quiero trabajar en un museo y ser un pintor famoso.

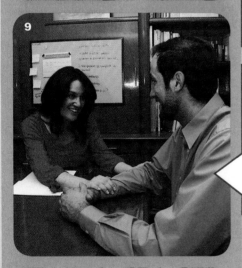

SRA. DÍAZ ¿Qué te hace especial, Miguel?

MIGUEL ¿Especial?

SRA. DÍAZ Bueno. Paremos un momento. Necesitas relajarte. Vamos a caminar.

MIGUEL Estamos esperando noticias del museo. (*al teléfono*) Hola. ¿Maru? ¡Genial! (*a la Sra. Díaz*) ¡La aceptaron!

SRA. DÍAZ Felicidades. Ahora quiero que tomes ese mismo entusiasmo y lo lleves a la entrevista.

Expresiones útiles

Talking about future plans

En menos de dos meses, ya habré regresado a mi casa en Wisconsin.
In less than two months, I'll have gone back home to Wisconsin.

¿Qué piensas hacer después de graduarte?
What do you think you'll be doing after graduation?

Vamos a crear una compañía de asesores de negocios.
We're going to open a consulting firm.

Les enseñaremos a las empresas a disminuir la cantidad de contaminación que producen.
We'll teach companies how to reduce the amount of pollution they produce.

No sé cómo vaya a ser mi vida a los treinta años.
I don't know what my life will be like when I am thirty.

Probablemente me habré ido de Wisconsin.
I'll probably have left Wisconsin.

Seré arqueóloga de un país exótico.
I'll be an archeologist in some exotic country.

Reactions

Estoy seguro/a de que tendrán mucho éxito.
I'm sure you'll be very successful.

¡Genial!
Great!

Additional Vocabulary

ejercer *to practice/exercise (a degree/profession)*
enterarse *to find out*
establecer *to establish*
extrañar *to miss*
por el porvenir *for/to the future*
el título *title*

¿Qué pasó?

1

¿Cierto o falso? Indica si lo que dicen estas oraciones es **cierto** o **falso**.
Corrige las oraciones falsas.

	Cierto	Falso
1. Juan Carlos y Felipe quieren crear su propia empresa.	○	○
2. En el futuro, Marissa va a viajar porque va a ser psicóloga.	○	○
3. La Sra. Díaz ayuda a Miguel con su currículum.	○	○
4. Miguel quiere seguir estudiando historia del arte.	○	○

2

Identificar Identifica quién puede decir estas oraciones.

1. Nosotros vamos a ayudar a que se reduzca la contaminación.
2. Me gustan los hospitales, por eso quiero ser doctora.
3. No imagino cómo será mi vida en el futuro.
4. Quiero ser un pintor famoso, como Salvador Dalí.
5. Lleva ese entusiasmo a la entrevista y serás el mejor candidato.

SRA. DÍAZ

MIGUEL

JIMENA

MARISSA

FELIPE

3

Profesiones Los protagonistas de la **Fotonovela** mencionan estas profesiones.
Define cada profesión.

1. arqueólogo/a
2. doctor(a)
3. administrador(a) de empresas
4. artista
5. hombre/mujer de negocios
6. abogado/a
7. pintor(a)
8. profesor(a)

4

Mis planes En parejas, hablen de sus planes para el futuro. Utilicen estas preguntas y frases.

- ¿Qué piensas hacer después de graduarte?
- ¿Quieres saber cuáles son mis planes para el futuro?
- ¿Cuáles son tus planes?
- ¿Dónde trabajarás?
- El próximo año/verano, voy a...
- Seré...
- Trabajaré en...

Ortografía
y, ll y h

The digraph **ll** and the letter **y** were not pronounced alike in Old Spanish. Nowadays, however, **ll** and **y** have the same or similar pronunciations in many parts of the Spanish-speaking world. This results in frequent misspellings. The letter **h**, as you already know, is silent in Spanish, and it is often difficult to know whether words should be written with or without it. Here are some of the word groups that are spelled with each letter.

talla	**sello**	**botella**	**amarillo**

The digraph **ll** is used in these endings: **-allo/a, -ello/a, -illo/a.**

llave	**llega**	**llorar**	**lluvia**

The digraph **ll** is used at the beginning of words in these combinations: **lla-, lle-, llo-, llu-.**

cayendo	**leyeron**	**oye**	**incluye**

The letter **y** is used in some forms of the verbs **caer, leer,** and **oír** and in verbs ending in **-uir.**

hiperactivo	**hospital**	**hipopótamo**	**humor**

The letter **h** is used at the beginning of words in these combinations: **hiper-, hosp-, hidr-, hipo-, hum-.**

hiato	**hierba**	**hueso**	**huir**

The letter **h** is also used in words that begin with these combinations: **hia-, hie-, hue-, hui-.**

Práctica Llena los espacios con **h, ll** o **y**. Después escribe una oración con cada una de las palabras.

1. cuchi___o
2. ___ielo
3. cue___o
4. estampi___a
5. estre___a
6. ___uésped
7. destru___ó
8. pla___a

Adivinanza Aquí tienes una adivinanza (*riddle*). Intenta descubrir de qué se trata.

Una cajita chiquita, blanca como la nieve: todos la saben abrir, nadie la sabe cerrar.[1]

Pista: Es una comida.

1. El huevo

Beneficios
en los empleos

¿Qué piensas si te ofrecen un trabajo que te da treinta días de vacaciones pagadas? Los beneficios laborales° en los Estados Unidos, España e Hispanoamérica son diferentes en varios sentidos°. En España, por ejemplo, todos los empleados, por ley, tienen treinta días de vacaciones pagadas al año. Otro ejemplo lo hallamos en las licencias por maternidad°. En los Estados Unidos se otorgan° doce semanas, dependiendo de la empresa si esos días son pagados o no. En muchos países hispanoamericanos, sin embargo, las leyes dictan que esta licencia sea pagada. Países como Chile y Venezuela ofrecen a las madres trabajadoras° dieciocho semanas de licencia pagada.

Otra diferencia está en los sistemas de jubilación° de los países hispanoamericanos. Hasta la década de 1990, la mayoría de los países de Centroamérica y Suramérica tenía un sistema de jubilación público. Es decir, las personas no tenían que pagar directamente por su jubilación, sino que el Estado la administraba. Sin embargo, en los últimos años las cosas han cambiado en Hispanoamérica: desde hace más de una década, casi todos los países han incorporado el sistema privado° de jubilación, y en muchos países podemos encontrar los dos sistemas (público y privado) funcionando al mismo tiempo, como en Colombia, Perú o Costa Rica.

El currículum vitae

- El currículum vitae contiene información personal y es fundamental que sea muy detallado°. En ocasiones, mientras más páginas tenga, mejor.

- Normalmente incluye° la educación completa del aspirante, todos los trabajos que ha tenido e incluso sus gustos personales y pasatiempos.

- Puede también incluir detalles que no se suelen incluir en los Estados Unidos: una foto del aspirante, su estado civil e incluso si tiene auto y de qué tipo.

beneficios laborales *job benefits* varios sentidos *many ways*
licencias por maternidad *maternity leave* se otorgan *are given*
madres trabajadoras *working mothers* jubilación *retirement*
privado *private* detallado *detailed* incluye *includes*

1 **¿Cierto o falso?** Indica si lo que dicen estas oraciones es **cierto** o **falso**. Corrige la información falsa.

1. Los trabajadores de los Estados Unidos y los de España tienen beneficios laborales diferentes.

2. La licencia por maternidad es igual en Hispanoamérica y los Estados Unidos.

3. En Venezuela, la licencia por maternidad es de cuatro meses y medio.

4. En España, los empleados tienen treinta días de vacaciones al año.

5. Hasta 1990, muchos países hispanoamericanos tenían un sistema de jubilación privado.

6. En Perú sólo tienen sistema de jubilación privado.

7. En general, el currículum vitae hispano y el estadounidense tienen contenido distinto.

8. En Hispanoamérica, es importante que el currículum vitae tenga pocas páginas.

El trabajo

la chamba (Méx.); el curro (Esp.); el laburo (Arg.); la pega (Chi.)	el trabajo
el/la cirujano/a	*surgeon*
la huelga	*strike*
el/la niñero/a	*babysitter*
el impuesto	*tax*

Igualdad° laboral

- **United Fruit Company** fue, por casi cien años, la mayor corporación estadounidense. Monopolizó las exportaciones de frutas de Hispanoamérica, e influenció enormemente la economía y la política de la región hasta 1970.

- **Fair Trade Coffee** trabaja para proteger a los agricultores° de café de los abusos de las grandes compañías multinacionales. Ahora, en lugares como Centroamérica, los agricultores pueden obtener mayores ganancias° a través del comercio directo y los precios justos°.

- **Oxfam International** trabaja en países como Guatemala, Ecuador, Nicaragua y Perú para concientizar a la opinión pública° de que la igualdad entre las personas es tan importante como el crecimiento° económico de las naciones.

Igualdad *Equality* agricultores *farmers* ganancias *profits* justos *fair* concientizar a la opinión pública *to make public opinion aware* crecimiento *growth*

César Chávez

César Estrada Chávez (1927–1993) nació cerca de Yuma, Arizona. De padres mexicanos, empezó a trabajar en el campo a los diez años de edad. Comenzó a luchar contra la discriminación en los años 40, mientras estaba en la Marina°. Fue en esos tiempos cuando se sentó en la sección para blancos en un cine segregacionista y se negó° a moverse.

Junto a su esposa, Helen Fabela, fundó° en 1962 la Asociación Nacional de Trabajadores del Campo° que después se convertiría en la coalición Trabajadores del Campo Unidos. Participó y organizó muchas huelgas en grandes compañías para lograr mejores condiciones laborales° y salarios más altos y justos para los trabajadores. Es considerado un héroe del movimiento laboral estadounidense. Desde el año 2000, la fecha de su cumpleaños es un día festivo pagado° en California y otros estados.

Marina *Navy* se negó *he refused* fundó *he established* Trabajadores del Campo *Farm Workers* condiciones laborales *working conditions* día festivo pagado *paid holiday*

Conexión Internet

¿Qué industrias importantes hay en los países hispanos?

Use the Web to find more cultural information related to this **Cultura** section.

2 **Comprensión** Contesta las preguntas.

1. ¿Cómo dice un argentino "perdí mi trabajo"?
2. ¿Cuál es el principio fundamental del Fair Trade Coffee?
3. ¿Para qué César Chávez organizó huelgas contra grandes compañías?
4. ¿Qué día es un día festivo pagado en California?

3 **Sus ambiciones laborales** Haz una lista con al menos tres ideas sobre las expectativas que tienes sobre tu futuro como trabajador(a). Puedes describir las ideas y ambiciones sobre el trabajo que quieres tener. ¿Conoces bien las reglas que debes seguir para conseguir un trabajo? ¿Te gustan? ¿Te disgustan?

The future

ANTE TODO You have already learned ways of expressing the near future in Spanish. You will now learn how to form and use the future tense. Compare the different ways of expressing the future in Spanish and English.

Present indicative

Voy al cine mañana.
I'm going to the movies tomorrow.

Present subjunctive

Ojalá **vaya al cine** mañana.
I hope I will go to the movies tomorrow.

ir a + [*infinitive*]

Voy a ir al cine.
I'm going to go to the movies.

Future

Iré al cine.
I will go to the movies.

CONSULTA
To review **ir a** + [*infinitive*], see **Estructura 4.1**, p. 126.

▶ In Spanish, the future is a simple tense that consists of one word, whereas in English it is made up of the auxiliary verb *will* or *shall*, and the main verb.

¡ATENCIÓN!
Note that -**ar**, -**er**, and -**ir** verbs all have the same endings in the future tense.

		estudiar	aprender	recibir
Future tense				
SINGULAR FORMS	yo	estudiar**é**	aprender**é**	recibir**é**
	tú	estudiar**ás**	aprender**ás**	recibir**ás**
	Ud./él/ella	estudiar**á**	aprender**á**	recibir**á**
PLURAL FORMS	nosotros/as	estudiar**emos**	aprender**emos**	recibir**emos**
	vosotros/as	estudiar**éis**	aprender**éis**	recibir**éis**
	Uds./ellos/ellas	estudiar**án**	aprender**án**	recibir**án**

▶ **¡Atención!** Note that all of the future endings have a written accent except the **nosotros/as** form.

¿Cuándo **recibirás** el ascenso?
*When **will you receive** the promotion?*

Mañana **aprenderemos** más.
*Tomorrow **we will learn** more.*

▶ The future endings are the same for regular and irregular verbs. For regular verbs, simply add the endings to the infinitive. For irregular verbs, add the endings to the irregular stem.

Irregular verbs in the future

INFINITIVE	STEM	FUTURE FORMS
decir	dir-	dir**é**
hacer	har-	har**é**
poder	podr-	podr**é**
poner	pondr-	pondr**é**
querer	querr-	querr**é**
saber	sabr-	sabr**é**
salir	saldr-	saldr**é**
tener	tendr-	tendr**é**
venir	vendr-	vendr**é**

▶ The future of **hay** (*inf.* **haber**) is **habrá** *(there will be)*.

La próxima semana **habrá** dos reuniones.	**Habrá** muchos gerentes en la videoconferencia.
Next week there will be two meetings.	*There will be many managers at the videoconference.*

▶ Although the English word *will* can refer to future time, it also refers to someone's willingness to do something. In this case, Spanish uses **querer** + [*infinitive*], not the future tense.

¿Quieres llamarme, por favor?	**¿Quieren ustedes escucharnos,** por favor?
Will you please call me?	*Will you please listen to us?*

COMPARE & CONTRAST

In Spanish, the future tense has an additional use: expressing conjecture or probability. English sentences involving expressions such as *I wonder, I bet, must be, may, might,* and *probably* are often translated into Spanish using the *future of probability*.

—¿Dónde **estarán** mis llaves?	—¿Qué hora **será**?
I wonder where my keys are.	*What time can it be? (I wonder what time it is.)*
—**Estarán** en la cocina.	—**Serán** las once o las doce.
They're probably in the kitchen.	*It must be (It's probably) eleven or twelve.*

Note that although the future tense is used, these verbs express conjecture about *present* conditions, events, or actions.

CONSULTA

To review these conjunctions of time, see **Estructura 13.3**, p. 461.

▶ The future may also be used in the main clause of sentences in which the present subjunctive follows a conjunction of time such as **cuando, después (de) que, en cuanto, hasta que,** and **tan pronto como.**

Cuando llegues a la oficina, **hablaremos**.	**Saldremos tan pronto como termine** su trabajo.
When you arrive at the office, we will talk.	*We will leave as soon as you finish your work.*

¡INTÉNTALO!   Conjuga en futuro los verbos entre paréntesis.

1. (dejar, correr, invertir) yo _____ *dejaré, correré, invertiré* _____
2. (renunciar, beber, vivir) tú _____
3. (hacer, poner, venir) Lola _____
4. (tener, decir, querer) nosotros _____
5. (ir, ser, estar) ustedes _____
6. (solicitar, comer, repetir) usted _____
7. (saber, salir, poder) yo _____
8. (encontrar, jugar, servir) tú _____

Práctica

1 **Planes** Celia está hablando de sus planes. Repite lo que dice, usando el tiempo futuro.

> **modelo**
>
> Voy a consultar el índice de Empresas 500 en la biblioteca.
> *Consultaré el índice de Empresas 500 en la biblioteca.*

1. Álvaro y yo nos vamos a casar pronto.
2. Julián me va a decir dónde puedo buscar trabajo.
3. Voy a buscar un puesto con un buen sueldo.
4. Voy a leer los anuncios clasificados todos los días.
5. Voy a obtener un puesto en mi especialización.
6. Mis amigos van a estar contentos por mí.

2 **La predicción inolvidable** Completa el párrafo con el futuro de los verbos.

asustarse	conseguir	estar	olvidar	tener
casarse	escribir	hacerse	ser	terminar

Nunca (1) _____ lo que me dijo la vidente (*clairvoyant*) antes de que se quedara sin batería mi teléfono celular: "En cinco años (2) _____ realidad todos tus deseos. (3) _____ tus estudios, (4) _____ un empleo rápidamente y tu éxito (5) _____ asombroso. (6) _____ con un hombre bueno y hermoso, del que (7) _____ enamorada. Pero en realidad (8) _____ una vida muy triste porque un día, cuando menos lo esperes..."

3 **Preguntas** Imagina que has aceptado uno de los puestos de los anuncios. Contesta las preguntas.

Laboratorios LUNA
Se busca científico con mucha imaginación para crear nuevos productos. Mínimo 3 años de experiencia. Puesto con buen sueldo y buenos beneficios.
Tel: 492-38-67

SE BUSCA CONTADOR(A)
Mínimo 5 años de experiencia. Debe hablar inglés, francés y alemán. Salario: 120.000 dólares al año. Envíen currículum por fax al: 924-90-34.

SE BUSCAN
Actores y actrices con experiencia para telenovela. Trabajarán por las noches. Salario: 40 dólares la hora. Soliciten puesto en persona. Calle El Lago n. 24, Managua.

SE NECESITAN
Jóvenes periodistas para el sitio web de un periódico nacional. Horario: 4:30 a 20:30. Comenzarán inmediatamente. Salario 20.000 dólares al año. Tel. contacto: 245-94-30.

1. ¿Cuál será el trabajo?
2. ¿Qué harás?
3. ¿Cuánto te pagarán?
4. ¿Sabes si te ofrecerán beneficios?
5. ¿Sabes el horario que tendrás? ¿Es importante saberlo?
6. ¿Crees que te gustará? ¿Por qué?
7. ¿Cuándo comenzarás a trabajar?
8. ¿Qué crees que aprenderás?

Comunicación

4

Nos mudamos Escucha la conversación entre Marisol y Fernando. Luego, indica si las conclusiones son **lógicas** o **ilógicas**, según lo que escuchaste.

	Lógico	Ilógico
1. Fernando vive en Managua.	○	○
2. Emilio comenzará a trabajar para otra empresa.	○	○
3. Marisol y Emilio quieren ver las playas y la selva de Nicaragua.	○	○
4. Julio y Mariana trabajan juntos.	○	○
5. Fernando no está totalmente contento con su sueldo.	○	○

5

Planear En parejas, hagan planes para formar una empresa privada. Usen las preguntas como guía.

1. ¿Cómo se llamará y qué tipo de empresa será?
2. ¿Cuántos empleados tendrá y cuáles serán sus oficios o profesiones?
3. ¿Qué tipo de beneficios se ofrecerán?
4. ¿Quién será el/la gerente y quién será el jefe/la jefa? ¿Por qué?
5. ¿Permitirá la empresa el teletrabajo? ¿Por qué?
6. ¿Dónde se pondrán anuncios para conseguir empleados?

6

Conversar Tú y tu compañero/a viajarán a la República Dominicana por siete días. Indiquen lo que harán y no harán. Digan dónde, cómo, con quién o en qué fechas lo harán, usando el anuncio como guía. Pueden usar sus propias ideas también.

> **modelo**
>
> **Estudiante 1:** ¿Qué haremos el martes?
> **Estudiante 2:** Visitaremos el Jardín Botánico.
> **Estudiante 1:** Pues, tú visitarás el Jardín Botánico y yo
> caminaré por el Mercado Modelo.

¡Bienvenido a la República Dominicana!

Se divertirá desde el momento en que llegue al **Aeropuerto Internacional de las Américas**.

• Visite la ciudad colonial de **Santo Domingo** con su interesante arquitectura.
• Vaya al **Jardín Botánico** y disfrute de nuestra abundante naturaleza.
• En el **Mercado Modelo** no va a poder resistir la tentación de comprar artesanías.
• No deje de escalar el **Pico Duarte** (se recomiendan 3 días).
• ¿Le gusta bucear? **Cabarete** tiene todo el equipo que usted necesita.
• ¿Desea nadar? **Punta Cana** le ofrece hermosas playas.

Síntesis

7

Predicciones Elige una persona que aparezca actualmente en las noticias (*news*). Escribe cinco predicciones sobre el futuro de esa persona. Usa el tiempo futuro.

16.2 The future perfect

ANTE TODO   Like other compound tenses you have learned, the future perfect (**el futuro perfecto**) is formed with a form of **haber** and the past participle. It is used to talk about what will have happened by some future point in time.

Future perfect

	hablar	**comer**	**vivir**
SINGULAR FORMS			
yo	**habré** hablado	**habré** comido	**habré** vivido
tú	**habrás** hablado	**habrás** comido	**habrás** vivido
Ud./él/ella	**habrá** hablado	**habrá** comido	**habrá** vivido
PLURAL FORMS			
nosotros/as	**habremos** hablado	**habremos** comido	**habremos** vivido
vosotros/as	**habréis** hablado	**habréis** comido	**habréis** vivido
Uds./ellos/ellas	**habrán** hablado	**habrán** comido	**habrán** vivido

¡ATENCIÓN!

As with other compound tenses, the past participle never varies in the future perfect; it always ends in **-o**.

En dos meses, ya habré regresado a Wisconsin.

Tendremos una compañía muy exitosa.

Sí, porque muchas empresas habrán solicitado nuestros servicios.

▶ The phrases **para** + [*time expression*] and **dentro de** + [*time expression*] are used with the future perfect to talk about what will have happened by some future point in time.

Para el lunes, habré hecho todas las preparaciones.
By Monday, I will have made all the preparations.

Dentro de un año, habré renunciado a mi trabajo.
Within a year, I will have resigned from my job.

¡INTÉNTALO!   Indica la forma apropiada del futuro perfecto.

1. Para el sábado, nosotros ___habremos obtenido___ (obtener) el dinero.
2. Yo _____ (terminar) el trabajo para cuando lleguen mis amigos.
3. Silvia _____ (hacer) todos los planes para el próximo fin de semana.
4. Para el cinco de junio, ustedes _____ (llegar) a Quito.
5. Para esa fecha, Ernesto y tú _____ (recibir) muchas ofertas.
6. Para el ocho de octubre, nosotros ya _____ (llegar) a Colombia.
7. Para entonces, yo _____ (volver) de la República Dominicana.
8. Para cuando yo te llame, ¿tú _____ (decidir) lo que vamos a hacer?
9. Para las nueve, mi hermana _____ (salir).
10. Para las ocho, tú y yo _____ (limpiar) el piso.

Práctica y Comunicación

1 **¿Qué habrá pasado?** Forma oraciones lógicas combinando ambas (*both*) columnas.

A

1. Para el año 2050, la población del mundo
2. Para la semana que viene, el profesor
3. Antes de cumplir los 40 años, yo
4. Dentro de una semana, ellos
5. Para cuando se dé cuenta, el científico
6. Para fin de año, las termitas

B

a. me habré jubilado.
b. habrá corregido los exámenes.
c. habrá aumentado un 47%.
d. habrán destruido su casa.
e. habrán atravesado el océano Pacífico.
f. habré escrito un libro, plantado un árbol y tenido tres hijos.
g. habrá hecho un gran daño a la humanidad.

2 **Escoger** Juan Luis habla de lo que habrá ocurrido en ciertos momentos del futuro. Escoge los verbos que mejor completen cada oración y ponlos en el futuro perfecto.

casarse	leer	solicitar
comprar	romperse	tomar
graduarse	ser	viajar

1. Para mañana por la tarde, yo ya _____ mi examen de economía.
2. Para la semana que viene, el profesor _____ nuestros exámenes.
3. Dentro de tres meses, Juan y Marisa _____ en Las Vegas.
4. Dentro de cinco meses, tú y yo _____ de la universidad.
5. Para finales (*end*) de mayo, yo _____ un trabajo en un banco.
6. Dentro de un año, tú _____ una casa nueva.
7. Antes de cumplir los 50 años, usted _____ a Europa.
8. Dentro de 25 años, Emilia ya _____ presidenta de los EE.UU.

3 **El futuro** Explica qué crees que habrá ocurrido en las vidas de cinco personas cercanas a ti dentro de diez años. Usa el futuro perfecto.

Síntesis

4 **Competir** En parejas, preparen una conversación hipotética (8 líneas o más) que ocurra en una fiesta. Una persona dice lo que habrá hecho para algún momento del futuro; la otra responde, diciendo cada vez algo más exagerado.

modelo

Estudiante 1: Cuando tenga 30 años, habré ganado un millón de dólares.
Estudiante 2: Y yo habré llegado a ser multimillonaria.
Estudiante 1: Para el 2025, me habrán escogido como la mejor escritora (*writer*) del país.
Estudiante 2: Pues, yo habré ganado el Premio Nobel de Literatura.

16.3 The past subjunctive

ANTE TODO You will now learn how to form and use the past subjunctive (**el pretérito imperfecto de subjuntivo**), also called the imperfect subjunctive. Like the present subjunctive, the past subjunctive is used mainly in multiple-clause sentences that express states and conditions such as will, influence, emotion, commands, indefiniteness, and non-existence.

The past subjunctive

		estudiar	aprender	recibir
SINGULAR FORMS	yo	estudia**ra**	aprendie**ra**	recibie**ra**
	tú	estudia**ras**	aprendie**ras**	recibie**ras**
	Ud./él/ella	estudia**ra**	aprendie**ra**	recibie**ra**
PLURAL FORMS	nosotros/as	estudiá**ramos**	aprendié**ramos**	recibié**ramos**
	vosotros/as	estudia**rais**	aprendie**rais**	recibie**rais**
	Uds./ellos/ellas	estudia**ran**	aprendie**ran**	recibie**ran**

▶ The past subjunctive endings are the same for all verbs.

-ra	**-ramos**
-ras	**-rais**
-ra	**-ran**

▶ The past subjunctive is formed using the **Uds./ellos/ellas** form of the preterite. By dropping the **-ron** ending from this preterite form, you establish the stem of all the past subjunctive forms. To this stem you then add the past subjunctive endings.

INFINITIVE	PRETERITE FORM	PAST SUBJUNCTIVE
hablar	ellos **habla**~~ron~~	habla**ra**, habla**ras**, hablá**ramos**
beber	ellos **bebie**~~ron~~	bebie**ra**, bebie**ras**, bebié**ramos**
escribir	ellos **escribie**~~ron~~	escribie**ra**, escribie**ras**, escribié**ramos**

▶ For verbs with irregular preterites, add the past subjunctive endings to the irregular stem.

INFINITIVE	PRETERITE FORM	PAST SUBJUNCTIVE
dar	**die**~~ron~~	die**ra**, die**ras**, dié**ramos**
decir	**dije**~~ron~~	dije**ra**, dije**ras**, dijé**ramos**
estar	**estuvie**~~ron~~	estuvie**ra**, estuvie**ras**, estuvié**ramos**
hacer	**hicie**~~ron~~	hicie**ra**, hicie**ras**, hicié**ramos**
ir/ser	**fue**~~ron~~	fue**ra**, fue**ras**, fué**ramos**
poder	**pudie**~~ron~~	pudie**ra**, pudie**ras**, pudié**ramos**
poner	**pusie**~~ron~~	pusie**ra**, pusie**ras**, pusié**ramos**
querer	**quisie**~~ron~~	quisie**ra**, quisie**ras**, quisié**ramos**
saber	**supie**~~ron~~	supie**ra**, supie**ras**, supié**ramos**
tener	**tuvie**~~ron~~	tuvie**ra**, tuvie**ras**, tuvié**ramos**
venir	**vinie**~~ron~~	vinie**ra**, vinie**ras**, vinié**ramos**

¡ATENCIÓN!

Note that the **nosotros/as** form of the past subjunctive always has a written accent.

¡LENGUA VIVA!

The past subjunctive has another set of endings:

-se	**-semos**
-ses	**-seis**
-se	**-sen**

It's a good idea to learn to recognize these endings because they are sometimes used in literary and formal contexts.

Deseaba que mi esposo recibiese un ascenso.

¡LENGUA VIVA!

Quisiera, the past subjunctive form of **querer**, is often used to make polite requests.

Quisiera hablar con Marco, por favor.
I would like to speak to Marco, please.

¿Quisieran ustedes algo más?
Would you like anything else?

▶ **-Ir** stem-changing verbs and other verbs with spelling changes follow a similar process to form the past subjunctive.

INFINITIVE	PRETERITE FORM	PAST SUBJUNCTIVE
preferir	prefirie~~ron~~	prefirie**ra**, prefirie**ras**, prefirié**ramos**
repetir	repitie~~ron~~	repitie**ra**, repitie**ras**, repitié**ramos**
dormir	durmie~~ron~~	durmie**ra**, durmie**ras**, durmié**ramos**
conducir	conduje~~ron~~	conduje**ra**, conduje**ras**, condujé**ramos**
creer	creye~~ron~~	creye**ra**, creye**ras**, creyé**ramos**
destruir	destruye~~ron~~	destruye**ra**, destruye**ras**, destruyé**ramos**
oír	oye~~ron~~	oye**ra**, oye**ras**, oyé**ramos**

▶ The past subjunctive is used in the same contexts and situations as the present subjunctive and the present perfect subjunctive, except that it generally describes actions, events, or conditions that have already happened.

Me pidieron que no
llegara tarde.
They asked me not to arrive late.

Me sorprendió que ustedes no
vinieran a la cena.
It surprised me that you didn't come to the dinner.

Salió antes de que yo **pudiera**
hablar contigo.
He left before I could talk to you.

Ellos querían que yo **escribiera**
una novela romántica.
They wanted me to write a romantic novel.

Cuando llegaste, no creí que tuviéramos muchas cosas en común.

No pensé que el año terminara tan pronto.

¡INTÉNTALO! Indica la forma apropiada del pretérito imperfecto de subjuntivo de los verbos entre paréntesis.

1. Quería que tú ___vinieras___ (venir) más temprano.
2. Esperábamos que ustedes _____ (hablar) mucho más en la reunión.
3. No creían que yo _____ (poder) hacerlo.
4. No deseaba que nosotros _____ (invertir) el dinero.
5. Sentí mucho que ustedes no _____ (estar) con nosotros anoche.
6. No era necesario que ellas _____ (hacer) todo.
7. Me pareció increíble que tú _____ (saber) dónde encontrarlo.
8. No había nadie que _____ (creer) tu historia.
9. Mis padres insistieron en que yo _____ (ir) a la universidad.
10. Queríamos salir antes de que ustedes _____ (llegar).

Práctica

1 **Diálogos** Completa los diálogos con el pretérito imperfecto de subjuntivo de los verbos entre paréntesis.

1. —¿Qué le dijo el consejero a Andrés? Quisiera saberlo.

—Le aconsejó que _____ (dejar) los estudios de arte y que _____ (estudiar) una carrera que _____ (pagar) mejor.

—Siempre el dinero. ¿No se enojó Andrés de que le _____ (aconsejar) eso?

—Sí, y le dijo que no creía que ninguna otra carrera le _____ (ir) a gustar más.

2. —Qué lástima que ellos no te _____ (ofrecer) el puesto de gerente.

—Querían a alguien que _____ (tener) experiencia en el sector público.

—Pero, ¿cómo? ¿Y tu maestría? ¿No te molestó que te _____ (decir) eso?

—No, no tengo experiencia en esa área, pero les gustó mucho mi currículum. Me pidieron que _____ (volver) en un año y _____ (solicitar) el puesto otra vez. Para entonces habré obtenido la experiencia que necesito y podré conseguir el puesto que quiera.

3. —Cuánto me alegré de que tus hijas _____ (venir) ayer a visitarte. ¿Cuándo se van?

—Bueno, yo esperaba que se _____ (quedar) dos semanas, pero no pueden. Ojalá _____ (poder). Hace mucho que no las veo.

2 **Año nuevo, vida nueva** El año pasado, Marta y Alberto querían cambiar de vida. Aquí tienen las listas con sus propósitos para el Año Nuevo (*New Year's resolutions*). Ellos no consiguieron hacer realidad ninguno. Lee las listas y escribe por qué crees que no los consiguieron. Usa el pretérito imperfecto de subjuntivo.

> **modelo**
>
> obtener un mejor puesto de trabajo
>
> *Era difícil que Alberto consiguiera un mejor puesto porque su novia le pidió que no cambiara de empleo.*

AYUDA

Puedes usar estas expresiones:

No era verdad que…
Era difícil que…
Era imposible que…
No era cierto que…
Su novio/a no queria que…

Alberto

pedir un aumento de sueldo
tener una vida más sana
visitar más a su familia
dejar de fumar

Marta

querer mejorar su relación de pareja
terminar los estudios con buenas notas
cambiar de casa
ahorrar más

_____

Comunicación

3

El mundo de los negocios Escucha la conversación entre Elisa y Carlota. Luego, indica si las conclusiones son **lógicas** o **ilógicas**, según lo que escuchaste.

	Lógico	Ilógico
1. Elisa ha pedido un aumento de sueldo.	○	○
2. A Carlota le sorprendió que Elisa renunciara a su puesto.	○	○
3. El jefe de Elisa es comunicativo con sus empleados.	○	○
4. Hoy, Elisa no ha trabajado.	○	○
5. Elisa ya solicitó otro puesto.	○	○

4

Reaccionar Ricardo acaba de llegar de Nicaragua. Reacciona a lo que te dice usando el pretérito imperfecto de subjuntivo.

> **modelo**
>
> El día que llegué, me esperaban mi abuela y tres primos.
>
> *¡Qué bien! Me alegré de que vieras a tu familia después de tantos años.*

1. Fuimos al volcán Masaya. ¡Y vimos la lava del volcán!
2. Visitamos la Catedral de Managua, que fue dañada por el terremoto (*earthquake*) de 1972.
3. No tuvimos tiempo de ir a la playa, pero pasamos unos días en el Hotel Dariense en Granada.
4. Fui a conocer el nuevo museo de arte y también fui al Teatro Rubén Darío.
5. Nos divertimos haciendo compras en Metrocentro.

Catedral de Managua, Nicaragua

5

Oraciones Escribe cinco oraciones sobre lo que otros esperaban de ti en el pasado y cinco más sobre lo que tú esperabas de ellos.

> **modelo**
>
> *Mi profesora quería que yo fuera a Granada para estudiar español.*
> *Yo deseaba que mis padres me enviaran a España.*

Síntesis

6

¡Vaya fiesta! Dos amigos/as fueron a una fiesta y se enojaron. Uno/a quería irse temprano, pero el/la otro/a quería irse más tarde porque estaba hablando con el/la chico/a que le gustaba. En parejas, inventen una conversación en la que esos/as amigos/as intentan arreglar todos los malentendidos (*misunderstandings*) que tuvieron en la fiesta. Usen el pretérito imperfecto de subjuntivo.

> **modelo**
>
> **Estudiante 1:** *¡Yo no pensaba que fueras tan aburrido/a!*
> **Estudiante 2:** *Yo no soy aburrido/a, sólo quería que nos fuéramos temprano.*

Recapitulación

SUBJECT
Javier
CONJUGATED FORM
empiezo
Main clause
dudan

Completa estas actividades para repasar los conceptos de gramática que aprendiste en esta lección.

1 Completar Completa el cuadro con el futuro. `12 pts.`

Infinitivo	yo	ella	nosotros
decir	diré		
poner			pondremos
salir		saldrá	

2 Verbos Completa el cuadro con el pretérito imperfecto de subjuntivo. `12 pts.`

Infinitivo	tú	nosotros	ustedes
dar			dieran
saber		supiéramos	
ir	fueras		

3 La oficina de empleo La nueva oficina de empleo está un poco desorganizada. Completa los diálogos con expresiones de probabilidad, utilizando el futuro perfecto de los verbos. `15 pts.`

SR. PÉREZ No encuentro el currículum de Mario Gómez.

SRA. MARÍN (1) _____ (Tomarlo) la secretaria.

LAURA ¿De dónde vienen estas ofertas de trabajo?

ROMÁN No estoy seguro. (2) _____ (Salir) en el periódico de hoy.

ROMÁN ¿Has visto la lista nueva de aspirantes?

LAURA No, (3) _____ (tú, ponerla) en el archivo.

SR. PÉREZ José Osorio todavía no ha recibido el informe.

LAURA (4) _____ (Nosotros, olvidarse) de enviarlo por correo.

SRA. MARÍN ¿Sabes dónde están las solicitudes de los aspirantes?

ROMÁN (5) _____ (Yo, dejarlas) en mi carro.

16.1 The future *pp. 552–553*

Future tense of **estudiar***	
estudiaré	estudiaremos
estudiarás	estudiaréis
estudiará	estudiarán

*Same endings for **-ar, -er,** and **-ir** verbs.

Irregular verbs in the future		
Infinitive	**Stem**	**Future forms**
decir	dir–	diré
hacer	har–	haré
poder	podr–	podré
poner	pondr–	pondré
querer	querr–	querré
saber	sabr–	sabré
salir	saldr–	saldré
tener	tendr–	tendré
venir	vendr–	vendré

► The future of **hay** is **habrá** (*there will be*).
► The future can also express conjecture or probability.

16.2 The future perfect *p. 556*

Future perfect of **vivir**	
habré vivido	**habremos** vivido
habrás vivido	**habréis** vivido
habrá vivido	**habrán** vivido

► The future perfect can also express probability in the past.

16.3 The past subjunctive *pp. 558–559*

Past subjunctive of **aprender***	
aprendiera	aprendiéramos
aprendieras	aprendierais
aprendiera	aprendieran

*Same endings for **-ar, -er,** and **-ir** verbs.

Irregular verbs in the future		
Infinitive	**Preterite form**	**Past subjunctive**
dar	dieron	diera
decir	dijeron	dijera
estar	estuvieron	estuviera
hacer	hicieron	hiciera
ir/ser	fueron	fuera
poder	pudieron	pudiera
poner	pusieron	pusiera
querer	quisieron	quisiera
saber	supieron	supiera
tener	tuvieron	tuviera
venir	vinieron	viniera

4   **Una decisión difícil** Completa el párrafo con el pretérito imperfecto de subjuntivo de los verbos. **27 pts.**

aceptar	graduarse	resolver
contratar	invertir	trabajar
dejar	ir	
estudiar	poder	

Cuando yo tenía doce años, me gustaba mucho pintar y mi profesor de dibujo me aconsejó que (1) _____ a una escuela de arte cuando (2) _____ de la escuela secundaria. Mis padres, por el contrario, siempre quisieron que sus hijos (3) _____ en la empresa familiar, y me dijeron que (4) _____ el arte y que (5) _____ una carrera con más futuro. Ellos no querían que yo (6) _____ mi tiempo y mi juventud en el arte. Mi madre en particular nos sugirió a mi hermana y a mí la carrera de administración de empresas, para que los dos (7) _____ ayudarlos con los negocios en el futuro. No fue fácil que mis padres (8) _____ mi decisión de dedicarme a la pintura, pero están muy felices de tener mis obras en su sala de reuniones. Me alegré de que todo se (9) _____ por fin.

5   **La semana de Rita** Con el futuro de los verbos, completa la descripción que hace Rita de lo que hará la semana próxima. **30 pts.**

El lunes por la mañana (1) _____ (llegar) el traje que pedí por Internet y por la tarde Luis (2) _____ (invitar, a mí) a ir al cine. El martes mi consejero y yo (3) _____ (comer) en La Delicia y a las cuatro (yo) (4) _____ (tener) una entrevista de trabajo en Industrias Levonox. El miércoles por la mañana (5) _____ (ir) a mi clase de inglés y por la tarde (6) _____ (visitar) a Luis. El jueves por la mañana, los gerentes de Levonox (7) _____ (llamar, a mí) por teléfono para decirme si conseguí el puesto. Por la tarde (yo) (8) _____ (cuidar) a mi sobrino Héctor. El viernes Ana y Luis (9) _____ (venir) a casa para trabajar conmigo y el sábado por fin (yo) (10) _____ (descansar).

6   **Canción** Escribe las palabras que faltan para completar este fragmento de la canción *Lo que pidas* de Julieta Venegas. **4 pts.**

daré	fuera	quisiera	saldré

❝ Lo que más (1) _____ pedirte
es que te quedes conmigo,
niño te (2) _____ lo que pidas
sólo no te vayas nunca. **❞**

Lectura

Antes de leer

A Julia de Burgos

Julia de Burgos

Julia de Burgos nació en 1914 en Carolina, Puerto Rico. Vivió también en La Habana, en Washington DC y en Nueva York, donde murió en 1953. Su poesía refleja temas como la muerte, la naturaleza, el amor y la patria°. Sus tres poemarios más conocidos se titulan *Poema en veinte surcos* (1938), *Canción de la verdad sencilla* (1939) y *El mar y tú* (publicado póstumamente).

Estrategia

Recognizing similes and metaphors

Similes and metaphors are figures of speech that are often used in literature to make descriptions more colorful and vivid.

In English, a simile (**símil**) makes a comparison using the words *as* or *like*. In Spanish, the words **como** and **parece** are most often used. Example: **Estoy tan feliz como un niño con zapatos nuevos.**

A metaphor (**metáfora**) is a figure of speech that identifies one thing with the attributes and qualities of another. Whereas a simile says one thing is like another, a metaphor says that one thing *is* another. In Spanish, **ser** is most often used in metaphors. Example: **La vida es sueño.** (*Life is a dream.*)

Examinar el texto

Lee el texto una vez usando las estrategias de lectura de las lecciones anteriores. ¿Qué te indican sobre el contenido de la lectura? Toma nota de las metáforas y los símiles que encuentres. ¿Qué significan? ¿Qué te dicen sobre el tema de la lectura?

¿Cómo son?

Escribe sobre las diferencias entre el **yo interior** de una persona y su **yo social**. ¿Hay muchas diferencias entre su forma de ser "privada" y su forma de ser cuando están con otras personas?

Después de leer

Comprensión

Contesta las preguntas.

1. ¿Quiénes son las dos "Julias" presentes en el poema?
2. ¿Qué características tiene cada una?
3. ¿Quién es la que habla de las dos?
4. ¿Qué piensas que ella siente por la otra Julia?
5. ¿Qué diferencias hay en el aspecto físico de una y otra mujer? ¿Qué simboliza esto?
6. ¿Cuáles son los temas más importantes del poema?

Las dos Fridas, de Frida Kahlo

Ya las gentes murmuran que yo soy tu enemiga
porque dicen que en verso doy al mundo tu yo.   25

Mienten°, Julia de Burgos. Mienten, Julia de Burgos.
La que se alza° en mis versos no es tu voz°: es mi voz;
porque tú eres ropaje° y la esencia soy yo;   5
y el más profundo abismo se tiende° entre las dos.

Tú eres fría muñeca° de mentira social,
y yo, viril destello° de la humana verdad.

Tú, miel° de cortesanas hipocresías; yo no;
que en todos mis poemas desnudo° el corazón.   10

Tú eres como tu mundo, egoísta; yo no;
que en todo me lo juego° a ser lo que soy yo.

Tú eres sólo la grave señora señorona°;
yo no; yo soy la vida, la fuerza°, la mujer.

Tú eres de tu marido, de tu amo°; yo no;   15
yo de nadie, o de todos, porque a todos, a todos,
en mi limpio sentir y en mi pensar me doy.

Tú te rizas° el pelo y te pintas°; yo no;
a mí me riza el viento; a mí me pinta el sol.

Tú eres dama casera°, resignada, sumisa,   20
atada° a los prejuicios de los hombres; yo no;
que yo soy Rocinante* corriendo desbocado°
olfateando° horizontes de justicia de Dios.

Tú en ti misma no mandas°; a ti todos te mandan;
en ti mandan tu esposo, tus padres, tus parientes,
el cura°, la modista°, el teatro, el casino,
el auto, las alhajas°, el banquete, el champán,
el cielo y el infierno, y el qué dirán social°.

En mí no, que en mí manda mi solo corazón,   30
mi solo pensamiento; quien manda en mí soy yo.

Tú, flor de aristocracia; y yo la flor del pueblo.
Tú en ti lo tienes todo y a todos se lo debes,
mientras que yo, mi nada a nadie se la debo.

Tú, clavada° al estático dividendo ancestral°,
y yo, un uno en la cifra° del divisor social,   35
somos el duelo a muerte° que se acerca° fatal.

Cuando las multitudes corran alborotadas°
dejando atrás cenizas° de injusticias quemadas,
y cuando con la tea° de las siete virtudes,
tras los siete pecados°, corran las multitudes,   40
contra ti, y contra todo lo injusto y lo inhumano,
yo iré en medio de ellas con la tea en la mano.

---

*Rocinante: El caballo de don Quijote, personaje literario de fama universal que se relaciona con el idealismo y el poder de la imaginación frente a la realidad.

patria *homeland* Mienten *They are lying* se alza *rises up* voz *voice* ropaje *apparel* se tiende *lies* muñeca *doll* destello *sparkle* miel *honey* desnudo *I uncover* me lo juego *I risk* señorona *matronly* fuerza *strength* amo *master* te rizas *curl* te pintas *put on makeup* dama casera *home-loving lady* atada *tied* desbocado *wildly* olfateando *sniffing* no mandas *are not the boss* cura *priest* modista *dressmaker* alhajas *jewelry* el qué dirán social *what society would say* clavada *stuck* ancestral *ancient* cifra *number* duelo a muerte *duel to the death* se acerca *approaches* alborotadas *rowdy* cenizas *ashes* tea *torch* pecados *sins*

Interpretación

Contesta las preguntas.

1. ¿Qué te resulta llamativo en el título de este poema?

2. ¿Por qué crees que se repite el "tú" y el "yo" en el poema? ¿Qué función tiene este desdoblamiento?

3. ¿Cómo interpretas los versos "tú eres fría muñeca de mentira social / y yo, viril destello de la humana verdad"? ¿Qué sustantivos (*nouns*) se contraponen en estos dos versos?

4. ¿Es positivo o negativo el comentario sobre la vida social: "miel de cortesanas hipocresías"?

5. Comenta la oposición entre "señorona" y "mujer" que aparece en los versos trece y catorce. ¿Podrías decir qué personas son las que dominan a la "señorona" y qué caracteriza, en cambio, a la mujer?

Monólogo

Imagina que eres un personaje famoso de la historia, la literatura o la vida actual. Escribe un monólogo breve. Debes escribirlo en segunda persona. Sigue el modelo.

modelo

Eres una mujer que vivió hace más de 150 años. La gente piensa que eres una gran poeta. Te gustaba escribir y pasar tiempo con tu familia y, además de poesías, escribías muchas cartas. Me gusta tu poesía porque es muy íntima y personal. (Emily Dickinson)

Escribe sobre estos temas:
▸ cómo lo/la ven las otras personas
▸ lo que te gusta y lo que no te gusta de él/ella
▸ lo que quieres o esperas que haga

Escritura

Estrategia

Using note cards

Note cards serve as valuable study aids in many different contexts. When you write, note cards can help you organize and sequence the information you wish to present.

Let's say you are going to write a personal narrative about a trip you took. You would jot down notes about each part of the trip on a different note card. Then you could easily arrange them in chronological order or use a different organization, such as the best parts and the worst parts, traveling and staying, before and after.

Here are some helpful techniques for using note cards to prepare for your writing:

▶ Label the top of each card with a general subject, such as **el avión** or **el hotel**.

▶ Number the cards in each subject category in the upper right corner to help you organize them.

▶ Use only the front side of each note card so that you can easily flip through them to find information.

Study the following example of a note card used to prepare a composition:

3

En el aeropuerto de Santo Domingo

Cuando llegamos al aeropuerto de Santo Domingo, después de siete horas de viaje, estábamos cansados pero felices. Hacía sol y viento.

Tema

Escribir una composición

Escribe una composición sobre tus planes profesionales y personales para el futuro. Utiliza el tiempo futuro. No te olvides de hacer planes para estas áreas de tu vida:

Lugar

▶ ¿Dónde vivirás?

▶ ¿Vivirás en la misma ciudad siempre? ¿Te mudarás mucho?

Familia

▶ ¿Te casarás? ¿Con quién?

▶ ¿Tendrás hijos? ¿Cuántos?

Empleo

▶ ¿En qué profesión trabajarás?

▶ ¿Tendrás tu propia empresa?

Finanzas

▶ ¿Ganarás mucho dinero?

▶ ¿Ahorrarás mucho? ¿Lo invertirás?

Termina tu composición con una lista de metas profesionales, utilizando el futuro perfecto.

Por ejemplo: **Para el año 2025, habré empezado mi propio negocio. Para el año 2035, habré ganado más dinero que Bill Gates.**

Escuchar

Preparación

Mira la foto. ¿De qué crees que van a hablar?
Haz una lista de la información que esperas oír
en este tipo de situación.

Ahora escucha

Ahora vas a oír una entrevista entre la señora
Sánchez y Rafael Ventura Romero. Antes
de escuchar la entrevista, haz una lista de la
información que esperas oír según tu conocimiento
previo° del tema.

1. _____
2. _____
3. _____
4. _____

Mientras escuchas la entrevista, llena el formulario
con la información necesaria. Si no oyes un dato°
que necesitas, escribe *Buscar en el currículum.*
¿Oíste toda la información que habías anotado
en tu lista?

Comprensión

Puesto solicitado _____
Nombre y apellidos del solicitante _____
Dirección _____ **Tel.** _____
- -
Educación _____
Experiencia profesional: Puesto _____
Empresa _____
¿Cuánto tiempo? _____
Referencias:
Nombre _____
Dirección _____ Tel. _____
Nombre _____
Dirección _____ Tel. _____

Preguntas

1. ¿Cuántos años hace que Rafael Ventura trabaja
   para Dulces González?

2. ¿Cuántas referencias tiene Rafael?

3. ¿Cuándo se gradúa Rafael?

4. ¿Cuál es la profesión de Armando Carreño?

5. ¿Cómo sabes si los resultados de la entrevista han
   sido positivos para Rafael Ventura?

conocimiento previo *prior knowledge* dato *fact; piece of information*

En pantalla

Ésta es la historia de un espantapájaros que trabaja en un campo de trigo°. Es un trabajo fácil, aunque muy solitario, y los días se le hacen muy largos. Para entretenerse°, mira a los pájaros, que parecen tenerle miedo. Pero, ¿por qué, si él es inofensivo° y amigable°? Sin embargo, un día algo cambia en la vida del espantapájaros. Él tomará entonces una decisión que lo llevará a un final inesperado°.

Preparación

Completar

Completa cada oración con la palabra correcta de **Expresiones útiles**. Haz los cambios necesarios.

1. Me pongo una _____ cuando estoy enfermo.

2. Como dijo Shakespeare, el amor es _____.

3. En un incendio (*fire*), todo se _____ y sólo quedan las _____.

4. El trabajo de un espantapájaros es _____ a las aves.

5. El _____ es un pájaro muy hábil (*skillful*) para _____.

¿Son buenos o son malos?

Escoge una de estas ocupaciones y escribe sobre los puntos positivos y negativos de esa área de trabajo.

> **modelo**
>
> árbitro (*referee*)
> Puede conocer a jugadores famosos. Y es quien hace que las reglas del juego se obedezcan (*be obeyed*). Pero si hace algo mal, todos lo odian.

- agente funerario (*mortician*)
- dentista
- ingeniero/a nuclear
- leñador(a) (*logger*)
- oficial de seguridad en un aeropuerto
- policía de tránsito (*traffic*)
- político/a
- recaudador(a) de impuestos (*tax collector*)

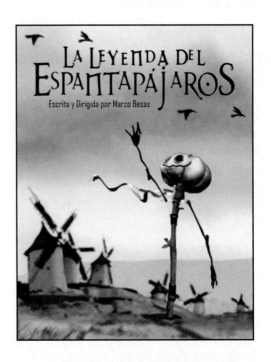

LA LEYENDA DEL ESPANTAPÁJAROS
Escrita y Dirigida por Marco Besas

Expresiones útiles

asustar	*to scare*
la bufanda	*scarf*
las cenizas	*ashes*
ciego	*blind*
el cuervo	*crow*
érase una vez	*once upon a time*
el espantapájaros	*scarecrow*
quemar	*to burn*
salvar	*to save*
solitario/a	*lonely*
volar	*to fly*

Para hablar del corto

la calabaza	*pumpkin*
el estereotipo	*stereotype*
incomprendido/a	*misunderstood*
la leyenda	*legend*
el luto	*mourning*
el molino	*windmill*
prejuzgar	*to prejudge*

campo de trigo *wheat field* **entretenerse** *to amuse itself* **inofensivo** *harmless*
amigable *friendly* **inesperado** *unexpected*

Escenas: La leyenda del espantapájaros

NARRADOR Érase una vez un espantapájaros que no tenía amigos.

NARRADOR Cada vez que [los pájaros] pasaban, él los saludaba, pero ellos nunca le respondían.

NARRADOR Y el cuervo explicó que el trabajo de los espantapájaros era asustar a los pobres pájaros que sólo querían comer.

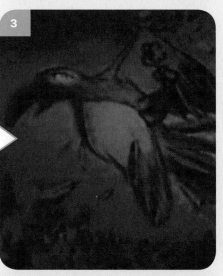

NARRADOR Una noche fría, cayó a sus pies un cuervo ciego.

NARRADOR El espantapájaros preguntó por qué los pájaros nunca querían hacerse amigos de los espantapájaros.

NARRADOR Esa misma noche decidió cambiar su vida.

Comprensión

Ordenar

Ordena las oraciones según (*as*) ocurrieron en el cortometraje.

_____ a. Los cuervos esparcieron (*scattered*) las cenizas del espantapájaros por toda la comarca (*region*).

_____ b. El amo (*owner*) se aterrorizó (*became terrified*) al ver que su espantapájaros hablaba.

_____ c. El cuervo ciego supo que lo había salvado un espantapájaros.

_____ d. El espantapájaros murió.

_____ e. Un cuervo ciego que tiritaba (*was shivering*) y moría de hambre cayó a los pies del espantapájaros.

_____ f. En memoria del espantapájaros, los cuervos decidieron vestirse de luto.

_____ g. Los vecinos quemaron el lugar donde estaba el espantapájaros.

_____ h. El amo pensó que si el espantapájaros podía hablar, era obra del diablo (*devil*).

_____ i. El espantapájaros quiso darle semillas (*seeds*) a un pájaro, pero éste no le hizo caso (*didn't pay attention to him*).

_____ j. Los cuervos quisieron salvar al espantapájaros.

_____ k. El espantapájaros se escondió (*hid*).

_____ l. El espantapájaros decidió que ya no quería trabajar asustando pájaros.

Preguntas

Contesta estas preguntas con oraciones completas.

1. ¿Qué fue lo que siempre deseó el espantapájaros? ¿Por qué?
2. ¿Qué hizo el cuervo ciego al escuchar la confesión del espantapájaros? ¿Por qué?
3. Al final, ¿qué pensaron los cuervos del espantapájaros? ¿Qué cambió en su actitud (*attitude*)? ¿Por qué?
4. ¿Cómo se cumplió (*came true*) finalmente el eterno deseo (*wish*) del espantapájaros?
5. ¿Qué haces si una responsabilidad de tu trabajo va en contra de lo que tú eres, de tus principios (*principles*) o de tus deseos?
6. ¿Te has sentido víctima de los prejuicios de los demás? ¿Cómo manejas esas situaciones?
7. ¿Alguna vez has juzgado a alguien sin conocerlo/la y después descubriste que estabas equivocado/a?
8. ¿Qué haces cuando eres injusto/a con alguien? ¿Admites tu error o no le dices nada?

Un final diferente

Escribe un final diferente para la historia del espantapájaros.

Vocabulario útil			
acercarse (a)	*to approach*	**la esperanza**	*hope*
las alas	*wings*	**el incendio**	*fire*
el amanecer	*dawn*	**llamar la atención**	*to call atention*
apagar (el fuego)	*to put out (the fire)*	**el monstruo**	*monster*
la armonía	*harmony*	**las plumas**	*feathers*
disfrazarse	*to disguise oneself*	**razonar**	*to reason*
escapar(se)	*to escape*	**transformarse (en)**	*to turn (into)*

Viernes en la tarde, llega el esperado fin de semana… y si el lunes es día festivo°, ¡mejor aún!° En varios países hispanos, además de tener entre quince y treinta días de vacaciones pagadas, hay bastantes días festivos. Por ejemplo, Puerto Rico tiene veintiún feriados°, Colombia tiene dieciocho y Argentina, México y Chile tienen más de trece. Aunque parece que se trabaja menos, no siempre es el caso: las jornadas laborales° suelen ser más largas en Latinoamérica. Así que la gente aprovecha° los **puentes**° para descansar e incluso para hacer viajes cortos.

Vocabulario útil

el desarrollo	*development*
el horario	*schedule*
promover	*to promote*
las ventas	*sales*

Preparación

¿Trabajas? ¿Cuáles son tus metas (*goals*) profesionales?

Escoger

Escoge la opción correcta de cada par de afirmaciones.
1. a. Todos los ecuatorianos son muy felices en su trabajo.
    b. En Ecuador, como en todos los países del mundo, hay personas que aman su trabajo y hay otras que lo odian.
2. a. El objetivo principal de la agencia Klein Tours es mostrar al mundo las maravillas de Ecuador.
    b. La agencia de viajes Klein Tours quiere mostrar al mundo que tiene los empleados más fieles y profesionales de toda Latinoamérica.

El mundo del trabajo

Gabriela, ¿qué es lo más difícil de ser una mujer policía?

Amo mi trabajo. Imagínate, tengo la sonrisa del mundo entre mis manos.

Nuestra principal estrategia de ventas es promover nuestra naturaleza...

día festivo *holiday* ¡mejor aún! *even better!* feriados *holidays* jornadas laborales *working days* aprovecha *make the most of* puentes *long weekends*

Nicaragua

El país en cifras

▸ **Área:** 129.494 km² (49.998 millas²), *aproximadamente el área de Nueva York. Nicaragua es el país más grande de Centroamérica. Su terreno es muy variado e incluye bosques tropicales, montañas, sabanas° y marismas°, además de unos 40 volcanes.*

▸ **Población:** 5.848.000

▸ **Capital:** Managua—934.000
Managua está en una región de una notable inestabilidad geográfica, con muchos volcanes y terremotos°. En décadas recientes, los nicaragüenses han decidido que no vale la pena° construir rascacielos° porque no resisten los terremotos.

▸ **Ciudades principales:** León, Masaya, Granada

▸ **Moneda:** córdoba

▸ **Idiomas:** español (oficial); lenguas indígenas y criollas (oficiales); inglés

Bandera de Nicaragua

Nicaragüenses célebres

▸ **Rubén Darío,** poeta (1867–1916)

▸ **Violeta Barrios de Chamorro,** política y expresidenta (1929–)

▸ **Daniel Ortega,** político y presidente (1945–)

▸ **Gioconda Belli,** poeta (1948–)

▸ **Luis Enrique,** cantante y compositor (1962–)

sabanas *grasslands* marismas *marshes* terremotos *earthquakes*
no vale la pena *it's not worthwhile* rascacielos *skyscrapers*
agua dulce *fresh water* Surgió *Emerged* maravillas *wonders*

Iglesia en León

Teatro Nacional Rubén Darío en Managua

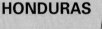

Calle en Granada

HONDURAS

Río Coco

Cordillera Isabelia

Chachagón · Saslaya · Piu

Río Tuma · Río Grande

Cordillera Dariense

Sierra Madre

León ·

Managua

Lago de Managua

Masaya · Lago de Nicaragua

· Granada

Isla Zapatera

Océano Pacífico

Concepción

Maderas · Isla Ometepe

Archipiélago de Solentiname

Río San Juan

COSTA RICA

ESTADOS UNIDOS

OCÉANO ATLÁNTICO

NICARAGUA

OCÉANO PACÍFICO

AMÉRICA DEL SUR

Violeta Barrios de Chamorro

¡Increíble pero cierto!

Ometepe, que en náhuatl significa "dos montañas", es la isla más grande del mundo en un lago de agua dulce°. Surgió° en el lago de Nicaragua por la actividad de los volcanes Maderas y Concepción. Por su valor natural y arqueológico, fue nominada para las siete nuevas maravillas° del mundo en 2009.

Historia • Las huellas° de Acahualinca

La región de Managua se caracteriza por tener un gran número de sitios prehistóricos. Las huellas de Acahualinca son uno de los restos° más famosos y antiguos°. Se formaron hace más de 6.000 años, a orillas° del lago de Managua. Las huellas, tanto de humanos como de animales, se dirigen° hacia una misma dirección, hacia el lago.

Artes • Ernesto Cardenal (1925–)

Ernesto Cardenal, poeta, escultor y sacerdote° católico, es uno de los escritores más famosos de Nicaragua, país conocido por sus grandes poetas. Ha escrito más de 35 libros y es considerado uno de los principales autores de Latinoamérica. Desde joven creyó en el poder de la poesía para mejorar la sociedad y trabajó por establecer la igualdad° y la justicia en su país. En los años 60, Cardenal estableció la comunidad artística del archipiélago de Solentiname en el lago de Nicaragua. Fue ministro de cultura del país desde 1979 hasta 1988 y participó en la fundación de Casa de los Tres Mundos, una organización creada para el intercambio cultural internacional.

Naturaleza • El lago de Nicaragua

El lago de Nicaragua, con un área de más de 8.000 km² (3.100 millas²), es el lago más grande de Centroamérica. Tiene más de 400 islas e islotes° de origen volcánico, entre ellas la isla Zapatera. Allí se han encontrado numerosos objetos de cerámica y estatuas prehispánicos. Se cree que la isla era un centro ceremonial indígena.

¿Qué aprendiste? Contesta cada pregunta con una oración completa.

1. ¿Por qué no hay muchos rascacielos en Managua?

2. Nombra dos poetas de Nicaragua.

3. Qué significa Ometepe en náhuatl?

4. ¿Cuándo y dónde se formaron las huellas de Acahualinca?

5. ¿Por qué es famoso el archipiélago de Solentiname?

6. ¿Qué cree Ernesto Cardenal acerca de la poesía?

7. ¿Cómo se formaron las islas del lago de Nicaragua?

8. ¿Qué hay de interés arqueológico en la isla Zapatera?

Conexión Internet Investiga estos temas en Internet.

1. ¿Dónde se habla inglés en Nicaragua y por qué?

2. ¿Qué información hay ahora sobre la economía y/o los derechos humanos en Nicaragua?

....

huellas *footprints* **restos** *remains* **antiguos** *ancient* **orillas** *shores* **se dirigen** *are headed* **sacerdote** *priest* **igualdad** *equality* **islotes** *islets*

La República Dominicana

El país en cifras

▶ **Área:** 48.730 km² (18.815 millas²), *el área combinada de New Hampshire y Vermont*

▶ **Población:** 10.349.000

La isla La Española, llamada así tras° el primer viaje de Cristóbal Colón, estuvo bajo el completo dominio de la corona° española hasta 1697, cuando la parte oeste de la isla pasó a ser propiedad° francesa. Hoy día está dividida políticamente en dos países, la República Dominicana en la zona este y Haití en el oeste.

▶ **Capital:** Santo Domingo—2.191.000

▶ **Ciudades principales:** Santiago de los Caballeros, La Vega, Puerto Plata, San Pedro de Macorís

▶ **Moneda:** peso dominicano

▶ **Idiomas:** español (oficial), criollo haitiano

Bandera de la República Dominicana

Dominicanos célebres

▶ **Juan Pablo Duarte,** político y padre de la patria° (1813–1876)

▶ **Celeste Woss y Gil,** pintora (1891–1985)

▶ **Juan Luis Guerra,** compositor y cantante de merengue (1957–)

▶ **Pedro Martínez,** beisbolista (1971–)

▶ **Marcos Díaz,** nadador de ultradistancia (1975–)

tras *after*   corona *crown*   propiedad *property*
padre de la patria *founding father*   restos *remains*
tumbas *graves*   navegante *sailor*   reemplazó *replaced*

Catedral de Santa María la Menor

Hombres tocando los palos en una misa en Nochebuena

Océano Atlántico

Isla La Española

Puerto Plata

Santiago

Bahía Escocesa

Río Yuna

Pico Duarte

La Vega

HAITÍ

Cordillera Central

Río San Juan

Sierra de Neiba

San Pedro de Macorís

Sierra de Baoruco

Bahía de Ocoa

Santo Domingo

Mar Caribe

ESTADOS UNIDOS

LA REPÚBLICA DOMINICANA

OCÉANO PACÍFICO

OCÉANO ATLÁNTICO

AMÉRICA DEL SUR

Trabajadores del campo recogen la cosecha de ajos

¡Increíble pero cierto!

Los restos° de Cristóbal Colón pasaron por varias ciudades desde su muerte en el siglo XVI hasta el siglo XIX. Por esto, se conocen dos tumbas° de este navegante°: una en la Catedral de Sevilla, España y otra en el Museo Faro a Colón en Santo Domingo, que reemplazó° la tumba inicial en la catedral de la capital dominicana.

Ciudades • Santo Domingo

La zona colonial de Santo Domingo, ciudad fundada en 1496, posee°
algunas de las construcciones más antiguas del hemisferio. Gracias a las
restauraciones°, la arquitectura de la ciudad es famosa no sólo por su belleza
sino también por el buen estado de sus edificios. Entre sus sitios más visitados
se cuentan° la Calle de las Damas, llamada así porque allí paseaban las
señoras de la corte del Virrey; el Alcázar de Colón, un palacio construido
entre 1510 y 1514 por Diego Colón, hijo de Cristóbal; y la Fortaleza Ozama,
la más vieja de las Américas, construida entre 1502 y 1508.

Deportes • El béisbol

El béisbol es un deporte muy practicado en el Caribe. Los primeros países
hispanos en tener una liga fueron Cuba y México, donde se empezó a jugar
al béisbol en el siglo° XIX. Hoy día este deporte es una afición° nacional en la
República Dominicana. Albert Pujols (foto, derecha), Carlos Gómez y David Ortiz
son sólo tres de los muchísimos beisbolistas dominicanos que han alcanzado° enorme
éxito e inmensa popularidad entre los aficionados.

Artes • El merengue

El merengue, un ritmo originario de la República Dominicana, tiene sus raíces°
en el campo. Tradicionalmente las canciones hablaban de los problemas sociales de
los campesinos°. Sus instrumentos eran la guitarra, el acordeón, el guayano° y la
tambora, un tambor° característico del lugar. Entre 1930 y 1960, el merengue se
popularizó en las ciudades; adoptó un tono más urbano, en el que se incorporaron
instrumentos como el saxofón y el bajo°, y empezaron a formarse grandes
orquestas. Uno de los cantantes y compositores de merengue más famosos
es Juan Luis Guerra.

¿Qué aprendiste? Contesta cada pregunta con una oración completa.

1. ¿Quién es Juan Luis Guerra?

2. ¿Cuándo se fundó la ciudad de Santo Domingo?

3. ¿Qué es el Alcázar de Colón?

4. Nombra dos beisbolistas famosos de la República Dominicana.

5. ¿De qué hablaban las canciones de merengue tradicionales?

6. ¿Qué instrumentos se utilizaban para tocar (*play*) el merengue?

7. ¿Cuándo se transformó el merengue en un estilo urbano?

8. ¿Qué cantante ha ayudado a internacionalizar el merengue?

Conexión Internet Investiga estos temas en Internet.

1. Busca más información sobre la isla La Española. ¿Cómo son las relaciones entre
   la República Dominicana y Haití?

2. Busca más información sobre la zona colonial de Santo Domingo: la Catedral de Santa María, la Casa de
   Bastidas o el Panteón Nacional. ¿Cómo son estos edificios? ¿Te gustan? Explica tus respuestas.

....

posee *possesses* **restauraciones** *restorations* **se cuentan** *are included* **siglo** *century* **afición** *pastime* **han alcanzado** *have reached*
raíces *roots* **campesinos** *rural people* **guayano** *metal scraper* **tambor** *drum* **bajo** *bass*

Las ocupaciones

el/la abogado/a	lawyer
el actor, la actriz	actor
el/la arqueólogo/a	archeologist
el/la arquitecto/a	architect
el/la bombero/a	firefighter
el/la carpintero/a	carpenter
el/la científico/a	scientist
el/la cocinero/a	cook; chef
el/la consejero/a	counselor; advisor
el/la contador(a)	accountant
el/la corredor(a) de bolsa	stockbroker
el/la diseñador(a)	designer
el/la electricista	electrician
el hombre/la mujer de negocios	businessperson
el/la maestro/a	teacher
el/la peluquero/a	hairdresser
el/la pintor(a)	painter
el/la político/a	politician
el/la psicólogo/a	psychologist
el/la reportero/a	reporter
el/la secretario/a	secretary
el/la técnico/a	technician

La entrevista

el anuncio	advertisement
el/la aspirante	candidate; applicant
los beneficios	benefits
el currículum	résumé
la entrevista	interview
el/la entrevistador(a)	interviewer
el puesto	position; job
el salario, el sueldo	salary
la solicitud (de trabajo)	(job) application
contratar	to hire
entrevistar	to interview
ganar	to earn
obtener	to obtain; to get
solicitar	to apply (for a job)

El mundo del trabajo

el ascenso	promotion
el aumento de sueldo	raise
la carrera	career
la compañía, la empresa	company; firm
el empleo	job; employment
el/la gerente	manager
el/la jefe/a	boss
los negocios	business; commerce
la ocupación	occupation
el oficio	trade
la profesión	profession
la reunión	meeting
el teletrabajo	telecommuting
el trabajo	job; work
la videoconferencia	videoconference
dejar	to quit; to leave behind
despedir (e:i)	to fire
invertir (e:ie)	to invest
renunciar (a)	to resign (from)
tener éxito	to be successful
comercial	commercial; business-related

Palabras adicionales

dentro de (diez años)	within (ten years)
próximo/a	next

Expresiones útiles	See page 547.

Un festival de arte

Communicative Goals

You will learn how to:

- Talk about and discuss the arts
- Express what you would like to do
- Express hesitation

A PRIMERA VISTA

- ¿Estará trabajando el hombre de la foto?
- ¿Es artista o arquitecto?
- ¿Tendrá un oficio?
- ¿Será una persona creativa o no?

Un festival de arte

Más vocabulario

el/la compositor(a)	composer
el/la director(a)	director; (musical) conductor
el/la dramaturgo/a	playwright
el/la escritor(a)	writer
el personaje (principal)	(main) character
las bellas artes	(fine) arts
el boleto	ticket
la canción	song
la comedia	comedy; play
el cuento	short story
la cultura	culture
el drama	drama; play
el espectáculo	show
el festival	festival
la historia	history; story
la obra	work (of art, music, etc.)
la obra maestra	masterpiece
la ópera	opera
la orquesta	orchestra
aburrirse	to get bored
dirigir	to direct
presentar	to present; to put on (a performance)
publicar	to publish
artístico/a	artistic
clásico/a	classical
dramático/a	dramatic
extranjero/a	foreign
folclórico/a	folk
moderno/a	modern
musical	musical
romántico/a	romantic
talentoso/a	talented

Variación léxica

banda ⟷ grupo musical (*Esp.*)

boleto ⟷ entrada (*Esp.*)

La Pintura

Pinta. (pintar)

la cerámica

el poeta

el poema

La Poesía

El músico toca un instrumento. (tocar)

La banda da un concierto. (dar)

la cantante

el baile

La Música

Práctica

1 **Escuchar** 🎧 Escucha la conversación y contesta las preguntas.

1. ¿Adónde fueron Ricardo y Juanita?
2. ¿Cuál fue el espectáculo que más le gustó a Ricardo?
3. ¿Qué le gustó más a Juanita?
4. ¿Qué dijo Ricardo del actor?
5. ¿Qué dijo Juanita del actor?
6. ¿Qué compró Juanita en el festival?
7. ¿Qué compró Ricardo?
8. ¿Qué poetas le interesaron a Ricardo?

2 **Artes** 🎧 Escucha las oraciones y escribe el número de cada oración debajo del arte correspondiente.

teatro	artesanía	poesía

música	danza

3 **¿Cierto o falso?** Indica si lo que dice cada oración es **cierto** o **falso**.

	Cierto	Falso
1. Las bellas artes incluyen la pintura, la escultura, la música, el baile y el drama.	○	○
2. Un boleto es un tipo de instrumento musical que se usa mucho en las óperas.	○	○
3. El tejido es un tipo de música.	○	○
4. Un cuento es una narración corta que puede ser oral o escrita.	○	○
5. Un compositor es el personaje principal de una obra de teatro.	○	○
6. Publicar es la acción de hablar en público a grandes grupos.	○	○

4 **Artistas** Indica la profesión de cada uno de estos artistas.

1. Javier Bardem
2. Frida Kahlo
3. Shakira
4. Octavio Paz
5. William Shakespeare
6. Miguel de Cervantes
7. Fernando Botero
8. Gustavo Dudamel
9. Toni Morrison
10. Fred Astaire

5 **Los favoritos** Indica cuál es tu película o programa favorito de cada categoría.

> *modelo*
> película musical
> Mi película musical favorita es *Les Misérables.*

1. película de ciencia ficción _____
2. programa de entrevistas _____
3. telenovela _____
4. película de horror _____
5. película de acción _____
6. concurso _____
7. programa de realidad _____
8. película de aventuras _____
9. documental _____
10. programa de dibujos animados _____

El cine y la televisión	
el canal	channel
el concurso	game show; contest
los dibujos animados	cartoons
el documental	documentary
la estrella (*m., f.*) de cine	movie star
el premio	prize; award
el programa de entrevistas/realidad	talk/reality show
la telenovela	soap opera
...de acción	action
...de aventuras	adventure
...de ciencia ficción	science fiction
...de horror	horror
...de vaqueros	western

6 **Completar** Completa las frases con las palabras adecuadas.

aburrirse	canal	estrella	musical
aplauden	de vaqueros	extranjera	romántica
artística	director	folclórica	talentosa

1. Una película que fue hecha en otro país es una película...
2. Si las personas que asisten a un espectáculo lo aprecian, ellos...
3. Una persona que puede hacer algo muy bien es una persona...
4. Una película que trata del amor y de las emociones es una película...
5. Una persona que pinta, esculpe y/o hace artesanía es una persona...
6. La música que refleja la cultura de una región o de un país es música...
7. Si la acción tiene lugar en el oeste de los EE.UU. durante el siglo XIX, probablemente es una película...
8. Una obra en la cual los actores presentan la historia por medio de (*by means of*) canciones y bailes es un drama...
9. Cuando una película no tiene una buena historia, el público empieza a...
10. Si quieres ver otro programa de televisión, es necesario que cambies de...

¡ATENCIÓN!

Apreciar means *to appreciate* only in the sense of evaluating what something is worth. Use **agradecer** to express the idea *to be thankful for.*

Ella **aprecia** la buena música.
She appreciates good music.

Le **agradezco** mucho su ayuda.
I thank you for your help.

7 **Analogías** Completa las analogías con las palabras adecuadas.

1. alegre ←→ triste ⊜ comedia ←→
2. escultor ←→ escultora ⊜ bailarín ←→
3. drama ←→ dramaturgo ⊜ pintura ←→
4. *Los Simpson* ←→ dibujos animados ⊜ *Jeopardy* ←→
5. de entrevistas ←→ programa ⊜ de vaqueros ←→
6. aplaudir ←→ público ⊜ hacer el papel ←→
7. poema ←→ literatura ⊜ tejido ←→
8. músico ←→ tocar ⊜ cantante ←→

¡LENGUA VIVA!

Remember that, in Spanish, last names do not have a plural form, although **los** may be used with a family name.

Los Simpson
The Simpsons

Comunicación

8 **Entrevista** Lee esta entrevista con un dramaturgo. Luego, indica si las conclusiones son **lógicas** o **ilógicas**, según lo que leíste.

Entrevista al dramaturgo Arturo Rodríguez

Entrevistadora: Díganos, ¿de qué trata (*is about*) su última obra?

Arturo Rodríguez: Bueno, básicamente trata de un escritor frustrado. El personaje principal es un joven muy talentoso, pero con muy mala suerte, al que le ocurren todo tipo de adversidades.

Entrevistadora: ¡Interesante! Y ¿podrá el público disfrutar de su obra en el teatro?

Arturo Rodríguez: Sí, se presentará a finales de este año, después de que se publique la obra.

Entrevistadora: ¡Muchas felicidades! Por último, todos sus fans se hacen la misma pregunta: ¿De dónde saca usted el tiempo para escribir? Para los espectadores que no lo sepan, Arturo Rodríguez se dedica a la escultura.

Arturo Rodríguez: La verdad es que no me aburro. Mi trabajo como escultor requiere que viaje a muchos países extranjeros, así que uso esas horas de avión para escribir. *El escritor frustrado* es el resultado de esos largos viajes.

Entrevistadora: ¡Impresionante! Aquí lo dejamos. Muchísimas gracias de nuevo. Y ahora el informe del tiempo...

	Lógico	Ilógico
1. Ésta es la primera obra de teatro de Arturo Rodríguez.	○	○
2. A Arturo Rodríguez le interesan diferentes tipos de arte.	○	○
3. *El escritor frustrado* se publicará este año.	○	○
4. Esta entrevista aparece en un periódico.	○	○

9 **Preguntas** Contesta las preguntas de tu compañero/a.

1. ¿Qué tipo de música prefieres? ¿Por qué?
2. ¿Tocas un instrumento? ¿Cuál?
3. ¿Hay algún instrumento que quisieras aprender a tocar?
4. ¿Con qué frecuencia vas al cine?
5. ¿Qué tipos de películas prefieres?
6. ¿Qué haces que se puede considerar artístico? ¿Pintas, dibujas, esculpes, haces artesanías, actúas en dramas, tocas un instrumento, cantas o escribes poemas?
7. ¿Con qué frecuencia vas a un museo de arte o asistes a conciertos, al teatro o a lecturas públicas de poesía?
8. ¿Es el arte una parte importante de tu vida? ¿Por qué?

10 **Un evento artístico** Escribe un anuncio para un evento artístico en tu comunidad: una exposición de arte, un concierto, una obra de teatro, una ópera, etc. Incluye la fecha, la hora, el lugar y una descripción del evento.

Una sorpresa para Maru

Miguel y Maru hacen una visita muy especial al Museo de Arte Popular.
Por otra parte, Jimena y Juan Carlos hablan sobre arte.

PERSONAJES JUAN CARLOS JIMENA

JUAN CARLOS Cuando era niño, iba con frecuencia a espectáculos culturales con mi mamá. A ella le gustan el teatro, los conciertos, la poesía y especialmente la danza.

MARU ¿Todo bien, Miguel? ¿Qué tienes allí?

MIGUEL ¿Podría pedirte algo?

MARU Claro.

JIMENA Mi mamá hubiera querido que tocara algún instrumento. Pero la verdad es que no tengo nada de talento musical, y Felipe tampoco.

JIMENA Aunque no tengamos talento artístico, mi mamá nos enseñó a apreciar la música.

JUAN CARLOS Creo que tu mamá y la mía se llevarían bien. Tal vez algún día lleguen a conocerse.

(*Mientras tanto, en el Museo de Arte Popular*)

MARU Siempre había querido venir aquí. Me encantan las artesanías de cerámica y sus tejidos. El arte folclórico nos cuenta la historia de su gente y su país.

MIGUEL María Eugenia Castaño Ricaurte, ¿me harías el honor de casarte conmigo?

MIGUEL **MARU** **FELIPE**

(*Juan Carlos y Jimena hablan de los espectáculos que les gustan.*)

JUAN CARLOS ¿Qué clase de espectáculos te gustan?

JIMENA Me gusta la música en vivo y el teatro. Además, me encantan las películas.

JIMENA ¿Cuáles son tus películas favoritas?

JUAN CARLOS Las de ciencia ficción y las de terror.

JUAN CARLOS ¿Te gustan las películas de acción?

JIMENA Sí, me fascinan, y también los documentales.

JUAN CARLOS Bueno, podríamos ir a verlos juntos.

(*Y... en el museo*)

MARU Sí. ¡Sí acepto casarme contigo! Qué anillo tan hermoso.

Expresiones útiles

Talking about the arts

Mi mamá hubiera querido que tocara algún instrumento.
My mother would have wanted me to play some instrument.
Pero la verdad es que no tengo nada de talento musical.
But the truth is I don't have any musical talent.
Me encantan las artesanías de cerámica y los tejidos.
I love ceramic crafts and weavings.
El arte folclórico nos cuenta la historia de su gente y su país.
Folkloric art tells us the history of its people and its country.

Getting engaged

¿Podría pedirte algo?
Could I ask you for something?
¿Me harías el honor de casarte conmigo?
Would you do me the honor of marrying me?
Sí. ¡Sí acepto casarme contigo!
Yes. Yes, I'll marry you!
Qué anillo tan hermoso.
What a beautiful ring.

Additional vocabulary

(No) Estoy de acuerdo.
I (dis)agree.

¿Qué pasó?

1 **Seleccionar** Selecciona la respuesta correcta.

1. Cuando era niño, Juan Carlos iba a los _____ culturales.
   a. premios   b. espectáculos   c. boletos
2. Jimena dice que no tiene talento _____.
   a. musical   b. moderno   c. folclórico
3. A Maru le encanta ver las _____ en cerámica y los tejidos.
   a. bailarinas   b. artesanías   c. bellas artes
4. A Jimena le gusta escuchar música en vivo e ir al _____.
   a. cine   b. festival   c. teatro
5. A Juan Carlos le gustan las películas de _____.
   a. acción y de vaqueros   b. aventuras y de drama   c. ciencia ficción y de terror

2 **Identificar** Identifica quién puede decir estas oraciones.

1. A mí mamá le gusta mucho la danza, pero también el teatro.
2. ¡Qué bonito es el arte folclórico que hay en este museo!
3. Me gustan mucho las películas.
4. Te voy a invitar a ver documentales, a mí también me gustan.
5. Nunca pude aprender a tocar un instrumento musical.
6. Me haces el hombre más feliz por querer casarte conmigo.

MARU

JIMENA

MIGUEL
JUAN CARLOS

3 **Correspondencias** ¿A qué eventos culturales asistirán juntos Jimena y Juan Carlos?

| una exposición de cerámica precolombina | un concierto | una ópera |
| una exposición de pintura española | una telenovela | una tragedia |

1. Escucharán música clásica y conocerán a un director muy famoso.
2. El público aplaudirá mucho a la señora que es soprano.
3. Como a Marissa le gusta la historia, la llevarán a ver esto.
4. Como a Miguel le gustaría ver arte, entonces irán con él.

4 **El fin de semana** Vas a asistir a dos eventos culturales el próximo fin de semana con un(a) compañero/a. Comenten entre ustedes por qué les gustan o les disgustan algunas de las actividades que van sugiriendo. Escojan al final dos actividades que puedan realizar juntos/as. Usen estas frases y expresiones en su conversación.

▶ ¿Qué te gustaría ver/hacer este fin de semana?
▶ ¿Te gustaría asistir a...?
▶ ¡Me encanta(n)... !
▶ Odio..., ¿qué tal si...?

Ortografía
Las trampas ortográficas

Some of the most common spelling mistakes in Spanish occur when two or more words have very similar spellings. This section reviews some of those words.

compro   **compró**   **hablo**   **habló**

There is no accent mark in the **yo** form of –**ar** verbs in the present tense. There is, however, an accent mark in the **Ud./él/ella** form of –**ar** verbs in the preterite.

------

este (adjective)   **éste** (pronoun)   **esté** (verb)

The demonstrative adjectives **esta** and **este** do not have an accent mark. The demonstrative pronouns **ésta** and **éste** have an accent mark on the first syllable. The verb forms **está** (*present indicative*) and **esté** (*present subjunctive*) have an accent mark on the last syllable.

------

jo-ven   **jó-ve-nes**   **bai-la-rín**   **bai-la-ri-na**

The location of the stressed syllable in a word determines whether or not a written accent mark is needed. When a plural or feminine form has more syllables than the singular or masculine form, an accent mark must sometimes be added or deleted to maintain the correct stress.

No me gusta la ópera, sino el teatro.
No quiero ir al festival si no vienes conmigo.

The conjunction **sino** (*but rather*) should not be confused with **si no** (*if not*). Note also the difference between **mediodía** (*noon*) and **medio día** (*half a day*) and between **por qué** (*why*) and **porque** (*because*).

Práctica Completa las oraciones con las palabras adecuadas para cada ocasión.

1. Javier me explicó que _____ lo invitabas, él no iba a venir. (sino/si no)
2. Me gustan mucho las _____ folclóricas. (canciones/canciónes)
3. Marina _____ su espectáculo en El Salvador. (presento/presentó)
4. Yo prefiero _____. (éste/esté)

Palabras desordenadas Ordena las letras para descubrir las palabras correctas. Después, ordena las letras indicadas para descubrir la respuesta a la pregunta.

¿Adónde va Manuel?

y u n a s e d ó   _ |O| _ |O| _ _ _ _

q u e r o p   _ |O| _ _ _ _

z o g a d e l a |O| _ _ |O| _ _ _ _

á s e t   _ |O| _ _

h a i t e s a b o n c i   _ _ _ _ |O| _ _ _ |O| _ _ _

Manuel va _ _ _ _ _ _ _ _ .[1]

[1] Manuel va al teatro.

Respuestas: desayunó, porque, adelgazo, está, habitaciones

Museo de Arte Contemporáneo de Caracas

Una visita al Museo de Arte Contemporáneo de Caracas (MACC) es una experiencia única. Su colección permanente incluye unas 3.000 obras de artistas de todo el mundo. Además, el museo organiza exposiciones temporales° de escultura, dibujo, pintura, fotografía, cine y video. En sus salas se pueden admirar obras de artistas como Matisse, Miró, Picasso, Chagall, Tàpies y Botero.

Exposición Cuerpo plural, MACC

La lección de esquí, de Joan Miró

En 2004 el museo tuvo que cerrar a causa de un incendio°. Entonces, su valiosa° colección fue trasladada al Museo de Bellas Artes, también en Caracas. Además se realizaron exposiciones en otros lugares, incluso al aire libre, en parques y bulevares.

Cuando el MACC reabrió° sus puertas, un año después, lo hizo con nuevos conceptos e ideas. Se dio más atención a las cerámicas y fotografías de la colección. También se creó una sala multimedia dedicada a las últimas tendencias° como video-arte y *performance*.

El MACC es un importante centro cultural. Además de las salas de exposición, cuenta con° un jardín de esculturas, un auditorio y una biblioteca especializada en arte. También organiza talleres° y recibe a grupos escolares. Un viaje a Caracas no puede estar completo sin una visita a este maravilloso museo.

Otros museos importantes

Museo del Jade (San José, Costa Rica): Tiene la colección de piezas de jade más grande del mundo. La colección tiene un gran valor° y una gran importancia histórica. Incluye muchas joyas° precolombinas.

Museo de Instrumentos Musicales (La Paz, Bolivia): Muestra más de 2.500 instrumentos musicales bolivianos y de otras partes del mundo. Tiene un taller de construcción de instrumentos musicales.

Museo Nacional de Culturas Populares (México, D.F., México): El museo investiga y difunde° las diferentes manifestaciones culturales de México, realiza exposiciones y organiza seminarios, cursos y talleres.

Museo del Cine Pablo Ducrós Hicken (Buenos Aires, Argentina): Dedicado a la historia del cine argentino, expone películas, libros, revistas, guiones°, carteles, fotografías, cámaras y proyectores antiguos.

exposiciones temporales *temporary exhibitions* incendio *fire*
valiosa *valuable* reabrió *reopened* tendencias *trends*
cuenta con *it has* talleres *workshops* valor *value* joyas *jewelry*
difunde *spreads* guiones *scripts*

ACTIVIDADES

1 **¿Cierto o falso?** Indica si lo que dice cada oración es **cierto** o **falso.** Corrige la información falsa.

1. La colección permanente del MACC tiene sólo obras de artistas venezolanos.

2. Durante el tiempo que el museo cerró a causa de un incendio, se realizaron exposiciones al aire libre.

3. Cuando el museo reabrió, se dio más atención a la pintura.

4. En el jardín del museo también pueden admirarse obras de arte.

5. La importancia del Museo del Jade se debe a las joyas europeas que se exponen en él.

6. En el Museo de Instrumentos Musicales de La Paz también se hacen instrumentos musicales.

7. En Buenos Aires hay un museo dedicado a la historia del cine de Hollywood.

Arte y espectáculos

las caricaturas (Col., El Salv., Méx.); los dibujitos (Arg.); los muñequitos (Cuba)	los dibujos animados
el coro	*choir*
el escenario	*stage*
el estreno	*debut, premiere*
el/la guionista	*scriptwriter*

EL MUNDO HISPANO

Artistas hispanos

- **Myrna Báez** (Santurce, Puerto Rico, 1931) Innovó las técnicas de la pintura y el grabado° en Latinoamérica. En 2001, el Museo de Arte de Puerto Rico le rindió homenaje° a sus cuarenta años de carrera artística.

- **Joaquín Cortés** (Córdoba, España, 1969) Bailarín y coreógrafo. En sus espectáculos une° sus raíces gitanas° a influencias musicales de todo el mundo.

- **Tania León** (La Habana, Cuba, 1943) Compositora y directora de orquesta. Ha sido cofundadora° y directora musical del *Dance Theater of Harlem*, y ha compuesto numerosas obras.

- **Rafael Murillo Selva** (Tegucigalpa, Honduras, 1936) Dramaturgo. En su obra refleja preocupaciones sociales y la cultura hondureña.

grabado *engraving* rindió homenaje *paid homage* une *combines* raíces gitanas *gypsy roots* cofundadora *co-founder*

PERFIL

Fernando Botero: un estilo único

El dibujante°, pintor y escultor **Fernando Botero** es un colombiano de fama internacional. Ha expuesto sus obras en galerías y museos de las Américas, Europa y Asia.

La pintura siempre ha sido su pasión. Su estilo se caracteriza por un cierto aire ingenuo° y unas proporciones exageradas. Mucha gente dice que Botero "pinta gordos", pero esto no es correcto. En su obra no sólo las personas son exageradas; los animales y los objetos también. Botero dice que empezó a pintar personas y cosas voluminosas por intuición. Luego, estudiando la pintura de los maestros italianos, se reafirmó su interés por el volumen y comenzó a usarlo conscientemente° en sus pinturas y esculturas, muchas de las cuales se exhiben en ciudades de todo el mundo. Botero es un trabajador incansable° y es que, para él, lo más divertido del mundo es pintar y crear.

El alguacil, de **Fernando Botero**

dibujante *drawer* ingenuo *naive* conscientemente *consciously* incansable *tireless*

Conexión Internet

¿Qué otros artistas de origen hispano son famosos?

Use the Web to find more cultural information related to this **Cultura** section.

ACTIVIDADES

2 **Comprensión** Contesta las preguntas.
1. ¿Cómo se dice en español "*The scriptwriter is on stage*"?
2. ¿Cuál fue la contribución de Myrna Báez al arte latinoamericano?
3. ¿En qué actividades artísticas trabaja Tania León?
4. ¿Qué tipo de obras realiza Fernando Botero?
5. ¿Cuáles son dos características del estilo de Botero?

3 **Sus artistas favoritos** En parejas, hablen sobre sus artistas favoritos (de cualquier disciplina artística). Hablen de la obra que más les gusta de estos artistas y expliquen por qué.

17.1 The conditional

ANTE TODO The conditional tense in Spanish expresses what you *would do* or what *would happen* under certain circumstances.

The conditional tense

		visitar	comer	aplaudir
SINGULAR FORMS	yo	visitar**ía**	comer**ía**	aplaudir**ía**
	tú	visitar**ías**	comer**ías**	aplaudir**ías**
	Ud./él/ella	visitar**ía**	comer**ía**	aplaudir**ía**
PLURAL FORMS	nosotros/as	visitar**íamos**	comer**íamos**	aplaudir**íamos**
	vosotros/as	visitar**íais**	comer**íais**	aplaudir**íais**
	Uds./ellos/ellas	visitar**ían**	comer**ían**	aplaudir**ían**

Creo que tu mamá y la mía se llevarían bien.

Pensé que te gustaría el Museo de Arte Popular.

▶ The conditional tense is formed much like the future tense. The endings are the same for all verbs, both regular and irregular. For regular verbs, you simply add the appropriate endings to the infinitive. **¡Atención!** All forms of the conditional have an accent mark.

▶ For irregular verbs, add the conditional endings to the irregular stems.

INFINITIVE	STEM	CONDITIONAL	INFINITIVE	STEM	CONDITIONAL
decir	dir-	dir**ía**	querer	querr-	querr**ía**
hacer	har-	har**ía**	saber	sabr-	sabr**ía**
poder	podr-	podr**ía**	salir	saldr-	saldr**ía**
poner	pondr-	pondr**ía**	tener	tendr-	tendr**ía**
haber	habr-	habr**ía**	venir	vendr-	vendr**ía**

▶ While in English the conditional is a compound verb form made up of the auxiliary verb *would* and a main verb, in Spanish it is a simple verb form that consists of one word.

Yo no me **pondría** ese vestido.
I would not put on that dress.

¿**Vivirían** ustedes en otro país?
Would you live in another country?

¡ATENCIÓN!

The polite expressions **Me gustaría...** (*I would like...*) and **Te gustaría...** (*You would like...*) are other examples of the conditional.

AYUDA

The infinitive of **hay** is **haber**, so its conditional form is **habría**.

▶ The conditional is commonly used to make polite requests.

¿**Podrías** abrir la ventana, por favor?
Would you open the window, please?

¿**Sería** tan amable de venir a mi oficina?
Would you be so kind as to come to my office?

▶ In Spanish, as in English, the conditional expresses the future in relation to a past action or state of being. In other words, the future indicates what *will happen* whereas the conditional indicates what *would happen*.

Creo que mañana **hará** sol.
I think it will be sunny tomorrow.

Creía que hoy **haría** sol.
I thought it would be sunny today.

▶ The English *would* is often used with a verb to express the conditional, but it can also mean *used to*, in the sense of past habitual action. To express past habitual actions, Spanish uses the imperfect, not the conditional.

Íbamos al parque los sábados.
We would go to the park on Saturdays.

De adolescentes, **comíamos** mucho.
As teenagers, we used to eat a lot.

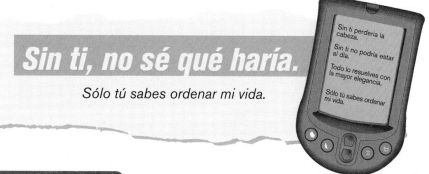
Keep in mind the two parallel combinations shown in the example sentences:

1) present tense in main clause → future tense in subordinate clause

2) past tense in main clause → conditional tense in subordinate clause

---

COMPARE & CONTRAST

In **Lección 16**, you learned the *future of probability*. Spanish also has the *conditional of probability*, which expresses conjecture or probability about a past condition, event, or action. Compare these Spanish and English sentences.

Serían las once de la noche
cuando Elvira me llamó.
*It must have been (It was probably)
11 p.m. when Elvira called me.*

Sonó el teléfono. ¿**Llamaría** Emilio
para cancelar nuestra cita?
*The phone rang. I wondered if it was
Emilio calling to cancel our date.*

Note that English conveys conjecture or probability with phrases such as *I wondered if*, *probably*, and *must have been*. In contrast, Spanish gets these same ideas across with conditional forms.

¡INTÉNTALO!   Indica la forma apropiada del condicional de los verbos.

1. Yo _____ escucharía, leería, esculpiría _____ (escuchar, leer, esculpir)
2. Tú _____ (apreciar, comprender, compartir)
3. Marcos _____ (poner, venir, querer)
4. Nosotras _____ (ser, saber, ir)
5. Ustedes _____ (presentar, deber, aplaudir)
6. Ella _____ (salir, poder, hacer)
7. Yo _____ (tener, tocar, aburrirse)
8. Tú _____ (decir, ver, publicar)

Práctica

1 **De viaje** A un grupo de artistas le gustaría hacer un viaje a Honduras. En estas oraciones nos cuentan sus planes de viaje. Complétalas con el condicional del verbo entre paréntesis.

1. Me _____ (gustar) llevar algunos libros de poesía de Leticia de Oyuela.
2. Ana _____ (querer) ir primero a Copán para conocer las ruinas mayas.
3. Yo _____ (decir) que fuéramos a Tegucigalpa primero.
4. Nosotras _____ (preferir) ver una obra del Grupo Dramático de Tegucigalpa. Luego _____ (poder) tomarnos un café.
5. Y nosotros _____ (ver) los cuadros del pintor José Antonio Velásquez. Y tú, Luisa, ¿qué _____ (hacer)?
6. Yo _____ (tener) interés en ver o comprar cerámica de José Arturo Machado. Y a ti, Carlos, ¿te _____ (interesar) ver la arquitectura colonial?

NOTA CULTURAL

Leticia de Oyuela (1935–2008) fue una escritora hondureña. En sus obras, Oyuela combinaba la historia con la ficción y, a través de sus personajes, cuestionaba y desafiaba (*used to challenge*) las normas sociales.

2 **¿Qué harías?** Indica qué harías en estas situaciones.

> Estás en un concierto de tu banda favorita y la persona que está sentada delante no te deja ver.

> Un amigo actor te invita a ver una película que acaba de hacer, y no te gusta nada cómo hace su papel.

> Estás invitado/a a los Premios Ariel. Es posible que te vayan a dar un premio, pero ese día estás muy enfermo/a.

> Te invitan, pagándote mucho dinero, a un programa de televisión para hablar de tu vida privada y pelearte (*to fight*) con tu novio/a durante el programa.

NOTA CULTURAL

Los Premios Ariel de México son el equivalente a los Premios Oscar en los Estados Unidos. Cada año los entrega la Academia Mexicana de Ciencias y Artes Cinematográficas. Algunas películas que han ganado un premio Ariel son *Amores perros* y *El laberinto del fauno*.

3 **Sugerencias** Matilde busca trabajo. Dile ocho cosas que tú harías si fueras ella. Usa el condicional.

modelo
> Si yo fuera tú, buscaría trabajo en la red.

AYUDA

Here are two ways of saying *If I were you*:
Si yo fuera tú...
Yo en tu lugar...

Comunicación

4

Cita Escucha la conversación telefónica entre José Antonio y Marcela. Luego, indica si las conclusiones son **lógicas** o **ilógicas**, según lo que escuchaste.

	Lógico	Ilógico
1. A José Antonio no le interesa el arte.	○	○
2. Marcela ya tiene planes hoy.	○	○
3. A Marcela no le gusta salir con José Antonio.	○	○
4. El hermano de José Antonio iría al cine también si no estuviera de vacaciones.	○	○
5. Marcela y José Antonio van a encontrarse en el cine primero para comprar los boletos.	○	○

5

¿Qué harías? Imagina que no tienes restricciones ni de dinero ni de tiempo y puedes hacer lo que quieras. Explica qué cosas harías. Utiliza un mínimo de cinco verbos en condicional.

> **modelo**
>
> *Escribiría cuentos para niños...*

6

Luces, cámara y acción En parejas, elijan una película que les guste y hablen sobre las cosas que habrían hecho de manera diferente si hubieran sido los directores.

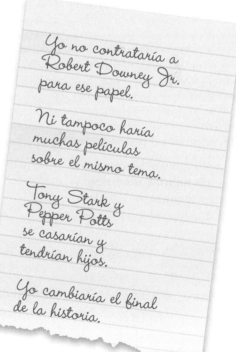

Yo no contrataría a Robert Downey Jr. para ese papel.

Ni tampoco haría muchas películas sobre el mismo tema.

Tony Stark y Pepper Potts se casarían y tendrían hijos.

Yo cambiaría el final de la historia.

Síntesis

7

Una vida diferente Piensa en un(a) artista famoso/a (cantante, actor/actriz, bailarín/bailarina, etc.). Escribe un párrafo en el que describas cómo sería tu vida si fueras esa persona. Utiliza el tiempo condicional.

17.2 | The conditional perfect

ANTE TODO Like other compound tenses you have learned—the present perfect, the past perfect, and the future perfect—the conditional perfect (**el condicional perfecto**) is formed with **haber** + [*past participle*].

Felipe habría venido con nosotros, pero sigue molesto.

Sí, pensé que ya se le había pasado el enojo.

The conditional perfect

		pintar	comer	vivir
SINGULAR FORMS	yo	**habría** pintado	**habría** comido	**habría** vivido
	tú	**habrías** pintado	**habrías** comido	**habrías** vivido
	Ud./él/ella	**habría** pintado	**habría** comido	**habría** vivido
PLURAL FORMS	nosotros/as	**habríamos** pintado	**habríamos** comido	**habríamos** vivido
	vosotros/as	**habríais** pintado	**habríais** comido	**habríais** vivido
	Uds./ellos/ellas	**habrían** pintado	**habrían** comido	**habrían** vivido

▶ The conditional perfect is used to express an action that would have occurred, but didn't.

¿No fuiste al espectáculo?
¡Te **habrías divertido**!
You didn't go to the show?
You would have had a good time!

Sandra **habría preferido** ir a la ópera, pero Omar prefirió ir al cine.
Sandra would have preferred to go to the opera, but Omar preferred to see a movie.

¡INTÉNTALO! Indica las formas apropiadas del condicional perfecto de los verbos.

1. Nosotros ___habríamos hecho___ (hacer) todos los quehaceres.
2. Tú _____ (apreciar) mi poesía.
3. Ellos _____ (pintar) un mural.
4. Usted _____ (tocar) el piano.
5. Ellas _____ (poner) la mesa.
6. Tú y yo _____ (resolver) los problemas.
7. Silvia y Alberto _____ (esculpir) una estatua.
8. Yo _____ (presentar) el informe.
9. Ustedes _____ (vivir) en el campo.
10. Tú _____ (abrir) la puerta.

Práctica

1 **Completar** Completa los diálogos con la forma apropiada del condicional perfecto de los verbos de la lista.

| divertirse | presentar | sentir | tocar |
| hacer | querer | tener | venir |

1. —Tú _____ el papel de Aída mejor que ella. ¡Qué lástima!
   —Sí, mis padres _____ desde California sólo para oírme cantar.
2. —Olga, yo esperaba algo más. Con un poco de dedicación y práctica la orquesta _____ mejor y los músicos _____ más éxito.
   —Menos mal que la compositora no los escuchó. Se _____ avergonzada.
3. —Tania _____ la comedia pero no pudo porque cerraron el teatro.
   —¡Qué lástima! Mi esposa y yo _____ ir a la presentación de la obra. Siempre veo tragedias y sé que _____.

2 **Combinar** Imagina qué harían estas personas en las situaciones presentadas. Combina elementos de cada una de las tres columnas para formar ocho oraciones usando el condicional perfecto.

 A **B** **C**

A	B	C
con talento artístico	yo	estudiar...
con más tiempo libre	tú	pintar...
en otro país	la gente	esculpir...
con más aprecio de las artes	mis compañeros y yo	viajar...
con más dinero	los artistas	escribir...
en otra película	Alejandro González Iñárritu	publicar...

3 **¿Qué habrías hecho?** Estos dibujos muestran situaciones poco comunes. No sabemos qué hicieron estas personas, pero tú, ¿qué habrías hecho?

1.

2.

3.

4.

Comunicación

4   **Pobre Mario** Lee la carta que Mario le escribió a Enrique. Luego, indica si las conclusiones son **lógicas** o **ilógicas**, según lo que leíste.

> Enrique:
>
>   Ya llegó el último día del musical. Yo creía que nunca iba a acabar. En general, los cantantes y actores eran bastante malos, pero no tuve tiempo de buscar otros, y además los buenos ya tenían trabajo en otras obras. Ayer todo salió muy mal. Como era la última noche, yo había invitado a unos críticos a ver la obra, pero no pudieron verla. El primer problema fue la cantante principal. Ella estaba enojada conmigo porque no quise pagarle todo el dinero que quería. Dijo que tenía problemas de garganta, y no salió a cantar. Conseguí otra cantante, pero los músicos de la orquesta todavía no habían llegado. Tenían que venir todos en un autobús no muy caro que yo había alquilado, pero el autobús salió a una hora equivocada. Entonces, el bailarín se enojó conmigo porque todo iba a empezar tarde. Quizás tenía razón mi padre. Seguramente soy mejor contador que director teatral.
>
>   Escríbeme,
>   Mario

	Lógico	Ilógico
1. Mario habría preferido no hacer el musical.	○	○
2. Mario no habría buscado otros cantantes y actores.	○	○
3. La cantante principal no habría aceptado más dinero.	○	○
4. El bailarín habría querido empezar antes.	○	○
5. Mario habría sido un contador malísimo.	○	○

5   **Este semestre** Escribe un párrafo de por lo menos cinco oraciones en el que expliques qué cosas habrías hecho de manera diferente este semestre. Utiliza el condicional perfecto.

> **modelo**
>
> Este semestre habría estudiado más para mi examen de economía; ¡me fue fatal!

Síntesis

6   **Yo en tu lugar** Primero, cada estudiante hace una lista con tres errores que ha cometido o tres problemas que ha tenido en su vida. Después, en parejas, túrnense para decirse qué habrían hecho en esas situaciones.

> **modelo**
>
> **Estudiante 1:** El año pasado saqué una mala nota en el examen de biología.
> **Estudiante 2:** Yo no habría sacado una mala nota. Habría estudiado más.

17.3 # The past perfect subjunctive

CONSULTA

To review the past perfect indicative, see **Estructura 15.2**, p. 522.

To review the present perfect subjunctive, see **Estructura 15.3**, p. 525.

ANTE TODO   The past perfect subjunctive (**el pluscuamperfecto de subjuntivo**), also called the pluperfect subjunctive, is formed with the past subjunctive of **haber** + [*past participle*]. Compare the following subjunctive forms.

Present subjunctive	Present perfect subjunctive
yo trabaje	yo haya trabajado

Past subjunctive	Past perfect subjunctive
yo trabajara	yo hubiera trabajado

Past perfect subjunctive

		pintar	comer	vivir
SINGULAR FORMS	yo	**hubiera** pintado	**hubiera** comido	**hubiera** vivido
	tú	**hubieras** pintado	**hubieras** comido	**hubieras** vivido
	Ud./él/ella	**hubiera** pintado	**hubiera** comido	**hubiera** vivido
PLURAL FORMS	nosotros/as	**hubiéramos** pintado	**hubiéramos** comido	**hubiéramos** vivido
	vosotros/as	**hubierais** pintado	**hubierais** comido	**hubierais** vivido
	Uds./ellos/ellas	**hubieran** pintado	**hubieran** comido	**hubieran** vivido

▶ The past perfect subjunctive is used in subordinate clauses under the same conditions that you have learned for other subjunctive forms, and in the same way the past perfect is used in English (*I had talked, you had spoken*, etc.). It refers to actions or conditions that had taken place before another action or condition in the past.

No había nadie que **hubiera dormido**.
There wasn't anyone who had slept.

Dudaba que ellos **hubieran llegado**.
I doubted that they had arrived.

Esperaba que Juan **hubiera ganado** el partido.
I hoped that Juan had won the game.

Llegué antes de que la clase **hubiera comenzado**.
I arrived before the class had begun.

¡INTÉNTALO!   Indica la forma apropiada del pluscuamperfecto de subjuntivo de cada verbo.

1. Esperaba que ustedes ___hubieran hecho___ (hacer) las reservaciones.
2. Dudaba que tú _____ (decir) eso.
3. No estaba seguro de que ellos _____ (ir).
4. No creían que nosotros _____ (hablar) con Ricardo.
5. No había nadie que _____ (poder) comer tanto como él.
6. No había nadie que _____ (ver) el espectáculo.
7. Me molestó que tú no me _____ (llamar) antes.
8. ¿Había alguien que no _____ (apreciar) esa película?
9. No creían que nosotras _____ (bailar) en el festival.
10. No era cierto que yo _____ (ir) con él al concierto.

Práctica

1 **Completar** Completa las oraciones con el pluscuamperfecto de subjuntivo de los verbos.

1. Me alegré de que mi familia _____ (irse) de viaje.
2. Me molestaba que Carlos y Miguel no _____ (venir) a visitarme.
3. Dudaba que la música que yo escuchaba _____ (ser) la misma que escuchaban mis padres.
4. No creían que nosotros _____ (poder) aprender español en un año.
5. Los músicos se alegraban de que su programa le _____ (gustar) tanto al público.
6. La profesora se sorprendió de que nosotros _____ (hacer) la tarea antes de venir a clase.

2 **Transformar** María está hablando de las emociones que ha sentido ante ciertos acontecimientos (*events*). Transforma sus oraciones según el modelo.

> **modelo**
>
> Me alegro de que hayan venido los padres de Micaela.
> *Me alegré de que hubieran venido los padres de Micaela.*

1. Es muy triste que haya muerto la tía de Miguel.

2. Dudo que Guillermo haya comprado una casa tan grande.

3. No puedo creer que nuestro equipo haya perdido el partido.

4. Me alegro de que mi novio me haya llamado.

5. Me molesta que el periódico no haya llegado.

6. Dudo que hayan cerrado el Museo de Arte.

¡LENGUA VIVA!

Both the preterite and the imperfect can be used to describe past thoughts or emotions. In general, the imperfect describes a particular action or mental state without reference to its beginning or end; the preterite refers to the occurrence of an action, thought, or emotion at a specific moment in time.

Pensaba que mi vida era aburrida.

Pensé que había dicho algo malo.

3 **El regreso** Durante 30 años, el astronauta Emilio Hernández estuvo en el espacio sin tener noticias de la Tierra. Usa el pluscuamperfecto de subjuntivo para indicar lo que Emilio esperaba que hubiera pasado.

> **modelo**
>
> su esposa / no casarse con otro hombre
> *Esperaba que su esposa no se hubiera casado con otro hombre.*

1. su hija Diana / conseguir ser una pintora famosa

2. los políticos / acabar con todas las guerras (*wars*)

3. su suegra / irse a vivir a El Salvador

4. su hermano Ramón / tener un empleo por más de dos meses

5. todos los países / resolver sus problemas económicos

6. su esposa / ya pagar el préstamo de la casa

Un festival de arte
quinientos noventa y siete
597

Comunicación

4

Una mala obra Escucha el mensaje telefónico que deja María Teresa, una espectadora, a una compañía de teatro. Luego, indica si las conclusiones son **lógicas** o **ilógicas**, según lo que escuchaste.

	Lógico	Ilógico
1. Era probable que María Teresa hubiera aplaudido mucho el martes.	○	○
2. La obra *La Celestina* fue gratis.	○	○
3. María Teresa fue sola al teatro.	○	○
4. Había una banda talentosa en el teatro.	○	○
5. María Teresa ha leído el libro *La Celestina*.	○	○

5

Reacciones Imagina que estos acontecimientos (*events*) ocurrieron la semana pasada. Indica cómo reaccionaste ante cada uno. Comparte tu reacción con un(a) compañero/a.

> **modelo**
> Vino a visitarte tu tía de El Salvador.
> *Me alegré de que hubiera venido a visitarme.*

1. Perdiste tu mochila con tus tarjetas de crédito y tus documentos.
2. Tu ex novio/a se casó con tu mejor amigo/a.
3. Encontraste cincuenta mil dólares cerca del banco.
4. Tus amigos/as te hicieron una fiesta sorpresa.

6

Opinión Escribe tu opinión sobre el último evento artístico al que asististe (un festival de cine, un concierto, una obra de teatro, etc.). Usa el pluscuamperfecto de subjuntivo.

> **modelo**
> *El sábado vi un documental sobre el flamenco. Me alegré de que mi hermana hubiera comprado los boletos...*

Síntesis

7

Noticias En parejas, lean estos titulares (*headlines*) e indiquen cuáles habrían sido sus reacciones si esto les hubiera ocurrido a ustedes. Utilicen el pluscuamperfecto de subjuntivo.

Un grupo de turistas se encuentra con Elvis en una gasolinera.
El cantante los saludó, les cantó unas canciones y después se marchó hacia las montañas, caminando tranquilamente.

Tres jóvenes estudiantes se perdieron en un bosque de Maine.
Después de estar tres horas perdidos, aparecieron en una gasolinera de un desierto de Australia.

Ayer, una joven hondureña, después de pasar tres años en coma, se despertó y descubrió que podía entender el lenguaje de los animales.
La joven, de momento, no quiere hablar con la prensa, pero una amiga suya nos dice que está deseando ir al zoológico.

Recapitulación

Completa estas actividades para repasar los conceptos de gramática que aprendiste en esta lección.

1 Completar Completa el cuadro con la forma correcta del condicional.
24 pts.

Infinitivo	tú	nosotros	ellas
pintar			
			querrían
		podríamos	
	habrías		

2 Diálogo Completa el diálogo con la forma adecuada del condicional de los verbos de la lista. **24 pts.**

dejar	gustar	llover	sorprender
encantar	ir	poder	volver

OMAR ¿Sabes? El concierto al aire libre fue un éxito. Yo creía que (1) _____ , pero hizo sol.

NIDIA Ah, me alegro. Te dije que Jaime y yo (2) _____, pero tuvimos un imprevisto (*something came up*) y no pudimos. Y a Laura, ¿la viste allí?

OMAR Sí, ella fue. Al contrario que tú, al principio me dijo que ella y su esposo no (3) _____ ir, pero al final aparecieron. Necesitaba relajarse un poco; está muy estresada con su trabajo.

NIDIA A mí no me (4) _____ que lo dejara. Yo, en su lugar, (5) _____ esa compañía y (6) _____ a escribir poesía. En realidad no necesita el dinero.

OMAR Estoy de acuerdo. Oye, esta noche voy a ir al teatro. ¿(7) _____ ir conmigo? Jaime también puede acompañarnos. Es una comedia familiar.

NIDIA A nosotros (8) _____ ir. ¿A qué hora es?

OMAR A las siete y media.

RESUMEN GRAMATICAL

17.1 The conditional *pp. 588–589*

The conditional tense* of aplaudir

aplaudiría	aplaudiríamos
aplaudirías	aplaudiríais
aplaudiría	aplaudirían

*Same endings for -ar, -er, and -ir verbs.

Irregular verbs

Infinitive	Stem	Conditional
decir	dir-	diría
hacer	har-	haría
poder	podr-	podría
poner	pondr-	pondría
haber	habr-	habría
querer	querr-	querría
saber	sabr-	sabría
salir	saldr-	saldría
tener	tendr-	tendría
venir	vendr-	vendría

17.2 The conditional perfect *p. 592*

pintar

habría pintado	habríamos pintado
habrías pintado	habríais pintado
habría pintado	habrían pintado

17.3 The past perfect subjunctive *p. 595*

cantar

hubiera cantado	hubiéramos cantado
hubieras cantado	hubierais cantado
hubiera cantado	hubieran cantado

► To form the past perfect subjunctive, take the **Uds./ellos/ellas** form of the preterite of **haber**, drop the ending (**-ron**), and add the past subjunctive endings (**-ra, -ras, -ra, -ramos, -rais, -ran**).

► Note that the **nosotros/as** form takes an accent.

3   **Fin de curso** El espectáculo de fin de curso de la escuela se canceló por falta de interés y ahora todos se arrepienten (*regret it*). Completa las oraciones con el condicional perfecto.   **24 pts.**

1. La profesora de danza _____ (convencer) a los mejores bailarines de que participaran.
2. Tú no _____ (escribir) en el periódico que el comité organizador era incompetente.
3. Los profesores _____ (animar) a todos a participar.
4. Nosotros _____ (invitar) a nuestros amigos y familiares.
5. Tú _____ (publicar) un artículo muy positivo sobre el espectáculo.
6. Los padres de los estudiantes _____ (dar) más dinero y apoyo.
7. Mis compañeros de drama y yo _____ (presentar) una comedia muy divertida.
8. El director _____ (hacer) del espectáculo su máxima prioridad.

4   **El arte** Estos estudiantes están decepcionados (*disappointed*) con sus estudios de arte. Escribe oraciones a partir de los elementos dados. Usa el imperfecto de indicativo y el pluscuamperfecto de subjuntivo. Sigue el modelo.   **24 pts.**

> **modelo**
>
> yo / esperar / la universidad / poner / más énfasis en el arte
> Yo esperaba que la universidad hubiera puesto más énfasis en el arte.

1. Sonia / querer / el departamento de arte / ofrecer / más clases

2. no haber nadie / oír / de ningún ex alumno / con éxito en el mundo artístico

3. nosotros / desear / haber / más exhibiciones de trabajos de estudiantes

4. ser una lástima / los profesores / no ser / más exigentes

5. Juanjo / dudar / nosotros / poder / escoger una universidad con menos recursos

6. ser increíble / la universidad / no construir / un museo más grande

5   **Adivinanza** Completa la adivinanza con la forma correcta del condicional del verbo **ser** y adivina la respuesta.   **4 pts.**

> **"** Me puedes ver en tu piso,
> y también en tu nariz;
> sin mí no habría ricos
> y nadie _____ (ser) feliz.
> ¿Quién soy? **"**
>
> _____

Lectura

Antes de leer

> ### Estrategia
> **Identifying stylistic devices**
>
> There are several stylistic devices (**recursos estilísticos**) that can be used for effect in poetic or literary narratives. *Anaphora* consists of successive clauses or sentences that start with the same word(s). *Parallelism* uses successive clauses or sentences with a similar structure. *Repetition* consists of words or phrases repeated throughout the text. *Enumeration* uses the accumulation of words to describe something. Identifying these devices can help you to focus on topics or ideas that the author chose to emphasize.

Contestar

1. ¿Cuál es tu instrumento musical favorito? ¿Sabes tocarlo? ¿Puedes describir su forma?

2. Compara el sonido de ese instrumento con algunos sonidos de la naturaleza. (Por ejemplo: El piano suena como la lluvia.)

3. ¿Qué instrumento es el "protagonista" de estos poemas de García Lorca?

4. Localiza en estos tres poemas algunos ejemplos de los recursos estilísticos que aparecen en la **Estrategia**. ¿Qué elementos o temas se enfatizan mediante esos recursos?

Resumen

Completa el párrafo con palabras de la lista.

artesanía	música	poeta
compositor	poemas	talento

Los _____ se titulan *La guitarra, Las seis cuerdas* y *Danza.* Son obras del _____ Federico García Lorca. Estos textos reflejan la importancia de la _____ en la poesía de este escritor. Lorca es conocido por su _____.

Federico García Lorca

El escritor español Federico García Lorca nació en 1898 en Fuente Vaqueros, Granada. En 1919 se mudó a Madrid y allí vivió en una residencia estudiantil donde se hizo° amigo del pintor Salvador Dalí y del cineasta° Luis Buñuel. En 1920 estrenó° su primera obra teatral, El maleficio° de la mariposa°. *En 1929 viajó a los Estados Unidos, donde asistió a clases en la Universidad de Columbia. Al volver a España, dirigió la compañía de teatro universitario "La Barraca", un proyecto promovido° por el gobierno de la República para llevar el teatro clásico a los pueblos españoles. Fue asesinado en agosto de 1936 en Víznar, Granada, durante la dictadura° militar de Francisco Franco. Entre sus obras más conocidas están* Poema del cante jondo *(1931) y* Bodas de sangre *(1933). El amor, la muerte y la marginación son algunos de los temas presentes en su obra.*

Danza

EN EL HUERTO° DE LA PETENERA°

En la noche del huerto,
seis gitanas°,
vestidas de blanco
bailan.

En la noche del huerto,
coronadas°,
con rosas de papel
y biznagas°.

En la noche del huerto,
sus dientes de nácar°,
escriben la sombra°
quemada.

Y en la noche del huerto,
sus sombras se alargan°,
y llegan hasta el cielo
moradas.

Las seis cuerdas

La guitarra,
hace llorar° a los sueños°.
El sollozo° de las almas°
perdidas,
se escapa por su boca
redonda°.
Y como la tarántula
teje° una gran estrella
para cazar suspiros°,
que flotan en su negro
aljibe° de madera°.

La guitarra

Empieza el llanto°
de la guitarra.
Se rompen las copas
de la madrugada°.
Empieza el llanto
de la guitarra.
Es inútil
callarla°.
Es imposible
callarla.
Llora monótona
como llora el agua,
como llora el viento
sobre la nevada°.
Es imposible
callarla.
Llora por cosas
lejanas°.
Arena° del Sur caliente
que pide camelias blancas.
Llora flecha sin blanco°,
la tarde sin mañana,
y el primer pájaro muerto
sobre la rama°.
¡Oh guitarra!
Corazón malherido°
por cinco espadas°.

Después de leer

Comprensión

Completa cada oración con la opción correcta.

1. En el poema *La guitarra* se habla del "llanto" de la guitarra. La palabra "llanto" se relaciona con el verbo _____.
   a. llover   b. cantar   c. llorar

2. El llanto de la guitarra en *La guitarra* se compara con _____.
   a. el viento   b. la nieve   c. el tornado

3. En el poema *Las seis cuerdas* se personifica a la guitarra como _____.
   a. una tarántula   b. un pájaro   c. una estrella

4. En *Danza*, las gitanas bailan en el _____.
   a. teatro   b. huerto   c. patio

Interpretación

Responde a las preguntas.

1. En los poemas *La guitarra* y *Las seis cuerdas* se personifica a la guitarra. Analicen esa personificación. ¿Qué cosas humanas puede hacer la guitarra? ¿En qué se parece a una persona?

2. ¿Creen que la música de *La guitarra* y *Las seis cuerdas* es alegre o triste? ¿En qué tipo de música te hace pensar?

3. ¿Puede existir alguna relación entre las seis cuerdas de la guitarra y las seis gitanas bailando en el huerto en el poema *Danza*? ¿Cuál?

Conversación

Primero, comenta con un(a) compañero/a tus gustos musicales (instrumentos favoritos, grupos, estilo de música, cantantes). Después, intercambien las experiencias más intensas o importantes que hayan tenido con la música (un concierto, un recuerdo asociado a una canción, etc.).

se hizo *he became* cineasta *filmmaker* estrenó *premiered* maleficio *curse; spell* mariposa *butterfly* promovido *promoted* dictadura *dictatorship* huerto *orchard* petenera *Andalusian song* gitanas *gypsies* coronadas *crowned* biznagas *type of plant* nácar *mother-of-pearl* sombra *shadow* se alargan *get longer* llorar *to cry* sueños *dreams* sollozo *sobbing* almas *souls* redonda *round* teje *spins* suspiros *sighs* aljibe *well* madera *wood* llanto *crying* madrugada *dawn* inútil callarla *useless to silence her* nevada *snowfall* lejanas *far-off* Arena *Sand* flecha sin blanco *arrow without a target* rama *branch* malherido *wounded* espadas *swords*

Escritura

Estrategia
Finding biographical information

Biographical information can be useful for a great variety of writing topics. Whether you are writing about a famous person, a period in history, or even a particular career or industry, you will be able to make your writing both more accurate and more interesting when you provide detailed information about the people who are related to your topic.

To research biographical information, you may wish to start with general reference sources, such as encyclopedias and periodicals. Additional background information on people can be found in biographies or in nonfiction books about the person's field or industry. For example, if you wanted to write about Sonia Sotomayor, you could find background information from periodicals, including magazine interviews. You might also find information in books or articles related to contemporary politics and Law.

Biographical information may also be available on the Internet, and depending on your writing topic, you may even be able to conduct interviews to get the information you need. Make sure to confirm the reliability of your sources whenever your writing includes information about other people.

You might want to look for the following kinds of information:

- date of birth
- date of death
- childhood experiences
- education
- family life
- place of residence
- life-changing events
- personal and professional accomplishments

Tema
¿A quién te gustaría conocer?

Si pudieras invitar a cinco personas famosas a cenar en tu casa, ¿a quiénes invitarías? Pueden ser de cualquier (*any*) época de la historia y de cualquier profesión. Algunas posibilidades son:

- el arte
- la música
- el cine
- las ciencias
- la religión
- la política

Escribe una composición breve sobre la cena. Explica por qué invitarías a estas personas y describe lo que harías, lo que preguntarías y lo que dirías si tuvieras la oportunidad de conocerlas. Utiliza el condicional.

Escuchar

Estrategia

**Listening for key words/
Using the context**

The comprehension of key words is vital
to understanding spoken Spanish. Use your
background knowledge of the subject
to help you anticipate what the key words
might be. When you hear unfamiliar words,
remember that you can use context to figure
out their meaning.

 To practice these strategies, you will now
listen to a paragraph from a letter sent to a job
applicant. Jot down key words, as well as any
other words you figured out from the context.

Preparación

Basándote en el dibujo, ¿qué palabras crees que
usaría un crítico en una reseña (*review*) de esta película?

Ahora escucha

Ahora vas a escuchar la reseña de la película.
Mientras escuches al crítico, recuerda que las
críticas de cine son principalmente descriptivas.
La primera vez que la escuches, identifica las
palabras clave (*key*) y escríbelas en la columna A.
Luego, escucha otra vez la reseña e identifica
el significado de las palabras en la columna B
mediante el contexto.

A	B
1. _____	1. estrenar
2. _____	2. a pesar de
3. _____	3. con reservas
4. _____	4. supuestamente
5. _____	5. la trama
6. _____	6. conocimiento

Comprensión

Cierto o falso

	Cierto	Falso
1. *El fantasma del lago Enriquillo* es una película de ciencia ficción.	O	O
2. Los efectos especiales son espectaculares.	O	O
3. Generalmente se ha visto a Jorge Verdoso en comedias románticas.	O	O
4. Jaime Rebelde es un actor espectacular.	O	O

Preguntas

1. ¿Qué aspectos de la película le gustaron al crítico?
2. ¿Qué no le gustó al crítico de la película?
3. ¿Irías a ver esta película? ¿Por qué?
4. Para ti, ¿cuáles son los aspectos más importantes de
   una película? Explica tu respuesta.

Ahora tú

Escoge una película con actores muy famosos que no fue lo
que esperabas. Escribe una reseña que describa el papel de
los actores, la trama, los efectos especiales, la cinematografía
u otros aspectos importantes de la película.

En pantalla

Este cortometraje°, escrito y dirigido por el español
Jorge Naranjo, fue el finalista de la novena edición
del concurso de Jameson Notodofilmfest. Es el
primero de la trilogía de cortometrajes que inspiró
el largometraje *Casting, la película,* del mismo
director. El protagonista de este corto, Javier
López, comparte sus experiencias en el mundo de
la actuación, un mundo casi impenetrable en el
que los actores se lo juegan todo° en esa prueba
inicial que es el casting. Con un toque° de humor
e ironía, Javi nos describe lo dura que es la vida de
los actores y lo absurdo y ridículo que puede llegar
a ser presentarse a un casting.

Vocabulario útil

aguantando	*hanging in there*
no te atreves	*you don't dare*
no te sale	*you can't do it*
quejarse	*to complain*
representante	*agent*

Preparación

¿Alguna vez te has presentado a un casting?
¿Cómo fue la experiencia?

Preguntas

Contesta las preguntas.

1. ¿Qué hace Javier en su trabajo de actor?

2. ¿Cómo está Javier al comenzar el casting?

3. Según Javier, ¿qué es lo peor que te pueden pedir en
   un casting?

4. ¿Dónde trabaja Javier? ¿Y dónde vive?

Una audición

En parejas, representen una audición original. Uno/a
de ustedes es director(a) de castings, la otra persona
se presenta a la prueba.

modelo

Director(a): *¿Podría usted representar el papel de una
mosca (fly) nerviosa dentro de una botella?*

cortometraje *short film* se lo juegan todo *they risk everthing* toque *touch*

Casting

Yo hago castings.

Ahora necesitamos que llores.

Eres muy bueno, buenísimo.

Todos los países hispanos cuentan con una gran variedad de museos, desde arte clásico o contemporáneo, hasta los que se especializan en la rica historia local que puede venir desde las antiguas° culturas prehispánicas. El Museo de Arte Popular, en la Ciudad de México, que viste en el episodio de **Fotonovela**, tiene como misión difundir°, preservar y continuar las técnicas tradicionales de elaborar artesanías mexicanas. Algunas de ellas son la cerámica, la joyería°, los textiles y el papel maché. A continuación vas a ver otro tipo de museos en España.

Vocabulario útil	
el lienzo	*canvas*
la muestra	*exhibit*
el primer plano	*foreground*

Preparación

¿Te interesa el arte? Cuando viajas, ¿visitas los museos del lugar al que vas? ¿Cuál es, de entre todas las artes, la que más te gusta o emociona?

¿Cierto o falso?

Indica si las oraciones son **ciertas** o **falsas**.

1. En Madrid, la oferta de arte es muy limitada.

2. En el Triángulo Dorado de los museos hay tres museos muy importantes de Madrid.

3. En la obra *Las meninas* de Velázquez, la perspectiva es muy real.

4. El Museo Reina Sofía está dedicado al arte contemporáneo y antiguo.

5. El lienzo *Guernica* de Picasso es pequeño.

6. La colección del Museo Thyssen era privada y luego fue donada (*donated*) al estado español.

7. El Greco era español.

Palacios del arte

... una ciudad [...] con una riquísima y selecta oferta de hoteles, restaurantes [...] y especialmente... ¡arte!

El edificio fue [...] un hospital. Hoy en día, está dedicado al arte contemporáneo.

Muchos aseguran° que es el primer surrealista.

antiguas *ancient* difundir *to spread* joyería *jewelry* aseguran *assure*

El Salvador

El país en cifras

▶ **Área:** 21.040 km² (8.124 millas²),
  el tamaño° de Massachusetts
▶ **Población:** 6.125.000

El Salvador es el país centroamericano más pequeño y el más densamente poblado. Su población, al igual que la de Honduras, es muy homogénea: casi el 90 por ciento es mestiza.

▶ **Capital:** San Salvador—1.605.000
▶ **Ciudades principales:** Soyapango, Santa Ana, San Miguel, Mejicanos
▶ **Moneda:** dólar estadounidense
▶ **Idiomas:** español (oficial), náhuatl, lenca

Bandera de El Salvador

Salvadoreños célebres

▶ **Óscar Romero,** arzobispo° y activista por los derechos humanos° (1917–1980)
▶ **Claribel Alegría,** poeta, novelista y cuentista (1924–)
▶ **Roque Dalton,** poeta, ensayista y novelista (1935–1975)
▶ **María Eugenia Brizuela,** política (1956–)
▶ **Francesca Miranda,** diseñadora (1957–)

Óscar Romero

tamaño *size* arzobispo *archbishop* derechos humanos *human rights*
laguna *lagoon* sirena *mermaid*

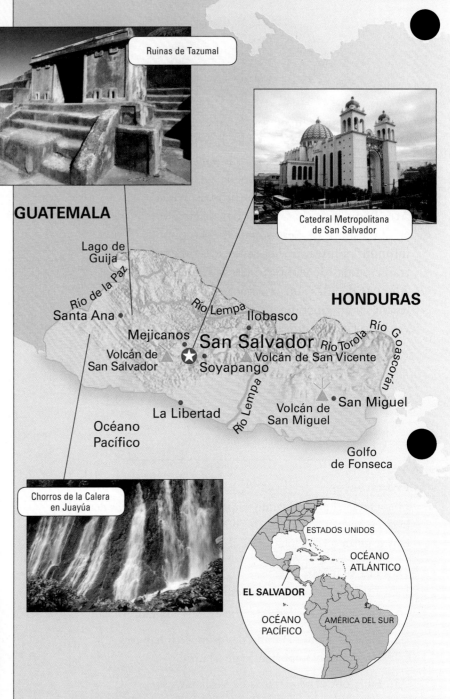

Ruinas de Tazumal

Catedral Metropolitana de San Salvador

GUATEMALA

Lago de Guija
Río de la Paz
Santa Ana
Río Lempa
Mejicanos
Volcán de San Salvador
San Salvador
Soyapango
Ilobasco
Río Torola
HONDURAS
Río Goascorán
Volcán de San Vicente
La Libertad
Río Lempa
Volcán de San Miguel
San Miguel
Océano Pacífico
Golfo de Fonseca

Chorros de la Calera en Juayúa

ESTADOS UNIDOS
OCÉANO ATLÁNTICO
EL SALVADOR
OCÉANO PACÍFICO
AMÉRICA DEL SUR

¡Increíble pero cierto!

El rico folclor salvadoreño se basa sobre todo en sus extraordinarios recursos naturales. Por ejemplo, según una leyenda, las muertes que se producen en la laguna° de Alegría tienen su explicación en la existencia de una sirena° solitaria que vive en el lago y captura a los jóvenes atractivos.

Deportes • El surfing

El Salvador es uno de los destinos favoritos en Latinoamérica para la práctica del surfing. Cuenta con 300 kilómetros de costa a lo largo del océano Pacífico y sus olas° altas son ideales para quienes practican este deporte. De sus playas, La Libertad es la más visitada por surfistas de todo el mundo, gracias a que está muy cerca de la capital salvadoreña. Sin embargo, los fines de semana muchos visitantes prefieren viajar a la Costa del Bálsamo, donde se concentra menos gente.

Naturaleza • El Parque Nacional Montecristo

El Parque Nacional Montecristo se encuentra en la región norte del país. Se le conoce también como El Trifinio porque se ubica° en el punto donde se unen las fronteras de Guatemala, Honduras y El Salvador. Este bosque reúne a muchas especies vegetales y animales, como orquídeas, monos araña°, pumas, quetzales y tucanes. Además, las copas° de sus enormes árboles forman una bóveda° que impide° el paso de la luz solar. Este espacio natural se encuentra a una altitud de 2.400 metros (7.900 pies) sobre el nivel del mar y recibe 200 centímetros (80 pulgadas°) de lluvia al año.

Artes • La artesanía de Ilobasco

Ilobasco es un pueblo conocido por sus artesanías. En él se elaboran objetos con arcilla° y cerámica pintada a mano, como juguetes°, adornos° y utensilios de cocina. Además, son famosas sus "sorpresas", que son pequeñas piezas° de cerámica en cuyo interior se representan escenas de la vida diaria. Los turistas realizan excursiones para ver la elaboración, paso a paso°, de estos productos.

¿Qué aprendiste? Contesta cada pregunta con una oración completa.

1. ¿Qué tienen en común las poblaciones de El Salvador y Honduras?

2. ¿Qué es el náhuatl?

3. ¿Quién es María Eugenia Brizuela?

4. Hay muchos lugares ideales para el surfing en El Salvador. ¿Por qué?

5. ¿A qué altitud se encuentra el Parque Nacional Montecristo?

6. ¿Cuáles son algunos de los animales y las plantas que viven en este parque?

7. ¿Por qué se le llama El Trifinio al Parque Nacional Montecristo?

8. ¿Por qué es famoso el pueblo de Ilobasco?

9. ¿Qué se puede ver en un viaje a Ilobasco?

10. ¿Qué son las "sorpresas" de Ilobasco?

Conexión Internet Investiga estos temas en Internet.

1. El Parque Nacional Montecristo es una reserva natural; busca información sobre otros parques o zonas protegidas en El Salvador. ¿Cómo son estos lugares? ¿Qué tipos de plantas y animales se encuentran allí?

2. Busca información sobre museos u otros lugares turísticos en San Salvador (u otra ciudad de El Salvador).

olas *waves* se ubica *it is located* monos araña *spider monkeys* copas *tops* bóveda *cap* impide *blocks* pulgadas *inches* arcilla *clay*
juguetes *toys* adornos *ornaments* piezas *pieces* paso a paso *step by step*

Honduras

El país en cifras

▸ **Área:** 112.492 km² (43.870 millas²),
un poco más grande que Tennessee

▸ **Población:** 8.598.000

Cerca del 90 por ciento de la población de Honduras es mestiza. Todavía hay pequeños grupos indígenas como los jicaque, los misquito y los paya, que han mantenido su cultura sin influencias exteriores y que no hablan español.

▸ **Capital:** Tegucigalpa—1.088.000

Tegucigalpa

▸ **Ciudades principales:** San Pedro Sula, El Progreso, La Ceiba

▸ **Moneda:** lempira

▸ **Idiomas:** español (oficial), lenguas indígenas, inglés

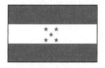

Bandera de Honduras

Hondureños célebres

▸ **José Antonio Velásquez,** pintor (1906–1983)

▸ **Argentina Díaz Lozano,** escritora (1912–1999)

▸ **Carlos Roberto Reina,** juez° y presidente del país (1926–2003)

▸ **Roberto Sosa,** escritor (1930–2011)

▸ **Salvador Moncada,** científico (1944–)

juez *judge* presos *prisoners* madera *wood* hamacas *hammocks*

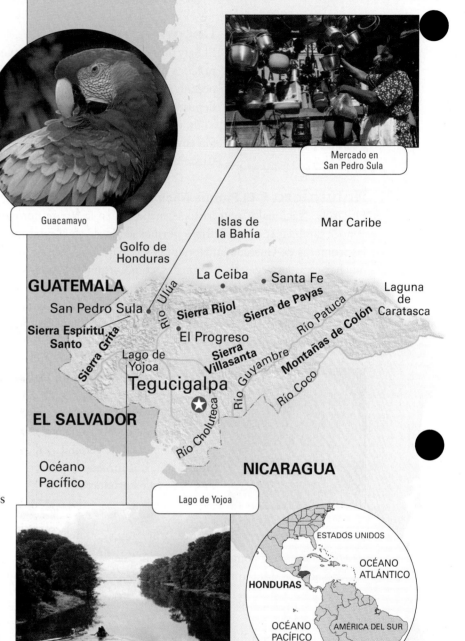

Guacamayo

Mercado en San Pedro Sula

Islas de la Bahía

Mar Caribe

Golfo de Honduras

GUATEMALA

La Ceiba

Santa Fe

Laguna de Caratasca

San Pedro Sula

Río Ulúa

Sierra Rijol

Sierra de Payas

Río Patuca

Sierra Espíritu Santo

Sierra Grita

El Progreso

Sierra Villasanta

Río Guyambre

Montañas de Colón

Lago de Yojoa

Tegucigalpa

Río Coco

EL SALVADOR

Río Choluteca

Océano Pacífico

NICARAGUA

Lago de Yojoa

ESTADOS UNIDOS

OCÉANO ATLÁNTICO

HONDURAS

OCÉANO PACÍFICO

AMÉRICA DEL SUR

¡Increíble pero cierto!

¿Irías de compras a una prisión? Hace un tiempo, cuando la Penitenciaría Central de Tegucigalpa aún funcionaba, los presos° hacían objetos de madera°, hamacas° y hasta instrumentos musicales y los vendían en una tienda dentro de la prisión. Allí, los turistas podían regatear con este especial grupo de artesanos.

Lugares • Copán

Copán es una zona arqueológica muy importante de Honduras. Fue construida por los mayas y se calcula que en el año 400 d. C. albergaba° a una ciudad con más de 150 edificios y una gran cantidad de plazas, patios, templos y canchas° para el juego de pelota°. Las ruinas más famosas del lugar son los edificios adornados con esculturas pintadas a mano, los cetros° ceremoniales de piedra y el templo Rosalila.

Economía • Las plantaciones de bananas

Desde hace más de cien años, las bananas son la exportación principal de Honduras y han tenido un papel fundamental en su historia. En 1899, la Standard Fruit Company empezó a exportar bananas del país centroamericano hacia Nueva Orleans. Esta fruta resultó tan popular en los Estados Unidos que generó grandes beneficios° para esta compañía y para la United Fruit Company, otra empresa norteamericana. Estas trasnacionales intervinieron muchas veces en la política hondureña debido° al enorme poder° económico que alcanzaron en la nación.

San Antonio de Oriente, 1957,
José Antonio Velásquez

Artes • José Antonio Velásquez (1906–1983)

José Antonio Velásquez fue un famoso pintor hondureño. Es catalogado como primitivista° porque sus obras representan aspectos de la vida cotidiana. En la pintura de Velásquez es notorio el énfasis en los detalles°, la falta casi total de los juegos de perspectiva y la pureza en el uso del color. Por todo ello, el artista ha sido comparado con importantes pintores europeos del mismo género° como Paul Gauguin o Emil Nolde.

¿Qué aprendiste? Contesta cada pregunta con una oración completa.

1. ¿Qué es el lempira?

2. ¿Por qué es famoso Copán?

3. ¿Dónde está el templo Rosalila?

4. ¿Cuál es la exportación principal de Honduras?

5. ¿Qué fue la Standard Fruit Company?

6. ¿Cómo es el estilo de José Antonio Velásquez?

7. ¿Qué temas trataba Velásquez en su pintura?

Conexión Internet Investiga estos temas en Internet.

1. ¿Cuáles son algunas de las exportaciones principales de Honduras, además de las bananas? ¿A qué países exporta Honduras sus productos?

2. Busca información sobre Copán u otro sitio arqueológico en Honduras. En tu opinión, ¿cuáles son los aspectos más interesantes del sitio?

....

albergaba *housed* canchas *courts* juego de pelota *pre-Columbian ceremonial ball game* cetros *scepters* beneficios *profits* debido a *due to* poder *power* primitivista *primitivist* detalles *details* género *genre*

Las bellas artes

el baile, la danza	dance
la banda	band
las bellas artes	(fine) arts
el boleto	ticket
la canción	song
la comedia	comedy; play
el concierto	concert
el cuento	short story
la cultura	culture
el drama	drama; play
la escultura	sculpture
el espectáculo	show
la estatua	statue
el festival	festival
la historia	history; story
la música	music
la obra	work (of art, music, etc.)
la obra maestra	masterpiece
la ópera	opera
la orquesta	orchestra
el personaje (principal)	(main) character
la pintura	painting
el poema	poem
la poesía	poetry
el público	audience
el teatro	theater
la tragedia	tragedy
aburrirse	to get bored
aplaudir	to applaud
apreciar	to appreciate
dirigir	to direct
esculpir	to sculpt
hacer el papel (de)	to play the role (of)
pintar	to paint
presentar	to present; to put on (a performance)
publicar	to publish
tocar (un instrumento musical)	to touch; to play (a musical instrument)
artístico/a	artistic
clásico/a	classical
dramático/a	dramatic
extranjero/a	foreign
folclórico/a	folk
moderno/a	modern
musical	musical
romántico/a	romantic
talentoso/a	talented

Los artistas

el bailarín, la bailarina	dancer
el/la cantante	singer
el/la compositor(a)	composer
el/la director(a)	director; (musical) conductor
el/la dramaturgo/a	playwright
el/la escritor(a)	writer
el/la escultor(a)	sculptor
la estrella (m., f.) de cine	movie star
el/la músico/a	musician
el/la poeta	poet

El cine y la televisión

el canal	channel
el concurso	game show; contest
los dibujos animados	cartoons
el documental	documentary
el premio	prize; award
el programa de entrevistas/realidad	talk /reality show
la telenovela	soap opera
… de acción	action
… de aventuras	adventure
… de ciencia ficción	science fiction
… de horror	horror
… de vaqueros	western

La artesanía

la artesanía	craftsmanship; crafts
la cerámica	pottery
el tejido	weaving

Expresiones útiles	See page 583.

Las actualidades

Communicative Goals

You will learn how to:

• Discuss current events and issues
• Talk about and discuss the media
• Reflect on experiences, such as travel

A PRIMERA VISTA
• ¿Qué profesión tendrán estas personas? ¿Son reporteros?
• ¿Es una videoconferencia?
• ¿Hacen entrevistas?
• ¿Es posible que hablen con estrellas de cine? ¿Con políticos?

Las actualidades

Más vocabulario

el acontecimiento	*event*
las actualidades	*news; current events*
el artículo	*article*
la encuesta	*poll; survey*
el informe	*report*
los medios de comunicación	*media; means of communication*
las noticias	*news*
la prensa	*press*
el reportaje	*report*
el desastre (natural)	*(natural) disaster*
el huracán	*hurricane*
la inundación	*flood*
el terremoto	*earthquake*
el desempleo	*unemployment*
la (des)igualdad	*(in)equality*
la discriminación	*discrimination*
la guerra	*war*
la libertad	*liberty; freedom*
la paz	*peace*
el racismo	*racism*
el sexismo	*sexism*
el SIDA	*AIDS*
anunciar	*to announce; to advertise*
comunicarse (con)	*to communicate (with)*
durar	*to last*
informar	*to inform*
luchar (por/contra)	*to fight; to struggle (for/against)*
transmitir, emitir	*to broadcast*
(inter)nacional	*(inter)national*
peligroso/a	*dangerous*

Variación léxica

informe ←→ trabajo (*Esp.*)

noticiero ←→ informativo (*Esp.*)

la tormenta

el ejército

el soldado

VOTA POR DÍAZ

el discurso

NO

NO

NO

la huelga

el crimen

el candidato

la violencia

el choque

el tornado

el incendio

La política

el/la ciudadano/a	citizen
el deber	responsibility; obligation
los derechos	rights
la dictadura	dictatorship
las elecciones	election
el impuesto	tax
la política	politics
el/la representante	representative
declarar	to declare
elegir (e:i)	to elect
obedecer	to obey
votar	to vote
político/a	political

BANCO

el diario

DIARIO

el noticiero

NOTICIAS CANAL 7

la locutora

Práctica

1 **Escuchar** 🎧 Escucha las noticias y selecciona la frase que mejor completa las oraciones.

1. Los ciudadanos creen que ____.
   a. hay un huracán en el Caribe
   b. hay discriminación en la imposición de los impuestos
   c. hay una encuesta en el Caribe
2. Los ciudadanos creen que los candidatos tienen ____.
   a. el deber de asegurar la igualdad en los impuestos
   b. el deber de hacer las encuestas
   c. los impuestos
3. La encuesta muestra que los ciudadanos ____.
   a. quieren desigualdad en las elecciones
   b. quieren hacer otra encuesta
   c. quieren igualdad en los impuestos
4. Hay ____ en el Caribe.
   a. un incendio grande b. una tormenta peligrosa c. un tornado
5. Los servicios de Puerto Rico predijeron anoche que ____ podrían destruir edificios y playas.
   a. los vientos b. los terremotos c. las inundaciones

2 **¿Cierto o falso?** 🎧 Escucha las oraciones e indica si lo que dice cada una es **cierto** o **falso**, según el dibujo.

1. _____
2. _____
3. _____
4. _____
5. _____
6. _____

3 **Categorías** Mira la lista e indica la categoría de cada uno de estos términos. Las categorías son: **desastres naturales, política** y **medios de comunicación**.

1. reportaje
2. inundación
3. incendio
4. candidato/a
5. encuesta
6. noticiero
7. prensa
8. elecciones
9. terremoto

4 **Definir** Define estas palabras.

1. guerra
2. crimen
3. ejército
4. desempleo
5. discurso
6. acontecimiento
7. sexismo
8. SIDA
9. huelga
10. racismo
11. locutor(a)
12. libertad

5 **Completar** Completa la noticia con los verbos adecuados para cada oración. Conjuga los verbos en el tiempo verbal correspondiente.

1. El grupo _____ a todos los medios de comunicación que iba a organizar una huelga general de los trabajadores.
   a. durar   b. votar   c. anunciar
2. Los representantes les pidieron a los ciudadanos que _____ al presidente.
   a. comer   b. obedecer   c. aburrir
3. La oposición, por otro lado, _____ a un líder para promover la huelga.
   a. publicar   b. emitir   c. elegir
4. El líder de la oposición dijo que si el gobierno ignoraba sus opiniones, la huelga iba a _____ mucho tiempo.
   a. transmitir   b. obedecer   c. durar
5. Hoy día, el líder de la oposición declaró que los ciudadanos estaban listos para _____ por sus derechos.
   a. informar   b. comunicarse   c. luchar

6 **Conversación** Completa esta conversación con las palabras adecuadas.

artículo	derechos	peligrosa
choque	dictaduras	transmitir
declarar	paz	violencia

RAÚL Oye, Agustín, ¿leíste el (1) _____ del diario *El País*?

AGUSTÍN ¿Cuál? ¿El del (2) _____ entre dos autobuses?

RAÚL No, el otro sobre…

AGUSTÍN ¿Sobre la tormenta (3) _____ que viene mañana?

RAÚL No, hombre, el artículo sobre política…

AGUSTÍN ¡Ay, claro! Un análisis de las peores (4) _____ de la historia.

RAÚL ¡Agustín! Deja de interrumpir. Te quería hablar del artículo sobre la organización que lucha por los (5) _____ humanos y la (6) _____.

AGUSTÍN Ah, no lo leí.

RAÚL Parece que te interesan más las noticias sobre la (7) _____, ¿eh?

7 **La vida civil** ¿Estás de acuerdo con estas afirmaciones?

1. Los medios de comunicación nos informan bien de las noticias.
2. Los medios de comunicación nos dan una visión global del mundo.
3. Los candidatos para las elecciones deben aparecer en todos los medios de comunicación.
4. Nosotros y nuestros representantes nos comunicamos bien.
5. Es importante que todos obedezcamos las leyes.
6. Es importante leer el diario todos los días.
7. Es importante mirar o escuchar un noticiero todos los días.
8. Es importante votar.

AYUDA
You may want to use these expressions:
En mi opinión…
Está claro que…
(No) Estoy de acuerdo.
Según mis padres…
Sería ideal que…

Comunicación

8 🎧

Noticias Escucha el fragmento de un noticiero. Luego, indica si las conclusiones son **lógicas** o **ilógicas**, según lo que escuchaste.

	Lógico	Ilógico
1. El gobierno del país es una dictadura.	○	○
2. Si gana el Partido Progreso y Avance, los ciudadanos tendrán más sueldo neto.	○	○
3. Si gana el Partido Progreso y Avance, habrá más personas sin trabajo.	○	○
4. Para la candidata del Partido Progreso y Avance, la igualdad de los ciudadanos es muy importante.	○	○
5. En el noticiero sólo se habla de política.	○	○

9

Las actualidades Describe lo que ves en las fotos. Luego, cuenta una historia para explicar qué pasó en cada foto.

10

Las elecciones Trabajen en parejas para representar una entrevista entre un(a) reportero/a de la televisión y un(a) político/a que va a ser candidato/a en las próximas elecciones.

Hasta pronto, Marissa

Marissa debe regresar a Wisconsin y quiere despedirse de sus amigos.

PERSONAJES   MARISSA   SR. DÍAZ

1

MARISSA ¡Hola, don Roberto! ¿Dónde están todos?

SR. DÍAZ Todos me dijeron que te pidiera una disculpa de su parte.

MARISSA (*triste*) Ah. No hay problema. ¿Puedo poner la tele?

SR. DÍAZ Claro.

MAITE FUENTES Un incendio en el centro ha ocasionado daños en tres edificios. Los representantes de la policía nos informan que no hay heridos. Aunque las elecciones son en pocas semanas, las encuestas no muestran un líder definido.

2

(*La familia Díaz y sus amigos sorprenden a Marissa en el restaurante.*)

MARISSA No tenía ni idea. (*a Jimena*) Tu papá me hizo creer que no podría despedirme de ustedes.

3

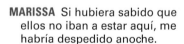

MARISSA Si hubiera sabido que ellos no iban a estar aquí, me habría despedido anoche.

SR. DÍAZ ¡Ánimo! No es un adiós, Marissa. Vamos a seguir en contacto. Pero, creo que tenemos algo de tiempo antes de que te vayas. Te llevo a comer tu última comida mexicana.

5

6

EMPLEADO Buenos días, señor Díaz. ¡Qué gusto verlo!

SR. DÍAZ Igualmente. Ella es Marissa. Pasó el año con nosotros. Quería que su última comida en México fuera la mejor de todas.

EMPLEADO Muy amable de su parte, señor. Su mesa está lista. Síganme, por favor.

4

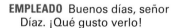

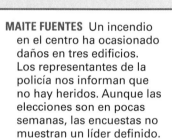

SR. DÍAZ Chicos, me dicen que se van a casar. Felicidades.

MIGUEL Nos casamos aquí en México el año que viene. Ojalá usted y su esposa puedan ir. (*a Marissa*) Si tú no estás harta de nosotros, nos encantaría que también vinieras.

 **MAITE FUENTES**   **DON DIEGO**   **EMPLEADO**   **SRA. DÍAZ**   **JIMENA**   **MIGUEL**   **FELIPE**   **MARU**   **JUAN CARLOS**

7

SRA. DÍAZ Marissa, ¿cuál fue tu experiencia favorita en México?

MARISSA Bueno, si tuviera que elegir una sola experiencia, tendría que ser el Día de Muertos. Chichén Itzá fue muy emocionante también. No puedo decidirme. ¡La he pasado de película!

8

SR. DÍAZ Mi hermana Ana María me pidió que te diera esto.

MARISSA *No way!*

JUAN CARLOS ¿Qué es?

MARISSA La receta del mole de la tía.

9

FELIPE Nosotros también tenemos algo para ti.

MARISSA ¡Mi diccionario! Lo dejo contigo, Felipe. Tenías razón. No lo necesito.

SR. DÍAZ Si queremos llegar a tiempo al aeropuerto, tenemos que irnos ya.

10

MARU Te veremos en nuestra boda.

MARISSA ¡Sí, seguro!

SR. DÍAZ Bueno, vámonos.

MARISSA (*a todos*) Cuídense. Gracias por todo.

Expresiones útiles

Expressing delight and surprise

¡Qué gusto verlo/la!
How nice to see you! (form.)
¡Qué gusto verte!
How nice to see you! (fam.)
¡No tenía ni idea!
I had no idea!
¡Felicidades!
Congratulations!

Playing a joke on someone

Todos me dijeron que te pidiera una disculpa de su parte.
They all told me to ask you to excuse them / forgive them.
Tu papá me hizo creer que no podría despedirme de ustedes.
Your dad made me think I wouldn't be able to say goodbye to you.

Talking about past and future trips

Si tuviera que elegir una sola experiencia, tendría que ser el Día de Muertos.
If I had to pick just one experience, it would have to be the Day of the Dead.
¡La he pasado de película!
I've had an awesome time!
Ojalá usted y su esposa puedan ir.
I hope you and your wife can come.
Si tú no estás harta de nosotros, nos encantaría que también vinieras.
If you aren't sick of us, we'd love you to come, too.
Si queremos llegar a tiempo al aeropuerto, tenemos que irnos ya.
If we want to get to the airport on time, we should go now.

Additional vocabulary

despedirse
to say goodbye

¿Qué pasó?

1   **¿Cierto o falso?** Decide si lo que se afirma en las oraciones es **cierto** o **falso**. Corrige las oraciones falsas.

	Cierto	Falso
1. Según la reportera, las elecciones son la próxima semana.	○	○
2. Marissa dice que una de sus experiencias favoritas en México fue el Día de Muertos.	○	○
3. La reportera dice que hay una inundación en el centro.	○	○
4. La Sra. Díaz le envía la receta de los tacos a Marissa.	○	○
5. Marissa le deja su diccionario a Jimena.	○	○

2   **Identificar** Identifica quién puede hacer estas afirmaciones.

1. Espero que disfrutes de tu última comida en México.

2. Los voy a extrañar mucho, ¡lo he pasado maravillosamente!

3. El presidente habló sobre los candidatos en estas elecciones.

4. ¿Qué fue lo que más te gustó de México?

5. No faltes a nuestra boda, nos dará mucho gusto verte de nuevo.

MAITE FUENTES

SR. DÍAZ

MARISSA

MARU

SRA. DÍAZ

3   **Preguntas** Contesta las preguntas.

1. ¿Dónde y cuándo se casarán Miguel y Maru?

2. ¿Por qué Marissa no imaginaba que vería a sus amigos en el restaurante?

3. Según lo que dice Maite Fuentes, ¿qué ha ocasionado el incendio en el centro?

4. ¿Por qué el Sr. Díaz le dice a Marissa que tienen que irse ya?

5. ¿Qué dice Marissa sobre la experiencia que vivió en Chichén Itzá?

4   **Las experiencias de Marissa** Trabajen en parejas para representar una conversación en español entre Marissa y un(a) amigo/a con quien se encuentra cuando ella acaba de regresar de México. Hablen de las experiencias buenas y malas que tuvieron durante ese tiempo. Utilicen estas frases y expresiones en la conversación:

▶ ¡Qué gusto volver a verte!
▶ Gusto de verte.
▶ Lo pasé de película/maravillosamente/muy bien.

▶ Me divertí mucho.
▶ Lo mejor fue...
▶ Lo peor fue...

Ortografía
Neologismos y anglicismos

As societies develop and interact, new words are needed to refer to inventions and discoveries, as well as to objects and ideas introduced by other cultures. In Spanish, many new terms have been invented to refer to such developments, and additional words have been "borrowed" from other languages.

bajar un programa *download*	**borrar** *to delete*	**correo basura** *junk mail*
en línea *online*	**enlace** *link*	**herramienta** *tool*
navegador *browser*	**pirata** *hacker*	**sistema operativo** *operating system*

Many Spanish neologisms, or "new words," refer to computers and technology. Due to the newness of these words, more than one term may be considered acceptable.

----

cederrón, CD-ROM	**escáner**	**fax**	**zoom**

In Spanish, many anglicisms, or words borrowed from English, refer to computers and technology. Note that the spelling of these words is often adapted to the sounds of the Spanish language.

----

jazz, yaz	**rap**	**rock**	**walkman**

Music and music technology are another common source of anglicisms.

----

gángster	**hippy, jipi**	**póquer**	**whisky, güisqui**

Other borrowed words refer to people or things that are strongly associated with another culture.

----

chárter	**esnob**	**estrés**	**flirtear**
gol	**hall**	**hobby**	**iceberg**
jersey	**júnior**	**récord**	**yogur**

There are many other sources of borrowed words. Over time, some anglicisms are replaced by new terms in Spanish, while others are accepted as standard usage.

Práctica Completa el diálogo usando las palabras de la lista.

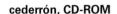

borrar	correo basura	esnob
chárter	en línea	estrés

GUSTAVO Voy a leer el correo electrónico.
REBECA Bah, yo sólo recibo _____. Lo único que hago con la computadora es _____ mensajes.
GUSTAVO Mira, cariño, hay un anuncio en Internet: un viaje barato a Punta del Este. Es un vuelo _____.
REBECA Últimamente tengo tanto _____. Sería buena idea que fuéramos de vacaciones. Pero busca un hotel muy bueno.
GUSTAVO Rebeca, no seas _____, lo importante es ir y disfrutar. Voy a comprar los boletos ahora mismo _____.

Dibujo Describe el dibujo utilizando por lo menos cinco anglicismos.

Protestas sociales

¿Cómo reaccionas ante° una situación injusta? ¿Protestas? Las huelgas y manifestaciones° son expresiones de protesta. Mucha gente asocia las huelgas con "no trabajar", pero no siempre es así. Hay huelgas donde los empleados del gobierno aplican las regulaciones escrupulosamente, demorando° los procesos administrativos; en otras, los trabajadores aumentan la producción. En países como España, las huelgas muchas veces se anuncian con anticipación° y, en los lugares que van a ser afectados, se ponen carteles con información como: "Esta oficina cerrará el día 14 con motivo de la huelga. Disculpen las molestias°".

Las manifestaciones son otra forma de protesta: la gente sale a la calle llevando carteles con frases y eslóganes. Una forma original de manifestación son los "cacerolazos", en los cuales la gente golpea° cacerolas y sartenes°. Los primeros cacerolazos tuvieron lugar en Chile y más tarde pasaron a otros países. Otras veces, el buen humor ayuda a confrontar temas serios y los manifestantes° marchan bailando, cantando eslóganes y tocando silbatos° y tambores°.

Actualmente° se puede protestar sin salir de casa. Lo único que necesitas es tener una computadora con conexión a Internet para poder participar en manifestaciones virtuales. Y no sólo de tu país, sino de todo el mundo.

Los eslóganes

El pueblo unido jamás será vencido°. Es el primer verso° de una canción que popularizó el grupo chileno Quilapayún.

Basta ya°. Se ha usado en el País Vasco en España durante manifestaciones en contra del terrorismo.

Agua para todos. Se ha gritado en manifestaciones contra la privatización del agua en varios países hispanos.

Ni guerra que nos mate°, ni paz que nos oprima°. Surgió° en la **Movilización Nacional de Mujeres contra la Guerra,** en Colombia (2002) para expresar un no rotundo° a la guerra.

Ni un paso° atrás. Ha sido usado en muchos países, como en Argentina por las Madres de la Plaza de Mayo*.

* Las Madres de la Plaza de Mayo es un grupo de mujeres que tiene hijos o familiares que desaparecieron durante la dictadura militar en Argentina (1976–1983).

ante *in the presence of* manifestaciones *demonstrations* demorando *delaying* con anticipación *in advance* Disculpen las molestias. *We apologize for any inconvenience.* golpea *bang* cacerolas y sartenes *pots and pans* manifestantes *demonstrators* silbatos *whistles* tambores *drums* Actualmente *Currently* vencido *defeated* verso *line* Basta ya. *Enough.* mate *kills* oprima *oppresses* Surgió *It arose* rotundo *absolute* paso *step*

1 **¿Cierto o falso?** Indica si lo que dice cada oración es cierto o falso. Corrige la información falsa.

1. En algunas huelgas las personas trabajan más de lo normal.

2. En España, las huelgas se hacen sin notificación previa.

3. En las manifestaciones virtuales se puede protestar sin salir de casa.

4. En algunas manifestaciones la gente canta y baila.

4. "Basta ya" es un eslogan que se ha usado en España en manifestaciones contra el terrorismo.

6. En el año 2002 se llevó a cabo la Movilización Nacional de Mujeres contra la Guerra en Argentina.

7. Los primeros "cacerolazos" se hicieron en Venezuela.

8. "Agua para todos" es un eslogan del grupo Quilapayún.

ASÍ SE DICE

Periodismo y política

la campaña	*campaign*
el encabezado	*headline*
la prensa amarilla	*tabloid press*
el sindicato	*(labor) union*
el suceso, el hecho	**el acontecimiento**

EL MUNDO HISPANO

Hispanos en la historia

- **Sonia Sotomayor** (Nueva York, EE.UU., 1954–) Doctora en Derecho de ascendencia puertorriqueña. Es la primera mujer hispana en ocupar el cargo de Jueza Asociada en la Corte Suprema de los Estados Unidos.

- **Che Guevara** (Rosario, Argentina, 1928–La Higuera, Bolivia, 1967) Ernesto "Che" Guevara es una de las figuras más controversiales del siglo° XX. Médico de profesión, fue uno de los líderes de la revolución cubana y participó en las revoluciones de otros países.

- **Rigoberta Menchú Tum** (Laj Chimel, Guatemala, 1959–) De origen maya, desde niña sufrió la pobreza y la represión, lo que la llevó muy pronto a luchar por los derechos humanos. En 1992 recibió el Premio Nobel de la Paz.

- **José Martí** (La Habana, Cuba, 1853–Dos Ríos, Cuba, 1895) Fue periodista, filósofo, poeta, diplomático e independentista°. Desde su juventud se opuso al régimen colonialista español. Murió luchando por la independencia de Cuba.

siglo *century* independentista *supporter of independence*

PERFIL

Dos líderes en Latinoamérica

En 2006, la chilena **Michelle Bachelet Jeria** y el boliviano **Juan Evo Morales Ayma** fueron proclamados presidentes de sus respectivos países. Para algunos, estos nombramientos fueron una sorpresa.

Michelle Bachelet estudió Medicina y se especializó en pediatría y salud pública. Fue víctima de la represión de Augusto Pinochet, quien gobernó el país de 1973 a 1990, y vivió varios años exiliada. Regresó a Chile y en 2000 fue nombrada Ministra de Salud. En 2002 fue Ministra de Defensa Nacional. Y en 2006 se convirtió en la primera presidenta de Chile, cargo que ocupó hasta 2010. En 2014 asumió nuevamente la presidencia de Chile.

Evo Morales es un indígena del altiplano andino°. Su lengua materna es el aimará. De niño, trabajó como pastor° de llamas. Luego, se trasladó a Cochabamba donde participó en asociaciones campesinas°. Morales reivindicó la forma tradicional de vida y los derechos de los campesinos indígenas. En 2006 ascendió a la presidencia de Bolivia. En 2009, la ONU lo nombró "Héroe Mundial de la Madre Tierra". Fue reelegido en 2009.

altiplano andino *Andean high plateau* pastor *shepherd* campesinas *farmers'*

Conexión Internet

¿Quiénes son otros líderes y pioneros hispanos?	Use the Web to find more cultural information related to this **Cultura** section.

ACTIVIDADES

2 **Comprensión** Contesta las preguntas.

1. ¿Cuáles son los sinónimos de acontecimiento?
2. ¿En qué es pionera Sonia Sotomayor?
3. ¿Qué cargos políticos ocupó Michelle Bachelet antes de ser presidenta?
4. ¿Por qué luchó Evo Morales en varias asociaciones campesinas?

3 **Líderes** ¿Quién es el/la líder de tu comunidad o región que más admiras? Escribe un breve párrafo explicando quién es, qué hace y por qué lo/la admiras.

18.1 **Si clauses**

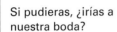 **Si** (*If*) clauses describe a condition or event upon which another condition or event depends. Sentences with **si** clauses consist of a **si** clause and a main (or result) clause.

Si pudieras, ¿irías a nuestra boda?

Sí, si tuviera la oportunidad, iría con mucho gusto.

▶ **Si** clauses can speculate or hypothesize about a current event or condition. They express what *would happen* if an event or condition *were to occur*. This is called a contrary-to-fact situation. In such instances, the verb in the **si** clause is in the past subjunctive while the verb in the main clause is in the conditional.

> Si **cambiaras** de empleo, **serías** más feliz.
> *If you changed jobs, you would be happier.*

> **Iría** de viaje a Suramérica si **tuviera** dinero.
> *I would travel to South America if I had money.*

▶ **Si** clauses can also describe a contrary-to-fact situation in the past. They can express what *would have happened* if an event or condition *had occurred*. In these sentences, the verb in the **si** clause is in the past perfect subjunctive while the verb in the main clause is in the conditional perfect.

> Si **hubiera sido** estrella de cine, **habría sido** rico.
> *If I had been a movie star, I would have been rich.*

> No **habrías tenido** hambre si **hubieras desayunado**.
> *You wouldn't have been hungry if you had eaten breakfast.*

▶ **Si** clauses can also express conditions or events that are possible or likely to occur. In such instances, the **si** clause is in the present indicative while the main clause uses a present, near future, future, or command form.

> Si **puedes** venir, **llámame**.
> *If you can come, call me.*

> Si **puedo** venir, **te llamo**.
> *If I can come, I'll call you.*

> Si **terminas** la tarea, **tendrás** tiempo para mirar la televisión.
> *If you finish your homework, you will have time to watch TV.*

> Si **terminas** la tarea, **vas a tener** tiempo para mirar la televisión.
> *If you finish your homework, you are going to have time to watch TV.*

¡ATENCIÓN!

Remember the difference between **si** (*if*) and **sí** (*yes*).

¡LENGUA VIVA!

Note that in Spanish the conditional is never used immediately following **si**.

▶ When the **si** clause expresses habitual past conditions or events, *not* a contrary-to-fact situation, the imperfect is used in both the **si** clause and the main (or result) clause.

Si Alicia me **invitaba** a una fiesta, yo siempre **iba**.
If (Whenever) Alicia invited me to a party, I would (used to) go.

Mis padres siempre **iban** a la playa si **hacía** buen tiempo.
My parents always went to the beach if the weather was good.

▶ The **si** clause may be the first or second clause in a sentence. Note that a comma is used only when the **si** clause comes first.

Si tuviera tiempo, iría contigo.
If I had time, I would go with you.

Iría contigo **si tuviera tiempo.**
I would go with you if I had time.

Summary of si clause sequences

Condition	Si clause	Main clause
Possible or likely	**Si** + present	Present Near future (**ir a** + infinitive) Future Command
Habitual in the past	**Si** + imperfect	Imperfect
Contrary-to-fact (present)	**Si** + past (imperfect) subjunctive	Conditional
Contrary-to-fact (past)	**Si** + past perfect (pluperfect) subjunctive	Conditional perfect

¡INTÉNTALO! Cambia los tiempos y modos de los verbos que aparecen entre paréntesis para practicar todos los tipos de oraciones con **si** que se muestran en la tabla anterior.

1. Si usted ___*va*___ (ir) a la playa, tenga cuidado con el sol.
2. Si tú _____ (querer), te preparo la merienda.
3. Si _____ (hacer) buen tiempo, voy a ir al parque.
4. Si mis amigos _____ (ir) de viaje, sacaban muchas fotos.
5. Si ella me _____ (llamar), yo la invitaría a la fiesta.
6. Si nosotros _____ (querer) ir al teatro, compraríamos los boletos antes.
7. Si tú _____ (levantarse) temprano, desayunarías antes de ir a clase.
8. Si ellos _____ (tener) tiempo, te llamarían.
9. Si yo _____ (ser) astronauta, habría ido a la Luna.
10. Si él _____ (ganar) un millón de dólares, habría comprado una mansión.
11. Si ustedes me _____ (decir) la verdad, no habríamos tenido este problema.
12. Si ellos _____ (trabajar) más, habrían tenido más éxito.

Práctica

1   **Emparejar** Empareja frases de la columna A con las de la columna B para crear oraciones lógicas.

A

1. Si aquí hubiera terremotos, _____
2. Si me informo bien, _____
3. Si te doy el informe, _____
4. Si la guerra hubiera continuado, _____
5. Si la huelga dura más de un mes, _____

B

a. ¿se lo muestras al director?
b. habrían muerto muchos más.
c. muchos van a pasar hambre.
d. podré explicar el desempleo.
e. no permitiríamos edificios altos.

AYUDA

Remember these forms of **haber**:

(si) hubiera
(if) there were

habría
there would be

2   **Minidiálogos** Completa los minidiálogos entre Teresa y Anita.

TERESA ¿Qué (1)_____ hecho tú si tu papá te (2)_____ regalado un carro?
ANITA Me (3)_____ muerto de la felicidad.

ANITA Si (4)_____ a Paraguay, ¿qué vas a hacer?
TERESA (5)_____ a visitar a mis parientes.

TERESA Si tú y tu familia (6)_____ un millón de dólares, ¿qué comprarían?
ANITA Si nosotros tuviéramos un millón de dólares, (7)_____ tres casas nuevas.

ANITA Si tú (8)_____ tiempo, ¿irías al cine con más frecuencia?
TERESA Sí, yo (9)_____ con más frecuencia si tuviera tiempo.

¡LENGUA VIVA!

Paraguay es conocido como "El Corazón de América" porque está en el centro de Suramérica. Sus lugares más visitados son la capital Asunción, que está situada a orillas (*on the banks*) del río Paraguay y la ciudad de Itauguá, en donde se producen muchos textiles.

3   **Completar** Completa las frases de una manera lógica.

1. Si tuviera un accidente de carro…
2. Me volvería loco/a (*I would go crazy*) si mi familia…
3. Me habría ido al Cuerpo de Paz (*Peace Corps*) si…
4. No volveré a ver las noticias en ese canal si…
5. Habría menos problemas si los medios de comunicación…
6. Si mis padres hubieran insistido en que fuera al ejército…
7. Si me ofrecen un viaje a la Luna…
8. Me habría enojado mucho si…
9. Si hubiera un desastre natural en mi ciudad…
10. Yo habría votado en las elecciones pasadas si…

Comunicación

4

Un robo Escucha la conversación entre Alicia y Fermín. Luego, indica quién diría con más probabilidad cada una de las afirmaciones, según lo que escuchaste.

	Alicia	Fermín
1. Si ocurre algo, yo soy la primera persona en llamar a la policía.	○	○
2. Si hubiéramos hecho las cosas de forma diferente, sería todo mucho mejor.	○	○
3. Si tomamos precauciones, no nos pasará nunca nada.	○	○
4. Si algo tiene que pasar, pasará. No importa lo que hagas para evitarlo.	○	○
5. Hoy tengo que trabajar.	○	○

5

¿Qué harían? En parejas, túrnense para hablar de lo que hacen, harían o habrían hecho en estas circunstancias.

1. si ves a tu novio/a con otro/a en el cine
2. si hubieras ganado un viaje a Uruguay
3. si mañana tuvieras el día libre
4. si te casaras y tuvieras ocho hijos
5. si tuvieras que cuidar a tus padres cuando sean mayores
6. si no tuvieras que preocuparte por el dinero
7. si te acusaran de cometer un crimen
8. si hubieras vivido bajo una dictadura

6

Escribir Piensa en cómo cambiaría tu vida diaria si no existiera Internet. ¿Cómo te informarías de las actualidades del mundo y de las noticias locales? ¿Cómo te llegarían noticias de tus amigos si no existiera el correo electrónico ni las redes sociales en línea (*social networking websites*)? Escribe un mínimo de siete oraciones con **si**.

Síntesis

7

Entrevista Prepara cinco preguntas para hacerle a un(a) candidato/a a la presidencia de tu país. Luego, en parejas, túrnense para hacer el papel de entrevistador(a) y de candidato/a. El/La entrevistador(a) reacciona a cada una de las respuestas del/de la candidato/a.

modelo

Entrevistador(a): ¿Qué haría usted en cuanto a la obesidad infantil?

Candidato/a: Pues, dudo que podamos decirles a los padres cómo alimentar a sus hijos. Creo que ellos deben preocuparse por darles comida saludable.

Entrevistador(a): ¿Entonces usted no haría nada para combatir la obesidad infantil?

Candidato/a: Si yo fuera presidente/a...

18.2 # Summary of the uses of the subjunctive

ANTE TODO Since **Lección 12**, you have been learning about subjunctive verb forms and practicing their uses. The following chart summarizes the subjunctive forms you have studied. The chart on the next page summarizes the uses of the subjunctive you have seen and contrasts them with uses of the indicative and the infinitive. These charts will help you review and synthesize what you have learned about the subjunctive in this book.

Espero que lo hayas pasado bien en México.

Sí, si hubiera podido, me habría quedado más tiempo.

Summary of subjunctive forms

-ar verbs		-er verbs		-ir verbs	
PRESENT SUBJUNCTIVE	PAST SUBJUNCTIVE	PRESENT SUBJUNCTIVE	PAST SUBJUNCTIVE	PRESENT SUBJUNCTIVE	PAST SUBJUNCTIVE
hable	hablara	beba	bebiera	viva	viviera
hables	hablaras	bebas	bebieras	vivas	vivieras
hable	hablara	beba	bebiera	viva	viviera
hablemos	habláramos	bebamos	bebiéramos	vivamos	viviéramos
habléis	hablarais	bebáis	bebierais	viváis	vivierais
hablen	hablaran	beban	bebieran	vivan	vivieran

PRESENT PERFECT SUBJUNCTIVE	PRESENT PERFECT SUBJUNCTIVE	PRESENT PERFECT SUBJUNCTIVE
haya hablado	haya bebido	haya vivido
hayas hablado	hayas bebido	hayas vivido
haya hablado	haya bebido	haya vivido
hayamos hablado	hayamos bebido	hayamos vivido
hayáis hablado	hayáis bebido	hayáis vivido
hayan hablado	hayan bebido	hayan vivido

PAST PERFECT SUBJUNCTIVE	PAST PERFECT SUBJUNCTIVE	PAST PERFECT SUBJUNCTIVE
hubiera hablado	hubiera bebido	hubiera vivido
hubieras hablado	hubieras bebido	hubieras vivido
hubiera hablado	hubiera bebido	hubiera vivido
hubiéramos hablado	hubiéramos bebido	hubiéramos vivido
hubierais hablado	hubierais bebido	hubierais vivido
hubieran hablado	hubieran bebido	hubieran vivido

CONSULTA

To review the subjunctive, refer to these sections:
Present subjunctive, **Estructura 12.3,** pp. 422–424.
Present perfect subjunctive, **Estructura 15.3,** p. 525.
Past subjunctive, **Estructura 16.3,** pp. 558–559.
Past perfect subjunctive, **Estructura 17.3,** p. 595.

The subjunctive is used...

1. After verbs and/or expressions of will and influence, when the subject of the subordinate clause is different from the subject of the main clause

   Los ciudadanos **desean** que el candidato presidencial los **escuche.**

2. After verbs and/or expressions of emotion, when the subject of the subordinate clause is different from the subject of the main clause

   Alejandra **se alegró** mucho de que le **dieran** el trabajo.

3. After verbs and/or expressions of doubt, disbelief, and denial

   Dudo que **vaya** a tener problemas para encontrar su maleta.

4. After the conjunctions **a menos que, antes (de) que, con tal (de) que, en caso (de) que, para que,** and **sin que**

   Cierra las ventanas **antes de que empiece** la tormenta.

5. After **cuando, después (de) que, en cuanto, hasta que,** and **tan pronto como** when they refer to future actions

   Tan pronto como haga la tarea, podrá salir con sus amigos.

6. To refer to an indefinite or nonexistent antecedent mentioned in the main clause

   Busco **un** empleado que **haya estudiado** computación.

7. After **si** to express something impossible, improbable, or contrary to fact

   Si hubieras escuchado el noticiero, te habrías informado sobre el terremoto.

The indicative is used...

1. After verbs and/or expressions of certainty and belief

   Es cierto que Uruguay **tiene** unas playas espectaculares.

2. After the conjunctions **cuando, después (de) que, en cuanto, hasta que,** and **tan pronto como** when they do not refer to future actions

   Hay más violencia **cuando hay** desigualdad social.

3. To refer to a definite or specific antecedent mentioned in the main clause

   Busco a **la** señora que me **informó** del crimen que ocurrió ayer.

4. After **si** to express something possible, probable, or not contrary to fact

   Pronto habrá más igualdad **si luchamos** contra la discriminación.

The infinitive is used...

1. After expressions of will and influence when there is no change of subject

   Martín **desea ir** a Montevideo este año.

2. After expressions of emotion when there is no change of subject

   Me alegro de conocer a tu esposo.

Práctica

1 **Conversación** Completa la conversación con los tiempos verbales adecuados.

EMA Busco al reportero que (1)_____ (publicar) el libro sobre la dictadura de Stroessner.

ROSA Ah, usted busca a Miguel Pérez. Ha salido.

EMA Le había dicho que yo vendría a verlo el martes, pero él me dijo que (2)_____ (venir) hoy.

ROSA No creo que a Miguel se le (3)_____ (olvidar) la cita. Si usted le (4)_____ (pedir) una cita, él me lo habría mencionado.

EMA Pues no, no pedí cita, pero si él me hubiera dicho que era necesario yo lo (5)_____ (hacer).

ROSA Creo que Miguel (6)_____ (ir) a cubrir un incendio hace media hora. No pensaba que nadie (7)_____ (ir) a venir esta tarde. Si quiere, le digo que la (8)_____ (llamar) tan pronto como (9)_____ (llegar). A menos que usted (10)_____ (querer) dejar un recado...

(*Entra Miguel.*)

EMA ¡Miguel! Amor, si hubieras llegado cinco minutos más tarde, no me (11)_____ (encontrar) aquí.

MIGUEL ¡Ema! ¿Qué haces aquí?

EMA Me dijiste que viniera hoy para que (12)_____ (poder) pasar más tiempo juntos.

ROSA (*En voz baja*) ¿Cómo? ¿Serán novios?

NOTA CULTURAL

El general **Alfredo Stroessner** es el dictador que más tiempo ha durado en el poder en un país de Suramérica. Stroessner se hizo presidente de Paraguay en 1954 y el 3 de febrero de 1989 fue derrocado (*overthrown*) en un golpe militar (*coup*). Después de esto, Stroessner se exilió a Brasil donde murió en 2006.

2 **Escribir** Escribe uno o dos párrafos sobre tu participación en las próximas elecciones. Usa por lo menos cuatro de estas frases.

- ▶ Votaré por... con tal de que...
- ▶ Quisiera saber...
- ▶ Si gana mi candidato/a...
- ▶ Espero que la economía...
- ▶ Estoy seguro/a de que...
- ▶ A menos que...

- ▶ Mis padres siempre me dijeron que...
- ▶ Si a la gente realmente le importara la familia...
- ▶ No habría escogido a ese/a candidato/a si...
- ▶ Si le preocuparan más los impuestos...
- ▶ Dudo que el/la otro/a candidato/a...
- ▶ En las próximas elecciones espero que...

3 **Explicar** Escribe una conversación breve sobre cada tema de la lista. Usa por lo menos un verbo en subjuntivo y otro en indicativo o en infinitivo. Sigue el modelo.

unas elecciones	una huelga	una inundación	la prensa
una guerra	un incendio	la libertad	un terremoto

modelo

un tornado

Persona 1: *Temo que este año haya tornados por nuestra zona.*

Persona 2: *No te preocupes. Creo que este año no va a haber muchos tornados.*

AYUDA

Some useful expressions:

Espero que...

Ojalá que...

Es posible que...

Es terrible que...

Es importante que...

Comunicación

4 **Guía turística** Lee esta guía turística de Uruguay. Luego, indica si las conclusiones son **lógicas** o **ilógicas**, según lo que leíste.

¡Conozca Uruguay!

La **Plaza Independencia** en **Montevideo**, con su **Puerta de la Ciudadela**, forma el límite entre la ciudad antigua y la nueva. Si le interesan las compras, desde este lugar puede comenzar su paseo por la **Avenida 18 de Julio**, la principal arteria comercial de la capital.

No deje de ir a **Punta del Este**. Conocerá uno de los lugares turísticos más fascinantes del mundo. No se pierda las maravillosas playas, el **Museo de Arte Americano** y la **Catedral de Maldonado** (1895) con su famoso altar, obra del escultor **Antonio Veiga**.

Sin duda, querrá conocer la famosa ciudad vacacional de **Piriápolis**, con su puerto que atrae cruceros, y disfrutar de sus playas y lindos paseos.

Tampoco se debe perder la **Costa de Oro**, junto al **Río de la Plata**. Para aquéllos interesados en la historia, dos lugares favoritos son la conocida iglesia **Nuestra Señora de Lourdes** y el chalet de **Pablo Neruda**.

	Lógico	Ilógico
1. La Puerta de la Ciudadela está en las afueras de Montevideo.	○	○
2. Si necesitaras comprar regalos, deberías ir a la Avenida 18 de Julio.	○	○
3. Cuando vayas a Piriápolis, lleva un traje de baño.	○	○
4. A Pablo Neruda le habría gustado mucho visitar Uruguay, pero nunca tuvo la oportunidad.	○	○

5 **Preguntas** Contesta las preguntas de tu compañero/a.

1. ¿Te irías a vivir a un lugar donde pudiera ocurrir un desastre natural? ¿Por qué?
2. ¿Te gustaría que tu vida fuera como la de tus padres? ¿Por qué? Y tus hijos, ¿preferirías que tuvieran experiencias diferentes a las tuyas? ¿Cuáles?
3. ¿Te parece importante que elijamos a una mujer como presidenta? ¿Por qué?
4. Si hubiera una guerra y te llamaran para entrar en el ejército, ¿obedecerías? ¿Lo considerarías tu deber? ¿Qué sentirías? ¿Qué pensarías?
5. Si sólo pudieras recibir noticias de un medio de comunicación, ¿cuál escogerías y por qué? Y si pudieras trabajar en un medio de comunicación, ¿escogerías el mismo?

Síntesis

6 **Desastres naturales** Escribe las instrucciones a seguir en caso de que hubiera una emergencia provocada por algún desastre natural. Escribe un mínimo de cinco instrucciones. Utiliza el subjuntivo.

Recapitulación

Completa estas actividades para repasar los conceptos de gramática que aprendiste en esta lección.

1 **Condicionales** Empareja las frases de la columna A con las de la columna B para crear oraciones lógicas. **24 pts.**

A

_____ 1. Todos estaríamos mejor informados

_____ 2. ¿Te sentirás mejor

_____ 3. Si esos locutores no tuvieran tanta experiencia,

_____ 4. ¿Votarías por un candidato como él

_____ 5. Si no te gusta este noticiero,

_____ 6. El candidato Díaz habría ganado las elecciones

_____ 7. Si la tormenta no se va pronto,

_____ 8. Ustedes se pueden ir

B

a. cambia el canal.

b. ya los habrían despedido.

c. si leyéramos el periódico todos los días.

d. la gente no podrá salir a protestar.

e. si no tienen nada más que decir.

f. si te digo que ya terminó la huelga?

g. Leopoldo fue a votar.

h. si supieras que no ha obedecido las leyes?

i. si hubiera hecho más entrevistas para la televisión.

2 **Escoger** Escoge la opción correcta para completar cada oración. **30 pts.**

1. Ojalá que aquí (hubiera/hay) un canal independiente.

2. Susana dudaba que (hubieras estudiado/estudias) medicina.

3. En cuanto (termine/terminé) mis estudios, buscaré trabajo.

4. Miguel me dijo que su familia nunca (veía/viera) los noticieros en la televisión.

5. Para estar bien informados, yo les recomiendo que (leen/lean) el diario *El Sol*.

6. Es terrible que en los últimos meses (haya habido/ha habido) tres desastres naturales.

7. Cuando (termine/terminé) mis estudios, encontré trabajo en un diario local.

8. El presidente no quiso (declarar/que declarara) la guerra.

9. Todos dudaban que la noticia (fuera/era) real.

10. Me sorprende que en el mundo todavía (exista/existe) la censura.

RESUMEN GRAMATICAL

18.1 **Si clauses**   *pp. 622–623*

Summary of **si** clause sequences		
Possible or likely	**Si** + present	+ present + **ir a** + infinitive + future + command
Habitual in the past	**Si** + imperfect	+ imperfect
Contrary-to-fact (present)	**Si** + past subjunctive	+ conditional
Contrary-to-fact (past)	**Si** + past perfect subjunctive	+ conditional perfect

18.2 **Summary of the uses of the subjunctive**

pp. 626–627

Summary of subjunctive forms

▶ **Present:** (-ar) hable, (-er) beba, (-ir) viva

▶ **Past:** (-ar) hablara, (-er) bebiera, (-ir) viviera

▶ **Present perfect: haya** + past participle

▶ **Past perfect: hubiera** + past participle

The subjunctive is used...
1. After verbs and/or expressions of: ▶ Will and influence (when subject changes) ▶ Emotion (when subject changes) ▶ Doubt, disbelief, denial
2. After **a menos que, antes (de) que, con tal (de) que, en caso (de) que, para que, sin que**
3. After **cuando, después (de) que, en cuanto, hasta que, tan pronto como** when they refer to future actions
4. To refer to an indefinite or nonexistent antecedent
5. After **si** to express something impossible, improbable, or contrary to fact

3

Las elecciones Completa el diálogo con la forma correcta del verbo entre paréntesis eligiendo entre el subjuntivo, el indicativo y el infinitivo, según el contexto. **42 pts.**

SERGIO ¿Ya has decidido por cuál candidato vas a votar en las elecciones del sábado?

MARINA No, todavía no. Es posible que no (1) _____ (yo, votar). Para mí es muy difícil (2) _____ (decidir) quién será el mejor representante. Y tú, ¿ya has tomado una decisión?

SERGIO Sí. Mi amigo Julio nos aconsejó que (3) _____ (leer) la entrevista que le hicieron al candidato Rodríguez en el diario *Tribuna*. En cuanto la (4) _____ (yo, leer), decidí votar por él.

MARINA ¿Hablas en serio? Espero que ya lo (5) _____ (tú, pensar) muy bien. El diario *Tribuna* no siempre es objetivo. Dudo que (6) _____ (ser) una fuente fiable *(reliable source)*. No vas a tener una idea clara de las habilidades de cada candidato a menos que (7) _____ (tú, comparar) información de distintas fuentes.

SERGIO Tienes razón, hoy día no hay ningún medio de comunicación que (8) _____ (decir) toda la verdad de forma independiente.

MARINA Tengo una idea. Sugiero que (9) _____ (nosotros, ir) esta noche a mi casa para (10) _____ (ver) juntos el debate de los candidatos por televisión. ¿Qué te parece?

SERGIO Es una buena idea, pero no creo que (11) _____ (yo, tener) tiempo.

MARINA No te preocupes. Voy a grabarlo para que (12) _____ (tú, poder) verlo.

SERGIO Gracias. Lo veré mañana tan pronto como (13) _____ (yo, llegar) a casa.

MARINA Me alegro de que (14) _____ (nosotros, aprender) más sobre los candidatos.

4

Canción Completa estos versos de una canción de Juan Luis Guerra con el pretérito imperfecto de subjuntivo de los verbos en la forma **nosotros/as**. **4 pts.**

❝ Y si aquí,
_____ (luchar) juntos
por la sociedad
y _____ (hablar) menos
resolviendo más. **❞**

Lectura

Antes de leer

Estrategia
Recognizing chronological order

Recognizing the chronological order of events in a narrative is key to understanding the cause-and-effect relationship between them. When you are able to establish the chronological chain of events, you will easily be able to follow the plot. In order to be more aware of the order of events in a narrative, you may find it helpful to prepare a numbered list of the events as you read.

Examinar el texto

Lee el texto usando las estrategias de lectura que has aprendido.

▶ ¿Ves palabras nuevas o cognados? ¿Cuáles son?

▶ ¿Qué te dice el dibujo sobre el contenido?

▶ ¿Tienes algún conocimiento previo° sobre don Quijote?

▶ ¿Cuál es el propósito° del texto?

▶ ¿De qué trata° la lectura?

Ordenar

Lee el texto otra vez para establecer el orden cronológico de los eventos. Luego ordena estos eventos según la historia.

_____ Don Quijote lucha contra los molinos de viento pensando que son gigantes.

_____ Don Quijote y Sancho toman el camino hacia Puerto Lápice.

_____ Don Quijote y Sancho descubren unos molinos de viento en un campo.

_____ El primer molino da un mal golpe a don Quijote, a su lanza y a su caballo.

_____ Don Quijote y Sancho Panza salen de su pueblo en busca de aventuras.

Don Quijote y los molinos de viento

Miguel de Cervantes
Fragmento adaptado de
El ingenioso hidalgo don Quijote de la Mancha

Miguel de Cervantes Saavedra, el escritor más universal de la literatura española, nació en Alcalá de Henares en 1547 y murió en Madrid en 1616, tras° haber vivido una vida llena de momentos difíciles, llegando a estar en la cárcel° más de una vez. Su obra, sin embargo, ha disfrutado a través de los siglos de todo el éxito que se merece. Don Quijote representa no sólo la locura° sino también la búsqueda° del ideal. En esta ocasión presentamos el famoso episodio de los molinos de viento°.

Entonces descubrieron treinta o cuarenta molinos de viento que había en aquel campo°. Cuando don Quijote los vio, dijo a su escudero°:

—La fortuna va guiando nuestras cosas mejor de lo que deseamos; porque allí, amigo Sancho Panza, se ven treinta, o pocos más, enormes gigantes con los que pienso hacer batalla y quitarles a todos las vidas, y comenzaremos a ser ricos; que ésta es buena guerra, y es gran servicio de Dios quitar tan malos seres° de la tierra.

—¿Qué gigantes?

—Aquéllos que ves allí —respondió su amo°— de los brazos largos, que algunos normalmente los tienen de casi dos leguas°.

Después de leer

¿Realidad o fantasía?

Indica si las afirmaciones sobre la lectura pertenecen a la realidad o la fantasía.

1. Don Quijote desea matar° a los enemigos.

2. Su escudero no ve a ningún ser sobrenatural.

3. El caballero ataca a unas criaturas cobardes y viles.

4. Don Quijote no ganó la batalla porque los gigantes fueron transformados en molinos de viento.

5. El sabio Frestón transformó los gigantes en molinos de viento.

conocimiento previo *prior knowledge* propósito *purpose*
¿De qué trata...? *What is... about?* matar *to kill*

—Mire usted —respondió Sancho— que aquéllos que allí están no son gigantes, sino molinos de viento, y lo que parecen brazos son las aspas°, que movidas por el viento, hacen andar la piedra del molino.

—Bien veo —respondió don Quijote— que no estás acostumbrado a las aventuras: ellos son gigantes; y si tienes miedo, quítate de ahí y reza° mientras yo voy a combatir con ellos en fiera° batalla.

Y diciendo esto, dio de espuelas° a su caballo Rocinante, sin oír las voces que su escudero Sancho le daba, diciéndole que, sin duda alguna, eran molinos de viento, y no gigantes, aquéllos que iba a atacar. Pero él iba tan convencido de que eran gigantes, que ni oía las voces de su escudero Sancho, ni se daba cuenta, aunque estaba ya muy cerca, de lo que eran; antes iba diciendo en voz alta:

—No huyáis°, cobardes° y viles criaturas, que sólo os ataca un caballero°.

Se levantó entonces un poco de viento, y las grandes aspas comenzaron a moverse, y cuando don Quijote vio esto, dijo:

—Pues aunque mováis más brazos que los del gigante Briareo, me lo vais a pagar.

Y diciendo esto, y encomendándose de todo corazón° a su señora Dulcinea, pidiéndole que le ayudase en esta difícil situación, bien cubierto de su rodela°, con la lanza en posición de ataque, fue a todo el galope de Rocinante y embistió° el primer molino que estaba delante: y dándole con la lanza en el aspa, el viento la giró con tanta furia, que la rompió en pequeños fragmentos, llevándose con ella al caballo y al caballero, que fue dando vueltas por el campo. Fue rápidamente Sancho Panza a ayudarle, todo lo rápido que podía correr su asno°, y cuando llegó encontró que no se podía mover: tan grande fue el golpe° que se dio con Rocinante.

—¡Por Dios! —dijo Sancho—. ¿No le dije yo que mirase bien lo que hacía, que sólo eran molinos de viento, y la única persona que podía equivocarse era alguien que tuviese otros molinos en la cabeza?

—Calla°, amigo Sancho —respondió don Quijote—, que las cosas de la guerra, más que otras, cambian continuamente; estoy pensando que aquel sabio° Frestón, que me robó el estudio y los libros, ha convertido estos gigantes en molinos por quitarme la gloria de su vencimiento°: tan grande es la enemistad que me tiene; pero al final, sus malas artes no van a poder nada contra la bondad de mi espada°.

—Dios lo haga como pueda —respondió Sancho Panza.

Y ayudándole a levantarse, volvió a subir sobre Rocinante, que medio despaldado estaba°. Y hablando de la pasada aventura, siguieron el camino del Puerto Lápice.

tras *after* **cárcel** *jail* **locura** *insanity* **búsqueda** *search* **molinos de viento** *windmills* **campo** *field* **escudero** *squire* **seres** *beings* **amo** *master* **leguas** *leagues (measure of distance)* **aspas** *sails* **reza** *pray* **fiera** *vicious* **dio de espuelas** *he spurred* **No huyáis** *Do not flee* **cobardes** *cowards* **caballero** *knight* **encomendándose de todo corazón** *entrusting himself with all his heart* **rodela** *round shield* **embistió** *charged* **asno** *donkey* **golpe** *blow (knock into)* **Calla** *Be quiet* **sabio** *magician* **vencimiento** *defeat* **espada** *sword* **que medio despaldado estaba** *whose back was half-broken*

Personajes

1. En este fragmento, se mencionan estos personajes. ¿Quiénes son?

   ▶ don Quijote
   ▶ Rocinante
   ▶ Dulcinea
   ▶ Sancho Panza
   ▶ los gigantes
   ▶ Frestón

2. ¿Qué puedes deducir de los personajes según la información que se da en este episodio?

3. ¿Quiénes son los personajes principales?

4. ¿Cuáles son las diferencias entre don Quijote y Sancho Panza? ¿Qué tienen en común?

¿Un loco o un héroe?

En un párrafo da tu opinión del personaje de don Quijote, basándote en la aventura de los molinos de viento. Ten en cuenta las acciones, los motivos y los sentimientos de don Quijote en su batalla contra los molinos de viento.

Una entrevista

Trabajen en parejas para preparar una entrevista sobre los acontecimientos de este fragmento de la novela de Cervantes. Un(a) estudiante representará el papel del/de la entrevistador(a) y el/la otro/a asumirá el papel de don Quijote o de Sancho Panza, quien comentará el episodio desde su punto de vista.

Escritura

Estrategia

Writing strong introductions and conclusions

Introductions and conclusions serve a similar purpose: both are intended to focus the reader's attention on the topic being covered. The introduction presents a brief preview of the topic. In addition, it informs your reader of the important points that will be covered in the body of your writing. The conclusion reaffirms those points and concisely sums up the information that has been provided. A compelling fact or statistic, a humorous anecdote, or a question directed to the reader are all interesting ways to begin or end your writing.

For example, if you were writing a biographical report on Miguel de Cervantes, you might begin your essay with the fact that his most famous work, *Don Quijote de la Mancha*, is the second most widely published book ever. The rest of your introductory paragraph would outline the areas you would cover in the body of your paper, such as Cervantes' life, his works, and the impact of *Don Quijote* on world literature. In your conclusion, you would sum up the most important information in the report and tie this information together in a way that would make your reader want to learn even more about the topic. You could write, for example: "Cervantes, with his wit and profound understanding of human nature, is without peer in the history of world literature."

Introducciones y conclusiones

Escribe una oración de introducción y otra de conclusión sobre estos temas.

1. el episodio de los molinos de viento de *Don Quijote de la Mancha*
2. la definición de la locura
3. la realidad y la fantasía en la literatura

Tema

Escribir una composición

Si tuvieras la oportunidad, ¿qué harías para mejorar el mundo? Escribe una composición sobre los cambios que harías en el mundo si tuvieras el poder° y los recursos necesarios. Piensa en lo que puedes hacer ahora y en lo que podrás hacer en el futuro. Considera estas preguntas:

▶ ¿Pondrías fin a todas las guerras? ¿Cómo?

▶ ¿Protegerías el medio ambiente? ¿Cómo?

▶ ¿Promoverías° la igualdad y eliminarías el sexismo y el racismo? ¿Cómo?

▶ ¿Eliminarías la corrupción en la política? ¿Cómo?

▶ ¿Eliminarías la escasez de viviendas° y el hambre?

▶ ¿Educarías a los demás sobre el SIDA? ¿Cómo?

▶ ¿Promoverías el fin de la violencia entre seres humanos?

▶ ¿Promoverías tu causa en los medios de comunicación? ¿Cómo?

▶ ¿Te dedicarías a alguna causa específica dentro de tu comunidad? ¿Cuál?

▶ ¿Te dedicarías a solucionar problemas nacionales o internacionales? ¿Cuáles?

poder *power*   Promoverías *Would you promote*   escasez de viviendas *homelessness*

Escuchar

Estrategia

Recognizing genre/
Taking notes as you listen

If you know the genre or type of discourse you are going to encounter, you can use your background knowledge to write down a few notes about what you expect to hear. You can then make additions and changes to your notes as you listen.

 To practice these strategies, you will now listen to a short toothpaste commercial. Before listening to the commercial, write down the information you expect it to contain. Then update your notes as you listen.

Preparación

Basándote en la foto, anticipa lo que vas a escuchar en el siguiente fragmento. Haz una lista y anota los diferentes tipos de información que crees que vas a oír.

Ahora escucha

Revisa la lista que hiciste para **Preparación.** Luego escucha el noticiero presentado por Sonia Hernández. Mientras escuchas, apunta los tipos de información que anticipaste y los que no anticipaste.

> **Tipos de información que anticipaste**

1. _____
2. _____
3. _____

> **Tipos de información que no anticipaste**

1. _____
2. _____
3. _____

Comprensión

Preguntas

1. ¿Dónde está Sonia Hernández?
   _____

2. ¿Quién es Jaime Pantufla?
   _____

3. ¿Dónde hubo una tormenta?
   _____

4. ¿Qué tipo de música toca el grupo Dictadura de Metal?
   _____

5. ¿Qué tipo de artista es Ugo Nespolo?
   _____

6. Además de lo que Sonia menciona, ¿de qué piensas que va a hablar en la próxima sección del programa?
   _____

Ahora tú

Usa la presentación de Sonia Hernández como modelo para escribir un breve noticiero para la comunidad donde vives. Incluye noticias locales, nacionales e internacionales.

En pantalla

Este anuncio corresponde a la campaña para las elecciones de consejeros regionales de Chile para el período 2014 a 2018. Estas elecciones se realizaron° en noviembre de 2013, junto a las elecciones presidenciales y parlamentarias. Por primera vez en la historia de Chile, los ciudadanos pudieron elegir a sus consejeros regionales. Anteriormente, los consejeros eran elegidos por los concejales° de cada región. Los consejeros regionales componen° el Consejo Regional y desempeñan° funciones regionales, como aprobar reglamentos° y planes de desarrollo° urbano y metropolitano.

Vocabulario útil	
avanza	*advances*
consejeros	*ministers*
crecer	*to grow*
voz	*voice*

Preparación

¿Votas? ¿Participas en política? ¿Crees que es necesario votar? ¿Por qué?

Preguntas

Contesta las preguntas.

1. Según la campaña, ¿por qué es tan importante el voto de los ciudadanos?
2. ¿Crees que el voto de un individuo puede mejorar la calidad de vida de sus vecinos? ¿Por qué?
3. ¿A quién pueden elegir los ciudadanos por primera vez en estas elecciones? ¿Qué importancia crees que tiene este cambio?
4. ¿Cuál piensas que es el objetivo de las imágenes que se muestran de trasfondo (*background*)?
5. ¿Crees que esta campaña es efectiva? ¿Por qué?

Campaña electoral

Escribe el guión de una campaña electoral para la televisión. Utiliza el subjuntivo y oraciones con **si**.

> **modelo**
>
> Si quieres que los precios de las viviendas bajen, vota por nuestro partido…

se realizaron *took place* concejales *councillors* componen *make up*
desempeñan *carry out* reglamentos *regulations* desarrollo *development*

Anuncio sobre elecciones chilenas

Tu voto puede mejorar la calidad de vida de tus vecinos.

Tu voto es tu voz.

No dejes que otros decidan por ti.

En los años veinte, menos de 5.000 puertorriqueños vivían en Nueva York. Para el 2010 eran casi 725.000. Además de Nueva York, ciudades como Chicago, Philadelphia, Newark y Providence tienen grandes comunidades puertorriqueñas. Ahora son un poco más de 4.600.000 los que viven en todos los estados, principalmente en el noreste° del país y en el centro de Florida. Los boricuas° en los EE.UU. han creado nuevas manifestaciones de su cultura, como la música salsa en la ciudad de Nueva York y los multitudinarios° desfiles° que se realizan cada año en todo el país, una gran muestra del orgullo° y la identidad de los puertorriqueños.

Vocabulario útil	
la estadidad	*statehood*
la patria	*homeland*
las relaciones exteriores	*foreign policy*
la soberanía	*sovereignty*

Preparación

¿Qué sabes de Puerto Rico? ¿Sabes qué territorios estadounidenses tienen un estatus especial? ¿En qué se diferencian de un estado normal?

¿Cierto o falso?

Indica si las oraciones son **ciertas** o **falsas**.

1. Los puertorriqueños sirven en el ejército de los EE.UU.

2. Puerto Rico es territorio de los EE.UU., pero el congreso estadounidense no tiene autoridad en la isla.

3. En Puerto Rico se usa la misma moneda que en los EE.UU.

4. En la isla se pagan sólo impuestos locales.

5. El comercio de la isla está a cargo del gobernador de Puerto Rico.

6. La mayoría de los puertorriqueños quieren que la isla sea una nación independiente.

noreste *northeast* boricuas *people from Puerto Rico*
multitudinarios *with mass participation* desfiles *parades* orgullo *pride*

Puerto Rico: ¿nación o estado?

Cuando estás aquí, no sabes si estás en un país latinoamericano o si estás en los EE.UU.

... todo lo relacionado a la defensa, las relaciones exteriores [...] está a cargo del gobierno federal de los EE.UU.

—**¿Cuál es su preferencia política?**
—**Yo quiero la estadidad...**

Paraguay

El país en cifras

▶ **Área:** 406.750 km² (157.046 millas²), *el tamaño° de California*
▶ **Población:** 6.703.000
▶ **Capital:** Asunción—2.139.000
▶ **Ciudades principales:** Ciudad del Este, San Lorenzo, Lambaré, Fernando de la Mora
▶ **Moneda:** guaraní
▶ **Idiomas:** español (oficial), guaraní (oficial)

Las tribus indígenas que habitaban la zona antes de la llegada de los españoles hablaban guaraní. Ahora el 90 por ciento de los paraguayos habla esta lengua, que se usa con frecuencia en canciones, poemas, periódicos y libros. Varios institutos y asociaciones, como el Teatro Guaraní, se dedican a preservar la cultura y la lengua guaraníes.

Bandera de Paraguay

Paraguayos célebres

▶ **Agustín Barrios,** guitarrista y compositor (1885–1944)
▶ **Josefina Plá,** escritora y ceramista (1903–1999)
▶ **Augusto Roa Bastos,** escritor (1917–2005)
▶ **Olga Blinder,** pintora (1921–2008)
▶ **Berta Rojas,** guitarrista (1966–)

tamaño *size* multara *fined*

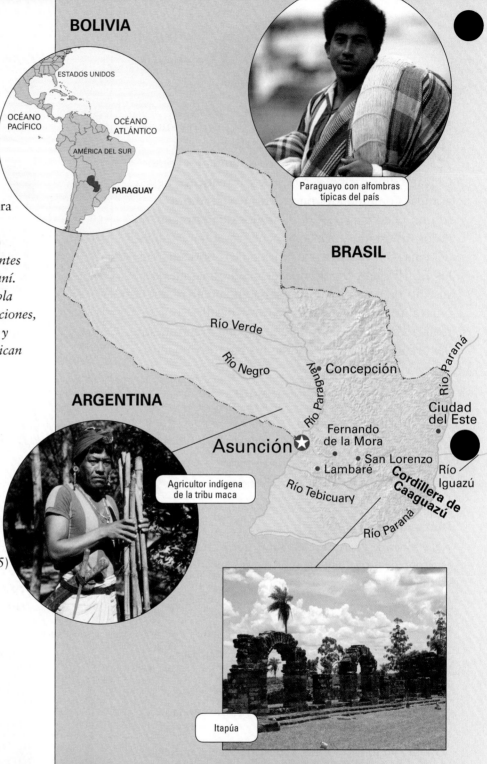

BOLIVIA

ESTADOS UNIDOS

OCÉANO PACÍFICO

OCÉANO ATLÁNTICO

AMÉRICA DEL SUR

PARAGUAY

Paraguayo con alfombras típicas del país

BRASIL

Río Verde

Río Negro

Río Paraguay

Concepción

Río Paraná

Ciudad del Este

ARGENTINA

Asunción

Fernando de la Mora

San Lorenzo

Lambaré

Río Iguazú

Agricultor indígena de la tribu maca

Río Tebicuary

Cordillera de Caaguazú

Río Paraná

Itapúa

¡Increíble pero cierto!

¿Te imaginas qué pasaría si el gobierno multara° a los ciudadanos que no van a votar? En Paraguay es una obligación. Ésta es una ley nacional, que otros países también tienen, para obligar a los ciudadanos a participar en las elecciones. En Paraguay los ciudadanos que no van a votar tienen que pagar una multa al gobierno.

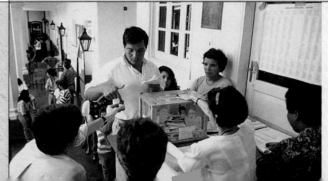

Artesanía • El ñandutí

La artesanía más famosa de Paraguay se llama ñandutí y es un encaje° hecho a mano originario de Itauguá. En guaraní, la palabra ñandutí significa telaraña° y esta pieza recibe ese nombre porque imita el trazado° que crean los arácnidos. Estos encajes suelen ser° blancos, pero también los hay de colores, con formas geométricas o florales.

Ciencias • La represa Itaipú

La represa° Itaipú es una instalación hidroeléctrica que se encuentra en la frontera entre Paraguay y Brasil. Su construcción inició en 1974 y duró 8 años. La cantidad de concreto que se utilizó durante los primeros cinco años de esta obra fue similar a la que se necesita para construir un edificio de 350 pisos. Cien mil trabajadores paraguayos participaron en el proyecto. En 1984 se puso en funcionamiento la Central Hidroeléctrica de Itaipú y gracias a su cercanía con las famosas cataratas del Iguazú, muchos turistas la visitan diariamente.

Naturaleza • Los ríos Paraguay y Paraná

Los ríos Paraguay y Paraná sirven de frontera natural entre Argentina y Paraguay, y son las principales rutas de transporte de este último país. El Paraná tiene unos 3.200 kilómetros navegables, y por esta ruta pasan barcos de más de 5.000 toneladas, los cuales viajan desde el estuario° del Río de la Plata hasta la ciudad de Asunción. El río Paraguay divide el Gran Chaco de la meseta° Paraná, donde vive la mayoría de los paraguayos.

¿Qué aprendiste? Contesta cada pregunta con una oración completa.

1. ¿Quién fue Augusto Roa Bastos?

2. ¿Cómo se llama la moneda de Paraguay?

3. ¿Qué es el ñandutí?

4. ¿De dónde es originario el ñandutí?

5. ¿Qué forma imita el ñandutí?

6. En total, ¿cuántos años tomó la construcción de la represa Itaipú?

7. ¿A cuántos paraguayos dio trabajo la construcción de la represa?

8. ¿Qué países separan los ríos Paraguay y Paraná?

9. ¿Qué distancia se puede navegar por el Paraná?

Conexión Internet Investiga estos temas en Internet.

1. Busca información sobre Alfredo Stroessner, el ex presidente de Paraguay. ¿Por qué se le considera un dictador?

2. Busca información sobre la historia de Paraguay. En tu opinión, ¿cuáles fueron los episodios decisivos en su historia?

encaje *lace* telaraña *spiderweb* trazado *outline; design* suelen ser *are usually* represa *dam* estuario *estuary* meseta *plateau*

Uruguay

El país en cifras

▶ **Área:** 176.220 km² (68.039 millas²),
el tamaño° del estado de Washington

▶ **Población:** 3.332.000

▶ **Capital:** Montevideo—1.672.000

*Casi la mitad° de la población de Uruguay vive
en Montevideo. Situada en la desembocadura° del
famoso Río de la Plata, esta ciudad cosmopolita
e intelectual es también un destino popular para
las vacaciones, debido a sus numerosas playas de
arena° blanca que se extienden hasta la ciudad
de Punta del Este.*

▶ **Ciudades principales:** Salto, Paysandú,
Las Piedras, Rivera

▶ **Moneda:** peso uruguayo

▶ **Idiomas:** español (oficial)

Bandera de Uruguay

Uruguayos célebres

▶ **Horacio Quiroga,** escritor (1878–1937)

▶ **Juana de Ibarbourou,** escritora (1892–1979)

▶ **Mario Benedetti,** escritor (1920–2009)

▶ **Cristina Peri Rossi,** escritora y profesora (1941–)

▶ **Jorge Drexler,** cantante y compositor (1964–)

tamaño *size* mitad *half* desembocadura *mouth* arena *sand*
avestruz *ostrich* no voladora *flightless* medir *measure* cotizado *valued*

Gaucho uruguayo

BRASIL

Río Arapey

Río Uruguay

• Salto

Cuchilla de Haedo

Rivera

• Paysandú

Río Negro

Embalse del
Río Negro

Río Negro

Cuchilla Grande

Laguna Merín

Río Yí

Cuchilla Grande
Inferior

Colonia

Río de la Plata

Las Piedras

☆ Montevideo

• Punta del
Este

ESTADOS UNIDOS

OCÉANO
PACÍFICO

OCÉANO
ATLÁNTICO

AMÉRICA DEL SUR

URUGUAY

Entrada a la Ciudad Vieja,
Colonia del Sacramento

¡Increíble pero cierto!

En Uruguay hay muchos animales curiosos,
entre ellos el ñandú. De la misma familia del
avestruz°, el ñandú es el ave no voladora° más
grande del hemisferio occidental. Puede llegar a
medir° dos metros. Normalmente, va en grupos
de veinte o treinta y vive en el campo. Es muy
cotizado° por su carne, sus plumas y sus huevos.

Costumbres • La carne y el mate

En Uruguay y Argentina, la carne es un elemento esencial de la dieta diaria. Algunos platillos representativos de estas naciones son el asado°, la parrillada° y el chivito°. El mate, una infusión similar al té, también es típico de la región. Esta bebida de origen indígena está muy presente en la vida social y familiar de estos países aunque, curiosamente, no se puede consumir en bares o restaurantes.

Deportes • El fútbol

El fútbol es el deporte nacional de Uruguay. El primer equipo de balompié uruguayo se formó en 1891 y en 1930 el país suramericano fue la sede° de la primera Copa Mundial de esta disciplina. El equipo nacional ha conseguido grandes éxitos a lo largo de los años: dos campeonatos olímpicos, en 1923 y 1928, y dos campeonatos mundiales, en 1930 y 1950. De hecho, Uruguay y Argentina han presentado su candidatura binacional para que la Copa Mundial de Fútbol de 2030 se celebre en sus países.

Costumbres • El Carnaval

El Carnaval de Montevideo es el de mayor duración en el mundo. A lo largo de 40 días, los uruguayos disfrutan de los desfiles° y la música que inundan las calles de su capital. La celebración más conocida es el Desfile de Llamadas, en el que participan bailarines al ritmo del candombe, una danza de tradición africana.

¿Qué aprendiste? Contesta cada pregunta con una oración completa.

1. ¿Qué tienen en común cuatro de los uruguayos célebres mencionados en la página anterior (*previous*)?

2. ¿Cuál es el elemento esencial de la dieta uruguaya?

3. ¿Qué es el ñandú?

4. ¿Qué es el mate?

5. ¿Cuándo se formó el primer equipo uruguayo de fútbol?

6. ¿Cuándo se celebró la primera Copa Mundial de fútbol?

7. ¿Cómo se llama la celebración más conocida del Carnaval de Montevideo?

8. ¿Cuántos días dura el Carnaval de Montevideo?

Edificio del Parlamento
en Montevideo

Conexión Internet Investiga estos temas en Internet.

1. Uruguay es conocido como un país de muchos escritores. Busca información sobre uno de ellos y escribe una biografía.

2. Investiga cuáles son las comidas y bebidas favoritas de los uruguayos. Descríbelas e indica cuáles te gustaría probar y por qué.

asado *barbecued beef* parrillada *barbecue* chivito *goat in Argentina; steak sandwich in Uruguay* sede *site* desfiles *parades*

Los medios de comunicación

el acontecimiento	*event*
las actualidades	*news; current events*
el artículo	*article*
el diario	*newspaper*
el informe	*report*
el/la locutor(a)	*(TV or radio) announcer*
los medios de comunicación	*media; means of communication*
las noticias	*news*
el noticiero	*newscast*
la prensa	*press*
el reportaje	*report*
anunciar	*to announce; to advertise*
comunicarse (con)	*to communicate (with)*
durar	*to last*
informar	*to inform*
ocurrir	*to occur; to happen*
transmitir, emitir	*to broadcast*
(inter)nacional	*(inter)national*
peligroso/a	*dangerous*

Las noticias

el choque	*collision*
el crimen	*crime; murder*
el desastre (natural)	*(natural) disaster*
el desempleo	*unemployment*
la (des)igualdad	*(in)equality*
la discriminación	*discrimination*
el ejército	*army*
la guerra	*war*
la huelga	*strike*
el huracán	*hurricane*
el incendio	*fire*
la inundación	*flood*
la libertad	*liberty; freedom*
la paz	*peace*
el racismo	*racism*
el sexismo	*sexism*
el SIDA	*AIDS*
el/la soldado	*soldier*
el terremoto	*earthquake*
la tormenta	*storm*
el tornado	*tornado*
la violencia	*violence*

La política

el/la candidato/a	*candidate*
el/la ciudadano/a	*citizen*
el deber	*responsibility; obligation*
los derechos	*rights*
la dictadura	*dictatorship*
el discurso	*speech*
las elecciones	*election*
la encuesta	*poll; survey*
el impuesto	*tax*
la política	*politics*
el/la representante	*representative*
declarar	*to declare*
elegir (e:i)	*to elect*
luchar (por/contra)	*to fight; to struggle (for/against)*
obedecer	*to obey*
votar	*to vote*
político/a	*political*

Expresiones útiles	*See page 617.*

Plan de escritura

1 **Ideas y organización**

Begin by organizing your writing materials. If you prefer to write by hand, you may want to have a few spare pens and pencils on hand, as well as an eraser or correction fluid. If you prefer to use a word-processing program, make sure you know how to type Spanish accent marks, the **tilde**, and Spanish punctuation marks. Then make a list of the resources you can consult while writing. Finally, make a list of the basic ideas you want to cover. Beside each idea, jot down a few Spanish words and phrases you may want to use while writing.

2 **Primer borrador**

Write your first draft, using the resources and ideas you gathered in **Ideas y organización.**

3 **Comentario**

Exchange drafts with another student and comment on each other's work, using these questions as a guide. Begin by mentioning what you like about the other student's writing.

a. How can the other student make his or her writing clearer, more logical, or more organized?

b. What suggestions do you have for making the writing more interesting or complete?

c. Do you see any spelling or grammatical errors?

4 **Redacción**

Revise your first draft, keeping in mind the other student's comments. Also, incorporate any new information you may have. Before handing in the final version, review your work using these guidelines:

a. Make sure each verb agrees with its subject. Then check the gender and number of each article, noun, and adjective.

b. Check your spelling and punctuation.

c. Consult your **Anotaciones para mejorar la escritura** (see description below) to avoid repetition of previous errors.

5 **Evaluación y progreso**

Review your instructor's comments and corrections. On a separate sheet of paper, write the heading **Anotaciones para mejorar** (*Notes for improving*) **la escritura** and list your most common errors. Place this list and your corrected document in your writing portfolio (**Carpeta de trabajos**) and consult it from time to time to gauge your progress.

Spanish Terms for Direction Lines and Instructions

Below is a list of useful terms that you might hear your instructor say. It also includes Spanish terms that appear in the direction lines of your textbook.

En las instrucciones — *In direction lines*

Cambia/Cambien...	*Change...*
Ciertas o falsas	*True or false*
Cierto o falso	*True or false*
Completa las oraciones de una manera lógica.	*Complete the sentences logically.*
Con un(a) compañero/a...	*With a partner...*
Contesta las preguntas.	*Answer the questions.*
Corrige las oraciones falsas.	*Correct the false statements.*
Cuenta/Cuenten...	*Tell...*
Di/Digan...	*Say...*
Discute/Discutan...	*Discuss...*
En parejas...	*In pairs...*
Entrevista...	*Interview...*
Escúchala	*Listen to it*
Forma oraciones completas.	*Create/Make complete sentences.*
Háganse preguntas.	*Ask each other questions.*
Haz el papel de...	*Play the role of...*
Haz los cambios necesarios.	*Make the necessary changes.*
Indica/Indiquen si las oraciones...	*Indicate if the sentences...*
Intercambia/Intercambien...	*Exchange...*
Lee/Lean en voz alta.	*Read aloud.*
Pon/Pongan...	*Put...*
... que mejor completa...	*...that best completes...*
Reúnete...	*Get together...*
... se da/dan como ejemplo.	*...is/are given as a model.*
Toma nota...	*Take note...*
Tomen apuntes.	*Take notes.*
Túrnense...	*Take turns...*

Palabras útiles — *Useful words*

la adivinanza	*riddle*
el anuncio	*advertisement/ad*
los apuntes	*notes*
el borrador	*draft*
la canción	*song*
la concordancia	*agreement*
el contenido	*contents*
el cortometraje	*short film*
eficaz	*efficient; effective*
la encuesta	*survey*
el equipo	*team*
el esquema	*outline*
el folleto	*brochure*
las frases	*phrases*
la hoja de actividades	*activity sheet/handout*
la hoja de papel	*piece of paper*
la información errónea	*incorrect information*
el/la lector(a)	*reader*
la lectura	*reading*
las oraciones	*sentences*
la ortografía	*spelling*
el papel	*role*
el párrafo	*paragraph*
el paso	*step*
la(s) persona(s) descrita(s)	*the person (people) described*
la pista	*clue*
por ejemplo	*for example*
el propósito	*purpose*
los recursos	*resources*
el reportaje	*report*
los resultados	*results*
según	*according to*
siguiente	*following*
la sugerencia	*suggestion*
el sustantivo	*noun*
el tema	*topic*
último	*last*
el último recurso	*last resort*

Verbos útiles *Useful verbs*

adivinar	*to guess*
anotar	*to jot down*
añadir	*to add*
apoyar	*to support*
averiguar	*to find out*
cambiar	*to change*
combinar	*to combine*
compartir	*to share*
comprobar (o:ue)	*to check*
contestar	*to answer*
corregir (e:i)	*to correct*
crear	*to create*
devolver (o:ue)	*to return*
doblar	*to fold*
dramatizar	*to act out*
elegir (e:i)	*to choose/select*
emparejar	*to match*
entrevistar	*to interview*
escoger	*to choose*
identificar	*to identify*
incluir	*to include*
informar	*to report*
intentar	*to try*
intercambiar	*to exchange*
investigar	*to research*
marcar	*to mark*
preguntar	*to ask*
recordar (o:ue)	*to remember*
responder	*to answer*
revisar	*to revise*
seguir (e:i)	*to follow*
seleccionar	*to select*
subrayar	*to underline*
traducir	*to translate*
tratar de	*to be about*

Expresiones útiles *Useful expressions*

Ahora mismo.	*Right away.*
¿Cómo no?	*But of course.*
¿Cómo se dice _____ en español?	*How do you say _____ in Spanish?*
¿Cómo se escribe _____?	*How do you spell _____?*
¿Comprende(n)?	*Do you understand?*
Con gusto.	*With pleasure.*
Con permiso.	*Excuse me.*
De acuerdo.	*Okay.*
De nada.	*You're welcome.*
¿De veras?	*Really?*
¿En qué página estamos?	*What page are we on?*
¿En serio?	*Seriously?*
Enseguida.	*Right away.*
hoy día	*nowadays*
Más despacio, por favor.	*Slower, please.*
Muchas gracias.	*Thanks a lot.*
No entiendo.	*I don't understand.*
No hay de qué.	*Don't mention it.*
No importa.	*No problem./It doesn't matter.*
¡No me digas!	*You don't say!*
No sé.	*I don't know.*
¡Ojalá!	*Hopefully!*
Perdone.	*Pardon me.*
Por favor.	*Please.*
Por supuesto.	*Of course.*
¡Qué bien!	*Great!*
¡Qué gracioso!	*How funny!*
¡Qué pena!	*What a shame/pity!*
¿Qué significa _____?	*What does _____ mean?*
Repite, por favor.	*Please repeat.*
Tengo una pregunta.	*I have a question.*
¿Tiene(n) alguna pregunta?	*Do you have any questions?*
Vaya(n) a la página dos.	*Go to page 2.*

Glossary of Grammatical Terms

ADJECTIVE A word that modifies, or describes, a noun or pronoun.

muchos libros	un hombre **rico**
many books	*a rich man*
las mujeres **altas**	
the tall women	

Demonstrative adjective An adjective that specifies which noun a speaker is referring to.

esta fiesta	**ese** chico
this party	*that boy*
aquellas flores	
those flowers	

Possessive adjective An adjective that indicates ownership or possession.

mi mejor vestido	Éste es **mi** hermano.
my best dress	*This is my brother.*

Stressed possessive adjective A possessive adjective that emphasizes the owner or possessor.

Es un libro **mío**.
It's my book./It's a book of mine.

Es amiga **tuya**; yo no la conozco.
She's a friend of yours; I don't know her.

ADVERB A word that modifies, or describes, a verb, adjective, or other adverb.

Pancho escribe **rápidamente**.
Pancho writes quickly.

Este cuadro es **muy** bonito.
This picture is very pretty.

ARTICLE A word that points out a noun in either a specific or a non-specific way.

Definite article An article that points out a noun in a specific way.

el libro	**la** maleta
the book	*the suitcase*
los diccionarios	**las** palabras
the dictionaries	*the words*

Indefinite article An article that points out a noun in a general, non-specific way.

un lápiz	**una** computadora
a pencil	*a computer*
unos pájaros	**unas** escuelas
some birds	*some schools*

CLAUSE A group of words that contains both a conjugated verb and a subject, either expressed or implied.

Main (or Independent) clause A clause that can stand alone as a complete sentence.

Pienso ir a cenar pronto.
I plan to go to dinner soon.

Subordinate (or Dependent) clause A clause that does not express a complete thought and therefore cannot stand alone as a sentence.

Trabajo en la cafetería **porque necesito dinero para la escuela**.
I work in the cafeteria because I need money for school.

COMPARATIVE A construction used with an adjective or adverb to express a comparison between two people, places, or things.

Este programa es **más interesante** que el otro.
This program is more interesting than the other one.

Tomás no es **tan alto como** Alberto.
Tomás is not as tall as Alberto.

CONJUGATION A set of the forms of a verb for a specific tense or mood or the process by which these verb forms are presented.

Preterite conjugation of **cantar**:

cant**é**	cant**amos**
cant**aste**	cant**asteis**
cant**ó**	cant**aron**

CONJUNCTION A word used to connect words, clauses, or phrases.

Susana es de Cuba **y** Pedro es de España.
Susana is from Cuba and Pedro is from Spain.

No quiero estudiar **pero** tengo que hacerlo.
I don't want to study, but I have to.

CONTRACTION The joining of two words into one. The only contractions in Spanish are **al** and **del**.

Mi hermano fue **al** concierto ayer.
*My brother went **to the** concert yesterday.*

Saqué dinero **del** banco.
*I took money **from the** bank.*

DIRECT OBJECT A noun or pronoun that directly receives the action of the verb.

Tomás lee **el libro.**   **La** pagó ayer.
*Tomás reads **the book.***   *She paid **it** yesterday.*

GENDER The grammatical categorizing of certain kinds of words, such as nouns and pronouns, as masculine, feminine, or neuter.

Masculine
articles el, un
pronouns él, lo, mío, éste, ése, aquél
adjective simpático

Feminine
articles la, una
pronouns ella, la, mía, ésta, ésa, aquélla
adjective simpática

IMPERSONAL EXPRESSION A third-person expression with no expressed or specific subject.

Es muy importante.   Llueve mucho.
It's very important.   *It's raining hard.*

Aquí se habla español.
Spanish is spoken here.

INDIRECT OBJECT A noun or pronoun that receives the action of the verb indirectly; the object, often a living being, to or for whom an action is performed.

Eduardo **le** dio un libro **a Linda.**
*Eduardo gave a book **to Linda.***

La profesora **me** puso una C en el examen.
*The professor gave **me** a C on the test.*

INFINITIVE The basic form of a verb. Infinitives in Spanish end in -ar, -er, or -ir.

hablar   correr   abrir
to speak   *to run*   *to open*

INTERROGATIVE An adjective, adverb, or pronoun used to ask a question.

¿**Quién** habla?   ¿**Cuántos** compraste?
***Who** is speaking?*   ***How many** did you buy?*

¿**Qué** piensas hacer hoy?
***What** do you plan to do today?*

INVERSION Changing the word order of a sentence, often to form a question.

Statement: Elena pagó la cuenta del restaurante.

Inversion: ¿Pagó Elena la cuenta del restaurante?

MOOD A grammatical distinction of verbs that indicates whether the verb is intended to make a statement or command or to express a doubt, emotion, or condition contrary to fact.

Imperative mood Verb forms used to make commands.

Di la verdad.   Caminen ustedes conmigo.
Tell the truth.   *Walk with me.*

¡**Comamos** ahora!
Let's eat now!

Indicative mood Verb forms used to state facts, actions, and states considered to be real.

Sé que **tienes** el dinero.
*I know that **you have** the money.*

Subjunctive mood Verb forms used principally in subordinate (dependent) clauses to express wishes, desires, emotions, doubts, and certain conditions, such as contrary-to-fact situations.

Prefieren que **hables** en español.
*They prefer that **you speak** in Spanish.*

Dudo que Luis **tenga** el dinero necesario.
*I doubt that Luis **has** the necessary money.*

NOUN A word that identifies people, animals, places, things, and ideas.

hombre	gato
man	*cat*
México	casa
Mexico	*house*
libertad	libro
freedom	*book*

NUMBER A grammatical term that refers to singular or plural. Nouns in Spanish and English have number. Other parts of a sentence, such as adjectives, articles, and verbs, can also have number.

Singular	Plural
una cosa	**unas** cosas
a thing	*some things*
el profesor	**los** profesores
the professor	*the professors*

NUMBERS Words that represent amounts.

Cardinal numbers Words that show specific amounts.

cinco minutos
five minutes

el año **dos mil veintitrés**
the year 2023

Ordinal numbers Words that indicate the order of a noun in a series.

el **cuarto** jugador	la **décima** hora
the fourth player	*the tenth hour*

PAST PARTICIPLE A past form of the verb used in compound tenses. The past participle may also be used as an adjective, but it must then agree in number and gender with the word it modifies.

Han **buscado** por todas partes.
They have searched everywhere.

Yo no había **estudiado** para el examen.
I hadn't studied for the exam.

Hay una **ventana abierta** en la sala.
There is an open window in the living room.

PERSON The form of the verb or pronoun that indicates the speaker, the one spoken to, or the one spoken about. In Spanish, as in English, there are three persons: first, second, and third.

Person	Singular	Plural
1st	**yo** *I*	**nosotros/as** *we*
2nd	**tú, Ud.** *you*	**vosotros/as, Uds.** *you*
3rd	**él, ella** *he, she*	**ellos, ellas** *they*

PREPOSITION A word or words that describe(s) the relationship, most often in time or space, between two other words.

Anita es **de** California.
Anita is from California.

La chaqueta está **en** el carro.
The jacket is in the car.

Marta se peinó **antes de** salir.
Marta combed her hair before going out.

PRESENT PARTICIPLE In English, a verb form that ends in *-ing*. In Spanish, the present participle ends in **-ndo**, and is often used with **estar** to form a progressive tense.

Mi hermana está **hablando** por teléfono ahora mismo.
My sister is talking on the phone right now.

PRONOUN A word that takes the place of a noun or nouns.

Demonstrative pronoun A pronoun that takes the place of a specific noun.

Quiero **ésta**.
I want this one.

¿Vas a comprar **ése**?
Are you going to buy that one?

Juan prefirió **aquéllos**.
Juan preferred those (over there).

Object pronoun A pronoun that functions as a direct or indirect object of the verb.

Te digo la verdad.
I'm telling you the truth.

Me lo trajo Juan.
Juan brought it to me.

Reflexive pronoun A pronoun that indicates that the action of a verb is performed by the subject on itself. These pronouns are often expressed in English with *-self: myself, yourself,* etc.

Yo **me** bañé antes de salir.
I bathed (myself) before going out.

Elena **se acostó** a las once y media.
Elena went to bed at eleven-thirty.

Relative pronoun A pronoun that connects a subordinate clause to a main clause.

El chico **que** nos escribió viene de visita mañana.
*The boy **who** wrote us is coming to visit tomorrow.*

Ya sé **lo que** tenemos que hacer.
*I already know **what** we have to do.*

Subject pronoun A pronoun that replaces the name or title of a person or thing, and acts as the subject of a verb.

Tú debes estudiar más.
***You** should study more.*

Él llegó primero.
***He** arrived first.*

SUBJECT A noun or pronoun that performs the action of a verb and is often implied by the verb.

María va al supermercado.
***María** goes to the supermarket.*

(Ellos) Trabajan mucho.
***They** work hard.*

Esos **libros** son muy caros.
*Those **books** are very expensive.*

SUPERLATIVE A word or construction used with an adjective or adverb to express the highest or lowest degree of a specific quality among three or more people, places, or things.

De todas mis clases, ésta es la **más interesante**.
*Of all my classes, this is the **most interesting**.*

Raúl es el **menos simpático** de los chicos.
*Raúl is the **least likeable** of the boys.*

TENSE A set of verb forms that indicates the time of an action or state: past, present, or future.

Compound tense A two-word tense made up of an auxiliary verb and a present or past participle. In Spanish, **estar** and **haber** are auxiliary verbs.

En este momento, **estoy estudiando**.
*At this time, **I am studying**.*

El paquete no **ha llegado** todavía.
*The package **has** not **arrived** yet.*

Simple tense A tense expressed by a single verb form.

María **estaba** enferma anoche.
*María **was** sick last night.*

Juana **hablará** con su mamá mañana.
*Juana **will speak** with her mom tomorrow.*

VERB A word that expresses actions or states of being.

Auxiliary verb A verb used with a present or past participle to form a compound tense. **Haber** is the most commonly used auxiliary verb in Spanish.

Los chicos **han** visto los elefantes.
*The children **have** seen the elephants.*

Espero que **hayas** comido.
*I hope you **have** eaten.*

Reflexive verb A verb that describes an action performed by the subject on itself and is always used with a reflexive pronoun.

Me compré un carro nuevo.
*I **bought myself** a new car.*

Pedro y Adela **se levantan** muy temprano.
*Pedro and Adela **get (themselves) up** very early.*

Spelling change verb A verb that undergoes a predictable change in spelling, in order to reflect its actual pronunciation in the various conjugations.

practicar	c→qu	practico	practiqué
dirigir	g→j	dirigí	dirijo
almorzar	z→c	almorzó	almorcé

Stem-changing verb A verb whose stem vowel undergoes one or more predictable changes in the various conjugations.

entender (e:ie)	entiendo
pedir (e:i)	piden
dormir (o:ue, u)	duermo, durmieron

Verb Conjugation Tables

The verb lists

The list of verbs below, and the model-verb tables that start on page A-11 show you how to conjugate the verbs taught in **PORTALES**. Each verb in the list is followed by a model verb conjugated according to the same pattern. The number in parentheses indicates where in the verb tables you can find the conjugated forms of the model verb. If you want to find out how to conjugate **divertirse**, for example, look up number 33, **sentir**, the model for verbs that follow the e:ie stem-change pattern.

How to use the verb tables

In the tables you will find the infinitive, present and past participles, and all the simple forms of each model verb. The formation of the compound tenses of any verb can be inferred from the table of compound tenses, pages A-11–12, either by combining the past participle of the verb with a conjugated form of **haber** or by combining the present participle with a conjugated form of **estar.**

---

abrazar (z:c) like cruzar (37)
abrir like vivir (3) *except* past participle is **abierto**
aburrir(se) like vivir (3)
acabar like hablar (1)
acampar like hablar (1)
acompañar like hablar (1)
aconsejar like hablar (1)
acordarse (o:ue) like contar (24)
acostarse (o:ue) like contar (24)
adelgazar (z:c) like cruzar (37)
afeitarse like hablar (1)
ahorrar like hablar (1)
alegrarse like hablar (1)
aliviar like hablar (1)
almorzar (o:ue) like contar (24) *except* (z:c)
alquilar like hablar (1)
andar like hablar (1) *except* preterite stem is anduv-
anunciar like hablar (1)
apagar (g:gu) like llegar (41)
aplaudir like vivir (3)
apreciar like hablar (1)
aprender like comer (2)
apurarse like hablar (1)
arrancar (c:qu) like tocar (44)
arreglar like hablar (1)

asistir like vivir (3)
aumentar like hablar (1)
ayudar(se) like hablar (1)
bailar like hablar (1)
bajar(se) like hablar (1)
bañarse like hablar (1)
barrer like comer (2)
beber like comer (2)
besar(se) like hablar (1)
borrar like hablar (1)
brindar like hablar (1)
bucear like hablar (1)
buscar (c:qu) like tocar (44)
caber (4)
caer(se) (5)
calentarse (e:ie) like pensar (30)
calzar (z:c) like cruzar (37)
cambiar like hablar (1)
caminar like hablar (1)
cantar like hablar (1)
casarse like hablar (1)
cazar (z:c) like cruzar (37)
celebrar like hablar (1)
cenar like hablar (1)
cepillarse like hablar (1)
cerrar (e:ie) like pensar (30)
chatear like hablar (1)
cobrar like hablar (1)
cocinar like hablar (1)
comenzar (e:ie) (z:c) like empezar (26)
comer (2)

compartir like vivir (3)
comprar like hablar (1)
comprender like comer (2)
comprometerse like comer (2)
comunicarse (c:qu) like tocar (44)
conducir (c:zc) (6)
confirmar like hablar (1)
conocer (c:zc) (35)
conseguir (e:i) (g:gu) like seguir (32)
conservar like hablar (1)
consumir like vivir (3)
contaminar like hablar (1)
contar (o:ue) (24)
contestar like hablar (1)
contratar like hablar (1)
controlar like hablar (1)
conversar like hablar (1)
correr like comer (2)
costar (o:ue) like contar (24)
creer (y) (36)
cruzar (z:c) (37)
cuidar like hablar (1)
dañar like hablar (1)
dar (7)
deber like comer (2)
decidir like vivir (3)
decir (e:i) (8)
declarar like hablar (1)
dejar like hablar (1)

depositar like hablar (1)
desarrollar like hablar (1)
desayunar like hablar (1)
descansar like hablar (1)
descargar like llegar (41)
describir like vivir (3) *except* past participle is descrito
descubrir like vivir (3) *except* past participle is descubierto
desear like hablar (1)
despedir(se) (e:i) like pedir (29)
despertarse (e:ie) like pensar (30)
destruir (y) (38)
dibujar like hablar (1)
dirigir (g:j) like vivir (3) *except* (g:j)
disfrutar like hablar (1)
divertirse (e:ie) like sentir (33)
divorciarse like hablar (1)
doblar like hablar (1)
doler (o:ue) like volver (34) *except* past participle is regular
dormir(se) (o:ue) (25)
ducharse like hablar (1)
dudar like hablar (1)
durar like hablar (1)
echar like hablar (1)
elegir (e:i) like pedir (29) *except* (g:j)

emitir like vivir (3)

empezar (e:ie) (z:c) (26)

enamorarse like hablar (1)

encantar like hablar (1)

encontrar(se) (o:ue) like contar (24)

enfermarse like hablar (1)

engordar like hablar (1)

enojarse like hablar (1)

enseñar like hablar (1)

ensuciar like hablar (1)

entender (e:ie) (27)

entrenarse like hablar (1)

entrevistar like hablar (1)

enviar (envío) (39)

escalar like hablar (1)

escanear like hablar (1)

escoger (g:j) like proteger (43)

escribir like vivir (3) *except* past participle is **escrito**

escuchar like hablar (1)

esculpir like vivir (3)

esperar like hablar (1)

esquiar (esquío) like enviar (39)

establecer (c:zc) like conocer (35)

estacionar like hablar (1)

estar (9)

estornudar like hablar (1)

estudiar like hablar (1)

evitar like hablar (1)

explicar (c:qu) like tocar (44)

faltar like hablar (1)

fascinar like hablar (1)

firmar like hablar (1)

fumar like hablar (1)

funcionar like hablar (1)

ganar like hablar (1)

gastar like hablar (1)

grabar like hablar (1)

graduarse (gradúo) (40)

guardar like hablar (1)

gustar like hablar (1)

haber (hay) (10)

hablar (1)

hacer (11)

importar like hablar (1)

imprimir like vivir (3)

indicar (c:qu) like tocar (44)

informar like hablar (1)

insistir like vivir (3)

interesar like hablar (1)

invertir (e:ie) like sentir (33)

invitar like hablar (1)

ir(se) (12)

jubilarse like hablar (1)

jugar (u:ue) (g:gu) (28)

lastimarse like hablar (1)

lavar(se) like hablar (1)

leer (y) like creer (36)

levantar(se) like hablar (1)

limpiar like hablar (1)

llamar(se) like hablar (1)

llegar (g:gu) (41)

llenar like hablar (1)

llevar(se) like hablar (1)

llover (o:ue) like volver (34) *except* past participle is regular

luchar like hablar (1)

mandar like hablar (1)

manejar like hablar (1)

mantener(se) (e:ie) like tener (20)

maquillarse like hablar (1)

mejorar like hablar (1)

merendar (e:ie) like pensar (30)

mirar like hablar (1)

molestar like hablar (1)

montar like hablar (1)

morir (o:ue) like dormir (25) *except* past participle is **muerto**

mostrar (o:ue) like contar (24)

mudarse like hablar (1)

nacer (c:zc) like conocer (35)

nadar like hablar (1)

navegar (g:gu) like llegar (41)

necesitar like hablar (1)

negar (e:ie) like pensar (30) *except* (g:gu)

nevar (e:ie) like pensar (30)

obedecer (c:zc) like conocer (35)

obtener (e:ie) like tener (20)

ocurrir like vivir (3)

odiar like hablar (1)

ofrecer (c:zc) like conocer (35)

oír (13)

olvidar like hablar (1)

pagar (g:gu) like llegar (41)

parar like hablar (1)

parecer (c:zc) like conocer (35)

pasar like hablar (1)

pasear like hablar (1)

patinar like hablar (1)

pedir (e:i) (29)

peinarse like hablar (1)

pensar (e:ie) (30)

perder (e:ie) like entender (27)

pescar (c:qu) like tocar (44)

pintar like hablar (1)

planchar like hablar (1)

poder (o:ue) (14)

poner(se) (15)

practicar (c:qu) like tocar (44)

preferir (e:ie) like sentir (33)

preguntar like hablar (1)

prender like comer (2)

preocuparse like hablar (1)

preparar like hablar (1)

presentar like hablar (1)

prestar like hablar (1)

probar(se) (o:ue) like contar (24)

prohibir (prohíbo) (42)

proteger (g:j) (43)

publicar (c:qu) like tocar (44)

quedar(se) like hablar (1)

querer (e:ie) (16)

quitar(se) like hablar (1)

recetar like hablar (1)

recibir like vivir (3)

reciclar like hablar (1)

recoger (g:j) like proteger (43)

recomendar (e:ie) like pensar (30)

recordar (o:ue) like contar (24)

reducir (c:zc) like conducir (6)

regalar like hablar (1)

regatear like hablar (1)

regresar like hablar (1)

reír(se) (e:i) (31)

relajarse like hablar (1)

renunciar like hablar (1)

repetir (e:i) like pedir (29)

resolver (o:ue) like volver (34)

respirar like hablar (1)

revisar like hablar (1)

rogar (o:ue) like contar (24) *except* (g:gu)

romper(se) like comer (2) *except* past participle is **roto**

saber (17)

sacar (c:qu) like tocar (44)

sacudir like vivir (3)

salir (18)

saludar(se) like hablar (1)

secar(se) (c:qu) like tocar (44)

seguir (e:i) (32)

sentarse (e:ie) like pensar (30)

sentir(se) (e:ie) (33)

separarse like hablar (1)

ser (19)

servir (e:i) like pedir (29)

solicitar like hablar (1)

sonar (o:ue) like contar (24)

sonreír (e:i) like reír(se) (31)

sorprender like comer (2)

subir like vivir (3)

sudar like hablar (1)

sufrir like vivir (3)

sugerir (e:ie) like sentir (33)

suponer like poner (15)

temer like comer (2)

tener (e:ie) (20)

terminar like hablar (1)

tocar (c:qu) (44)

tomar like hablar (1)

torcerse (o:ue) like volver (34) *except* (c:z) and past participle is regular; e.g., yo tuerzo

toser like comer (2)

trabajar like hablar (1)

traducir (c:zc) like conducir (6)

traer (21)

transmitir like vivir (3)

tratar like hablar (1)

usar like hablar (1)

vender like comer (2)

venir (e:ie) (22)

ver (23)

vestirse (e:i) like pedir (29)

viajar like hablar (1)

visitar like hablar (1)

vivir (3)

volver (o:ue) (34)

votar like hablar (1)

Regular verbs: simple tenses

Infinitive	INDICATIVE Present	Imperfect	Preterite	Future	Conditional	SUBJUNCTIVE Present	Past	IMPERATIVE
1 hablar Participles: hablando, hablado	hablo	hablaba	hablé	hablaré	hablaría	hable	hablara	
	hablas	hablabas	hablaste	hablarás	hablarías	hables	hablaras	habla tú (no hables)
	habla	hablaba	habló	hablará	hablaría	hable	hablara	hable Ud.
	hablamos	hablábamos	hablamos	hablaremos	hablaríamos	hablemos	habláramos	hablemos
	habláis	hablabais	hablasteis	hablaréis	hablaríais	habléis	hablarais	hablad (no habléis)
	hablan	hablaban	hablaron	hablarán	hablarían	hablen	hablaran	hablen Uds.
2 comer Participles: comiendo, comido	como	comía	comí	comeré	comería	coma	comiera	
	comes	comías	comiste	comerás	comerías	comas	comieras	come tú (no comas)
	come	comía	comió	comerá	comería	coma	comiera	coma Ud.
	comemos	comíamos	comimos	comeremos	comeríamos	comamos	comiéramos	comamos
	coméis	comíais	comisteis	comeréis	comeríais	comáis	comierais	comed (no comáis)
	comen	comían	comieron	comerán	comerían	coman	comieran	coman Uds.
3 vivir Participles: viviendo, vivido	vivo	vivía	viví	viviré	viviría	viva	viviera	
	vives	vivías	viviste	vivirás	vivirías	vivas	vivieras	vive tú (no vivas)
	vive	vivía	vivió	vivirá	viviría	viva	viviera	viva Ud.
	vivimos	vivíamos	vivimos	viviremos	viviríamos	vivamos	viviéramos	vivamos
	vivís	vivíais	vivisteis	viviréis	viviríais	viváis	vivierais	vivid (no viváis)
	viven	vivían	vivieron	vivirán	vivirían	vivan	vivieran	vivan Uds.

All verbs: compound tenses

PERFECT TENSES

INDICATIVE

Present Perfect		Past Perfect		Future Perfect		Conditional Perfect	
he	hablado	había	hablado	habré	hablado	habría	hablado
has	comido	habías	comido	habrás	comido	habrías	comido
ha	vivido	había	vivido	habrá	vivido	habría	vivido
hemos		habíamos		habremos		habríamos	
habéis		habíais		habréis		habríais	
han		habían		habrán		habrían	

SUBJUNCTIVE

Present Perfect		Past Perfect	
haya	hablado	hubiera	hablado
hayas	comido	hubieras	comido
haya	vivido	hubiera	vivido
hayamos		hubiéramos	
hayáis		hubierais	
hayan		hubieran	

PROGRESSIVE TENSES

INDICATIVE

Present Progressive	Past Progressive		Future Progressive		Conditional Progressive	
estoy	estaba		estaré		estaría	
estás	estabas	hablando	estarás	hablando	estarías	hablando
está	estaba	comiendo	estará	comiendo	estaría	comiendo
estamos	estábamos	viviendo	estaremos	viviendo	estaríamos	viviendo
estáis	estabais		estaréis		estaríais	
están	estaban		estarán		estarían	

SUBJUNCTIVE

Present Progressive		Past Progressive	
esté		estuviera	
estés	hablando	estuvieras	hablando
esté	comiendo	estuviera	comiendo
estemos	viviendo	estuviéramos	viviendo
estéis		estuvierais	
estén		estuvieran	

Irregular verbs

Infinitive	INDICATIVE					SUBJUNCTIVE		IMPERATIVE
	Present	Imperfect	Preterite	Future	Conditional	Present	Past	
4 caber	**quepo**	cabía	**cupe**	**cabré**	**cabría**	**quepa**	**cupiera**	
	cabes	cabías	**cupiste**	**cabrás**	**cabrías**	**quepas**	**cupieras**	cabe tú (no **quepas**)
	cabe	cabía	**cupo**	**cabrá**	**cabría**	**quepa**	**cupiera**	**quepa** Ud.
Participles:	cabemos	cabíamos	**cupimos**	**cabremos**	**cabríamos**	**quepamos**	**cupiéramos**	**quepamos**
cabiendo	cabéis	cabíais	**cupisteis**	**cabréis**	**cabríais**	**quepáis**	**cupierais**	cabed (no **quepáis**)
cabido	caben	cabían	**cupieron**	**cabrán**	**cabrían**	**quepan**	**cupieran**	**quepan** Uds.
5 caer(se)	**caigo**	caía	caí	caeré	caería	**caiga**	**cayera**	
	caes	caías	**caíste**	caerás	caerías	**caigas**	**cayeras**	cae tú (no **caigas**)
	cae	caía	**cayó**	caerá	caería	**caiga**	**cayera**	**caiga** Ud.
Participles:	caemos	caíamos	**caímos**	caeremos	caeríamos	**caigamos**	**cayéramos**	**caigamos**
cayendo	caéis	caíais	**caísteis**	caeréis	caeríais	**caigáis**	**cayerais**	caed (no **caigáis**)
caído	caen	caían	**cayeron**	caerán	caerían	**caigan**	**cayeran**	**caigan** Uds.
6 conducir	**conduzco**	conducía	**conduje**	conduciré	conduciría	**conduzca**	**condujera**	
(c:zc)	conduces	conducías	**condujiste**	conducirás	conducirías	**conduzcas**	**condujeras**	conduce tú (no **conduzcas**)
	conduce	conducía	**condujo**	conducirá	conduciría	**conduzca**	**condujera**	**conduzca** Ud.
Participles:	conducimos	conducíamos	**condujimos**	conduciremos	conduciríamos	**conduzcamos**	**condujéramos**	**conduzcamos**
conduciendo	conducís	conducíais	**condujisteis**	conduciréis	conduciríais	**conduzcáis**	**condujerais**	conducid (no **conduzcáis**)
conducido	conducen	conducían	**condujeron**	conducirán	conducirían	**conduzcan**	**condujeran**	**conduzcan** Uds.

7. dar — Participles: dando, dado

	INDICATIVE					SUBJUNCTIVE		IMPERATIVE
Infinitive	Present	Imperfect	Preterite	Future	Conditional	Present	Past	
dar	doy	daba	di	daré	daría	dé	diera	
	das	dabas	diste	darás	darías	des	dieras	da tú (no des)
	da	daba	dio	dará	daría	dé	diera	dé Ud.
	damos	dábamos	dimos	daremos	daríamos	demos	diéramos	demos
	dais	dabais	disteis	daréis	daríais	deis	dierais	dad (no deis)
	dan	daban	dieron	darán	darían	den	dieran	den Uds.

8. decir (e:i) — Participles: diciendo, dicho

	Present	Imperfect	Preterite	Future	Conditional	Present	Past	IMPERATIVE
decir	digo	decía	dije	diré	diría	diga	dijera	
	dices	decías	dijiste	dirás	dirías	digas	dijeras	di tú (no digas)
	dice	decía	dijo	dirá	diría	diga	dijera	diga Ud.
	decimos	decíamos	dijimos	diremos	diríamos	digamos	dijéramos	digamos
	decís	decíais	dijisteis	diréis	diríais	digáis	dijerais	decid (no digáis)
	dicen	decían	dijeron	dirán	dirían	digan	dijeran	digan Uds.

9. estar — Participles: estando, estado

	Present	Imperfect	Preterite	Future	Conditional	Present	Past	IMPERATIVE
estar	estoy	estaba	estuve	estaré	estaría	esté	estuviera	
	estás	estabas	estuviste	estarás	estarías	estés	estuvieras	está tú (no estés)
	está	estaba	estuvo	estará	estaría	esté	estuviera	esté Ud.
	estamos	estábamos	estuvimos	estaremos	estaríamos	estemos	estuviéramos	estemos
	estáis	estabais	estuvisteis	estaréis	estaríais	estéis	estuvierais	estad (no estéis)
	están	estaban	estuvieron	estarán	estarían	estén	estuvieran	estén Uds.

10. haber — Participles: habiendo, habido

	Present	Imperfect	Preterite	Future	Conditional	Present	Past	IMPERATIVE
haber	he	había	hube	habré	habría	haya	hubiera	
	has	habías	hubiste	habrás	habrías	hayas	hubieras	
	ha	había	hubo	habrá	habría	haya	hubiera	
	hemos	habíamos	hubimos	habremos	habríamos	hayamos	hubiéramos	
	habéis	habíais	hubisteis	habréis	habríais	hayáis	hubierais	
	han	habían	hubieron	habrán	habrían	hayan	hubieran	

11. hacer — Participles: haciendo, hecho

	Present	Imperfect	Preterite	Future	Conditional	Present	Past	IMPERATIVE
hacer	hago	hacía	hice	haré	haría	haga	hiciera	
	haces	hacías	hiciste	harás	harías	hagas	hicieras	haz tú (no hagas)
	hace	hacía	hizo	hará	haría	haga	hiciera	haga Ud.
	hacemos	hacíamos	hicimos	haremos	haríamos	hagamos	hiciéramos	hagamos
	hacéis	hacíais	hicisteis	haréis	haríais	hagáis	hicierais	haced (no hagáis)
	hacen	hacían	hicieron	harán	harían	hagan	hicieran	hagan Uds.

12. ir — Participles: yendo, ido

	Present	Imperfect	Preterite	Future	Conditional	Present	Past	IMPERATIVE
ir	voy	iba	fui	iré	iría	vaya	fuera	
	vas	ibas	fuiste	irás	irías	vayas	fueras	ve tú (no vayas)
	va	iba	fue	irá	iría	vaya	fuera	vaya Ud.
	vamos	íbamos	fuimos	iremos	iríamos	vayamos	fuéramos	vamos
	vais	ibais	fuisteis	iréis	iríais	vayáis	fuerais	id (no vayáis)
	van	iban	fueron	irán	irían	vayan	fueran	vayan Uds.

13. oír (y) — Participles: oyendo, oído

	Present	Imperfect	Preterite	Future	Conditional	Present	Past	IMPERATIVE
oír	oigo	oía	oí	oiré	oiría	oiga	oyera	
	oyes	oías	oíste	oirás	oirías	oigas	oyeras	oye tú (no oigas)
	oye	oía	oyó	oirá	oiría	oiga	oyera	oiga Ud.
	oímos	oíamos	oímos	oiremos	oiríamos	oigamos	oyéramos	oigamos
	oís	oíais	oísteis	oiréis	oiríais	oigáis	oyerais	oíd (no oigáis)
	oyen	oían	oyeron	oirán	oirían	oigan	oyeran	oigan Uds.

14. poder (o:ue)
Participles: pudiendo, podido

	INDICATIVE					SUBJUNCTIVE		IMPERATIVE
	Present	Imperfect	Preterite	Future	Conditional	Present	Past	
	puedo	podía	pude	podré	podría	pueda	pudiera	
	puedes	podías	pudiste	podrás	podrías	puedas	pudieras	puede tú (no puedas)
	puede	podía	pudo	podrá	podría	pueda	pudiera	pueda Ud.
	podemos	podíamos	pudimos	podremos	podríamos	podamos	pudiéramos	podamos
	podéis	podíais	pudisteis	podréis	podríais	podáis	pudierais	poded (no podáis)
	pueden	podían	pudieron	podrán	podrían	puedan	pudieran	puedan Uds.

15. poner
Participles: poniendo, puesto

	INDICATIVE					SUBJUNCTIVE		IMPERATIVE
	Present	Imperfect	Preterite	Future	Conditional	Present	Past	
	pongo	ponía	puse	pondré	pondría	ponga	pusiera	
	pones	ponías	pusiste	pondrás	pondrías	pongas	pusieras	pon tú (no pongas)
	pone	ponía	puso	pondrá	pondría	ponga	pusiera	ponga Ud.
	ponemos	poníamos	pusimos	pondremos	pondríamos	pongamos	pusiéramos	pongamos
	ponéis	poníais	pusisteis	pondréis	pondríais	pongáis	pusierais	poned (no pongáis)
	ponen	ponían	pusieron	pondrán	pondrían	pongan	pusieran	pongan Uds.

16. querer (e:ie)
Participles: queriendo, querido

	INDICATIVE					SUBJUNCTIVE		IMPERATIVE
	Present	Imperfect	Preterite	Future	Conditional	Present	Past	
	quiero	quería	quise	querré	querría	quiera	quisiera	
	quieres	querías	quisiste	querrás	querrías	quieras	quisieras	quiere tú (no quieras)
	quiere	quería	quiso	querrá	querría	quiera	quisiera	quiera Ud.
	queremos	queríamos	quisimos	querremos	querríamos	queramos	quisiéramos	queramos
	queréis	queríais	quisisteis	querréis	querríais	queráis	quisierais	quered (no queráis)
	quieren	querían	quisieron	querrán	querrían	quieran	quisieran	quieran Uds.

17. saber
Participles: sabiendo, sabido

	INDICATIVE					SUBJUNCTIVE		IMPERATIVE
	Present	Imperfect	Preterite	Future	Conditional	Present	Past	
	sé	sabía	supe	sabré	sabría	sepa	supiera	
	sabes	sabías	supiste	sabrás	sabrías	sepas	supieras	sabe tú (no sepas)
	sabe	sabía	supo	sabrá	sabría	sepa	supiera	sepa Ud.
	sabemos	sabíamos	supimos	sabremos	sabríamos	sepamos	supiéramos	sepamos
	sabéis	sabíais	supisteis	sabréis	sabríais	sepáis	supierais	sabed (no sepáis)
	saben	sabían	supieron	sabrán	sabrían	sepan	supieran	sepan Uds.

18. salir
Participles: saliendo, salido

	INDICATIVE					SUBJUNCTIVE		IMPERATIVE
	Present	Imperfect	Preterite	Future	Conditional	Present	Past	
	salgo	salía	salí	saldré	saldría	salga	saliera	
	sales	salías	saliste	saldrás	saldrías	salgas	salieras	sal tú (no salgas)
	sale	salía	salió	saldrá	saldría	salga	saliera	salga Ud.
	salimos	salíamos	salimos	saldremos	saldríamos	salgamos	saliéramos	salgamos
	salís	salíais	salisteis	saldréis	saldríais	salgáis	salierais	salid (no salgáis)
	salen	salían	salieron	saldrán	saldrían	salgan	salieran	salgan Uds.

19. ser
Participles: siendo, sido

	INDICATIVE					SUBJUNCTIVE		IMPERATIVE
	Present	Imperfect	Preterite	Future	Conditional	Present	Past	
	soy	era	fui	seré	sería	sea	fuera	
	eres	eras	fuiste	serás	serías	seas	fueras	sé tú (no seas)
	es	era	fue	será	sería	sea	fuera	sea Ud.
	somos	éramos	fuimos	seremos	seríamos	seamos	fuéramos	seamos
	sois	erais	fuisteis	seréis	seríais	seáis	fuerais	sed (no seáis)
	son	eran	fueron	serán	serían	sean	fueran	sean Uds.

20. tener (e:ie)
Participles: teniendo, tenido

	INDICATIVE					SUBJUNCTIVE		IMPERATIVE
	Present	Imperfect	Preterite	Future	Conditional	Present	Past	
	tengo	tenía	tuve	tendré	tendría	tenga	tuviera	
	tienes	tenías	tuviste	tendrás	tendrías	tengas	tuvieras	ten tú (no tengas)
	tiene	tenía	tuvo	tendrá	tendría	tenga	tuviera	tenga Ud.
	tenemos	teníamos	tuvimos	tendremos	tendríamos	tengamos	tuviéramos	tengamos
	tenéis	teníais	tuvisteis	tendréis	tendríais	tengáis	tuvierais	tened (no tengáis)
	tienen	tenían	tuvieron	tendrán	tendrían	tengan	tuvieran	tengan Uds.

21 traer
Participles: trayendo, traído

Infinitive	INDICATIVE					SUBJUNCTIVE		IMPERATIVE
	Present	Imperfect	Preterite	Future	Conditional	Present	Past	
traer	traigo	traía	traje	traeré	traería	traiga	trajera	
	traes	traías	trajiste	traerás	traerías	traigas	trajeras	trae tú (no traigas)
	trae	traía	trajo	traerá	traería	traiga	trajera	traiga Ud.
	traemos	traíamos	trajimos	traeremos	traeríamos	traigamos	trajéramos	traigamos
	traéis	traíais	trajisteis	traeréis	traeríais	traigáis	trajerais	traed (no traigáis)
	traen	traían	trajeron	traerán	traerían	traigan	trajeran	traigan Uds.

22 venir (e:ie)
Participles: viniendo, venido

Infinitive	INDICATIVE					SUBJUNCTIVE		IMPERATIVE
	Present	Imperfect	Preterite	Future	Conditional	Present	Past	
venir	vengo	venía	vine	vendré	vendría	venga	viniera	
	vienes	venías	viniste	vendrás	vendrías	vengas	vinieras	ven tú (no vengas)
	viene	venía	vino	vendrá	vendría	venga	viniera	venga Ud.
	venimos	veníamos	vinimos	vendremos	vendríamos	vengamos	viniéramos	vengamos
	venís	veníais	vinisteis	vendréis	vendríais	vengáis	vinierais	venid (no vengáis)
	vienen	venían	vinieron	vendrán	vendrían	vengan	vinieran	vengan Uds.

23 ver
Participles: viendo, visto

Infinitive	INDICATIVE					SUBJUNCTIVE		IMPERATIVE
	Present	Imperfect	Preterite	Future	Conditional	Present	Past	
ver	veo	veía	vi	veré	vería	vea	viera	
	ves	veías	viste	verás	verías	veas	vieras	ve tú (no veas)
	ve	veía	vio	verá	vería	vea	viera	vea Ud.
	vemos	veíamos	vimos	veremos	veríamos	veamos	viéramos	veamos
	veis	veíais	visteis	veréis	veríais	veáis	vierais	ved (no veáis)
	ven	veían	vieron	verán	verían	vean	vieran	vean Uds.

Stem-changing verbs

24 contar (o:ue)
Participles: contando, contado

Infinitive	INDICATIVE					SUBJUNCTIVE		IMPERATIVE
	Present	Imperfect	Preterite	Future	Conditional	Present	Past	
contar	cuento	contaba	conté	contaré	contaría	cuente	contara	
	cuentas	contabas	contaste	contarás	contarías	cuentes	contaras	cuenta tú (no cuentes)
	cuenta	contaba	contó	contará	contaría	cuente	contara	cuente Ud.
	contamos	contábamos	contamos	contaremos	contaríamos	contemos	contáramos	contemos
	contáis	contabais	contasteis	contaréis	contaríais	contéis	contarais	contad (no contéis)
	cuentan	contaban	contaron	contarán	contarían	cuenten	contaran	cuenten Uds.

25 dormir (o:ue)
Participles: durmiendo, dormido

Infinitive	INDICATIVE					SUBJUNCTIVE		IMPERATIVE
	Present	Imperfect	Preterite	Future	Conditional	Present	Past	
dormir	duermo	dormía	dormí	dormiré	dormiría	duerma	durmiera	
	duermes	dormías	dormiste	dormirás	dormirías	duermas	durmieras	duerme tú (no duermas)
	duerme	dormía	durmió	dormirá	dormiría	duerma	durmiera	duerma Ud.
	dormimos	dormíamos	dormimos	dormiremos	dormiríamos	durmamos	durmiéramos	durmamos
	dormís	dormíais	dormisteis	dormiréis	dormiríais	durmáis	durmierais	dormid (no durmáis)
	duermen	dormían	durmieron	dormirán	dormirían	duerman	durmieran	duerman Uds.

26 empezar (e:ie) (z:c)
Participles: empezando, empezado

Infinitive	INDICATIVE					SUBJUNCTIVE		IMPERATIVE
	Present	Imperfect	Preterite	Future	Conditional	Present	Past	
empezar	empiezo	empezaba	empecé	empezaré	empezaría	empiece	empezara	
	empiezas	empezabas	empezaste	empezarás	empezarías	empieces	empezaras	empieza tú (no empieces)
	empieza	empezaba	empezó	empezará	empezaría	empiece	empezara	empiece Ud.
	empezamos	empezábamos	empezamos	empezaremos	empezaríamos	empecemos	empezáramos	empecemos
	empezáis	empezabais	empezasteis	empezaréis	empezaríais	empecéis	empezarais	empezad (no empecéis)
	empiezan	empezaban	empezaron	empezarán	empezarían	empiecen	empezaran	empiecen Uds.

27. entender (e:ie) — Participles: entendiendo, entendido

	INDICATIVE					SUBJUNCTIVE		IMPERATIVE
	Present	Imperfect	Preterite	Future	Conditional	Present	Past	
	entiendo	entendía	entendí	entenderé	entendería	entienda	entendiera	
	entiendes	entendías	entendiste	entenderás	entenderías	entiendas	entendieras	entiende tú (no entiendas)
	entiende	entendía	entendió	entenderá	entendería	entienda	entendiera	entienda Ud.
	entendemos	entendíamos	entendimos	entenderemos	entenderíamos	entendamos	entendiéramos	entendamos
	entendéis	entendíais	entendisteis	entenderéis	entenderíais	entendáis	entendierais	entended (no entendáis)
	entienden	entendían	entendieron	entenderán	entenderían	entiendan	entendieran	entiendan Uds.

28. jugar (u:ue) (g:gu) — Participles: jugando, jugado

	INDICATIVE					SUBJUNCTIVE		IMPERATIVE
	Present	Imperfect	Preterite	Future	Conditional	Present	Past	
	juego	jugaba	jugué	jugaré	jugaría	juegue	jugara	
	juegas	jugabas	jugaste	jugarás	jugarías	juegues	jugaras	juega tú (no juegues)
	juega	jugaba	jugó	jugará	jugaría	juegue	jugara	juegue Ud.
	jugamos	jugábamos	jugamos	jugaremos	jugaríamos	juguemos	jugáramos	juguemos
	jugáis	jugabais	jugasteis	jugaréis	jugaríais	juguéis	jugarais	jugad (no juguéis)
	juegan	jugaban	jugaron	jugarán	jugarían	jueguen	jugaran	jueguen Uds.

29. pedir (e:i) — Participles: pidiendo, pedido

	INDICATIVE					SUBJUNCTIVE		IMPERATIVE
	Present	Imperfect	Preterite	Future	Conditional	Present	Past	
	pido	pedía	pedí	pediré	pediría	pida	pidiera	
	pides	pedías	pediste	pedirás	pedirías	pidas	pidieras	pide tú (no pidas)
	pide	pedía	pidió	pedirá	pediría	pida	pidiera	pida Ud.
	pedimos	pedíamos	pedimos	pediremos	pediríamos	pidamos	pidiéramos	pidamos
	pedís	pedíais	pedisteis	pediréis	pediríais	pidáis	pidierais	pedid (no pidáis)
	piden	pedían	pidieron	pedirán	pedirían	pidan	pidieran	pidan Uds.

30. pensar (e:ie) — Participles: pensando, pensado

	INDICATIVE					SUBJUNCTIVE		IMPERATIVE
	Present	Imperfect	Preterite	Future	Conditional	Present	Past	
	pienso	pensaba	pensé	pensaré	pensaría	piense	pensara	
	piensas	pensabas	pensaste	pensarás	pensarías	pienses	pensaras	piensa tú (no pienses)
	piensa	pensaba	pensó	pensará	pensaría	piense	pensara	piense Ud.
	pensamos	pensábamos	pensamos	pensaremos	pensaríamos	pensemos	pensáramos	pensemos
	pensáis	pensabais	pensasteis	pensaréis	pensaríais	penséis	pensarais	pensad (no penséis)
	piensan	pensaban	pensaron	pensarán	pensarían	piensen	pensaran	piensen Uds.

31. reír(se) (e:i) — Participles: riendo, reído

	INDICATIVE					SUBJUNCTIVE		IMPERATIVE
	Present	Imperfect	Preterite	Future	Conditional	Present	Past	
	río	reía	reí	reiré	reiría	ría	riera	
	ríes	reías	reíste	reirás	reirías	rías	rieras	ríe tú (no rías)
	ríe	reía	rió	reirá	reiría	ría	riera	ría Ud.
	reímos	reíamos	reímos	reiremos	reiríamos	riamos	riéramos	riamos
	reís	reíais	reísteis	reiréis	reiríais	riáis	rierais	reíd (no riáis)
	ríen	reían	rieron	reirán	reirían	rían	rieran	rían Uds.

32. seguir (e:i) (gu:g) — Participles: siguiendo, seguido

	INDICATIVE					SUBJUNCTIVE		IMPERATIVE
	Present	Imperfect	Preterite	Future	Conditional	Present	Past	
	sigo	seguía	seguí	seguiré	seguiría	siga	siguiera	
	sigues	seguías	seguiste	seguirás	seguirías	sigas	siguieras	sigue tú (no sigas)
	sigue	seguía	siguió	seguirá	seguiría	siga	siguiera	siga Ud.
	seguimos	seguíamos	seguimos	seguiremos	seguiríamos	sigamos	siguiéramos	sigamos
	seguís	seguíais	seguisteis	seguiréis	seguiríais	sigáis	siguierais	seguid (no sigáis)
	siguen	seguían	siguieron	seguirán	seguirían	sigan	siguieran	sigan Uds.

33. sentir (e:ie) — Participles: sintiendo, sentido

	INDICATIVE					SUBJUNCTIVE		IMPERATIVE
	Present	Imperfect	Preterite	Future	Conditional	Present	Past	
	siento	sentía	sentí	sentiré	sentiría	sienta	sintiera	
	sientes	sentías	sentiste	sentirás	sentirías	sientas	sintieras	siente tú (no sientas)
	siente	sentía	sintió	sentirá	sentiría	sienta	sintiera	sienta Ud.
	sentimos	sentíamos	sentimos	sentiremos	sentiríamos	sintamos	sintiéramos	sintamos
	sentís	sentíais	sentisteis	sentiréis	sentiríais	sintáis	sintierais	sentid (no sintáis)
	sienten	sentían	sintieron	sentirán	sentirían	sientan	sintieran	sientan Uds.

34

Infinitive	INDICATIVE					SUBJUNCTIVE		IMPERATIVE
	Present	Imperfect	Preterite	Future	Conditional	Present	Past	
volver (o:ue)	vuelvo	volvía	volví	volveré	volvería	vuelva	volviera	
	vuelves	volvías	volviste	volverás	volverías	vuelvas	volvieras	vuelve tú (no vuelvas)
	vuelve	volvía	volvió	volverá	volvería	vuelva	volviera	vuelva Ud.
Participles:	volvemos	volvíamos	volvimos	volveremos	volveríamos	volvamos	volviéramos	volvamos
volviendo	volvéis	volvíais	volvisteis	volveréis	volveríais	volváis	volvierais	volved (no volváis)
vuelto	vuelven	volvían	volvieron	volverán	volverían	vuelvan	volvieran	vuelvan Uds.

Verbs with spelling changes only

35

Infinitive	INDICATIVE					SUBJUNCTIVE		IMPERATIVE
	Present	Imperfect	Preterite	Future	Conditional	Present	Past	
conocer (c:zc)	conozco	conocía	conocí	conoceré	conocería	conozca	conociera	
	conoces	conocías	conociste	conocerás	conocerías	conozcas	conocieras	conoce tú (no conozcas)
	conoce	conocía	conoció	conocerá	conocería	conozca	conociera	conozca Ud.
Participles:	conocemos	conocíamos	conocimos	conoceremos	conoceríamos	conozcamos	conociéramos	conozcamos
conociendo	conocéis	conocíais	conocisteis	conoceréis	conoceríais	conozcáis	conocierais	conoced (no conozcáis)
conocido	conocen	conocían	conocieron	conocerán	conocerían	conozcan	conocieran	conozcan Uds.

36

Infinitive	INDICATIVE					SUBJUNCTIVE		IMPERATIVE
	Present	Imperfect	Preterite	Future	Conditional	Present	Past	
creer (y)	creo	creía	creí	creeré	creería	crea	creyera	
	crees	creías	creíste	creerás	creerías	creas	creyeras	cree tú (no creas)
	cree	creía	creyó	creerá	creería	crea	creyera	crea Ud.
Participles:	creemos	creíamos	creímos	creeremos	creeríamos	creamos	creyéramos	creamos
creyendo	creéis	creíais	creísteis	creeréis	creeríais	creáis	creyerais	creed (no creáis)
creído	creen	creían	creyeron	creerán	creerían	crean	creyeran	crean Uds.

37

Infinitive	INDICATIVE					SUBJUNCTIVE		IMPERATIVE
	Present	Imperfect	Preterite	Future	Conditional	Present	Past	
cruzar (z:c)	cruzo	cruzaba	crucé	cruzaré	cruzaría	cruce	cruzara	
	cruzas	cruzabas	cruzaste	cruzarás	cruzarías	cruces	cruzaras	cruza tú (no cruces)
	cruza	cruzaba	cruzó	cruzará	cruzaría	cruce	cruzara	cruce Ud.
Participles:	cruzamos	cruzábamos	cruzamos	cruzaremos	cruzaríamos	crucemos	cruzáramos	crucemos
cruzando	cruzáis	cruzabais	cruzasteis	cruzaréis	cruzaríais	crucéis	cruzarais	cruzad (no crucéis)
cruzado	cruzan	cruzaban	cruzaron	cruzarán	cruzarían	crucen	cruzaran	crucen Uds.

38

Infinitive	INDICATIVE					SUBJUNCTIVE		IMPERATIVE
	Present	Imperfect	Preterite	Future	Conditional	Present	Past	
destruir (y)	destruyo	destruía	destruí	destruiré	destruiría	destruya	destruyera	
	destruyes	destruías	destruiste	destruirás	destruirías	destruyas	destruyeras	destruye tú (no destruyas)
	destruye	destruía	destruyó	destruirá	destruiría	destruya	destruyera	destruya Ud.
Participles:	destruimos	destruíamos	destruimos	destruiremos	destruiríamos	destruyamos	destruyéramos	destruyamos
destruyendo	destruís	destruíais	destruisteis	destruiréis	destruiríais	destruyáis	destruyerais	destruid (no destruyáis)
destruido	destruyen	destruían	destruyeron	destruirán	destruirían	destruyan	destruyeran	destruyan Uds.

39

Infinitive	INDICATIVE					SUBJUNCTIVE		IMPERATIVE
	Present	Imperfect	Preterite	Future	Conditional	Present	Past	
enviar (envío)	envío	enviaba	envié	enviaré	enviaría	envíe	enviara	
	envías	enviabas	enviaste	enviarás	enviarías	envíes	enviaras	envía tú (no envíes)
	envía	enviaba	envió	enviará	enviaría	envíe	enviara	envíe Ud.
Participles:	enviamos	enviábamos	enviamos	enviaremos	enviaríamos	enviemos	enviáramos	enviemos
enviando	enviáis	enviabais	enviasteis	enviaréis	enviaríais	enviéis	enviarais	enviad (no enviéis)
enviado	envían	enviaban	enviaron	enviarán	enviarían	envíen	enviaran	envíen Uds.

Infinitive	INDICATIVE					SUBJUNCTIVE		IMPERATIVE
	Present	Imperfect	Preterite	Future	Conditional	Present	Past	
40 graduarse (gradúo)	**gradúo**	graduaba	gradué	graduaré	graduaría	**gradúe**	graduara	
	gradúas	graduabas	graduaste	graduarás	graduarías	**gradúes**	graduaras	**gradúa** tú (no **gradúes**)
	gradúa	graduaba	graduó	graduará	graduaría	**gradúe**	graduara	**gradúe** Ud.
Participles:	graduamos	graduábamos	graduamos	graduaremos	graduaríamos	graduemos	graduáramos	graduemos
graduando	graduáis	graduabais	graduasteis	graduaréis	graduaríais	graduéis	graduarais	graduad (no graduéis)
graduado	**gradúan**	graduaban	graduaron	graduarán	graduarían	**gradúen**	graduaran	**gradúen** Uds.
41 llegar (g:gu)	llego	llegaba	**llegué**	llegaré	llegaría	**llegue**	llegara	
	llegas	llegabas	llegaste	llegarás	llegarías	**llegues**	llegaras	llega tú (no **llegues**)
	llega	llegaba	llegó	llegará	llegaría	**llegue**	llegara	**llegue** Ud.
Participles:	llegamos	llegábamos	llegamos	llegaremos	llegaríamos	**lleguemos**	llegáramos	**lleguemos**
llegando	llegáis	llegabais	llegasteis	llegaréis	llegaríais	**lleguéis**	llegarais	llegad (no **lleguéis**)
llegado	llegan	llegaban	llegaron	llegarán	llegarían	**lleguen**	llegaran	**lleguen** Uds.
42 prohibir (prohíbo)	**prohíbo**	prohibía	prohibí	prohibiré	prohibiría	**prohíba**	prohibiera	
	prohíbes	prohibías	prohibiste	prohibirás	prohibirías	**prohíbas**	prohibieras	**prohíbe** tú (no **prohíbas**)
	prohíbe	prohibía	prohibió	prohibirá	prohibiría	**prohíba**	prohibiera	**prohíba** Ud.
Participles:	prohibimos	prohibíamos	prohibimos	prohibiremos	prohibiríamos	prohibamos	prohibiéramos	prohibamos
prohibiendo	prohibís	prohibíais	prohibisteis	prohibiréis	prohibiríais	prohibáis	prohibierais	prohibid (no prohibáis)
prohibido	**prohíben**	prohibían	prohibieron	prohibirán	prohibirían	**prohíban**	prohibieran	**prohíban** Uds.
43 proteger (g:j)	**protejo**	protegía	protegí	protegeré	protegería	**proteja**	protegiera	
	proteges	protegías	protegiste	protegerás	protegerías	**protejas**	protegieras	protege tú (no **protejas**)
	protege	protegía	protegió	protegerá	protegería	**proteja**	protegiera	**proteja** Ud.
Participles:	protegemos	protegíamos	protegimos	protegeremos	protegeríamos	**protejamos**	protegiéramos	**protejamos**
protegiendo	protegéis	protegíais	protegisteis	protegeréis	protegeríais	**protejáis**	protegierais	proteged (no **protejáis**)
protegido	protegen	protegían	protegieron	protegerán	protegerían	protejan	protegieran	**protejan** Uds.
44 tocar (c:qu)	toco	tocaba	**toqué**	tocaré	tocaría	**toque**	tocara	
	tocas	tocabas	tocaste	tocarás	tocarías	**toques**	tocaras	toca tú (no **toques**)
	toca	tocaba	tocó	tocará	tocaría	**toque**	tocara	**toque** Ud.
Participles:	tocamos	tocábamos	tocamos	tocaremos	tocaríamos	**toquemos**	tocáramos	**toquemos**
tocando	tocáis	tocabais	tocasteis	tocaréis	tocaríais	**toquéis**	tocarais	tocad (no **toquéis**)
tocado	tocan	tocaban	tocaron	tocarán	tocarían	**toquen**	tocaran	**toquen** Uds.

Guide to Vocabulary

Note on alphabetization

For purposes of alphabetization, **ch** and **ll** are not treated as separate letters, but **ñ** follows **n**. Therefore, in this glossary you will find that **año**, for example, appears after **anuncio**.

Abbreviations used in this glossary

adj.	adjective	*form.*	formal	*pl.*	plural
adv.	adverb	*indef.*	indefinite	*poss.*	possessive
art.	article	*interj.*	interjection	*prep.*	preposition
conj.	conjunction	*i.o.*	indirect object	*pron.*	pronoun
def.	definite	*m.*	masculine	*ref.*	reflexive
d.o.	direct object	*n.*	noun	*sing.*	singular
f.	feminine	*obj.*	object	*sub.*	subject
fam.	familiar	*p.p.*	past participle	*v.*	verb

Spanish-English

A

a *prep.* at; to 1
  ¿A qué hora...? At what time...? 1
  a bordo aboard
  a dieta on a diet 15
  a la derecha de to the right of 2
  a la izquierda de to the left of 2
  a la plancha grilled 8
  a la(s) + *time* at + *time* 1
  a menos que *conj.* unless 13
  a menudo *adv.* often 10
  a nombre de in the name of 5
  a plazos in installments 14
  A sus órdenes. At your service.
  a tiempo *adv.* on time 10
  a veces *adv.* sometimes 10
  a ver let's see
abeja *f.* bee
abierto/a *adj.* open 5, 14
abogado/a *m., f.* lawyer 16
abrazar(se) *v.* to hug; to embrace (each other) 11
abrazo *m.* hug
abrigo *m.* coat 6
abril *m.* April 5
abrir *v.* to open 3
abuelo/a *m., f.* grandfather/ grandmother 3
abuelos *pl.* grandparents 3
aburrido/a *adj.* bored; boring 5
aburrir *v.* to bore 7
aburrirse *v.* to get bored 17
acabar de (+ *inf.*) *v.* to have just *done something* 6
acampar *v.* to camp 5
accidente *m.* accident 10
acción *f.* action 17
  de acción action (genre) 17

aceite *m.* oil 8
aceptar: ¡Acepto casarme contigo! I'll marry you! 17
acompañar *v.* to accompany 14
aconsejar *v.* to advise 12
acontecimiento *m.* event 18
acordarse (de) (o:ue) *v.* to remember 7
acostarse (o:ue) *v.* to go to bed 7
activo/a *adj.* active 15
actor *m.* actor 16
actriz *f.* actress 16
actualidades *f., pl.* news; current events 18
adelgazar *v.* to lose weight; to slim down 15
además (de) *adv.* furthermore; besides 10
adicional *adj.* additional
adiós *m.* goodbye 1
adjetivo *m.* adjective
administración de empresas *f.* business administration 2
adolescencia *f.* adolescence 9
¿adónde? *adv.* where (to)? (destination) 2
aduana *f.* customs
aeróbico/a *adj.* aerobic 15
aeropuerto *m.* airport 5
afectado/a *adj.* affected 13
afeitarse *v.* to shave 7
aficionado/a *m., f.* fan 4
afirmativo/a *adj.* affirmative
afuera *adv.* outside 5
afueras *f., pl.* suburbs; outskirts 12
agencia de viajes *f.* travel agency 5
agente de viajes *m., f.* travel agent 5
agosto *m.* August 5
agradable *adj.* pleasant

agua *f.* water 8
  agua mineral mineral water 8
aguantar *v.* to endure, to hold up 14
ahora *adv.* now 2
  ahora mismo right now 5
ahorrar *v.* to save (money) 14
ahorros *m., pl.* savings 14
aire *m.* air 13
ajo *m.* garlic 8
al (*contraction of* **a** + **el**) 4
  al aire libre open-air 6
  al contado in cash 14
  (al) este (to the) east 14
  al lado de next to; beside 2
  (al) norte (to the) north 14
  (al) oeste (to the) west 14
  (al) sur (to the) south 14
alcoba *f.* bedroom
alcohol *m.* alcohol 15
alcohólico/a *adj.* alcoholic 15
alegrarse (de) *v.* to be happy 13
alegre *adj.* happy; joyful 5
alegría *f.* happiness 9
alemán, alemana *adj.* German 3
alérgico/a *adj.* allergic 10
alfombra *f.* carpet; rug 12
algo *pron.* something; anything 7
algodón *m.* cotton 6
alguien *pron.* someone; somebody; anyone 7
algún, alguno/a(s) *adj.* any; some 7
alimento *m.* food
  alimentación *f.* diet
aliviar *v.* to reduce 15
  aliviar el estrés/la tensión to reduce stress/tension 15
allá *adv.* over there 2
allí *adv.* there 2
alma *f.* soul 9
almacén *m.* department store 6

almohada *f.* pillow 12
almorzar (o:ue) *v.* to have lunch 4
almuerzo *m.* lunch 4, 8
aló *interj.* hello (*on the telephone*) 11
alquilar *v.* to rent 12
alquiler *m.* rent (payment) 12
altar *m.* altar 9
altillo *m.* attic 12
alto/a *adj.* tall 3
aluminio *m.* aluminum 13
ama de casa *m., f.* housekeeper; caretaker 12
amable *adj.* nice; friendly 5
amarillo/a *adj.* yellow 6
amigo/a *m., f.* friend 3
amistad *f.* friendship 9
amor *m.* love 9
  amor a primera vista love at first sight 9
anaranjado/a *adj.* orange 6
ándale *interj.* come on 14
andar *v.* **en patineta** to skateboard 4
ángel *m.* angel 9
anillo *m.* ring 17
animal *m.* animal 13
aniversario (de bodas) *m.* (wedding) anniversary 9
anoche *adv.* last night 6
anteayer *adv.* the day before yesterday 6
antes *adv.* before 7
  antes (de) que *conj.* before 13
  antes de *prep.* before 7
antibiótico *m.* antibiotic 10
antipático/a *adj.* unpleasant 3
anunciar *v.* to announce; to advertise 18
anuncio *m.* advertisement 16
año *m.* year 5
  año pasado last year 6
apagar *v.* to turn off 11
aparato *m.* appliance
apartamento *m.* apartment 12
apellido *m.* last name 3
apenas *adv.* hardly; scarcely 10
aplaudir *v.* to applaud 17
aplicación *f.* app 11
apreciar *v.* to appreciate 17
aprender (a + *inf.*) *v.* to learn 3
apurarse *v.* to hurry; to rush 15
aquel, aquella *adj.* that (over there) 6
aquél, aquélla *pron.* that (over there) 6
aquello *neuter, pron.* that; that thing; that fact 6
aquellos/as *pl. adj.* those (over there) 6
aquéllos/as *pl. pron.* those (ones) (over there) 6
aquí *adv.* here 1
  Aquí está(n)... Here is/are... 5
árbol *m.* tree 13

archivo *m.* file 11
arete *m.* earring 6
argentino/a *adj.* Argentine 3
armario *m.* closet 12
arqueología *f.* archeology 2
arqueólogo/a *m., f.* archeologist 16
arquitecto/a *m., f.* architect 16
arrancar *v.* to start (*a car*) 11
arreglar *v.* to fix; to arrange 11; to neaten; to straighten up 12
arreglarse *v.* to get ready 7; to fix oneself (*clothes, hair, etc. to go out*) 7
arroba *f.* @ symbol 11
arroz *m.* rice 8
arte *m.* art 2
artes *f., pl.* arts 17
artesanía *f.* craftsmanship; crafts 17
artículo *m.* article 18
artista *m., f.* artist 3
artístico/a *adj.* artistic 17
arveja *f.* pea 8
asado/a *adj.* roast 8
ascenso *m.* promotion 16
ascensor *m.* elevator 5
así *adv.* like this; so (*in such a way*) 10
asistir (a) *v.* to attend 3
aspiradora *f.* vacuum cleaner 12
aspirante *m., f.* candidate; applicant 16
aspirina *f.* aspirin 10
atún *m.* tuna 8
aumentar *v.* to grow; to get bigger 13
aumentar *v.* **de peso** to gain weight 15
aumento *m.* increase
  aumento de sueldo pay raise 16
aunque although
autobús *m.* bus 1
automático/a *adj.* automatic
auto(móvil) *m.* auto(mobile) 5
autopista *f.* highway 11
ave *f.* bird 13
avenida *f.* avenue
aventura *f.* adventure 17
  de aventuras adventure (genre) 17
avergonzado/a *adj.* embarrassed 5
avión *m.* airplane 5
¡Ay! *interj.* Oh!
  ¡Ay, qué dolor! Oh, what pain!
ayer *adv.* yesterday 6
ayudar(se) *v.* to help (each other) 11
azúcar *m.* sugar 8
azul *adj. m., f.* blue 6

B

bailar *v.* to dance 2
bailarín/bailarina *m., f.* dancer 17
baile *m.* dance 17
bajar(se) de *v.* to get off of/out of (a vehicle) 11
bajo/a *adj.* short (*in height*) 3
balcón *m.* balcony 12
balde *m.* bucket 5
ballena *f.* whale 13
baloncesto *m.* basketball 4
banana *f.* banana 8
banco *m.* bank 14
banda *f.* band 17
bandera *f.* flag
bañarse *v.* to bathe; to take a bath 7
baño *m.* bathroom 7
barato/a *adj.* cheap 6
barco *m.* boat 5
barrer *v.* to sweep 12
  barrer el suelo *v.* to sweep the floor 12
barrio *m.* neighborhood 12
bastante *adv.* enough; rather 10
basura *f.* trash 12
baúl *m.* trunk 11
beber *v.* to drink 3
bebida *f.* drink 8
  bebida alcohólica *f.* alcoholic beverage 15
béisbol *m.* baseball 4
bellas artes *f., pl.* fine arts 17
belleza *f.* beauty 14
beneficio *m.* benefit 16
besar(se) *v.* to kiss (each other) 11
beso *m.* kiss 9
biblioteca *f.* library 2
bicicleta *f.* bicycle 4
bien *adv.* well 1
bienestar *m.* well-being 15
bienvenido(s)/a(s) *adj.* welcome 1
billete *m.* paper money; ticket
billón *m.* trillion
biología *f.* biology 2
bisabuelo/a *m., f.* great-grandfather/great-grandmother 3
bistec *m.* steak 8
blanco/a *adj.* white 6
blog *m.* blog 11
(blue)jeans *m., pl.* jeans 6
blusa *f.* blouse 6
boca *f.* mouth 10
boda *f.* wedding 9
boleto *m.* ticket 2, 17
bolsa *f.* purse, bag 6
bombero/a *m., f.* firefighter 16
bonito/a *adj.* pretty 3
borrador *m.* eraser 2
borrar *v.* to erase 11
bosque *m.* forest 13
  bosque tropical tropical forest; rain forest 13

bota *f.* boot 6
botella *f.* bottle 9
  botella de vino bottle of wine 9
botones *m., f. sing.* bellhop 5
brazo *m.* arm 10
brindar *v.* to toast (*drink*) 9
bucear *v.* to scuba dive 4
buen, bueno/a *adj.* good 3, 6
  buena forma good shape (*physical*) 15
  Buenas noches. Good evening; Good night. 1
  Buenas tardes. Good afternoon. 1
  Bueno. Hello. (*on telephone*) 11
  Buenos días. Good morning. 1
bulevar *m.* boulevard
buscador *m.* browser 11
buscar *v.* to look for 2
buzón *m.* mailbox 14

C

caballero *m.* gentleman, sir 8
caballo *m.* horse 5
cabe: no cabe duda de there's no doubt 13
cabeza *f.* head 10
cada *adj. m., f.* each 6
caerse *v.* to fall (down) 10
café *m.* café 4; *adj. m., f.* brown 6; *m.* coffee 8
cafeína *f.* caffeine 15
cafetera *f.* coffee maker 12
cafetería *f.* cafeteria 2
caído/a *p.p.* fallen 14
caja *f.* cash register 6
cajero/a *m., f.* cashier
  cajero automático *m.* ATM 14
calavera de azúcar *f.* skull made out of sugar 9
calcetín (calcetines) *m.* sock(s) 6
calculadora *f.* calculator 2
calentamiento global *m.* global warming 13
calentarse (e:ie) *v.* to warm up 15
calidad *f.* quality 6
calle *f.* street 11
calor *m.* heat
caloría *f.* calorie 15
calzar *v.* to take size... shoes 6
cama *f.* bed 5
cámara de video *f.* video camera 11
cámara digital *f.* digital camera 11
camarero/a *m., f.* waiter/waitress 8
camarón *m.* shrimp 8
cambiar (de) *v.* to change 9
cambio: de cambio in change 2
cambio *m.* **climático** climate change 13

cambio *m.* **de moneda** currency exchange
caminar *v.* to walk 2
camino *m.* road
camión *m.* truck; bus
camisa *f.* shirt 6
camiseta *f.* t-shirt 6
campo *m.* countryside 5
canadiense *adj.* Canadian 3
canal *m.* (TV) channel 11; 17
canción *f.* song 17
candidato/a *m., f.* candidate 18
canela *f.* cinnamon 10
cansado/a *adj.* tired 5
cantante *m., f.* singer 17
cantar *v.* to sing 2
capital *f.* capital city
capó *m.* hood 11
cara *f.* face 7
caramelo *m.* caramel 9
cargador *m.* charger 11
carne *f.* meat 8
  carne de res *f.* beef 8
carnicería *f.* butcher shop 14
caro/a *adj.* expensive 6
carpintero/a *m., f.* carpenter 16
carrera *f.* career 16
carretera *f.* highway; (main) road 11
carro *m.* car; automobile 11
carta *f.* letter 4; (playing) card 5
cartel *m.* poster 12
cartera *f.* wallet 4, 6
cartero *m.* mail carrier 14
casa *f.* house; home 2
casado/a *adj.* married 9
casarse (con) *v.* to get married (to) 9
casi *adv.* almost 10
catorce fourteen 1
cazar *v.* to hunt 13
cebolla *f.* onion 8
cederrón *m.* CD-ROM
celebrar *v.* to celebrate 9
cementerio *m.* cemetery 9
cena *f.* dinner 8
cenar *v.* to have dinner 2
centro *m.* downtown 4
  centro comercial shopping mall 6
cepillarse los dientes/el pelo *v.* to brush one's teeth/one's hair 7
cerámica *f.* pottery 17
cerca de *prep.* near 2
cerdo *m.* pork 8
cereales *m., pl.* cereal; grains 8
cero *m.* zero 1
cerrado/a *adj.* closed 5
cerrar (e:ie) *v.* to close 4
cerveza *f.* beer 8
césped *m.* grass
ceviche *m.* marinated fish dish 8
  ceviche de camarón *m.* lemon-marinated shrimp 8
  chaleco *m.* vest
champán *m.* champagne 9
champiñón *m.* mushroom 8

champú *m.* shampoo 7
chaqueta *f.* jacket 6
chatear *v.* to chat 11
chau *fam. interj.* bye 1
cheque *m.* (bank) check 14
  cheque (de viajero) *m.* (traveler's) check 14
chévere *adj., fam.* terrific
chico/a *m., f.* boy/girl 1
chino/a *adj.* Chinese 3
chocar (con) *v.* to run into
chocolate *m.* chocolate 9
choque *m.* collision 18
chuleta *f.* chop (*food*) 8
  chuleta de cerdo *f.* pork chop 8
cibercafé *m.* cybercafé 11
ciclismo *m.* cycling 4
cielo *m.* sky 13
cien(to) one hundred 2
ciencias *f., pl.* sciences 2
  ciencias ambientales environmental science 2
  de ciencia ficción *f.* science fiction (genre) 17
científico/a *m., f.* scientist 16
cierto/a *adj.* certain 13
  es cierto it's certain 13
  no es cierto it's not certain 13
cima *f.* top, peak 15
cinco five 1
cincuenta fifty 2
cine *m.* movie theater 4
cinta *f.* (audio)tape
cinta caminadora *f.* treadmill 15
cinturón *m.* belt 6
circulación *f.* traffic 11
cita *f.* date; appointment 9
ciudad *f.* city
ciudadano/a *m., f.* citizen 18
Claro (que sí). *fam.* Of course.
clase *f.* class 2
  clase de ejercicios aeróbicos *f.* aerobics class 15
clásico/a *adj.* classical 17
cliente/a *m., f.* customer 6
clínica *f.* clinic 10
cobrar *v.* to cash (a check) 14
coche *m.* car; automobile 11
cocina *f.* kitchen; stove 9, 12
cocinar *v.* to cook 12
cocinero/a *m., f.* cook, chef 16
cofre *m.* hood 14
cola *f.* line 14
colesterol *m.* cholesterol 15
color *m.* color 6
comedia *f.* comedy; play 17
comedor *m.* dining room 12
comenzar (e:ie) *v.* to begin 4
comer *v.* to eat 3
comercial *adj.* commercial; business-related 16
comida *f.* food; meal 4, 8
como like; as 8
¿cómo? what?; how? 1, 2
  ¿Cómo es...? What's... like?

¿Cómo está usted? *form.* How are you? 1
¿Cómo estás? *fam.* How are you? 1
¿Cómo se llama usted? *(form.)* What's your name? 1
¿Cómo te llamas? *fam.* What's your name? 1
cómoda *f.* chest of drawers 12
cómodo/a *adj.* comfortable 5
compañero/a de clase *m., f.* classmate 2
compañero/a de cuarto *m., f.* roommate 2
compañía *f.* company; firm 16
compartir *v.* to share 3
compositor(a) *m., f.* composer 17
comprar *v.* to buy 2
compras *f., pl.* purchases
  ir de compras to go shopping 5
comprender *v.* to understand 3
comprobar *v.* to check
comprometerse (con) *v.* to get engaged (to) 9
computación *f.* computer science 2
computadora *f.* computer 1
computadora portátil *f.* portable computer; laptop 11
comunicación *f.* communication 18
comunicarse (con) *v.* to communicate (with) 18
comunidad *f.* community 1
con *prep.* with 2
  Con él/ella habla. Speaking. *(on telephone)* 11
  con frecuencia *adv.* frequently 10
  Con permiso. Pardon me; Excuse me. 1
  con tal (de) que *conj.* provided (that) 13
concierto *m.* concert 17
concordar *v.* to agree
concurso *m.* game show; contest 17
conducir *v.* to drive 6, 11
conductor(a) *m., f.* driver 1
conexión *f.* **inalámbrica** wireless connection 11
confirmar *v.* to confirm 5
confirmar *v.* **una reservación** *f.* to confirm a reservation 5
confundido/a *adj.* confused 5
congelador *m.* freezer 12
congestionado/a *adj.* congested; stuffed-up 10
conmigo *pron.* with me 4, 9
conocer *v.* to know; to be acquainted with 6
conocido/a *adj.; p.p.* known
conseguir (e:i) *v.* to get; to obtain 4
consejero/a *m., f.* counselor; advisor 16
consejo *m.* advice
conservación *f.* conservation 13
conservar *v.* to conserve 13
construir *v.* to build
consultorio *m.* doctor's office 10
consumir *v.* to consume 15

contabilidad *f.* accounting 2
contador(a) *m., f.* accountant 16
contaminación *f.* pollution 13
  contaminación del aire/del agua air/water pollution 13
contaminado/a *adj.* polluted 13
contaminar *v.* to pollute 13
contar (o:ue) *v.* to count; to tell 4
contento/a *adj.* content 5
contestadora *f.* answering machine
contestar *v.* to answer 2
contigo *fam. pron.* with you 5, 9
contratar *v.* to hire 16
control *m.* **remoto** remote control 11
controlar *v.* to control 13
conversación *f.* conversation 1
conversar *v.* to converse, to chat 2
copa *f.* wineglass; goblet 12
corazón *m.* heart 10
corbata *f.* tie 6
corredor(a) *m., f.* **de bolsa** stockbroker 16
correo *m.* mail; post office 14
  correo de voz *m.* voice mail 11
  correo electrónico *m.* e-mail 4
correr *v.* to run 3
cortesía *f.* courtesy
cortinas *f., pl.* curtains 12
corto/a *adj.* short *(in length)* 6
cosa *f.* thing 1
costar (o:ue) *v.* to cost 6
costarricense *adj.* Costa Rican 3
cráter *m.* crater 13
creer *v.* to believe 3, 13
  creer (en) *v.* to believe (in) 3
  no creer *v.* not to believe 13
creído/a *adj., p.p.* believed 14
crema de afeitar *f.* shaving cream 5, 7
crimen *m.* crime; murder 18
cruzar *v.* to cross 14
cuaderno *m.* notebook 1
cuadra *f.* (city) block 14
¿cuál(es)? which?; which one(s)? 2
  ¿Cuál es la fecha de hoy? What is today's date? 5
cuadro *m.* picture 12
cuando *conj.* when 7; 13
¿cuándo? when? 2
¿cuánto(s)/a(s)? how much/how many? 1, 2
  ¿Cuánto cuesta...? How much does... cost? 6
  ¿Cuántos años tienes? How old are you?
cuarenta forty 2
cuarto de baño *m.* bathroom 7
cuarto *m.* room 2; 7
cuarto/a *adj.* fourth 5
  menos cuarto quarter to (time) 1
  y cuarto quarter after (time) 1
cuatro four 1
cuatrocientos/as four hundred 2
cubano/a *adj.* Cuban 3
cubiertos *m., pl.* silverware

cubierto/a *p.p.* covered
cubrir *v.* to cover
cuchara *f.* (table or large) spoon 12
cuchillo *m.* knife 12
cuello *m.* neck 10
cuenta *f.* bill 8; account 14
  cuenta corriente *f.* checking account 14
  cuenta de ahorros *f.* savings account 14
cuento *m.* short story 17
cuerpo *m.* body 10
cuidado *m.* care
cuidar *v.* to take care of 13
cultura *f.* culture 2, 17
cumpleaños *m., sing.* birthday 9
cumplir años *v.* to have a birthday
cuñado/a *m., f.* brother-in-law/ sister-in-law 3
currículum *m.* résumé 16
curso *m.* course 2

D

danza *f.* dance 17
dañar *v.* to damage; to break down 10
dar *v.* to give 6
  dar un consejo *v.* to give advice
  darse con *v.* to bump into; to run into (something) 10
  darse prisa *v.* to hurry; to rush 15
de *prep.* of; from 1
  ¿De dónde eres? *fam.* Where are you from? 1
  ¿De dónde es usted? *form.* Where are you from? 1
  ¿De parte de quién? Who is speaking/calling? *(on telephone)* 11
  ¿de quién...? whose...? *(sing.)* 1
  ¿de quiénes...? whose...? *(pl.)* 1
  de algodón (made) of cotton 6
  de aluminio (made) of aluminum 13
  de buen humor in a good mood 5
  de compras shopping 5
  de cuadros plaid 6
  de excursión hiking 4
  de hecho in fact
  de ida y vuelta roundtrip 5
  de la mañana in the morning; A.M. 1
  de la noche in the evening; at night; P.M. 1
  de la tarde in the afternoon; in the early evening; P.M. 1
  de lana (made) of wool 6
  de lunares polka-dotted 6
  de mal humor in a bad mood 5
  de moda in fashion 6
  De nada. You're welcome. 1
  de niño/a as a child 10
  de parte de on behalf of 11

de plástico (made) of plastic 13
de rayas striped 6
de repente suddenly 6
de seda (made) of silk 6
de vaqueros western (genre) 17
de vez en cuando from time to time 10
de vidrio (made) of glass 13
debajo de *prep.* below; under 2
deber (+ *inf.*) *v.* should; must; ought to 3
deber *m.* responsibility; obligation 18
debido a due to (the fact that)
débil *adj.* weak 15
decidir (+ *inf.*) *v.* to decide 3
décimo/a *adj.* tenth 5
decir (e:i) *v.* **(que)** to say (that); to tell (that) 4
decir la respuesta to say the answer 4
decir la verdad to tell the truth 4
decir mentiras to tell lies 4
declarar *v.* to declare; to say 18
dedo *m.* finger 10
dedo del pie *m.* toe 10
deforestación *f.* deforestation 13
dejar *v.* to let; to quit; to leave behind 16
dejar de (+ *inf.*) *v.* to stop (*doing something*) 13
dejar una propina *v.* to leave a tip
del (*contraction of* de + el) of the; from the 1
delante de *prep.* in front of 2
delgado/a *adj.* thin; slender 3
delicioso/a *adj.* delicious 8
demás *adj.* the rest
demasiado *adv.* too much 6
dentista *m., f.* dentist 10
dentro de (diez años) within (ten years) 16; inside
dependiente/a *m., f.* clerk 6
deporte *m.* sport 4
deportista *m.* sports person
deportivo/a *adj.* sports-related 4
depositar *v.* to deposit 14
derecha *f.* right 2
a la derecha de to the right of 2
derecho *adv.* straight (ahead) 14
derechos *m., pl.* rights 18
desarrollar *v.* to develop 13
desastre (natural) *m.* (natural) disaster 18
desayunar *v.* to have breakfast 2
desayuno *m.* breakfast 8
descafeinado/a *adj.* decaffeinated 15
descansar *v.* to rest 2
descargar *v.* to download 11
descompuesto/a *adj.* not working; out of order 11
describir *v.* to describe 3
descrito/a *p.p.* described 14
descubierto/a *p.p.* discovered 14

descubrir *v.* to discover 13
desde *prep.* from 6
desear *v.* to wish; to desire 2
desempleo *m.* unemployment 18
desierto *m.* desert 13
desigualdad *f.* inequality 18
desordenado/a *adj.* disorderly 5
despacio *adv.* slowly 10
despedida *f.* farewell; goodbye
despedir (e:i) *v.* to fire 16
despedirse (de) (e:i) *v.* to say goodbye (to) 18
despejado/a *adj.* clear (*weather*)
despertador *m.* alarm clock 7
despertarse (e:ie) *v.* to wake up 7
después *adv.* afterwards; then 7
después de after 7
después de que *conj.* after 13
destruir *v.* to destroy 13
detrás de *prep.* behind 2
día *m.* day 1
día de fiesta holiday 9
diario *m.* diary 1; newspaper 18
diario/a *adj.* daily 7
dibujar *v.* to draw 2
dibujo *m.* drawing
dibujos animados *m., pl.* cartoons 17
diccionario *m.* dictionary 1
dicho/a *p.p.* said 14
diciembre *m.* December 5
dictadura *f.* dictatorship 18
diecinueve nineteen 1
dieciocho eighteen 1
dieciséis sixteen 1
diecisiete seventeen 1
diente *m.* tooth 7
dieta *f.* diet 15
comer una dieta equilibrada to eat a balanced diet 15
diez ten 1
difícil *adj.* difficult; hard 3
Diga. Hello. (*on telephone*) 11
diligencia *f.* errand 14
dinero *m.* money 6
dirección *f.* address 14
dirección electrónica *f.* e-mail address 11
director(a) *m., f.* director; (*musical*) conductor 17
dirigir *v.* to direct 17
disco compacto compact disc (CD) 11
discriminación *f.* discrimination 18
discurso *m.* speech 18
diseñador(a) *m., f.* designer 16
diseño *m.* design
disfraz *m.* costume 9
disfrutar (de) *v.* to enjoy; to reap the benefits (of) 15
disminuir *v.* to reduce 16
diversión *f.* fun activity; entertainment; recreation 4
divertido/a *adj.* fun
divertirse (e:ie) *v.* to have fun 9
divorciado/a *adj.* divorced 9

divorciarse (de) *v.* to get divorced (from) 9
divorcio *m.* divorce 9
doblar *v.* to turn 14
doble *adj.* double 5
doce twelve 1
doctor(a) *m., f.* doctor 3; 10
documental *m.* documentary 17
documentos de viaje *m., pl.* travel documents
doler (o:ue) *v.* to hurt 10
dolor *m.* ache; pain 10
dolor de cabeza *m.* headache 10
doméstico/a *adj.* domestic 12
domingo *m.* Sunday 2
don *m.* Mr.; sir 1
doña *f.* Mrs.; ma'am 1
donde *adv.* where
¿Dónde está...? Where is...? 2
¿dónde? where? 1, 2
dormir (o:ue) *v.* to sleep 4
dormirse (o:ue) *v.* to go to sleep; to fall asleep 7
dormitorio *m.* bedroom 12
dos two 1
dos veces *f.* twice; two times 6
doscientos/as two hundred 2
drama *m.* drama; play 17
dramático/a *adj.* dramatic 17
dramaturgo/a *m., f.* playwright 17
droga *f.* drug 15
drogadicto/a *m., f.* drug addict 15
ducha *f.* shower 7
ducharse *v.* to shower; to take a shower 7
duda *f.* doubt 13
dudar *v.* to doubt 13
no dudar not to doubt 13
dueño/a *m., f.* owner 8
dulces *m., pl.* sweets; candy 9
durante *prep.* during 7
durar *v.* to last 18

E

e *conj.* (*used instead of* **y** *before words beginning with* **i** *and* **hi**) and
echar *v.* to throw
echar (una carta) al buzón *v.* to put (a letter) in the mailbox; to mail 14
ecología *f.* ecology 13
ecológico/a *adj.* ecological 13
ecologista *m., f.* ecologist 13
economía *f.* economics 2
ecoturismo *m.* ecotourism 13
ecuatoriano/a *adj.* Ecuadorian 3
edad *f.* age 9
edificio *m.* building 12
edificio de apartamentos apartment building 12
(en) efectivo *m.* cash 6

ejercer *v.* to practice/exercise (a degree/profession) 16

ejercicio *m.* exercise 15
  ejercicios aeróbicos aerobic exercises 15
  ejercicios de estiramiento stretching exercises 15

ejército *m.* army 18

el *m., sing., def. art.* the 1

él *sub. pron.* he 1; *obj. pron.* him

elecciones *f., pl.* election 18

electricista *m., f.* electrician 16

electrodoméstico *m.* electric appliance 12

elegante *adj. m., f.* elegant 6

elegir (e:i) *v.* to elect 18

ella *sub. pron.* she 1; *obj. pron.* her

ellos/as *sub. pron.* they 1; *obj. pron.* them

embarazada *adj.* pregnant 10

emergencia *f.* emergency 10

emitir *v.* to broadcast 18

emocionante *adj. m., f.* exciting

empezar (e:ie) *v.* to begin 4

empleado/a *m., f.* employee 5

empleo *m.* job; employment 16

empresa *f.* company; firm 16

en *prep.* in; on 2
  en casa at home
  en caso (de) que *conj.* in case (that) 13
  en cuanto *conj.* as soon as 13
  en efectivo in cash 14
  en exceso in excess; too much 15
  en línea in-line 4
  en punto on the dot; exactly; sharp (*time*) 1
  en qué in what; how
  ¿En qué puedo servirles? How can I help you? 5
  en vivo live 7

enamorado/a (de) *adj.* in love (with) 5

enamorarse (de) *v.* to fall in love (with) 9

encantado/a *adj.* delighted; pleased to meet you 1

encantar *v.* to like very much; to love (*inanimate objects*) 7

encima de *prep.* on top of 2

encontrar (o:ue) *v.* to find 4

encontrar(se) (o:ue) *v.* to meet (each other); to run into (each other) 11
  encontrarse con to meet up with 7

encuesta *f.* poll; survey 18

energía *f.* energy 13
  energía nuclear nuclear energy 13
  energía solar solar energy 13

enero *m.* January 5

enfermarse *v.* to get sick 10

enfermedad *f.* illness 10

enfermero/a *m., f.* nurse 10

enfermo/a *adj.* sick 10

enfrente de *adv.* opposite; facing 14

engordar *v.* to gain weight 15

enojado/a *adj.* angry 5

enojarse (con) *v.* to get angry (with) 7

ensalada *f.* salad 8

ensayo *m.* essay 3

enseguida *adv.* right away

enseñar *v.* to teach 2

ensuciar *v.* to get (something) dirty 12

entender (e:ie) *v.* to understand 4

enterarse *v.* to find out 16

entonces *adv.* so, then 5, 7

entrada *f.* entrance 12; ticket

entre *prep.* between; among 2

entregar *v.* to hand in 11

entremeses *m., pl.* hors d'oeuvres; appetizers 8

entrenador(a) *m., f.* trainer 15

entrenarse *v.* to practice; to train 15

entrevista *f.* interview 16

entrevistador(a) *m., f.* interviewer 16

entrevistar *v.* to interview 16

envase *m.* container 13

enviar *v.* to send; to mail 14

equilibrado/a *adj.* balanced 15

equipaje *m.* luggage 5

equipo *m.* team 4

equivocado/a *adj.* wrong 5

eres *fam.* you are 1

es he/she/it is 1
  Es bueno que... It's good that... 12
  es cierto it's certain 13
  es extraño it's strange 13
  es igual it's the same 5
  Es importante que... It's important that... 12
  es imposible it's impossible 13
  es improbable it's improbable 13
  Es malo que... It's bad that... 12
  Es mejor que... It's better that... 12
  Es necesario que... It's necessary that... 12
  es obvio it's obvious 13
  es posible it's possible 13
  es probable it's probable 13
  es ridículo it's ridiculous 13
  es seguro it's certain 13
  es terrible it's terrible 13
  es triste it's sad 13
  Es urgente que... It's urgent that... 12
  Es la una. It's one o'clock. 1
  es una lástima it's a shame 13
  es verdad it's true 13

esa(s) *f., adj.* that; those 6

ésa(s) *f., pron.* that (one); those (ones) 6

escalar *v.* to climb 4
  escalar montañas to climb mountains 4

escalera *f.* stairs; stairway 12

escalón *m.* step 15

escanear *v.* to scan 11

escoger *v.* to choose 8

escribir *v.* to write 3
  escribir un mensaje electrónico to write an e-mail 4
  escribir una carta to write a letter 4

escrito/a *p.p.* written 14

escritor(a) *m., f.* writer 17

escritorio *m.* desk 2

escuchar *v.* to listen (to) 2
  escuchar la radio to listen to the radio 2
  escuchar música to listen to music 2

escuela *f.* school 1

esculpir *v.* to sculpt 17

escultor(a) *m., f.* sculptor 17

escultura *f.* sculpture 17

ese *m., sing., adj.* that 6

ése *m., sing., pron.* that one 6

eso *neuter, pron.* that; that thing 6

esos *m., pl., adj.* those 6

ésos *m., pl., pron.* those (ones) 6

España *f.* Spain

español *m.* Spanish (*language*) 2

español(a) *adj. m., f.* Spanish 3

espárragos *m., pl.* asparagus 8

especialidad: las especialidades del día today's specials 8

especialización *f.* major 2

espectacular *adj.* spectacular

espectáculo *m.* show 17

espejo *m.* mirror 7

esperar *v.* to hope; to wish 13
  esperar (+ inf.) *v.* to wait (for); to hope 2

esposo/a *m., f.* husband/wife; spouse 3

esquí (acuático) *m.* (water) skiing 4

esquiar *v.* to ski 4

esquina *f.* corner 14

está he/she/it is, you are
  Está bien. That's fine.
  Está (muy) despejado. It's (very) clear. (*weather*)
  Está lloviendo. It's raining. 5
  Está nevando. It's snowing. 5
  Está (muy) nublado. It's (very) cloudy. (*weather*) 5

esta(s) *f., adj.* this; these 6
  esta noche tonight

ésta(s) *f., pron.* this (one); these (ones) 6

establecer *v.* to establish 16

estación *f.* station; season 5
  estación de autobuses bus station 5
  estación del metro subway station 5
  estación de tren train station 5

estacionamiento *m.* parking lot 14

estacionar *v.* to park 11

estadio *m.* stadium 2

estado civil *m.* marital status 9

Estados Unidos *m., pl.* (EE.UU.; E.U.) United States

estadounidense *adj. m., f.* from the United States 3

estampilla *f.* stamp 14

estante *m.* bookcase; bookshelves 12

estar *v.* to be 2
 estar a dieta to be on a diet 15
 estar aburrido/a to be bored 5
 estar afectado/a (por) to be affected (by) 13
 estar cansado/a to be tired 5
 estar contaminado/a to be polluted 13
 estar de acuerdo to agree 17
 Estoy de acuerdo. I agree. 17
 No estoy de acuerdo. I don't agree. 17
 estar de moda to be in fashion 6
 estar de vacaciones *f., pl.* to be on vacation 5
 estar en buena forma to be in good shape 15
 estar enfermo/a to be sick 10
 estar harto/a de... to be sick of... 18
 estar listo/a to be ready 5
 estar perdido/a to be lost 14
 estar roto/a to be broken
 estar seguro/a to be sure 5
 estar torcido/a to be twisted; to be sprained 10
 No está nada mal. It's not bad at all. 5

estatua *f.* statue 17

este *m.* east 14

este *m., sing., adj.* this 6

éste *m., sing., pron.* this (one) 6

estéreo *m.* stereo 11

estilo *m.* style

estiramiento *m.* stretching 15

esto *neuter pron.* this; this thing 6

estómago *m.* stomach 10

estornudar *v.* to sneeze 10

estos *m., pl., adj.* these 6

éstos *m., pl., pron.* these (ones) 6

estrella *f.* star 13
 estrella de cine *m., f.* movie star 17

estrés *m.* stress 15

estudiante *m., f.* student 1, 2

estudiantil *adj. m., f.* student 2

estudiar *v.* to study 2

estufa *f.* stove 12

estupendo/a *adj.* stupendous 5

etapa *f.* stage 9

evitar *v.* to avoid 13

examen *m.* test; exam 2

examen médico physical exam 10

excelente *adj. m., f.* excellent 5

exceso *m.* excess 15

excursión *f.* hike; tour; excursion 4

excursionista *m., f.* hiker

éxito *m.* success

experiencia *f.* experience

explicar *v.* to explain 2

explorar *v.* to explore

expresión *f.* expression

extinción *f.* extinction 13

extranjero/a *adj.* foreign 17

extrañar *v.* to miss 16

extraño/a *adj.* strange 13

F

fábrica *f.* factory 13

fabuloso/a *adj.* fabulous 5

fácil *adj.* easy 3

falda *f.* skirt 6

faltar *v.* to lack; to need 7

familia *f.* family 3

famoso/a *adj.* famous

farmacia *f.* pharmacy 10

fascinar *v.* to fascinate 7

favorito/a *adj.* favorite 4

fax *m.* fax (machine)

febrero *m.* February 5

fecha *f.* date 5

¡Felicidades! Congratulations! 9

¡Felicitaciones! Congratulations! 9

feliz *adj.* happy 5
 ¡Feliz cumpleaños! Happy birthday! 9

fenomenal *adj.* great, phenomenal 5

feo/a *adj.* ugly 3

festival *m.* festival 17

fiebre *f.* fever 10

fiesta *f.* party 9

fijo/a *adj.* fixed, set 6

fin *m.* end 4
 fin de semana weekend 4

finalmente *adv.* finally

firmar *v.* to sign (*a document*) 14

física *f.* physics 2

flan (de caramelo) *m.* baked (caramel) custard 9

flexible *adj.* flexible 15

flor *f.* flower 13

folclórico/a *adj.* folk; folkloric 17

folleto *m.* brochure

forma *f.* shape 15

formulario *m.* form 14

foto(grafía) *f.* photograph 1

francés, francesa *adj. m., f.* French 3

frecuentemente *adv.* frequently

frenos *m., pl.* brakes

frente (frío) *m.* (cold) front 5

fresco/a *adj.* cool

frijoles *m., pl.* beans 8

frío/a *adj.* cold

frito/a *adj.* fried 8

fruta *f.* fruit 8

frutería *f.* fruit store 14

fuera *adv.* outside

fuerte *adj. m., f.* strong 15

fumar *v.* to smoke 15
 (no) fumar *v.* (not) to smoke 15

funcionar *v.* to work 11; to function

fútbol *m.* soccer 4

fútbol americano *m.* football 4

futuro/a *adj.* future
 en el futuro in the future

G

gafas (de sol) *f., pl.* (sun)glasses 6

gafas (oscuras) *f., pl.* (sun)glasses

galleta *f.* cookie 9

ganar *v.* to win 4; to earn (money) 16

ganga *f.* bargain 6

garaje *m.* garage; (mechanic's) repair shop 11; garage (*in a house*) 12

garganta *f.* throat 10

gasolina *f.* gasoline 11

gasolinera *f.* gas station 11

gastar *v.* to spend (*money*) 6

gato *m.* cat 13

gemelo/a *m., f.* twin 3

genial *adj.* great 16

gente *f.* people 3

geografía *f.* geography 2

gerente *m., f.* manager 8, 16

gimnasio *m.* gymnasium 4

gobierno *m.* government 13

golf *m.* golf 4

gordo/a *adj.* fat 3

grabar *v.* to record 11

gracias *f., pl.* thank you; thanks 1
 Gracias por invitarme. Thanks for inviting me. 9

graduarse (de/en) *v.* to graduate (from/in) 9

grande *adj.* big; large 3

grasa *f.* fat 15

gratis *adj. m., f.* free of charge 14

grave *adj.* grave; serious 10

gripe *f.* flu 10

gris *adj. m., f.* gray 6

gritar *v.* to scream, to shout

grito *m.* scream 5

guantes *m., pl.* gloves 6

guapo/a *adj.* handsome; good-looking 3

guardar *v.* to save (on a computer) 11

guerra *f.* war 18

guía *m., f.* guide

gustar *v.* to be pleasing to; to like 2
 Me gustaría... I would like...

gusto *m.* pleasure 1
 El gusto es mío. The pleasure is mine. 1

Mucho gusto. Pleased to meet you. 1
¡Qué gusto verlo/la! *(form.) How nice to see you!* 18
¡Qué gusto verte! *(fam.) How nice to see you!* 18

H

haber *(auxiliar) v.* to have (done something) 15
habitación *f.* room 5
  habitación doble double room 5
  habitación individual single room 5
hablar *v.* to talk; to speak 2
hacer *v.* to do; to make 4
  Hace buen tiempo. The weather is good. 5
  Hace (mucho) calor. It's (very) hot. *(weather)* 5
  Hace fresco. It's cool. *(weather)* 5
  Hace (mucho) frío. It's (very) cold. *(weather)* 5
  Hace mal tiempo. The weather is bad. 5
  Hace (mucho) sol. It's (very) sunny. *(weather)* 5
  Hace (mucho) viento. It's (very) windy. *(weather)* 5
  hacer cola to stand in line 14
  hacer diligencias to run errands 14
  hacer ejercicio to exercise 15
  hacer ejercicios aeróbicos to do aerobics 15
  hacer ejercicios de estiramiento to do stretching exercises 15
  hacer el papel (de) to play the role (of) 17
  hacer gimnasia to work out 15
  hacer juego (con) to match (with) 6
  hacer la cama to make the bed 12
  hacer las maletas to pack (one's) suitcases 5
  hacer quehaceres domésticos to do household chores 12
  hacer (wind)surf to (wind)surf 5
  hacer turismo to go sightseeing
  hacer un viaje to take a trip 5
  ¿Me harías el honor de casarte conmigo? Would you do me the honor of marrying me? 17
hacia *prep.* toward 14
hambre *f.* hunger
hamburguesa *f.* hamburger 8
hasta *prep.* until 6; toward
  Hasta la vista. See you later. 1
  Hasta luego. See you later. 1
  Hasta mañana. See you tomorrow. 1

Hasta pronto. See you soon. 1
hasta que *conj.* until 13
hay there is; there are 1
  Hay (mucha) contaminación. It's (very) smoggy.
  Hay (mucha) niebla. It's (very) foggy.
  Hay que It is necessary that
  No hay de qué. You're welcome. 1
  No hay duda de There's no doubt 13
hecho/a *p.p.* done 14
heladería *f.* ice cream shop 14
helado/a *adj.* iced 8
helado *m.* ice cream 9
hermanastro/a *m., f.* stepbrother/stepsister 3
hermano/a *m., f.* brother/sister 3
hermano/a mayor/menor *m., f.* older/younger brother/sister 3
hermanos *m., pl.* siblings (brothers and sisters) 3
hermoso/a *adj.* beautiful 6
hierba *f.* grass 13
hijastro/a *m., f.* stepson/stepdaughter 3
hijo/a *m., f.* son/daughter 3
  hijo/a único/a *m., f.* only child 3
  hijos *m., pl.* children 3
híjole *interj.* wow 6
historia *f.* history 2; story 17
hockey *m.* hockey 4
hola *interj.* hello; hi 1
hombre *m.* man 1
  hombre de negocios *m.* businessman 16
hora *f.* hour 1; the time
horario *m.* schedule 2
horno *m.* oven 12
  horno de microondas *m.* microwave oven 12
horror *m.* horror 17
  de horror horror (genre) 17
hospital *m.* hospital 10
hotel *m.* hotel 5
hoy *adv.* today 2
  hoy día *adv.* nowadays
  Hoy es... Today is... 2
hueco *m.* hole 4
huelga *f.* strike *(labor)* 18
hueso *m.* bone 10
huésped *m., f.* guest 5
huevo *m.* egg 8
humanidades *f., pl.* humanities 2
huracán *m.* hurricane 18

I

ida *f.* one way *(travel)*
idea *f.* idea 18
iglesia *f.* church 4
igualdad *f.* equality 18
igualmente *adv.* likewise 1
impermeable *m.* raincoat 6

importante *adj. m., f.* important 3
importar *v.* to be important to; to matter 7
imposible *adj. m., f.* impossible 13
impresora *f.* printer 11
imprimir *v.* to print 11
improbable *adj. m., f.* improbable 13
impuesto *m.* tax 18
incendio *m.* fire 18
increíble *adj. m., f.* incredible 5
indicar cómo llegar *v.* to give directions 14
individual *adj.* single *(room)* 5
infección *f.* infection 10
informar *v.* to inform 18
informe *m.* report; paper *(written work)* 18
ingeniero/a *m., f.* engineer 3
inglés *m.* English *(language)* 2
inglés, inglesa *adj.* English 3
inodoro *m.* toilet 7
insistir (en) *v.* to insist (on) 12
inspector(a) de aduanas *m., f.* customs inspector 5
inteligente *adj. m., f.* intelligent 3
intento *m.* attempt 11
intercambiar *v.* to exchange
interesante *adj. m., f.* interesting 3
interesar *v.* to be interesting to; to interest 7
internacional *adj. m., f.* international 18
Internet Internet 11
inundación *f.* flood 18
invertir (e:ie) *v.* to invest 16
invierno *m.* winter 5
invitado/a *m., f.* guest 9
invitar *v.* to invite 9
inyección *f.* injection 10
ir *v.* to go 4
  ir a (+ inf.) to be going to do something 4
  ir de compras to go shopping 5
  ir de excursión (a las montañas) to go on a hike (in the mountains) 4
  ir de pesca to go fishing
  ir de vacaciones to go on vacation 5
  ir en autobús to go by bus 5
  ir en auto(móvil) to go by auto(mobile); to go by car 5
  ir en avión to go by plane 5
  ir en barco to go by boat 5
  ir en metro to go by subway
  ir en moto(cicleta) to go by motorcycle 5
  ir en taxi to go by taxi 5
  ir en tren to go by train
irse *v.* to go away; to leave 7
italiano/a *adj.* Italian 3
izquierda *f.* left 2
  a la izquierda de to the left of 2

J

jabón *m.* soap 7
jamás *adv.* never; not ever 7
jamón *m.* ham 8
japonés, japonesa *adj.* Japanese 3
jardín *m.* garden; yard 12
jefe, jefa *m., f.* boss 16
jengibre *m.* ginger 10
joven *adj. m., f., sing.* (**jóvenes** *pl.*)
  young 3
  joven *m., f., sing.* (**jóvenes** *pl.*)
  young person 1
joyería *f.* jewelry store 14
jubilarse *v.* to retire (*from work*) 9
juego *m.* game
jueves *m., sing.* Thursday 2
jugador(a) *m., f.* player 4
jugar (u:ue) *v.* to play 4
  jugar a las cartas *f., pl.* to
  play cards 5
jugo *m.* juice 8
  jugo de fruta *m.* fruit juice 8
julio *m.* July 5
jungla *f.* jungle 13
junio *m.* June 5
juntos/as *adj.* together 9
juventud *f.* youth 9

K

kilómetro *m.* kilometer 11

L

la *f., sing., def. art.* the 1; *f., sing.,*
  d.o. pron. her, it, *form.* you 5
laboratorio *m.* laboratory 2
lago *m.* lake 13
lámpara *f.* lamp 12
lana *f.* wool 6
langosta *f.* lobster 8
lápiz *m.* pencil 1
largo/a *adj.* long 6
las *f., pl., def. art.* the 1; *f., pl., d.o.*
  pron. them; you 5
lástima *f.* shame 13
lastimarse *v.* to injure oneself 10
  lastimarse el pie to injure
  one's foot 10
lata *f.* (*tin*) can 13
lavabo *m.* sink 7
lavadora *f.* washing machine 12
lavandería *f.* laundromat 14
lavaplatos *m., sing.* dishwasher 12
lavar *v.* to wash 12
  lavar (el suelo, los platos) to
  wash (the floor, the dishes) 12
lavarse *v.* to wash oneself 7
  lavarse la cara to wash one's
  face 7
  lavarse las manos to wash
  one's hands 7
le *sing., i.o. pron.* to/for him, her,
  form. you 6

Le presento a... *form.* I would
  like to introduce you to (name). 1
lección *f.* lesson 1
leche *f.* milk 8
lechuga *f.* lettuce 8
leer *v.* to read 3
  leer el correo electrónico
  to read e-mail 4
  leer un periódico to read a
  newspaper 4
  leer una revista to read a
  magazine 4
leído/a *p.p.* read 14
lejos de *prep.* far from 2
lengua *f.* language 2
  lenguas extranjeras *f., pl.*
  foreign languages 2
lentes de contacto *m., pl.*
  contact lenses
  lentes (de sol) (sun)glasses
lento/a *adj.* slow 11
les *pl., i.o. pron.* to/for them,
  you 6
letrero *m.* sign 14
levantar *v.* to lift 15
  levantar pesas to lift
  weights 15
levantarse *v.* to get up 7
ley *f.* law 13
libertad *f.* liberty; freedom 18
libre *adj. m., f.* free 4
librería *f.* bookstore 2
libro *m.* book 2
licencia de conducir *f.* driver's
  license 11
limón *m.* lemon 8
limpiar *v.* to clean 12
  limpiar la casa *v.* to clean the
  house 12
limpio/a *adj.* clean 5
línea *f.* line 4
listo/a *adj.* ready; smart 5
literatura *f.* literature 2
llamar *v.* to call 11
  llamar por teléfono to call on
  the phone
llamarse *v.* to be called; to be
  named 7
llanta *f.* tire 11
llave *f.* key 5; wrench 11
llegada *f.* arrival 5
llegar *v.* to arrive 2
llenar *v.* to fill 11, 14
  llenar el tanque to fill the
  tank 11
  llenar (un formulario) to fill
  out (a form) 14
lleno/a *adj.* full 11
llevar *v.* to carry 2; to wear;
  to take 6
  llevar una vida sana to lead
  a healthy lifestyle 15
  llevarse bien/mal (con) to
  get along well/badly (with) 9
llorar *v.* to cry 15
llover (o:ue) *v.* to rain 5

Llueve. It's raining. 5
lluvia *f.* rain
lo *m., sing. d.o. pron.* him, it, *form.*
  you 5
  ¡Lo he pasado de película!
  I've had a fantastic time! 18
  lo mejor the best (thing)
  lo que that which; what 12
  Lo siento. I'm sorry. 1
loco/a *adj.* crazy 6
locutor(a) *m., f.* (TV or radio)
  announcer 18
lodo *m.* mud
los *m., pl., def. art.* the 1; *m. pl.,*
  d.o. pron. them, you 5
luchar (contra/por) *v.* to fight;
  to struggle (against/for) 18
luego *adv.* then 7; later 1
lugar *m.* place 2, 4
luna *f.* moon 13
lunares *m.* polka dots
lunes *m., sing.* Monday 2
luz *f.* light; electricity 12

M

madrastra *f.* stepmother 3
madre *f.* mother 3
madurez *f.* maturity; middle age 9
maestro/a *m., f.* teacher 16
magnífico/a *adj.* magnificent 5
maíz *m.* corn 8
mal, malo/a *adj.* bad 3
maleta *f.* suitcase 1
mamá *f.* mom
mandar *v.* to order 12; to send;
  to mail 14
manejar *v.* to drive 11
manera *f.* way
mano *f.* hand 1
manta *f.* blanket 12
mantener *v.* to maintain 15
  mantenerse en forma to stay
  in shape 15
mantequilla *f.* butter 8
manzana *f.* apple 8
mañana *f.* morning, a.m. 1;
  tomorrow 1
mapa *m.* map 1, 2
maquillaje *m.* makeup 7
maquillarse *v.* to put on
  makeup 7
mar *m.* sea 5
maravilloso/a *adj.* marvelous 5
mareado/a *adj.* dizzy; nauseated
  10
margarina *f.* margarine 8
mariscos *m., pl.* shellfish 8
marrón *adj. m., f.* brown 6
martes *m., sing.* Tuesday 2
marzo *m.* March 5
más *adv.* more 2
  más de (+ *number*) more
  than 8
  más tarde later (on) 7
  más... que more... than 8

masaje *m.* massage 15
matemáticas *f., pl.* mathematics 2
materia *f.* course 2
matrimonio *m.* marriage 9
máximo/a *adj.* maximum 11
mayo *m.* May 5
mayonesa *f.* mayonnaise 8
mayor *adj.* older 3
 el/la mayor *adj.* oldest 8
me *sing., d.o. pron.* me 5; *sing. i.o. pron.* to/for me 6
 Me gusta... I like... 2
 Me gustaría(n)... I would like... 15
 Me llamo... My name is... 1
 Me muero por... I'm dying to (for)...
mecánico/a *m., f.* mechanic 11
mediano/a *adj.* medium
medianoche *f.* midnight 1
medias *f., pl.* pantyhose, stockings 6
medicamento *m.* medication 10
medicina *f.* medicine 10
médico/a *m., f.* doctor 3; *adj.* medical 10
medio/a *adj.* half 3
 medio ambiente *m.* environment 13
 medio/a hermano/a *m., f.* half-brother/half-sister 3
 mediodía *m.* noon 1
 medios de comunicación *m., pl.* means of communication; media 18
 y media thirty minutes past the hour (time) 1
mejor *adj.* better 8
 el/la mejor *m., f.* the best 8
mejorar *v.* to improve 13
melocotón *m.* peach 8
menor *adj.* younger 3
 el/la menor *m., f.* youngest 8
menos *adv.* less 10
 menos cuarto..., menos quince... quarter to... (*time*) 1
 menos de (+ *number*) fewer than 8
 menos... que less... than 8
mensaje *m.* **de texto** text message 11
mensaje electrónico *m.* e-mail message 4
mentira *f.* lie 4
menú *m.* menu 8
mercado *m.* market 6
 mercado al aire libre open-air market 6
merendar (e:ie) *v.* to snack 8; to have an afternoon snack
merienda *f.* afternoon snack 15
mes *m.* month 5
mesa *f.* table 2
mesita *f.* end table 12
 mesita de noche night stand 12
meterse en problemas *v.* to get into trouble 13

metro *m.* subway 5
mexicano/a *adj.* Mexican 3
mí *pron., obj. of prep.* me 9
mi(s) *poss. adj.* my 3
microonda *f.* microwave 12
 horno de microondas *m.* microwave oven 12
miedo *m.* fear
miel *f.* honey 10
mientras *conj.* while 10
miércoles *m., sing.* Wednesday 2
mil *m.* one thousand 2
 mil millones billion
milla *f.* mile
millón *m.* million 2
millones (de) *m.* millions (of)
mineral *m.* mineral 15
minuto *m.* minute
mío(s)/a(s) *poss.* my; (of) mine 11
mirar *v.* to look (at); to watch 2
 mirar (la) televisión to watch television 2
mismo/a *adj.* same 3
mochila *f.* backpack 2
moda *f.* fashion 6
moderno/a *adj.* modern 17
molestar *v.* to bother; to annoy 7
monitor *m.* (computer) monitor 11
 monitor(a) *m., f.* trainer
mono *m.* monkey 13
montaña *f.* mountain 4
montar *v.* **a caballo** to ride a horse 4
montón: un montón de a lot of 4
monumento *m.* monument 4
morado/a *adj.* purple 6
moreno/a *adj.* brunet(te) 3
morir (o:ue) *v.* to die 8
mostrar (o:ue) *v.* to show 4
moto(cicleta) *f.* motorcycle 5
motor *m.* motor
muchacho/a *m., f.* boy/girl 3
mucho/a *adj.*, a lot of; much; many 3
 (Muchas) gracias. Thank you (very much); Thanks (a lot). 1
 muchas veces *adv.* a lot; many times 10
 Mucho gusto. Pleased to meet you. 1
mudarse *v.* to move (from one house to another) 12
muebles *m., pl.* furniture 12
muerte *f.* death 9
muerto/a *p.p.* died 14
mujer *f.* woman 1
 mujer de negocios *f.* business woman 16
 mujer policía *f.* female police officer
multa *f.* fine
mundial *adj. m., f.* worldwide
mundo *m.* world 8
muro *m.* wall 15
músculo *m.* muscle 15
museo *m.* museum 4
música *f.* music 2, 17

musical *adj. m., f.* musical 17
músico/a *m., f.* musician 17
muy *adv.* very 1
 (Muy) bien, gracias. (Very) well, thanks. 1

N

nacer *v.* to be born 9
nacimiento *m.* birth 9
nacional *adj. m., f.* national 18
nacionalidad *f.* nationality 1
nada nothing 1; not anything 7
 nada mal not bad at all 5
nadar *v.* to swim 4
nadie *pron.* no one, nobody, not anyone 7
naranja *f.* orange 8
nariz *f.* nose 10
natación *f.* swimming 4
natural *adj. m., f.* natural 13
naturaleza *f.* nature 13
navegador *m.* **GPS** GPS 11
navegar (en Internet) *v.* to surf (the Internet) 11
Navidad *f.* Christmas 9
necesario/a *adj.* necessary 12
necesitar (+ *inf.*) *v.* to need 2
negar (e:ie) *v.* to deny 13
 no negar (e:ie) *v.* not to deny 13
negocios *m., pl.* business; commerce 16
negro/a *adj.* black 6
nervioso/a *adj.* nervous 5
nevar (e:ie) *v.* to snow 5
 Nieva. It's snowing. 5
ni...ni neither... nor 7
niebla *f.* fog
nieto/a *m., f.* grandson/granddaughter 3
nieve *f.* snow
ningún, ninguno/a(s) *adj.* no; none; not any 7
niñez *f.* childhood 9
niño/a *m., f.* child 3
no no; not 1
 ¿no? right? 1
 no cabe duda de there is no doubt 13
 no es seguro it's not certain 13
 no es verdad it's not true 13
 No está nada mal. It's not bad at all. 5
 no estar de acuerdo to disagree
 No estoy seguro. I'm not sure.
 no hay there is not; there are not 1
 No hay de qué. You're welcome. 1
 no hay duda de there is no doubt 13
 ¡No me diga(s)! You don't say!
 No me gustan nada. I don't like them at all. 2

no muy bien not very well 1
No quiero. I don't want to. 4
No sé. I don't know.
No te preocupes. (*fam.*) Don't worry. 7
no tener razón to be wrong 3
noche *f.* night 1
nombre *m.* name 1
norte *m.* north 14
norteamericano/a *adj.* (North) American 3
nos *pl., d.o. pron.* us 5; *pl., i.o. pron.* to/for us 6
Nos vemos. See you. 1
nosotros/as *sub. pron.* we 1; *obj. pron.* us
noticia *f.* news 11
noticias *f., pl.* news 18
noticiero *m.* newscast 18
novecientos/as nine hundred 2
noveno/a *adj.* ninth 5
noventa ninety 2
noviembre *m.* November 5
novio/a *m., f.* boyfriend/girlfriend 3
nube *f.* cloud 13
nublado/a *adj.* cloudy 5
Está (muy) nublado. It's very cloudy. 5
nuclear *adj. m. f.* nuclear 13
nuera *f.* daughter-in-law 3
nuestro(s)/a(s) *poss. adj.* our 3; our, (of) ours 11
nueve nine 1
nuevo/a *adj.* new 6
número *m.* number 1; (shoe) size 6
nunca *adv.* never; not ever 7
nutrición *f.* nutrition 15
nutricionista *m., f.* nutritionist 15

O

o or 7
o... o ; either... or 7
obedecer *v.* to obey 18
obra *f.* work (*of art, literature, music, etc.*) 17
obra maestra *f.* masterpiece 17
obtener *v.* to obtain; to get 16
obvio/a *adj.* obvious 13
océano *m.* ocean
ochenta eighty 2
ocho eight 1
ochocientos/as eight hundred 2
octavo/a *adj.* eighth 5
octubre *m.* October 5
ocupación *f.* occupation 16
ocupado/a *adj.* busy 5
ocurrir *v.* to occur; to happen 18
odiar *v.* to hate 9
oeste *m.* west 14
oferta *f.* offer
oficina *f.* office 12

oficio *m.* trade 16
ofrecer *v.* to offer 6
oído *m.* (sense of) hearing; inner ear 10
oído/a *p.p.* heard 14
oír *v.* to hear 4
ojalá (que) *interj.* I hope (that); I wish (that) 13
ojo *m.* eye 10
olvidar *v.* to forget 10
once eleven 1
ópera *f.* opera 17
operación *f.* operation 10
ordenado/a *adj.* orderly 5
ordinal *adj.* ordinal (*number*)
oreja *f.* (outer) ear 10
organizarse *v.* to organize oneself 12
orquesta *f.* orchestra 17
ortografía *f.* spelling
ortográfico/a *adj.* spelling
os *fam., pl. d.o. pron.* you 5; *fam., pl. i.o. pron.* to/for you 6
otoño *m.* autumn 5
otro/a *adj.* other; another 6
otra vez again

P

paciente *m., f.* patient 10
padrastro *m.* stepfather 3
padre *m.* father 3
padres *m., pl.* parents 3
pagar *v.* to pay 6
pagar a plazos to pay in installments 14
pagar al contado to pay in cash 14
pagar en efectivo to pay in cash 14
pagar la cuenta to pay the bill
página *f.* page 11
página principal *f.* home page 11
país *m.* country 1
paisaje *m.* landscape 5
pájaro *m.* bird 13
palabra *f.* word 1
paleta helada *f.* popsicle 4
pálido/a *adj.* pale 14
pan *m.* bread 8
pan tostado *m.* toasted bread 8
panadería *f.* bakery 14
pantalla *f.* screen 11
pantalla táctil *f.* touch screen
pantalones *m., pl.* pants 6
pantalones cortos *m., pl.* shorts 6
pantuflas *f.* slippers 7
papa *f.* potato 8
papas fritas *f., pl.* fried potatoes; French fries 8
papá *m.* dad
papás *m., pl.* parents
papel *m.* paper 2; role 17

papelera *f.* wastebasket 2
paquete *m.* package 14
par *m.* pair 6
par de zapatos pair of shoes 6
para *prep.* for; in order to; by; used for; considering 11
para que *conj.* so that 13
parabrisas *m., sing.* windshield 11
parar *v.* to stop 11
parecer *v.* to seem 6
pared *f.* wall 12
pareja *f.* (married) couple; partner 9
parientes *m., pl.* relatives 3
parque *m.* park 4
párrafo *m.* paragraph
parte: de parte de on behalf of 11
partido *m.* game; match (*sports*) 4
pasado/a *adj.* last; past 6
pasado *p.p.* passed
pasaje *m.* ticket 5
pasaje de ida y vuelta *m.* roundtrip ticket 5
pasajero/a *m., f.* passenger 1
pasaporte *m.* passport 5
pasar *v.* to go through
pasar la aspiradora to vacuum 12
pasar por la aduana to go through customs
pasar tiempo to spend time
pasarlo bien/mal to have a good/bad time 9
pasatiempo *m.* pastime; hobby 4
pasear *v.* to take a walk; to stroll 4
pasear en bicicleta to ride a bicycle 4
pasear por to walk around
pasillo *m.* hallway 12
pasta *f.* **de dientes** toothpaste 7
pastel *m.* cake; pie 9
pastel de chocolate *m.* chocolate cake 9
pastel de cumpleaños *m.* birthday cake
pastelería *f.* pastry shop 14
pastilla *f.* pill; tablet 10
patata *f.* potato 8
patatas fritas *f., pl.* fried potatoes; French fries 8
patinar (en línea) *v.* to (inline) skate 4
patineta *f.* skateboard 4
patio *m.* patio; yard 12
pavo *m.* turkey 8
paz *f.* peace 18
pedir (e:i) *v.* to ask for; to request 4; to order (*food*) 8
pedir prestado *v.* to borrow 14
pedir un préstamo *v.* to apply for a loan 14
Todos me dijeron que te pidiera una disculpa de su parte. They all told me to ask you to excuse them/forgive them. 18
peinarse *v.* to comb one's hair 7

película *f.* movie 4
peligro *m.* danger 13
peligroso/a *adj.* dangerous 18
pelirrojo/a *adj.* red-haired 3
pelo *m.* hair 7
pelota *f.* ball 4
peluquería *f.* beauty salon 14
peluquero/a *m., f.* hairdresser 16
penicilina *f.* penicillin
pensar (e:ie) *v.* to think 4
  pensar (+ inf.) *v.* to intend to;
    to plan to (*do something*) 4
  pensar en *v.* to think about 4
pensión *f.* boardinghouse
peor *adj.* worse 8
  el/la peor *adj.* the worst 8
pequeño/a *adj.* small 3
pera *f.* pear 8
perder (e:ie) *v.* to lose; to miss 4
perdido/a *adj.* lost 13, 14
Perdón. Pardon me.;
  Excuse me. 1
perezoso/a *adj.* lazy
perfecto/a *adj.* perfect 5
periódico *m.* newspaper 4
periodismo *m.* journalism 2
periodista *m., f.* journalist 3
permiso *m.* permission
pero *conj.* but 2
perro *m.* dog 13
persona *f.* person 3
personaje *m.* character 17
  personaje principal *m.*
    main character 17
pesas *f. pl.* weights 15
pesca *f.* fishing
pescadería *f.* fish market 14
pescado *m.* fish (*cooked*) 8
pescar *v.* to fish 5
peso *m.* weight 15
pez *m., sing.* (**peces** *pl.*) fish (*live*) 13
pie *m.* foot 10
piedra *f.* stone 13
pierna *f.* leg 10
pimienta *f.* black pepper 8
pintar *v.* to paint 17
pintor(a) *m., f.* painter 16
pintura *f.* painting; picture 12, 17
piña *f.* pineapple
piscina *f.* swimming pool 4
piso *m.* floor (*of a building*) 5
pizarra *f.* blackboard 2
placer *m.* pleasure
planchar la ropa *v.* to iron the
  clothes 12
planes *m., pl.* plans
planta *f.* plant 13
  planta baja *f.* ground floor 5
plástico *m.* plastic 13
plato *m.* dish (*in a meal*) 8; *m.*
  plate 12
  plato principal *m.* main dish 8
playa *f.* beach 5
plaza *f.* city or town square 4
plazos *m., pl.* periods; time 14
pluma *f.* pen 2
plumero *m.* duster 12
población *f.* population 13

pobre *adj. m., f.* poor 6
pobrecito/a *adj.* poor thing 3
pobreza *f.* poverty
poco *adv.* little 5, 10
poder (o:ue) *v.* to be able to; can 4
  ¿Podría pedirte algo? Could I
    ask you something? 17
  ¿Puedo dejar un recado?
    May I leave a message? 11
poema *m.* poem 17
poesía *f.* poetry 17
poeta *m., f.* poet 17
policía *f.* police (force) 11
política *f.* politics 18
político/a *m., f.* politician 16; *adj.*
  political 18
pollo *m.* chicken 8
  pollo asado *m.* roast chicken 8
poner *v.* to put; to place 4; to turn
  on (*electrical appliances*) 11
  poner la mesa to set the
    table 12
  poner una inyección to give
    an injection 10
  ponerle el nombre to name
  someone/something 9
ponerse (+ adj.) *v.* to become
  (+ *adj.*) 7; to put on 7
por *prep.* in exchange for; for;
  by; in; through; around; along;
  during; because of; on account
  of; on behalf of; in search of;
  by way of; by means of 11
  por aquí around here 11
  por ejemplo for example 11
  por eso that's why;
    therefore 11
  por favor please 1
  por fin finally 11
  por la mañana in the
    morning 7
  por la noche at night 7
  por la tarde in the afternoon 7
  por lo menos *adv.* at least 10
  ¿por qué? why? 2
  Por supuesto. Of course.
  por teléfono by phone; on the
    phone
  por último finally 7
porque *conj.* because 2
portátil *adj.* portable 11
portero/a *m., f.* doorman/
  doorwoman 1
porvenir *m.* future 16
  por el porvenir for/to the
    future 16
posesivo/a *adj.* possessive
posible *adj.* possible 13
  es posible it's possible 13
  no es posible it's not
    possible 13
postal *f.* postcard
postre *m.* dessert 9
practicar *v.* to practice 2
  practicar deportes *m., pl.* to
    play sports 4
precio (fijo) *m.* (fixed; set)
  price 6

preferir (e:ie) *v.* to prefer 4
pregunta *f.* question
preguntar *v.* to ask (*a question*) 2
premio *m.* prize; award 17
prender *v.* to turn on 11
prensa *f.* press 18
preocupado/a (por) *adj.* worried
  (about) 5
preocuparse (por) *v.* to worry
  (about) 7
preparar *v.* to prepare 2
preposición *f.* preposition
presentación *f.* introduction
presentar *v.* to introduce; to
  present 17; to put on (*a
  performance*) 17
  Le presento a… I would like
    to introduce you to (name).
    (*form.*) 1
  Te presento a… I would like
    to introduce you to (name).
    (*fam.*) 1
presiones *f., pl.* pressures 15
prestado/a *adj.* borrowed
préstamo *m.* loan 14
prestar *v.* to lend; to loan 6
primavera *f.* spring 5
primer, primero/a *adj.* first 5
primero *adv.* first 2
primo/a *m., f.* cousin 3
principal *adj. m., f.* main 8
prisa *f.* haste
  darse prisa *v.* to hurry;
    to rush 15
probable *adj. m., f.* probable 13
  es probable it's probable 13
  no es probable it's not
    probable 13
probar (o:ue) *v.* to taste; to try 8
probarse (o:ue) *v.* to try on 7
problema *m.* problem 1
profesión *f.* profession 3; 16
profesor(a) *m., f.* teacher 1, 2
programa *m.* program 1
  programa de computación
    m. software 11
  programa de entrevistas *m.*
    talk show 17
  programa de realidad *m.*
    reality show 17
programador(a) *m., f.* computer
  programmer 3
prohibir *v.* to prohibit 10;
  to forbid
pronombre *m.* pronoun
pronto *adv.* soon 10
propina *f.* tip 8
propio/a *adj.* own
proteger *v.* to protect 13
proteína *f.* protein 15
próximo/a *adj.* next 3, 16
proyecto *m.* project 11
prueba *f.* test; quiz 2
psicología *f.* psychology 2
psicólogo/a *m., f.*
  psychologist 16
publicar *v.* to publish 17

público *m.* audience 17
pueblo *m.* town
puerta *f.* door 2
puertorriqueño/a *adj.* Puerto Rican 3
pues *conj.* well
puesto *m.* position; job 16
puesto/a *p.p.* put 14
puro/a *adj.* pure 13

Q

que *pron.* that; which; who 12
   ¿En qué...? In which...?
   ¡Qué...! How...!
   ¡Qué dolor! What pain!
   ¡Qué ropa más bonita! What pretty clothes! 6
   ¡Qué sorpresa! What a surprise!
   ¿qué? what? 1, 2
   ¿Qué día es hoy? What day is it? 2
   ¿Qué hay de nuevo? What's new? 1
   ¿Qué hora es? What time is it? 1
   ¿Qué les parece? What do you (*pl.*) think?
   ¿Qué onda? What's up? 14
   ¿Qué pasa? What's happening? What's going on? 1
   ¿Qué pasó? What happened?
   ¿Qué precio tiene? What is the price?
   ¿Qué tal...? How are you?; How is it going? 1
   ¿Qué talla lleva/usa? What size do you wear? 6
   ¿Qué tiempo hace? How's the weather? 5
quedar *v.* to be left over; to fit (*clothing*) 7; to be located 14
quedarse *v.* to stay; to remain 7
quehaceres domésticos *m., pl.* household chores 12
quemar (un CD/DVD) *v.* to burn (a CD/DVD)
querer (e:ie) *v.* to want; to love 4
queso *m.* cheese 8
quien(es) *pron.* who; whom; that 12
¿quién(es)? who?; whom? 1, 2
   ¿Quién es...? Who is...? 1
   ¿Quién habla? Who is speaking/calling? (*telephone*) 11
química *f.* chemistry 2
quince fifteen 1
   menos quince quarter to (time) 1
   y quince quarter after (time) 1
quinceañera *f.* young woman celebrating her fifteenth birthday 9
quinientos/as five hundred 2
quinto/a *adj.* fifth 5
quisiera *v.* I would like

quitar el polvo *v.* to dust 12
quitar la mesa *v.* to clear the table 12
quitarse *v.* to take off 7
quizás *adv.* maybe 5

R

racismo *m.* racism 18
radio *f.* radio (*medium*) 2; *m.* radio (set) 11
radiografía *f.* X-ray 10
rápido *adv.* quickly 10
ratón *m.* mouse 11
ratos libres *m., pl.* spare (free) time 4
raya *f.* stripe
razón *f.* reason
rebaja *f.* sale 6
receta *f.* prescription 10
recetar *v.* to prescribe 10
recibir *v.* to receive 3
reciclaje *m.* recycling 13
reciclar *v.* to recycle 13
recién casado/a *m., f.* newlywed 9
recoger *v.* to pick up 13
recomendar (e:ie) *v.* to recommend 8, 12
recordar (o:ue) *v.* to remember 4
recorrer *v.* to tour an area
recorrido *m.* tour 13
recuperar *v.* to recover 11
recurso *m.* resource 13
   recurso natural *m.* natural resource 13
red *f.* network; Web 11
reducir *v.* to reduce 13
refresco *m.* soft drink 8
refrigerador *m.* refrigerator 12
regalar *v.* to give (a gift) 9
regalo *m.* gift 6
regatear *v.* to bargain 6
región *f.* region; area
regresar *v.* to return 2
regular *adv.* so-so; OK 1
reído *p.p.* laughed 14
reírse (e:i) *v.* to laugh 9
relaciones *f., pl.* relationships
relajarse *v.* to relax 9
reloj *m.* clock; watch 2
renovable *adj.* renewable 13
renunciar (a) *v.* to resign (from) 16
repetir (e:i) *v.* to repeat 4
reportaje *m.* report 18
reportero/a *m., f.* reporter 16
representante *m., f.* representative 18
reproductor de CD *m.* CD player 11
reproductor de DVD *m.* DVD player 11
reproductor de MP3 *m.* MP3 player 11
resfriado *m.* cold (*illness*) 10
residencia estudiantil *f.* dormitory 2

resolver (o:ue) *v.* to resolve; to solve 13
respirar *v.* to breathe 13
responsable *adj.* responsible 8
respuesta *f.* answer
restaurante *m.* restaurant 4
resuelto/a *p.p.* resolved 14
reunión *f.* meeting 16
revisar *v.* to check 11
   revisar el aceite *v.* to check the oil 11
revista *f.* magazine 4
rico/a *adj.* rich 6; *adj.* tasty; delicious 8
ridículo/a *adj.* ridiculous 13
río *m.* river 13
rodilla *f.* knee 10
rogar (o:ue) *v.* to beg; to plead 12
rojo/a *adj.* red 6
romántico/a *adj.* romantic 17
romper *v.* to break 10
   romperse la pierna *v.* to break one's leg 10
romper (con) *v.* to break up (with) 9
ropa *f.* clothing; clothes 6
   ropa interior *f.* underwear 6
rosado/a *adj.* pink 6
roto/a *adj.* broken 14
rubio/a *adj.* blond(e) 3
ruso/a *adj.* Russian 3
rutina *f.* routine 7
   rutina diaria *f.* daily routine 7

S

sábado *m.* Saturday 2
saber *v.* to know; to know how 6
   saber a to taste like 8
sabrosísimo/a *adj.* extremely delicious 8
sabroso/a *adj.* tasty; delicious 8
sacar *v.* to take out
   sacar buenas notas to get good grades 2
   sacar fotos to take photos 5
   sacar la basura to take out the trash 12
   sacar(se) un diente to have a tooth removed 10
sacudir *v.* to dust 12
   sacudir los muebles to dust the furniture 12
sal *f.* salt 8
sala *f.* living room 12; room
   sala de emergencia(s) emergency room 10
salario *m.* salary 16
salchicha *f.* sausage 8
salida *f.* departure; exit 5
salir *v.* to leave 4; to go out
   salir con to go out with; to date 4, 9
   salir de to leave from 4
   salir para to leave for (a place) 4
salmón *m.* salmon 8

salón de belleza *m.* beauty salon 14
salud *f.* health 10
saludable *adj.* healthy 10
saludar(se) *v.* to greet (each other) 11
saludo *m.* greeting 1
   saludos a... greetings to... 1
sandalia *f.* sandal 6
sandía *f.* watermelon
sándwich *m.* sandwich 8
sano/a *adj.* healthy 10
se *ref. pron.* himself, herself, itself, *form.* yourself, themselves, yourselves 7
se *impersonal* one 10
   Se hizo... He/she/it became...
secadora *f.* clothes dryer 12
secarse *v.* to dry (oneself) 7
sección de (no) fumar *f.* (non)smoking section 8
secretario/a *m., f.* secretary 16
secuencia *f.* sequence
sed *f.* thirst
seda *f.* silk 6
sedentario/a *adj.* sedentary; related to sitting 15
seguir (e:i) *v.* to follow; to continue 4
según according to
segundo/a *adj.* second 5
seguro/a *adj.* sure; safe; confident 5
seis six 1
seiscientos/as six hundred 2
sello *m.* stamp 14
selva *f.* jungle 13
semáforo *m.* traffic light 14
semana *f.* week 2
   fin *m.* **de semana** weekend 4
   semana *f.* **pasada** last week 6
semestre *m.* semester 2
sendero *m.* trail; path 13
sentarse (e:ie) *v.* to sit down 7
sentir (e:ie) *v.* to be sorry; to regret 13
sentirse (e:ie) *v.* to feel 7
señor (Sr.); don *m.* Mr.; sir 1
señora (Sra.); doña *f.* Mrs.; ma'am 1
señorita (Srta.) *f.* Miss 1
separado/a *adj.* separated 9
separarse (de) *v.* to separate (from) 9
septiembre *m.* September 5
séptimo/a *adj.* seventh 5
ser *v.* to be 1
   ser aficionado/a (a) to be a fan (of)
   ser alérgico/a (a) to be allergic (to) 10
   ser gratis to be free of charge 14
serio/a *adj.* serious
servicio *m.* service 15
servilleta *f.* napkin 12
servir (e:i) *v.* to serve 8; to help 5
sesenta sixty 2
setecientos/as seven hundred 2

setenta seventy 2
sexismo *m.* sexism 18
sexto/a *adj.* sixth 5
sí *adv.* yes 1
si *conj.* if 4
SIDA *m.* AIDS 18
siempre *adv.* always 7
siete seven 1
silla *f.* seat 2
sillón *m.* armchair 12
similar *adj. m., f.* similar
simpático/a *adj.* nice; likeable 3
sin *prep.* without 13
   sin duda without a doubt
   sin embargo however
   sin que *conj.* without 13
sino but (rather) 7
síntoma *m.* symptom 10
sitio *m.* place 3
sitio *m.* **web** website 11
situado/a *p.p.* located
sobre *m.* envelope 14; *prep.* on; over 2
   sobre todo above all 13
(sobre)población *f.* (over)population 13
sobrino/a *m., f.* nephew/niece 3
sociología *f.* sociology 2
sofá *m.* couch; sofa 12
sol *m.* sun 13
solar *adj. m., f.* solar 13
soldado *m., f.* soldier 18
soleado/a *adj.* sunny
solicitar *v.* to apply (*for a job*) 16
solicitud (de trabajo) *f.* (job) application 16
sólo *adv.* only 6
solo/a *adj.* alone
soltero/a *adj.* single 9
solución *f.* solution 13
sombrero *m.* hat 6
Son las dos. It's two o'clock. 1
sonar (o:ue) *v.* to ring 11
sonreído *p.p.* smiled 14
sonreír (e:i) *v.* to smile 9
sopa *f.* soup 8
sorprender *v.* to surprise 9
sorpresa *f.* surprise 9
sótano *m.* basement; cellar 12
soy I am 1
   Soy de... I'm from... 1
su(s) *poss. adj.* his; her; its; *form.* your; their 3
subir(se) a *v.* to get on/into (*a vehicle*) 11
sucio/a *adj.* dirty 5
sudar *v.* to sweat 15
suegro/a *m., f.* father-in-law/mother-in-law 3
sueldo *m.* salary 16
suelo *m.* floor 12
sueño *m.* sleep
suerte *f.* luck
suéter *m.* sweater 6
sufrir *v.* to suffer 10
   sufrir muchas presiones to be under a lot of pressure 15
   sufrir una enfermedad to suffer an illness 10

sugerir (e:ie) *v.* to suggest 12
supermercado *m.* supermarket 14
suponer *v.* to suppose 4
sur *m.* south 14
sustantivo *m.* noun
suyo(s)/a(s) *poss.* (of) his/her; (of) hers; its; *form.* your, (of) yours, (of) theirs, their 11

T

tabla de (wind)surf *f.* surf board/sailboard 5
tal vez *adv.* maybe 5
talentoso/a *adj.* talented 17
talla *f.* size 6
   talla grande *f.* large
taller *m.* **mecánico** garage; mechanic's repair shop 11
también *adv.* also; too 2; 7
tampoco *adv.* neither; not either 7
tan *adv.* so 5
   tan... como as... as 8
   tan pronto como *conj.* as soon as 13
tanque *m.* tank 11
tanto *adv.* so much
   tanto... como as much... as 8
tantos/as... como as many... as 8
tarde *adv.* late 7; *f.* afternoon; evening; P.M. 1
tarea *f.* homework 2
tarjeta *f.* (post) card
tarjeta de crédito *f.* credit card 6
tarjeta postal *f.* postcard
taxi *m.* taxi 5
taza *f.* cup 12
te *sing., fam., d.o. pron.* you 5; *sing., fam., i.o. pron.* to/for you 6
   Te presento a... *fam.* I would like to introduce you to (name). 1
   ¿Te gustaría? Would you like to?
   ¿Te gusta(n)...? Do you like...? 2
té *m.* tea 8
   té helado *m.* iced tea 8
teatro *m.* theater 17
teclado *m.* keyboard 11
técnico/a *m., f.* technician 16
tejido *m.* weaving 17
teleadicto/a *m., f.* couch potato 15
(teléfono) celular *m.* (cell) phone 11
telenovela *f.* soap opera 17
teletrabajo *m.* telecommuting 16
televisión *f.* television 2
televisión por cable *f.* cable television
televisor *m.* television set 11
temer *v.* to fear; to be afraid 13
temperatura *f.* temperature 10
temporada *f.* period of time 5
temprano *adv.* early 7

tenedor *m.* fork 12
tener *v.* to have 3
  tener... años to be... years old 3
  tener (mucho) calor to be (very) hot 3
  tener (mucho) cuidado to be (very) careful 3
  tener dolor to have pain 10
  tener éxito to be successful 16
  tener fiebre to have a fever 10
  tener (mucho) frío to be (very) cold 3
  tener ganas de (+ *inf.*) to feel like (*doing something*) 3
  tener (mucha) hambre *f.* to be (very) hungry 3
  tener (mucho) miedo (de) to be (very) afraid (of); to be (very) scared (of) 3
  tener miedo (de) que to be afraid that
  tener planes *m., pl.* to have plans
  tener (mucha) prisa to be in a (big) hurry 3
  tener que (+ *inf.*) *v.* to have to (*do something*) 3
  tener razón *f.* to be right 3
  tener (mucha) sed *f.* to be (very) thirsty 3
  tener (mucho) sueño to be (very) sleepy 3
  tener (mucha) suerte to be (very) lucky 3
  tener tiempo to have time 14
  tener una cita to have a date; to have an appointment 9
tenis *m.* tennis 4
tensión *f.* tension 15
tercer, tercero/a *adj.* third 5
terco/a *adj.* stubborn 10
terminar *v.* to end; to finish 2
  terminar de (+ *inf.*) *v.* to finish (*doing something*)
terremoto *m.* earthquake 18
terrible *adj. m., f.* terrible 13
ti *obj. of prep., fam.* you 9
tiempo *m.* time 14; weather 5
  tiempo libre free time
tienda *f.* store 6
tierra *f.* land; soil 13
tinto/a *adj.* red (wine) 8
tío/a *m., f.* uncle/aunt 3
tíos *m., pl.* aunts and uncles 3
título *m.* title 16
tiza *f.* chalk 2
toalla *f.* towel 7
tobillo *m.* ankle 10
tocar *v.* to play (*a musical instrument*) 17; to touch 17
todavía *adv.* yet; still 3, 5
todo *m.* everything 5
todo(s)/a(s) *adj.* all
todos *m., pl.* all of us; *m., pl.* everybody; everyone
todos los días *adv.* every day 10
tomar *v.* to take; to drink 2

tomar clases *f., pl.* to take classes 2
tomar el sol to sunbathe 4
tomar en cuenta to take into account
tomar fotos *f., pl.* to take photos 5
tomar la temperatura to take someone's temperature 10
tomar una decisión to make a decision 15
tomate *m.* tomato 8
tonto/a *adj.* foolish 3
torcerse (o:ue) (el tobillo) *v.* to sprain (one's ankle) 10
tormenta *f.* storm 18
tornado *m.* tornado 18
tortuga (marina) *f.* (sea) turtle 13
tos *f., sing.* cough 10
toser *v.* to cough 10
tostado/a *adj.* toasted 8
tostadora *f.* toaster 12
trabajador(a) *adj.* hard-working 3
trabajar *v.* to work 2
trabajo *m.* job; work 16
traducir *v.* to translate 6
traer *v.* to bring 4
tráfico *m.* traffic 11
tragedia *f.* tragedy 17
traído/a *p.p.* brought 14
traje *m.* suit 6
  traje de baño *m.* bathing suit 6
trajinera *f.* type of barge 3
tranquilo/a *adj.* calm; quiet 15
  Tranquilo/a. Relax. 7
  Tranquilo/a, cariño. Relax, sweetie. 11
transmitir *v.* to broadcast 18
tratar de (+ *inf.*) *v.* to try (*to do something*) 15
trece thirteen 1
treinta thirty 1, 2
  y treinta thirty minutes past the hour (time) 1
tren *m.* train 5
tres three 1
trescientos/as three hundred 2
trimestre *m.* trimester; quarter 2
triste *adj.* sad 5
tú *fam. sub. pron.* you 1
tu(s) *fam. poss. adj.* your 3
turismo *m.* tourism
turista *m., f.* tourist 1
turístico/a *adj.* touristic
tuyo(s)/a(s) *fam. poss. pron.* your; (of) yours 11

U

Ud. *form. sing.* you 1
Uds. *pl.* you 1
último/a *adj.* last 7
  la última vez the last time 7
un, uno/a *indef. art.* a; one 1
  a la una at one o'clock 1
  una vez once 6
  una vez más one more time

uno one 1
único/a *adj.* only 3; unique 9
universidad *f.* university; college 2
unos/as *m., f., pl. indef. art.* some 1
urgente *adj.* urgent 12
usar *v.* to wear; to use 6
usted (Ud.) *form. sing.* you 1
ustedes (Uds.) *pl.* you 1
útil *adj.* useful
uva *f.* grape 8

V

vaca *f.* cow 13
vacaciones *f. pl.* vacation 5
valle *m.* valley 13
vamos let's go 4
vaquero *m.* cowboy 17
  de vaqueros *m., pl.* western (genre) 17
varios/as *adj. m. f., pl.* various; several
vaso *m.* glass 12
veces *f., pl.* times 6
vecino/a *m., f.* neighbor 12
veinte twenty 1
veinticinco twenty-five 1
veinticuatro twenty-four 1
veintidós twenty-two 1
veintinueve twenty-nine 1
veintiocho twenty-eight 1
veintiséis twenty-six 1
veintisiete twenty-seven 1
veintitrés twenty-three 1
veintiún, veintiuno/a *adj.* twenty-one 1
veintiuno twenty-one 1
vejez *f.* old age 9
velocidad *f.* speed 11
  velocidad máxima *f.* speed limit 11
vencer *v.* to expire 14
vendedor(a) *m., f.* salesperson 6
vender *v.* to sell 6
venir *v.* to come 3
ventana *f.* window 2
ver *v.* to see 4
  a ver *v.* let's see
  ver películas *f., pl.* to see movies 4
verano *m.* summer 5
verbo *m.* verb
verdad *f.* truth 4
  (no) es verdad it's (not) true 13
  ¿verdad? right? 1
verde *adj., m. f.* green 6
verduras *pl., f.* vegetables 8
vestido *m.* dress 6
vestirse (e:i) *v.* to get dressed 7
vez *f.* time 6
viajar *v.* to travel 2
viaje *m.* trip 5
viajero/a *m., f.* traveler 5

vida *f.* life 9
video *m.* video 1
videoconferencia *f.* videoconference 16
videojuego *m.* video game 4
vidrio *m.* glass 13
viejo/a *adj.* old 3
viento *m.* wind
viernes *m., sing.* Friday 2
vinagre *m.* vinegar 8
vino *m.* wine 8
   vino blanco *m.* white wine 8
   vino tinto *m.* red wine 8
violencia *f.* violence 18
visitar *v.* to visit 4
   visitar monumentos *m., pl.* to visit monuments 4
visto/a *p.p.* seen 14
vitamina *f.* vitamin 15
viudo/a *adj.* widower/widow 9
vivienda *f.* housing 12
vivir *v.* to live 3
vivo/a *adj.* clever; living
volante *m.* steering wheel 11
volcán *m.* volcano 13
vóleibol *m.* volleyball 4
volver (o:ue) *v.* to return 4
volver a ver(te, lo, la) *v.* to see (you, him, her) again
vos *pron.* you

vosotros/as *fam., pl.* you 1
votar *v.* to vote 18
vuelta *f.* return trip
vuelto/a *p.p.* returned 14
vuestro(s)/a(s) *poss. adj.* your 3; your, (of) yours *fam., pl.* 11

Y

y *conj.* and 1
   y cuarto quarter after (time) 1
   y media half-past (time) 1
   y quince quarter after (time) 1
   y treinta thirty (minutes past the hour) 1
   ¿Y tú? *fam.* And you? 1
   ¿Y usted? *form.* And you? 1
ya *adv.* already 6
yerno *m.* son-in-law 3
yo *sub. pron.* I 1
yogur *m.* yogurt 8

Z

zanahoria *f.* carrot 8
zapatería *f.* shoe store 14
zapatos de tenis *m., pl.* tennis shoes, sneakers 6

English-Spanish

A

a **un/a** *m., f., sing.; indef. art.* 1
@ (*symbol*) **arroba** *f.* 1
a.m. **de la mañana** *f.* 1
able: be able to **poder (o:ue)** *v.* 4
aboard **a bordo**
above all **sobre todo** 13
accident **accidente** *m.* 10
accompany **acompañar** *v.* 14
account **cuenta** *f.* 14
   on account of **por** *prep.* 11
accountant **contador(a)** *m., f.* 16
accounting **contabilidad** *f.* 2
ache **dolor** *m.* 10
acquainted: be acquainted with
   conocer *v.* 6
action (genre) **de acción** *f.* 17
active **activo/a** *adj.* 15
actor **actor** *m.,* **actriz** *f.* 16
addict (*drug*) **drogadicto/a**
   m., f. 15
additional **adicional** *adj.*
address **dirección** *f.* 14
adjective **adjetivo** *m.*
adolescence **adolescencia** *f.* 9
adventure (genre) **de aventuras**
   f. 17
advertise **anunciar** *v.* 18
advertisement **anuncio** *m.* 16
advice **consejo** *m.*
   give advice **dar consejos** 6
advise **aconsejar** *v.* 12
advisor **consejero/a** *m., f.* 16
aerobic **aeróbico/a** *adj.* 15
   aerobics class **clase de**
      ejercicios aeróbicos 15
   to do aerobics **hacer ejercicios**
      aeróbicos 15
affected **afectado/a** *adj.* 13
   be affected (by) **estar** *v.*
      afectado/a (por) 13
affirmative **afirmativo/a** *adj.*
afraid: be (very) afraid (of) **tener**
   (mucho) miedo (de) 3
   be afraid that **tener miedo**
      (de) que
after **después de** *prep.* 7;
   después de que *conj.* 13
afternoon **tarde** *f.* 1
afterward **después** *adv.* 7
again **otra vez**
age **edad** *f.* 9
agree **concordar** *v.*
agree **estar** *v.* **de acuerdo** 17
   I agree. **Estoy de acuerdo.** 17
   I don't agree. **No estoy de**
      acuerdo. 17
agreement **acuerdo** *m.*
AIDS **SIDA** *m.* 18
air **aire** *m.* 13
   air pollution **contaminación**
      del aire 13
airplane **avión** *m.* 5
airport **aeropuerto** *m.* 5
alarm clock **despertador** *m.* 7

alcohol **alcohol** *m.* 15
   to consume alcohol **consumir**
      alcohol 15
alcoholic **alcohólico/a** *adj.* 15
all **todo(s)/a(s)** *adj.*
   all of us **todos**
allergic **alérgico/a** *adj.* 10
   be allergic (to) **ser alérgico/a**
      (a) 10
alleviate **aliviar** *v.*
almost **casi** *adv.* 10
alone **solo/a** *adj.*
along **por** *prep.* 11
already **ya** *adv.* 6
also **también** *adv.* 2; 7
altar **altar** *m.* 9
aluminum **aluminio** *m.* 13
   (made) of aluminum **de**
      aluminio 13
always **siempre** *adv.* 7
American (*North*)
   norteamericano/a *adj.* 3
among **entre** *prep.* 2
amusement **diversión** *f.*
and **y** 1, **e** (*before words beginning*
   with i or hi)
   And you?**¿Y tú?** *fam.* 1;
      ¿Y usted? *form.* 1
angel **ángel** *m.* 9
angry **enojado/a** *adj.* 5
   get angry (with) **enojarse** *v.*
      (con) 7
animal **animal** *m.* 13
ankle **tobillo** *m.* 10
anniversary **aniversario** *m.* 9
   (wedding) anniversary
      aniversario *m.* **(de bodas)** 9
announce **anunciar** *v.* 18
announcer (*TV/radio*) **locutor(a)**
   m., f. 18
annoy **molestar** *v.* 7
another **otro/a** *adj.* 6
answer **contestar** *v.* 2;
   respuesta *f.*
answering machine **contestadora** *f.*
antibiotic **antibiótico** *m.* 10
any **algún, alguno/a(s)** *adj.* 7
anyone **alguien** *pron.* 7
anything **algo** *pron.* 7
apartment **apartamento** *m.* 12
apartment building **edificio de**
   apartamentos 12
app **aplicación** *f.* 11
appear **parecer** *v.*
appetizers **entremeses** *m., pl.* 8
applaud **aplaudir** *v.* 17
apple **manzana** *f.* 8
appliance (electric)
   electrodoméstico *m.* 12
applicant **aspirante** *m., f.* 16
application **solicitud** *f.* 16
   job application **solicitud de**
      trabajo 16
apply (*for a job*) **solicitar** *v.* 16
   apply for a loan **pedir (e:i)** *v.*
      un préstamo 14
appointment **cita** *f.* 9
   have an appointment **tener** *v.*
      una cita 9
appreciate **apreciar** *v.* 17

April **abril** *m.* 5
archeologist **arqueólogo/a**
   m., f. 16
archeology **arqueología** *f.* 2
architect **arquitecto/a** *m., f.* 16
area **región** *f.*
Argentine **argentino/a** *adj.* 3
arm **brazo** *m.* 10
armchair **sillón** *m.* 12
army **ejército** *m.* 18
around **por** *prep.* 11
   around here **por aquí** 11
arrange **arreglar** *v.* 11
arrival **llegada** *f.* 5
arrive **llegar** *v.* 2
art **arte** *m.* 2
   (fine) arts **bellas artes** *f., pl.* 17
article **artículo** *m.* 18
artist **artista** *m., f.* 3
artistic **artístico/a** *adj.* 17
arts **artes** *f., pl.* 17
as **como** 8
   as a child **de niño/a** 10
   as... as **tan... como** 8
   as many... as **tantos/as...**
      como 8
   as much... as **tanto...**
      como 8
   as soon as **en cuanto** *conj.* 13;
      tan pronto como *conj.* 13
ask (*a question*) **preguntar** *v.* 2
   ask for **pedir (e:i)** *v.* 4
asparagus **espárragos** *m., pl.* 8
aspirin **aspirina** *f.* 10
at **a** *prep.* 1; **en** *prep.* 2
   at + *time* **a la(s)** + *time* 1
   at home **en casa**
   at least **por lo menos** 10
   at night **por la noche** 7
   At what time...? **¿A qué**
      hora...? 1
   At your service. **A sus**
      órdenes.
ATM **cajero automático** *m.* 14
attempt **intento** *m.* **11**
attend **asistir (a)** *v.* 3
attic **altillo** *m.* 12
audience **público** *m.* 17
August **agosto** *m.* 5
aunt **tía** *f.* 3
   aunts and uncles **tíos** *m., pl.* 3
automobile **automóvil** *m.* 5;
   carro *m.;* **coche** *m.* 11
autumn **otoño** *m.* 5
avenue **avenida** *f.*
avoid **evitar** *v.* 13
award **premio** *m.* 17

B

backpack **mochila** *f.* 2
bad **mal, malo/a** *adj.* 3
   It's bad that... **Es malo**
      que... 12
   It's not bad at all. **No está**
      nada mal. 5
bag **bolsa** *f.* 6
bakery **panadería** *f.* 14

balanced **equilibrado/a** *adj.* 15
  to eat a balanced diet **comer una dieta equilibrada** 15
balcony **balcón** *m.* 12
ball **pelota** *f.* 4
banana **banana** *f.* 8
band **banda** *f.* 17
bank **banco** *m.* 14
bargain **ganga** *f.* 6; **regatear** *v.* 6
baseball (*game*) **béisbol** *m.* 4
basement **sótano** *m.* 12
basketball (*game*) **baloncesto** *m.* 4
bathe **bañarse** *v.* 7
bathing suit **traje** *m.* **de baño** 6
bathroom **baño** *m.* 7; **cuarto de baño** *m.* 7
be **ser** *v.* 1; **estar** *v.* 2
  be... years old **tener... años** 3
  be sick of... **estar harto/a de...** 18
beach **playa** *f.* 5
beans **frijoles** *m., pl.* 8
beautiful **hermoso/a** *adj.* 6
beauty **belleza** *f.* 14
  beauty salon **peluquería** *f.* 14; **salón** *m.* **de belleza** 14
because **porque** *conj.* 2
  because of **por** *prep.* 11
become (+ *adj.*) **ponerse (+ adj.)** 7; **convertirse** *v.*
bed **cama** *f.* 5
  go to bed **acostarse (o:ue)** *v.* 7
bedroom **alcoba** *f.*, **recámara** *f.*; **dormitorio** *m.* 12
beef **carne de res** *f.* 8
beer **cerveza** *f.* 8
before **antes** *adv.* 7; **antes de** *prep.* 7; **antes (de) que** *conj.* 13
beg **rogar (o:ue)** *v.* 12
begin **comenzar (e:ie)** *v.* 4; **empezar (e:ie)** *v.* 4
behalf: on behalf of **de parte de** 11
behind **detrás de** *prep.* 2
believe (in) **creer** *v.* **(en)** 3; **creer** *v.* 13
  not to believe **no creer** 13
believed **creído/a** *p.p.* 14
bellhop **botones** *m., f. sing.* 5
below **debajo de** *prep.* 2
belt **cinturón** *m.* 6
benefit **beneficio** *m.* 16
beside **al lado de** *prep.* 2
besides **además (de)** *adv.* 10
best **mejor** *adj.*
  the best **el/la mejor** *m., f.* 8
  lo mejor *neuter*
better **mejor** *adj.* 8
  It's better that... **Es mejor que...** 12
between **entre** *prep.* 2
beverage **bebida** *f.* 8
  alcoholic beverage **bebida alcohólica** *f.* 15
bicycle **bicicleta** *f.* 4

big **grande** *adj.* 3
bill **cuenta** *f.* 8
billion **mil millones**
biology **biología** *f.* 2
bird **ave** *f.* 13; **pájaro** *m.* 13
birth **nacimiento** *m.* 9
birthday **cumpleaños** *m., sing.* 9
  have a birthday **cumplir** *v.* **años**
black **negro/a** *adj.* 6
blackboard **pizarra** *f.* 2
blanket **manta** *f.* 12
block (city) **cuadra** *f.* 14
blog **blog** *m.* 11
blond(e) **rubio/a** *adj.* 3
blouse **blusa** *f.* 6
blue **azul** *adj. m., f.* 6
boarding house **pensión** *f.*
boat **barco** *m.* 5
body **cuerpo** *m.* 10
bone **hueso** *m.* 10
book **libro** *m.* 2
bookcase **estante** *m.* 12
bookshelves **estante** *m.* 12
bookstore **librería** *f.* 2
boot **bota** *f.* 6
bore **aburrir** *v.* 7
bored **aburrido/a** *adj.* 5
  be bored **estar** *v.* **aburrido/a** 5
  get bored **aburrirse** *v.* 17
boring **aburrido/a** *adj.* 5
born: be born **nacer** *v.* 9
borrow **pedir (e:i)** *v.* **prestado** 14
borrowed **prestado/a** *adj.*
boss **jefe** *m.*, **jefa** *f.* 16
bother **molestar** *v.* 7
bottle **botella** *f.* 9
  bottle of wine **botella de vino** 9
bottom **fondo** *m.*
boulevard **bulevar** *m.*
boy **chico** *m.* 1; **muchacho** *m.* 3
boyfriend **novio** *m.* 3
brakes **frenos** *m., pl.*
bread **pan** *m.* 8
break **romper** *v.* 10
  break (one's leg) **romperse (la pierna)** 10
  break down **dañar** *v.* 10
  break up (with) **romper** *v.* **(con)** 9
breakfast **desayuno** *m.* 8
  have breakfast **desayunar** *v.* 2
breathe **respirar** *v.* 13
bring **traer** *v.* 4
broadcast **transmitir** *v.* 18; **emitir** *v.* 18
brochure **folleto** *m.*
broken **roto/a** *adj.* 14
  be broken **estar roto/a**
brother **hermano** *m.* 3
brother-in-law **cuñado** *m.* 3
brothers and sisters **hermanos** *m., pl.* 3
brought **traído/a** *p.p.* 14

brown **café** *adj.* 6; **marrón** *adj.* 6
browser **buscador** *m.* 11
brunet(te) **moreno/a** *adj.* 3
brush **cepillar(se)** *v.* 7
  brush one's hair **cepillarse el pelo** 7
  brush one's teeth **cepillarse los dientes** 7
bucket **balde** *m.* 5
build **construir** *v.*
building **edificio** *m.* 12
bump into (*something accidentally*) **darse con** 10; (*someone*) **encontrarse** *v.* 11
burn (a CD/DVD) **quemar** *v.* **(un CD/DVD)**
bus **autobús** *m.* 1
  bus station **estación** *f.* **de autobuses** 5
business **negocios** *m. pl.* 16
  business administration **administración** *f.* **de empresas** 2
  business-related **comercial** *adj.* 16
businessperson **hombre** *m.* **/ mujer** *f.* **de negocios** 16
busy **ocupado/a** *adj.* 5
but **pero** *conj.* 2; (*rather*) **sino** *conj.* (*in negative sentences*) 7
butcher shop **carnicería** *f.* 14
butter **mantequilla** *f.* 8
buy **comprar** *v.* 2
by **por** *prep.* 11; **para** *prep.* 11
  by means of **por** *prep.* 11
  by phone **por teléfono**
  by plane **en avión** 5
  by way of **por** *prep.* 11
bye **chau** *interj. fam.* 1

C

cable television **televisión** *f.* **por cable** *m.*
café **café** *m.* 4
cafeteria **cafetería** *f.* 2
caffeine **cafeína** *f.* 15
cake **pastel** *m.* 9
  chocolate cake **pastel de chocolate** *m.* 9
calculator **calculadora** *f.* 2
call **llamar** *v.* 11
  be called **llamarse** *v.* 7
  call on the phone **llamar por teléfono**
calm **tranquilo/a** *adj.* 15
calorie **caloría** *f.* 15
camera **cámara** *f.* 11
camp **acampar** *v.* 5
can (*tin*) **lata** *f.* 13
can **poder (o:ue)** *v.* 4
  Could I ask you something? **¿Podría pedirte algo?** 17
Canadian **canadiense** *adj.* 3

candidate **aspirante** *m., f.* 16;
  candidato/a *m., f.* 18
candy **dulces** *m., pl.* 9
capital city **capital** *f.*
car **coche** *m.* 11; **carro** *m.* 11;
  auto(móvil) *m.* 5
caramel **caramelo** *m.* 9
card **tarjeta** *f.*; (*playing*)
  carta *f.* 5
care **cuidado** *m.*
  take care of **cuidar** *v.* 13
career **carrera** *f.* 16
careful: be (very) careful **tener** *v.*
  (mucho) cuidado 3
caretaker **ama** *m., f.* **de casa** 12
carpenter **carpintero/a** *m., f.* 16
carpet **alfombra** *f.* 12
carrot **zanahoria** *f.* 8
carry **llevar** *v.* 2
cartoons **dibujos** *m, pl.*
  animados 17
case: in case (that) **en caso (de)**
  que 13
cash (a check) **cobrar** *v.* 14;
  cash **(en) efectivo** 6
  cash register **caja** *f.* 6
  pay in cash **pagar** *v.* **al contado**
    14; **pagar en efectivo** 14
cashier **cajero/a** *m., f.*
cat **gato** *m.* 13
CD **disco compacto** *m.* 11
CD player **reproductor de CD**
  m. 11
CD-ROM **cederrón** *m.*
celebrate **celebrar** *v.* 9
celebration **celebración** *f.*
cellar **sótano** *m.* 12
(cell) phone **(teléfono)**
  celular *m.* 11
cemetery **cementerio** *m.* 9
cereal **cereales** *m., pl.* 8
certain **cierto/a** *adj.*; **seguro/a**
  adj. 13
  it's (not) certain **(no) es**
    cierto/seguro 13
chalk **tiza** *f.* 2
champagne **champán** *m.* 9
change **cambiar** *v.* **(de)** 9
change: in change **de cambio** 2
channel (*TV*) **canal** *m.* 11; 17
character (*fictional*) **personaje**
  m. 17
  (main) character *m.* **personaje**
    (principal) 17
charger **cargador** *m.* 11
chat **conversar** *v.* 2; **chatear** *v.* 11
cheap **barato/a** *adj.* 6
check **comprobar (o:ue)** *v.*;
  revisar *v.* 11; (*bank*) **cheque**
  m. 14
  check the oil **revisar el aceite** 11
checking account **cuenta** *f.*
  corriente 14
cheese **queso** *m.* 8
chef **cocinero/a** *m., f.* 16
chemistry **química** *f.* 2
chest of drawers **cómoda** *f.* 12
chicken **pollo** *m.* 8

child **niño/a** *m., f.* 3
childhood **niñez** *f.* 9
children **hijos** *m., pl.* 3
Chinese **chino/a** *adj.* 3
chocolate **chocolate** *m.* 9
  chocolate cake **pastel** *m.* **de**
    chocolate 9
cholesterol **colesterol** *m.* 15
choose **escoger** *v.* 8
chop (*food*) **chuleta** *f.* 8
Christmas **Navidad** *f.* 9
church **iglesia** *f.* 4
cinnamon **canela** *f.* 10
citizen **ciudadano/a** *m., f.* 18
city **ciudad** *f.*
class **clase** *f.* 2
  take classes **tomar clases** 2
classical **clásico/a** *adj.* 17
classmate **compañero/a** *m., f.* **de**
  clase 2
clean **limpio/a** *adj.* 5;
  limpiar *v.* 12
  clean the house *v.* **limpiar la**
    casa 12
clear (*weather*) **despejado/a** *adj.*
  clear the table **quitar la**
    mesa 12
  It's (very) clear. (*weather*)
    Está (muy) despejado.
clerk **dependiente/a** *m., f.* 6
climate change **cambio climático**
  m. 13
climb **escalar** *v.* 4
  climb mountains **escalar**
    montañas 4
clinic **clínica** *f.* 10
clock **reloj** *m.* 2
close **cerrar (e:ie)** *v.* 4
closed **cerrado/a** *adj.* 5
closet **armario** *m.* 12
clothes **ropa** *f.* 6
  clothes dryer **secadora** *f.* 12
clothing **ropa** *f.* 6
cloud **nube** *f.* 13
cloudy **nublado/a** *adj.* 5
  It's (very) cloudy. **Está (muy)**
    nublado. 5
coat **abrigo** *m.* 6
coffee **café** *m.* 8
  coffee maker **cafetera** *f.* 12
cold **frío** *m.* 5;
  (*illness*) **resfriado** *m.* 10
  be (*feel*) (very) cold **tener**
    (mucho) frío 3
  It's (very) cold. (*weather*) **Hace**
    (mucho) frío. 5
college **universidad** *f.* 2
collision **choque** *m.* 18
color **color** *m.* 6
comb one's hair **peinarse** *v.* 7
come **venir** *v.* 3
come on **ándale** *interj.* 14
comedy **comedia** *f.* 17
comfortable **cómodo/a** *adj.* 5
commerce **negocios** *m., pl.* 16
commercial **comercial** *adj.* 16
communicate (with) **comunicarse**
  v. **(con)** 18

communication **comunicación**
  f. 18
  means of communication
    medios *m. pl.* **de**
    comunicación 18
community **comunidad** *f.* 1
company **compañía** *f.* 16;
  empresa *f.* 16
comparison **comparación** *f.*
composer **compositor(a)** *m., f.* 17
computer **computadora** *f.* 1
  computer disc **disco** *m.*
  computer monitor **monitor**
    m. 11
  computer programmer
    programador(a) *m., f.* 3
  computer science **computación**
    f. 2
concert **concierto** *m.* 17
conductor (*musical*) **director(a)**
  m., f. 17
confident **seguro/a** *adj.* 5
confirm **confirmar** *v.* 5
  confirm a reservation **confirmar**
    una reservación 5
confused **confundido/a** *adj.* 5
congested **congestionado/a**
  adj. 10
Congratulations! **¡Felicidades!**;
  ¡Felicitaciones! *f., pl.* 9
conservation **conservación** *f.* 13
conserve **conservar** *v.* 13
considering **para** *prep.* 11
consume **consumir** *v.* 15
container **envase** *m.* 13
contamination **contaminación** *f.*
content **contento/a** *adj.* 5
contest **concurso** *m.* 17
continue **seguir (e:i)** *v.* 4
control **control** *m.*; **controlar** *v.* 13
conversation **conversación** *f.* 1
converse **conversar** *v.* 2
cook **cocinar** *v.* 12; **cocinero/a**
  m., f. 16
cookie **galleta** *f.* 9
cool **fresco/a** *adj.* 5
  It's cool. (*weather*) **Hace**
    fresco. 5
corn **maíz** *m.* 8
corner **esquina** *f.* 14
cost **costar (o:ue)** *v.* 6
Costa Rican **costarricense** *adj.* 3
costume **disfraz** *m.* 9
cotton **algodón** *f.* 6
  (made of) cotton **de algodón** 6
couch **sofá** *m.* 12
couch potato **teleadicto/a**
  m., f. 15
cough **tos** *f.* 10; **toser** *v.* 10
counselor **consejero/a** *m., f.* 16
count **contar (o:ue)** *v.* 4
country (*nation*) **país** *m.* 1
countryside **campo** *m.* 5
(married) couple **pareja** *f.* 9
course **curso** *m.* 2; **materia** *f.* 2
courtesy **cortesía** *f.*
cousin **primo/a** *m., f.* 3

cover **cubrir** *v.*
covered **cubierto/a** *p.p.*
cow **vaca** *f.* 13
crafts **artesanía** *f.* 17
craftsmanship **artesanía** *f.* 17
crater **cráter** *m.* 13
crazy **loco/a** *adj.* 6
create **crear** *v.*
credit **crédito** *m.* 6
    credit card **tarjeta** *f.* **de crédito** 6
crime **crimen** *m.* 18
cross **cruzar** *v.* 14
cry **llorar** *v.* 15
Cuban **cubano/a** *adj.* 3
culture **cultura** *f.* 2, 17
cup **taza** *f.* 12
currency exchange **cambio** *m.* **de moneda**
current events **actualidades** *f.,* *pl.* 18
curtains **cortinas** *f., pl.* 12
custard (*baked*) **flan** *m.* 9
custom **costumbre** *f.*
customer **cliente/a** *m., f.* 6
customs **aduana** *f.*
    customs inspector **inspector(a)** *m., f.* **de aduanas** 5
cybercafé **cibercafé** *m.* 11
cycling **ciclismo** *m.* 4

D

dad **papá** *m.*
daily **diario/a** *adj.* 7
    daily routine **rutina** *f.* **diaria** 7
damage **dañar** *v.* 10
dance **bailar** *v.* 2; **danza** *f.* 17; **baile** *m.* 17
dancer **bailarín/bailarina** *m., f.* 17
danger **peligro** *m.* 13
dangerous **peligroso/a** *adj.* 18
date (*appointment*) **cita** *f.* 9; (*calendar*) **fecha** *f.* 5; (*someone*) **salir** *v.* **con (alguien)** 9
    have a date **tener una cita** 9
daughter **hija** *f.* 3
daughter-in-law **nuera** *f.* 3
day **día** *m.* 1
    day before yesterday **anteayer** *adv.* 6
death **muerte** *f.* 9
decaffeinated **descafeinado/a** *adj.* 15
December **diciembre** *m.* 5
decide **decidir** *v.* (+ *inf.*) 3
declare **declarar** *v.* 18
deforestation **deforestación** *f.* 13
delicious **delicioso/a** *adj.* 8; **rico/a** *adj.* 8; **sabroso/a** *adj.* 8
delighted **encantado/a** *adj.* 1
dentist **dentista** *m., f.* 10
deny **negar (e:ie)** *v.* 13
    not to deny **no negar** 13

department store **almacén** *m.* 6
departure **salida** *f.* 5
deposit **depositar** *v.* 14
describe **describir** *v.* 3
described **descrito/a** *p.p.* 14
desert **desierto** *m.* 13
design **diseño** *m.*
designer **diseñador(a)** *m., f.* 16
desire **desear** *v.* 2
desk **escritorio** *m.* 2
dessert **postre** *m.* 9
destroy **destruir** *v.* 13
develop **desarrollar** *v.* 13
diary **diario** *m.* 1
dictatorship **dictadura** *f.* 18
dictionary **diccionario** *m.* 1
die **morir (o:ue)** *v.* 8
died **muerto/a** *p.p.* 14
diet **dieta** *f.* 15; **alimentación** *f.*
    balanced diet **dieta equilibrada** 15
    be on a diet **estar a dieta** 15
difficult **difícil** *adj. m., f.* 3
digital camera **cámara** *f.* **digital** 11
dining room **comedor** *m.* 12
dinner **cena** *f.* 8
    have dinner **cenar** *v.* 2
direct **dirigir** *v.* 17
director **director(a)** *m., f.* 17
dirty **ensuciar** *v.*; **sucio/a** *adj.* 5
    get (something) dirty **ensuciar** *v.* 12
disagree **no estar de acuerdo**
disaster **desastre** *m.* 18
discover **descubrir** *v.* 13
discovered **descubierto/a** *p.p.* 14
discrimination **discriminación** *f.* 18
dish **plato** *m.* 8, 12
    main dish *m.* **plato principal** 8
dishwasher **lavaplatos** *m., sing.* 12
disk **disco** *m.*
disorderly **desordenado/a** *adj.* 5
divorce **divorcio** *m.* 9
divorced **divorciado/a** *adj.* 9
    get divorced (from) **divorciarse** *v.* **(de)** 9
dizzy **mareado/a** *adj.* 10
do **hacer** *v.* 4
    do aerobics **hacer ejercicios aeróbicos** 15
    do household chores **hacer quehaceres domésticos** 12
    do stretching exercises **hacer ejercicios de estiramiento** 15
    (I) don't want to. **No quiero.** 4
doctor **doctor(a)** *m., f.* 3; 10; **médico/a** *m., f.* 3
documentary (*film*) **documental** *m.* 17
dog **perro** *m.* 13
domestic **doméstico/a** *adj.*
    domestic appliance **electrodoméstico** *m.*
done **hecho/a** *p.p.* 14
door **puerta** *f.* 2

doorman/doorwoman **portero/a** *m., f.* 1
dormitory **residencia** *f.* **estudiantil** 2
double **doble** *adj.* 5
    double room **habitación** *f.* **doble** 5
doubt **duda** *f.* 13; **dudar** *v.* 13
    not to doubt **no dudar** 13
    there is no doubt that **no cabe duda de** 13; **no hay duda de** 13
download **descargar** *v.* 11
downtown **centro** *m.* 4
drama **drama** *m.* 17
dramatic **dramático/a** *adj.* 17
draw **dibujar** *v.* 2
drawing **dibujo** *m.*
dress **vestido** *m.* 6
    get dressed **vestirse (e:i)** *v.* 7
drink **beber** *v.* 3; **bebida** *f.* 8; **tomar** *v.* 2
drive **conducir** *v.* 6; **manejar** *v.* 11
driver **conductor(a)** *m., f.* 1
drug **droga** *f.* 15
    drug addict **drogadicto/a** *m., f.* 15
dry (oneself) **secarse** *v.* 7
during **durante** *prep.* 7; **por** *prep.* 11
dust **sacudir** *v.* 12; **quitar** *v.* **el polvo** 12
    dust the furniture **sacudir los muebles** 12
duster **plumero** *m.* 12
DVD player **reproductor** *m.* **de DVD** 11

E

each **cada** *adj.* 6
ear (outer) **oreja** *f.* 10
early **temprano** *adv.* 7
earn **ganar** *v.* 16
earring **arete** *m.* 6
earthquake **terremoto** *m.* 18
ease **aliviar** *v.*
east **este** *m.* 14
    to the east **al este** 14
easy **fácil** *adj. m., f.* 3
eat **comer** *v.* 3
ecological **ecológico/a** *adj.* 13
ecologist **ecologista** *m., f.* 13
ecology **ecología** *f.* 13
economics **economía** *f.* 2
ecotourism **ecoturismo** *m.* 13
Ecuadorian **ecuatoriano/a** *adj.* 3
effective **eficaz** *adj. m., f.*
egg **huevo** *m.* 8
eight **ocho** 1
eight hundred **ochocientos/as** 2
eighteen **dieciocho** 1
eighth **octavo/a** 5
eighty **ochenta** 2
either... or **o... o** *conj.* 7
elect **elegir (e:i)** *v.* 18
election **elecciones** *f. pl.* 18

electric appliance
electrodoméstico *m.* 12
electrician **electricista** *m.*, *f.* 16
electricity **luz** *f.* 12
elegant **elegante** *adj. m.*, *f.* 6
elevator **ascensor** *m.* 5
eleven **once** 1
e-mail **correo** *m.* **electrónico** 4
e-mail address **dirección** *f.*
electrónica 11
e-mail message **mensaje** *m.*
electrónico 4
read e-mail **leer** *v.* **el correo**
electrónico 4
embarrassed **avergonzado/a**
adj. 5
embrace (each other) **abrazar(se)**
v. 11
emergency **emergencia** *f.* 10
emergency room **sala** *f.* **de**
emergencia(s) 10
employee **empleado/a** *m.*, *f.* 5
employment **empleo** *m.* 16
end **fin** *m.* 4; **terminar** *v.* 2
end table **mesita** *f.* 12
endure **aguantar** *v.* 14
energy **energía** *f.* 13
engaged: get engaged (to)
comprometerse *v.* **(con)** 9
engineer **ingeniero/a** *m.*, *f.* 3
English (*language*) **inglés** *m.* 2;
inglés, inglesa *adj.* 3
enjoy **disfrutar** *v.* **(de)** 15
enough **bastante** *adv.* 10
entertainment **diversión** *f.* 4
entrance **entrada** *f.* 12
envelope **sobre** *m.* 14
environment **medio ambiente**
m. 13
environmental science **ciencias**
ambientales 2
equality **igualdad** *f.* 18
erase **borrar** *v.* 11
eraser **borrador** *m.* 2
errand **diligencia** *f.* 14
essay **ensayo** *m.* 3
establish **establecer** *v.* 16
evening **tarde** *f.* 1
event **acontecimiento** *m.* 18
every day **todos los días** 10
everything **todo** *m.* 5
exactly **en punto** 1
exam **examen** *m.* 2
excellent **excelente** *adj.* 5
excess **exceso** *m.* 15
in excess **en exceso** 15
exchange **intercambiar** *v.*
in exchange for **por** 11
exciting **emocionante** *adj. m.*, *f.*
excursion **excursión** *f.*
excuse **disculpar** *v.*
Excuse me. (*May I?*) **Con**
permiso. 1; (*I beg your*
pardon.) **Perdón.** 1
exercise **ejercicio** *m.* 15;
hacer *v.* **ejercicio** 15;
(*a degree/profession*) **ejercer**
v. 16
exit **salida** *f.* 5

expensive **caro/a** *adj.* 6
experience **experiencia** *f.*
expire **vencer** *v.* 14
explain **explicar** *v.* 2
explore **explorar** *v.*
expression **expresión** *f.*
extinction **extinción** *f.* 13
eye **ojo** *m.* 10

F

fabulous **fabuloso/a** *adj.* 5
face **cara** *f.* 7
facing **enfrente de** *prep.* 14
fact: in fact **de hecho**
factory **fábrica** *f.* 13
fall (down) **caerse** *v.* 10
fall asleep **dormirse (o:ue)** *v.* 7
fall in love (with) **enamorarse**
v. **(de)** 9
fall (season) **otoño** *m.* 5
fallen **caído/a** *p.p.* 14
family **familia** *f.* 3
famous **famoso/a** *adj.*
fan **aficionado/a** *m.*, *f.* 4
be a fan (of) **ser aficionado/a (a)**
far from **lejos de** *prep.* 2
farewell **despedida** *f.*
fascinate **fascinar** *v.* 7
fashion **moda** *f.* 6
be in fashion **estar de moda** 6
fast **rápido/a** *adj.*
fat **gordo/a** *adj.* 3; **grasa** *f.* 15
father **padre** *m.* 3
father-in-law **suegro** *m.* 3
favorite **favorito/a** *adj.* 4
fax (*machine*) **fax** *m.*
fear **miedo** *m.*; **temer** *v.* 13
February **febrero** *m.* 5
feel **sentir(se) (e:ie)** *v.* 7
feel like (*doing something*) **tener**
ganas de (+ *inf.*) 3
festival **festival** *m.* 17
fever **fiebre** *f.* 10
have a fever **tener** *v.* **fiebre** 10
few **pocos/as** *adj. pl.*
fewer than **menos de**
(+ *number*) 8
field: major field of study
especialización *f.*
fifteen **quince** 1
fifteen-year-old girl celebrating her
birthday **quinceañera** *f.*
fifth **quinto/a** 5
fifty **cincuenta** 2
fight (for/against) **luchar** *v.* **(por/**
contra) 18
figure (*number*) **cifra** *f.*
file **archivo** *m.* 11
fill **llenar** *v.* 11
fill out (a form) **llenar (un**
formulario) 14
fill the tank **llenar el**
tanque 11

finally **finalmente** *adv.*; **por**
último 7; **por fin** 11
find **encontrar (o:ue)** *v.* 4
find (each other) **encontrar(se)**
find out **enterarse** *v.* 16
fine **multa** *f.*
That's fine. **Está bien.**
(fine) arts **bellas artes** *f.*, *pl.* 17
finger **dedo** *m.* 10
finish **terminar** *v.* 2
finish (*doing something*)
terminar *v.* **de (+ *inf.*)**
fire **incendio** *m.* 18; **despedir**
(e:i) *v.* 16
firefighter **bombero/a** *m.*, *f.* 16
firm **compañía** *f.* 16; **empresa**
f. 16
first **primer, primero/a** 2, 5
fish (*food*) **pescado** *m.* 8;
pescar *v.* 5; (*live*) **pez** *m.*, *sing.*
(**peces** *pl.*) 13
fish market **pescadería** *f.* 14
fishing **pesca** *f.*
fit (*clothing*) **quedar** *v.* 7
five **cinco** 1
five hundred **quinientos/as** 2
fix (*put in working order*) **arreglar**
v. 11; (*clothes, hair, etc. to*
go out) **arreglarse** *v.* 7
fixed **fijo/a** *adj.* 6
flag **bandera** *f.*
flexible **flexible** *adj.* 15
flood **inundación** *f.* 18
floor (*of a building*) **piso** *m.* 5;
suelo *m.* 12
ground floor **planta baja** *f.* 5
top floor **planta** *f.* **alta**
flower **flor** *f.* 13
flu **gripe** *f.* 10
fog **niebla** *f.*
folk **folclórico/a** *adj.* 17
follow **seguir (e:i)** *v.* 4
food **comida** *f.* 4, 8
foolish **tonto/a** *adj.* 3
foot **pie** *m.* 10
football **fútbol** *m.* **americano** 4
for **para** *prep.* 11; **por** *prep.* 11
for example **por ejemplo** 11
for me **para mí** 8
forbid **prohibir** *v.*
foreign **extranjero/a** *adj.* 17
foreign languages **lenguas**
f., *pl.* **extranjeras** 2
forest **bosque** *m.* 13
forget **olvidar** *v.* 10
fork **tenedor** *m.* 12
form **formulario** *m.* 14
forty **cuarenta** 2
four **cuatro** 1
four hundred **cuatrocientos/as** 2
fourteen **catorce** 1
fourth **cuarto/a** *m.*, *f.* 5

free **libre** *adj. m., f.* 4
  be free (of charge) **ser gratis** 14
  free time **tiempo libre**; spare (free) time **ratos libres** 4
freedom **libertad** *f.* 18
freezer **congelador** *m.* 12
French **francés, francesa** *adj.* 3
  French fries **papas** *f., pl.* **fritas** 8; **patatas** *f., pl.* **fritas** 8
frequently **frecuentemente** *adv.*; **con frecuencia** *adv.* 10
Friday **viernes** *m., sing.* 2
fried **frito/a** *adj.* 8
  fried potatoes **papas** *f., pl.* **fritas** 8; **patatas** *f., pl.* **fritas** 8
friend **amigo/a** *m., f.* 3
friendly **amable** *adj. m., f.* 5
friendship **amistad** *f.* 9
from **de** *prep.* 1; **desde** *prep.* 6
  from the United States **estadounidense** *m., f. adj.* 3
  from time to time **de vez en cuando** 10
  I'm from… **Soy de…** 1
front: (cold) front **frente (frío)** *m.* 5
fruit **fruta** *f.* 8
  fruit juice **jugo** *m.* **de fruta** 8
  fruit store **frutería** *f.* 14
full **lleno/a** *adj.* 11
fun **divertido/a** *adj.*
  fun activity **diversión** *f.* 4
  have fun **divertirse (e:ie)** *v.* 9
function **funcionar** *v.*
furniture **muebles** *m., pl.* 12
furthermore **además (de)** *adv.* 10
future **porvenir** *m.* 16
  for/to the future **por el porvenir** 16
  in the future **en el futuro**

G

gain weight **aumentar** *v.* **de peso** 15; **engordar** *v.* 15
game **juego** *m.*; (match) **partido** *m.* 4
  game show **concurso** *m.* 17
garage (in a house) **garaje** *m.* 12; **garaje** *m.* 11; **taller (mecánico)** 11
garden **jardín** *m.* 12
garlic **ajo** *m.* 8
gas station **gasolinera** *f.* 11
gasoline **gasolina** *f.* 11
gentleman **caballero** *m.* 8
geography **geografía** *f.* 2
German **alemán, alemana** *adj.* 3

get **conseguir (e:i)** *v.* 4; **obtener** *v.* 16
  get along well/badly (with) **llevarse bien/mal (con)** 9
  get bigger **aumentar** *v.* 13
  get bored **aburrirse** *v.* 17
  get good grades **sacar buenas notas** 2
  get into trouble **meterse en problemas** *v.* 13
  get off of (a vehicle) **bajar(se)** *v.* **de** 11
  get on/into (a vehicle) **subir(se)** *v.* **a** 11
  get out of (a vehicle) **bajar(se)** *v.* **de** 11
  get ready **arreglarse** *v.* 7
  get up **levantarse** *v.* 7
gift **regalo** *m.* 6
ginger **jengibre** *m.* 10
girl **chica** *f.* 1; **muchacha** *f.* 3
girlfriend **novia** *f.* 3
give **dar** *v.* 6; (as a gift) **regalar** 9
  give directions **indicar cómo llegar** 14
glass (drinking) **vaso** *m.* 12; **vidrio** *m.* 13
  (made) of glass **de vidrio** 13
glasses **gafas** *f., pl.* 6
  sunglasses **gafas** *f., pl.* **de sol** 6
global warming **calentamiento global** *m.* 13
gloves **guantes** *m., pl.* 6
go **ir** *v.* 4
  go away **irse** 7
  go by boat **ir en barco** 5
  go by bus **ir en autobús** 5
  go by car **ir en auto(móvil)** 5
  go by motorcycle **ir en moto(cicleta)** 5
  go by plane **ir en avión** 5
  go by taxi **ir en taxi** 5
  go down **bajar(se)** *v.*
  go on a hike **ir de excursión** 4
  go out (with) **salir** *v.* **(con)** 9
  go up **subir** *v.*
  Let's go. **Vamos.** 4
goblet **copa** *f.* 12
going to: be going to (do something) **ir a (+ inf.)** 4
golf **golf** *m.* 4
good **buen, bueno/a** *adj.* 3, 6
  Good afternoon. **Buenas tardes.** 1
  Good evening. **Buenas noches.** 1
  Good morning. **Buenos días.** 1
  Good night. **Buenas noches.** 1
  It's good that… **Es bueno que…** 12

goodbye **adiós** *m.* 1
  say goodbye (to) **despedirse** *v.* **(de) (e:i)** 18
good-looking **guapo/a** *adj.* 3
government **gobierno** *m.* 13
GPS **navegador GPS** *m.* 11
graduate (from/in) **graduarse** *v.* **(de/en)** 9
grains **cereales** *m., pl.* 8
granddaughter **nieta** *f.* 3
grandfather **abuelo** *m.* 3
grandmother **abuela** *f.* 3
grandparents **abuelos** *m., pl.* 3
grandson **nieto** *m.* 3
grape **uva** *f.* 8
grass **hierba** *f.* 13
grave **grave** *adj.* 10
gray **gris** *adj. m., f.* 6
great **fenomenal** *adj. m., f.* 5; **genial** *adj.* 16
great-grandfather **bisabuelo** *m.* 3
great-grandmother **bisabuela** *f.* 3
green **verde** *adj. m., f.* 6
greet (each other) **saludar(se)** *v.* 11
greeting **saludo** *m.* 1
  Greetings to… **Saludos a…** 1
grilled **a la plancha** 8
ground floor **planta baja** *f.* 5
grow **aumentar** *v.* 13
guest (at a house/hotel) **huésped** *m., f.* 5 (invited to a function) **invitado/a** *m., f.* 9
guide **guía** *m., f.*
gymnasium **gimnasio** *m.* 4

H

hair **pelo** *m.* 7
hairdresser **peluquero/a** *m., f.* 16
half **medio/a** *adj.* 3
  half-brother **medio hermano** *m.* 3
  half-past… (time) **…y media** 1
  half-sister **media hermana** *f.* 3
hallway **pasillo** *m.* 12
ham **jamón** *m.* 8
hamburger **hamburguesa** *f.* 8
hand **mano** *f.* 1
hand in **entregar** *v.* 11
handsome **guapo/a** *adj.* 3
happen **ocurrir** *v.* 18
happiness **alegría** *v.* 9
Happy birthday! **¡Feliz cumpleaños!** 9
happy **alegre** *adj.* 5; **contento/a** *adj.* 5; **feliz** *adj. m., f.* 5
  be happy **alegrarse** *v.* **(de)** 13
hard **difícil** *adj. m., f.* 3
hard-working **trabajador(a)** *adj.* 3
hardly **apenas** *adv.* 10
hat **sombrero** *m.* 6

hate **odiar** *v.* 9
have **tener** *v.* 3
  have time **tener tiempo** 14
  have to (*do something*) **tener que** (+ *inf.*) 3
  have a tooth removed **sacar(se) un diente** 10
he **él** 1
head **cabeza** *f.* 10
headache **dolor** *m.* **de cabeza** 10
health **salud** *f.* 10
healthy **saludable** *adj. m., f.* 10; **sano/a** *adj.* 10
  lead a healthy lifestyle **llevar** *v.* **una vida sana** 15
hear **oír** *v.* 4
heard **oído/a** *p.p.* 14
hearing: sense of hearing **oído** *m.* 10
heart **corazón** *m.* 10
heat **calor** *m.*
Hello. **Hola.** 1; (*on the telephone*) **Aló.** 11; **Bueno.** 11; **Diga.** 11
help **ayudar** *v.*; **servir (e:i)** *v.* 5
  help each other **ayudarse** *v.* 11
her **su(s)** *poss. adj.* 3; (of) hers **suyo(s)/a(s)** *poss.* 11
  her **la** *f., sing., d.o. pron.* 5
  to/for her **le** *f., sing., i.o. pron.* 6
here **aquí** *adv.* 1
  Here is/are... **Aquí está(n)...** 5
Hi. **Hola.** 1
highway **autopista** *f.* 11; **carretera** *f.* 11
hike **excursión** *f.* 4
  go on a hike **ir de excursión** 4
hiker **excursionista** *m., f.*
hiking **de excursión** 4
him *m., sing., d.o. pron.* **lo** 5; to/for him **le** *m., sing., i.o. pron.* 6
hire **contratar** *v.* 16
his **su(s)** *poss. adj.* 3; (of) his **suyo(s)/a(s)** *poss. pron.* 11
history **historia** *f.* 2; 17
hobby **pasatiempo** *m.* 4
hockey **hockey** *m.* 4
hold up **aguantar** *v.* 14
hole **hueco** *m.* 4
holiday **día** *m.* **de fiesta** 9
home **casa** *f.* 2
  home page **página** *f.* **principal** 11
homework **tarea** *f.* 2
honey **miel** *f.* 10
hood **capó** *m.* 11; **cofre** *m.* 11
hope **esperar** *v.* (+ *inf.*) 2; **esperar** *v.* 13
  I hope (that) **ojalá (que)** 13
horror (genre) **de horror** *m.* 17
hors d'oeuvres **entremeses** *m., pl.* 8
horse **caballo** *m.* 5
hospital **hospital** *m.* 10

hot: be (*feel*) (very) hot **tener (mucho) calor** 3
  It's (very) hot. **Hace (mucho) calor.** 5
hotel **hotel** *m.* 5
hour **hora** *f.* 1
house **casa** *f.* 2
household chores **quehaceres** *m. pl.* **domésticos** 12
housekeeper **ama** *m., f.* **de casa** 12
housing **vivienda** *f.* 12
How...! **¡Qué...!**
  how **¿cómo?** *adv.* 1, 2
  How are you? **¿Qué tal?** 1
  How are you? **¿Cómo estás?** *fam.* 1
  How are you? **¿Cómo está usted?** *form.* 1
  How can I help you? **¿En qué puedo servirles?** 5
  How is it going? **¿Qué tal?** 1
  How is the weather? **¿Qué tiempo hace?** 5
  How much/many? **¿Cuánto(s)/a(s)?** 1
  How much does... cost? **¿Cuánto cuesta...?** 6
  How old are you? **¿Cuántos años tienes?** *fam.*
however **sin embargo**
hug (each other) **abrazar(se)** *v.* 11
humanities **humanidades** *f., pl.* 2
hundred **cien, ciento** 2
hunger **hambre** *f.*
hungry: be (very) hungry **tener** *v.* **(mucha) hambre** 3
hunt **cazar** *v.* 13
hurricane **huracán** *m.* 18
hurry **apurarse** *v.* 15; **darse prisa** *v.* 15
  be in a (big) hurry **tener** *v.* **(mucha) prisa** 3
hurt **doler (o:ue)** *v.* 10
husband **esposo** *m.* 3

I

I **yo** 1
  I hope (that) **Ojalá (que)** *interj.* 13
  I wish (that) **Ojalá (que)** *interj.* 13
ice cream **helado** *m.* 9
  ice cream shop **heladería** *f.* 14
iced **helado/a** *adj.* 8
  iced tea **té** *m.* **helado** 8
idea **idea** *f.* 18
if **si** *conj.* 4
illness **enfermedad** *f.* 10

important **importante** *adj.* 3
  be important to **importar** *v.* 7
  It's important that... **Es importante que...** 12
impossible **imposible** *adj.* 13
  it's impossible **es imposible** 13
improbable **improbable** *adj.* 13
  it's improbable **es improbable** 13
improve **mejorar** *v.* 13
in **en** *prep.* 2; **por** *prep.* 11
  in the afternoon **de la tarde** 1; **por la tarde** 7
  in a bad mood **de mal humor** 5
  in the direction of **para** *prep.* 11
  in the early evening **de la tarde** 1
  in the evening **de la noche** 1; **por la tarde** 7
  in a good mood **de buen humor** 5
  in the morning **de la mañana** 1; **por la mañana** 7
  in love (with) **enamorado/a (de)** 5
  in search of **por** *prep.* 11
in front of **delante de** *prep.* 2
increase **aumento** *m.*
incredible **increíble** *adj.* 5
inequality **desigualdad** *f.* 18
infection **infección** *f.* 10
inform **informar** *v.* 18
injection **inyección** *f.* 10
  give an injection *v.* **poner una inyección** 10
injure (oneself) **lastimarse** 10
  injure (one's foot) **lastimarse** *v.* **(el pie)** 10
inner ear **oído** *m.* 10
inside **dentro** *adv.*
insist (on) **insistir** *v.* **(en)** 12
installments: pay in installments **pagar** *v.* **a plazos** 14
intelligent **inteligente** *adj.* 3
intend to **pensar** *v.* (+ *inf.*) 4
interest **interesar** *v.* 7
interesting **interesante** *adj.* 3
  be interesting to **interesar** *v.* 7
international **internacional** *adj. m., f.* 18
Internet **Internet** 11
interview **entrevista** *f.* 16; interview **entrevistar** *v.* 16
interviewer **entrevistador(a)** *m., f.* 16
introduction **presentación** *f.*
  I would like to introduce you to (name). **Le presento a...** *form.* 1; **Te presento a...** *fam.* 1
invest **invertir (e:ie)** *v.* 16
invite **invitar** *v.* 9
iron (clothes) **planchar** *v.* **la ropa** 12

it **lo/la** *sing., d.o., pron.* 5
Italian **italiano/a** *adj.* 3
its **su(s)** *poss. adj.* 3;
   suyo(s)/a(s) *poss. pron.* 11
it's the same **es igual** 5

J

jacket **chaqueta** *f.* 6
January **enero** *m.* 5
Japanese **japonés, japonesa**
   adj. 3
jeans **(blue)jeans** *m., pl.* 6
jewelry store **joyería** *f.* 14
job **empleo** *m.* 16; **puesto**
   m. 16; **trabajo** *m.* 16
   job application **solicitud** *f.* **de**
      trabajo 16
jog **correr** *v.*
journalism **periodismo** *m.* 2
journalist **periodista** *m., f.* 3
joy **alegría** *f.* 9
juice **jugo** *m.* 8
July **julio** *m.* 5
June **junio** *m.* 5
jungle **selva, jungla** *f.* 13
just **apenas** *adv.*
   have just done something
      acabar de (+ *inf.*) 6

K

key **llave** *f.* 5
keyboard **teclado** *m.* 11
kilometer **kilómetro** *m.* 11
kiss **beso** *m.* 9
   kiss each other **besarse** *v.* 11
kitchen **cocina** *f.* 9, 12
knee **rodilla** *f.* 10
knife **cuchillo** *m.* 12
know **saber** *v.* 6; **conocer** *v.* 6
know how **saber** *v.* 6

L

laboratory **laboratorio** *m.* 2
lack **faltar** *v.* 7
lake **lago** *m.* 13
lamp **lámpara** *f.* 12
land **tierra** *f.* 13
landscape **paisaje** *m.* 5
language **lengua** *f.* 2
laptop (computer) **computadora**
   f. **portátil** 11
large **grande** *adj.* 3
large (*clothing size*) **talla**
   grande
last **durar** *v.* 18; **pasado/a**
   adj. 6; **último/a** *adj.* 7
   last name **apellido** *m.* 3
   last night **anoche** *adv.* 6
   last week **semana** *f.* **pasada** 6
   last year **año** *m.* **pasado** 6
   the last time **la última vez** 7

late **tarde** *adv.* 7
later (on) **más tarde** 7
   See you later. **Hasta la vista.** 1;
      Hasta luego. 1
laugh **reírse (e:i)** *v.* 9
laughed **reído** *p.p.* 14
laundromat **lavandería** *f.* 14
law **ley** *f.* 13
lawyer **abogado/a** *m., f.* 16
lazy **perezoso/a** *adj.*
learn **aprender** *v.* **(a + *inf.*)** 3
least, at **por lo menos** *adv.* 10
leave **salir** *v.* 4; **irse** *v.* 7
   leave a tip **dejar una**
      propina
   leave behind **dejar** *v.* 16
   leave for (*a place*) **salir para**
   leave from **salir de**
left **izquierda** *f.* 2
   be left over **quedar** *v.* 7
   to the left of **a la izquierda de** 2
leg **pierna** *f.* 10
lemon **limón** *m.* 8
lend **prestar** *v.* 6
less **menos** *adv.* 10
   less… than **menos… que** 8
   less than **menos de (+ *number*)**
lesson **lección** *f.* 1
let **dejar** *v.*
let's see **a ver**
letter **carta** *f.* 4, 14
lettuce **lechuga** *f.* 8
liberty **libertad** *f.* 18
library **biblioteca** *f.* 2
license (*driver's*) **licencia** *f.* **de**
   conducir 11
lie **mentira** *f.* 4
life **vida** *f.* 9
lifestyle: lead a healthy lifestyle
   llevar una vida sana 15
lift **levantar** *v.* 15
   lift weights **levantar pesas** 15
light **luz** *f.* 12
like **como** *prep.* 8; **gustar** *v.* 2
   I like… **Me gusta(n)…** 2
   like this **así** *adv.* 10
   like very much **encantar** *v.;*
      fascinar *v.* 7
   Do you like…? **¿Te**
      gusta(n)…? 2
likeable **simpático/a** *adj.* 3
likewise **igualmente** *adv.* 1
line **línea** *f.* 4; **cola** (*queue*) *f.* 14
listen (to) **escuchar** *v.* 2
   listen to music **escuchar**
      música 2
   listen to the radio **escuchar la**
      radio 2
literature **literatura** *f.* 2
little (*quantity*) **poco** *adv.* 10
live **vivir** *v.* 3; **en vivo** *adj.* 7
living room **sala** *f.* 12
loan **préstamo** *m.* 14; **prestar**
   v. 6, 14
lobster **langosta** *f.* 8
located **situado/a** *adj.*
   be located **quedar** *v.* 14

long **largo/a** *adj.* 6
look (at) **mirar** *v.* 2
look for **buscar** *v.* 2
lose **perder (e:ie)** *v.* 4
   lose weight **adelgazar** *v.* 15
lost **perdido/a** *adj.* 13, 14
   be lost **estar perdido/a** 14
lot, a **muchas veces** *adv.* 10
lot of, a **mucho/a** *adj.* 3; **un**
   montón de 4
love (*another person*) **querer**
   (e:ie) *v.* 4; (*inanimate objects*)
   encantar *v.* 7; **amor** *m.* 9
   in love **enamorado/a** *adj.* 5
   love at first sight **amor a**
      primera vista 9
luck **suerte** *f.*
lucky: be (very) lucky **tener**
   (mucha) suerte 3
luggage **equipaje** *m.* 5
lunch **almuerzo** *m.* 4, 8
   have lunch **almorzar (o:ue)**
      v. 4

M

ma'am **señora (Sra.); doña** *f.* 1
mad **enojado/a** *adj.* 5
magazine **revista** *f.* 4
magnificent **magnífico/a** *adj.* 5
mail **correo** *m.* 14; **enviar** *v.,*
   mandar *v.* 14; **echar (una**
   carta) al buzón 14
   mail carrier **cartero** *m.* 14
mailbox **buzón** *m.* 14
main **principal** *adj. m., f.* 8
maintain **mantener** *v.* 15
major **especialización** *f.* 2
make **hacer** *v.* 4
   make a decision **tomar una**
      decisión 15
   make the bed **hacer la**
      cama 12
makeup **maquillaje** *m.* 7
   put on makeup **maquillarse** *v.* 7
man **hombre** *m.* 1
manager **gerente** *m., f.* 8, 16
many **mucho/a** *adj.* 3
   many times **muchas veces** 10
map **mapa** *m.* 1, 2
March **marzo** *m.* 5
margarine **margarina** *f.* 8
marinated fish **ceviche** *m.* 8
   lemon-marinated shrimp
      ceviche *m.* **de camarón** 8
marital status **estado** *m.* **civil** 9
market **mercado** *m.* 6
   open-air market **mercado al**
      aire libre 6
marriage **matrimonio** *m.* 9
married **casado/a** *adj.* 9
   get married (to) **casarse** *v.*
      (con) 9
   I'll marry you! **¡Acepto**
      casarme contigo! 17

marvelous **maravilloso/a** *adj.* 5
massage **masaje** *m.* 15
masterpiece **obra maestra** *f.* 17
match (*sports*) **partido** *m.* 4
match (with) **hacer** *v.*
   juego (con) 6
mathematics **matemáticas**
   f., pl. 2
matter **importar** *v.* 7
maturity **madurez** *f.* 9
maximum **máximo/a** *adj.* 11
May **mayo** *m.* 5
May I leave a message? **¿Puedo**
   dejar un recado? 11
maybe **tal vez** 5; **quizás** 5
mayonnaise **mayonesa** *f.* 8
me **me** *sing., d.o. pron.* 5
   to/for me **me** *sing., i.o. pron.* 6
meal **comida** *f.* 8
means of communication **medios**
   m., pl. **de comunicación** 18
meat **carne** *f.* 8
mechanic **mecánico/a** *m., f.* 11
   mechanic's repair shop **taller**
     mecánico 11
media **medios** *m., pl.* **de**
   comunicación 18
medical **médico/a** *adj.* 10
medication **medicamento** *m.* 10
medicine **medicina** *f.* 10
medium **mediano/a** *adj.*
meet (each other) **encontrar(se)**
   v. 11; **conocer(se)** *v.* 8
   meet up with **encontrarse con** 7
meeting **reunión** *f.* 16
menu **menú** *m.* 8
message **mensaje** *m.*
Mexican **mexicano/a** *adj.* 3
microwave **microonda** *f.* 12
   microwave oven **horno** *m.* **de**
     microondas 12
middle age **madurez** *f.* 9
midnight **medianoche** *f.* 1
mile **milla** *f.*
milk **leche** *f.* 8
million **millón** *m.* 2
   million of **millón de** 2
mine **mío(s)/a(s)** *poss.* 11
mineral **mineral** *m.* 15
   mineral water **agua** *f.*
     mineral 8
minute **minuto** *m.*
mirror **espejo** *m.* 7
Miss **señorita (Srta.)** *f.* 1
miss **perder (e:ie)** *v.* 4; **extrañar**
   v. 16
mistaken **equivocado/a** *adj.*
modern **moderno/a** *adj.* 17
mom **mamá** *f.*
Monday **lunes** *m., sing.* 2
money **dinero** *m.* 6
monitor **monitor** *m.* 11
monkey **mono** *m.* 13
month **mes** *m.* 5
monument **monumento** *m.* 4

moon **luna** *f.* 13
more **más** 2
   more... than **más... que** 8
   more than **más de (+**
     number) 8
morning **mañana** *f.* 1
mother **madre** *f.* 3
mother-in-law **suegra** *f.* 3
motor **motor** *m.*
motorcycle **moto(cicleta)** *f.* 5
mountain **montaña** *f.* 4
mouse **ratón** *m.* 11
mouth **boca** *f.* 10
move (*from one house to another*)
   mudarse *v.* 12
movie **película** *f.* 4
   movie star **estrella** *f.*
     de cine 17
   movie theater **cine** *m.* 4
MP3 player **reproductor** *m.* **de**
   MP3 11
Mr. **señor (Sr.)**; **don** *m.* 1
Mrs. **señora (Sra.)**; **doña** *f.* 1
much **mucho/a** *adj.* 3
mud **lodo** *m.*
murder **crimen** *m.* 18
muscle **músculo** *m.* 15
museum **museo** *m.* 4
mushroom **champiñón** *m.* 8
music **música** *f.* 2, 17
musical **musical** *adj., m., f.* 17
musician **músico/a** *m., f.* 17
must **deber** *v.* (+ *inf.*) 3
my **mi(s)** *poss. adj.* 3; **mío(s)/a(s)**
   poss. pron. 11

N

name **nombre** *m.* 1
   be named **llamarse** *v.* 7
   in the name of **a nombre de** 5
   last name **apellido** *m.* 3
   My name is... **Me llamo...** 1
   name someone/something
     ponerle el nombre 9
napkin **servilleta** *f.* 12
national **nacional** *adj. m., f.* 18
nationality **nacionalidad** *f.* 1
natural **natural** *adj. m., f.* 13
   natural disaster **desastre** *m.*
     natural 18
   natural resource **recurso** *m.*
     natural 13
nature **naturaleza** *f.* 13
nauseated **mareado/a** *adj.* 10
near **cerca de** *prep.* 2
neaten **arreglar** *v.* 12
necessary **necesario/a** *adj.* 12
   It is necessary that... **Es**
     necesario que... 12
neck **cuello** *m.* 10
need **faltar** *v.* 7; **necesitar** *v.* (+
   inf.) 2
neighbor **vecino/a** *m., f.* 12
neighborhood **barrio** *m.* 12

neither **tampoco** *adv.* 7
neither... nor **ni... ni** *conj.* 7
nephew **sobrino** *m.* 3
nervous **nervioso/a** *adj.* 5
network **red** *f.* 11
never **nunca** *adj.* 7; **jamás** 7
new **nuevo/a** *adj.* 6
newlywed **recién casado/a**
   m., f. 9
news **noticias** *f., pl.* 18;
   actualidades *f., pl.* 18; **noticia**
   f. 11
newscast **noticiero** *m.* 18
newspaper **periódico** 4; **diario**
   m. 18
next **próximo/a** *adj.* 3, 16
   next to **al lado de** *prep.* 2
nice **simpático/a** *adj.* 3; **amable**
   adj. 5
niece **sobrina** *f.* 3
night **noche** *f.* 1
   night stand **mesita** *f.* **de**
     noche 12
nine **nueve** 1
nine hundred **novecientos/as** 2
nineteen **diecinueve** 1
ninety **noventa** 2
ninth **noveno/a** 5
no **no** 1; **ningún, ninguno/a(s)**
   adj. 7
   no one **nadie** *pron.* 7
nobody **nadie** 7
none **ningún, ninguno/a(s)**
   adj. 7
noon **mediodía** *m.* 1
nor **ni** *conj.* 7
north **norte** *m.* 14
   to the north **al norte** 14
nose **nariz** *f.* 10
not **no** 1
   not any **ningún, ninguno/a(s)**
     adj. 7
   not anyone **nadie** *pron.* 7
   not anything **nada** *pron.* 7
   not bad at all **nada mal** 5
   not either **tampoco** *adv.* 7
   not ever **nunca** *adv.* 7; **jamás**
     adv. 7
   not very well **no muy bien** 1
   not working **descompuesto/a**
     adj. 11
notebook **cuaderno** *m.* 1
nothing **nada** 1; 7
noun **sustantivo** *m.*
November **noviembre** *m.* 5
now **ahora** *adv.* 2
nowadays **hoy día** *adv.*
nuclear **nuclear** *adj. m., f.* 13
   nuclear energy **energía**
     nuclear 13
number **número** *m.* 1
nurse **enfermero/a** *m., f.* 10
nutrition **nutrición** *f.* 15
nutritionist **nutricionista** *m.,*
   f. 15

O

o'clock: It's… o'clock **Son las…** 1
It's one o'clock. **Es la una.** 1
obey **obedecer** v. 18
obligation **deber** m. 18
obtain **conseguir (e:i)** v. 4; **obtener** v. 16
obvious **obvio/a** adj. 13
it's obvious **es obvio** 13
occupation **ocupación** f. 16
occur **ocurrir** v. 18
October **octubre** m. 5
of **de** prep. 1
Of course. **Claro que sí.; Por supuesto.**
offer **oferta** f.; **ofrecer (c:zc)** v. 6
office **oficina** f. 12
doctor's office **consultorio** m. 10
often **a menudo** adv. 10
Oh! **¡Ay!**
oil **aceite** m. 8
OK **regular** adj. 1
It's okay. **Está bien.**
old **viejo/a** adj. 3
old age **vejez** f. 9
older **mayor** adj. m., f. 3
older brother, sister **hermano/a mayor** m., f. 3
oldest **el/la mayor** 8
on **en** prep. 2; **sobre** prep. 2
on behalf of **por** prep. 11
on the dot **en punto** 1
on time **a tiempo** 10
on top of **encima de** 2
once **una vez** 6
one **uno** 1
one hundred **cien(to)** 2
one million **un millón** m. 2
one more time **una vez más**
one thousand **mil** 2
one time **una vez** 6
onion **cebolla** f. 8
only **sólo** adv. 6; **único/a** adj. 3
only child **hijo/a único/a** m., f. 3
open **abierto/a** adj. 5, 14; **abrir** v. 3
open-air **al aire libre** 6
opera **ópera** f. 17
operation **operación** f. 10
opposite **enfrente de** prep. 14
or **o** conj. 7
orange **anaranjado/a** adj. 6; **naranja** f. 8
orchestra **orquesta** f. 17
order **mandar** 12; (food) **pedir (e:i)** v. 8
in order to **para** prep. 11
orderly **ordenado/a** adj. 5
ordinal (numbers) **ordinal** adj.
organize oneself **organizarse** v. 12
other **otro/a** adj. 6

ought to **deber** v. (+ inf.) adj. 3
our **nuestro(s)/a(s)** poss. adj. 3; poss. pron. 11
out of order **descompuesto/a** adj. 11
outside **afuera** adv. 5
outskirts **afueras** f., pl. 12
oven **horno** m. 12
over **sobre** prep. 2
(over)population **(sobre)población** f. 13
over there **allá** adv. 2
own **propio/a** adj.
owner **dueño/a** m., f. 8

P

p.m. **de la tarde, de la noche** f. 1
pack (one's suitcases) **hacer** v. **las maletas** 5
package **paquete** m. 14
page **página** f. 11
pain **dolor** m. 10
have pain **tener** v. **dolor** 10
paint **pintar** v. 17
painter **pintor(a)** m., f. 16
painting **pintura** f. 12, 17
pair **par** m. 6
pair of shoes **par** m. **de zapatos** 6
pale **pálido/a** adj. 14
pants **pantalones** m., pl. 6
pantyhose **medias** f., pl. 6
paper **papel** m. 2; (report) **informe** m. 18
Pardon me. (May I?) **Con permiso.** 1; (Excuse me.) Pardon me. **Perdón.** 1
parents **padres** m., pl. 3; **papás** m., pl.
park **estacionar** v. 11; **parque** m. 4
parking lot **estacionamiento** m. 14
partner (one of a married couple) **pareja** f. 9
party **fiesta** f. 9
passed **pasado/a** p.p.
passenger **pasajero/a** m., f. 1
passport **pasaporte** m. 5
past **pasado/a** adj. 6
pastime **pasatiempo** m. 4
pastry shop **pastelería** f. 14
path **sendero** m. 13
patient **paciente** m., f. 10
patio **patio** m. 12
pay **pagar** v. 6
pay in cash **pagar** v. **al contado; pagar en efectivo** 14
pay in installments **pagar** v. **a plazos** 14
pay the bill **pagar la cuenta**
pea **arveja** m. 8
peace **paz** f. 18
peach **melocotón** m. 8

peak **cima** f. 15
pear **pera** f. 8
pen **pluma** f. 2
pencil **lápiz** m. 1
penicillin **penicilina** f.
people **gente** f. 3
pepper (black) **pimienta** f. 8
per **por** prep. 11
perfect **perfecto/a** adj. 5
period of time **temporada** f. 5
person **persona** f. 3
pharmacy **farmacia** f. 10
phenomenal **fenomenal** adj. 5
photograph **foto(grafía)** f. 1
physical (exam) **examen** m. **médico** 10
physician **doctor(a), médico/a** m., f. 3
physics **física** f. sing. 2
pick up **recoger** v. 13
picture **cuadro** m. 12; **pintura** f. 12
pie **pastel** m. 9
pill (tablet) **pastilla** f. 10
pillow **almohada** f. 12
pineapple **piña** f.
pink **rosado/a** adj. 6
place **lugar** m. 2, 4; **sitio** m. 3; **poner** v. 4
plaid **de cuadros** 6
plans **planes** m., pl.
have plans **tener planes**
plant **planta** f. 13
plastic **plástico** m. 13
(made) of plastic **de plástico** 13
plate **plato** m. 12
play **drama** m. 17; **comedia** f. 17 **jugar (u:ue)** v. 4; (a musical instrument) **tocar** v. 17; (a role) **hacer el papel de** 17; (cards) **jugar a (las cartas)** 5; (sports) **practicar deportes** 4
player **jugador(a)** m., f. 4
playwright **dramaturgo/a** m., f. 17
plead **rogar (o:ue)** v. 12
pleasant **agradable** adj.
please **por favor** 1
Pleased to meet you. **Mucho gusto.** 1; **Encantado/a.** adj. 1
pleasing: be pleasing to **gustar** v. 7
pleasure **gusto** m. 1; **placer** m.
The pleasure is mine. **El gusto es mío.** 1
poem **poema** m. 17
poet **poeta** m., f. 17
poetry **poesía** f. 17
police (force) **policía** f. 11
political **político/a** adj. 18
politician **político/a** m., f. 16
politics **política** f. 18
polka-dotted **de lunares** 6
poll **encuesta** f. 18
pollute **contaminar** v. 13

polluted **contaminado/a** *m., f.* 13
  be polluted **estar contaminado/a** 13
pollution **contaminación** *f.* 13
pool **piscina** *f.* 4
poor **pobre** *adj., m., f.* 6
  poor thing **pobrecito/a** *adj.* 3
popsicle **paleta helada** *f.* 4
population **población** *f.* 13
pork **cerdo** *m.* 8
  pork chop **chuleta** *f.* **de cerdo** 8
portable **portátil** *adj.* 11
  portable computer **computadora** *f.* **portátil** 11
position **puesto** *m.* 16
possessive **posesivo/a** *adj.*
possible **posible** *adj.* 13
  it's (not) possible **(no) es posible** 13
post office **correo** *m.* 14
postcard **postal** *f.*
poster **cartel** *m.* 12
potato **papa** *f.* 8; **patata** *f.* 8
pottery **cerámica** *f.* 17
practice **entrenarse** *v.* 15; **practicar** *v.* 2; (a degree/ profession) **ejercer** *v.* 16
prefer **preferir (e:ie)** *v.* 4
pregnant **embarazada** *adj. f.* 10
prepare **preparar** *v.* 2
preposition **preposición** *f.*
prescribe (medicine) **recetar** *v.* 10
prescription **receta** *f.* 10
present **regalo** *m.*; **presentar** *v.* 17
press **prensa** *f.* 18
pressure **presión** *f.*
  be under a lot of pressure **sufrir muchas presiones** 15
pretty **bonito/a** *adj.* 3
price **precio** *m.* 6
  (fixed, set) price **precio** *m.* **fijo** 6
print **imprimir** *v.* 11
printer **impresora** *f.* 11
prize **premio** *m.* 17
probable **probable** *adj.* 13
  it's (not) probable **(no) es probable** 13
problem **problema** *m.* 1
profession **profesión** *f.* 3; 16
professor **profesor(a)** *m., f.*
program **programa** *m.* 1
programmer **programador(a)** *m., f.* 3
prohibit **prohibir** *v.* 10
project **proyecto** *m.* 11
promotion (career) **ascenso** *m.* 16
pronoun **pronombre** *m.*
protect **proteger** *v.* 13
protein **proteína** *f.* 15
provided (that) **con tal (de) que** *conj.* 13
psychologist **psicólogo/a** *m., f.* 16

psychology **psicología** *f.* 2
publish **publicar** *v.* 17
Puerto Rican **puertorriqueño/a** *adj.* 3
purchases **compras** *f., pl.*
pure **puro/a** *adj.* 13
purple **morado/a** *adj.* 6
purse **bolsa** *f.* 6
put **poner** *v.* 4; **puesto/a** *p.p.* 14
  put (a letter) in the mailbox **echar (una carta) al buzón** 14
  put on (a performance) **presentar** *v.* 17
  put on (clothing) **ponerse** *v.* 7
  put on makeup **maquillarse** *v.* 7

Q

quality **calidad** *f.* 6
quarter (academic) **trimestre** *m.* 2
  quarter after (time) **y cuarto** 1; **y quince** 1
  quarter to (time) **menos cuarto** 1; **menos quince** 1
question **pregunta** *f.*
quickly **rápido** *adv.* 10
quiet **tranquilo/a** *adj.* 15
quit **dejar** *v.* 16
quiz **prueba** *f.* 2

R

racism **racismo** *m.* 18
radio (medium) **radio** *f.* 2
  radio (set) **radio** *m.* 11
rain **llover (o:ue)** *v.* 5; **lluvia** *f.*
  It's raining. **Llueve.** 5; **Está lloviendo.** 5
raincoat **impermeable** *m.* 6
rain forest **bosque** *m.* **tropical** 13
raise (salary) **aumento de sueldo** 16
rather **bastante** *adv.* 10
read **leer** *v.* 3; **leído/a** *p.p.* 14
  read e-mail **leer el correo electrónico** 4
  read a magazine **leer una revista** 4
  read a newspaper **leer un periódico** 4
ready **listo/a** *adj.* 5
reality show **programa de realidad** *m.* 17
reap the benefits (of) *v.* **disfrutar** *v.* **(de)** 15
receive **recibir** *v.* 3
recommend **recomendar (e:ie)** *v.* 8; 12
record **grabar** *v.* 11
recover **recuperar** *v.* 11
recreation **diversión** *f.* 4

recycle **reciclar** *v.* 13
recycling **reciclaje** *m.* 13
red **rojo/a** *adj.* 6
red-haired **pelirrojo/a** *adj.* 3
reduce **reducir** *v.* 13; **disminuir** *v.* 16
  reduce stress/tension **aliviar el estrés/la tensión** 15
refrigerator **refrigerador** *m.* 12
region **región** *f.*
regret **sentir (e:ie)** *v.* 13
relatives **parientes** *m., pl.* 3
relax **relajarse** *v.* 9
  Relax. **Tranquilo/a**. 7
  Relax, sweetie. **Tranquilo/a, cariño.** 11
remain **quedarse** *v.* 7
remember **acordarse (o:ue)** *v.* **(de)** 7; **recordar (o:ue)** *v.* 4
remote control **control remoto** *m.* 11
renewable **renovable** *adj.* 13
rent **alquilar** *v.* 12; (payment) **alquiler** *m.* 12
repeat **repetir (e:i)** *v.* 4
report **informe** *m.* 18; **reportaje** *m.* 18
reporter **reportero/a** *m., f.* 16
representative **representante** *m., f.* 18
request **pedir (e:i)** *v.* 4
reservation **reservación** *f.* 5
resign (from) **renunciar (a)** *v.* 16
resolve **resolver (o:ue)** *v.* 13
resolved **resuelto/a** *p.p.* 14
resource **recurso** *m.* 13
responsibility **deber** *m.* 18; **responsabilidad** *f.*
responsible **responsable** *adj.* 8
rest **descansar** *v.* 2
restaurant **restaurante** *m.* 4
résumé **currículum** *m.* 16
retire (from work) **jubilarse** *v.* 9
return **regresar** *v.* 2; **volver (o:ue)** *v.* 4
returned **vuelto/a** *p.p.* 14
rice **arroz** *m.* 8
rich **rico/a** *adj.* 6
ride a bicycle **pasear** *v.* **en bicicleta** 4
ride a horse **montar** *v.* **a caballo** 5
ridiculous **ridículo/a** *adj.* 13
  it's ridiculous **es ridículo** 13
right **derecha** *f.* 2
  be right **tener razón** 3
  right? (question tag) **¿no?** 1; **¿verdad?** 1
  right away **enseguida** *adv.*
  right now **ahora mismo** 5
  to the right of **a la derecha de** 2
rights **derechos** *m.* 18
ring **anillo** *m.* 17

ring (*a doorbell*) **sonar (o:ue)**
    v. 11
river **río** *m.* 13
road **carretera** *f.* 11; **camino** *m.*
roast **asado/a** *adj.* 8
roast chicken **pollo** *m.* **asado** 8
rollerblade **patinar en línea** *v.*
romantic **romántico/a** *adj.* 17
room **habitación** *f.* 5; **cuarto**
    m. 2; 7
    living room **sala** *f.* 12
roommate **compañero/a**
    m., f. **de cuarto** 2
roundtrip **de ida y vuelta** 5
    roundtrip ticket **pasaje** *m.* **de**
    ida y vuelta 5
routine **rutina** *f.* 7
rug **alfombra** *f.* 12
run **correr** *v.* 3
    run errands **hacer**
    diligencias 14
    run into (*have an accident*)
    chocar (con) *v.*; (*meet*
    accidentally) **encontrar(se)**
    (o:ue) *v.* 11; (*run into*
    something) **darse (con)** 10
    run into (each other)
    encontrar(se) (o:ue) *v.* 11
rush **apurarse, darse prisa** *v.* 15
Russian **ruso/a** *adj.* 3

S

sad **triste** *adj.* 5; 13
    it's sad **es triste** 13
safe **seguro/a** *adj.* 5
said **dicho/a** *p.p.* 14
sailboard **tabla de windsurf** *f.* 5
salad **ensalada** *f.* 8
salary **salario** *m.* 16; **sueldo**
    m. 16
sale **rebaja** *f.* 6
salesperson **vendedor(a)** *m., f.* 6
salmon **salmón** *m.* 8
salt **sal** *f.* 8
same **mismo/a** *adj.* 3
sandal **sandalia** *f.* 6
sandwich **sándwich** *m.* 8
Saturday **sábado** *m.* 2
sausage **salchicha** *f.* 8
save (*on a computer*) **guardar**
    v. 11; save (*money*) **ahorrar**
    v. 14
savings **ahorros** *m.* 14
    savings account **cuenta** *f.* **de**
    ahorros 14
say **decir** *v.* 4; **declarar** *v.* 18
say (that) **decir (que)** *v.* 4
    say the answer **decir la**
    respuesta 4
scan **escanear** *v.* 11
scarcely **apenas** *adv.* 10
scared: be (very) scared (of) **tener**
    (mucho) miedo (de) 3
schedule **horario** *m.* 2
school **escuela** *f.* 1
sciences *f., pl.* **ciencias** 2

science fiction (genre) **de**
    ciencia ficción *f.* 17
scientist **científico/a** *m., f.* 16
scream **grito** *m.* 5; **gritar** *v.*
screen **pantalla** *f.* 11
scuba dive **bucear** *v.* 4
sculpt **esculpir** *v.* 17
sculptor **escultor(a)** *m., f.* 17
sculpture **escultura** *f.* 17
sea **mar** *m.* 5
    (sea) turtle **tortuga (marina)**
    f. 13
season **estación** *f.* 5
seat **silla** *f.* 2
second **segundo/a** 5
secretary **secretario/a** *m., f.* 16
sedentary **sedentario/a** *adj.* 15
see **ver** *v.* 4
    see (you, him, her) again **volver**
    a ver(te, lo, la)
    see movies **ver películas** 4
    See you. **Nos vemos.** 1
    See you later. **Hasta la vista.** 1;
    Hasta luego. 1
    See you soon. **Hasta pronto.** 1
    See you tomorrow. **Hasta**
    mañana. 1
seem **parecer** *v.* 6
seen **visto/a** *p.p.* 14
sell **vender** *v.* 6
semester **semestre** *m.* 2
send **enviar; mandar** *v.* 14
separate (from) **separarse** *v.*
    (de) 9
separated **separado/a** *adj.* 9
September **septiembre** *m.* 5
sequence **secuencia** *f.*
serious **grave** *adj.* 10
serve **servir (e:i)** *v.* 8
service **servicio** *m.* 15
set (*fixed*) **fijo/a** *adj.* 6
    set the table **poner la mesa** 12
seven **siete** 1
seven hundred **setecientos/as** 2
seventeen **diecisiete** 1
seventh **séptimo/a** 5
seventy **setenta** 2
several **varios/as** *adj. pl.*
sexism **sexismo** *m.* 18
shame **lástima** *f.* 13
    it's a shame **es una lástima** 13
shampoo **champú** *m.* 7
shape **forma** *f.* 15
    be in good shape **estar en**
    buena forma 15
    stay in shape **mantenerse en**
    forma 15
share **compartir** *v.* 3
sharp (*time*) **en punto** 1
shave **afeitarse** *v.* 7
shaving cream **crema** *f.* **de**
    afeitar 5, 7
she **ella** 1
shellfish **mariscos** *m., pl.* 8
ship **barco** *m.*
shirt **camisa** *f.* 6
shoe **zapato** *m.* 6
    shoe size **número** *m.* 6
    shoe store **zapatería** *f.* 14

tennis shoes **zapatos** *m., pl.* **de**
    tenis 6
shop **tienda** *f.* 6
shopping, to go **ir de compras** 5
    shopping mall **centro**
    comercial *m.* 6
short (*in height*) **bajo/a** *adj.* 3; (*in*
    length) **corto/a** *adj.* 6
short story **cuento** *m.* 17
shorts **pantalones cortos**
    m., pl. 6
should (*do something*) **deber** *v.*
    (+ *inf.*) 3
shout **gritar** *v.*
show **espectáculo** *m.* 17;
    mostrar (o:ue) *v.* 4
    game show **concurso** *m.* 17
shower **ducha** *f.* 7; **ducharse** *v.* 7
shrimp **camarón** *m.* 8
siblings **hermanos/as** *pl.* 3
sick **enfermo/a** *adj.* 10
    be sick **estar enfermo/a** 10
    get sick **enfermarse** *v.* 10
sign **firmar** *v.* 14; **letrero** *m.* 14
silk **seda** *f.* 6
    (made of) silk **de seda** 6
since **desde** *prep.*
sing **cantar** *v.* 2
singer **cantante** *m., f.* 17
single **soltero/a** *adj.* 9
    single room **habitación** *f.*
    individual 5
sink **lavabo** *m.* 7
sir **señor (Sr.), don** *m.* 1;
    caballero *m.* 8
sister **hermana** *f.* 3
sister-in-law **cuñada** *f.* 3
sit down **sentarse (e:ie)** *v.* 7
six **seis** 1
six hundred **seiscientos/as** 2
sixteen **dieciséis** 1
sixth **sexto/a** 5
sixty **sesenta** 2
size **talla** *f.* 6
    shoe size *m.* **número** 6
(in-line) skate **patinar (en línea)** 4
skateboard **andar en patineta**
    v. 4
ski **esquiar** *v.* 4
skiing **esquí** *m.* 4
    water-skiing **esquí** *m.*
    acuático 4
skirt **falda** *f.* 6
skull made out of sugar **calavera**
    de azúcar *f.* 9
sky **cielo** *m.* 13
sleep **dormir (o:ue)** *v.* 4; **sueño** *m.*
    go to sleep **dormirse**
    (o:ue) *v.* 7
sleepy: be (very) sleepy **tener**
    (mucho) sueño 3
slender **delgado/a** *adj.* 3
slim down **adelgazar** *v.* 15
slippers **pantuflas** *f.* 7
slow **lento/a** *adj.* 11
slowly **despacio** *adv.* 10
small **pequeño/a** *adj.* 3
smart **listo/a** *adj.* 5
smile **sonreír (e:i)** *v.* 9
smiled **sonreído** *p.p.* 14

smoggy: It's (very) smoggy. **Hay (mucha) contaminación.**
smoke **fumar** *v.* 15
  (not) to smoke **(no) fumar** 15
smoking section **sección** *f.* **de fumar** 8
  (non) smoking section *f.* **sección de (no) fumar** 8
snack **merendar (e:ie)** *v.* 8
  afternoon snack **merienda** *f.* 15
  have a snack **merendar** *v.* 8
sneakers **los zapatos de tenis** 6
sneeze **estornudar** *v.* 10
snow **nevar (e:ie)** *v.* 5; **nieve** *f.*
snowing: It's snowing. **Nieva.** 5; **Está nevando.** 5
so (*in such a way*) **así** *adv.* 10; **tan** *adv.* 5
  so much **tanto** *adv.*
  so-so **regular** 1
  so that **para que** *conj.* 13
soap **jabón** *m.* 7
soap opera **telenovela** *f.* 17
soccer **fútbol** *m.* 4
sociology **sociología** *f.* 2
sock(s) **calcetín (calcetines)** *m.* 6
sofa **sofá** *m.* 12
soft drink **refresco** *m.* 8
software **programa** *m.* **de computación** 11
soil **tierra** *f.* 13
solar **solar** *adj., m., f.* 13
  solar energy **energía solar** 13
soldier **soldado** *m., f.* 18
solution **solución** *f.* 13
solve **resolver (o:ue)** *v.* 13
some **algún, alguno/a(s)** *adj.* 7; **unos/as** *indef. art.* 1
somebody **alguien** *pron.* 7
someone **alguien** *pron.* 7
something **algo** *pron.* 7
sometimes **a veces** *adv.* 10
son **hijo** *m.* 3
song **canción** *f.* 17
son-in-law **yerno** *m.* 3
soon **pronto** *adv.* 10
  See you soon. **Hasta pronto.** 1
sorry: be sorry **sentir (e:ie)** *v.* 13
  I'm sorry. **Lo siento.** 1
soul **alma** *f.* 9
soup **sopa** *f.* 8
south **sur** *m.* 14
  to the south **al sur** 14
Spain **España** *f.*
Spanish (*language*) **español** *m.* 2; **español(a)** *adj.* 3
spare (free) time **ratos libres** 4
speak **hablar** *v.* 2
  Speaking. (*on the telephone*) **Con él/ella habla.**
special: today's specials **las especialidades del día** 8
spectacular **espectacular** *adj. m., f.*
speech **discurso** *m.* 18
speed **velocidad** *f.* 11
  speed limit **velocidad** *f.* **máxima** 11

spelling **ortografía** *f.*, **ortográfico/a** *adj.*
spend (*money*) **gastar** *v.* 6
spoon (*table or large*) **cuchara** *f.* 12
sport **deporte** *m.* 4
  sports-related **deportivo/a** *adj.* 4
spouse **esposo/a** *m., f.* 3
sprain (one's ankle) **torcerse (o:ue)** *v.* **(el tobillo)** 10
spring **primavera** *f.* 5
(city or town) square **plaza** *f.* 4
stadium **estadio** *m.* 2
stage **etapa** *f.* 9
stairs **escalera** *f.* 12
stairway **escalera** *f.* 12
stamp **estampilla** *f.* 14; **sello** *m.* 14
stand in line **hacer** *v.* **cola** 14
star **estrella** *f.* 13
start (*a vehicle*) **arrancar** *v.* 11
station **estación** *f.* 5
statue **estatua** *f.* 17
status: marital status **estado** *m.* **civil** 9
stay **quedarse** *v.* 7
  stay in shape **mantenerse en forma** 15
steak **bistec** *m.* 8
steering wheel **volante** *m.* 11
step **escalón** *m.* 15
stepbrother **hermanastro** *m.* 3
stepdaughter **hijastra** *f.* 3
stepfather **padrastro** *m.* 3
stepmother **madrastra** *f.* 3
stepsister **hermanastra** *f.* 3
stepson **hijastro** *m.* 3
stereo **estéreo** *m.* 11
still **todavía** *adv.* 5
stockbroker **corredor(a)** *m., f.* **de bolsa** 16
stockings **medias** *f., pl.* 6
stomach **estómago** *m.* 10
stone **piedra** *f.* 13
stop **parar** *v.* 11
  stop (*doing something*) **dejar de** (+ *inf.*) 13
store **tienda** *f.* 6
storm **tormenta** *f.* 18
story **cuento** *m.* 17; **historia** *f.* 17
stove **cocina, estufa** *f.* 12
straight **derecho** *adv.* 14
  straight (ahead) **derecho** 14
straighten up **arreglar** *v.* 12
strange **extraño/a** *adj.* 13
  it's strange **es extraño** 13
street **calle** *f.* 11
stress **estrés** *m.* 15
stretching **estiramiento** *m.* 15
  do stretching exercises **hacer ejercicios** *m. pl.* **de estiramiento** 15
strike (*labor*) **huelga** *f.* 18
striped **de rayas** 6
stroll **pasear** *v.* 4
strong **fuerte** *adj. m., f.* 15

struggle (for/against) **luchar** *v.* **(por/contra)** 18
student **estudiante** *m., f.* 1; 2; **estudiantil** *adj.* 2
study **estudiar** *v.* 2
stupendous **estupendo/a** *adj.* 5
style **estilo** *m.*
suburbs **afueras** *f., pl.* 12
subway **metro** *m.* 5
  subway station **estación** *f.* **del metro** 5
success **éxito** *m.*
successful: be successful **tener éxito** 16
such as **tales como**
suddenly **de repente** *adv.* 6
suffer **sufrir** *v.* 10
  suffer an illness **sufrir una enfermedad** 10
sugar **azúcar** *m.* 8
suggest **sugerir (e:ie)** *v.* 12
suit **traje** *m.* 6
suitcase **maleta** *f.* 1
summer **verano** *m.* 5
sun **sol** *m.* 13
sunbathe **tomar** *v.* **el sol** 4
Sunday **domingo** *m.* 2
(sun)glasses **gafas** *f., pl.* **(de sol)** 6
sunny: It's (very) sunny. **Hace (mucho) sol.** 5
supermarket **supermercado** *m.* 14
suppose **suponer** *v.* 4
sure **seguro/a** *adj.* 5
  be sure **estar seguro/a** 5
surf **hacer** *v.* surf 5; (*the Internet*) **navegar** *v.* **(en Internet)** 11
surfboard **tabla de surf** *f.* 5
surprise **sorprender** *v.* 9; **sorpresa** *f.* 9
survey **encuesta** *f.* 18
sweat **sudar** *v.* 15
sweater **suéter** *m.* 6
sweep the floor **barrer el suelo** 12
sweets **dulces** *m., pl.* 9
swim **nadar** *v.* 4
swimming **natación** *f.* 4
  swimming pool **piscina** *f.* 4
symptom **síntoma** *m.* 10

T

table **mesa** *f.* 2
tablespoon **cuchara** *f.* 12
tablet (*pill*) **pastilla** *f.* 10
take **tomar** *v.* 2; **llevar** *v.* 6
  take care of **cuidar** *v.* 13
  take someone's temperature **tomar** *v.* **la temperatura** 10
  take (*wear*) a shoe size **calzar** *v.* 6
  take a bath **bañarse** *v.* 7
  take a shower **ducharse** *v.* 7
  take off **quitarse** *v.* 7

take out the trash *v.* **sacar la basura** 12
take photos **tomar** *v.* **fotos** 5; **sacar** *v.* **fotos** 5
talented **talentoso/a** *adj.* 17
talk **hablar** *v.* 2
   talk show **programa** *m.* **de entrevistas** 17
tall **alto/a** *adj.* 3
tank **tanque** *m.* 11
taste **probar (o:ue)** *v.* 8
   taste like **saber a** 8
tasty **rico/a** *adj.* 8; **sabroso/a** *adj.* 8
tax **impuesto** *m.* 18
taxi **taxi** *m.* 5
tea **té** *m.* 8
teach **enseñar** *v.* 2
teacher **profesor(a)** *m., f.* 1, 2; **maestro/a** *m., f.* 16
team **equipo** *m.* 4
technician **técnico/a** *m., f.* 16
telecommuting **teletrabajo** *m.* 16
telephone **teléfono** 11
television **televisión** *f.* 2
   television set **televisor** *m.* 11
tell **contar** *v.* 4; **decir** *v.* 4
tell (that) **decir** *v.* **(que)** 4
   tell lies **decir mentiras** 4
   tell the truth **decir la verdad** 4
temperature **temperatura** *f.* 10
ten **diez** 1
tennis **tenis** *m.* 4
   tennis shoes **zapatos** *m., pl.* **de tenis** 6
tension **tensión** *f.* 15
tent **tienda** *f.* **de campaña**
tenth **décimo/a** 5
terrible **terrible** *adj. m., f.* 13
   it's terrible **es terrible** 13
terrific **chévere** *adj.*
test **prueba** *f.* 2; **examen** *m.* 2
text message **mensaje** *m.* **de texto** 11
Thank you. **Gracias.** *f., pl.* 1
   Thank you (very much). **(Muchas) gracias.** 1
   Thanks (a lot). **(Muchas) gracias.** 1
   Thanks for inviting me. **Gracias por invitarme.** 9
that **que, quien(es)** *pron.* 12
   that (one) **ése, ésa, eso** *pron.* 6; **ese, esa,** *adj.* 6
   that (*over there*) **aquél, aquélla, aquello** *pron.* 6; **aquel, aquella** *adj.* 6
   that which **lo que** 12
   that's why **por eso** 11
the **el** *m.,* **la** *f. sing.,* **los** *m.,* **las** *f., pl.* 1
theater **teatro** *m.* 17
their **su(s)** *poss. adj.* 3; **suyo(s)/a(s)** *poss. pron.* 11
them **los/las** *pl., d.o. pron.* 5
   to/for them **les** *pl., i.o. pron.* 6
then (*afterward*) **después** *adv.* 7; (*as a result*) **entonces** *adv.* 5, 7; (*next*) **luego** *adv.* 7

there **allí** *adv.* 2
   There is/are... **Hay...** 1
   There is/are not... **No hay...** 1
therefore **por eso** 11
these **éstos, éstas** *pron.* 6; **estos, estas** *adj.* 6
they **ellos** *m.,* **ellas** *f. pron.* 1
   They all told me to ask you to excuse them/forgive them. **Todos me dijeron que te pidiera una disculpa de su parte.** 18
thin **delgado/a** *adj.* 3
thing **cosa** *f.* 1
think **pensar (e:ie)** *v.* 4; (believe) **creer** *v.*
   think about **pensar en** *v.* 4
third **tercero/a** 5
thirst **sed** *f.*
thirsty: be (very) thirsty **tener (mucha) sed** 3
thirteen **trece** 1
thirty **treinta** 1; thirty (*minutes past the hour*) **y treinta; y media** 1
this **este, esta** *adj.;* **éste, ésta, esto** *pron.* 6
those **ésos, ésas** *pron.* 6; **esos, esas** *adj.* 6
those (over there) **aquéllos, aquéllas** *pron.* 6; **aquellos, aquellas** *adj.* 6
thousand **mil** *m.* 2
three **tres** 1
   three hundred **trescientos/as** 2
throat **garganta** *f.* 10
through **por** *prep.* 11
Thursday **jueves** *m., sing.* 2
thus (*in such a way*) **así** *adv.*
ticket **boleto** *m.* 2, 17; **pasaje** *m.* 5
tie **corbata** *f.* 6
time **vez** *f.* 6; **tiempo** *m.* 14
   have a good/bad time **pasarlo bien/mal** 9
   I've had a fantastic time. **Lo he pasado de película.** 18
   What time is it? **¿Qué hora es?** 1
   (At) What time...? **¿A qué hora...?** 1
times **veces** *f., pl.* 6
   many times **muchas veces** 10
   two times **dos veces** 6
tip **propina** *f.* 8
tire **llanta** *f.* 11
tired **cansado/a** *adj.* 5
   be tired **estar cansado/a** 5
title **título** *m.* 16
to **a** *prep.* 1
toast (*drink*) **brindar** *v.* 9
   toast **pan** *m.* **tostado** 8
toasted **tostado/a** *adj.* 8
   toasted bread **pan tostado** *m.* 8
toaster **tostadora** *f.* 12
today **hoy** *adv.* 2
   Today is... **Hoy es...** 2
toe **dedo** *m.* **del pie** 10
together **juntos/as** *adj.* 9
toilet **inodoro** *m.* 7

tomato **tomate** *m.* 8
tomorrow **mañana** *f.* 1
   See you tomorrow. **Hasta mañana.** 1
tonight **esta noche** *adv.*
too **también** *adv.* 2; 7
   too much **demasiado** *adv.* 6; **en exceso** 15
tooth **diente** *m.* 7
toothpaste **pasta** *f.* **de dientes** 7
top **cima** *f.* 15
tornado **tornado** *m.* 18
touch **tocar** *v.* 17
touch screen **pantalla táctil** *f.*
tour **excursión** *f.* 4; **recorrido** *m.* 13
tour an area **recorrer** *v.*
tourism **turismo** *m.*
tourist **turista** *m., f.* 1; **turístico/a** *adj.*
toward **hacia** *prep.* 14; **para** *prep.* 11
towel **toalla** *f.* 7
town **pueblo** *m.*
trade **oficio** *m.* 16
traffic **circulación** *f.* 11; **tráfico** *m.* 11
   traffic light **semáforo** *m.* 14
tragedy **tragedia** *f.* 17
trail **sendero** *m.* 13
train **entrenarse** *v.* 15; **tren** *m.* 5
   train station **estación** *f.* **de tren** *m.* 5
trainer **entrenador(a)** *m., f.* 15
translate **traducir** *v.* 6
trash **basura** *f.* 12
travel **viajar** *v.* 2
   travel agency **agencia** *f.* **de viajes** 5
   travel agent **agente** *m., f.* **de viajes** 5
traveler **viajero/a** *m., f.* 5
   (traveler's) check **cheque (de viajero)** 14
treadmill **cinta caminadora** *f.* 15
tree **árbol** *m.* 13
trillion **billón** *m.*
trimester **trimestre** *m.* 2
trip **viaje** *m.* 5
   take a trip **hacer un viaje** 5
tropical forest **bosque** *m.* **tropical** 13
true: it's (not) true **(no) es verdad** 13
trunk **baúl** *m.* 11
truth **verdad** *f.* 4
try **intentar** *v.;* **probar (o:ue)** *v.* 8
   try (*to do something*) **tratar de (+ inf.)** 15
   try on **probarse (o:ue)** *v.* 7
t-shirt **camiseta** *f.* 6
Tuesday **martes** *m., sing.* 2
tuna **atún** *m.* 8
turkey **pavo** *m.* 8
turn **doblar** *v.* 14
   turn off (*electricity/appliance*) **apagar** *v.* 11
   turn on (*electricity/appliance*) **poner** *v.* 11; **prender** *v.* 11

twelve **doce** 1
twenty **veinte** 1
twenty-eight **veintiocho** 1
twenty-five **veinticinco** 1
twenty-four **veinticuatro** 1
twenty-nine **veintinueve** 1
twenty-one **veintiuno** 1;
  veintiún, veintiuno/a *adj.* 1
twenty-seven **veintisiete** 1
twenty-six **veintiséis** 1
twenty-three **veintitrés** 1
twenty-two **veintidós** 1
twice **dos veces** 6
twin **gemelo/a** *m., f.* 3
two **dos** 1
  two hundred **doscientos/as** 2
  two times **dos veces** 6

U

ugly **feo/a** *adj.* 3
uncle **tío** *m.* 3
under **debajo de** *prep.* 2
understand **comprender** *v.* 3;
  entender (e:ie) *v.* 4
underwear **ropa interior** 6
unemployment **desempleo** *m.* 18
unique **único/a** *adj.* 9
United States **Estados Unidos
  (EE.UU.)** *m. pl.*
university **universidad** *f.* 2
unless **a menos que** *conj.* 13
unmarried **soltero/a** *adj.* 9
unpleasant **antipático/a** *adj.* 3
until **hasta** *prep.* 6; **hasta que**
  conj. 13
urgent **urgente** *adj.* 12
  It's urgent that... **Es urgente
  que...** 12
us **nos** *pl., d.o. pron.* 5
  to/for us **nos** *pl., i.o. pron.* 6
use **usar** *v.* 6
used for **para** *prep.* 11
useful **útil** *adj. m., f.*

V

vacation **vacaciones** *f., pl.* 5
  be on vacation **estar de
  vacaciones** 5
  go on vacation **ir de
  vacaciones** 5
vacuum **pasar** *v.* **la aspiradora** 12
  vacuum cleaner **aspiradora** *f.* 12
valley **valle** *m.* 13
various **varios/as** *adj. m., f. pl.*
vegetables **verduras** *pl., f.* 8
verb **verbo** *m.*
very **muy** *adv.* 1
  (Very) well, thank you. **(Muy)
  bien, gracias.** 1
video **video** *m.* 1
  video camera **cámara** *f.* **de
  video** 11
  video game **videojuego** *m.* 4

videoconference
  videoconferencia *f.* 16
vinegar **vinagre** *m.* 8
violence **violencia** *f.* 18
visit **visitar** *v.* 4
  visit monuments **visitar
  monumentos** 4
vitamin **vitamina** *f.* 15
voice mail **correo de voz** *m.* 11
volcano **volcán** *m.* 13
volleyball **vóleibol** *m.* 4
vote **votar** *v.* 18

W

wait (for) **esperar** *v.* **(+** *inf.***)** 2
waiter/waitress **camarero/a**
  m., f. 8
wake up **despertarse (e:ie)** *v.* 7
walk **caminar** *v.* 2
  take a walk **pasear** *v.* 4
  walk around **pasear por** 4
wall **pared** *f.* 12; **muro** *m.* 15
wallet **cartera** *f.* 4, 6
want **querer (e:ie)** *v.* 4
war **guerra** *f.* 18
warm up **calentarse (e:ie)** *v.* 15
wash **lavar** *v.* 12
  wash one's face/hands **lavarse
  la cara/las manos** 7
  wash (the floor, the dishes)
  **lavar (el suelo, los
  platos)** 12
  wash oneself **lavarse** *v.* 7
washing machine **lavadora** *f.* 12
wastebasket **papelera** *f.* 2
watch **mirar** *v.* 2; **reloj** *m.* 2
  watch television **mirar (la)
  televisión** 2
water **agua** *f.* 8
  water pollution **contaminación
  del agua** 13
  water-skiing **esquí** *m.*
  acuático 4
way **manera** *f.*
we **nosotros(as)** *m., f.* 1
weak **débil** *adj. m., f.* 15
wear **llevar** *v.* 6; **usar** *v.* 6
weather **tiempo** *m.*
  The weather is bad. **Hace mal
  tiempo.** 5
  The weather is good. **Hace
  buen tiempo.** 5
weaving **tejido** *m.* 17
Web **red** *f.* 11
website **sitio** *m.* **web** 11
wedding **boda** *f.* 9
Wednesday **miércoles** *m., sing.* 2
week **semana** *f.* 2
weekend **fin** *m.* **de semana** 4
weight **peso** *m.* 15
  lift weights **levantar** *v.* **pesas**
  f., pl. 15
welcome **bienvenido(s)/a(s)**
  adj. 1

well: (Very) well, thanks. **(Muy)
  bien, gracias.** 1
well-being **bienestar** *m.* 15
well organized **ordenado/a** *adj.* 5
west **oeste** *m.* 14
  to the west **al oeste** 14
western (*genre*) **de vaqueros** 17
whale **ballena** *f.* 13
what **lo que** *pron.* 12
what? **¿qué?** 1
  At what time...? **¿A qué
  hora...?** 1
  What a pleasure to...! **¡Qué
  gusto (+** *inf.***)...!** 18
  What day is it? **¿Qué día es
  hoy?** 2
  What do you guys think? **¿Qué
  les parece?**
  What happened? **¿Qué
  pasó?**
  What is today's date? **¿Cuál
  es la fecha de hoy?** 5
  What nice clothes! **¡Qué ropa
  más bonita!** 6
  What size do you wear? **¿Qué
  talla lleva (usa)?** 6
  What time is it? **¿Qué hora
  es?** 1
  What's going on? **¿Qué pasa?** 1
  What's happening? **¿Qué
  pasa?** 1
  What's... like? **¿Cómo es...?**
  What's new? **¿Qué hay de
  nuevo?** 1
  What's the weather like? **¿Qué
  tiempo hace?** 5
  What's up? **¿Qué onda?** 14
  What's wrong? **¿Qué pasó?**
  What's your name? **¿Cómo se
  llama usted?** *form.* 1;
  ¿Cómo te llamas (tú)? *fam.* 1
when **cuando** *conj.* 7; 13
When? **¿Cuándo?** 2
where **donde**
where (to)? (*destination*)
  ¿adónde? 2; (*location*)
  ¿dónde? 1, 2
  Where are you from? **¿De
  dónde eres (tú)?** (*fam.*) 1;
  ¿De dónde es (usted)?
  (*form.*) 1
  Where is...? **¿Dónde está...?** 2
which **que** *pron.*, **lo que** *pron.* 12
which? **¿cuál?** 2; **¿qué?** 2
  In which...? **¿En qué...?**
  which one(s)? **¿cuál(es)?** 2
while **mientras** *conj.* 10
white **blanco/a** *adj.* 6
  white wine **vino blanco** 8
who **que** *pron.* 12; **quien(es)**
  pron. 12
who? **¿quién(es)?** 1, 2
Who is...? **¿Quién es...?** 1
  Who is speaking/calling? (*on
  telephone*)
  ¿De parte de quién? 11
  Who is speaking? (*on telephone*)
  ¿Quién habla? 11
whole **todo/a** *adj.*

whom **quien(es)** *pron.* 12
whose? **¿de quién(es)?** 1
why? **¿por qué?** 2
widower/widow **viudo/a** *adj.* 9
wife **esposa** *f.* 3
win **ganar** *v.* 4
wind **viento** *m.*
window **ventana** *f.* 2
windshield **parabrisas** *m.,*
   sing. 11
windsurf **hacer** *v.* **windsurf** 5
windy: It's (very) windy. **Hace**
   (mucho) viento. 5
wine **vino** *m.* 8
   red wine **vino tinto** 8
   white wine **vino blanco** 8
wineglass **copa** *f.* 12
winter **invierno** *m.* 5
wireless connection **conexión**
   inalámbrica *f.* 11
wish **desear** *v.* 2; **esperar** *v.* 13
   I wish (that) **ojalá (que)** 13
with **con** *prep.* 2
   with me **conmigo** 4; 9
   with you **contigo** *fam.* 5, 9
within (ten years) **dentro de (diez**
   años) *prep.* 16
without **sin** *prep.* 2; **sin que**
   conj. 13
woman **mujer** *f.* 1
wool **lana** *f.* 6
   (made of) wool **de lana** 6
word **palabra** *f.* 1
work **trabajar** *v.* 2; **funcionar**
   v. 11; **trabajo** *m.* 16
   work (*of art, literature, music,*
      etc.) **obra** *f.* 17
   work out **hacer gimnasia** 15
world **mundo** *m.* 8
worldwide **mundial** *adj. m., f.*
worried (about) **preocupado/a**
   (por) *adj.* 5
worry (about) **preocuparse** *v.*
   (por) 7
   Don't worry. **No te preocupes.**
      fam. 7
worse **peor** *adj. m., f.* 8
worst **el/la peor** 8
Would you like to...? **¿Te**
   gustaría...? *fam.*
Would you do me the honor of
   marrying me? **¿Me harías**
   el honor de casarte
   conmigo? 17
wow **híjole** *interj.* 6
wrench **llave** *f.* 11
write **escribir** *v.* 3
   write a letter/an e-mail
      escribir una carta/un
      mensaje electrónico 4

writer **escritor(a)** *m., f* 17
written **escrito/a** *p.p.* 14
wrong **equivocado/a** *adj.* 5
   be wrong **no tener razón** 3

X

X-ray **radiografía** *f.* 10

Y

yard **jardín** *m.* 12; **patio** *m.* 12
year **año** *m.* 5
   be... years old **tener...**
      años 3
yellow **amarillo/a** *adj.* 6
yes **sí** *interj.* 1
yesterday **ayer** *adv.* 6
yet **todavía** *adv.* 5
yogurt **yogur** *m.* 8
you **tú** *fam.* **usted (Ud.)** *form.*
   sing. **vosotros/as** *m., f. fam. pl.*
   ustedes (Uds.) *pl.* 1; (to, for)
   you *fam. sing.* **te** *pl.* **os** 6; *form.*
   sing. **le** *pl.* **les** 6
   you **te** *fam., sing.,* **lo/la** *form.,*
      sing., **os** *fam., pl.,* **los/las**
      pl, d.o. pron. 5
You don't say! **¡No me digas!**
   fam.; **¡No me diga!** *form.*
You're welcome. **De nada.** 1; **No**
   hay de qué. 1
young **joven** *adj., sing.* (**jóvenes**
   pl.) 3
   young person **joven** *m., f., sing.*
      (**jóvenes** *pl.*) 1
   young woman **señorita**
      (Srta.) *f.*
younger **menor** *adj. m., f.* 3
younger: younger brother, sister *m.,*
   f. **hermano/a menor** 3
youngest **el/la menor** *m., f.* 8
your **su(s)** *poss. adj. form.* 3;
   tu(s) *poss. adj. fam. sing.* 3;
   vuestro/a(s) *poss. adj. fam.*
   pl. 3
your(s) *form.* **suyo(s)/a(s)** *poss.*
   pron. form. 11; **tuyo(s)/a(s)**
   poss. fam. sing. 11; **vuestro(s)**
   /a(s) *poss. fam.* 11
youth *f.* **juventud** 9

Z

zero **cero** *m.* 1

Text Credits

498 ©Denevi, Marco, *Cartas peligrosas y otros cuentos. Obras Completas, Tomo 5*, Buenos Aires, Corregidor, 1999, pags. 192-193.
530 Gabriel García Márquez, "Un día de estos", LOS FUNERALES DE LA MAMA GRANDE ©Gabriel García Márquez, 1962 y Herederos de Gabriel García Márquez, 2014.
565 de Burgos, Julia. "Julia de Burgos: yo misma fui mi ruta" from *Song of the Simple Truth: The Complete Poems of Julia de Burgos*. Willimantic: Curbstone Press, 1995.
600 © Herederos de Federico García Lorca.

Film Credits

110 By permission of Xochitl Dorsey.
534 By permission of Instituto Mexicano de Cinematografía (IMCINE).
568 By permission of Elemental Films.
604 By Jorge Naranjo and Nana Films (http://vimeo.com/35170814).

Comic Credits

31 © Joaquin Salvador Lavado (QUINO) Toda Mafalda - Ediciones de La Flor, 1993.
394 TUTE.

Photography Credits

All images © Vista Higher Learning unless otherwise noted.

Cover: © Massimo Ripani/SIME/eStockphoto

Front matter: © GM Visuals/Media Bakery.

Lesson 1: 1: Paula Díez; **2:** © John Henley/Corbis; **3:** Martín Bernetti; **4:** Martín Bernetti; **10:** (l) Rachel Distler; (r) Ali Burafi; **11:** (l) © Matt Sayles/AP/Corbis; (tr) © Hans Georg Roth/Corbis; (br) Paola Ríos-Schaaf; **12:** (l) Janet Dracksdorf; (r) © Tom Grill/Corbis; **16:** (l) © José Girarte/iStockphoto; (r) © Blend Images/Alamy; **19:** (l) Dario Eusse Tobón; (m) Anne Loubet; (r) © Digital Vision/Getty Images; **27:** Trevor Lush/Purestock; **28:** (all) Martín Bernetti; **31:** (tl) Ana Cabezas Martín; (tml) Martín Bernetti; (tmr) © Serban Enache/Dreamstime; (tr) Vanessa Bertozzi; (bl) © Corey Hochachka/Design Pics/Corbis; (bm) VHL; (br) Ramiro Isaza/Fotocolombia; **32:** Carolina Zapata; **33:** Paula Díez; **36:** (t) © Robert Holmes/Corbis; (m) © Jon Arnold Images/Alamy; (b) © Andres R/Shutterstock; **37:** (tl) © PhotoLink/Getty Images; (tr) © Tony Arruza/Corbis; (bl) © Shaul Schwarz/Sygma/Corbis; (br) Marta Mesa.

Lesson 2: 39: © Radius Images/Maxx Images; **42:** Martín Bernetti; **43:** © Chris Schmidt/iStockphoto; **48:** (l) Mauricio Arango; (r) © Pablo Corral V/Corbis; **49:** (t) © Murle/Dreamstime; (b) © Paul Almasy/Corbis; **57:** © Stephen Coburn/Shutterstock; **59:** (l) Paola Rios-Schaaf; (r) © Image Source/Corbis; **67:** (l) © Rick Gomez/Corbis; (r) © Hola Images/Workbook.com; **68:** José Blanco; **69:** © PNC/Media Bakery; **70:** (all) Martín Bernetti; **71:** Nora y Susana/Fotocolombia; **74:** (tl) José Blanco; (tr) José Blanco; (m) © Elke Stolzenberg/Corbis; (b) © Reuters/Corbis; **75:** (t) Courtesy of Charles Ommanney; (ml) José Blanco; (mr) José Blanco; (bl) © Iconotec/Fotosearch; (br) VHL.

Lesson 3: 77: © Paul Bradbury/Age Fotostock; **79:** Martín Bernetti; **80:** (tl) Anne Loubet; (tr) © Blend Images/Alamy; (mtl) Ana Cabezas Martín; (mtr) Ventus Pictures; (mbl) Martín Bernetti; (mbr) Martín Bernetti; (bl) Martín Bernetti; (br) Martín Bernetti; **86:** (tl) © David Cantor/AP Images; (tr) © Rafael Perez/Reuters/Corbis; (b) © Martial Trezzini/EPA/Corbis; **87:** (t) © Dani Cardona/Reuters/Corbis; (b) © LOTE/Splash News/Corbis; **90:** (l) Martín Bernetti; (r) José Blanco; **92:** © Andres Rodriguez/Alamy; **95:** Monkey Business Images/Shutterstock; **97:** (l) © Tyler Olson/Fotolia; (r) Martín Bernetti; **98:** Martín Bernetti; **103:** © Fotoluminate/123RF; **106:** (t) Martín Bernetti; (m) Martín Bernetti; (b) Martín Bernetti; **107:** (t) Nora y Susana/Fotocolombia; (m) © Chuck Savage/Corbis; (b) Martín Bernetti; **108:** © Tom & Dee Ann McCarthy/Corbis; **109:** Martín Bernetti; **112:** (t) Martín Bernetti; (ml) Martín Bernetti; (mm) Iván Mejía; (mr) Lauren Krolick; (b) Martín Bernetti; **113:** (tl) Martín Bernetti; (tr) © Pablo Corral V/Corbis; (ml) Martín Bernetti; (mr) © Gerardo Mora; (b) Martín Bernetti.

Lesson 4: 115: © Digital Vision/Getty Images; **117:** © George Shelley/Corbis; **124:** (l) © Javier Soriano/AFP/Getty Images; (r) © Fernando Bustamante/AP Images; **125:** (t) © Photo Works/Shutterstock; (b) © Zuma Press/Alamy; **128:** Rafael Rios; **139:** © Media Bakery; **142:** Martín Bernetti; **143:** © Fernando Llano/AP Images; **144:** Martín Bernetti; **145:** © Rick Gomez/Corbis; **148:** (tl) © Randy Miramontez/Shutterstock; (tr) © Albright-Knox Art Gallery/Corbis; (ml) Ruben Varela; (mr) Carolina Zapata; (b) © Henry Romero/Reuters/Corbis; **149:** (tl) © Radius Images/Alamy; (tr) © Bettmann/Corbis; (m) © Corel/Corbis; (b) © David R. Frazier Photolibrary/Alamy.

Lesson 5: 151: © Gavin Hellier/Getty Images; **162:** © Gary Cook/Alamy; **163** (t): © AFP/Getty Images; **163** (b): © Mark A. Johnson/Corbis; **167:** © Ronnie Kaufman/Corbis; **180:** Carlos Gaudier; **181** (tl): © Corel/Corbis; **181** (tr): Carlos Gaudier; **181** (m): Carlos Gaudier; **181** (b): Carlos Gaudier; **182:** Carolina Zapata; **186** (tl): © Nanniqui/Dreamstime; **186** (tr): José Blanco; **186** (ml): Carlos Gaudier; **186** (mr): © Capricornis Photographic/Shutterstock; **186** (b): © Dave G. Houser/Corbis; **187** (tl): Carlos Gaudier; **187** (tr): © Lawrence Manning/Corbis; **187** (m): © Stocktrek/Getty Images; **187** (b): Carlos Gaudier.

Lesson 6: 189: © Asiapix RF/Inmagine; **198:** (l) © Jose Caballero Digital Press Photos/Newscom; (r) Janet Dracksdorf; **199:** (t) © Carlos Alvarez/Getty Images; (bl) © Guiseppe Carace/Getty Images; (br) © Mark Mainz/Getty Images; **204:** (all) Pascal Pernix; **209:** (all) Martín Bernetti; **210:** (all) Paula Díez; **211:** Paula Díez; **216-217:** (all) Shutterstock and Paula Diez; **218:** © Noam/Fotolia; **219:** Martín Bernetti; **222:** (tl) Pascal Pernix; (tr) Pascal Pernix; (mt) Pascal Pernix; (mb) Pascal Pernix; (b) © PhotoLink/Getty Images; **223:** (tl) © Don Emmert/AFP/Getty Images; (tr) Pascal Pernix; (bl) Pascal Pernix; (br) The Kobal Collection at Art Resource, NY.

Lesson 7: 225: © Media Bakery; **234:** © Stewart Cohen/Blend Images/Corbis; **235:** (t) Ali Burafi; (b) Janet Dracksdorf; **237:** (l) Martín Bernetti; (r) Martín Bernetti; **239:** (l) Martín Bernetti; (r) © Ariel Skelley/Corbis; **242:** José Blanco; **243:** Martín Bernetti; **245:** Purestock/Alamy; **252–253:** © Didem Hizar/Fotolia; **254:** © I love images/Alamy; **255:** Martín Bernetti; **258:** (t) Martín Bernetti; (mtl) VHL; (mtr) Martín Bernetti; (mbl) © Richard Franck Smith/Sygma/Corbis; (mbr) © Charles & Josette Lenars/Corbis; (b) © Yann Arthus-Bertrand/Corbis; **259:** (tl) Martín Bernetti; (tr) © Mick Roessler/Corbis; (bl) © Jeremy Horner/Corbis; (br) © Marshall Bruce/iStockphoto.

Television Credits

34 By permission of Edgardo Tettamanti.
72 By permission of Cencosud.
146 By permission of Diego Reves.
184 By permission of Univision.com.
220 ©Comercial Mexicana.
256 By permission of Asepxia, Genommalab and Kepel & Mata.
294 By permission of Andres Felipe Roa.
326 By permission of Javier Ugarte (director).
362 By permission of Getting Better Creative Studio.
398 By permission of Davivienda.
436 By permission of Carrefour.
470 By permission of Ecovidrio.
502 By permission of Banco Ficensa.
636 By permission of Subdirector de la Secretaria de Comunicaciones, Gobierno de Chile.

About the Author

José A. Blanco founded Vista Higher Learning in 1998. A native of Barranquilla, Colombia, Mr. Blanco holds a B.A. in Literature from the University of California, Santa Cruz, and a M.A. in Hispanic Studies from Brown University. He has worked as a writer, editor, and translator for Houghton Mifflin and D.C. Heath and Company and has taught Spanish at the secondary and university levels. Mr. Blanco is also the co-author of several other Vista Higher Learning programs: **Vistas, Panorama, Aventuras,** and **¡Viva!** at the introductory level, **Ventanas, Facetas, Enfoques, Imagina,** and **Sueña** at the intermediate level, and **Revista** at the advanced conversation level.

About the Illustrators

Yayo, an internationally acclaimed illustrator, was born in Colombia. He has illustrated children's books, newspapers, and magazines, and has been exhibited around the world. He currently lives in Montreal, Canada.

Pere Virgili lives and works in Barcelona, Spain. His illustrations have appeared in textbooks, newspapers, and magazines throughout Spain and Europe.

Born in Caracas, Venezuela, **Hermann Mejía** studied illustration at the *Instituto de Diseño de Caracas*. Hermann currently lives and works in the United States.

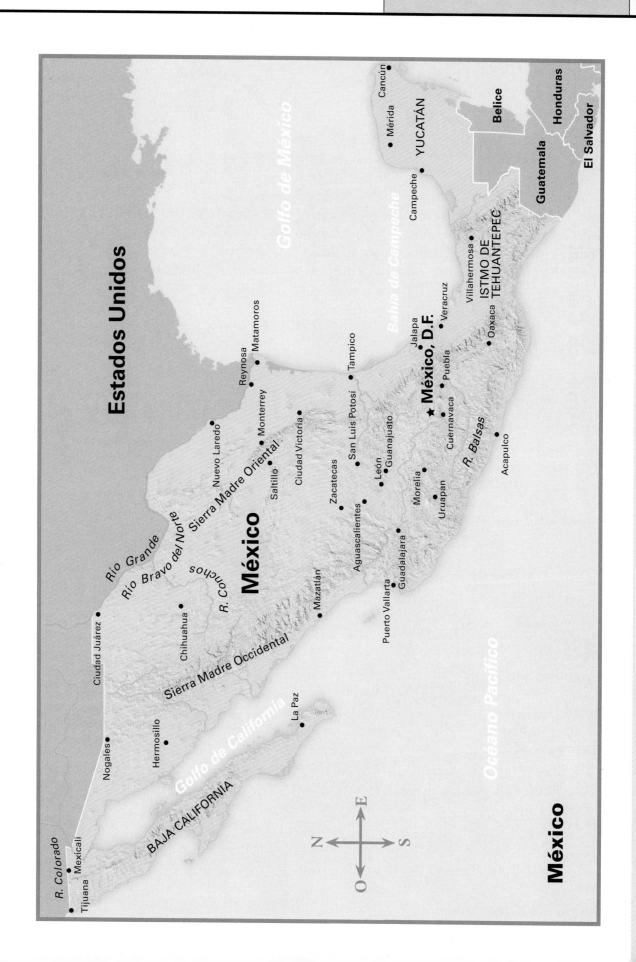

Estados Unidos

Golfo de México

México

Océano Pacífico

Golfo de California

BAJA CALIFORNIA

Bahía de Campeche

YUCATÁN

ISTMO DE TEHUANTEPEC

R. Balsas

Sierra Madre Occidental

Sierra Madre Oriental

Río Grande

Río Bravo del Norte

R. Conchos

R. Colorado

Tijuana
Mexicali
Nogales
Hermosillo
La Paz
Ciudad Juárez
Chihuahua
Mazatlán
Puerto Vallarta
Guadalajara
Morelia
Uruapan
Cuernavaca
Acapulco
Aguascalientes
León
Guanajuato
Zacatecas
Saltillo
Ciudad Victoria
San Luis Potosí
Tampico
Nuevo Laredo
Monterrey
Reynosa
Matamoros
México, D.F.
Puebla
Jalapa
Veracruz
Villahermosa
Oaxaca
Campeche
Mérida
Cancún

Belice
Guatemala
Honduras
El Salvador

N
E
S
O

México

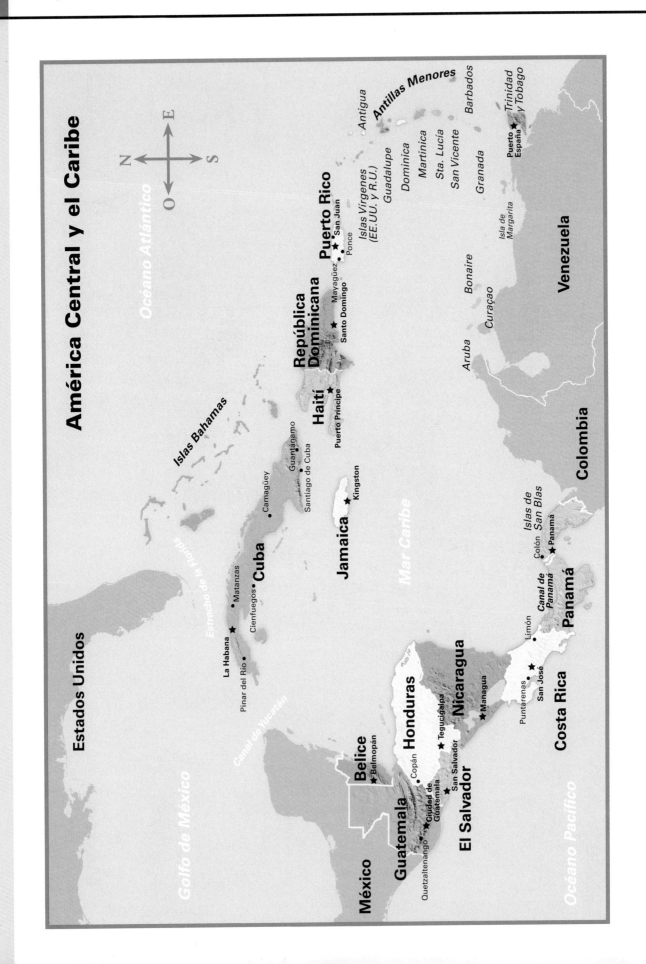

América Central y el Caribe

Mar Caribe

Barranquilla   Maracaibo
Caracas
Puerto España
Venezuela   **Trinidad y Tobago**

Medellín
Colombia   Bogotá
Cali

Pasto

Ecuador   Quito
Guayaquil

R. Orinoco

Georgetown
Guyana   Paramaribo
Surinam   Cayena
Guayana Francesa

Iquitos

Perú

R. Negro

R. Amazonas
Manaus   Belém

R. Madeira

Cordillera de los Andes

Recife

Lima
Cuzco
Arequipa   Lago Titicaca
Arica   La Paz
Bolivia   Sucre
Iquique

Antofagasta

Brasil   Salvador
Brasilia

R. Paraguay

R. Paraná   Belo Horizonte

São Paulo   Río de Janeiro
Santos

Paraguay
Salta   Asunción

Chile

R. Paraná
R. Uruguay

Porto Alegre

Córdoba

Valparaíso   Mendoza   Rosario
Santiago   **Uruguay**
Buenos Aires   Montevideo

Concepción   **Argentina**

Bahía Blanca

Océano Pacífico

Océano Atlántico

Cordillera de los Andes

Puerto Montt

N
O ← → E
S

Estrecho de Magallanes
Punta Arenas   Islas Malvinas

Tierra del Fuego

América del Sur

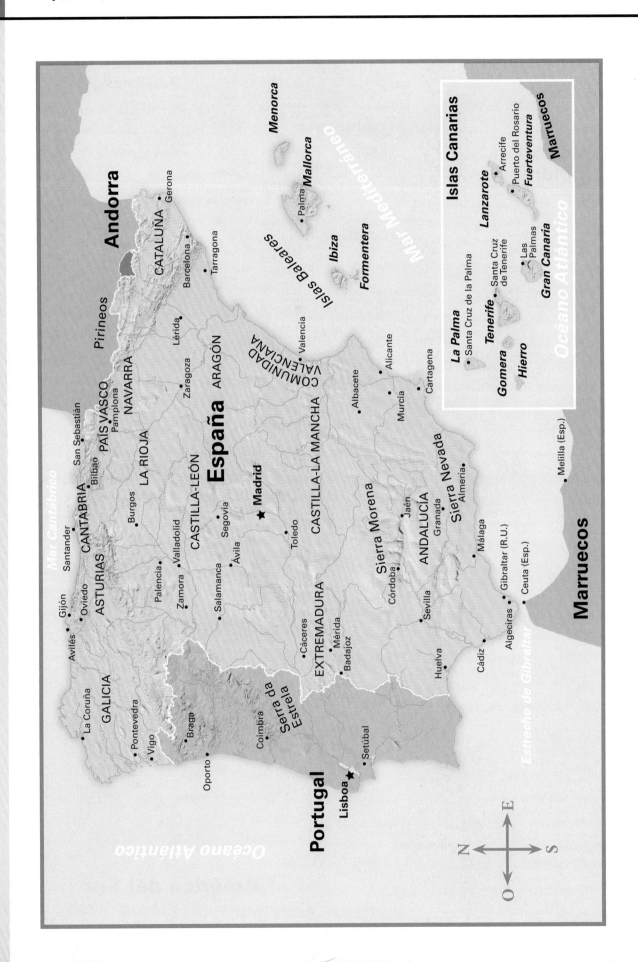